From PIXELS to ANIMATION

An Introduction to Graphics Programming

LIMITED WARRANTY AND DISCLAIMER OF LIABILITY

ACADEMIC PRESS, INC. ("AP") AND ANYONE ELSE WHO HAS BEEN INVOLVED IN THE CREATION OR PRODUCTION OF THE ACCOMPANYING CODE ("THE PRODUCT") CANNOT AND DO NOT WARRANT THE PERFORMANCE OR RESULTS THAT MAY BE OBTAINED BY USING THE PRODUCT. THE PRODUCT IS SOLD "AS IS" WITHOUT WARRANTY OF ANY KIND (EXCEPT AS HEREAFTER DESCRIBED), EITHER EXPRESSED OR IMPLIED, INCLUDING, BUT NOT LIMITED TO, ANY WARRANTY OF PERFORMANCE OR ANY IMPLIED WARRANTY OF MERCHANTABILITY OR FITNESS FOR ANY PARTICULAR PURPOSE. AP WARRANTS ONLY THAT THE MAGNETIC DISKETTE(S) ON WHICH THE CODE IS RECORDED IS FREE FROM DEFECTS IN MATERIAL AND FAULTY WORKMANSHIP UNDER THE NORMAL USE AND SERVICE FOR A PERIOD OF NINETY (90) DAYS FROM THE DATE THE PRODUCT IS DELIVERED. THE PURCHASER'S SOLE AND EXCLUSIVE REMEDY IN THE EVENT OF A DEFECT IS EXPRESSLY LIMITED TO EITHER REPLACEMENT OF THE DISKETTE(S) OR REFUND OF THE PURCHASE PRICE, AT AP'S SOLE DISCRETION.

IN NO EVENT, WHETHER AS A RESULT OF BREACH OF CONTRACT, WARRANTY OR TORT (INCLUDING NEGLIGENCE), WILL AP OR ANYONE WHO HAS BEEN INVOLVED IN THE CREATION OR PRODUCTION OF THE PRODUCT BE LIABLE TO PURCHASER FOR ANY DAMAGES, INCLUDING ANY LOST PROFITS, LOST SAVINGS OR OTHER INCIDENTAL OR CONSEQUENTIAL DAMAGES ARISING OUT OF THE USE OR INABILITY TO USE THE PRODUCT OR ANY MODIFICATIONS THEREOF, OR DUE TO THE CONTENTS OF THE CODE, EVEN IF AP HAS BEEN ADVISED OF THE POSSIBILITY OF SUCH DAMAGES, OR FOR ANY CLAIM BY ANY OTHER PARTY.

Any request for replacement of a defective diskette must be postage prepaid and must be accompanied by the original defective diskette, your mailing address and telephone number, and proof of date of purchase and purchase price. Send such requests, stating the nature of the problem, to Academic Press Customer Service, 6277 Sea Harbor Drive, Orlando, FL 32887, 1-800-321-5068. AP shall have no obligation to refund the purchase price or to replace a diskette based on claims of defects in the nature or operation of the Product.

Some states do not allow limitation on how long an implied warranty lasts, nor exclusions or limitations of incidental or consequential damage, so the above limitations and exclusions may not apply to you. This Warranty gives you specific legal rights, and you may also have other rights which vary from jurisdiction to jurisdiction.

THE RE-EXPORT OF UNITED STATES ORIGIN SOFTWARE IS SUBJECT TO THE UNITED STATES LAWS UNDER THE EXPORT ADMINISTRATION ACT OF 1969 AS AMENDED. ANY FURTHER SALE OF THE PRODUCT SHALL BE IN COMPLIANCE WITH THE UNITED STATES DEPARTMENT OF COMMERCE ADMINISTRATION REGULATIONS. COMPLIANCE WITH SUCH REGULATIONS IS YOUR RESPONSIBILITY AND NOT THE RESPONSIBILITY OF AP.

From PIXELS to ANIMATION

An Introduction to Graphics Programming

James Alan Farrell

AP PROFESSIONAL

Boston San Diego New York
London Sydney Tokyo Toronto

This book is printed on acid-free paper. ♾

AP PROFESSIONAL
955 Massachusetts Avenue, Cambridge, Massachusetts 02139

An imprint of ACADEMIC PRESS
A Division of HARCOURT BRACE & COMPANY

United Kingdom edition published by
ACADEMIC PRESS LIMITED
24–28 Oval Road, London NW1 7DX

Library of Congress Cataloging-in-Publication Data
Farrell, James Alan.
From pixels to animation : an introduction to graphics programming / James Alan Farrell.
p. cm.
Includes index.
ISBN 0-12-249710-4 (acid-free paper)
1. Computer graphics. I. Title.
T385.F39 1994 94-28379
006.6—dc20 CIP

Printed in the United States of America
94 95 96 97 98 IP 9 8 7 6 5 4 3 2 1

Contents

Table of Figures

Table of Figures

Table of Tables

Table of Tables

Preface

This book got it's start in the fall of 1992, when a local tech school asked me to teach a class on computer graphics in Pascal. I investigated what books were available for as texts and found all of two, neither of which was entirely suitable. It turns out that the class was never held, so I decided to take the time I would have spent teaching to write a suitable Pascal graphics book. Although the basic outline of this book was developed from that class it should be noted here that this book it not a text book. It is instead a thorough introduction to the topic. It contains no exercises as a text would, but it does contain plenty of examples, and a number of ideas for interesting programs. Nearly all of the examples and several other interesting programs can also be found on the companion disk supplied with this book.

When it came time to find a publisher for the book, AP Professional told me they were interested, but only if I rewrote it for C, since Pascal is rarely used by professional graphics programmers. C is just much better suited for graphics. As it turns out, many of the examples shrank drastically in size when they were rewritten. Although this book is designed primarily for the Borland C user, Microsoft C is presented quite solidly. One full chapter is devoted to using Microsoft C for graphics, and an appendix is provided as a reference for Microsoft graphics functions. The SVGA library on the distribution disk is compatible with both Borland and Microsoft compilers

This book is based on the outline I would have used to teach that class, only much expanded. As such it starts at the very beginning, with the basic workings of graphics hardware, and progresses through all aspects of graphics programming, up to advanced topics such as ray tracing and fractals. The basics are covered thoroughly before moving on, so that the student of graphics programming has a solid base on which to build. Computer graphics programming is a huge field, and a single introductory book cannot hope to cover everything in detail, so this book spends most of its time covering the basics, then gives a smattering of advanced topics. This will give the student a taste for which topics he/she wishes to pursue.

One problem with teaching graphics is that two separate approaches must be covered. One is a low-level approach that teaches how to draw dots on the screen, how to draw lines, etc. The other is a high-level approach that teaches what to do with those lines and dots. The one is not necessarily incompatible with the other, but most beginning graphics students do not want to spend a lot of time covering the intricate functions needed to draw lines, circles, etc. They would rather just be able to draw the lines, and learn how to use them first. Only after the student becomes more sophisticated and starts running into limitations, does he or she usually become interested in creating his/her own line drawing functions.

Fortunately most compilers provide graphics functions. This makes the approach alluded to in the previous paragraph possible. This book starts by introducing the basic concepts, including a detailed description of the graphics functions supplied with two of the most popular C compilers, Borland and Microsoft, and such things as making graphs and charts, and basic perspective and color handling. Once the student is familiar and comfortable with these concepts, and starts finding the limitations of them, then he/she can move on.

One limitation of many C compilers is that they do not yet provide functions for programming SVGA monitors. Within the description of low-level programming is a thorough description of how to program SVGA monitors. A library of functions is included with the book to demonstrate the functions outlined in these chapters, and also to provide an extension to the high-level graphics capabilities provided by most compilers. This library can be used with Microsoft C, Borland C, and most other C compilers.

The next part of the book gives a quick introduction to some of the more advanced graphics programming topics. This section is meant to give a feel for where the graphics programming student can "go from here." Topics are introduced such as animation, ray tracing, and fractals. Many books have been written on each of these topics, and one cannot hope to thoroughly cover any of them in a book of this scope. One can, however, give much practical information and a feel for these topics.

The last section, the appendices, is a reference, in which I attempted to put the information I have most often needed in one place over the years. To sum up, this book can be divided into four sections:

- The basics of graphics programming, which covers graphics hardware, high-level functions provided by Borland and Microsoft C and also making graphs and charts, changing colors, and 3D graphics
- Low-level graphics, which covers getting around the limitations of standard graphics libraries, SVGA programming, and creating graphics functions.
- Advanced topics, which covers animation, linear transformations, ray tracing, and fractals.
- Reference, which covers many topics

I have made every attempt to make this book as useful as possible. It is my sincere wish that you find it so.

JAF, 4/28/94

Acknowledgements

There are quite a number of people who have helped to make this book a success. Without their help this project would have failed long before it was even started. I would like to thank each of them individually, but if I were to do that I would have to write another entire book. I'm sure this is a common problem with projects of this scope. There are several individuals, however, that especially need to be mentioned.

Tim Christian, who gave me a tremendous amount of invaluable advice on SVGA and mouse programming.

Arthur Weinburger, who was always available for consulting on math problems, and who provided the one example of calculus that appears in this book.

Magnus Rimvall, who was instrumental in finding a publisher.

Jenifer Niles, who is a very patient editor.

And of course my family, for always putting up with me.

1

Graphics Displays

Overview of Graphics Video Displays

This chapter discusses how graphics video displays work in a theoretical way. This chapter should be read as a quick overview. An in-depth understanding of this material is not needed at this time. Some of the material is confusing, so developing an in-depth understanding now, before using the hardware, will be difficult. If you find yourself becoming confused don't be too concerned; you will understand when you start using these devices in later chapters. A brief look at the workings behind the screen now, however, will make understanding graphics programming easier.

The Basic Monochrome Monitor

The first computer monitors [also known as cathode-ray tubes (CRT's), or video display tubes (VDT's)] were only capable of displaying a single color. Thus they are called monochrome (see fig. 1.1.1). These are the simplest type of monitor, so we will use them as a starting point in explaining how monitors work.

The central component of a monitor is a large glass tube. This tube is the cathode-ray tube itself, although when most people talk of a CRT they usually mean the whole monitor. The air in this tube is evacuated, to make this a vacuum tube. At one end of the tube is a sort of gun, which shoots a beam of electrons at the other end. This is called an electron gun or cathode. At the other end of the tube is a large flat area coated with phosphors. Phosphors glow when hit with electrons. This surface is the viewing area or the screen itself. After the electron gun but before the screen is a series of magnets that focus the electrons into a tight beam, and steer the electron beam to a certain point on the screen.

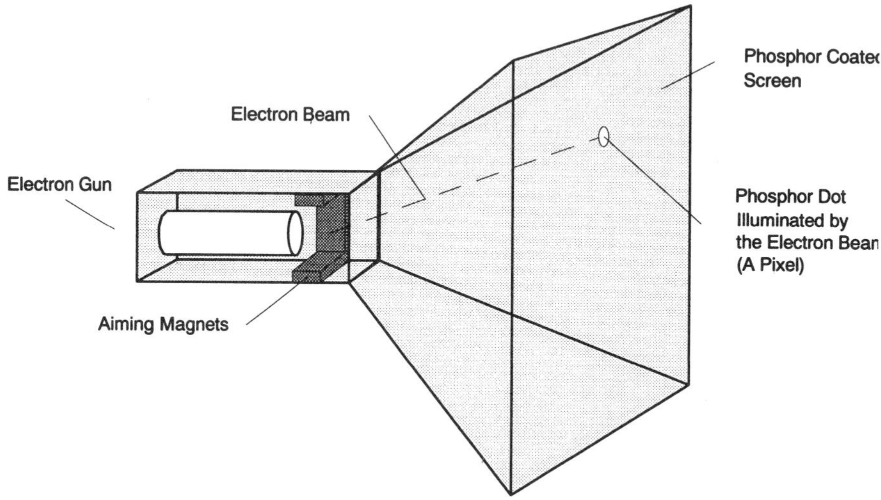

Fig. 1.1.1 Cutaway of a Monochrome Monitor

Pixels and the Frame Buffer

The electron beam sweeps across the screen in a series of lines. The beam sweeps from the top left to the top right, then moves down a fraction of an inch and sweeps across again. The area on the screen covered as the beam sweeps once is a *scan line.* This process is repeated until the entire screen is covered.

As the beam sweeps the electron gun is turned on and off. Any phosphors on the screen that are hit by electrons glow. Any that are not remain dark. These small area that glow or do not glow are called *picture elements*, or *pixels* for short.

Whether the gun is turned on or not for a certain pixel is determined by a piece of memory called the *frame buffer* (see fig. 1.1.2). There is a bit in the frame buffer for each pixel. If that bit is set the electron gun is turned when the beam is sweeping over that pixel, and that pixel glows. If that bit is not set, then that pixel does not glow. The largest portion of graphics programming is loading the frame buffer in a way that causes meaningful pictures to appear on the screen.

There are a number of different phosphors, which light up with different colors. By using different phosphors monitors can be made that display in white, amber, green, or any other color.

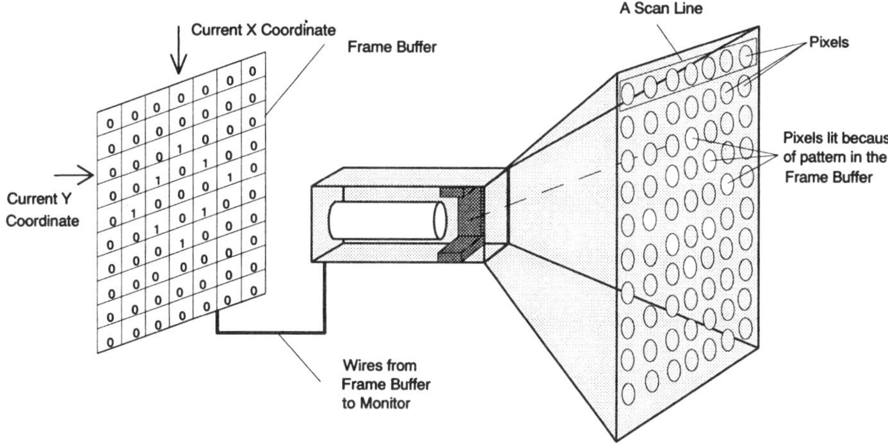

Fig. 1.1.2 Very Low Resolution Monitor with Frame Buffer

Other Things That Are Good to Know

After the phosphors are hit with the electron beam they light up brightly. But as soon as the electrons stop hitting them they start to fade. Therefore the beam must keep retracing over the screen. If the beam is too slow the phosphors will fade a noticeable amount, and the screen will flicker. The fact that phosphors do fade allows for things to be taken off the screen. Simply clear the appropriate bits in the frame buffer. The electron beam now will not hit those pixels, and the pixels will fade so that the item will no longer appear on the screen.

Considering how quickly phosphors need to fade in order for an item to disappear off the screen in a reasonable time, and considering that the screen needs to be refreshed quick enough that this same fading does not cause flickering, we realize that the screen must be refreshed quite quickly. The time needed for the electron beam to completely cover the screen and return to its starting point is called the *refresh rate.* This time is usually 70 to 80 milliseconds. The lower the time the better.

Some systems have frame buffers with more bits than are needed to control the display. The bits are grouped together into sets. The computer can decide which set of bits to display. A new picture can be drawn on one set while another set is used to control the electron gun. In this way, all the processing needed to draw a new picture is invisible to the user. The set being used is switched, and a new picture appears! These sets of bits are called *pages.* This is because switching pages on the computer is supposed to be like turning pages in a book. Page switching is often used in animation. The page being displayed on the monitor is called the *active page.*

The method of programming a monitor covered in this section is called *raster scan.* This is the method used by all PC monitors. Other graphics systems sometimes use a method called v*ector scan.* With a vector scan monitor, commands are given to steer the electron beam to draw the desired pattern. This method gives very clear, crisp looking lines, but can flicker and be quite slow if a complex pattern is drawn. With the raster scan technique all pixels are covered each time the screen is refreshed. This means the amount of time needed to refresh the screen is constant, no matter what is displayed. The screen won't flicker just because there is a lot being displayed.

Raster scan monitors cannot draw lines as crisply as vector scan monitors (see fig. 1.1.3). The screen behaves almost like a piece of graph paper. Images are created by color in squares of the graph paper. When you try to draw a line this way, squares are just not located in convenient locations. So the square nearest the correct location is chosen. The fact that squares are so often not where you need one gives a line on a raster scan monitor a jagged appearance. This can be improved by raising the number of pixels.

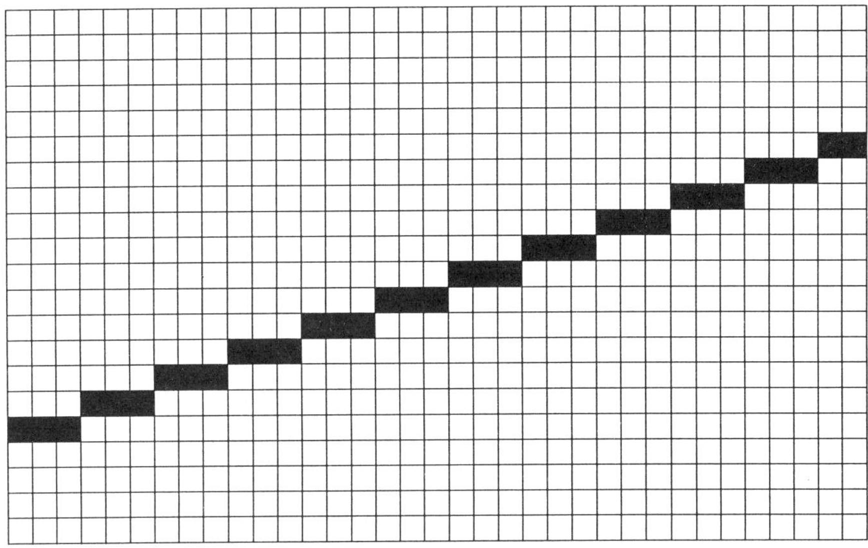

Fig. 1.1.3 Magnified Line on a Raster Scan Monitor

A More Advanced Monochrome Monitor

The monitor described in the last section can only display one color. Moreover, it can only display one intensity, or brightness of color. It would be useful to be able to display different brightnesses, or shades. This can be done by setting the electron gun to different intensity levels. If the gun has four levels of intensity – off, low, medium, and high, then four shades can be displayed: black, dark gray, bright gray, and white. But now the frame buffer has to be larger. For each pixel we now need 2 bits. Remember with 2 bits we can describe four levels – 0 (00b), 1 (01b), 2 (10b) and 3 (11b). This monitor is more flexible, and can display things the first one can not, but it requires more memory. If there are 4 bits per pixel then 16 shades of gray can be displayed, and with 6 bits per pixel 64 shades can be displayed.

Dot Pitch

Monitor advertisements often list the dot pitch of the monitor. The electron gun can actually be turned on and off a number of times for each pixel. The dot pitch is a measure of how much space is needed to turn the electron gun on then off again. The less space needed the clearer and sharper things will appear on the screen. Common dot pitches are 0.28 and 0.31.

Color Monitors

Color Mixing

Before understanding how a color monitor works, it is necessary to know how color mixing works. Color mixing is the combining of two or three colors to get a different color. With color mixing only three primary colors are needed to produce almost all the colors that the eye can see. These colors are called the *primary colors.*

Additive and Subtractive Color Mixing

There are two types of color mixing, *additive* and *subtractive.* Subtractive color mixing is probably what most people are more familiar with. Paint mixing uses subtractive color mixing. For mixing light, additive color mixing is used, which is what a computer does. The primary colors for additive and subtractive mixing are different. For additive mixing the primary colors are red, green and blue. Mixing red and green makes yellow, mixing red and blue makes magenta, and mixing green and blue makes a color called cyan, which, surprisingly enough, is a blue-green color. White is obtained by mixing all three primary colors. By using different amounts of the three primary colors nearly all shades of all colors can be obtained. Monitors with these three primary colors are often called RGB monitors.

This type of color mixing may seem strange at first. After all, how do you make orange by mixing red, green, and blue? But it does work. We will be covering it in detail in Chapter 6. After a little practice it will become clear that orange is mostly red, with blue and green added in an equal but smaller amount.

How Color Monitors Work

In color monitors the pixels are divided into three separate dots. One dot is green, one red, and the other blue. These dots are close enough together that they look like a single pixel. The color of each dot blends together to make the color you see when you look at that pixel. There are three electron guns, one for each color (see fig. 1.2.1). By varying the intensity of each gun, a large number of colors can be displayed.

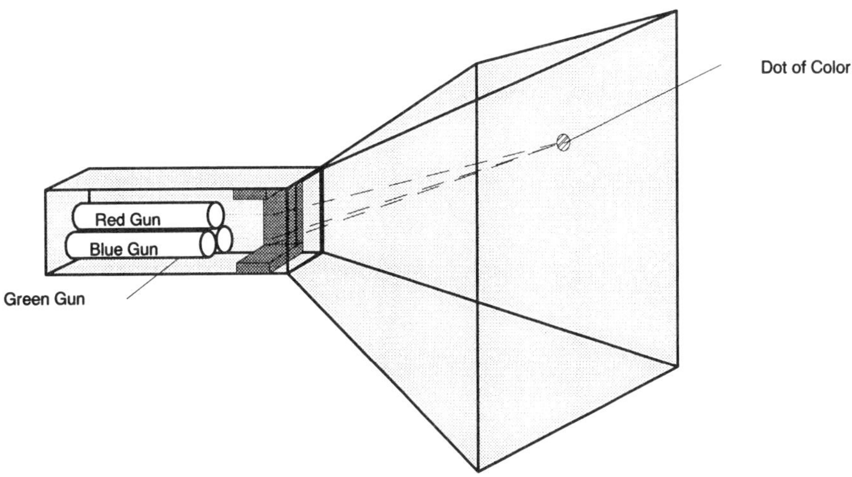

Fig. 1.2.1 Color Monitor with three Electron Guns

Color Palettes and the Color Frame Buffer

Now with three guns the frame buffer needs to be quite a lot larger. If each color can display 64 shades, then we need to have 6 bits per color per pixel, or 18 bits per pixel. If there are 640 pixels across the screen, and 480 pixels down the screen then there are 640 × 480 or 307,200 pixels on the screen. The memory needed would be 5,529,600 bits or 691 kilobytes. Nowadays, with the price of RAM dropping like a stone, that does not sound like a prohibitive amount. But not too long ago a system with this much memory dedicated to the display would have cost hundreds of thousands of dollars! To lessen the amount of memory needed, the concept of color palettes was devised. A special array of memory is set aside. Each entry in this array contains three values. Each value is the intensity level of the one of the electron guns – blue, red or green. This is called the *palette array* or (in the case of the PC) the *palette registers*. The number in the frame buffer is an index into this array. When a certain pixel is being lit the system looks in the frame buffer. The number it finds there tells it which entry in the palette array to use. The entry in the palette array tells the system how to set the electron guns to get the desired color. This system is confusing, but it saves RAM and so is cheaper. Also only one number has to be set in the frame buffer for each pixel instead of three, one for each gun. This saves time. The best way to understand the idea of palettes is to use them, although looking at the fig 1.2.2 might also help. We will cover them again down the road.

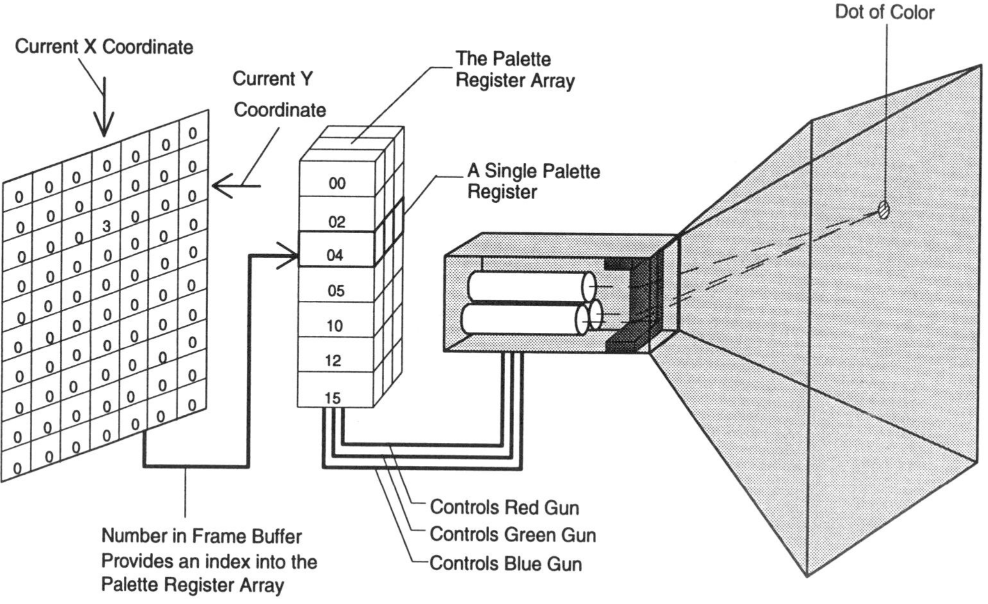

Fig. 1.2.2 Color Monitor with Frame Buffer and Palette Array

IBM PC Monitors

A number of monitors are available for the IBM PC. We will be dealing mostly with the VGA and SVGA monitors, which at the time of this writing are the most common. In addition we need to mention several other monitors, including the Hercules monochrome monitor, and several older monitors from which the VGA derives its capabilities.

In the past few years a number of new monitor types, SVGA monitors, have become available, with more types being added all the time. Until recently these newer types were all programmed differently. Brand X's monitor was programmed differently from Brand Z's. Fortunately in 1989 the Video Electronic Standards

Association (VESA)[1] developed a standard that is both powerful and flexible. This standard defines how monitors built today, and those that will be built in the future, might be programmed. The Standard, referred to as the Video BIOS Extension (VBE), allows all monitors that support it to be programmed the same way. This greatly simplifies the task of programming today's powerful monitors. While this standard was first set in 1989, it is only now beginning to really catch on. At the time this is being written most new monitor types do support the standard, but only a year ago that was not true. At that time those monitor manufacturers that did support the standard would often provide a disk with software on it to make the monitor look VESA VBE compliant. But the software was often buggy and things were not very satisfactory. This situation looks like it is changing and more and more manufacturers are producing video cards with the VBE built in. The capabilities defined by this standard are shown at the end of this chapter, but actually using the standard to program graphics is covered in detail in Chapter 9.

IBM monitor systems come in two parts. There is the monitor itself, and a card that contains circuitry for controlling the monitor and the memory for the frame buffer. Most of the time when referring to a PC monitor, both the card and the monitor are being referred to.

The Hercules Monitor

The Hercules monitor is a high quality monochrome graphics monitor made by the Hercules company for IBM PC clones. It is the simplest of the PC graphics monitors. In most ways it is very much like the monochrome monitor discussed earlier. It has 720 pixels across by 348 pixels down and four shades of gray. Therefore it has $720 \times 348 \times 2$ or 501120 bits, or 31,320 bytes of RAM per page. It has two pages.

The Hercules monitor does not enjoy the full support of the operating system (BIOS), and thus many of the things we will be doing later in this book will be difficult to do on this card. The Hercules is supported by Turbo C, however, which allows most of its features to be used.

---

[1] The Video Electronics Standards Association is the international, non-profit organization which sets and supports industry-wide video graphics standards for the benefit of the end user. VESA's membership consists of manufacturers of monitors, peripherals, systems and software products. The VESA offices are located at 2150 North First Street, Suite 440, San Jose, CA 95131-2029, and can be reached at (408) 435-0333, FAX (408) 435-8225.

Graphics Displays

The CGA Monitor

The CGA monitor was IBM's first PC color graphics monitor. Because it was the first it is crude, hard to use, and the colors it produces are not very good. This is not because monitor technology in the early 1980s was so bad. This is because the price of RAM was quite high and things were done to save as much RAM as possible. This means that there was not enough to hold the data needed to make a good looking display or to make it easier to program.

With the CGA monitor we have to introduce the idea of modes. The IBM color monitors have different modes, which allow for different functionality from a single monitor. One mode might allow for only text to be displayed while saving on memory. Another mode might allow for graphics, but need far more memory, be more limited in the colors it can display, and be much slower when displaying text. Modes allow application software to get the most out of a monitor. Not all programs need the same monitor capabilities. Modes allow the program to "customize" the monitor. All monitors are downward compatible, that is, they all support the modes of the monitors that came before. Since the Hercules is not really an IBM monitor, no other monitor shares the same graphics modes. Table 1.3.1 gives the modes of the CGA monitor.

Table 1.3.1 CGA Modes

Mode Number	Description
0x00	Text, 16 colors, 40 characters per line, 25 lines
0x01	Text, 16 colors, 40 characters per line, 25 lines
0x02	Text, 16 colors, 80 characters per line, 25 lines
0x03	Text, 16 colors, 80 characters per line, 25 lines
0x04	Graphics, 4 Colors, 320 pixels by 200 pixels, low resolution, 1 page
0x05	Graphics, 4 Colors, 320 pixels by 200 pixels low resolution, 1 page
0x06	Graphics, 2 colors, 640 pixels by 200 pixels medium resolution, 1 page

CGA Text Modes

Table 1.3.1 needs some explanation. The first two modes, 0 and 1, look the same. They are. And so are modes 2 and 3, and so are 4 and 5. The reason for having these modes is not entirely clear. It probably seemed like a good idea at the time.

Notice that some modes are text and some are graphics. In the text modes only text can be displayed. In graphics modes both text and graphics can be displayed. The first four modes display text in 16 colors, and 8 colors are available for the background. These 16 foreground colors are (in order) BLACK, BLUE, GREEN, CYAN, RED, MAGENTA, BROWN, LIGHTGRAY, DARKGRAY, LIGHTBLUE, LIGHTGREEN, LIGHTCYAN, LIGHTRED, LIGHTMAGENTA, YELLOW, and WHITE. Turbo and Microsoft C define constants for each color exactly as shown here, with the light red as one word, and all in caps. The background color can be any one of the first eight.

Also notice that the information given for the types of modes is different. Text modes do not give the number of pixels, colors, or pages. That is because for text modes you cannot access individual pixels, only characters; the colors are the same for all text modes, and there is only one page. In graphics mode you can change any single pixel on the screen. The screen in text mode is called *all points addressable.* Different graphics modes handle colors differently. The palette registers are larger for some modes than for others. Finally, with CGA monitors there is only one page for any graphics mode, but other monitors have modes that support more pages. Details of the graphics modes are given next.

CGA Low Resolution Modes (4 Colors)

The CGA in low resolution is a strange beast. While it behaves similar to the general color graphics monitor described earlier, it does some things in an unusual way. There are four available colors in this mode; that is, there are four palette registers, but what colors might appear on the screen together is predefined. That is, if you want the color red to appear on your screen, the other colors that you can use are limited to green, brown, and a background color that you can choose. Each combination of colors in CGA terms is called a *palette.* Note that this use of the term *palette* is somewhat different than how it is used elsewhere in this book. Here a palette is the set of all colors that can appear on the screen at one time. Change the palette, and all colors on the screen change. Elsewhere in this book the term *palette* is used to mean a description of a single color or one palette register. Change that type of palette and only one color on the screen changes. In CGA terms a palette is a set of predefined palette registers.

When the monitor is put into this mode you have a choice of two palettes. Each palette has three predefined colors and a background color, which is chosen by the programmer. This color defaults to black. The first palette has green, red, and brown; the second palette has cyan, magenta, and light gray. In addition to these two palettes, a bit can be set that tells the monitor to set the electron guns on high. When this is done the color combinations become light green, light red, and yellow; or light cyan, light magenta, and white. If these choices of colors sound annoying, they are. Fortunately the CGA monitor is becoming rather rare, and we can spend most of our time studying more sophisticated monitors with better colors and easier methods for programming.

In this mode there are 320 pixels horizontally across the monitor, and 200 vertically down the monitor.

The CGA Medium Resolution Mode (Two Colors)

The CGA monitor supports a mode that allows for two colors. In this mode there are 640 pixels across and 200 down. This is a great improvement in resolution over the low res modes, but this improvement is offset by the fact that only two colors can be displayed – normally black and white – and that these colors only have a single intensity. This is similar to the simple monochrome monitor describe in the first section of this chapter.

The EGA Monitor

The Enhanced Graphics Monitor was the next step forward from the CGA monitor. As such, this monitor supports the same modes as the CGA. It also supports a number of new modes, which operate much more like our general monitor. Table 1.3.2 introduces these modes.

Table 1.3.2 EGA Modes

Mode Number	Description
0x06	Graphics, 2 colors out of 64, 640 pixels by 200 pixels medium resolution, 1 page
0x07	Text, 4 colors, 80 characters per line, 25 lines
0x0D	Graphics, 16 colors out of 64, 320 pixels by 200 pixels low resolution, 1 page
0x0E	Graphics, 16 colors out of 64, 640 pixels by 200 pixels medium resolution, 4 pages.
0x0F	Graphics, 4 colors, 640 pixels by 350 pixels medium resolution, 1 page
0x10	Graphics, 16 colors out of 64, 640 pixels by 350 pixels medium resolution, 2 pages

Not all of these modes will be covered in detail. Turbo C supports modes 6, 13, 14, 15, and 16. Since mode 16 allows for 16 colors in medium resolution, while mode 15 only supports 4 colors with the same resolution, it seems likely that mode 16 will be used far more often. In fact, mode 16 is really the only important mode from our point of view.

EGA Mode 16 Medium Resolution (16 Colors)

Mode 16 on the EGA makes use of 16 palette registers. Each register is 6 bits wide. The first 2 bits control the red gun, the next 2 bits the green gun, and the final 2 bits control the blue gun. Each gun has four levels of brightness. With all possible combinations of these levels, 64 colors are possible. There are 16 of these registers and therefore 16 colors can be displayed on the monitor at one time. Of the modes listed in table 1.3.2, modes 13 and 14 work basically the same, only with a different number of pixels on the screen. Mode 6 has fewer pixels and only two palette registers, so only 2 colors can appear on the screen at one time.

The MCGA Monitor

The MCGA monitor was developed by IBM at about the same time as the EGA. The EGA is not actually an IBM product, but, fortunately, there was enough industry support for it to become a standard. The MCGA never caught on as an industry standard, and is mostly found on low-end PS/2s (models 25 and 30). This is important to know for two reasons. The MCGA does not support EGA modes because it is not a newer, improved monitor. It was developed more or less in parallel with the EGA. Also, Turbo C does not support the MCGA. The MCGA does support CGA modes, however, and when programming this monitor using Turbo C these modes are the easiest to use. Microsoft does a better job at supporting this monitor.

There is one new mode introduced by the MCGA. Mode 19 makes use of 256 palette registers, each of which is 18 bits wide. This allows for 256 colors to be displayed from a possible 262,144. This is a low resolution mode with 320 pixels by 200 pixels. This mode can be used to make very colorful displays, and even though it is a low resolution mode, it can be used to make very realistic looking displays.

The VGA Monitor

This is the last monitor standard set by IBM. This monitor supports all the modes of the CGA, EGA and MCGA. In addition it supports a high resolution 16 color mode, mode 18. This mode has 16 palette registers. Each register is 18 bits wide, 6 bits for each color. This allows for 16 colors from a possible 262,144. The resolution in this mode is 640 pixels by 480 pixels. This mode is supported by Turbo C and Microsoft C, and will be the mode most commonly used in this book. Remember that while this monitor does support the MCGA 256 color mode, Turbo C does not. The later chapters in this book talk about getting around Turbo's limitation to take full advantage of this mode. Table 1.3.3 lists the modes supported by the VGA monitor. This table can also be found in Appendix D.

Table 1.3.3 All Modes CGA - VGA

Mode	Minimu m Adapter	Text/ Graphics	Pixels/ Characters	Colors	Pages
0x0	CGA	Text	40 × 25	16 fore/ 8 back	
0x0	CGA	Text	40 × 25	16 fore/ 8 back	
0x0	CGA	Text	80 × 25	16 fore/ 8 back	
0x0	CGA	Text	80 × 25	16 fore/ 8 back	
0x04	CGA	Graphics	320 × 200	4 (CGA palette)	1
0x05	CGA	Graphics	320 × 200	4 (CGA palette)	1
0x06	CGA	Graphics	640 × 200	2	1
0x07	EGA	Text	80 × 25	4 (CGA palette)	
0x0D	EGA	Graphics	320 × 200	16 out of 64 16/256K (VGA)	1
0x0E	EGA	Graphics	640 × 200	16 out of 64 16/256K (VGA)	4
0x0F	EGA	Graphics	640 × 350	4	1
0x10	EGA	Graphics	640 × 350	16 out of 64 16/256K (VGA)	2
0x11	VGA	Graphics	640 × 480	16 out of 256K	1
0x12	VGA	Graphics	640 × 480	16 out of 256K	1
0x13	VGA	Graphics	320 × 200	256 out of 256K	1

SVGA Monitors

It was 1987 when IBM defined its last monitor standard, the VGA. Since then technology has grown tremendously, and the need for newer, more powerful monitor types was seen many years ago. But IBM had lost its ability to control the market. So a number of manufacturers started producing monitors with more advanced capabilities, but none of these monitors had the same capabilities, nor were they programmed the same way, which made these monitors difficult to use from a programmer's standpoint. The programmer had to know a great deal about the hardware each monitor used, and provide code to support each type.

Then in 1989 VESA was organized by a number of manufacturers and "interested parties" to develop standards that are simple to program, and yet powerful and flexible enough to support the monitors that were then being developed and those yet to be developed. They released their first standard, the Video BIOS Extension, version 1.0 in October of that year. This standard has slowly gained acceptance. When VESA was first formed it was fairly small, but gradually it gained more members, and as it did, its work gained more acceptance. The time has now finally arrived when the programmer can expect an SVGA graphics card to support the VBE.

The original version of the VBE, released in 1989, defined seven modes, starting with mode 0x100 (100 hex, throughout this book we will use the C standard notation for hex.). The latest update, version 1.2, which was released in 1991, defines 20 more modes. Today only the best and most expensive monitors are capable of supporting the best of these modes. It looks like this standard will be the standard for some years to come.

The original modes defined by VBE 1.0 used 256 palette registers, the same as the MCGA, while VBE 1.2 defined more powerful text modes, and modes that have done away with the palette registers. As RAM has become cheaper it has now become possible to use a large number of bits for each electron gun and for each pixel in the frame buffer. The graphics modes defined by VBE 1.2 do this. Modes of this type are referred to throughout this book as "direct color modes," since the colors are represented directly in the frame buffer, rather than in indirectly accessed palette registers. Table 1.3.4 shows the modes defined by the VBE, along with the VBE version number where the mode was defined.

Table 1.3.4 SVGA Monitor modes

VESA VBE Version	Mode	Graphics/ Text	Pixels/ Characters	Colors
1.0	0x100	Graphics	640 × 400	256 out of 256K
	0x101	Graphics	640 × 480	256 out of 256K
	0x102	Graphics	800 × 600	16 out of 256K
	0x103	Graphics	800 × 600	256 out of 256K
	0x104	Graphics	1024 × 768	16 out of 256K
	0x105	Graphics	1024 × 768	256 out of 256K
	0x106	Graphics	1280 × 1024	16 out of 256K
	0x107	Graphics	1280 × 1024	256 out of 256K
1.1	0x108	Text	80 × 60	8
	0x109	Text	132 × 25	8
	0x10A	Text	132 × 43	8
	0x10B	Text	132 × 50	8
	0x10C	Text	132 × 60	8
1.2	0x10D	Graphics	320 × 200	15 bit
	0x10E	Graphics	320 × 200	16 bit
	0x10F	Graphics	320 × 200	24 bit
	0x110	Graphics	640 × 480	15 bit
	0x111	Graphics	640 × 480	16 bit
	0x112	Graphics	640 × 480	24 bit
	0x113	Graphics	800 × 600	15 bit
	0x114	Graphics	800 × 600	16 bit
	0x115	Graphics	800 × 600	24 bit
	0x116	Graphics	1024 × 768	15 bit
	0x117	Graphics	1024 × 768	16 bit
	0x118	Graphics	1024 × 768	24 bit
	0x119	Graphics	1280 × 1024	15 bit
	0x11A	Graphics	1280 × 1024	16 bit
	0x11B	Graphics	1280 × 1024	24 bit

2

The Borland Graphics Interface

Graphics programming is a complex task. The graphics programmer needs to be able to create a number of shapes, colors, and patterns on the monitor. Different monitors have different characteristics. Different code is needed for each monitor type on which a graphics program will run. Fortunately, Borland has done quite a bit to lighten the load.

Borland C provides a set of routines that are automatically linked into programs when they are needed. This set of routines is called the *run-time library*. The run-time library contains interfaces to a set of graphics routines. The code for the routines is not kept in the run-time library, but in separate files on the disk. This allows the program to figure out the monitor type AT RUN TIME, and bring in only the code needed for the monitor being used. This allows the executable file to be much smaller, saving valuable RAM. This graphics system is called the *Borland Graphics Interface*, or *BGI*.

To use the graphics library, it is necessary to include a header file named "graphics.h". This file contains constant definitions and function prototypes needed by the graphics library and the BGI. At this point you might be wondering what the difference is between the graphics library and the BGI. In this text, *graphics library* refers to code contained in the run-time library. Nothing special needs to be done to load this code. *BGI* refers to the code that is kept on the disk until needed. This is the code that is loaded as the program is running.

Each monitor type has its own file, which contains the code needed for that monitor. The Borland Graphics Interface files have the extension ".BGI". The graphics library provides routines to detect the type of monitor, load the correct .BGI file, set the monitor to graphics mode, and draw graphics. The run-time library code makes calls to the BGI. It should be noted here that when referring to this system BGI means the system itself, and .BGI means the files where code is kept.

Sometimes it can be annoying to need a file separate from the program. If you are writing a program for distribution, such as to a customer, the needed .BGI file can be easily misplaced. To avoid this the .BGI file can be linked into your program to create one executable file. The method for doing this is covered at the end of this chapter.

Graphics programs often need text. With graphics, not only can you create text, you have a variety of styles and sizes from which to choose. You can even write text sideways! This is accomplished in Borland C programs in a manner similar to the way that graphics are programmed. There is a set of separate files, the .CHR files, that hold code for making text. There are separate .CHR files for each style. Calls are made to routines in the graphics unit to load the .CHR file and write text on the screen. Text is covered in detail in Chapter 3.

Setting Up to do Graphics

initgraph( ) and detectgraph( )

Before any graphics can be put on the screen, the monitor must be changed from text to graphics mode. Different monitors support different modes. The first graphics monitors (the CGA monitor) were not very capable. Later monitors had better capabilities, but needed to support programs that only ran on older monitors. All graphics monitors support more than one mode, and the more advanced monitors, such as the VGA, support many modes. After practicing graphics programming for a while you will become familiar with the different modes, how they look, and how they act. Until then, the mode with the highest resolution is usually the easiest to use for good looking results.

The BGI has a routine that will detect what type of monitor the program is running on and set it to its highest resolution. This routine is called detectgraph( ). It has two parameters. The first one is an integer that represents the monitor type. A preferred monitor type can be selected by using a predefined constant. By telling this routine that you have a CGA monitor when you really have a VGA monitor you can "fake it out." The graphics system will think it really is a CGA, and use the CGA modes. Of course, you lose the abilities of the more powerful monitors when you do this. If this parameter is zero then Borland C will determine the type of monitor on the system. Table 2.1.1, on the next page, shows the constants and their meanings. The second parameter passes back an integer representing the best mode to use for the selected monitor. Here is the prototype for this function:

```
void far detectgraph (int far *graphdriver,
                      int far *mode);
  /*
   * detectgraph() will determine what type of
   *   monitor the system has.  It will then
   *   determine the mode with the highest
   *   resolution.
   *
   * Parameters:
   *   graphdriver - The type of monitor being
   *     used.  If DETECT (0) is used, the type
   *     of monitor is detected and passed
   *     back.
   *   mode - The mode with the highest
   *     resolution for the selected monitor.
   */
```

Now that Borland C knows what mode to use, the monitor needs to be put into graphics mode. The initgraph( ) function does this. This function also loads the appropriate .BGI file. Function initgraph( ) takes three parameters. One for the monitor type, one for the mode, and the third is a path name telling it where the .BGI file can be found on the disk. The monitor type is the same as the monitor type for detectgraph( ), with the exception that DETECT cannot be used. The mode is also the same as that returned by detectgraph( ). It's kind of neat that they work together that way. Table 2.1.1 on the next page gives the modes for each monitor type. The path is the DOS path; that is the directories under the root directory where the .BGI file is located. If the directory will be the default directory a null string can be used.

DOS path names use the backslash character, as do C strings, to represent an escape character. If you need to represent a backslash inside a C string use two back slashes; thus, "\\" means the root directory.

Here is initgraph( ) defined:

```
void far initgraph (int  far *graphdriver,
                    int  far *mode,
                    char far *pathtodriver);
  /*
   * initgraph() will load the proper BGI
   *   driver, then set the monitor to the
   *   proper mode.
   *
   * Parameters:
   *   graphdriver  - BGI driver to be used
   *   mode         - What mode should be used.
   *   pathtodriver - location of BGI file on
   *                  the hard disk.
   */
```

The parameters to detectgraph( ) and initgraph( ) are all pointers. This means constants cannot be passed in, only addresses of variables. When the function needs a value, it is placed into a variable, and the address of that variable is passed.

The graphics library defines a set of integer constants that the preceeding routines can use as monitor types. Table 2.1.1 gives the constant name, its numeric value, and the .BGI file needed for that monitor.

Table 2.1.1 Monitor Types Defined by the BGI

Constant Name	Numeric Value	BGI Driver Needed
DETECT	0 (Request Autodetection)	Depends on Monitor Type
CGA	1	CGA.BGI
MCGA	2	CGA.BGI
EGA	3	EGAVGA.BGI
EGA64	4	EGAVGA.BGI
EGAMONO	5	EGAVGA.BGI
IBM8514	6	IBM8514.BGI
HERCMONO	7	HERC.BGI
ATT400	8	ATT.BGI
VGA	9	EGAVGA.BGI
PC3270	10	PC3270.BGI

Considering that Chapter 1 talks about five monitor types, there is a surprising variety of monitor types in this table. The first one, DETECT, tells detectgraph( ) to determine which constant to use. EGA monitors can use several different constants. All these modes will work on any EGA card with a color monitor. At one time laptop computers with EGA cards and monochrome LCD monitors were common. EGAMONO is the preferred constant for these monitors. The IBM8514, the ATT400, and the PC3270 are three monitor types that have different capabilities than the VGA. These monitors are not standard, and so will not be discussed further in this book. Once the basic concepts of graphics programming are understood they can be applied to these or any other monitor types.

Table 2.1.2 is a table of constants for each mode. The numeric values are used over again with different monitor types. If you intend to use these constants directly, rather than using detectgraph( ), make sure that the monitor is in the correct mode. If the monitor does not support the mode passed to initgraph( ), the call will fail.

Table 2.1.2 Monitor Modes Supported by the BGI

Driver	**Mode Name**	**Numeric Value**	**Cols**	**Rows**	**Palette**	**Pages**
CGA	CGAC0	0	320	200	C0	1
	CGAC1	1	320	200	C1	1
	CGAC2	2	320	200	C2	1
	CGAC3	3	320	200	C3	1
	CGAHI	4	640	200	2 Colors	1
MCGA	MCGAC0	0	320	200	C0	1
	MCGAC1	1	320	200	C0	1
	MCGAC2	2	320	200	C0	1
	MCGAC3	3	320	200	C0	1
	MCGAMED	4	640	200	2 Colors	1
	MCGAHI	5	640	480	2 Colors	1
EGA	EGALO	0	640	200	16 Colors	4
	EGAHI	1	640	350	16 Colors	2

Driver	Mode Name	Numeric Value	Cols	Rows	Palette	Pages
EGA64	EGA64LO	0	640	200	16 color	1
	EGA64HI	1	640	350	4 color	1
EGA-MONO	EGAMONOHI	3	640	350	2 color	1
	EGAMONOHI	3	640	350	2 color	2
HERC	HERCMONOHI	0	720	348	2 color	2
ATT400	ATT400C0	0	320	200	C0	1
	ATT400C1	1	320	200	C1	1
	ATT400C2	2	320	200	C2	1
	ATT400C3	3	320	200	C3	1
	ATT400MED	4	640	200	2 Color	1
	ATT400HI	5	640	400	2 Color	1
VGA	VGALO	0	640	200	16 Color	2
	VGAMED	1	640	350	16 Color	2
	VGAHI	2	640	480	16 Color	1
PC3270	PC3270HI	0	720	350	2 Color	1
IBM8514	IBM8514LO	0	640	480	256 Color	1
	IBM8514HI	1	1024	768	256 Color	1

Here is an example of code for detecting the monitor type and setting it to the highest resolution mode:

```
#include <graphics.h>

void main(void) {
    int Mode, Driver, GraphError;

    Driver = DETECT;
    detectgraph(&Driver, &Mode);
    initgraph(&Driver, &Mode, '');
```

```
                    .
                    .
                    .
}
```

The integer variable Driver is given the value DETECT. This tells detectgraph( ) to determine what type of monitor to use. The detected monitor type is passed back in Driver. The mode with the highest resolution for the detected monitor type is passed back in Mode. The monitor type and the selected mode are then passed to initgraph( ). An empty string is passed as the path for the .BGI file. This tells initgraph( ) to look at the current directory for the .BGI file. The preceeding code is a good way to start any graphics program that might run on more than one monitor. You will see it used quite often throughout this book.

graphresult( ) and grapherrormsg( )

A call to initgraph( ) will fail if the proper .BGI file is not on the given path. What happens when it fails? This does not cause the program to "crash" or stop running. Instead the program will continue until the next call to a graphics routine is made. Then a run-time error will occur causing the program to stop running. The message `"BGI Error:  Graphics not initialized (use initgraph)"` will be displayed. This can be confusing. The initgraph( ) function was called. Borland provides a function just for such an occasion. Function graphresult( ) returns an error code. Table 2.1.3 gives the possible return values and what they mean.

Table 2.1.3 Error Codes Used by the BGI

Error Code	Constant	Meaning
0	grOk	No error
-1	grNoInitGraph	(BGI) graphics not installed (use InitGraph)
-2	grNotDetected	Graphics hardware not detected
-3	grFileNotFound	Device driver not found
-4	grInvalidDriver	Invalid device driver file
-5	grNoLoadMem	Not enough memory to load driver
-6	grNoScanMem	Out of memory in scan fill
-7	grNoFloodMem	Out of memory in flood fill
-8	grFontNotFound	Font file not found
-9	grNoFontMem	Not enough memory to load font
-10	grInvalidMode	Invalid graphics mode for selected driver
-11	grError	Graphics Error
-12	grIOerror	Graphics I/O error
-13	grInvalidFont	Invalid font file
-14	grInvalidFontNum	Invalid font number
-15	grInvalidDeviceNum	Invalid device number
-18	grInvalidVersion	Invalid version number

If a call to graphresult( ) returns grOk then the last graphics call was successful, otherwise it failed. This function also resets the error level, so a second call will always return grOk. As you can see by a quick glance at the table, this function covers a wide range of graphics routines, not just initgraph( ).

Suppose a call to a graphics routine just failed. It would be handy to print an error message on the screen, relevant to the error that occurred. Borland has provided a function for this. The function grapherrormsg( ) will return a string describing the error, which can be printed. The program can then take the appropriate corrective action without terminating.

Here are definitions for graphresult( ) and grapherrormsg( ):

```
int far graphresult(void);
```

```
  /*
   * graphresult() returns an error code for
   *   the last graphics routine called, and
   *   resets the error level to grOk.
   */

char * far grapherrormsg (int errorcode);
  /*
   * grapherrormsg() returns a string
   *   describing the error associated with the
   *   error code passed in.
   *
   * Parameter:
   *   errorcode - integer of error returned by
   *     graphresult.
   */
```

An example using these routines follows the section on closegraph( ).

getgraphmode( ), setgraphmode( )

After setting the monitor with initgraph( ), the mode that the monitor is in can be found using the function getgraphmode( ). This mode can be changed without calling initgraph( ) and reloading the .BGI file, by using setgraphmode( ). Here are definitions for these two routines:

```
int far getgraphmode(void);
  /*
   * getgraphmode() returns the mode that the
   *   monitor is currently in.
   */

void far setgraphmode (int Mode);
  /*
   * setgraphmode() will change the mode that
   *   the monitor is currently in.
   */
```

Function setgraphmode( ) will not change the .BGI driver that is currently loaded. In order to do that another call to initgraph( ) is needed. This means that the modes setgraphmode( ) can use are limited to those supported by the currently loaded .BGI file.

closegraph( )

Before exiting a program it would be nice to set the monitor back to text mode. This is accomplished using closegraph( ). Here is its definition:

```
void closegraph(void);
    /*
     * closegraph() sets the monitor to text
     *   mode.
     */
```

By using initgraph( ) and closegraph( ) repeatedly you can toggle between text and graphics modes.

Here is an example program to demonstrate some of the functions we have discussed. It does not print any graphics on the screen, but it does do the following: detects what monitor the computer has using detectgraph( ); sets the monitor to graphics mode using initgraph( ); determines if the call to initgraph( ) was successful using graphresult( ); if not it prints an error message, otherwise it returns the screen to text mode and exits. This program is a good template from which to build graphics programs. Place calls to functions under the comment "/* Do Graphics Stuff Here */". A good way to write you first graphics program would be to type in this program with one of the procedures given in the next section.

```
/*
 * Shell for graphics programs
 */

#include <graphics.h>

void main(void) {
    int Mode, Driver, GraphError;

    Driver = DETECT;
    detectgraph(&Driver, &Mode);
    initgraph(&Driver, &Mode, '');

    GraphError = graphresult();
    if (GraphError != grOk) {
        printf("%s\n",
                grapherrormsg(GraphError));
        exit(-1);
    }

    /* Do Graphics Stuff Here */
```

```
closegraph();
}
```

Graphics Primitives

Pixels and putpixel( )

What is a pixel? Pixel stands for *picture element*, which is the smallest dot that can be drawn on the screen. Chapter 1 gives a detailed explanation of how a pixel is generated, and why nothing smaller can be drawn.

Pixels are placed on the screen in a grid, something like the spaces on graph paper. Drawing pictures on the screen is something like making a drawing on graph paper by filling in the squares. Cartesian coordinates are used to specify pixels on the screen. The origin of our Cartesian plane is the upper left-hand corner of the screen. This is somewhat unexpected. One would expect (0,0) to be the lower left-hand corner, where it usually is when drawing a graph. Another likely location is the center of the screen, as when drawing a graph with negative coordinates. This arrangement is not hard to get used to, however.

When drawing on a screen the programmer must be concerned with how many pixels will fit on the screen. On the VGA monitor in VGAHI mode there are 640 pixels across the screen and 480 down the screen. This is called the *resolution*. The resolution changes with the mode. VGAMED is 640 × 350, and VGALO is 320 × 200.

One would think that pixels are round or square. This would simplify the problem of drawing shapes on the screen. But because of the different number of pixels available in different modes, pixels cannot be square in all modes. The pixels in VGAHI mode are square, but in all other modes they are rectangular. The ratio of the length to the width of a pixel is called the *aspect ratio*. To be precise, the aspect ratio is the size of the pixel in the X dimension divided by its size in the Y dimension. A square pixel has an aspect ratio of 1. In a mode where the aspect ratio is not 1, this must be taken into account. If a circle is drawn without considering the aspect ratio, it will turn into an oval. Fortunately Borland's graphics routines automatically take the aspect ratio into account. There are two functions for dealing with the aspect ratio – getaspectratio( ) and setaspectratio( ) – but they are rarely ever needed, since BGI routines automatically adjust for aspect ratio. These routines are not discussed here.

In addition to resolution and aspect ratio, pixels have color. The VGAHI mode allows for 16 colors to be displayed at one time. These 16 colors have predefined constants associated with them, as shown in Table 2.2.1.

Table 2.2.1 Color Constants Defined by the BGI

Dark Colors	Numeric Value	Light Colors	Numeric Value
BLACK	0	DARKGRAY	8
BLUE	1	LIGHTBLUE	9
GREEN	2	LIGHTGREEN	10
CYAN	3	LIGHTCYAN	11
RED	4	LIGHTRED	12
MAGENTA	5	LIGHTMAGENTA	13
BROWN	6	YELLOW	14
LIGHTGRAY	7	WHITE	15

Any time the screen is in a 16-color mode, whether it is an EGA or a VGA, it can use the constants in this table. For more discussion on how colors are displayed or modes that support 16 colors, see Chapter 1. It is possible to change the available colors. Chapter 5 explains how this is done.

The function for displaying a pixel is called putpixel( ). Its definition is :

```
void far putpixel (int x, int y, int color);
  /*
   * putpixel() lights a pixel on the screen
   *
   * Parameters:
   *   x     - the x coordinate of the pixel.
   *   y     - the Y coordinate of the pixel.
   *   color - the color the pixel will be
   *           displayed in.
   */
```

getmaxx( ), getmaxy( ) and getmaxcolor( )

If a pixel is put at a coordinate that is off the screen nothing happens. That's not to bad when only one pixel does not show up, but this also happens with many other routines. When a circle or line doesn't show up the picture might be completely altered. Oftentimes when using detectgraph( ), the programmer does not know where the edge of the screen is. On the VGA in high-res mode (VGAHI) the bottom-most pixel is at 480, but on the CGA in two-color mode the bottom most pixel is at 200. The getmaxx( ) and getmaxy( ) functions return the maximum X and Y coordinates, respectively.

A program that is written to run on a number of monitor systems will not know what mode the monitor is in until it is running. We do not know when we are writing such a program how many pixels the monitor has, or how many colors it can use. The functions getmaxx( ) and getmaxy( ) will return the number of pixels in the X and Y dimensions, respectively. The getmaxcolor( ) function returns the number of colors available in the current mode. Here are prototypes for these functions:

```
int far getmaxx(void);
    /*
     * getmaxx() returns the maximum X
     *   coordinate.
     */

int far getmaxy(void);
    /*
     * getmaxy() returns the maximum Y
     *   coordinate.
     */

int far getmaxcolor(void);
    /*
     * getmaxcolor() returns the number of the
     *   highest color available
     */
```

cleardevice( )

After drawing a picture on the screen it is sometimes handy to clear the screen. The function clearscr( ) is used in text mode, but it doesn't work in graphics mode. The function cleardevice( ) is used instead:

```
void cleardevice(void);
    /*
     * cleardevice() clears the graphics screen
     */
```

Here is an example using putpixel( ), getmaxx( ) and getmaxy( ), getmaxcolor( ), and cleardevice( ):

```
#include <graphics.h>
#include <stdio.h>
#include <stdlib.h>
```

```
#include <conio.h>

void PutPixel_Demo() {

/*
 * This procedure puts a number of pixels on
 *   the screen at random locations
 */

    int  MaxX, MaxY, Count;

    randomize();
    MaxX = getmaxx();
    MaxY = getmaxy();
    for (Count=0; Count < 5000; Count++)
        putpixel (random(MaxX), random(MaxY),
        Count % getmaxcolor());

    /* Read a keypress from the keyboard. Some
       keys (such as F1) return 2 characters.
       If one of these was pressed, read the
       second character.  Finally clear the
       screen.  These three lines appear
       constantly throughout the book.
    */
    getch();
    if (kbhit()) getch();
    closegraph();

} /* end function PutPixel_Demo() */
```

This procedure lights 5000 pixels on the screen in different colors, then waits for the user to press a key. Random is used to set the X and Y coordinates. The third parameter to putpixel( ) is "Count % getmaxcolor( )". This will take the value of count and perform a modulo using the maximum number of colors. This way the pixels being displayed will cycle through all the available colors.

A word should be said about the two lines before the call to closegraph( ). The call to getch( ) waits for the user to press a key. This is a simple enough way to cause the program to wait until the user is ready to go on. But there is a quirk with the PC keyboard. Certain keys, such as the function keys or the cursor keys, return two characters. The kbhit( ) function is used to determine if one of these of keys was pressed. If so the extra character is read. If this is not done the next time getch( ) is called the program will not pause. This method is used throughout the book, whenever there is a need for the program to pause for the user.

Lines

Writing a good line drawing procedure is not easy. One must draw lines that have a constant thickness, meet both endpoints, and work with any slope. It must also be very quick. If a large number of lines have to be drawn the difference between a good line procedure and a poor one is all too apparent. Of course Borland has provided us with a good line drawing routine. Here is the function prototype:

```
void far line (int x1, int y1, int x2, int y2);
  /*
   * line() will draw a line from one
   *   coordinate to another
   *
   * Parameters:
   *  x1 - X of the first coordinate.
   *  y1 - Y of the first coordinate.
   *  x2 - X of the second coordinate.
   *  y2 - Y of the second coordinate.
   */
```

This function is fairly straightforward. There are two endpoints, and each one has an X and Y coordinate. A line will be drawn between them. But the color is missing! There is a default color used by line( ) and a number of other procedures. The function getcolor( ) returns what this default color is, and the procedure setcolor( ) will set a new one.

```
int far getcolor(void) : Word;
  /*
   * getcolor() will return the default
   *   drawing color
   */

void far setcolor (int Color);
  /*
   * setcolor will set the default drawing
   *  color
   *
   * Parameters:
   *   Color - The color that the default
   *           will be set to
   */
```

The related routines getbkcolor( ) and setbkcolor( ) do the same for the background color. Note that the constant BLACK means the background color. When the background color is changed to something other than black, a pixel plotted with the color constant BLACK will not appear black, but as whatever color the background is set to. When this pixel is plotted directly on the background it will not show up at all! This can be frustrating, since graphresult( ) returns grOk. Everything worked correctly, but nothing showed up on the screen! In most cases DARKGRAY can be substituted for BLACK. DARKGRAY looks black against most other colors.

A procedure is given at the end of the next section to demonstrate these.

```
int far getbkcolor(void);
  /*
   * getbkcolor() returns the background color
   */

void setbkcolor (int Color);
  /*
   * setcolor() sets the background color
   *
   * Parameters:
   *   Color - The color that the background
   *           will be set to
   */
```

lineto( ), linerel( ), moveto( ), moverel( )

Oftentimes it is convenient to draw a line from the point where the last line ended to a new point. The function moveto( ) will set a current point on the screen. The function lineto( ) will draw a line from the current point to another point, then make the second point the new current point. Function moverel( ) will move the current point to a position relative to the current point. If the current point is (50, 50) and the command moverel (-10, 10) is given the new current point will be (40, 60). Function linerel( ) will draw a line from the current point to a position relative to the current position, then set the new current position there. Always start with moveto( ) to make sure that the current point is where you think it is.

```
void far moveto (int x, int y);
  /*
   * moveto() will set the current drawing
   *   location
   *
   * Parameters:
   *   x - X coordinate to start drawing at
   *   y - Y coordinate to start drawing at
   */

void far lineto (int x, int y);
```

```
  /*
   * lineto() draws a line from the current
   *  position to coordinates (X,Y) then sets
   *  the current position to (X, Y)
   *
   * Parameters:
   *   x - X coordinate to start drawing at
   *   y - Y coordinate to start drawing at
   */

void far moverel (int x, int y);
  /*
   * moverel() changes the current drawing
   *   position by the number of pixels
   *   specified by X and Y
   *
   * Parameters:
   *   x - Number of pixels to move the
   *        current position in X dimension.
   *   y - Number of pixels to move the
   *        current position in Y dimension.
   */

void far linerel (int x, int y);
  /*
   * linerel() draws a line from the current
   *   position to a position specified by
   *   x, y; relative to the current
   *   position.  This is then made the new
   *   current position.
   *
   * Parameters:
   *   x - distance in the X dimension.
   *   y - distance in the Y dimension.
   */
```

To demonstrate, here is how a box can be drawn with these functions:

```
moveto  (1,1);     /* Set Start Position */
linerel (50, 0);   /* Draw a line 50 pixels to
                      to the right */
linerel (0, 50);   /* Draw a line 50 pixels
                      Down */
linerel (-50, 0); /* Draw a line 50 to the
                      left */
lineto  (1, 1);    /* Close the figure from
                      wherever I am */
```

Here is a function that will draw a series of lines in a diamond shape using line( ), then outlines the diamond using moveto( ), lineto( ) and linerel( ):

```
#include <graphics.h>
#include <stdio.h>
#include <stdlib.h>
#include <conio.h>

void Line_Demo() {

/*
 * This procedure draws lines on the screen in
 *   a diamond pattern, in various colors, then
 *   outlines the pattern with a white line.
 */

    int      X_Coord, Y_Coord, X_Center,
             Y_Center;
    unsigned int Color;

    X_Center = getmaxx() / 2;
    Y_Center = getmaxy() / 2;

    /* Draw lines in first quadrant */
    X_Coord  = X_Center;
    Y_Coord  = 1;
    while (Y_Coord < Y_Center) {
        Color = (Color + 1) % getmaxcolor();
        setcolor(Color);
        line (X_Center, Y_Center,
              X_Coord,  Y_Coord);
        Y_Coord += 3;
        X_Coord -= 3;
    } /* end while loop */

    /* Draw lines in Second quadrant */
    while (X_Coord < X_Center) {
        Color = (Color + 1) % getmaxcolor();
        setcolor(Color);
        line (X_Center, Y_Center,
              X_Coord, Y_Coord);
        Y_Coord += 3;
        X_Coord += 3;
    } /* end while loop */

    /* Draw lines in Third quadrant */
    while (Y_Coord > Y_Center) {
        Color = (Color + 1) % getmaxcolor();
```

```
        setcolor(Color);
        line (X_Center, Y_Center,
              X_Coord, Y_Coord);
        Y_Coord -= 3;
        X_Coord += 3;
    } /* end while loop */

    /* Draw lines in Fourth quadrant */
    while (X_Coord > X_Center) {
        Color = (Color + 1) % getmaxcolor();
        setcolor(Color);
        line (X_Center, Y_Center,
              X_Coord, Y_Coord);
        Y_Coord -= 3;
        X_Coord -= 3;
    } /* end while loop */

    /* Draw Border with LineTo and LineRel
       commands */
    setcolor(WHITE);
    moveto  (X_Center, 1);
    lineto  (X_Center+Y_Center, Y_Center);
    lineto  (X_Center, getmaxy());
    linerel (-Y_Center, -Y_Center);
    linerel (Y_Center, -Y_Center);

    getch();
    if (kbhit()) getch();
    cleardevice();

} /* end function Line_Demo() */
```

This function will draw a series of lines radiating from the center of the screen outward in a diamond shape, one quadrant at a time. It will then draw a white border around the diamond.

Circles, Ellipses, Arcs, and Sectors

Lines are not all there is to graphics. Many pictures contain circles, arcs, and other shapes, as well as lines. It is difficult to come up with a good efficient line algorithm. It is much more difficult to devise a good algorithm for drawing arcs. Again the BGI comes to the rescue. The function circle( ) is used to draw circles. Simply specify the center and the radius.

The function arc( ) draws a portion of a circle, using the same parameters, plus a start angle and an end angle. This function draws arcs in the counterclockwise direction; 0 degrees is at the right-hand side of the circle, and 90 degrees is at the top. A complete circle can be drawn by using a start angle of 0 and an end angle of 360.

Function ellipse( ) works like arc( ), but draws the arc of an ellipse rather than that of a circle. The ellipse( ) function uses the same parameters as arc( ), with the exception that instead of one radius parameter there are two, one for the X direction, one for Y. An entire ellipse can be drawn by making the start angle 0 and the end angle 360. This function is somewhat limited in that the major axis must be aligned with the X axis or the Y axis. If the X and Y radii are equal an arc of a circle is drawn.

It seems as if this procedure will handle all the work of the above routines. So why not just use it? Drawing an ellipse, even if the two radii are equal, requires more calculations than drawing a circle. If a number of circles are being drawn using this procedure it can be significantly slower than using the circle routine.

The sector( ) function draws an arc, then draws two lines connecting the edges to the center. This makes a pie slice shape on the screen. This function is useful for making pie charts, such as those found on spread sheets.

```
void far circle (int x, int y, int radius);
  /*
   * circle() draws a circle on the screen
   *
   * Parameters:
   *   x - X coordinate of the center
   *   y - Y coordinate of the center
   *   radius - the radius of the circle
   */

void far arc (int x, int y, int stangle,
              int endangle, int radius);
  /*
   * arc() draws an arc of a circle
   *
   * Parameters:
   *   x - X coordinate of the center
   *   y - Y coordinate of the center
   *   stangle - angle to start at - 0 is at 3
   *             o'clock
   *   endangle - angle to stop at - arc is
   *              drawn counterclockwise
   *   radius - the radius of the circle
   */

void far Ellipse (int x, int y,
                  int stangle, int endangle,
                  int xradius, int yradius);
```

```
    /*
     * ellipse() draws an arc of an ellipse
     *
     * Parameters:
     *   x - X coordinate of the center
     *   y - Y coordinate of the center
     *   stangle - angle to start at - 0 is at
     *             3 o'clock
     *   endangle - angle to stop at - arc is
     *              drawn counter-clockwise
     *   XRadius - the radius of the ellipse in
     *             the X dimension
     *   YRadius - the radius of the ellipse in
     *             the Y dimension
     */

void far sector (int x, int y,
                 int stangle, int endangle,
                 int xradius, int yradius);
    /*
     * sector() draws and fills an arc of an
     *   ellipse
     *
     * Parameters:
     *   x - X coordinate of the center
     *   y - Y coordinate of the center
     *   stangle - angle to start at - 0 is at
     *             3 o'clock
     *   endangle - angle to stop at - arc is
     *              drawn counter-clockwise
     *   XRadius - the radius of the ellipse in
     *             the X dimension
     *   YRadius - the radius of the ellipse in
     *             the Y dimension
     */
```

Here is an example of circles:

```
#include <graphics.h>
#include <stdio.h>
#include <stdlib.h>
#include <conio.h>

void Circle_Demo() {

/*
 * This procedure places circles of various
 *   sizes and colors on the screen
```

```
    */

        int  MaxX, MaxY, MaxRadius, MaxColor,
             Count;

        randomize();
        MaxX         = getmaxx();
        MaxY         = getmaxy();
        MaxRadius    = MaxY / 2;
        MaxColor     = getmaxcolor();

        for (Count = 0; Count < 50; Count++) {
            setcolor (Count % MaxColor);
            circle (random(MaxX), random(MaxY),
                    random(MaxRadius));
        } /* end for loop */

        getch();
        if (kbhit()) getch();
        cleardevice();

    } /* end function Circle_Demo() */
```

This is a simple procedure that draws a series of circles on the screen in random locations and with random sizes. Here is a demonstration of ellipses:

```
#include <graphics.h>
#include <stdio.h>
#include <stdlib.h>
#include <conio.h>

void Ellipse_Demo() {

/*
 * This procedure places a series of ellipses
 *   on the screen, centered at the same point,
 *   but with varying x and y radii
 */

    int  X_Center, Y_Center, MaxRadius,
         MaxColor, Color,
         X_Rad,    Y_Rad;

    X_Center  = getmaxx() / 2;
    Y_Center  = getmaxy() / 2;
    MaxRadius = Y_Center;
    MaxColor  = getmaxcolor();
    X_Rad     = MaxRadius;
```

```
    Y_Rad      = 0;
    Color      = 0;

    while (X_Rad > 1) {
        Color = (Color + 1) % MaxColor;
        setcolor (Color);
        X_Rad -= 3;
        Y_Rad += 3;
        ellipse (X_Center, Y_Center, 0, 360,
                 X_Rad, Y_Rad);
    } /* end while loop */

    getch();
    if (kbhit()) getch();
    cleardevice();

} /* end function Ellipse_Demo() */
```

This procedure makes a series of ellipses on the screen, all centered on the center of the screen, and varying the X and Y radii inversely. That is, as the X radius gets smaller the Y radius gets larger. This is one of the prettier procedures in this chapter. Try changing the 3's to 1's on the lines that say X_Rad -= 3; and Y_Rad += 3; the effect is rather interesting (although rather slow).

drawpoly( ) and rectangle( )

A polygon is any closed shape made entirely of straight lines. A regular polygon is a polygon where all sides are the same length and all angles point to the outside of the shape. The function drawpoly( ) can draw any polygon, either regular or irregular. It takes two parameters. The first is the number of vertices, or angles, in the polygon. The second parameter is a pointer to an array of integers. This array contains the X and Y coordinates of the vertices. The first location in the array is the first X coordinate, the next location is the first Y, the next location is the next X, etc.

Since the second parameter is simply a pointer to an array, the number of vertices that the function can handle is arbitrary. The only way that drawpoly( ) knows how many points are in the array is by the first parameter. If more vertices are in the array than the number indicated by the first parameter, the leftovers are ignored. If there are not enough points in the array, the procedure will keep reading from memory adjacent to the point array. Whatever happens to be there will be interpreted as point coordinates. This can lead to lines being drawn at wild angles, going off the screen, and other strange effects.

The function rectangle( ) can be used to draw rectangles aligned with the X and Y axes. This is handy, since these are particularly common polygons and not as much information is needed to draw them. Not every vertex needs to be given, only the upper right and the lower left.

```
void far drawpoly (int numpoints;
                   int far *polypoints);
  /*
   * drawpoly() draws a polygon
   *
   * Parameters:
   *   numpoints  - The number of vertices in
   *     the polygon.
   *   polypoints - array of integers
   *     containing the coordinates of the
   *     vertices.
   */


void far rectangle (int x1, int y1,
                    int x2, int y2);
  /*
   * rectangle() draws a rectangle on the
   *   screen
   *
   * Parameters:
   *   x1 - The X coordinate of the upper
   *        left corner
   *   y1 - The Y coordinate of the upper
   *        left corner
   *   x2 - The X coordinate of the lower
   *        right corner
   *   y2 - The Y coordinate of the lower right
   *        corner
   */
```

Here is a procedure demonstrating drawpoly( ):

```
/*
 * Demonstrate the drawpoly() function
 */

#include <graphics.h>
#include <conio.h>
#include <stdio.h>
#include <stdlib.h>
```

```
void DrawPoly_Demo(){

/*
 * Draw a kind of arrow head shaped thing using
 *   Borland's DrawPoly routine
 */

    int  Poly[10];

    /* Define the Polygon */
    Poly[0] = getmaxx() / 3;
    Poly[1] = 1;
    Poly[2] = getmaxx() / 2;
    Poly[3] = getmaxy() / 3;
    Poly[4] = (getmaxx() / 3) * 2;
    Poly[5] = 1;
    Poly[6] = getmaxx() / 2;
    Poly[7] = (getmaxy() / 3) * 2;
    Poly[8] = getmaxx() / 3;
    Poly[9] = 1;

    /* Fill the Polygon - it does not have to
       be on the screen first */
    drawpoly (5, Poly);

    getch();
    if (kbhit()) getch();
    cleardevice();

} /* end function DrawPoly_Demo() */

void main (void) {
    int Mode, Driver, GraphError;

    Driver = DETECT;
    detectgraph(&Driver, &Mode);
    initgraph(&Driver, &Mode, '');

    GraphError = graphresult();
    if (GraphError != grOk) {
        printf("%s\n",
                grapherrormsg(GraphError));
        exit(-1);
    }

    /* Do Graphics Stuff Here */
    DrawPoly_Demo();

    closegraph();
}
```

This program will draw an irregular polygon with a shape similar to an arrowhead. Since C is an untyped language, the array can be redefined to make the program more readable. The following program substitutes an array of structures, each structure containing one vertex, for the array. This is more readable, but when compiled, gives a warning message about a suspicious pointer conversion. It does work, however.

```
/*
 * Demonstrate the drawpoly() function with an
 *   alternate data structure
 */

#include <graphics.h>
#include <conio.h>
#include <stdio.h>
#include <stdlib.h>

void DrawPoly_Demo(void) {

/*
 * Draw a kind of arrow head shaped thing using
 *   Borland's DrawPoly routine.
 */

    struct {
        int X, Y;
    } Poly[10];

    /* Define the Polygon */
    /* This is more readeable than the last
       program - it is obvious which numbers
       are x and which are y coordinates */
    Poly[0].X = getmaxx() / 3;
    Poly[0].Y = 1;
    Poly[1].X = getmaxx() / 2;
    Poly[1].Y = getmaxy() / 3;
    Poly[2].X = (getmaxx() / 3) * 2;
    Poly[2].Y = 1;
    Poly[3].X = getmaxx() / 2;
    Poly[3].Y = (getmaxy() / 3) * 2;
    Poly[4].X = getmaxx() / 3;
    Poly[4].Y = 1;

    /* Fill the Polygon.  This line gives a
       warning about a suspicious pointer
```

```
        conversion.  It does work. */
    drawpoly (5, Poly);

    getch();
    if (kbhit()) getch();
    cleardevice();

} /* end function DrawPoly_Demo() */

void main (void) {
    int Mode, Driver, GraphError;

    Driver = DETECT;
    detectgraph(&Driver, &Mode);
    initgraph(&Driver, &Mode, '');

    GraphError = graphresult();
    if (GraphError != grOk) {
        printf("%s\n",
                grapherrormsg(GraphError));
        exit(-1);
    }

    /* Do Graphics Stuff Here */
    DrawPoly_Demo();

    closegraph();
}
```

More Advanced Primitives

We have just covered a number of basic graphics primitives for creating dots on the screen, lines, and arcs. These are important, and when used wisely, can do just about everything. But life would be easier with certain other capabilities. It would be nice if there were a way to draw a dotted line other than with line segments, or to fill a shape other than figuring out the boundaries, then drawing lines between them. This section covers a number of primitives that make life easier.

Line Styles

Lines can be thick or thin. Lines can be dotted, dashed, or a combination of dotted and dashed. The setlinestyle( ) function provides control over how lines are drawn. This function can be used to set the thickness and the pattern of dots and dashes.

This procedure allows the programmer to draw lines with predefined patterns, or design his/her own patterns.

```
void far setlinestyle (int linestyle,
                       unsigned upattern,
                       int thickness);
  /*
   * setlinestyle() will set the thickness
   *   and patterns of dots and dashes used
   *   to draw a line.
   *
   * Parameters:
   *   lineStyle - Identifies the style the
   *     line is drawn in.
   *   upattern  - User defined bit pattern
   *     used to draw lines if LineStyle is 4
   *     (User defined Style)
   *   thickness - The thickness of the line.
   */
```

The LineStyle parameter is a number which tells the procedure which style is wanted. Table 2.3.1 gives the possible values.

Table 2.3.1 Line Styles Defined by the BGI

Name	Value	Description
SOLID_LINE	0	Solid line
DOTTED_LINE	1	Dotted line
CENTER_LINE	2	Centered line
DASHED_LINE	3	Dashed line
USERBIT_LINE	4	User-defined line style

The UPattern parameter is only used if LineStyle equals 4. This is a bit pattern of 16 bits. When the line is drawn, it is drawn as series of 16 dots, repeated over and over again. If a bit is set in UPattern then the matching dot is lit on the line. If the bit is cleared, then the matching dot is not lit.

This would be a good time to review the relation between hexadecimal and binary. Hex makes a handy way to initialize bit patterns. One digit in hex is equivalent to four digits in binary, or four bits in a word. This means that every number that can be made from four bits can be made with one hex digit. Also, any number that can be represented with one hex digit can be represented with four bits. This one-to-one mapping is what makes hex so handy in computer science. To initialize a byte, 2 hex digits are needed. To initialize a word, 4 hex digits are needed.

Now if you want to draw a line with a dash and two dots, the first thing to do is figure out the bit pattern needed. Remember, there are 16 bits in a word. The following bit pattern will give a dash then two dots: 1111 1100 1100 1100. This can be easily represented in hex as 0xFCCC. Now you can make a call like:

```
setlinestyle (USERBIT_LINE, 0xFCCC,
              NORM_WIDTH);
```

The next time that line( ) is called the line that is drawn will have a dash then two dots. Remember this only works if the LineStyle parameter is USERBIT_LINE. Otherwise the second parameter is ignored.

The third parameter to setlinestyle( ) sets the thickness. A "3" will set the thickness to 3 pixels. Any other number will set the thickness to 1 pixel. A "1" is usually used for readability.

This program demonstrates the use of setlinestyle( ):

```
/*
 * Program to demonstrate line styles
 * Remember that the setlinestyle() routine
 *   also sets the style for lineto(),
 *   rectangle(), and drawpoly().  The
 *   Thickness parameter sets the thickness for
 *   arcs, circles, ellipses and pie slices.
 */

#include <graphics.h>
#include <conio.h>
#include <stdio.h>
#include <stdlib.h>

void Line_Thickness(void) {
/*
 * Draw lines with 2 different thicknesses
 */

    /* Draw a thin line */
    setcolor(GREEN);
    setlinestyle (SOLID_LINE, 0, NORM_WIDTH);
    line (1, 40, getmaxx(), 40);

    /* Draw a Thick line */
    setcolor(YELLOW);
    setlinestyle (SOLID_LINE, 0, THICK_WIDTH);
```

```
    line (1, 50, getmaxx(), 50);

    getch();
    if (kbhit()) getch();

} /* end function Line_Thickness() */

/*----------------------------------------------*/

void Line_Style1(void) {
/*
 * Draw lines in 4 predefined styles:
 *   SOLID_LINE = 0;  DOTTED_LINE = 1;
 *   CENTER_LINE = 2; DASHED_LINE = 3.
 */

    int  i;

    for (i = 0; i <= 3; i++) {
        setcolor(i+2);
        setlinestyle (i, 0, THICK_WIDTH);
        line (1, 80+(i*20), getmaxx(),
                 80+(i*20));
    } /* end for loop */

    getch();
    if (kbhit()) getch();

} /* end function Line_Style1() */

/*----------------------------------------------*/

void Line_Style2(void) {
/*
 * Draw lines in styles defined by the
 *   programmer.
 */

    /* Draw a line with bit pattern
       0000 0000 1111 1111 */
    /* A dashed line */
    /* Remember that each hex number is 4 bits
       in binary. */
    setcolor(RED);
    setlinestyle (USERBIT_LINE, 0x00FF,
                  THICK_WIDTH);
    line (1, 180, getmaxx(), 180);

    /* Draw a line with bit pattern
```

```
       0011 1100 0011 0000 */
    /* A Dash then a Dot */
    setcolor(GREEN);
    setlinestyle (USERBIT_LINE, 0x3C30,
                  THICK_WIDTH);
    line (1, 200, getmaxx(), 200);

    /* Draw a line with bit pattern
       1111 1100 1100 1100 */
    /* A dash then 2 dots */
    setcolor(BLUE);
    setlinestyle (USERBIT_LINE, 0xFCCC,
                  THICK_WIDTH);
    line (1, 220, getmaxx(), 220);

    /* Got the idea? */

    getch();
    if (kbhit()) getch();
    cleardevice();

} /* end function Line_Style2() */

/*------------------------------------------*/

/* Remember - the most common use of cut and
     paste is for automated error production */

void main (void) {
    int Mode, Driver, GraphError;

    Driver = DETECT;
    detectgraph(&Driver, &Mode);
    initgraph(&Driver, &Mode, '');

    GraphError = graphresult();
    if (GraphError != grOk) {
         printf("%s\n",
                grapherrormsg(GraphError));
         exit(-1);
    }

    /* Do Graphics Stuff Here */
    Line_Thickness();
    Line_Style1();
    Line_Style2();

    closegraph();
}
```

The preceeding program contains three functions. The first one demonstrates the two different line thicknesses, The next one demonstrates the four predefined styles, and the last one shows how the programmer can define two patterns him/herself.

Filling Things: fillpoly( ), fillellipse( ), floodfill( )

Another common task in graphics is filling shapes. Borland C provides three primitives for filling shapes: fillpoly( ), fillellipse( ), and floodfill( ). The fillpoly( ) function uses a highly efficient algorithm for filling polygons. The polygon does not need to be on the screen. The vertices are passed to the procedure in an array, the same way that they are passed to drawpoly( ). Function fillpoly( ) can then figure out where the borders of the polygon are. This function is the most efficient of the filling procedures, and it is recommended that it is used where possible. Unfortunately not all shapes are polygons.

```
void far fillpoly(int numpoints,
                  int far *polypoints);
  /*
   * fillpoly() draws a filled polygon.
   *
   * Parameters:
   *   numpoints  - The number of vertices in
   *     the polygon.
   *   polypoints - array of integers
   *     containing the coordinates of the
   *     vertices.
   */
```

Function fillellipse( ) can be used for filling ellipses. Like fillpoly( ), fillellipse( ) does not need to have the ellipse on the screen before it is filled. This function takes the same parameters as ellipse( ), except for the start and end angles, and so can be used to create the same ellipses. It also has the same limitation that the major axis must be on the X or Y axis. Remember that a circle is an ellipse with the X and Y axes the same length, so this procedure is used to fill circles also.

```
void far fillellipse (int x, int y,
                      int xradius,
                      int yradius);
  /*
   * fillellipse() draws a filled ellipse on
```

```
 *   the screen
 *
 * Parameters:
 *   x       - X coordinate of the center
 *   y       - Y coordinate of the center
 *   xradius - the radius of the ellipse in
 *     the X dimension
 *   yradius - the radius of the ellipse in
 *     the Y dimension
 */
```

Some shapes are not ellipses or polygons. If a shape is made from both straight lines and curves, neither of the preceeding functions can be used. The floodfill( ) function can be used in these circumstances. This procedure works by setting a point inside the shape to be filled. It then fills in one direction until it finds an edge. Then it tries another direction, then the third direction, and then the fourth. At each point it tries all directions. Function floodfill( ) needs to be able to find the border of the shape it is filling, so, unlike the two procedures above, the shape needs to be on the screen before it can be filled.

The floodfill( ) function uses a recursive algorithm that is rather slow and uses a lot of memory. In addition, this function suffers from several other shortcomings. For these reasons the two previous filling functions are preferred. Use them whenever possible.

```
void far floodfill (int x, int y, int border);
  /*
   * floodfill() fills an irregularly shaped
   *   closed shape.
   *
   * Parameters:
   *   x      - X coordinate of the seed
   *            point.
   *   Y      - Y coordinate of the seed
   *            point.
   *   Border - Border color of the shape to
   *            be filled.
   */
```

Here is a program demonstrating these filling functions. A word of warning: The function that demonstrates floodfill( ) draws an irregular shape on the screen. This function was tested on a VGA monitor. On other monitors this shape might have an opening in it due to a difference in aspect ratios. If this is the case the floodfill( ) will "leak out" and fill the entire screen. This is one of those annoying problems with floodfill( ) mentioned above.

```
/*
 * Program to demonstrate fill routines
 */

#include <graphics.h>
#include <conio.h>
#include <stdio.h>
#include <stdlib.h>

void FillPoly_Demo (void) {

/*
 * Fill a kind of arrow head shaped thing using
 * Borland's PolyFill routine.  If you really
 * read these comments you'd realize this
 * comment keeps changing
 */

    int  Poly[8];

    /* Define the Polygon */
    Poly[0] = getmaxx() / 3;
    Poly[1] = 1;
    Poly[2] = getmaxx() / 2;
    Poly[3] = getmaxy() / 3;
    Poly[4] = (getmaxx() / 3) * 2;
    Poly[5] = 1;
    Poly[6] = getmaxx() / 2;
    Poly[7] = (getmaxy() / 3) * 2;

    /* Fill the Polygon - it does not have to
       be on the screen first */
    fillpoly (4, Poly);

    getch();
    if (kbhit()) getch();
    cleardevice();

} /* end function FillPoly_Demo() */

/*---------------------------------------*/

void FillEllipse_Demo(void) {

/*
 * Fill randomly generated ellipses, using a
 * solid fill and different colors.
```

```
 */

    int  count, X_Center, Y_Center, Color,
         X_Rad, Y_Rad;

    randomize();
    for (count = 0; count < 30; count++) {
        X_Center  = random(getmaxx());
        Y_Center  = random(getmaxy());
        X_Rad     = random(getmaxx() / 2);
        Y_Rad     = random(getmaxy() / 2);
        Color     = random(15) + 1;
                /* Set Fill Color   */
        setfillstyle (1,Color);
               /* Set Border Color */
        setcolor     (16 - Color);
        fillellipse  (X_Center, Y_Center,
                      X_Rad, Y_Rad);
    } /* end for loop */

    getch();
    if (kbhit()) getch();
    cleardevice();

} /* end function FillEllipse_Demo() */

/*-------------------------------------------*/

void FloodFill_Demo(void) {
/*
 * Procedure to demonstrate FloodFill
 *
 * Things to remember:
 *
 *   FloodFill uses lots of memory - only use
 *     it when other fill methods won't work
 *     (ie:  filling nonpolygons that are also
 *           nonellipses)
 *
 *   This routine was designed and tested on a
 *     VGA monitor. If your monitor does not
 *     support VGA Hi Res mode (ie: CGA or
 *     Monochrome) you might have to modify
 *     this routine to make sure the shape is
 *     closed.
 */

    /* Draw NON Polygon first */
    setcolor (WHITE);
```

```
    arc (getmaxx() / 2, getmaxy() / 2, 0, 90,
         getmaxy() / 2);
    moveto (getmaxx() / 2, 1);
    lineto (getmaxx() / 2, getmaxy() / 3);
    lineto (getmaxx() / 3, getmaxy() / 3);
    lineto (getmaxx() / 3, getmaxy() / 2);
    lineto (getmaxx() / 2, getmaxy() / 2);
    lineto (getmaxx() / 2,
            (getmaxy() / 3) * 2);
    lineto ((getmaxx() / 3) * 2,
            (getmaxy() / 3) * 2);
    lineto ((getmaxx() / 3) * 2,
             getmaxy() / 2);
    lineto (558, getmaxy() / 2);

    /* Fill the Non Polygon */
    setfillstyle  (1, MAGENTA);
         /* Make sure we have a point */
         /* inside the shape */
    floodfill     ((getmaxx() / 2) + 5,
                   (getmaxy() / 2) + 5,
                   WHITE);

    getch();
    if (kbhit()) getch();
    cleardevice();

} /* end function FloodFill_Demo() */

/*---------------------------------------------*/

void main (void) {
    int Mode, Driver, GraphError;

    Driver = DETECT;
    detectgraph(&Driver, &Mode);
    initgraph(&Driver, &Mode, '');

    GraphError = graphresult();
    if (GraphError != grOk) {
        printf("%s\n",
                grapherrormsg(GraphError));
        exit(-1);
    }

    /* Do Graphics Stuff Here */
    FillPoly_Demo();
    FillEllipse_Demo();
    FloodFill_Demo();
```

```
    closegraph();
}
```

Changing Fill Styles and the Fill Color

The last section described how to fill graphics with a single solid color. Oftentimes the fill needs to be different colors. The fill color is not changed by setcolor( ). Other times filling with a pattern will make graphics more clear. Borland has supplied a method of changing colors and the fill pattern used by the various filling routines. A single function, setfillstyle( ), can be used to select any of the 16 colors, and a number of predefined fill patterns. Another procedure, setfillpattern( ), is used to design a new fill pattern. Function setfillpattern( ) is described below. Function setfillstyle( )'s definition is:

```
void far setfillstyle (int Pattern, int Color);
  /*
   * setfillstyle() sets the fill pattern used
   *   by fillpoly(), fillellipse() and
   *   floodfill().
   *
   * Parameters:
   *   Pattern - Number of the pattern used to
   *             fill things.
   *   Color   - Color that will be used to
   *             fill things.
   */
```

The first parameter takes a number that designates the pattern to be used. Table 2.3.2 describes what each of the numbers means.

Table 2.3.2 Fill Patterns defined by the BGI

Name	Value	Description
EMPTY_FILL	0	Fill with the background color
SOLID_FILL	1	Solid fill
LINE_FILL	2	Fill with horizontal lines
LTSLASH_FILL	3	Fill with ///
SLASH_FILL	4	Fill with ///, thick lines
BKSLASH_FILL	5	Fill with \\\, thick lines
LTBKSLASH_FILL	6	Fill with \\\, thin lines
HATCH_FILL	7	Light hatch fill
XHATCH_FILL	8	Heavy crosshatch fill
INTERLEAVE_FILL	9	Interleaving line fill
WIDE_DOT_FILL	10	Widely spaced dot fill
CLOSE_DOT_FILL	11	Closely spaced dot fill
USER_FILL	12	User-defined fill patterns

Some of these patterns deserve particular attention. The first one, EMPTY_FILL, will fill an object with the background color. This is useful for making an object look like it has a hole through it. The same thing can be accomplished by using the SOLID_FILL pattern with the color BLACK. Remember that when the background color is changed the filled section will change to match. When the last pattern, USER_FILL, is used, setfillpattern( ) needs to be called to set up the user-defined pattern.

Here is a function that demonstrates setfillstyle( ):

```
/*
 * Program to demonstrate fill routines
 */

#include <graphics.h>
#include <conio.h>
#include <stdio.h>
#include <stdlib.h>

void FillStyle_Demo(void) {

/*
 * Demonstrate different predefined fill
```

```
 *   styles.  Same as the fill ellipse routine,
 *   but uses more than just solid fill.
 */

   int  count, X_Center, Y_Center, Color,
        X_Rad, Y_Rad;

   randomize();
   for (count = 0; count < 50; count++) {
       X_Center  = random(getmaxx());
       Y_Center  = random(getmaxy());
       X_Rad     = random(getmaxx() / 2);
       Y_Rad     = random(getmaxy() / 2);
       Color     = random(15) + 1;
           /* Set Fill Style and Color */
       setfillstyle (random(10)+1,Color);
           /* Set Border Color */
       setcolor     (16 - Color);
       fillellipse  (X_Center, Y_Center,
                      X_Rad, Y_Rad);
   } /* end for loop */

   getch();
   if (kbhit()) getch();
   cleardevice();

} /* end function FillStyle_Demo() */

/*-------------------------------------------*/

void main (void) {
    int Mode, Driver, GraphError;

    Driver = DETECT;
    detectgraph(&Driver, &Mode);
    initgraph(&Driver, &Mode, '');

    GraphError = graphresult();
    if (GraphError != grOk) {
        printf("%s\n",
                grapherrormsg(GraphError));
        exit(-1);
    }

    /* Do Graphics Stuff Here */
    FillStyle_Demo();

    closegraph();
}
```

This procedure will draw a series of ellipses at random locations on the screen with randomly sized X and Y axes. These ellipses are filled using patterns supplied by Borland.

User-Defined Fill Patterns

Creating a user-defined fill pattern is similar to creating a user-defined line style, only now there are two dimensions to deal with. Therefore we need a two-dimensional array of bits. This array is created by using an array of 8 bytes. Each byte can be thought of as an array of 8 bits, so this is an array of 8 by 8 bits. The easiest way of setting the bits is to assign hex values to each byte, just as with linestyle( ).

So then what is done with this array? As the shape is filled, the pattern is referenced so that when a bit is set in the pattern the matching pixel is set to the fill color. When a bit is cleared in the pattern, the matching pixel is set to the background color. When a bit is set in the pattern, the corresponding pixel is set to the fill color. Next to that pattern another is placed, so that the pattern repeats in a series. If the shape being filled does not end at the end of the pattern, the fill pattern is cut off so that the entire shape is filled, but the pattern does not spill outside.

The easiest way to come up with a fill pattern is to use a piece of graph paper. Make the desired pattern on the graph paper, in an 8 by 8 grid. Then convert each row across to a hex number.

Here is an example: Suppose the fill pattern shown in fig. 2.3.1 is desired.

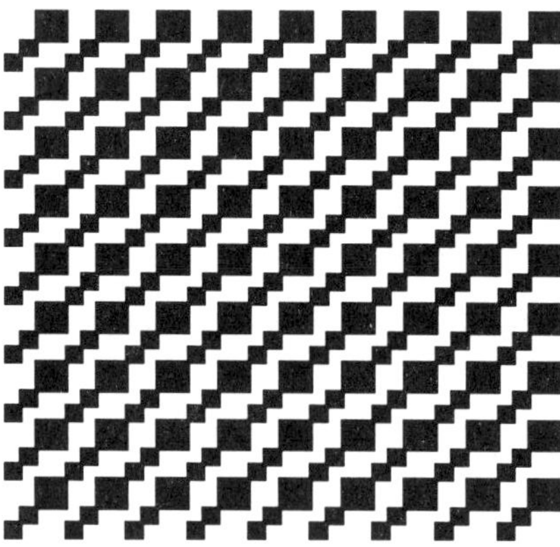

Fig 2.3.1 A User-Defined Fill Pattern

This is a rather complicated pattern. It might help to take a close look at it on graph paper (see Fig. 2.3.2).

Fig 2.3.2 Blowup of a User-Defined Fill Pattern

It might help even more to look at just an 8 × 8 section of the graph paper (Fig 2.3.2).

Fig 2.3.2 An 8x8 section of a user-defined fill pattern

Now we can see that this is really the following bit pattern (where one row of bits, a byte that is, is one row on the above graph paper):

```
1100 0011
1100 0011
0000 1100
```

```
0000 1111
0011 0000
0011 0000
1100 0011
1100 0011
```

And from that we can see that the array should be filled with the values:

```
0xC3 = 1100 0011
0xC3 = 1100 0011
0x0C = 0000 1100
0x0C = 0000 1100
0x30 = 0011 0000
0x30 = 0011 0000
0xC3 = 1100 0011
0xC3 = 1100 0011
```

And now that you know how to use this procedure here is its definition:

```
void setfillpattern (char far *pattern,
                     int color);
  /*
   * setfillpattern() defines a pattern to be
   *   used by the fill procedures
   *
   * Parameters:
   *   pattern - array of 8 bytes, used as a
   *     2D array of bits. The pattern in the
   *     array is used as the fill pattern
   *   color   - Color used for filling
   */
```

The following program demonstrates the pattern described above, as well as the patterns supplied by Borland and three other user-defined patterns.

```
/*
 * Program to demonstrate fill routines
 */

#include <graphics.h>
#include <conio.h>
#include <stdio.h>
#include <stdlib.h>

void SetFillPattern_Demo(void) {
/*
 * Procedure to demonstrate setfillpattern()
```

```
*
* Hint - setfillpattern() is easier to use if
*   you lay out the pattern with graph paper
*   first
*
* It might be good exercise to see if you can
* figure out why the patterns used by this
* procedure look the way they do.
*/

   char Pattern[8];
   int  Rectangle[8];

   /* Pattern 1 - Upper Left corner */
   Pattern[0] = 0x0E;
   Pattern[1] = 0x0E;
   Pattern[2] = 0x0E;
   Pattern[3] = 0x0E;
   Pattern[4] = 0x70;
   Pattern[5] = 0x70;
   Pattern[6] = 0x70;
   Pattern[7] = 0x70;
   setfillpattern (Pattern, 10);

   Rectangle[0] = getmaxx() / 4;
   Rectangle[1] = 0;
   Rectangle[2] = getmaxx() / 2;
   Rectangle[3] = 0;
   Rectangle[4] = getmaxx() / 2;
   Rectangle[5] = getmaxy() / 2;
   Rectangle[6] = getmaxx() / 4;
   Rectangle[7] = getmaxy() / 2;
   fillpoly(4, Rectangle);

   /* Pattern 2 - Upper Right corner */
   Pattern[0] = 0x00;
   Pattern[1] = 0x00;
   Pattern[2] = 0x00;
   Pattern[3] = 0x0F;
   Pattern[4] = 0x0F;
   Pattern[5] = 0x0F;
   Pattern[6] = 0x00;
   Pattern[7] = 0x00;
   setfillpattern (Pattern, 11);

   Rectangle[0] = (getmaxx() / 4) * 3;
   Rectangle[1] = 0;
   Rectangle[2] = getmaxx() / 2;
   Rectangle[3] = 0;
```

```
Rectangle[4] = getmaxx() / 2;
Rectangle[5] = getmaxy() / 2;
Rectangle[6] = (getmaxx() / 4) * 3;
Rectangle[7] = getmaxy() / 2;
fillpoly(4, Rectangle);

/* Pattern 3 - Lower Left corner */
Pattern[0] = 0xC3;
Pattern[1] = 0xC3;
Pattern[2] = 0x0C;
Pattern[3] = 0x0C;
Pattern[4] = 0x30;
Pattern[5] = 0x30;
Pattern[6] = 0xC3;
Pattern[7] = 0xC3;
setfillpattern (Pattern, 12);

Rectangle[0] = getmaxx() / 4;
Rectangle[1] = getmaxy() / 2;
Rectangle[2] = getmaxx() / 2;
Rectangle[3] = getmaxy() / 2;
Rectangle[4] = getmaxx() / 2;
Rectangle[5] = getmaxy();
Rectangle[6] = getmaxx() / 4;
Rectangle[7] = getmaxy();
fillpoly(4, Rectangle);

/* Pattern 4 - Lower Right corner */
Pattern[0] = 0x00;
Pattern[1] = 0x00;
Pattern[2] = 0x06;
Pattern[3] = 0x0C;
Pattern[4] = 0x18;
Pattern[5] = 0x30;
Pattern[6] = 0x60;
Pattern[7] = 0xC0;
setfillpattern (Pattern, 13);

Rectangle[0] = (getmaxx() / 4) * 3;
Rectangle[1] = getmaxy() / 2;
Rectangle[2] = getmaxx() / 2;
Rectangle[3] = getmaxy() / 2;
Rectangle[4] = getmaxx() / 2;
Rectangle[5] = getmaxy();
Rectangle[6] = (getmaxx() / 4) * 3;
Rectangle[7] = getmaxy();
fillpoly(4, Rectangle);

getch();
```

```
    if (kbhit()) getch();
    cleardevice();

} /* end function SetFillPattern_Demo() */

/*--------------------------------------------*/

void main (void) {
    int Mode, Driver, GraphError;

    Driver = DETECT;
    detectgraph(&Driver, &Mode);
    initgraph(&Driver, &Mode, '');

    GraphError = graphresult();
    if (GraphError != grOk) {
        printf("%s\n",
                grapherrormsg(GraphError));
        exit(-1);
    }

    /* Do Graphics Stuff Here */
    FillPoly_Demo();
    FillEllipse_Demo();
    FloodFill_Demo();
    FillStyle_Demo();
    SetFillPattern_Demo();

    closegraph();
}
```

The program will draw four boxes on the screen, each one filled with a different user-defined fill pattern. See if you can figure out how each pattern is generated. By the way, the pattern in the lower left corner is the one described in the text.

Linking .BGI Files into a Program

It is often desirable to put the code from the .BGI files directly into the executable file. Thus, only one file will be needed to run the program. The size of this program, however, is larger than if the BGI code is kept on the disk. This section describes how BGI code can be linked into the .EXE file. Most of the information given in this section can be found in the UTIL.DOC. This is a very useful file that is distributed with Borland C. It covers a number of utility programs provided with the compiler and not well documented elsewhere. If you have not already, you might want to take the time to skim this file. It contains a great deal of useful information.

BGIOBJ.EXE

.BGI files can be converted to object files by using the utility BGIOBJ.EXE. This program is called from the DOS commandline, with the name of the .BGI file as a commandline parameter. The following line will convert EGAVGA.BGI to EGAVGA.OBJ:

```
C> BGIOBJ EGAVGA
```

Now that the graphics driver is in the form of an object file, it can be linked into your program like any other object file. In case you are unfamiliar with this procedure, a brief description of how to link is given at the end of this section.

Once the graphics driver is linked with the program, it needs to be registered. This is done by calling the function registerbgidriver( ). This function takes one parameter, which is a constant defined for the driver being registered. The function returns a 0 if the call was successful, or a negative value if unsuccessful. Here is the function prototype:

```
int registerbgidriver(void (*driver)(void));
    /*
     * registerbgidriver will register a
     *   graphics driver that has been linked
     *   into the executable file.
     *
     * Parameters:
     *   driver - symbolic constant for the
     *            driver being registered.
     */
```

Table 2.4.1 gives the constants for the .BGI files.

Table 2.4.1 Constants for Linking .BGI Files into a Program

Driver File	Constant Name
CGA	CGA_driver
EGAVGA	EGAVGA_driver
HERC	Herc_driver
ATT (for the AT&T 400 monitor)	ATT_driver
PC3270	PC3270_driver
IBM8514	IBM8514_driver

Here is an example call to registerbgidriver( ):

```
if (registerbgidriver(EGAVGA_driver) < 0) {
    printf("An error was detected\n");
    exit(-1);
}
```

Your program will need a driver for each monitor type on which it will run. If the program will only run on VGA monitors, then only the EGAVGA driver needs to be linked in and registered. If the program will run on a number of monitor types, then all the correct drivers will need to be linked and registered.

Sometimes, when linking a number of drivers, the linker will give the error "Segment exceeds 64K". This problem has to do with the architecture of the 8086 microprocessor. The address space is divided into segments. The largest a segment can be is 65,536 bytes, or 64 kilobytes. When linking the graphics driver object files, the linker attempts to put them all in the same segment. If there are too many of them, they do not fit in 64K. This problem can be solved by using the "/F" option with BGIOBJ:

```
C> BGIOBJ /F EGAVGA
```

This option tells BGIOBJ that the driver belongs in its own segment. When this is done a different function is needed to register the driver: registerfarbgidriver( ). The definition is almost the same as for the last function:

```
int far registerfarbgidriver(void *__driver);
    /*
     * registerfarbgidriver will register a
     *   graphics driver that has been linked
     *   into the executable file, but only
```

```
        *   when it has been converted using
        *   BGIOBJ's /F option
        *
        * Parameters:
        *   driver - symbolic constant for the
        *            driver being registered.
        */
```

The names of the drivers are the same as for the other function, with "_far" appended to the end. With this function the above example becomes:

```
if (registerfarbgidriver(EGAVGA_driver_far)
                                            < 0) {
    printf("An error was detected\n");
    exit(-1);
}
```

Methods of Linking

The normal method of having separate object files linked into your program is to include them in the project file. This file is used by the Integrated Development Environment (IDE) to determine what files should be linked together to form the executable file. Setting this file up from within the IDE is straightforward, and is covered in the TC Getting Started manual that comes with the compiler.

The second method of linking the graphics driver into your program is to place it into the graphics run-time library. The run-time libraries are automatically searched at link time for functions being called. If a function is called and is not in one of the object files listed in the project file, TC will automatically look in the run-time library. If the function with the correct name is in the run-time library, that function will be used. Otherwise an error will be raised announcing that the function could not be found.

The TLIB utility is used for putting object files into libraries. Specify the name of the library the object is to be entered into and the name of the object file with a plus sign before it:

```
C> TLIB GRAPHICS +EGAVGA
```

Several object files can be added to a library with one call. For more information on TLIB, read the UTIL.DOC file provided with the compiler.

The final method of linking graphics drivers into your program is to do so manually with TLINK. This program is also covered in UTIL.DOC.

3

Text in Graphics Modes

Fonts

When the screen is in text mode, the characteristics of text are rather restricted. All characters are the same size, orientation, and font. In graphics mode there is a lot more freedom. Text can be all different sizes. Borland C allows text to run horizontally or vertically. In graphics mode the character set is not limited to a single font.

What is a font? Basically, it is the shape of characters. When letters are written they should all look like they belong together. This Sentence does not look good, because it uses a number of mixed fonts. If one letter in the font is fancy, then they should all be fancy. If one letter is plain, then they should all be plain.

Text in Graphics Modes

Fonts have several characteristics. One is whether or not the font is *proportional.* A proportional font will space the characters according to the width of the character. An "i" will take less space than an "m". In a nonproportional font all, letters take the same amount of space.

A proportional font: abcdefghijklmnopqrstuvwxyz
A nonproportional font: `abcdefghijklmnopqrstuvwxyz`

Compare how much space there is for the "i" in both examples.

Another characteristic of a font is whether it is *bitmapped* or *stroked.* With a bitmapped font the characters are made by placing dots in a grid. A stroked font is made by drawing lines to make each letter. Bitmapped fonts are easier to create and take less work for the computer to put on the screen, but they usually do not look as good as a stroked font.

Fig. 3.1.1 A Closeup of a Bitmapped Letter

Bitmapped fonts are usually nonproportional. With most bitmapped fonts the designer selects a grid size, then designs all letters to fit into the same size grid. The example in Fig. 3.1.1 shows an 8 × 8 grid. Another common size is 14 × 14. The more pixels in a grid, the better the letter looks. A problem with bitmapped fonts is that they do not scale well. When the letter is enlarged it starts to appear "chunky." This is due to the method by which bitmapped fonts are stored in the computer. Stroked fonts can be resized over a wide range and will still look good (see Fig. 3.1.2).

Fig. 3.1.2 A Closeup of a Stroked Letter

Some stroked fonts are *outline fonts.* Lines are drawn around the outside of the character, and the middle is left blank. It is the job of the programmer to fill the character with the desired color. A font that is filled in is called a *filled font.* Some stroked fonts are simple enough that they do not require filling.

A number of fonts come with Borland C. One is bitmapped, the rest are stroked. The bitmapped font is the default, and is loaded when the monitor is put into graphics mode. Other fonts need to be loaded from the disk before they are used. They reside in files with the extension .CHR. The function settextstyle( ) will load the font. This function does not take a path name like initgraph( ). Instead all the .CHR files present are loaded with the .BGI files. This means all the .CHR files used must be present in the same directory as the .BGI files when initgraph( ) is called. If the call to settextstyle( ) fails, the default font will be loaded, so things can always be written on the screen, they just might not look as expected. In addition to setting the font, settextstyle( ) also sets the size and orientation. Table 3.1.1 shows the five fonts that come with Borland C.

Table 3.1.1 Borland Supplied Fonts

Font Name	Value	Description
DEFAULT_FONT	0	8 × 8 bitmapped font
TRIPLEX_FONT	1	Stroked triplex font
SMALL_FONT	2	Stroked small font
SANS_SERIF_FONT	3	Stroked sans-serif font
GOTHIC_FONT	4	Stroked gothic font

Function settextstyle( ) is also used to set the direction that text will run. Text can be set so that it runs up and down, with the tops of letters towards the left of the screen. The other choice, of course, is right to left, as text normally runs.

```
void settextstyle (int font, int direction,
                   int charsize);
  /*
   * settextstyle() will set the font,
   *   direction and size for graphics text.
   *   The proper .CHR file must be present.
   *
   * Parameters:
   *   font      - What font will be loaded.
   *   direction - 0 for horizontal, 1 for
   *               vertical.
```

```
     *   charsize   - Size to multiply character
     */
```

This function has a parameter to set the size of the text being written. This size is multiplied by the base size of the font, so that the size of each character as it is written might be 7 times the base size of the font, or 4 times, or 19 times, etc. Sometime whole number sizes are not adequate. In certain circumstances the 8 might be to large, while 7 is to small. The function setusercharsize( ) can be used to exactly specify text size. This procedure takes four parameters. The first two control the size in the X dimension, the other two in the Y dimension. The first parameter is an integer, which is multiplied by base size of the font for the X dimension. The next parameter then divides this number. The resulting number is used as a scale factor for the X dimension. The procedure is then applied to the parameters for the Y dimension. This way a size of 7.5 can be obtained by using a multiply factor of 15 and a divide factor of 2. The X and Y dimensions are scaled independently, so letters can be made short and fat or tall and thin.

```
void setusercharsize (int multx, int divx,
                      int multy, int divy);
  /*
   * setusercharsize() will set the size that
   *   graphics text will be written, and
   *   reproportion graphics text.
   *
   * Parameters:
   *   multx - Multiply value for X
   *   divx  - Divide value for X
   *   multy - Multiply value for Y
   *   divy  - Divide value for Y
   */
```

The output function printf( ) is not used to put graphics text on the screen. This function, while powerful, does not have enough flexibility for graphics. Instead two functions, called outtext( ) and outtextxy( ), are used. Function outtext( ) will write a string at the current cursor position. Function outtextxy( ) has parameters to give the screen position, in XY coordinates, as well as the text to be written. These functions will not work for integers, characters, or reals. They only work on strings. To print formatted text as printf( ) does, write the string to a buffer using sprintf( ), then print the buffer using one of these functions.

```
void outtext (char far *textstring);
  /*
   * outtext() will write a string of text to
```

```
    *   the screen at the current position using
    *   parameters selected by SelectTextStyle.
    *
    * Parameter:
    *   textstring - String of text to be
    *                written.
    */

void outtextxy (int x, int y,
                char far *textstring);
  /*
    * outtext() will write a string of text to
    *   the screen using parameters selected by
    *   SelectTextStyle, at the screen
    *   coordinates given by X and Y.
    *
    * Parameters:
    *   x          - X coordinate of text
    *   y          - Y coordinate of text
    *   textstring - String of text to be
    *                written.
    */
```

Normally text is left justified. That is, it is written starting at the X coordinate given by outtextxy( ). Often it is easier to find where the middle or end of the text should be. When drawing a graph, the axes must be labeled. These labels should be centered. If we could center the text it would be a lot easier than determining where to start writing left-justified text. The settextjustify( ) routine will allow horizontal text to be left justified, centered, or right justified. Vertical text can be top justified (default), centered, or bottom justified. This procedure uses the constants shown in Table 3.1.2.

Table 3.1.2 Text Justifications for settextjustify( )

Text Direction	Name	Value	Action
Horizontal	LEFT_TEXT	0	Left justify text
	CENTER_TEXT	1	Center text
	RIGHT_TEXT	2	Right justify text
Vertical	BOTTOM_TEXT	0	Justify from the bottom
	CENTER_TEXT	1	Center text
	TOP_TEXT	2	Justify from the top

```
void settextjustify (int horiz, int vert);
    /*
     * settextjustify() will set the text
     *   justification for vertical or
     *   horizontal text.
     *
     * Parameters:
     *   horiz - Text justification for
     *           horizontal text.
     *   vert  - Text justification for
     *           vertical text.
     */
```

If a program needs to find the current text settings use gettextsettings( ). The settings are returned in a data structure called textsettingstype. Here are definitions for these:

```
void gettextsettings (struct textsettingstype
                                    far *texttypeinfo);
  /*
   * gettextsettings() will return the various
   *   parameters for graphics text settings
   *
   * Parameter:
   *   texttypeinfo - Data structure holding
   *     parameters for graphics text.
   */

struct textsettingstype {
  int font;
  int direction;
  int charsize;
  int horiz;
  int vert;
};
```

The function textheight( ) will take a string of text and determine how much space in pixels it needs in the Y dimension, given the current settings. The similar function textwidth( ) will do the same for the X dimension. These functions are useful when a lot of graphics text needs to be placed on the screen. They can be used to determine if there is enough room on the screen, and to make sure the text does not overlap.

```
int far textheight (char far *textstring);
    /*
     * textheight() will return the height of a
     *   string in pixels, given the current
     *   graphics text settings
     *
     * Parameter:
     *   textstring - String to be measured.
     */

int far textwidth (char far *textstring);
    /*
     * textwidth() will return the width of a
     *   string in pixels, given the current
     *   graphics text settings
     *
     * Parameter:
     *   textstring - String to be measured.
     */
```

The program at the end of the next section demonstrates most of these procedures and functions.

Borland Supplied Fonts

What follows is a description of the fonts supplied with the Borland C compiler. Ideally an example of the text would provided with each description. Unfortunately the word processing software this text is being written on does not support the same fonts. A demonstration of the fonts can be found in one of the programs on the distribution disk; program BK0301.C.

Bitmapped

The bitmapped font is the default font. When the system is put into graphics mode this font is loaded automatically. When a call to settextstyle( ) fails, this font is loaded, with a size of 4. This is, of course, a bitmapped font, so it does not scale well. At large sizes it starts to look "chunky." It is a nonproportional font.

Triplex

Triplex is a fancy stroked font. It looks like three strokes are used for each letter, thus the name. It scales well, and in fact looks best when scaled to large size. Triplex can be used for writing that needs to be seen from a distance, such as for advertising. This font, as well as the rest of the supplied fonts, are proportional. Triplex is a filled font. All fonts except for the bitmapped font need a .CHR file. If this file is not present, the call to settextstyle( ) will fail, and the bitmapped font will be loaded instead. The .CHR file for Triplex is TRIP.CHR.

Small

The small font is a simple stroked font. Each letter is made of a single stroke, so that it does not need filling. It scales well, but looks best when scaled to a medium size. When scaled to a large size it looks rather insubstantial. The small font takes it's name from the fact that it can be scaled to a very small size – much smaller than can be easily read, in fact. It can be very bad for the eyes. It is proportional. This font is easiest to use for most purposes, and is the most commonly used in this book. Its file is LITT.CHR.

SanSerif

SanSerif looks like block letters. This font is made by outlining the shapes of the letters. At large sizes it needs to be filled by the programmer. This can be tedious and annoying. At smaller sizes the lines are thick enough that the letters appear filled, so hand filling is not needed. This font is not recommended for large text, although sometimes the other fonts at large size just do not look right. At small sizes it looks "chunky." At medium sizes this font looks good, and does not need filling. The .CHR file is SANS.CHR.

Gothic

The gothic font is a really fancy font, like the lettering in an old book. It looks best at a large size, and at a small size can be quite unreadable. It might be good for headlines or as an attention grabber. It is proportional, filled, and can be found in the file GOTH.CHR.

The following program might look rather large, but it is really quite simple. A separate procedure is given to demonstrate each font, using various sizes plus horizontal and vertical text. The procedures are quite similar, and make use of most of the procedures and functions described in the last section.

```
/*
 * Program to demonstrate graphics text
 */

#include <graphics.h>
#include <stdio.h>
#include <stdlib.h>
#include <conio.h>

/*-------------------------------------------*/

void Default_Font_Demo(void) {

/*
 * Write text on the screen with the
 * Default_font.  This procedure is self
 *  documenting.
 */

    setbkcolor    (BLUE);
    setcolor      (YELLOW);

    settextjustify (CENTER_TEXT, CENTER_TEXT);
    settextstyle (DEFAULT_FONT, HORIZ_DIR, 4);
    outtextxy  (getmaxx() / 2,
                textheight("Horizontal Default"
                "Horizontal Default");

    settextstyle (DEFAULT_FONT, VERT_DIR, 2);
    outtextxy (textheight ("Vertical Default"),
               getmaxy() / 2,
               "Vertical Default");

    settextjustify (LEFT_TEXT, TOP_TEXT);
    settextstyle (DEFAULT_FONT, HORIZ_DIR, 1);
    setcolor      (WHITE);
    outtextxy     (40, 80,
       "Default_Font is a Bitmapped font. \
 When it is scaled it becomes");
    outtextxy     (40, 90,
       "\'chunky\'.  It is non proportional - \
meaning all letters take the");
    outtextxy     (40, 100,
```

```
            "same horizontal space.");

        getch();
        if (kbhit()) getch();
        cleardevice();

    } /* end Default_Font_Demo */

    /*-------------------------------------------*/

    void Triplex_Font_Demo(void) {

    /*
     * Write text on the screen with the
     * Triplex_font.  This procedure is self
     * documenting
     */

        setbkcolor    (BLUE);
        setcolor      (YELLOW);

        settextjustify (CENTER_TEXT, CENTER_TEXT);
        settextstyle(TRIPLEX_FONT, HORIZ_DIR, 6);
        outtextxy    (getmaxx() / 2, 20,
                      "Horizontal Triplex");

        settextstyle(TRIPLEX_FONT, VERT_DIR, 4);
        outtextxy    (16, getmaxy() / 2,
                     "Vertical Triplex");

        settextjustify (LEFT_TEXT, TOP_TEXT);
        settextstyle (TRIPLEX_FONT, HORIZ_DIR, 1);
        setcolor      (WHITE);
        outtextxy     (45, 80,
         "Triplex_font is a fancy font. \
    It is a stroked font so that it");
        outtextxy     (45, 100,
         "will scale well.  Triplex looks \
    best when scaled to a large size,");
        outtextxy     (45, 120,
         "therefore it works well when a monitor \
    is to be read from a");
        outtextxy     (45, 140,
         "distance, such as for advertising. \
    It is a proportional font, so");
        outtextxy     (45, 160,
         "not all characters take the same amount \
    of space.");
```

```
    getch();
    if (kbhit()) getch();
    cleardevice();

} /* end Triplex_Font_Demo */

/*------------------------------------------*/

void Small_Font_Demo(void) {

/*
 * Write text on the screen with the
 * Small_font.  This procedure is self
 * documenting
 */

    setbkcolor    (BLUE);
    setcolor      (YELLOW);

    settextjustify (CENTER_TEXT, CENTER_TEXT);
    settextstyle (SMALL_FONT, HORIZ_DIR, 8);
    outtextxy     (getmaxx() / 2, 20,
                   "Horizontal Small Font");

    settextstyle (SMALL_FONT, VERT_DIR, 8);
    outtextxy     (16, getmaxy() / 2,
                   "Vertical Small Font");

    settextjustify (LEFT_TEXT, TOP_TEXT);
    settextstyle (SMALL_FONT, HORIZ_DIR, 6);
    setcolor      (WHITE);
    outtextxy     (45, 80,
       "Small Font is a simple stroked font \
that can be made");
    settextstyle (SMALL_FONT, HORIZ_DIR, 1);
    outtextxy     (545, 80, "really Tiny.");
    settextstyle (SMALL_FONT, HORIZ_DIR, 6);
    outtextxy     (45, 100,
       "This small size gives a great deal of \
scaling flexibility.");
    outtextxy     (45, 120,
       "Small Font is a proportional font \
that scales well.  This");
    outtextxy     (45, 140,
       "font is often useful when making \
graphs and charts.");

    getch();
    if (kbhit()) getch();
```

```
    cleardevice();

} /* end Small_Font_Demo */

/*---------------------------------------------*/

void Sans_Serif_Font_Demo(void) {

/*
 * Write text on the screen with the
 * Sans_Serif_font.  This procedure is self
 * documenting
 */

    setbkcolor    (BLUE);
    setcolor      (YELLOW);

    settextjustify (CENTER_TEXT, CENTER_TEXT);
    settextstyle  (SANS_SERIF_FONT,
                   HORIZ_DIR, 7);
    outtextxy     (getmaxx() / 2, 20,
                   "Horizontal Sans Serif");

    settextstyle  (SANS_SERIF_FONT, VERT_DIR,4);
    outtextxy     (16, getmaxy() / 2,
                   "Vertical Sans Serif");

    settextjustify (LEFT_TEXT, TOP_TEXT);
    settextstyle  (SANS_SERIF_FONT,
                   HORIZ_DIR, 1);
    setcolor      (WHITE);
    outtextxy     (50, 80,
      "Sans Serif is a proportional stroked \
font.  It looks good when");
    outtextxy     (50, 100,
      "scaled to medium sizes, but at small \
sizes it looks \'chunky\',");
    outtextxy     (50, 120,
      "and at large sizes it needs filling. \
Because of the odd shapes");
    outtextxy     (50, 140,
      "of the letters, filling is annoying.");

    getch();
    if (kbhit()) getch();
    cleardevice();

} /* end Sans_Serif_Font_Demo */
```

```
/*-------------------------------------------*/

void Gothic_Font_Demo(void) {

/*
 * Write text on the screen with the
 * Gothic_font.  This procedure is self
 * documenting
 */

    setbkcolor    (BLUE);
    setcolor      (YELLOW);

    settextjustify (CENTER_TEXT, CENTER_TEXT);
    settextstyle (GOTHIC_FONT, HORIZ_DIR, 6);
    outtextxy     (getmaxx() / 2, 20,
                   "Horizontal Gothic");

    settextstyle (GOTHIC_FONT, VERT_DIR, 4);
    outtextxy     (16, getmaxy() / 2,
                   "Vertical Gothic");

    settextjustify (LEFT_TEXT, TOP_TEXT);
    settextstyle (GOTHIC_FONT, HORIZ_DIR, 2);
    setcolor      (WHITE);
    outtextxy     (55, 80,
      "Gothic font is a really fancy font.  \
It is stroked, so it");
    outtextxy     (55, 100,
      "scales well, and it is proportional. \
At small scales it is");
    outtextxy     (55, 120,
      "hard to read.  It can be used for \
headlines, or as an");
    outtextxy     (55, 140,
      "attention grabber.");

    getch();
    if (kbhit()) getch();
    cleardevice();

} /* end Gothic_Font_Demo */

/*-------------------------------------------*/

void main(void) {
    int Mode, Driver, GraphError;

    Driver = DETECT;
```

```
        detectgraph(&Driver, &Mode);
        initgraph(&Driver, &Mode, '');

        GraphError = graphresult();
        if (GraphError != grOk) {
            printf("%s\n",
                grapherrormsg(GraphError));
            exit(-1);
        }

        /* Do Graphics Stuff Here */
        Default_Font_Demo();
        Triplex_Font_Demo();
        Small_Font_Demo();
        Sans_Serif_Font_Demo();
        Gothic_Font_Demo();

        closegraph();
    }
```

Creating New Fonts

Creating a new font can be a long and tedious process. A great deal of detail goes into each individual character. In addition you must create capital letters, lowercase letters, punctuation characters, and any other character that you will need in your font. An entire font can consist of more than 250 characters, each of which must look good and look appropriate with the other characters in the font. If none of Borland C's fonts suits your needs, then you might want to look at Bulletin Board Services to find a suitable font that someone else has already developed.

Once a font is created it can be placed into its own .CHR file, and used with Borland C's graphics text routines. The method for doing this is rather involved, and beyond the scope of a beginning graphics book. It will not be covered here. Two simpler methods will be covered for creating a user defined-font, one for a bitmapped font, and the other for a stroked font.

Creating a Bitmapped Font

Creating a Bitmap

Creating a bitmapped font takes less work than creating a stroked font. First a bitmap must be created for each letter. For an 8 × 8 bitmap an array of 8 bytes might be used. For a 14 × 14 bitmap an array of 14 words could be used. This means that 2 bits for each word will be wasted. There are 14 words per character, and 256 characters in the complete character set. This means that a total of 896 bits will be wasted. This is really not a whole lot when running on a computer with a megabyte or more of RAM. Also the entire character set does not need to be created, only the characters that will be used. This not only saves RAM, but saves the programmer's time as well.

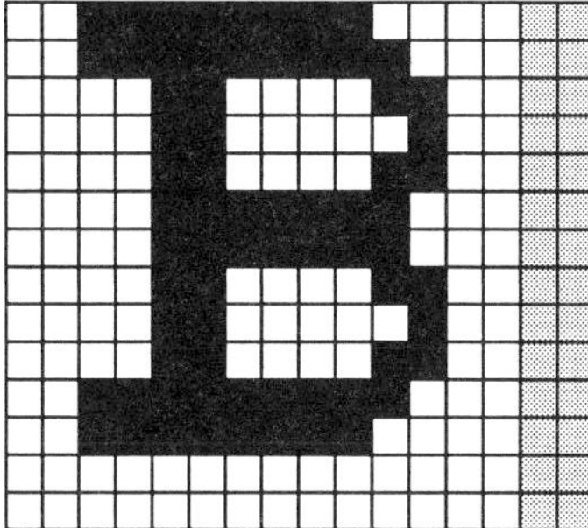

Fig. 3.3.1 A Closeup of a Bitmapped Letter

Fig. 3.3.1 is an example of a 14 × 14 bitmap made up of an array of words. The shaded columns are left over, and not used. The bottom two rows are also blank. These rows are for letters such as "p," that "go below the line." The code below shows how the bitmap is defined and initialed for the letter "A".

```
unsigned One_Letter[14] = {0x0300, /* 'A' */
                           0x0780,
                           0x0CC0,
                           0x1860,
                           0x3030,
                           0x7FF8,
                           0x7FF8,
                           0x6018,
                           0x6018,
                           0x6018,
                           0x6018,
```

```
                                0x0000,
                                0x0000,
                                0x0000 };
```

Each character in the bitmap array will have to be initialized. This process is much like creating a user-defined fill pattern. The design for the letter can be created on graph paper. Then the pixel patterns are read and converted to hex. These pixel patterns are placed into the bitmap for the correct letter. See Changing Fill Styles and Fill Color, in Chapter 2, for a more detailed description of how this is done.

It is handy to put all the character bitmaps into a single array, indexed by the characters. This will simplify writing a procedure to display the text. A string can be passed to the procedure, and the procedure will loop through the string using each character as an index into the array.

```
unsigned bitmap_array[256][14] = { ...
```

Of course the real bitmap will need all characters that might be used, including punctuation and special characters. There are 256 characters in the complete set, on the IBM PC.

A Procedure for Writing Strings

Once we have this array and a string that needs printing, we can loop through the string and use each character as an index into the bitmap array. It is then a simple thing to pull out the correct bitmap for printing.

```
for (i = 0; My_String[i]; i++)
    write_char(BitMap[My_String[i]]);
```

Fig. 3.3.2 is a picture of what the above lines actually mean:

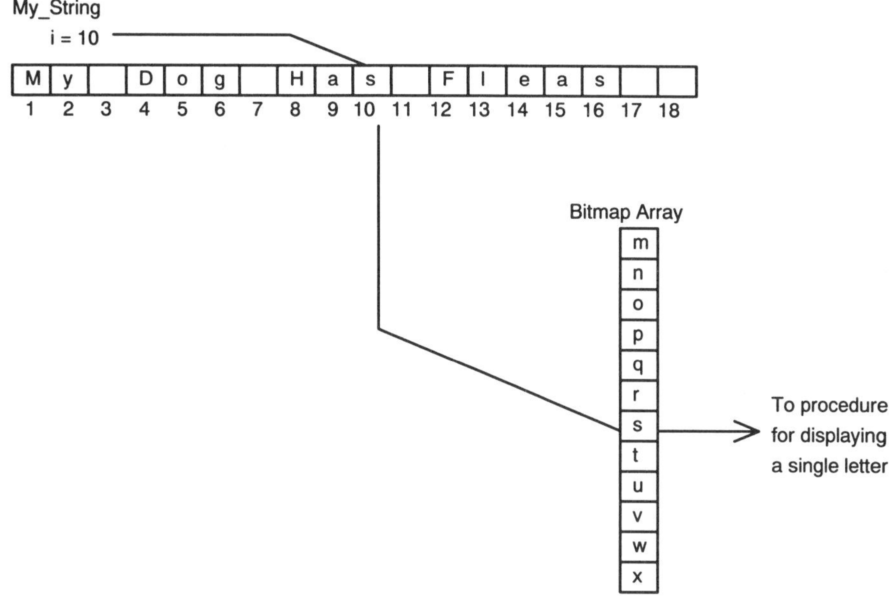

Fig. 3.3.2 Finding a Letter in the Bitmap Array

Now it would be nice to put the above into a procedure, so that it can be called with a string, the same way that outtext( ) is. It would also be useful to make the procedure generic, so that different programs can make use of it. The trouble is that a string that is the correct length for this program might be to long or short for another. Fortunately there is a trick. Declare the string parameter as a pointer to a character. Now strings of any size can be passed. Just make sure that all strings end with a null character (ASCII 0). All strings should do this anyway.

How to Write a Character

Now we need to write the procedure to write an individual letter. The concept is pretty straightforward. Take a starting point on the screen and the array of bits. Have a loop that loops through the words in the array. Inside of this loop have a second loop that loops through each bit. If the bit is set, light the pixel on the screen. Here is some psuedocode:

```
for (Word_Number = 0; Word_Number < 14;
                              Word_Number++)
  for (Bit_Number = 1; Bit_Number < 15;
                              Bit_Number++)
    if(Bit_Array[Word_Number][Bit_Number]) then
```

```
put_pixel (X + Bit_Number,
           Y + Word_Number, Color);
```

Notice that Word_Number is given an initial value of 0, and Bit_Number is given an initial value of 1. This is because of the way we initialized the bitmap and of how Intel microprocessors store data. Bits are stored in reverse order. The two leftover columns in the bitmap picture above are actually bits 0 and 1. The way that the call to putpixel( ) is done, however, makes up for this, so that letters appear correctly on the screen. The X and Y variables were not explained above. These are simply the locations where each letter starts.

Simple? But we cannot access the bits in a word this way. The assembler programmer will immediately see that bit-wise logical operations are what is needed here. Bit-wise operators will perform a logical operation on all bits in a word. For instance the value 0x0072 ANDed with the value 0x8F03 will return a value of 0x0002, because the only bit set in both words is the second one. We can use this operation to pick off individual bits in a word. To get the first bit, AND the word with the value 0x0001. This is called a *bit mask*. To get the second use 0x0002, and for the third, 0x0004. Notice that the first number in binary is 0000 0000 0000 0001. The second is 0000 0000 0000 0010, and the third is 0000 0000 0000 0100. Each one has only one bit set, and that bit is moved one place each time. By continually shifting the bit that is set each individual bit can be detected.

But what value will be returned each time? If 0x000F is ANDed with 0x0004, the 0x0004 will be returned. Does this mean we have to look for a different value each time? No, a simpler test can be devised. The operation will always return 0 if the bit is not set. So all we have to test is whether the answer is 0 or not.

It sounds like we need a separate test for each bit: Word & 0x0001 for the first bit, then 0x0002 for the next, etc., until all bits are tested. Can we do this with a loop? Yes, we can shift the bit mask the needed number of bits, so that the set bit is in the correct position. Here it is all put together:

```
for (Word_Number = 0; Word_Number < 14;
                             Word_Number++) {
  for (Bit_Number = 1; Bit_Number < 15;
                              Bit_Number++) {
    if (Bit_Array[Word_Number] &
                   (0x01 << Bit_Number)) {
      put_pixel (X + Bit_Number,
                 Y + Word_Number, Color);
    } /* end if */
  } /* end inner for */
} /* end outer for */
X += 14;
```

This is actual Borland C code and will work. X is updated after the letter is written so that the next letter will not be written over it.

Scaling Characters

Now we have a fairly straightforward procedure for writing a character on the screen. This function can be used by the string writing function described above. But so far text can only be written in one size. A function can be written similar to Borland C's setusercharsize( ). This function will set variables, called X_Scale and Y_Scale in the text, that are used to make letters larger when written on the screen. X scaling and Y scaling are independent, so letters can be made tall and thin or short and fat. Of course, this is a bitmapped font, so it suffers from "chunkiness" when scaled. The setusercharsize( ) function has four parameters. Two are division factors to allow characters to be sized to fractional sizes. With a bitmapped font it is fairly straightforward to deal with whole number scale factors, but fractional scale factors cause problems.

What is done with the scale factors to make the letters appear to be different sizes? The text writing procedure needs to be modified. Two loops need to be added at strategic locations, one for the X scale and the other for the Y scale. The X scale loop is placed inside the if statement. This loop simply counts from 1 to X_Scale, so that more bits are put. If the scale factor is 3 then 3 bits are put where 1 would have been put otherwise. The other loop is placed just inside the loop for the word. This loop counts from 1 to Y_Scale This will repeat the byte the correct number of times. The indexes for these loops are X_Size and Y_Size, respectively. Something else needs to be done. With what's given above the same pixel will keep getting re-lit. The call to putpixel( ) needs to be modified. The X coordinate is now X_Position + (X_Size * (<Number of bits> - Bit_Number)), where <Number of bits> is the 8 if an 8 × 8 bitmap is used, or 14 if a 14 × 14 bitmap is used. The Y coordinate is now Current_Y + (Word_Number * Y_Size). Finally the current X position must be updated taking into account the X scale factor. This is done by multiplying the number of bits, 8 or 14, by the scale factor and adding it to the X position. This is the width of the character in pixels. Now here is the updated code:

```
for (Word_Number = 0; Word_Number < 14;
                                Word_Number++) {

  for (Y_Size = Y_Scale-1; Y_Size >= 0;
                                    Y_Size--) {
    Word_From_Bitmap =
                 BitMap_array[ch][Word_Number];
```

```
      for (Bit_Number = 1; Bit_Number < 15;
                                 Bit_Number++) {

        if (Word_From_Bitmap &
                          (0x01 << Bit_Number)) {

          for (X_Size = 0; X_Size < X_Scale;
                                     X_Size++) {

            /* this is hard to read there are */
            /* three parameters to PutPixel */
            putpixel
              (X_Position+X_Size+
                    (X_Scale*(14 - Bit_Number)),
               Y_Position+Y_Size+
                    (Y_Scale*Word_Number),
               Letter_Color);

          } /* end for (X_Size...          */
        }   /* end if ((Word_From_Bit...   */
      }     /* end for (Bit_Number...      */
    }       /* end for (Y_Size...          */
  }         /* end for (Word_Number        */
  X_Position += X_Scale * 14;
```

Miscellaneous Other Procedures

Several other functions are needed. It would be handy to have a function to set X_Position and Y_Position. This way text can be written wherever needed. This function is called set_location( ). The write_str_xy( ) routine will set these variables and then write a string. Finally a procedure is needed to set X_Scale and Y_Scale. This is called set_scalefactor( ). Now that we have all these functions they can be put into their own file, so that any graphics program you write can link them in. Files BK0302.C and BK0302.H provide the beginnings of a bitmapped text library. They are not complete, and are not a full program. They only give an example that can be built on. Here is the header file to give function prototypes:

```
#ifndef __MYGRAPHICSINCLUDED__

#define __MYGRAPHICSINCLUDED__

void set_location    (int X, int Y);
void set_scalefactor (int MultX, int MultY);
void set_textcolor   (unsigned color);
void write_char      (char ch);
void write_str       (char *str);
```

```
void write_str_xy    (int X, int Y, char *str);

#endif
```

The file uses the __MYGRAPHICSINCLUDED__ macro to determine if these prototypes have already been declared. It is a good idea to do this whenever you write a file that will be used in separate projects. Here is the code file:

```
#include "bk0302.h"
  /* demo programs are named for the chapter
     and example number in that chapter.  This
     is book - chapter 3, second example.  the
     header file contains function prototypes
     for functions coded here */

#include <graphics.h>


unsigned letter[14];
  /* This is really a 14 X 14 bit array.  The
   * last 2 bits in each word are ignored.
   */

  /* Wimping out for the example - This should
     be [0 .. 255] in which case it might be
     accessed like BitMap['A'] */
unsigned BitMap_array[3][14] = { 0x0300,
                                 0x0780,
                                 0x0CC0,
                                 0x1860,
                                 0x3030,
                                 0x7FF8,
     /* Letter 'A' */            0x7FF8,
                                 0x6018,
                                 0x6018,
                                 0x6018,
                                 0x6018,
                                 0x0000,
                                 0x0000,
                                 0x0000,

                                 0x3FC0,
                                 0x3FE0
                                 0x0C30,
                                 0x0C10,
                                 0x0C30,
    /* Letter 'B' */             0x0FE0,
                                 0x0FE0,
```

```
                                        0x0C30,
                                        0x0C10,
                                        0x0C30,
                                        0x3FE0,
                                        0x3FC0,
                                        0x0000,
                                        0x0000,

                                        0x03E0,
                                        0x07F0,
                                        0x0C18,
                                        0x1818,
                                        0x1800
                                        0x1800,
     /* Letter 'C' */                   0x1800,
                                        0x1818,
                                        0x0C18,
                                        0x07F0,
                                        0x03E0,
                                        0x0000,
                                        0x0000,
                                        0x0000 };


unsigned X_Scale      = 1,
         Y_Scale      = 1,
         X_Position   = 0,
         Y_Position   = 0,
         Letter_Color = LIGHTGRAY;

/*------------------------------------------*/

void set_location    (int X, int Y) {

    X_Position = X;
    Y_Position = Y;

} /* end set_location() */

/*------------------------------------------*/

void set_scalefactor (int MultX, int MultY) {

    X_Scale = MultX;
    Y_Scale = MultY;

} /* end set_scalefactor() */

/*------------------------------------------*/
```

```
void set_textcolor   (unsigned color) {

    Letter_Color = color;

} /* end set_textcolor() */

/*------------------------------------------*/

void write_char      (char ch) {
    unsigned Word_From_Bitmap;
    int      Word_Number,
             Bit_Number,
             X_Size,
             Y_Size;

 /* our array starts at 'A', for a full
    character array with all 256 characters,
    remove this line */
    ch = ch - 'A';
    for (Word_Number = 0; Word_Number < 14;
                          Word_Number++) {

      for (Y_Size = Y_Scale-1; Y_Size >= 0;
                               Y_Size--) {
        Word_From_Bitmap =
                 BitMap_array[ch][Word_Number];

        for (Bit_Number = 1; Bit_Number < 15;
                             Bit_Number++) {

          if (Word_From_Bitmap &
                     (0x01 << Bit_Number)) {

            for (X_Size = 0; X_Size < X_Scale;
                             X_Size++) {

           /* this is hard to read there are */
           /* three parameters to PutPixel */
            putpixel
              (X_Position+X_Size+
                   (X_Scale*(14 - Bit_Number)),
               Y_Position+Y_Size+
                   (Y_Scale*Word_Number),
               Letter_Color);

          } /* end for (X_Size...        */
        }   /* end if ((Word_From_Bit... */
      }     /* end for (Bit_Number...    */
```

```
    }        /* end for (Y_Size...          */
  }          /* end for (Word_Number        */
} /* end write_char() */

/*------------------------------------------------*/

void write_str       (char *str) {
    int i;
    for (i=0; str[i]; i++)
      write_char(str[i]);
} /* end write_str() */

/*------------------------------------------------*/

void write_str_xy   (int X, int Y, char *str) {
    int i;

    X_Position = X;
    Y_Position = Y;
    for (i=0; str[i]; i++) write_char(str[i]);
} /* end write_str_xy */
```

Other Suggestions

Setting up the bitmap is by far the largest portion of work involved with creating a bitmapped font. It might be a good idea to keep all the bitmaps in a file that can be read in at run time. This will make your source code smaller and easier to understand, and will allow the same routines to be used with different fonts. If you expect to be creating many bitmapped fonts, you might also want to write an interactive program for creating the font. One such program I've seen used the cursor keys to move around a grid. The space bar is used to toggle a square in the grid on or off. The letter was displayed to the side of the grid showing what it looked like at its normal size. Such a tool would be quite valuable for creating consistent looking fonts.

It might be useful to add some other functions to these. For instance a newline( ) function could use the current Y scale factor to set the current position to the beginning of the next line.

Creating a Stroked Font

The idea behind creating a stroked font is quite simple. A bitmapped font writes letters a pixel at a time. A bitmapped font uses the line drawing and arc commands to draw the letters. Implementing a stroked font takes quite a bit of work. Making arcs match up with lines in a letter is a tricky proposition, especially when the letters are scaled. Instead of using arcs, you might consider using a large number of line segments. If the font is to be scaled to large sizes, a letter might require quite a few line segments to look smooth.

There is little left to say on creating stroked fonts, so here is an example. The header file is almost the same as for the bitmapped font. The only difference is that the set_scale( ) function accepts divisor factors. This is because a stroked font can be scaled to sizes that are not integer multipliers of the base size. To see why this can be done here and not with a bitmapped font, compare the code here with the code in the last section. You will have a difficult time making this code work on the bitmapped font. Here is the header file:

```
#ifndef __MYGRAPHICSINCLUDED2__

#define __MYGRAPHICSINCLUDED2__

void set_location    (int X, int Y);
void set_scalefactor (int MultX, int DivX,
                      int MultY, int DivY);
void set_textcolor   (unsigned color);
void write_char      (char ch);
void write_str       (char *str);
void write_str_xy    (int X, int Y, char *str);

#endif
```

Since most of the routines are named the same as with the bitmapped font, these are not compatible. If you attempt to link both fonts to a program you will get an error claiming that set_scalefactor( ) has been redefined. To avoid this you might append the name of the font to the beginning of each function. Another method might be to create a new file that determines which font is being used and calls the correct function. This function is closer to Borland C's.

Most of the code in the actual file is the same as for the bitmapped font. One difference is that the scale factors are stored as floats. It might be more efficient to store the multiply and divide factors separately as integers. Then each time they are used, multiply then divide to find the scale factor. These are two integer operations as opposed to a single floating point operation (a multiply). On machines without a coprocessor this will be faster.

Of course the way the letters are written is different here from the last example. With stroked fonts there is a function for each character in the font. Well, actually there are two characters in the example. We need an efficient method of calling these functions based on a character variable. The first thing that comes to mind is a switch statement. With 256 cases, this would be one ugly switch! So we take advantage of a feature that is unique to C. We create an array of pointers to functions. Load the array with the address of the character writing functions. Now the correct function can be called by indexing the array with the letter to be written. Any good introductory C text will give a detailed description of, and the syntax for, pointers to functions. The syntax we need can be gotten from the example below:

```
#include "bk0303.h"

#include <graphics.h>

/* internal global variables */
unsigned X_Position    = 14,
         Y_Position    = 14,
         Letter_Color = LIGHTGRAY;
float    X_Scale       = 1.0,
         Y_Scale       = 1.0;

/* function prototypes, 1 for each letter */
/* for this example only 'A' and 'P' are
   implemented */

void A_funct();
void P_funct();

/* Array of function pointers, one for each
   letter. */
/* (256 for the full character set) */

void (*char_array[2])() = { A_funct, P_funct };

/*------------------------------------------*/

void set_location    (int X, int Y) {

    X_Position = X;
    Y_Position = Y;

} /* end set_location() */

/*-------------------------------------------*/

void set_scalefactor (int MultX, int DivX,
                      int MultY, int DivY) {

    X_Scale = MultX/DivX;
    Y_Scale = MultY/DivY;
```

```
} /* end set_scalefactor() */

/*------------------------------------------*/

void set_textcolor   (unsigned color) {

    Letter_Color = color;

} /* end set_textcolor() */

/*------------------------------------------*/

void A_funct() {

/*
 * Procedure to write a simple block letter 'A'
 *  on the screen.  This procedure allows the
 *  letter to be scaled by different amounts in
 *  the X and Y dimensions
 */

    moveto  (X_Position,    Y_Position);
    linerel ( 4 * X_Scale, -8 * Y_Scale);
    linerel ( 4 * X_Scale,  8 * Y_Scale);
    linerel (-1 * X_Scale,  0);
    linerel ((-1.5 * X_Scale), -3 * Y_Scale);
    linerel (-3 * X_Scale,  0);
    linerel ((-1.5 * X_Scale),  3 * Y_Scale);
    linerel (-1 * X_Scale,  0);

    moveto  (X_Position + (4 * X_Scale),
             Y_Position - (6 * Y_Scale));
    linerel (     X_Scale, 2 * Y_Scale);
    linerel (-2 * X_Scale, 0);
    linerel (     X_Scale, -2 * Y_Scale);

    /* using floodfill because letters often
       are non polygons */
    floodfill (X_Position + 2,
               Y_Position - 2,
               getcolor());

    /* update X_Position */

    X_Position += X_Scale * 12;

} /* end A_funct() */
```

```
/*---------------------------------------------*/

void P_funct () {
/*
 * Procedure to write a simple block letter 'A'
 *   on the screen.  This procedure allows the
 *   letter to be scaled by different amounts
 *   in the X and Y dimensions
 */

    moveto  (X_Position, Y_Position);
    linerel ( 0,            -8 * Y_Scale);
    linerel ( 4 * X_Scale,  0);
    moveto  (X_Position + 4 * X_Scale,
             Y_Position - 4 * Y_Scale);
    linerel (-3 * X_Scale,  0);
    linerel ( 0,            4 * Y_Scale);
    linerel (-1 * X_Scale,  0);
    arc     (X_Position + 4 * X_Scale,
             Y_Position - 6 * Y_Scale,
             270, 90, Y_Scale * 2);
    moveto  (X_Position + 4 * X_Scale,
             Y_Position - 7 * Y_Scale);
    linerel (-3 * X_Scale,  0);
    linerel ( 0,            2 * Y_Scale);
    linerel ( 3 * X_Scale,  0);
    arc     (X_Position + 4 * X_Scale,
             Y_Position - 6 * Y_Scale,
             270, 90, Y_Scale);

    floodfill (X_Position + 1,
               Y_Position - 1,
               getcolor());

    X_Position += X_Scale * 8;

} /* end P_funct */

/*--------------------------------------------*/

void write_char      (char ch) {
/*
  this is what this function should really look
  like :

    void write_char      (char ch) {
        (char_array[ch])();
    }
```

```
  it really is that simple!
  it has been changed because of the
    abbreviated example
*/

    if (ch == 'A')
        (char_array[0])();
    else if (ch == 'P')
        (char_array[1])();
    else {
        closegraph();
        printf(
           "Programmer defined font error: ");
        printf("Unimplemented letter/n");
        exit();
    }
}


/*-------------------------------------------*/

void write_str       (char *str) {
    int i;
    for (i=0; str[i]; i++)
      write_char(str[i]);
} /* end write_str() */

/*------------------------------------------*/

void write_str_xy   (int X, int Y, char *str) {
    int i;

    X_Position = X;
    Y_Position = Y;
    for (i=0; str[i]; i++)
      write_char(str[i]);
} /* end write_str_xy */
```

4

Microsoft C Graphics

Graphics programming is a complex task. The graphics programmer needs to be able to create a number of shapes, colors and patterns on the monitor. Different monitors have different characteristics. Graphics programs have to be able to detect the monitor type and make adjustments for different characteristics. Fortunately Microsoft has done quite a bit to lighten the load.

Microsoft C provides a set of routines that are automatically linked into programs when they are needed. This set of routines is called the *run-time library*. The run-time library contains a set of graphics routines. To use the graphics library, it is necessary to include a header file named "graph.h", which contains constant definitions and function prototypes needed by the graphics library.

This chapter covers the most commonly used of these functions. First we need to be able to change the monitor's mode, then we need to be able to draw dots, or pixels, on the screen. Functions to do this are covered first. Microsoft C gives us the ability to partition off a section of the screen, and create a window in the sectioned-off partition. These functions are discussed after the basic commands. Next we cover functions for drawing lines and shapes, especially ellipses and polygons. When we draw closed shapes, such as ellipses and polygons, we can fill them. They can be filled either with a solid color or with patterns. How this is done is presented after the basic functions. Graphics programs often need text. With graphics, not only can you create text, you have a variety of styles and sizes from which to choose. You can even write sideways! Text in graphics programming is covered thoroughly at the end of the chapter.

To say this book was written with Microsoft graphics in mind would not be true. Most of the examples in Chapters 5, 6 and 7, and in the Chapters 11 and after use Borland graphics routines. The chapters between 7 and 11 present a programming library for SVGA monitors. Every attempt has been made to make this library compatible with both Microsoft and Borland compilers, and any other C compiler that uses the same DOS interface functions.[1] Since 8 out of 15 chapters use examples oriented more towards Borland graphics routines, most of the functions presented in this chapter give a brief description of the equivalent Borland function.

Setting Up to do Graphics

_setvideomode( ) and _getvideoconfig( )

Before any graphics can be put on the screen, the monitor must be changed from text to graphics mode. Different monitors support different modes. The first graphics monitor type, the CGA monitor, was not very capable. Later monitors had better capabilities, but needed to support programs that only ran on older monitors. To provide better capabilities and at the same time remain compatible, different modes have been provided. One mode is compatible with a previous generation, while another provides new and better capabilities.

All graphics monitors support more than one mode, and the more advanced monitors, such as the VGA, support many modes. After practicing graphics programming for awhile you will become familiar with the different modes, how they look, and how they act. Until then, the mode with the highest resolution is usually the easiest to use for good looking results.

---

[1] int86( ) and other functions in the same family. For details see Chapter 8.

Microsoft C provides the function _setvideomode( ) for setting the screen to different video modes. An integer parameter tells it what mode to use. The header file graph.h defines a number of constants to use with this routine. Table 4.1.1 gives the constants.

Table 4.1.1 Modes Supported by Microsoft Graphics

Constant	Value	Number of Pixels	Number of Colors	Monitor Types
_MAXRESMODE	-3	depends on monitor	depends on monitor	All
_MAXCOLORMODE	-2	depends on monitor	depends on monitor	All
_DEFAULTMODE	-1	restore to original	restore to original	All
_TEXTBW40	0	40 col text	16 grey	All
_TEXTC40	1	40 col text	16 for/8 back	Color only
_TEXTBW80	2	80 col text	16 grey	All except PCjr.
_TEXTC80	3	80 col text	16 for/8 back	All color exc. PCjr.
_MRES4COLOR	4	320 × 200	4	CGA
_MRESNOCOLOR	5	320 × 200	4 grey	CGA
_HRESBW	6	640 × 200	2 (B&W)	CGA
_TEXTMONO	7	80 col text	2 (B&W)	Hercules
_HERCMONO	8	720 × 348	2 (B&W)	Hercules
_MRES16COLOR	13	320 × 200	16	EGA
_HRES16COLOR	14	640 × 200	16	EGA
_ERESNOCOLOR	15	640 × 350	2 (B&W)	EGA
_ERESCOLOR	16	640 × 350	4 or 16	EGA
_VRES2COLOR	17	640 × 480	2 (B&W)	VGA
_VRES16COLOR	18	640 × 480	16	VGA
_VRES256COLOR	19	320 × 200	256	VGA
_ORESCOLOR	64	640 × 400	1/16	Olivetti

Any of these constants can be used on a downwardly compatible monitor. In other words the modes available on CGA monitors are also available on a VGA monitor. For information on what is downwardly compatible see Chapter 1. This is the first time the Olivetti monitor has been mentioned in this text. Since it is not in the main stream of monitor technology and is not compatible with VGA and SVGA monitors it is not covered in detail. Here is the definition of _setvideomode( ).

```
short _far _setvideomode(short mode);
  /*
   * Function to set video mode
   *
   * Parameter:
   *   mode - the number desired mode
   *
   * Returns: 0 on error
   */
```

The first two modes, _MAXRESMODE and _MAXCOLORMODE, are the most interesting. When the program does not know what monitor type it is working on these two constants can be used to find the highest resolution or the highest number of colors. As of this writing Microsoft C has not been extended to support SVGA monitors, so when such a monitor is being used it will appear as a VGA monitor to the graphics system. It is rumored that Microsoft plans to support SVGA monitors soon, and may well do so before this book appears on the market.

When the monitor mode is set using one of these constants, the program will not know how many pixels or colors are available. The _getvideoconfig( ) function is used to find this information. Its parameter is a pointer to a structure defined in graph.h, called videoconfig. Here are the function prototype and the definition of the videoconfig structure.

```
struct videoconfig _far * _getvideoconfig
             (struct videoconfig _far *config);
  /*
   * Function to get the current video
   *   configuration
   *
   * Parameter:
   *   config - information on the current
   *     video configuration
   *
   * Returns: information on the current
   *     video configuration
   */

struct videoconfig {
  short numxpixels;
  short numypixels;
  short numtextcols;
```

```
    short numtextrows;
    short numcolors;
    short bitsperpixel;
    short numvideopages;
    short mode;
    short adapter;
    short monitor;
    short memory;
};
```

The fields numxpixels and numypixels give the number of pixels in the appropriate dimension, if the monitor is in graphics mode. If the monitor is in text mode, numtextcols and numtextrows give the number of columns and rows, respectively. The field numcolors gives the number of available colors. The next field, bitsperpixel, gives the color resolution, or number of bits needed to define the color of a pixel. This is discussed in more detail in Chapter 6 on the use of color. The field after that, numvideopages, is a little more complicated. The concept of video pages is introduced in Chapter 1 on graphics hardware, and expanded in Chapter 12 on animation. The field mode is the mode that the monitor was in when the call to _getvideoconfig( ) was made. The number in this field should correspond to one of the positive values in Table 4.1.1. The field adapter gives the type of video adapter the computer is equipped with, and monitor is the type of monitor. Microsoft has defined constants for each of these fields. The adapter constants are given in Table 4.1.2 and the monitor constants are given in Table 4.1.3. The last field, memory, gives the amount of memory the video card has.

Table 4.1.2 Adapter Types Supported by Microsoft Graphics

Constant	Value	Adapter Type
_MDPA	0x0001	Monochrome Display Adapter
_CGA	0x0002	Color Graphics Adapter
_EGA	0x0004	Enhanced Graphics Adapter
_VGA	0x0008	Video Graphics Array
_MCGA	0x0010	MultiColor Graphics Array
_HGC	0x0020	Hercules Graphics Adapter
_OCGA	0x0042	Olivetti Color Graphics Adapter
_OEGA	0x0044	Olivetti Enhanced Graphics Adapter
_OVGA	0x0048	Olivetti Video Array

Table 4.1.3 Monitor Types Supported by Microsoft Graphics

Constant	Value	Monitor Type
_MONO	0x0001	Monochrome
_COLOR	0x0002	Color or enhanced monochrome emulating color
_ENHCOLOR	0x0004	Enhanced Color
_ANALOGMONO	0x0008	Analog Monochrome only
_ANALOGCOLOR	0x0010	Analog Color only
_ANALOG	0x0018	Analog Monochrome and Color modes

The values in Tables 4.1.2 and 4.1.3 are meant to be tested with bit-wise AND operations. Notice that if _ANALOGMONO and _ANALOGCOLOR are ORed together the result is _ANALOG.

With the fields in the videoconfig structure, a program can find out everything it needs to know about the monitor on which the program is running.

Microsoft recommends for graphics programming that a call to _getvideoconfig( ) be made, then the adapter field of the videoconfig structure be tested to determine what modes are supported. After this is done the monitor is set to the best mode. A simpler procedure is to set the mode using either _MAXRESMODE or _MAXCOLORMODE, depending on the graphics being displayed, then calling _getvideoconfig( ) to determine what mode was set. I have found this method effective for nearly all Microsoft C graphics program I've written. I generally find the _MAXRESMODE is the easiest to work with. The color selection is limited, at least on VGA monitors, but it is easier to make good looking graphics when using better resolution with fewer colors than the other way around.

Once the graphics program is finished, the monitor should be returned back to its native mode. It is annoying for a program to finish and leave the screen in graphics mode. Text in most graphics modes looks quite ugly and the cursor disappears, and someone who is less familiar with a PC might have a difficult time returning it to text mode. The way to reset the monitor to its native mode is to call _setvideomode( ) with _DEFAULTMODE.

The following piece of code is a shell for a graphics program. It does not make any graphics on the screen, it is just for demonstrating how to set the monitor to graphics mode and how to set it back when you are done. Function _setvideomode( ) attempts to set the monitor to its best resolution mode. If it fails for some reason the program exits with an error message. If the mode with the most number of colors is desired replace _MAXRESMODE with _MAXCOLORMODE. After the mode is set a call to _getvideoconfig( ) is used to get information on what mode the monitor is in. After this, calls can be made to functions that actually draw the graphics on the screen. The last thing this program does is set the monitor back to text mode. This program can be found in file BK0401.C on the distribution disk.

```
#include <graph.h>

struct videoconfig adapter_info;

void main () {

  if (_setvideomode(_MAXRESMODE) == 0) {
    printf("error in setting graphics mode\n\n");
    exit(-1);
  }
  _getvideoconfig(&adapter_info);

  /* do graphics stuff here */

  _setvideomode(_DEFAULTMODE);
}
```

Borland supplies functions to perform the same jobs, but these functions work rather differently. You might want to review functions detectgraph( ), initgraph( ), and closegraph( ) in Chapter 2, so that you will understand examples in future chapters more easily.

Graphics Primitives

_setpixel( ), _setcolor( )

The term *pixel* has been used a number of times in this chapter already. What is a pixel? Pixel stands for *picture element*. A picture element is the smallest dot that can be drawn on the screen. Chapter 1 gives a detailed explanation of how a pixel is generated, and why nothing smaller can be drawn.

Pixels are placed on the screen in a grid, something like the spaces in graph paper. Drawing pictures on the screen is something like making a drawing on graph paper by filling in the squares. Cartesian coordinates are used to specify pixels on the screen. The origin of our Cartesian plane is the upper left-hand corner of the screen, which is somewhat unexpected. One would expect (0,0) to be the lower left-hand corner, where it usually is when drawing a graph. This arrangement is not hard to get used to, however.

When drawing on a screen the programmer must be concerned with how many pixels will fit on the screen. On the VGA monitor in _VRES16COLOR mode there are 640 pixels across the screen, and 480 down. This is called the *resolution.* The resolution changes with the mode. _ERESCOLOR is 640 × 350, and _MRES256COLOR is 320 × 200.

One would think that pixels must be square. This would simplify the problem of drawing shapes on the screen. But because of the different number of pixels available in different modes, pixels cannot be square in all modes. The pixels in _VRES16COLOR mode are square, but in all other modes they are rectangular. The ratio of the length to the width of a pixel is called the *aspect ratio.* To be precise, the aspect ratio is the size of the pixel in the X dimension divided by its size in the Y dimension. A square pixel has an aspect ratio of 1. In a mode where the aspect ratio is not 1, this must be taken into account. If a circle is drawn without considering the aspect ratio it will turn into an oval. Fortunately for us, most Microsoft C graphics routines automatically take aspect ratio into account. Circles appear round in all modes.

The Microsoft function for drawing a pixel is _setpixel( ). Here is its prototype:

```
short far _setpixel(short x, short y);
  /*
   * function for setting a pixel
   *
   * parameters:
   *   x - x coordinate of pixel being set
   *   y - y coordinate of pixel being set
   */
```

Borland supplies an equivalent function, putpixel( ). A code fragment demonstrating this function is given after the next section on setting the color. This code fragment can be found on the distribution disk on program BK0402.C.

Many graphics functions take X and Y coordinates as parameters. To simplify matters, the file graph.h defines a structure, xycoord, which contains both these fields. Many graphics functions, including _setpixel( ), have an alternate function to accept this structure. To use the alternate function append _xy to the end of the function name.

```
struct xycoord {
  short xcoord;
  short ycoord;
```

```
};

short far _setpixel_xy(struct xycoord);
  /*
   * function for setting a pixel
   *
   * parameter:
   *   the location of the pixel being set
   */
```

Note that the Microsoft documentation says that these alternate functions are not documented and may not be supported in future versions. Check your manual to determine if they are supported by your version of the compiler, and do not use them if you plan to maintain your program on future versions.

In addition to resolution and aspect ratio, pixels have color. The VRES16COLOR mode allows for 16 colors to be displayed at one time. These colors can are numbered 0 through 15. The color that each number stands for can be changed, as described in Chapter 6. Table 4.2.1 gives the default values.

Table 4.2.1 Colors Available in VGA 16-Color Mode (see appendix B for colors defined for 256 color mode)

Dark Colors	**Numeric Value**	**Light Colors**	**Numeric Value**
BLACK	0	GRAY	8
BLUE	1	LIGHTBLUE	9
GREEN	2	LIGHTGREEN	10
CYAN	3	LIGHTCYAN	11
RED	4	LIGHTRED	12
MAGENTA	5	LIGHTMAGENTA	13
BROWN	6	YELLOW	14
WHITE	7	BRIGHTWHITE	15

Any time the screen is in a 16-color mode, whether it is an EGA or a VGA monitor, it can use the numeric constants in this table. Note that, unlike Borland C, named constants or macros do not exist for these 16 colors, **you must use the number itself for 16-color modes**. There are named constants for 256 color mode, but those constants will not work for other modes. Borland gets around this problem by not supporting 256 color mode. For more discussion on how colors are displayed on modes that support 16 colors, see Chapter 1.

The function _setpixel( ) needs to know what color to set the pixel to. There is a variable in the graphics library that holds a value used by all drawing functions. This value, the color that pixels are set to, is referred to as the current drawing color. Microsoft provides the function _setcolor( ) for setting the current drawing color. Here is the prototype for this function:

```
short far _setcolor(short color);
  /*
   * function for setting the current drawing
   *   color.
   *
   * Parameters:
   *   color - color the current drawing color
   *           will be set to.
   */
```

Once this function is called all graphics functions will use the color passed in. At times the color of a pixel on the screen needs to be found. Use the function _getpixel( ):

```
short _far _getpixel(short x, short y);
  /*
   * function for finding the color of a pixel
   *
   * parameters:
   *   x - x coordinate of pixel being gotten
   *   y - y coordinate of pixel being gotten
   *
   * returns:
   *   The color of the pixel
   */
```

The function _getcolor( ) returns the current drawing color:

```
short far _getcolor(void);
  /*
   * function for getting the current drawing
   *   color.
   *
   * returns:
   *   The current drawing color
   */
```

The following function demonstrates _setpixel( ) and _setcolor( ).

```
void setpixel_demo() {
  int i;

  for (i=0; i<10000; i++) {
    _setcolor((short)i%adapter_info.numcolors);
    _setpixel(rand()%adapter_info.numxpixels,
              rand()%adapter_info.numxpixels);
  } /* end for loop */

  getch();
  if(kbhit()) getch();
  _clearscreen(_GCLEARSCREEN);

} /* setpixel_demo() */
```

This function, which can be found in BK0402.C on the distribution disk, will light 10,000 pixels at random locations, using different colors, then pause until the user presses a key. Notice the if statement at the end of the function. This is needed because certain keys on the PC keyboard, such as the function keys and the cursor keys, return more than one character. Once a character is read, the keyboard must be tested to see if one of these special keys has been pressed. If this is the case the second character is read. This is discussed more fully in second program in Chapter 6 (on colors) .

To set the background color use _setbkcolor( ). As long as the screen is in 16-color mode it uses the same color constants defined for _setcolor( ). The function _getbkcolor( ) is used to find the background color.

```
long far _setbkcolor(long color);
  /*
   * function for setting the background color
   *   in graphics mode.
   *
   * Parameters
   *   color - the color the background will be
   *           set to
   */

long far _getbkcolor(void);
  /*
   * function to get the background color in
   *   graphics mode
   */
```

Viewports and Windows

Ordinarily the origin of the screen is at the upper left corner of the screen. This can be adjusted with the _setvieworg( ) function:

```
struct xycoord far _setvieworg (short x,
                                 short y);
  /*
   * function for moving the origin to another
   *   part of the screen
   *
   * Parameters:
   *   x - x coordinate of the origin, as
   *       measured from the upper left corner
   *   y - y coordinate of the origin, as
   *       measured from the upper left corner
   */
```

This can be handy when drawing graphs, since the origin can be placed on the screen where it should be in the graph. All programs in this book keep the origin in the upper left corner to remain compatible with Borland C, which does not support this function.

A region can be set up on the screen such that only items drawn in the region will appear on the screen. Any item drawn outside this region will not appear. Such a region is called a *clipping region.* The function for defining a clipping region is _setcliprgn( ).

```
void far _setcliprgn(short x1, short y1,
                     short x2, short y2);
  /*
   * function for setting a clipping region
   *
   * Parameters:
   *   x1 - left side of clipping region
   *   y1 - top of clipping region
   *   x2 - right side of clipping region
   *   y2 - bottom of clipping region
   */
```

A viewport is a clipping region with the origin in the upper left-hand corner. A viewport can be created by calling _setvieworg ( ) followed by _setcliprgn( ). Microsoft provides a short cut, the _setviewport( ) function. One call to _setviewport( ) has the same effect as calling both of the above functions.

```
void far _viewport (short x1, short y1,
                    short x2, short y2);
  /*
   * function for setting a view port
   *
   * Parameters:
   *   x1 - left side of view port
   *   y1 - top of view port
   *   x2 - right side of view port
   *   y2 - bottom of view port
   */
```

One extremely useful function provided by Microsoft C is the _setwindow( ) function. This function allows the viewport coordinates to be scaled to fit the task at hand. This function also allows the Y coordinates to be reversed, so that they are more natural. Here is the function prototype:

```
void far _setwindow (short finvert,
                     double wx1, double wy1,
                     double wx2, double wy2);
  /*
   * function for setting a graphics window
   *
   * Parameters:
   *   finvert - should the y coordinates be
   *     reversed from the normal screen.  A
   *     value of 1 reverses the coordinates,
   *     0 does not.
   *   wx1 - the new x coordinate of the left-hand side of
   *     the window.
   *   wy1 - the new y coordinate of the top
   *     of the window.
   *   wx2 - the new x coordinate of the right-hand side of
   *     the window.
   *   wy2 - the new y coordinate of the bottom
   *     of the window.
   */
```

This function takes double precision floating point values as parameters, so the window can be scaled to fractional values. In this case we need functions for drawing on the screen that also use double precision floating point numbers. Most of the graphics output routines have alternate functions defined for using the window. To use these functions append a _w to the function name:

```
short far _setpixel_w(double x, double y);
  /*
   * function for setting a pixel, using
   *   scaled window coordinates
   *
   * parameters:
   *   x - x coordinate of pixel being set
   *   y - y coordinate of pixel being set
   */
```

If a viewport is set before the call to _setwindow( ) the window will fill the viewport. Otherwise the entire screen is used. To see what functions support viewports, or what functions use the xycoord structure see Appendix B on Microsoft C graphics functions.

Note that this is one interpretation of what a window is. MS-Windows is a different type of windows. The chapters that cover SVGA programming use window to mean something still different. This is confusing, but cannot really be helped.

Borland C does not have any functions equivalent to the ones in this section, and therefore they are not used in any of the examples in this book. These functions can make drawing graphs and charts much easier. Once you have looked at Chapter 5 on graphing and charting, you may wish to try rewriting the functions presented there using these routines. You will find they get much smaller and simpler.

_clearscreen( )

Now that we can put graphics on the screen, we might want to erase them so we can start over. This is done with _clearscreen( ).

```
void far _clearscreen(short area);
  /*
   * function for clearing all or part of the
   *   screen
   *
   * Parameter:
   *   area - part of the screen to be cleared.
   */
```

Three constants are defined for use with this function: _GCLEARSCREEN, _GVIEWPORT, and GWINDOW. Use the correct one for clearing the area you wish to have cleared.

Drawing Lines

The next thing we'd like to do is draw lines. We need two functions to do this – _moveto( ) and _lineto( ). The _moveto( ) function sets a location on the screen. The _lineto( ) function draws a line from that location to another. The function _lineto( ) can then be called again without calling _moveto( ), and a line is drawn from the end of the original line to a new location. The location where the line will start is referred to as the current location. Here are the prototypes for these functions:

```
struct xycoord far _moveto(short x, short y);
  /*
   * function for setting the current location
   *   where the next line will be drawn from.
   *
   * Parameters:
   *   x - x coordinate of current location
   *   y - y coordinate of current location
   */

struct xycoord far _lineto(short x, short y);
  /*
   * function for drawing a line.  The start
   *   of line is the set with _moveto()
   *
   * Parameters:
   *   x - x coordinate where the line will end
   *   y - y coordinate where the line will end
   */
```

The following program fragment shows how to use these functions. It draws a series of lines on the screen in a diamond shape. Again this piece of code can be found in BK0402.C.

```
void line_demo() {

/*
 * This function draws lines on the screen in a
 * diamond pattern, in various colors, then
 * outlines the pattern with a white line.
 */

  int      X_Coord,  Y_Coord,
           X_Center, Y_Center;
  unsigned int Color = 1;
  char     junk;
```

```
X_Center = adapter_info.numxpixels / 2;
Y_Center = adapter_info.numypixels / 2;

/* Draw lines in first quadrant */
X_Coord  = X_Center;
Y_Coord  = 1;
while (Y_Coord < Y_Center) {
  Color = (Color+1)%adapter_info.numcolors;
  _setcolor(Color);
  _moveto (X_Center, Y_Center);
  _lineto (X_Coord, Y_Coord);
  Y_Coord++;
  X_Coord--;
} /* end while loop */

/* Draw lines in Second quadrant */
while (X_Coord < X_Center) {
  Color = (Color+1)%adapter_info.numcolors;
  _setcolor(Color);
  _moveto (X_Center, Y_Center);
  _lineto (X_Coord, Y_Coord);
  Y_Coord++;
  X_Coord++;
} /* end while loop */

/* Draw lines in Third quadrant */
while (Y_Coord > Y_Center) {
  Color = (Color+1)%adapter_info.numcolors;
  _setcolor(Color);
  _moveto (X_Center, Y_Center);
  _lineto (X_Coord, Y_Coord);
  Y_Coord--;
  X_Coord++;
} /* end while loop */

/* Draw lines in Fourth quadrant */
while (X_Coord > X_Center) {
  Color = (Color+1)%adapter_info.numcolors;
  _setcolor(Color);
  _moveto (X_Center, Y_Center);
  _lineto (X_Coord, Y_Coord);
  Y_Coord--;
  X_Coord--;
} /* end while loop */

getch();
if (kbhit()) getch();
_clearscreen(_GCLEARSCREEN);
```

```
} /* end function Line_Demo() */
```

There are also _line_w( ) and _line_xy( ) functions. Borland supports a moveto( ) and lineto( ) functions, but also supports a line( ) function that has two endpoints as parameters. Unless there is an overriding reason, this is the function that is used for most examples.

Drawing Circles, Ellipses, Arcs, and Pie Slices

For drawing circles and ellipses, Microsoft provides the _ellipse( ) function. This function takes 2 x values and 2 y values as parameters. You can think of these as the upper-left and lower-right corner of a rectangle that the ellipse will fit inside of. Figure 4.2.1 shows this, but the ellipse routine does not draw the rectangle on the screen. The rectangle is known as a *bounding rectangle* or *bounding box.*

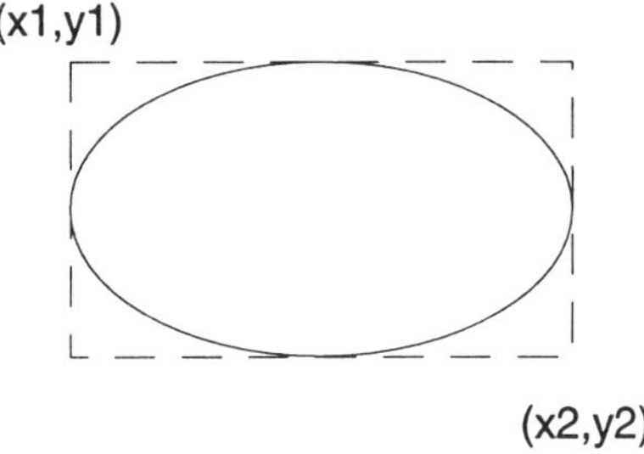

Fig 4.2.1. The Bounding Box of an Ellipse

To draw a circle use a square bounding rectangle. Here is the prototype for the ellipse routine:

```
short far _ellipse (short control,
                    short x1, short y1,
                    short x2, short y2);
  /*
   * function for drawing ellipses.
   *
   * Parameters:
   *   control - whether the ellipse should be
   *             filled or not.
   *   x1, y1  - coordinates of upper left
   *             corner
   *   x1, y1  - coordinates of lower right
   *             corner
   */
```

The first parameter is whether to fill the shape or not. The file graph.h defines the constants _GFILLINTERIOR and _GBORDER to be used here. Other Microsoft C routines for filling shapes have the same parameter and use the same constants. Here is an example of _ellipse:

```
void ellipse_demo() {
  /*
   * Note - Microsoft C does not contain a
   *  circle routine.  Use the _ellipse()
   *  function.
   */

    int  X_Center, Y_Center, MaxRadius,
         MaxColor, Color, X_Rad, Y_Rad;

    X_Center  = adapter_info.numxpixels / 2;
    Y_Center  = adapter_info.numypixels / 2;
    MaxRadius = Y_Center;
    MaxColor  = adapter_info.numcolors;
    X_Rad     = Y_Center;
    Y_Rad     = 0;
    Color     = 0;

    while (X_Rad > 1) {
      Color = (Color + 1) % MaxColor;
      _setcolor (Color);
      X_Rad -= 3;
      Y_Rad += 3;
      _ellipse (_GBORDER,
               X_Center-X_Rad, Y_Center-Y_Rad,
               X_Center+X_Rad, Y_Center+Y_Rad);
    } /* end while loop */

    getch();
    if (kbhit())  getch();
    _clearscreen(_GCLEARSCREEN);

} /* end function Ellipse_Demo() */
```

This function draws a series of ellipses, changing the length and width to form a pattern on the screen. It is a very interesting effect. This code can be found on the distribution disk in BK0402.C.

Microsoft supplies the _ellipse_w( ) and _ellipse_wxy( ) functions for use with the _setwindow( ) function and with the xycoord structure. Borland supports an ellipse( ) function that is somewhat different. Since the Borland ellipse( ) function is used in some examples, it might be a good idea to review it. The Borland routine does not have a parameter equivalent to the control parameter, nor does it use a bounding box. Instead it uses two lengths, one for the X dimension, the other for the Y dimension. This routine only draws the outline, while a separate fill_ellipse( ) function is used to draw a filled ellipse.

To draw an arc that is not a complete circle or ellipse use _arc( ).

```
short far _arc(short x1, short y1,
               short x2, short y2,
               short x3, short y3,
               short x4, short y4);
  /*
   * function for drawing an arc
   *
   * Parameters:
   *   x1, y1 - the upper left corner of the
   *            bounding box
   *   x2, y2 - the lower right corner of the
   *            bounding box
   *   x3, y3 - start vector
   *   x4, y4 - end vector
   */
```

The start of the arc is marked by a line from the center of the bounding rectangle to the point (x3,y3). Where this line crosses the bounding rectangle the arc begins. A line from the center to (x4, y4) is used to mark the end of the arc. Figure 4.2.2 shows how this works pictorially. If you wish the arc to appear on the other side of these lines reverse the order of points (x3,y3) and (x4,y4).

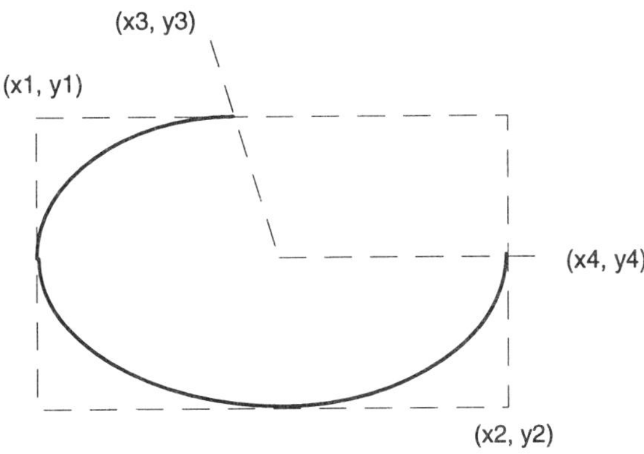

Fig 4.2.2. Parameters to the _arc( ) Function

The _pie( ) function is a similar function for drawing pie slices, only the start and end vectors are drawn in from the center of the bounding rectangle up to the edges. This function is useful for creating pie charts.

```
short far _pie(short control,
               short x1, short y1,
               short x2, short y2,
               short x3, short y3,
               short x4, short y4);
  /*
   * function for drawing pie slices.
   *
   * Parameters:
   *   control - whether the pie slice should
   *             be filled or not
   *   x1, y1 - the upper left corner of the
   *            bounding box
   *   x2, y2 - the lower right corner of the
   *            bounding box
   *   x3, y3 - start vector
   *   x4, y4 - end vector
   */
```

Microsoft supplies _wxy versions of the _arc( ) and _pie( ) functions, but not the _w versions. Borland supplies a function called pieslice( ), which is equivalent to Microsoft's _pie( ). This function is used in Chapter 5, in the section on pie charts. Borland's function arc( ) only draws circular arcs. The Borland function ellipse( ) is used to drawing elliptical arcs.

Drawing Rectangles and Polygons

Microsoft C provides routines for creating rectangles and polygons. The _rectangle( ) routine has a parameter to tell whether the rectangle should be filled or not, and parameters for the upper left corner and the lower right corner.

```
short far _rectangle(short control,
                     short x1, short y1,
                     short x1, short y1);
  /*
   * function for drawing rectangles
   *
   * Parameters:
   *   control - whether the rectangle is
```

```
 *             filled
 *   x1, y1  - the upper left corner
 *   x2, y2  - the lower right corner
 */
```

The _polygon( ) function is a little more complicated. It has the same parameter for whether the shape should be filled, then it takes a pointer to an array of xycoord structures, and finally the number of points in the polygon. Here is the prototype:

```
short far _polygon(short control,
                   struct xycoord far *points,
                   short numpoints);
  /*
   * function for drawing polygons
   *
   * Parameters:
   *   control   - whether the polygon should
   *               be filled
   *   points    - array of points, each is a
   *               corner of the polygon
   *   numpoints - the number of corner points
   */
```

Here is an example of the _polygon( ) function:

```
void poly_demo() {
/*
 * Draw a kind of arrow head-shaped thing using
 * Microsoft's _polygon() routine
 */
    struct xycoord Poly[4];

    Poly[0].xcoord=adapter_info.numxpixels/3;
    Poly[0].ycoord=1;
    Poly[1].xcoord=adapter_info.numxpixels/2;
    Poly[1].ycoord=adapter_info.numypixels/3;
    Poly[2].xcoord=
           (adapter_info.numxpixels/3)*2;
    Poly[2].ycoord=1;
    Poly[3].xcoord=adapter_info.numxpixels/2;
    Poly[3].ycoord=
           (adapter_info.numypixels/3)*2;
    Poly[4].xcoord=adapter_info.numxpixels/3;
    Poly[4].ycoord=1;
```

```
    /* draw the Polygon */
    _polygon (_GFILLINTERIOR, Poly, 4);

    getch();
    if (kbhit())  getch();

} /* end function DrawPoly_Demo() */
```

Patterned Lines

Patterned lines are dashed lines, dotted lines, or other lines that are not solid. Microsoft provides the _setlinestyle( ) function for setting the pattern of the line to whatever the programmers wants.

```
void _setlinestyle(unsigned short mask);
  /*
   * Function to set the style that future
   * lines will be drawn with.
   *
   * Parameter:
   *   mask - bit pattern to describe pattern
   *          of line
   */
```

The mask parameter is a bit map. When the line is drawn, this bit map is referenced. For every bit set in the mask a pixel is lit on the line. For every bit cleared a pixel is not lit. So by setting the bit pattern 1010 1010 1010 1010, the next call to _lineto( ) will result in a dotted line. This can be accomplished with the hex value 0xAAAA. The following lines of code draw a dotted line across the screen. This is in BK0403.C on the distribution disk.

```
_setlinestyle(0xAAAA);
_moveto(0,5);
_lineto(adapter_info.numxpixels);
```

This would be a good time to review the relation between hexadecimal and binary. Hex makes a handy way to initialize bit patterns. One digit in hex is equivalent to four digits in binary, or four bits in a word. This means that every number that can be made from four bits can be made with one hex digit. Also, any number that can be represented with one hex digit can be represented with four bits. This one-to-one mapping is what makes hex so handy in computer science. To initialize a byte, two hex digits are needed. To initialize a word, four hex digits are needed.

The hex number 0xF0F0 can be used to draw dashed lines. More complex patterns can be created. The number 0xAAFF will result in four dots then a long dash; 0xAA00 will result in four dots then a space. To get back to a solid line use 0xFFFF. Examples are given on the distribution disk in the file BK0403.C.

Filling Shapes

Filling shapes with solid fill is simple. The various functions provided for drawing shapes have a control parameter. If the constant _GBORDER is used the border of the object is drawn. If the constant _GFILLINTERIOR is used the object is filled, but no border is drawn. If you want the object filled and a border drawn then two function calls are needed.

Sometimes there are shapes on the screen that need to be filled, but that cannot be obtained by one of the provided routines. To fill these use the _floodfill( ) routine.

```
short _floodfill (short x, short y,
                  short boundary);
  /*
   * Routine for filling shapes that are not
   *   ellipses or polygons
   *
   * Parameters:
   *   x, y - location of any point inside the
   *          object being filled
   *   boundary - the color of the border of
   *              the shape
   */
```

The _floodfill( ) function starts at a pixel in the interior of the shape and fills outward from there until a pixel the color of the boundary parameter is encountered. It keeps trying different directions until the entire shape is filled. The flood fill algorithm is a well-known algorithm. Source code for one version is given in Chapter 11 on filling. This routine has a shortcoming, in that the border must be made entirely of a single color. If one part of the border is a different color from the rest _floodfill will "leak" out and fill the entire screen.

Filling with Patterns

Filling with patterns requires a little more thought. The method is similar to setting line patterns described in the last section. A bit pattern is set up that describes the pattern the object will be filled with. The _setfillmask( ) function is used to set the pattern.

```
void _setfillmask(unsigned char *mask);
  /*
   * Function to set fill pattern
   *
   * Parameter:
   *   mask - array of 8 characters giving
   *          bit pattern for filling
   */
```

This function uses an array of 8 characters for the pattern. There is a certain amount of subtlety in setting this bit mask. The programmer must be aware of how the edges will look when the pattern repeats.

A good example of setting up this bit mask, and also a good example of the subtleties involved, is an example given by Microsoft. The pattern shown in Fig. 4.2.3 is used to fill with a series of diagonal lines.

Fig 4.2.3. Portion of a Fill Pattern

Looking at this pattern, it looks as if it will make a rather interesting series of diagonals. The following code can be used to set this pattern:

```
char fillmask[8];

fillmask[0] = 0x93;
fillmask[1] = 0xC9;
fillmask[2] = 0x64;
fillmask[3] = 0xB2;
fillmask[4] = 0x59;
fillmask[5] = 0x2C;
fillmask[6] = 0x96;
fillmask[7] = 0x4B;

_setfillmask(fillmask);
```

But will this really do what we expect when we fill something? Let's take a look at what happens when we put several of these patterns close together (see Fig. 4.2.4)

Fig. 4.2.4 An Area Filled with Pattern in Fig. 4.2.3

The spaces are there only so the reader can see where one pattern ends and the next begins. Now it is easy to see that a rather complex pattern is created, not the diagonal lines expected. It is also easy to see how to change it so diagonal lines are created. By moving the line in the lower left corner over one pixel, eliminating the next line over, and making the triangle of pixels in the upper right corner into one pixel we get the pattern in Fig. 4.2.5.

Fig 4.2.5. Fill Pattern for Diagonal Lines (Fancy)

We can create this with the following:

```
fillmask[0] = 0x91;
fillmask[1] = 0xC8;
fillmask[2] = 0x64;
fillmask[3] = 0x32;
fillmask[4] = 0x19;
fillmask[5] = 0x8C;
fillmask[6] = 0x46;
fillmask[7] = 0x23;
```

This gives the pattern in Fig. 4.2.6:

Fig.4.2.6 Area Filled with Pattern in Fig 4.2.5

When the gaps are closed this makes a nice pattern with a thin diagonal line and a thick diagonal line. To create your own patterns it is useful to draw them on graph paper to see what will happen when the edges interact. This next piece of code is found on the distribution disk in the file BK0403.C. It contains both the patterns given above, plus a solid fill [the first call to _rectangle( ) since _setfillmask( ) is not called first] and a third pattern not described here. It might be instructive to see if you can figure out what this pattern will look like.

```
void fill_pattern_demo() {
  char fillmask[8];

  _setcolor  (9);
  _rectangle (_GFILLINTERIOR,
              adapter_info.numxpixels/4,
              0,
              adapter_info.numxpixels/2,
              adapter_info.numypixels/2);
  _setcolor  (15);
  _rectangle (_GBORDER,
              adapter_info.numxpixels/4,
              0,
              adapter_info.numxpixels/2,
              adapter_info.numypixels/2);

  fillmask[0] = 0x93;
  fillmask[1] = 0xC9;
  fillmask[2] = 0x64;
  fillmask[3] = 0xB2;
  fillmask[4] = 0x59;
  fillmask[5] = 0x2C;
  fillmask[6] = 0x96;
  fillmask[7] = 0x4B;

  _setcolor  (14);
  _setfillmask(fillmask);
  _rectangle (_GFILLINTERIOR,
              adapter_info.numxpixels*3/4,
              0,
              adapter_info.numxpixels/2,
              adapter_info.numypixels/2);
  _setcolor  (15);
  _rectangle (_GBORDER,
              adapter_info.numxpixels*3/4,
              0,
              adapter_info.numxpixels/2,
              adapter_info.numypixels/2);

  fillmask[0] = 0x91;
  fillmask[1] = 0xC8;
  fillmask[2] = 0x64;
  fillmask[3] = 0x32;
  fillmask[4] = 0x19;
  fillmask[5] = 0x8C;
  fillmask[6] = 0x46;
  fillmask[7] = 0x23;
```

```
    _setcolor  (12);
    _setfillmask(fillmask);
    _rectangle (_GFILLINTERIOR,
                adapter_info.numxpixels/4,
                adapter_info.numypixels/2,
                adapter_info.numxpixels/2,
                adapter_info.numypixels-1);
    _setcolor  (15);
    _rectangle (_GBORDER,
                adapter_info.numxpixels/4,
                adapter_info.numypixels/2,
                adapter_info.numxpixels/2,
                adapter_info.numypixels-1);

    fillmask[0] = 0xC3;
    fillmask[1] = 0xC3;
    fillmask[2] = 0x0C;
    fillmask[3] = 0x0C;
    fillmask[4] = 0x30;
    fillmask[5] = 0x30;
    fillmask[6] = 0xC3;
    fillmask[7] = 0xC3;

    _setcolor  (13);
    _setfillmask(fillmask);
    _rectangle (_GFILLINTERIOR,
                adapter_info.numxpixels*3/4,
                adapter_info.numypixels/2,
                adapter_info.numxpixels/2,
                adapter_info.numypixels-1);
    _setcolor  (15);
    _rectangle (_GBORDER,
                adapter_info.numxpixels*3/4,
                adapter_info.numypixels/2,
                adapter_info.numxpixels/2,
                adapter_info.numypixels-1);

    getch();
    if (kbhit()) getch();
}
```

Text in Graphics Mode

Using the monitor in graphics mode gives a great deal of flexibility to text. The programmer is no longer bound by one style of text or by a single size.

The style of text is called the *typeface.* Different typefaces can be presented in different sizes. The combination of size and typeface is called a font.

Fonts have several characteristics. One is whether or not the font is *proportional.* A proportional font will space the characters according to the width of each character. An "i" will take less space than an "m". In a nonproportional font all letters take the same amount of space.

A proportional font: abcdefghijklmnopqrstuvwxyz
A nonproportional font: `abcdefghijklmnopqrstuvwxyz`

Compare how much space there is for the "i" in both examples.

Another characteristic of a font is whether is *bitmapped* or *stroked.* With a bitmapped font the characters are made by placing dots in a grid. A stroked font is made by drawing lines to make each letter. Bitmapped fonts are easier to create and take less work for the computer to put on thc screen, but they usually do not look as good as a stroked font. Stroked fonts take more work for the font designer, but they can be resized easily, and generally look good at different sizes. When a bitmapped font is resized it will often look "chunky. Microsoft refers to stroked fonts as "vector mapped" fonts.

Fig. 4.3.1 A Closeup of a Bitmapped Letter

Bitmapped fonts are usually nonproportional. With most bitmapped fonts the designer selects a grid size, then designs all letters to fit into the same size grid. The example in Fig 4.3.1 is an 8 × 8 grid. Another common size is 14 × 14. The more pixels in a grid the better the letter looks.

B

Fig. 4.3.2 Closeup of a Stroked Letter

Some stroked fonts are *outline fonts*. Lines are drawn around the outside of the character, and the middle is left blank. It is the job of the programmer to fill the character with the desired color. A font that is filled in is called a *filled font*. Some stroked fonts are simple enough that they do not require filling.

Microsoft C provides six fonts, which are supplied in files with the extension .FON. In addition to these six fonts, Microsoft Windows™ .FON files can also be used. Table 4.3.1 shows the six fonts provided by Microsoft.

Table 4.3.1 Microsoft Graphics Fonts

Font	Mapping	Sizes	Spacing	File Name
Courier	Bit	13×8, 16×9, 20×12	Fixed	COURB.FON
Helv	Bit	13×5, 16x7, 20×8, 13×15, 16×6, 19×8	Fixed	HELVB.FON
Tms Rmn	Bit	10×5, 12×6, 15x8 16×9, 20×12, 26×16	Fixed	TMSRB.FON
Modern	Stroked	Scaled	Proportional	MODERN.FON
Script	Stroked	Scaled	Proportional	SCRIPT.FON
Roman	Stroked	Scaled	Proportional	ROMAN.FON

The bitmapped fonts can only be used in the sizes shown, which are given as number of pixels. The stroked fonts can be scaled to any size.

Tto use text in a graphics program, the different fonts to be used need to be registered, then a font needs to be chosen. Once a font is chosen the _outgtext( ) function needs to be used to output text, since the standard C screen output functions [printf( ), putch( ), etc.] will not work with graphics fonts.

Registering Fonts

The _registerfonts( ) function is used to register the available fonts. This tells the program what fonts are available in .FON files for use. It does not bring the fonts into the program from the disk. This is important to note. The .FON files must be kept available on the disk where the program can read them. If these are on a floppy disk and the disk is changed, or if the program changes directories and cannot find these files, future calls to set the font will fail.

The _registerfonts( ) function takes a path name in the form of a string. This path contains the name of a font file. Wild cards are accepted, so a number of font files can be registered in a single call.

```
short _registerfonts(unsigned char *filename)
  /*
   * Function to register available fonts for
   *   using text in graphics modes
   *
   * Parameter:
   *   filename - path of font files.  Wild
   *              cards are accepted.
   *
   * Returns:
   *   A value less than 0 if an error occurs,
   *   otherwise the number of fonts registered.
   */
```

Here is an example of registering fonts:

```
if (_registerfonts("\\font_dir\\*.fon") < 0) {
  printf ("Error - Fonts not registered\n");
}
```

This code segment will look in a directory called \font_dir, for all font files. The reason for the double back slash (\\) is that a single backslash is read as an escape character. Two back slashes tell the compiler that a backslash is the intended character.

Setting the Current Font

The _setfont( ) function is used to set the font. Setting the font sets the typeface and the size. The _setfont( ) function takes a string as an argument. Embedded within the string are character codes to describe the font to be set. Below is the function prototype, then a table of character codes. After the table is an explanation of the code and examples of how they are used.

```
short _setfont (unsigned char *options)
  /*
   * Function for setting the current font
   *
   * Parameter:
   *   options - String describing font desired
   *
   * Returns:
   *   Number of the font when successful, or a
   *   negative value otherwise.
   */
```

Table 4.3.2 Option codes for use with _setfont( )

Option Code	Meaning
b	Select best fit
f	Fixed space font only
h*y*	Character Height – y is height in pixels
n*x*	Font number, where x is less than the number returned by _registerfonts( )
p	Proportional font only
r	Raster mapped (bitmapped) font only
t'fontname'	Name typeface, in single quotes
v	Vector-mapped (stroked) font only
w*x*	Character Width – x is the width in pixels

As you can see, there are a number of ways to select a font. Usually the most convenient is by the font name. If a stroked font is specified and sizes are given with the "h" or "w" option codes, the font is scaled to those sizes. If a bitmapped font is selected and sizes are specified, the font will only be loaded if it is available in the given sizes. If the best fit "b" option is specified, then the font most closely matching the one specified will be loaded, using the sizes that are closest to those given.

If the "b" option is used a font will always be loaded, but it might not be the font expected. If this option is not used it is possible that no font will be loaded. If an attempt to write using graphics fonts is made when no font is loaded, garbage will be written on the screen.

You do not need to use the font name to load the font. A font number can be specified with the "n" option. This is the number where the font is in the register. This is not always convenient, since, if a call to _registerfonts( ) is made with wild cards, it is likely that the programmer will not know the order in which the fonts were loaded. The font can also be selected by size, by specifying bitmapped or stroked, or by specifying proportional or fixed space.

Here are some examples.

```
_setfont("t'roman'h30w24);
```

This command will load the roman font, scaled to a height of 30 pixels and a width of 24 pixels. This font can be scaled since it is a stroked font.

The string format shown here is difficult to read. The _setfont( ) function will ignore any unknown characters, so the command may be rewritten in a more readable format. The spaces and commas in the following example are ignored by _setfont( ).

```
_setfont("t'roman', h30, w24");
```

The order of the option codes in the string is not important. The size could be placed before the typeface.

Bitmapped fonts cannot be scaled. If a size is specified for a bitmapped font, the font must be available in that size. The following will not work, since tms rmn is not scalable and not available with a height of 30 or a width of 24 (see table 4.3.1).

```
_setfont("t'tms rmn', h30, w24");
```

The "b" option tells _setfont( ) to make the best fit. The following will load the tms rmn typeface, but it might not be the exact size expected.

```
_setfont("t'tms rmn', h30, w24, b");
```

The following will load the first font in the register that comes in a size, or can be scaled to, 40 pixels in height.

```
_setfont("h40");
```

This shows that the name or number of a font does not need to be specified to load a font. This is useful if you do not know what fonts will be available when the program is run.

Writing Text in Graphics Mode

Before you can experiment with _setfont( ) you need to be able to write text to the screen, using the selected font. The normal C output functions [putch( ), printf( ), etc.] will not work with the special graphics fonts. They only use the blocky bitmapped font that is native to the monitor. The function _outgtext( ) is used to write text using graphics fonts.

```
void _outgtext(unsigned char *text);
  /*
   * function for outputting text using
   *   graphics fonts
   *
   * Parameter:
   *   text - string of text
   */
```

This function will not format text the way printf( ) does. To do this use sprintf( ) to format a buffer, then use _outgtext( ) to write the buffer. Borland C's output routine has the same shortcoming. Examples of formatting a buffer then writing can be seen in the next chapter, on making graphs and charts. This function does not have parameters to give it a screen location. To set the location where text will be written use _moveto( ). After the text is output,the current location is updated to the position on the screen at the end of the string.

The following example sets the font to roman, or the closest font to roman, then writes "I Love MicroSoft C!" on the center of the screen.

```
#include <graph.h>
#include <stdlib.h>

struct videoconfig adapter_info;

void text_demo() {
  if (_registerfonts("*.FON") < 0) {
    printf("No font files found");
    exit(-1);
  }

  _setfont("t'roman', b, h170, w30");

  _moveto(60,165);

  _outgtext("I Love MicroSoft C!");

  getch();
```

```
  if (kbhit()) getch();
}

void main () {

  if (_setvideomode(_MAXRESMODE) == 0) {
    printf
      ("error in setting graphics mode\n\n");
    exit(-1);
  }
  _getvideoconfig(&adapter_info);

  /* do graphics stuff here */
  _setbkcolor(_BLUE);
  text_demo();

  _setvideomode(_DEFAULTMODE);
}
```

Oftentimes, the fonts available are just not what the situation calls for. For information on how to create your own fonts, see Chapter 3, which covers this in detail.

5

Graphs and Charts

One of the most common uses of computer graphics is for drawing charts and graphs. Many programs are written to process data. The results of this processing are then shown graphically using graphs, bar charts, or pie charts. Such a display makes it easy for the user to tell at a glance the results of the processing. Unfortunately, coming up with a function to graph data is not as easy as it would seem. Oftentimes the work outweighs the gains. To overcome this, this chapter develops general functions that can be placed in a separate file and called any time data need to be graphed or charted.

Graphing Data

Two methods commonly used for graphing are Cartesian coordinates and polar coordinates. The cartesian coordinates method is the familiar grid type of graphing used by most high school math and science courses. The second is useful for plotting certain types of scientific data. It places the origin in the center of the graph. The position of a point is determined by an angle and a distance from the origin. There are other methods for graphing. Once the basic methods for drawing a graph are understood, it should be a simple matter to figure out these other methods.

Cartesian Coordinates

First, in order to understand what is going on, we develop a Borland C function that graphs two trig functions (sine and cosine), then graphs the product of the two. After that, a set of functions is developed to graph arrays of data.

Graphing Functions "By Hand"

Drawing the trace of a graph on the screen is fairly straightforward. Start with a for loop. The loop variable is passed to the function that is being plotted. The loop variable is used as the X coordinate, and the result of the function call is used as the Y coordinate. The code for doing this looks like:

```
for (i = 0; i < n; i++)
    putpixel (i, function(i));
```

This is easy enough in theory, but of course the practical reality of the computer system adds complexity. In plain English, this just won't work. First of all we don't want the plot to appear on a blank screen. We need axes that are clearly labeled. In addition there is a problem with scale. Imagine that we are plotting a sine function. Any call to the sine function will return between -1 and 1. When this is plotted using the code above, it makes a very flat trace across the top of the screen. The trace must be scaled to fit on the screen.

One easy way to accomplish scaling is to set up multiply factors for the X and Y dimensions. The largest and smallest values for the dimension need to be found. For the X dimension this is easy. Subtract the largest from the smallest to find the range of the data. Divide the number of pixels that the plot should cover by the range. Now when a point is plotted, multiply by this scale factor. The scale factors for the X and Y dimensions must be found separately, because the number of pixels used and the range of the data are different for each dimension.

The first step is to figure the number of pixels to be used in each direction. The trace should not take up the whole screen. Room should be left for labeling the axes. On the VGA monitor leave 25 pixels below the trace and 75 pixels to the left for labeling. Once the trace is drawn these values can be adjusted to make the best looking graph. The rest of the screen can now be used for the trace. It is useful to set up variables that give the high and low pixel values for each dimension. The screen coordinates halfway between these are also found, for labeling purposes. Now that the high and low pixel values for each dimension are known, the scale factors can be found. Here is an example of code to set up these variables:

```
Y_High   = getmaxy() - 50;
Y_Low    = 20;
Y_Center = ((Y_High - Y_Low) / 2) + Y_Low;
DY       = (Y_Low - Y_High)/(1 - (-1));

X_High   = getmaxx() - 50;
X_Low    = 75;
X_Center = ((X_High - X_Low) / 2) + X_Low;
DX       = (X_High - X_Low)/(360 - 0);
```

In this example DX and DY are the scale factors. The function being plotted is the sine function. The plot will go from 0 to 360 in the X direction, and -1 to 1 in the Y direction. This is where the values in the denominators come from. The code for finding DY shows the high value of the Y dimension being subtracted from the low value. One might think this is backward, but in reality it is the PC monitor that is backward. The subtraction is done because the Y coordinates start at the top of the screen.

The code in the denominators seems clumsy. Since these values are constants we can rewrite these two lines as:

```
DY       = (Y_Low - Y_High)/2;
DX       = (X_High - X_Low)/360;
```

The next job is to draw the axes. Since the high, low, and center screen coordinates for the graph have already been found, this is straightforward:

```
setcolor (LIGHTGRAY);
line     (X_Low, Y_Low,    X_Low,  Y_High);
line     (X_Low, Y_Center,
          X_High, Y_Center);
```

This code draws the Y axis then the X axis. Notice that Y_Center is used when drawing the X axis. This is because the origin happens to lie on this line. If the origin appears on the graph, the axes should be drawn through it.

Labeling is not quite as easy. Each axis should have a title, and the axes should have units. Adding titles is fairly straightforward. First set text justification to CENTER in both dimensions. For the Y label set text direction to VERT_DIR, or for the X label set it to HORIZ_DIR. Use outtextxy( ) to write the label at the center of the axis, with enough room between it and the axis so that it does not hit the axis. The amount of space needed can be found using textheight( ). Here is an example:

```
settextstyle (SMALL_FONT, VERT_DIR, 9);
settextjustify (CENTER_TEXT, CENTER_TEXT);

outtextxy (X_Low-textheight("Y Label")*2-10,
            Y_Center,
           "Y Label");

settextstyle (SMALL_FONT, HORIZ_DIR, 9);

outtextxy (X_Center,
           Y_High + textheight("X Label") + 5,
           "X Label");
```

The small font looks good on graphs. It can be made small enough for units and comments that might be placed on the graph later, and it is not too fancy. Gothic simply would not look appropriate on a graph.

Next the units have to be placed on the axes. Each unit step need not be labeled. Often there are just too many, as in our example of the sine wave. Labeling each degree from 0 to 360 would make for a very crowded display. Generally, eight or nine labels are sufficient for the units.

The outtextxy( ) function is again called to write the label. Unfortunately this function will not handle integers or reals, only strings. The sprintf( ) function is used to convert integers and reals to strings. Its syntax is similar to fprintf( ), only the file is replaced with a pointer to a string.

Now how do we find the number to convert to a string? Decide how many unit labels you want. Then a for loop can be used. Take the total number of units, divide that by the number of labels, multiply by the loop variable, and that is the number to be written.

```
for (i = 0; i <= 8; i++)
  sprintf(Label_Str,"%1f",(float)i*(360 / 8));
```

Note the float type casting. This is because i is an integer, so the whole operation is assumed to be integer, and integer instructions are used for the whole operation. This is more efficient for the computer, but the decimal part is truncated. We need the decimal part, so we need to tell Borland C to use floating point math. Type casts like this appear in various places throughout the code in this chapter.

And now outtextxy( ) can be used to output the text. The numbers should appear just below the X axis and just to the left of the Y axis, far enough away so that it does not write over the axis. The spacing between labels is the number of units divided by the number of labels, multiplied by the scale factor, multiplied by the loop variable. The border of the graph then has to be added on so that the numbers will start at the beginning of the graph, not the edge of the screen.

```
outtextxy(X_Low + (i*(360/8)*DX),
          Y_Center + textheight("Label_Str"),
          Label_Str);
```

Here is the complete code for writing units for our example:

```
settextstyle (SMALL_FONT, HORIZ_DIR, 4);
for(i = 0; i <= 8; i++) {
  sprintf(Label_Str,"%.1f",(float)i*(360/8));
  outtextxy(X_Low+(i*(360/8)*DX),
            Y_Center + textheight("1"),
            Label_Str);
}

for(i = -4; i <= 4; i++) {
  sprintf(Label_Str, "%.2f", (float) i / 4);
  outtextxy(X_Low-textwidth("1.00"),
            i*(DY/4)+Y_Center,
            Label_Str);
}
```

Now the trace can be drawn. The easiest method would be to use a loop from the lowest unit on the X axis to the highest. Place a call to putpixel( ) in the loop. The X coordinate will be the loop variable multiplied by the X scale factor, with X_Low added on. The Y coordinate will be the result of a function call with the loop variable as the parameter to the function. The result must be multiplied by the Y_Scale factor. The result is then added to Y_Center to center the trace on the graph.

There is a problem with the method described above. If there is a large difference between the Y values of two successive plots, the plotted pixels will not touch. The plot looks like a dotted line. To avoid this problem the lineto( ) function can be used. The moveto( ) function is called with the starting point, then the call to putpixel( ) is replaced with a call to lineto( ). The result is a good looking graph:

```
moveto ((0*DX)+X_Low,
        (sin(0*M_PI/180*3)*DY)+Y_Center);

for(i = 1; i <= 360; i++)
  lineto ((i*DX)+X_Low,
          (sin(i*M_PI/180*3)*DY)+Y_Center);
```

Notice in the above code that the loop variable is multiplied by M_PI/180. This is because C's trig functions operate in radians. To convert degrees to radians multiply by pi/180. We are now ready to put the whole thing together. This is done in file BK0501.C. This is a stand-alone program that can be compiled using Borland C, and when it is run it will plot the function sin(i*3), then on top of that plot cos(i), then sin(i*3) * cos(i). This program will require some modification for those using compilers other than Borland C, as will most programs in Chapters 5 to 10.

A Generic Function for Graphing Functions

Now that we have an example of a program for making a graph, wouldn't it be nice if we could make a general plotting function? All we have to do is pass in data and it will be graphed automatically. Then we don't have to go through all the work to set up a graph each time. Let the computer do the work.

The function will work basically the same as the one developed in the last section. Variables will be set up that define the edges of the graph, then these will be used, along with the data, to find scale factors. The axes will be drawn, titles added, and units marked on each axis. Then the plot will be drawn.

To make this work, we need an array of data. To make the function as generic as possible, the array is unsized. Only a pointer to the array is passed. So we need a parameter to give the number of data points in the array. The array hold the Y values. To label the graph correctly, we need the high and low values for the X axis. Finally we need titles for the X and Y axes. So here is the function prototype:

```
void draw_graph (int    Data_Points,
                 float  X_Lo_Val,
                 float  X_Hi_Val,
                 float *Data,
                 char  *X_Label,
                 char  *Y_Label);
```

Data_Points is the number of data points in the data array. X_Lo_Val and X_Hi_Val are the low and high values for the X axis, respectively. Data is a pointer to the data array. X_Label and Y_Label are the labels for the X and Y axes.

The first thing to do is set up the boundaries. This is accomplished the same way as in the last section. Allow space for titles on the left and bottom, use getmaxx( ) to find the right, getmaxy( ) minus space for labels for the lower boundary, 0 for the top, and the space needed for the axis title and units for the left. Now we need to find DX and DY. For DX we have parameters that give the number of X values and the high and low X values. So all we have to do is:

```
DX = (X_Hi - X_Lo) / Data_Points;
```

For DY we need to find the range. This is the highest value in the data array minus the lowest value. A function that loops through the array and finds the highest and lowest values is handy here:

```
void get_lo_and_hi_vals (int    Data_Points,
                         float *Data,
                         float *Y_Lo_Val,
                         float *Y_Hi_Val) {

  int i;

  *Y_Lo_Val = Data[0];
  *Y_Hi_Val = Data[0];
  for (i = 1; i <= Data_Points; i++)
    if (Data[i] < *Y_Lo_Val)
        *Y_Lo_Val = Data[i];
    else if (Data[i] > *Y_Hi_Val)
        *Y_Hi_Val = Data[i];
} /* end get_lo_and_hi_vals */
```

Now that we have this information we can find DY the same way we did in the last section:

```
DY = (Y_Lo - Y_Hi) / (Y_Hi_Val - Y_Lo_Val);
```

where Y_Lo and Y_Hi are screen coordinates, and Y_Hi_Val and Y_Lo_Val are the highest and lowest data elements to be plotted.

Now we need to draw the axes. This is not quite as easy as when done "by hand." There you could figure out where the origin was, and draw the axis. With this function we cannot count on the origin being nicely at the center of the data, or being nicely at the side. Instead we have to determine where the origin is and put the axis there, or put the axis at the edge if the origin is not on the graph.

One way of setting the axes is to set two variables, X_of_Y_axis and Y_of_X_axis, then use them for drawing the axes. X_of_Y_axis holds the X coordinate of the Y axis, and Y_of_X_axis the Y coordinate of the X axis. An if statement is used to determine if the origin is on the graph in a particular dimension. If the highest value is less than 0 the origin is not on the graph, and the axis should be drawn at the top of the graph. If the lowest value is greater than 0, the origin is again off the graph, and the axis should be drawn at the bottom.

Otherwise the location of the origin must be found. There is a neat trick to do this. The lowest value in the range can be thought of as the distance from the lowest point in the range to the origin. So if we take this number and multiply by the scale factor we have the number of pixels from the boundary to the origin. This only works if the lowest point is negative, otherwise this gives us the number of pixels in the wrong direction. The if statement described above will take care of this. If the origin is on the graph the lower bound must be negative, so the result of multiplying this by the scale factor will be negative.

But if we move a certain number of pixels from the boundary in the negative direction we will be moving off the graph. So take the negative of the low value. Then add the boundary to the result and this is where the axis is located. Here is the code for drawing the axes:

```
X0 = X_Lo + (-X_Lo_Val*DX);
Y0 = Y_Hi + (-Y_Lo_Val*DY);

/* Draw X Axis */
if (0 < Y_Lo_Val)
  Y_of_X_Axis = Y_Hi;
else if (0 > Y_Hi_Val)
  Y_of_X_Axis = Y_Lo;
else
  Y_of_X_Axis = Y0;

line (X_Lo, Y_of_X_Axis, X_Hi, Y_of_X_Axis);

/* Draw Y Axis */
if (0 < X_Lo_Val)
  X_of_Y_Axis = X_Lo;
else if (0 > X_Hi_Val)
  X_of_Y_Axis = X_Hi;
else
  X_of_Y_Axis = X_Lo +
    (X_Lo_Val*((float)(X_Hi - X_Lo) /
                        (X_Lo_Val - X_Hi_Val)));
```

```
line (X_of_Y_Axis, Y_Lo, X_of_Y_Axis, Y_Hi);
```

Now that the axes are drawn, the rest of the function is much like the one in the last section. Titles are written the same way, axes are numbered the same, and the trace is plotted the same way. Here is all the code put together:

```
void draw_graph (int    Data_Points,
                 float  X_Lo_Val,
                 float  X_Hi_Val,
                 float *Data,
                 char  *X_Label,
                 char  *Y_Label) {

  int  i;
  char Label_Str[8];
  int  X_of_Y_Axis,   /* X value where the Y
                           axis is drawn */
       Y_of_X_Axis;   /* same for X axis */

  G_Data_Points = Data_Points;  /* save this
                           for add_trace() */

  get_lo_and_hi_vals (Data_Points, Data,
                      &G_Y_Lo_Val, &G_Y_Hi_Val);

  G_X_Hi = getmaxx() - 25;
  G_X_Lo = 100;
  G_Y_Hi = getmaxy() - 75;
  G_Y_Lo = 10;
  G_DX   = (float)(G_X_Hi - G_X_Lo) /
                        (G_Data_Points - 1);
  G_DY   = (G_Y_Lo - G_Y_Hi) /
                    (G_Y_Hi_Val - G_Y_Lo_Val);
  G_X0   = G_X_Lo + (-X_Lo_Val*G_DX);
  G_Y0   = G_Y_Hi + (-G_Y_Lo_Val*G_DY );

  setcolor (G_Axis_Color);

  /* Draw X Axis */
  /* Axis is drawn at the 0 coordinate if the 0
     coordinate is on the chart.  Otherwise it
     is drawn on the edge closer to the 0
     coordinate */
  if (0 < G_Y_Lo_Val)
    Y_of_X_Axis = G_Y_Hi;
  else if (0 > G_Y_Hi_Val)
    Y_of_X_Axis = G_Y_Lo;
```

```
else
  Y_of_X_Axis = G_Y0;

line (G_X_Lo, Y_of_X_Axis,
      G_X_Hi, Y_of_X_Axis);

/* Draw Y Axis */
if (0 < X_Lo_Val)
  X_of_Y_Axis = G_X_Lo;
else if (0 > X_Hi_Val)
  X_of_Y_Axis = G_X_Hi;
else
  X_of_Y_Axis = G_X_Lo + (X_Lo_Val*
              ((float)(G_X_Hi - G_X_Lo) /
                  (X_Lo_Val - X_Hi_Val)));

line (X_of_Y_Axis, G_Y_Lo,
      X_of_Y_Axis, G_Y_Hi);

/* Now label the axes */

settextstyle (SMALL_FONT, VERT_DIR, 8);
settextjustify (CENTER_TEXT, CENTER_TEXT);
outtextxy (textheight(Y_Label),
           ((G_Y_Lo - G_Y_Hi) / 2) + G_Y_Hi,
             Y_Label);

settextstyle (SMALL_FONT, HORIZ_DIR, 8);
outtextxy (((G_X_Hi - G_X_Lo) / 2) + G_X_Lo,
             getmaxy()-textheight(X_Label),
             X_Label);

settextstyle (SMALL_FONT, HORIZ_DIR, 4);

for(i = 0; i <= 8; i++) {
  sprintf (Label_Str, "%.2f",
           X_Lo_Val+((float)i*
           ((X_Hi_Val-X_Lo_Val)/8)));
  outtextxy((i*(G_X_Hi-G_X_Lo)/8)+G_X_Lo,
             Y_of_X_Axis+textheight("1"),
             Label_Str);

  sprintf  (Label_Str, "%.2f",
            G_Y_Lo_Val + ((float)i *
            ((G_Y_Hi_Val-G_Y_Lo_Val) / 8)));
  outtextxy(X_of_Y_Axis-textwidth("00.00"),
           (i*(G_Y_Lo-G_Y_Hi) / 8) + G_Y_Hi,
            Label_Str);
}
```

```
/* And finally, draw the graph */

setcolor (G_Trace_Color);
moveto (G_X_Lo, G_Y0 + (Data[0]*G_DY ));

for(i = 1; i < G_Data_Points; i++)
  lineto(G_X_Lo + (i*G_DX),
         G_Y0 + (Data[i]*G_DY));

} /* end draw_graph () */
```

This function makes graphing much easier. The only work involved is that of putting data into the array. The computer can now figure out all the annoying details of finding the boundaries and numbering the axes. But it does have drawbacks. Only one trace can be made. The program given in the last section had three traces on it. Well, if you look carefully at the listing just given you will notice that some variables are not declared. The variables that start with "G_" are global variables. These can be used by another function to add traces to a graph that is already drawn. This function is quite simple since the hard work of setting things up is already done. It just plots a new trace on the screen.

```
void Add_Trace (float *Data) {
  int i;

  setcolor (Trace_Color);
  moveto (X_Lo, Y0 + Data[0]*DY);
  for (i = 1; i < G_Data_Points; i++)
    lineto (X_Lo+(float)i*DX, Y0 + Data[i]*DY);
} /* Add_Trace */
```

This function plots data the same way as the last one, and should not need any more explanation. It is handy to place these two functions into their own file, so that they are available to programs down the line. Other useful functions would be ones for setting the trace color and the color of the axes and labels. This has in fact been done. The code is in file BK0502.C, with the header information, function prototypes, etc., in BK0502.H. The header file can be included and the C source file linked with your programs. Similar files are also included for polar coordinate graphing, as well as bar and pie charts. These files are described later.

There is one problem with the above code. The high and low values are set with the first trace. If any traces are added that have higher or lower values, they will not fit. To prevent this a function might be added to set the highest and lowest values that will be displayed. Either that, or they could be added as parameters to draw_graph( ).

Polar Coordinates

What Are Polar Coordinates?

In high school the Cartesian coordinate system of graphing is covered quite thoroughly. There are many other methods of graphing. One other method that is quite common, and quite useful, is the *polar coordinate* method. With polar coordinates, the origin is at the center of the graph. A point is plotted by giving a distance from the origin, and an angle with a line drawn from the origin straight to the right. The distance is usually referred to as "r", for radius, and the angle is usually called Theta (see Fig. 5.1.1).

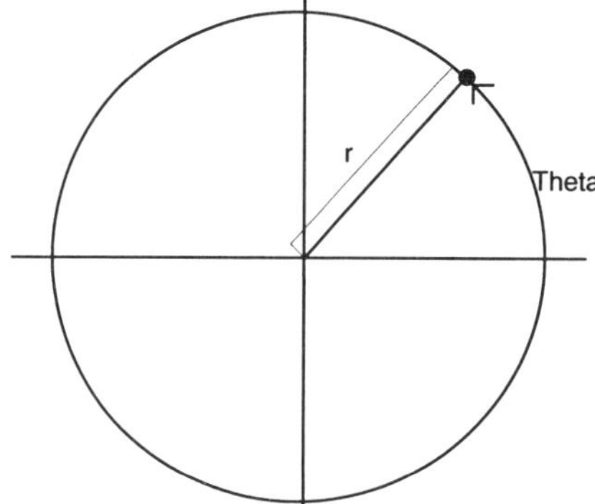

Fig. 5.1.1 A Point Plotted a Distance r and Angle Theta

While polar coordinates makes drawing a square more difficult, it makes many shapes easier. A circle can be drawn by making r a constant value, and incrementing theta from 0 to 360. Many interesting shapes can be created easily with polar coordinates.

How to Plot Polar Coordinates on a PC Monitor

The PC monitor is set up in Cartesian coordinates. To plot polar coordinates they must be translated to Cartesian coordinates. To find X, take the cosine of theta and multiply by the distance. To find Y take the sine of theta and multiply by the distance. Remember to adjust for the origin. In C:

```
X = r * cos(Theta);
Y = r * sin(Theta);
putpixel (X + (getmaxx() / 2),
          (getmaxy() / 2) - Y, Color);
```

The "getmaxx( ) / 2" and "getmaxy( ) / 2" place the origin in the center of the screen.

Now we run into a problem. If you use the above method to plot something like (cos(4*Theta), Theta), you will find a very small trace on the screen. This is a scale problem, similar to the one encountered in the last two sections. The largest cos(Theta*4) ever gets is 1, and the smallest is -1. This value needs to be multiplied by a scale factor so that it will fit properly on the screen. Cos(Theta*4) is a distance from the origin. So multiplying by the scale factor should put the largest value returned by the function at the edge of the graph. In this example we know that the largest value we will encounter is 1. We also know that the nearest edges are the top and bottom of the screen, and the origin is halfway between. So for an adjustment we would probably use (getmaxy( ) / 2). In general, the adjustment, when multiplied by the largest or smallest value returned by the trig function, should put the pixel at the edge of the screen.

A Function for Graphing Polar Coordinates

The code developed in this section is quite similar to the one for Cartesian coordinates. An array of data is passed in. The procedure finds the maximum value in the array, and this value is used to compute an adjustment factor. Axes and labels are drawn, and the function is plotted.

The array that is passed in now runs from 0 to 360, which is (of course) the number of degrees in a circle. If more than 360 degrees needs to be plotted, there is (again) a function for adding traces. This can be called with the data going from 360 to 720 degrees, and again with the data going from 720 to 1080 degrees. This process can repeat until all data are plotted.

The Cartesian procedure provided for two axis labels. This no longer makes sense. The axes in polar coordinates are always the number of degrees. In addition, the array of data always goes from 0 degrees to 360 degrees. So there is no need for low and high values, or for the number of data points to be passed in. No labels are passed in. If desired, the programmer can add a title after the plot is drawn.

So now the function prototype can be made quite simple. The only data passed in is the data array:

```
void Polar_draw_graph(float Radii[NUMOFDEGREES]);
```

The constant NUMOFDEGREES is 361, so this array is indexed from 0 to 360.

Now, on to the procedure! The first thing to do is to find a scale factor. To find the correct scale factor, we need to find the largest value in the data array. These values represent distance from the origin. A positive value is a distance in a direction given by angle theta. (In this case theta is equal to the position in the array, i.e., the value plotted at angle 85 degrees is in Radii[85].) A negative value is the same distance from the origin, but in the opposite direction. In polar coordinates the point (r, Theta) is equal to the point (-r, Theta+180). So we need to find the largest magnitude, or absolute value, in the array. A simple function can find this value:

```
void get_hi_val (float  Data[NUMOFDEGREES],
                 float *Hi_Val) {
  int i;

  *Hi_Val = Data[0];
  for(i=1; i<NUMOFDEGREES; i++)
    if (abs(Data[i]) > *Hi_Val)
      *Hi_Val = abs(Data[i]);
} /* end get_hi_val() */
```

This function is simple enough that it does not need explanation. Now that the largest value in the array is found, the scale factor can be found by dividing the maximum radius that fits on the screen by this value. The maximum radius is the distance, in screen pixels, from the origin to the edge of the plot. The origin is the center of the screen. The edge of the plot is the edge of the screen minus 25 pixels, to allow for text labels to be added later. In the example that follows the scale value is called DR. To plot a point, multiply r by DR, then translate to screen coordinates.

Now axes should be drawn to show the origin, 0, 90, 180, and 270 degrees. Also, a reference circle should be drawn to indicate distance from the origin. This circle should be centered on the origin and have a radius the same as the maximum radius of the graph. Another reference circle can also be drawn with half the radius. Since the graph is scaled, these circles should be sized to fit the screen. The plot will be sized to match the reference circles.

```
setcolor (G_Axis_Color);
line (G_X_Center - Max_Radius - 20,G_Y_Center,
      G_X_Center + Max_Radius + 20,G_Y_Center);
line (G_X_Center,G_Y_Center - Max_Radius - 20,
      G_X_Center,G_Y_Center + Max_Radius + 20);

circle (G_X_Center, G_Y_Center,
```

```
        (getmaxy()-25) / 2);
circle (G_X_Center, G_Y_Center,
        (getmaxy()-25) / 4);
```

It is not necessary to label the axes, because these always stand for degrees. The reference circles should be given values, so magnitude can be seen by looking at the graph. The label for the outer circle is the maximum value in the array. The label for the inner circle is half this value. A good location for the labels is just outside the reference circle at the 45, degree mark. This location can be found using a method similar to plotting the points. Multiply the maximum radius by cos(45) to find the X value, and sin(45) to find the Y value. Add a little on to each so the label will not be right on the circle. Sin(45) and cos(45) are both constants, so they do not need to be figured out each time the procedure is called. The value, which happens to 0.7071 for both, is adjusted to 0.75, to make the label appear above the reference circle. This value is then placed directly in the program. Here is the code:

```
settextstyle(SMALL_FONT, HORIZ_DIR, 4);
sprintf  (Label_String,"%.2f",G_MaxVal);
outtextxy(G_X_Center+((float)Max_Radius*0.75),
          G_Y_Center-((float)Max_Radius*0.75),
          Label_String);
sprintf  (Label_String,"%.2f",G_MaxVal/2.0);
outtextxy(
        G_X_Center+(((float)Max_Radius*0.8)/2),
        G_Y_Center-(((float)Max_Radius*0.8)/2),
        Label_String);
```

The value used to place the inner label is 0.8. This seems to look better on the inner circle than 0.75.

Now we are ready to plot the trace. Function lineto( ) is used to avoid spaces in the plot. Use moveto( ) to move the current drawing point to the proper location. Remember to translate from polar coordinates to screen coordinates. Here is the code for making the trace:

```
moveto   (Return_X(0, Radii[0]*G_DR),
          Return_Y(0, Radii[0]*G_DR));
for(Theta=1; Theta<NUMOFDEGREES; Theta++)
  lineto (Return_X(Theta*Pi_Over_180,
                   Radii[Theta]*G_DR),
          Return_Y(Theta*Pi_Over_180,
                   Radii[Theta]*G_DR));
```

All the code is here for the function. As with the routine for Cartesian coordinates, several auxiliary routines are useful. Functions are needed for adding additional traces and for changing the color of the trace. The following example also gives a function for setting the origin. This might also be done internally. This function is given so that the plot does not have to be exactly centered, allowing for titles or other text.

You now have all the pieces necessary for a generic polar graphing function. The pieces are all put together in the file BK0503.C on the distribution disk. There are function prototypes and constants defined in BK0503.H. It might be worth your while to review these two files, or at least the header file, at this time.

As with Cartesian coordinates, this unit does have problems. If Polar_Add_Trace( ) is used with data that have a higher magnitude than the first trace plotted, the new trace will go off the graph. The following program shows how to set up calls to this procedure and some interesting things to plot:

```
#include <graphics.h>
#include <stdio.h>
#include <stdlib.h>
#include <conio.h>
#include <math.h>
#include "bk0403.h"

void main(void) {
  float *Data;
  int   i,
        Driver,
        Mode;

  Driver = DETECT;
  detectgraph(&Driver, &Mode);
  initgraph(&Driver, &Mode, '');

  GraphError = graphresult();
  if (GraphError != grOk) {
    printf("%s\n",grapherrormsg(GraphError));
    exit(-1);
  }

  /* Do Graphics Stuff Here */

  Polar_Set_Center_Coords (getmaxx() / 2,
                           getmaxy() / 2);
  Polar_Set_Axis_Color (LIGHTGRAY);

  /* Fill Data with something */
```

```
    for(i=0; i<NUMOFDEGREES; i++)
      Data[i] = i*2;

    /* call graph function to display */
    Polar_Set_Trace_Color (YELLOW);
    Polar_Draw_Graph (Data);
    Polar_Set_Trace_Color (GREEN);
    for(i=0; i<NUMOFDEGREES; i++)
      Data[i] = 650;

    Polar_Add_Trace (Data);

    Polar_Set_Trace_Color (RED);
    for(i=0; i<NUMOFDEGREES; i++)
      Data[i] = cos((float)(4*i)*M_PI/180)*720;

    Polar_Add_Trace (Data);

    /* wait for user */
    getch();
    if (kbhit()) getch();

    closegraph();
  }
```

Drawing Charts

As with graphs, there are many types of charts. Two of the more common types, bar charts and pie charts, are presented here. Other types of charts are similar to these. Once the methods for creating these types of charts are understood, it should not be difficult to develop other forms of charts.

Bar charts and pie charts require some specialized graphics routines. Namely, routines that can draw filled-in bars and filled-in pie slices. Borland has supplied routines to do these things with Borland C.

```
void far bar (int left,  int top,
              int right, int bottom);
  /*
   * bar() will draw a filled in rectangle.
   *
   * Parameters:
   *   left   - coordinate of left side
   *   top    - coordinate of top
```

```
     *   right  - coordinate of right side
     *   bottom - coordinate of bottom
     */

  void far pieslice (int x, int y,
                     int stangle, int endangle,
                     int Radius);
    /*
     * pieslice() will draw a filled portion of a
     *   pie chart
     *
     * Parameters:
     *   x        - X coordinate of center
     *   y        - Y coordinate of center
     *   stangle  - angle to start drawing at
     *   endangle - angle to stop drawing at
     *   radius   - radius of arc
     */
```

The bar( ) function draws a filled bar, but does not outline it, so this procedure is often used in conjunction with the rectangle( ) function described in Chapter 2.

Bar Charts

To write a bar charting function, it is necessary to determine what data the function will need. The bar chart will need data, title for the axes, and labels for each bar. It is possible to obtain values for the Y axis from the data. It would be nice if bars could be grouped together. Then the groups need to be labeled. Now we know what the function prototype should look like:

```
  void draw_bar_chart(int    Data_Points,
                      float *Data,
                      int    Bars_Per_Group,
                      char  *X_Label,
                      char  *Y_Label,
                      char  *Bar_Labels[],
                      char  *Group_Labels[])
```

Some charts do not group bars. If there are no groups then the group labels can be ignored. If Bars_Per_Group is 0 or equal to Data_Points then Bar_Labels is ignored. It would make no sense to have Bars_Per_Group greater than Data_Points.

This is not checked, however. If this situation does occur the function will behave in an unpredictable manner.

Writing this procedure is rather involved. A good place to start is how wide should the bars be and how much space should there be between them? We can look at how many bars there are, then use this to find the answers. The more bars, the narrower they should be, and the less space there should be between them. This is complicated by the fact that groups should have some extra space between them. Trying to come up with a good rule for relating the size of bars and the space between them to the number of bars and groups, while considering the space between groups, gets quite complicated. The procedure given simply sets a constant width to the bars, and adjusts the spacing. The number of pixels between each bar is then determined. Twice the number of pixels is used to separate groups of bars.

So, in order to find the number of pixels, we must first determine the number of groups. This is the total number of bars divided by the bars in each group. The number of bars is held in Data_Points for consistency with the previous sections. The number of bars in a group is in Bars_Per_Group.

Next we have to determine a size for the bars. I've found a bar width of 30 to look good on the VGA monitor. A thinner bar might be desirable for a monitor with lower resolution, or a thicker bar might be better if not too many bars will be used most of the time.

One last thing needs to be found. To determine the number of spaces, we need to know how much room the entire chart should take up. This is determined in the same way as for graphing Cartesian coordinates. Determine how wide the screen is, then leave room for margins and text. Now that we know how much room we are supposed to take up, along with all the information found above, we can figure out how many pixels to place between the bars.

Subtract the space taken up by the bars from the total amount of space. This gives the total amount of space that goes between all bars. Now take the number of bars and add the number of groups to find the total number of spaces between bars. Subtract one from this, since there is no space on the end of the graph. Remember that the number of groups is Data_Points / Bars_Per_Group. Finally divide the total amount of space by the number of gaps. This gives the number of pixels for each space between the bars. Here is the code:

```
if (Bars_Per_Group == 0)
       Bars_Per_Group = Data_Points;

get_lo_and_hi_vals (Data_Points, Data,
                     &Y_Lo_Val, &Y_Hi_Val);

X_Hi = getmaxx() - 10;
```

```
X_Lo = 100;

Width = 30;
Space_Betw_Bars =
   ((X_Hi - X_Lo) - (Data_Points * Width)) /
                Data_Points + (Data_Points /
                Bars_Per_Group) - 1);
```

Now we need to scale the bars (data) to fit on the screen. As with the Cartesian graphing function, we find a scale factor. To find the scale factor we first need to determine how many pixels we will be using in the Y dimension. We do not use the whole screen, because we need room for labels and titles. Once the number of useful pixels is found, the largest value in the data array needs to be found. Put the first value of the array into a variable, then loop through the array. Whenever a value is higher than the one in the variable, replace it. Now divide the number of pixels by the highest value.

```
Y_Hi = getmaxy() - 75;
Y_Lo = 10;

DY = (float)(Y_Hi - Y_Lo) / Y_Hi_Val;
```

But wait–we have one slight problem. Groups need to be labeled. Since the X axis will be used to label individual bars it might look better if groups are labeled at the top. Using the code described above, there will be no room. A small modification will solve that problem. If the scale factor is multiplied by 7/8 to make a new scale factor, then there will be enough room at the top to place text. It is easy to throw this multiplication into the code given above:

```
Y_Hi = getmaxy() - 75;
Y_Lo = 10;

DY = ((float)(Y_Hi-Y_Lo)*7.0) / (Y_Hi_Val*8);
```

Now we draw the X and Y axes:

```
if ((getbkcolor() != LIGHTGRAY) &&
                    (getbkcolor() != WHITE))
  setcolor(LIGHTGRAY);
else
  setcolor(DARKGRAY);

line (X_Lo, Y_Hi, X_Hi, Y_Hi);
line (X_Lo, Y_Lo, X_Lo, Y_Hi);
```

The if statement makes sure that when the background color has been changed the axes will still stand out.

Labeling is also much like it is in Cartesian graphing. The titles for the axes are the easiest place to start. Set text justification to center, set text style to the small font, set direction to vertical, find the center of the Y axis, and print the Y label. Next set text direction to horizontal, find the center of the X axis, and print the X label.

```
/* Label Axes */
settextstyle (SMALL_FONT, VERT_DIR, 8);
settextjustify (CENTER_TEXT, CENTER_TEXT);
outtextxy (textheight(Y_Label),
          ((Y_Lo - Y_Hi) / 2) + Y_Hi,
          Y_Label);

settextstyle (SMALL_FONT, HORIZ_DIR, 8);
outtextxy (((X_Hi - X_Lo) / 2) + X_Lo,
          getmaxy()-textheight(X_Label),
          X_Label);
```

That's the easy part of labeling. Now units need to be put on the Y axis. Again, this is the same as with Cartesian coordinates.

The outtextxy function is used to write the label. Unfortunately this function will not handle integers or reals, only strings. The sprintf( ) function is used to convert numbers to strings. Its syntax is similar to fprintf( ), only the file is replaced by a pointer to a string.

Now how do we find the number to convert to a string? Decide how many unit labels you want. Then a for loop can be used. Take the total number of units, divide that by the number of labels, multiply by the loop variable, and that is the number to be written out:

```
for(i = 0; i <= 8; i++) {
  sprintf (Label_Str, "%.3f",
          ((i * ((Y_Hi_Val - Y_Lo_Val) / 8))));
```

Now outtextxy( ) can be used to output the text. The numbers should appear just to the left of the Y axis, far enough away so that they do not write over the axis. The spacing between labels is the number of units divided by the number of labels, multiplied by the scale factor, multiplied by the loop variable. Finally the border of the graph has to be added on so that the numbers will start at the bottom of the chart, not the edge of the screen.

```
for(i = 0; i <= 8; i++) {
```

```
    sprintf (Label_Str, "%.3f",
        (Y_Lo_Val+(i*((Y_Hi_Val-Y_Lo_Val)/8))));
```

Here is the complete code for writing units for our example:

```
  settextstyle (SMALL_FONT, HORIZ_DIR, 4);
  for(i = 0; i <= 8; i++) {
    sprintf (Label_Str, "%.3f",
         (Y_Lo_Val+(i*((Y_Hi_Val-Y_Lo_Val)/8))));
    outtextxy (X_Lo - textwidth("00.00"),
               (i*((Y_Lo-Y_Hi)*7)/64)+Y_Hi,
               Label_Str);
  }
```

Bars are not labeled here. Because of the uneven spacing caused by groups, it is easier to label bars as they are drawn. Group labels are put in last.

Now we need to draw the bars. Charts look fancier when the bars are filled with different patterns and colors. Making this happen is an interesting problem. The simplest way to do this is to set up functions that will rotate the colors and patterns. The colors and fill patterns should start over whenever a new group starts. Also there are some undesirable colors and patterns that need to be avoided. The background color should be avoided. There is a fill pattern that fills in the background color, and another that fills in the current fill color solidly, and there is the user-defined pattern, which is undefined. All three of these are best avoided.

It is easiest to set up four functions to help with the color and pattern management chores. The first two functions set up the current color and pattern, and store information about what colors and patterns should not be used. The next two functions rotate through the acceptable colors and patterns, either starting over when a new group starts or when all the colors or patterns are used.

The first function is the one for setting up the color rotation. It sets up a variable that will be used to determine if the rotation should start over. This variable is called G_Number_Of_Colors. G indicates the variable is global. It is hidden within the file, however, so no outside procedures can change it. In professional programming such protected use of global variables is common. G_Number_Of_Variables is set to either the maximum number of colors on the system or Bars_Per_Group, whichever is lower. This way the rotation will start over at the beginning of each group. Another global variable, G_Cur_Color is set to 1. This is the current color being used. It is then checked to make sure that 1 is not the background color. If it is, G_Cur_Color is incremented.

Here is a source of confusion. G_Cur_Color cannot be set to color 0, because 0 is always the background color. So why check to see if 1 is the background color? After all 0 cannot equal 1. Well, if you read Chapter 1 you might remember something about palette registers and mapping one color into another. The color that is represented by 1 might be the same as the color represented by 0. This needs to be checked. How colors are handled on the PC is explained more fully in the next chapter. Here is the code:

```
unsigned G_Number_Of_Colors,
         G_Cur_Color,
         G_Number_Of_Patterns,
         G_Cur_Pattern;

void setup_colors (int Bars_Per_Group) {

  if (Bars_Per_Group < getmaxcolor())
    G_Number_Of_Colors = Bars_Per_Group;
  else
    G_Number_Of_Colors = getmaxcolor();

  G_Cur_Color = 0;

} /* end setup_colors() */
```

The procedure for setting up the pattern rotation is a little simpler because there is no remapping of patterns as with this business of the background color being equal to another color. Fill pattern 0 fills in the background color, fill pattern 1 fills in solid with the current fill color. Fill pattern 2 fills with thin lines. This light pattern clashes with other, heavier patterns, so it is not used. So G_Cur_Pattern is set to 3. Setting G_Number_Of_Patterns is the same as with the setting G_Number_Of_Colors in the last procedure, only the number of patterns is a constant 12, and not system dependent.

```
void setup_patterns (int Bars_Per_Group) {

  if (Bars_Per_Group < 12)
    G_Number_Of_Patterns = Bars_Per_Group + 3;
  else
    G_Number_Of_Patterns = 11;

  G_Cur_Pattern = 2;

} /* end setup_patterns() */
```

Next we have two functions to provide color and pattern rotation. The function Return_Next_Color( ) provides the color rotation. To start, increment G_Cur_Color. If the color is now the background color, it needs to be incremented again. If it is now too large, it needs to be set back to the beginning. But resetting it could set it to the background color. So this check is made again.

```
unsigned Return_Next_Color() {

  G_Cur_Color++;

  if (G_Cur_Color == getbkcolor())
    G_Cur_Color++;
  if (G_Cur_Color > G_Number_Of_Colors)
    G_Cur_Color = 1;
  if (G_Cur_Color == getbkcolor())
    G_Cur_Color++;
  return (G_Cur_Color);

} /* end Return_Next_Color */
```

Return_Next_Pattern( ) handles the pattern rotation. Again, this function is simpler than the one dealing with colors. It increments G_Cur_Pattern, checks to see if G_Cur_Pattern is out of range, and returns it.

```
unsigned Return_Next_Pattern() {

  G_Cur_Pattern++;
  if (G_Cur_Pattern > G_Number_Of_Patterns-1)
    G_Cur_Pattern = 3;
  return (G_Cur_Pattern);

} /* end Return_Next_Pattern() */
```

Now with a fairly simple, straightforward set of function calls we can control the colors and patterns of the bars.

And finally we are ready to draw bars. A variable called Next_Position is used to find the X coordinate of the left-hand side of the bar. Next_Position + Width gives the right-hand side. Next position needs a value before anything can start. Its initial value is the left-hand side of the graph, plus the width of a space, so the first bar will not be right up against the edge of the graph. Y_Hi is the bottom of the bar. Remember that on the PC, Y coordinates are reversed. The top of the bar is found by taking the value in the data array and multiplying by the scale factor DY, then subtracting from Y_Hi.

Loop through the data array. The first thing to do in the loop is to call setfillstyle( ). The parameters are the functions Return_Next_Pattern and Return_Next_Color. Then a bar can be drawn with the bar( ) function. This function will create a filled-in bar using the color and pattern set by the call to setfillstyle( ). It will not outline the bar. So a call to rectangle( ) needs to be made.

In the example function there is a check to see if Data[i] is 0 before drawing the bar. This is because the bar( ) function will make a small but visible piece of a bar even when the difference in the Y coordinates is 0. It is assumed that if a 0 is in the data array the programmer did not want any bar to appear.

```
Next_Position = X_Lo + Space_Betw_Bars;

/* Draw Bars */
for (i = 0; i < Data_Points; i++) {
  setfillstyle (Return_Next_Pattern(),
                Return_Next_Color());
  if (Data[i] != 0.0) {
    bar(Next_Position,      Y_Hi,
        Next_Position+Width,Y_Hi-(Data[i]*DY));
    rectangle(Next_Position,         Y_Hi,
              Next_Position+Width,
              Y_Hi-(Data[i]*DY));
```

Notice that the loop is not closed. That is because we are not done yet. The bars need to labeled. We did not do that with the rest of the labels because it is easier to find the correct X coordinate for the label here, while drawing the bars. Next_Position gives the left-hand side of the bar. If we add half a bar width then we have the middle of the bar.

The code for the Y position looks a little complicated. This is because if all the labels are put at the same Y value, not much text can be used before labels start running into each other. Code is put in that alternately adds to the Y value so every other label is written lower on the screen. This is done by taking the height of a typical string, plus 5 pixels, and multiplying it by (i % 2) + 1. If i is even the height will be multiplied by 1, otherwise it will be multiplied by 2.

```
outtextxy (Next_Position + (Width / 2),
           Y_Hi + (textheight("Height") + 5) *
                               (((i+1)%2) + 1),
           Bar_Labels[i]);
```

Now we have to update Next_Position. Add the width of a bar, plus the width of a space between bars. If this is the end of a group, add another space.

```
if ((i+1) % Bars_Per_Group == 0)
  Next_Position += Space_Betw_Bars;
next_Position += Space_Betw_Bars + Width;
```

Now here is the whole code for drawing the bars:

```
Next_Position = X_Lo + Space_Betw_Bars;

/* Draw Bars */
for (i = 0; i < Data_Points; i++) {
  setfillstyle (Return_Next_Pattern(),
                Return_Next_Color());
  if (Data[i] != 0.0) {
    bar(Next_Position,Y_Hi,
        Next_Position+Width,Y_Hi-(Data[i]*DY));
    rectangle (Next_Position,Y_Hi,
               Next_Position + Width,
               Y_Hi - (Data[i] * DY));
    outtextxy (Next_Position + (Width / 2),
          Y_Hi + (textheight("Height") + 5) *
                                (((i+1)%2) + 1),
          Bar_Labels[i]);
  } /* end if */
  if ((i+1) % Bars_Per_Group == 0)
    Next_Position += Space_Betw_Bars;
    Next_Position += Space_Betw_Bars + Width;
} /* end for loop */
```

There is still one more thing to be done with this function. Groups are not yet labeled. First of all we have to check to see if the bars are grouped. There is a line of code at the beginning of the procedure that checks if Bars_Per_Group is 0. If it is then Bars_Per_Group is set to Data_Points, so now we only have the one check to do.

Now, assuming that we do indeed need to label groups, we need to find where to put each label. The best place would be centered over the group, just above the highest bar. First we need to find the center of a group. This can be done by determining how wide a group is, multiplying by the group number, then adding half the width of a group. As always, X_Lo must also be added. To get the width of a group, start with the number of bars in a group multiplied by the width of each bar. To this number add the number of spaces multiplied by the width of a space. The number of spaces is the number of bars plus one, since there is an extra space between groups. In the code below the number of spaces in a group and the number of bars in a group have been factored out, since they are both the same. Then the width of the extra space is added on the end.

The Y coordinate is found by looping through the data array and looking at the data in the group. The largest value is saved. Here is the code:

```
/* Label Groups */
settextstyle (SMALL_FONT, HORIZ_DIR, 6);
if (Bars_Per_Group != Data_Points) {
  /* pixels per group so we can center the
     label over the group */
  Pixels_Per_Group = ((Width+Space_Betw_Bars)*
             Bars_Per_Group) + Space_Betw_Bars;

  /* loop through the label array */
  for (i = 0;
       i < Data_Points / Bars_Per_Group; i++) {
    Y_Hi_Val = Data[(i*Bars_Per_Group)+1];

    /* find highest value in current group */
    for (j = 0; j < Bars_Per_Group; j++) {
      if (Y_Hi_Val<Data[(i*Bars_Per_Group)+j]){
        Y_Hi_Val = Data[(i*Bars_Per_Group)+j];
      }
    }

    /* write label */
    outtextxy((Pixels_Per_Group * (i+1)) -
                (Pixels_Per_Group / 2) + X_Lo,
              Y_Hi - ((Y_Hi_Val*DY)+25),
              Group_Labels[i]);
  } /* end for loop */
} /* end if (Bars_Per_Group ... */
```

Now you have all the parts and pieces to write a bar graph procedure. To see the code all put together please view file BK0504.C on the distribution disk. Function prototypes and any needed constants are in BK0504.H.

Pie Charts

Pie charts are useful for giving values as percentages, or as parts in relation to the whole. To do this, the slices of the chart need to be sized correctly. It is difficult to tell by looking at a pie chart if a slice is 41% or 43% of the whole, so labeling is important. The programmer should have the ability to emphasize a slice by pulling it out from the rest of the pie, or "exploding" it.

To make the above happen, the following parameters are needed: a data array and the number of points in the data array; an array of titles, one for each slice; an array of booleans (or logicals) to determine if a slice should be exploded or not;

and a string for the title. Booleans are handled as characters for simplicity. Here is the function prototype:

```
void draw_pie_chart(int    Data_Points,
                    float *Data,
                    char  *Title,
                    char  *Slice_Labels[],
                    char  *Exploded);
```

Pie charts represent data in terms of percentage of the whole. So the first thing to be done is to determine what the whole is. All the values in the array are added and stored in a variable called Total. At the same time, the number of array elements that are not zero are added and the total is put into a variable called Actual_Data. The function we are developing simply ignores data containing zeroe. For some applications this will be inadequate, but it is somewhat simpler, and sufficient for learning purposes.

```
for(i = 0; i < Data_Points; i++) {
  if (Data[i] != 0) {
    Actual_Data++;
    Total += Data[i];
  } /* end if */
} /* end for loop */
```

To translate the value of each slice to degrees, divide Total by 360.

Next we have to find the location of the center of the graph. It should be halfway from left to right, but a little above the center to allow room for the title. The radius should be a little less than the distance from the center of the graph to the nearest edge, to allow for additional text to be added later.

The pie slices are filled, the same as the bars in the last section. The same concerns are raised about appropriate fill patterns and colors. The background color should not be used. Neither should the background or solid fill patterns. A detailed explanation, with code, is given in the last section.

The title should be centered at the bottom of the screen. Each section of code described above is pretty simple. But together they are substantial enough to warrant an example:

```
/* Find number of degrees per data point */
/* Note - There must be data, or this will
   die with a divide by zero error */
Mx = 360.0/Total;

X_Center = getmaxx() / 2;
```

```
Y_Center = (getmaxy() / 2) - 32;
Radius   = (getmaxy() / 2) - 50;

setup_colors(Data_Points);
setup_patterns(Data_Points);

/* write title */
settextjustify (CENTER_TEXT, CENTER_TEXT);
settextstyle (SMALL_FONT, HORIZ_DIR, 8);
outtextxy (X_Center,
           getmaxy()-textheight(Title), Title);
```

Now into the meat of the problem – putting the slices on the screen. First we will go over how to place ordinary unexploded slices on the screen. It is helpful to keep a running total of degrees. This is called Current_Total. Current_Total is initialized to 0, because no slices have yet been drawn. Elements of the data array that contain zeros are not drawn, so a check must be made for these. A call is made to setfillstyle( ), with calls to functions Return_Next_Pattern( ) and Return_Next_Color( ). These two functions are described in the last section on bar charts. Now a call to pieslice( ) is made. The center coordinates have been found previously. The start angle is Current_Total. The end angle is Current_Total, plus the value in the data array for the current slice multiplied by the scale factor.

The result of the multiplication must be rounded. Normally, the value will be truncated before the addition takes place. If this is allowed to happen gaps will appear in the chart. To prevent this, 0.5 is added to the value before it is truncated. This gives the effect of rounding, although it is not entirely accurate. It is good enough for pie charts, but this method is not recommended for sophisticated numerical analysis.

Update Current_Total by adding the value in the data array for the current slice multiplied by the scale factor, plus 0.5.

```
Current_Total = 0;
for(i = 0; i < Data_Points-1; i++)
  if (Data[i] != 0) {
    setfillstyle (Return_Next_Pattern(),
                  Return_Next_Color());
    pieslice (X_Center, Y_Center,
              Current_Total,
              Current_Total + (Data[i]*Mx+0.5),
              Radius);
    current_total += (Data[i]*Mx+0.5);
  } /* end if */
```

The above code does not allow for exploded slices. An if statement needs to be added to check the "exploded" array. If a slice is exploded then the center coordinates given to pieslice( ) need to be moved out from the center of the circle. But what does "out" mean? At one part of the circle, adding to the X coordinate will move the slice in the correct direction, while on the other side of the circle it would move the slice exactly in the wrong direction! A little trigonometry can be used to tell us how to correctly explode a slice. Bet you never knew trig was actually useful!

If we add the cosine of the angle at the middle of the slice to the X value, and subtract the sine from the Y value, the slice will nicely move in the correct direction. Of course sine and cosine return a value between 0 and 1. This does not move the slice very far. Multiplying by 15 seems to move the slice a good distance. Remember to convert the angle to radians before calling trig functions.

```
Angle_Center = Current_Total +
        (Current_Total+((Data[i]*Mx)+0.5)) / 2;
Cur_X_Center = X_Center +
               (15*cos(Angle_Center*M_PI/180));
Cur_Y_Center = Y_Center -
               (15*sin(Angle_Center*M_PI/180));
pieslice (Cur_X_Center, Cur_Y_Center,
          Current_Total,
          Current_Total + (Data[i]*Mx+0.5),
          Radius);
```

Now we come across a problem. As we draw each slice, the current total is updated with a rounded value. Current total is the value used for start and end angles of each slice. It should equal 360 at the end. If it ends up a little short a crack will appear between the last slice and the first. If the value is too high, pieslice( ) has a bit of a problem. It wraps the value so that it is in the range 0 to 360. It then gets confused and swaps the start and end angles. The slice is drawn over the entire graph! Since the simple rounding method we used is not overly accurate these problems occur more often than not. The cure is to end the loop one slice early, then draw the last slice outside the loop. The final call to pieslice is hard coded to end at 360 degrees.

```
for(i = 0; i < Data_Points-1; i++) {
  if (Data[i] != 0) {
    Angle_Center =
      (Current_Total + Current_Total +
                    (int)(Data[i]*Mx+0.5)) / 2;

    setfillstyle (Return_Next_Pattern(),
                  Return_Next_Color());
    if (Exploded[i] == 0)
      pieslice (X_Center, Y_Center,
                Current_Total,
                Current_Total+(Data[i]*Mx+0.5),
```

```
                Radius);
      else {
        Cur_X_Center =
                X_Center + (15*cos(Angle_Center*
                                       M_PI/180));
        Cur_Y_Center =
                Y_Center - (15*sin(Angle_Center*
                                       M_PI/180));
        pieslice (Cur_X_Center, Cur_Y_Center,
                  Current_Total,
                  Current_Total+(Data[i]*Mx+0.5),
                  Radius);
      } /* end else */
      Current_Total += (Data[i]*Mx+0.5);
    } /* end if */
  }   /* end for loop */

  /* Draw the final piece */
  /* it must end on precisely 360 degrees,
     or trouble occurs */
  Angle_Center = (Current_Total + 360) / 2;

  setfillstyle (Return_Next_Pattern(),
                Return_Next_Color());
  if (Exploded[i] == 0)
    pieslice (X_Center, Y_Center, Current_Total,
              360, Radius);
  else {
    Cur_X_Center =
        X_Center+(15*cos(Angle_Center*M_PI/180));
    Cur_Y_Center =
        Y_Center-(15*sin(Angle_Center*M_PI/180));
    pieslice (Cur_X_Center, Cur_Y_Center,
              Current_Total, 360, Radius);
  } /* end else */
```

The last thing to do is add slice labels. We need to traverse the data array again so we know where the slices are. The labels look best centered on the slice, about two-thirds the distance to the edge of the graph. The centerline of the slice is found the same way as the direction of an exploded slice. Instead of multiplying by 15, multiply by Radius * 2/3.

```
  Text_X = ((Radius * 2.0/3) *
              cos(Angle_Center*M_PI/180)) + 0.5;
  Text_X = ((Radius * 2.0/3) *
              sin(Angle_Center*M_PI/180)) + 0.5;
```

A little above this location write the slice label. A little below, write the percentage for the slice. The percentage is found by taking the data element from the data array, multiplying by 100, and dividing by Total. Here is the code for accomplishing this:

```
outtextxy(X_Center + Text_X,
          Y_Center - (Text_Y +
                  textheight(Slice_Labels[i])),
          Slice_Labels[i]);
sprintf(Temp_Str,"%d%%",
               (int)((Data[i]*100)/Total+0.5));
outtextxy(X_Center + Text_X,
        Y_Center-(Text_Y-textheight(Temp_Str)),
          Temp_Str);
```

The complete code for this is in BK0505.C on the distribution disk. Function prototypes and constants are in BK0505.H.

6

Color Models and Programming Colors

To make good looking graphics, the programmer needs complete control over the colors being displayed. This chapter discusses the basics of color manipulation on the PC. In addition, the first section of this chapter covers color theory, and develops the idea of a color model. A color model allows a large number of colors to be expressed in terms of a few primary colors. Several color models are presented.

The VGA monitor has modes where a certain number of colors or shades can be selected from out of 256,000. One mode, the high-resolution mode, allows for 16 colors to be selected from 256,000. This mode is covered in the second section of this chapter, the section titled "Changing the Color Palette". Another mode, which only has medium resolution, allows for 256 colors to be displayed. This mode, unfortunately, is not supported by the BGI. To use this mode with Borland's graphics system, calls to the operating system must be made. The same is true for SVGA modes, where higher numbers of pixels and more colors are available. This technique is covered in Chapter 8.

Sixteen colors sounds like a lot, but the computer handles each shade as a separate color. Sixteen shades is not much at all. Half-toning and dithering are methods to simulate having more shades.

When two shades that are as close to each other appear next to each other on the screen, a visible line appears between them. Even if the shades are as close as possible, that is if two color guns are set the same and the third gun is only different by 1 bit, the line will still appear. With 6 bits per gun the color resolution is not good enough to make shading appear smooth to the human eye. If the effect of a smooth shading is desired dithering is used.

Half-toning is a similar technique for creating new shades that are between shades available on the system. This works by blending available shades to produce shades that otherwise would not be available. Dithering and half-toning methods are covered in the third section of the chapter. This section uses the 16-color mode described in the section titled "Changing the Color Palette", and assumes that the programmer is using a VGA or better monitor. If you do not have access to such a monitor, the example programs will not work. The information in this chapter is still useful, however, as well as quite interesting.

The final section of this chapter is on the CGA monitor. Information presented in the first section of the chapter describes how most color monitor systems work. Even graphics systems on main frames and workstations use hardware similar to that described in the section titled "Changing the Color Palette". They only differ in details, such as number of bits used to describe a color. The CGA, however, is quite a different animal altogether. At the time the CGA was designed cost was a big consideration. As technology has improved, parts have become less expensive. Now a VGA system costs less than the CGA did when it was introduced. To.save costs, the engineers that designed the CGA did things that make it unlike any other monitor system. Therefore a separate section is needed to cover this strange beast.

Color Mixing and Color Models

The CMY and RGB Color Models

To understand how to control colors on a monitor, it is necessary to first understand color in general. Color comes from light, which is a wave. Different colors come from light of different wavelengths. Light has many possible frequencies, most of which cannot be seen. Radio waves and microwaves are frequencies of light that cannot be seen. Of course, in this chapter we are only concerned with frequencies that can be seen, the frequencies called *visible light*.

The eye has receptors that pick up certain frequencies. Signals are sent from these receptors to the brain, where the signals are compared. By comparing these signals the brain can build a picture. The eye is quite amazing for its ability to discern colors accurately in varying light conditions.

There are three sets of receptors in the eye, each one keyed to a different frequency. One receptor detects red, one green, and other blue. A color that is between two wavelengths that the receptors detect will stimulate each of the two proportionally. If the wave is halfway between red and green, both sets of receptors will be stimulated equally. If the color is closer to red, the red receptor will be stimulated more than the green. Because of this, the eye can be fooled. If red and green light is shown at the same time, the red and green receptors will both be stimulated and the eye will see yellow. If all receptors are stimulated white is seen. A color computer monitor has phosphors that are red, green, and blue. By varying the intensities of the phosphors almost any color can be displayed. Note here that the mechanism of the eye is not completely understood. The information in the last section does work, but there are colors that the eye can see that cannot be produced with an RGB color monitor. The section on the CIE color model discusses this in detail.

Most people are familiar with color mixing, but not what is described above. The color mixing most people know uses yellow and blue to make green. But now we have red, blue, and green. How do we make orange? Well, first let's talk about the difference between these methods.

White light is made up of all visible colors. When white light hits a surface, some of the colors are absorbed. The color that is reflected is the one that the eye detects, so this is seen as the color of the surface. When we say paint is a certain color what we are really saying is that it absorbs certain frequencies of light, and reflects others. By mixing in other colors more frequencies are absorbed. This is called subtractive color mixing, since frequencies are being subtracted out of the light that gets reflected.

A color model based on subtractive mixing is the CMY color model. The primaries used by this model are cyan, magenta, and yellow. With this color model white is the absence of color, and black is the result of mixing all three primaries. This model is used by color printers and other hardcopy devices. On many of these devices the primary colors used are not dark enough to give black, so black is added as a fourth primary. When this is done the model is referred to as CMYK.

Color Models and Programming Colors

Computer monitors do not use reflected light, they are a light source themselves. So they use the additive color model, which is called RGB, for its primaries, red, green, and blue. These three color models can be displayed as a graph, where the amount of each primary is plotted along each axis. These graphs are cube shaped, and so are called *color cubes*. The graph of the RGB color model is shown in Fig. 6.1.1.

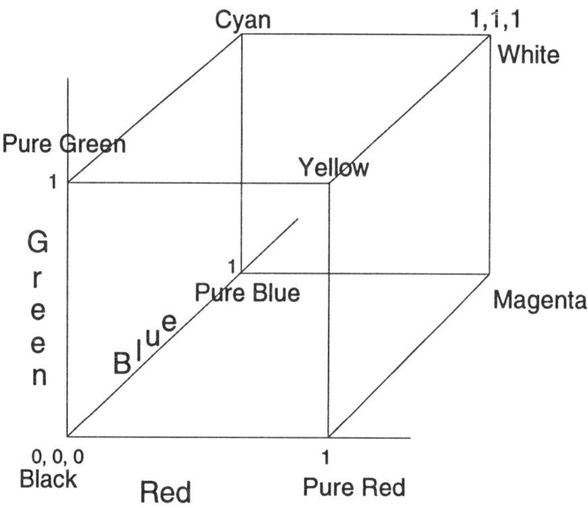

Fig. 6.1.1 The RGB Color Cube

The graph in Fig 6.1.1 is called the *RGB color cube*. Black is at the origin. The intensity of each color increases along each axis. One is the highest intensity for each color. The point (1, 1, 1) is white. The line from the origin to this point is the gray scale. Other vertices are magenta (the intersection of red and blue), yellow (the intersection of red and green), and a color called cyan (the intersection of blue and green). These three colors, called the secondary colors, are the primaries for the subtractive color model. This is a fundamental relation between the two models. The primary colors of the one are the secondary colors of the other.

Other Color Models

It is often useful to understand other color models. This section presents several different models: The CIE color model, which is a mathematical model useful in color research, and HSV and HLS color models, which are more intuitive.

The CIE Color Model

This color model was developed by the International Commission on Illumination (CIE), based in France, in 1931. It is a mathematical model used for studying colors. Three theoretical primary colors are used as a basis for all colors the eye can detect. There really are no such colors, but since this is a theoretical model that does not matter. All the visible colors are plotted on a two dimensional graph as a mixture of these three primaries, with white in the middle. This sounds like the result should be a triangle. But the human eye does not really develop its picture of color based on three primaries. So the resulting graph looks like Fig. 6.1.2.

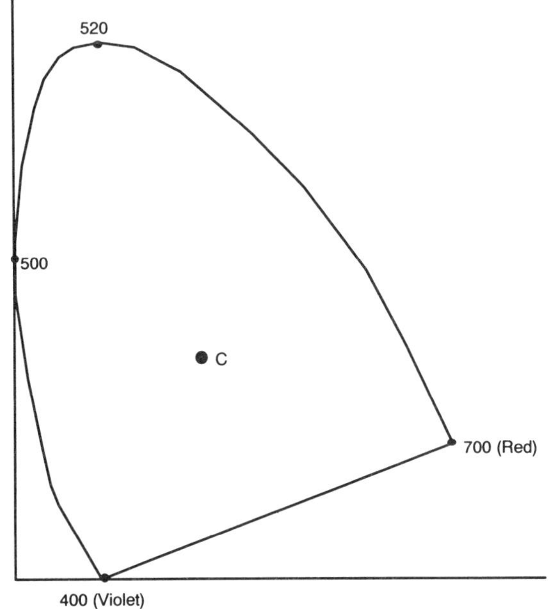

Fig. 6.1.2 The CIE Chromaticity Diagram

This diagram is known as the *CIE chromaticity diagram*. Each point on the edge of the diagram represents a pure color of one specific wavelength. The point labeled C is white, where all colors combine equally. A line drawn from a point on the edge to C will start out as a pure color and will become less pure until at the center all colors are combined. In this way we can measure the purity of a color. If the color appears on a line halfway between C and the edge, that color is 50% pure. By tracing that line to the edge we can find the dominant wavelength of a color. If the line is drawn through C to an equal distance on the other side, the complement of the color is found. The complement can be viewed as missing the color, or from the CIE chromaticity diagram we can find the dominant wavelength of the complement. The diagram in Fig. 6.1.3 shows how to find purity, dominant wavelength, and the complement on the CIE chromaticity diagram. Fig. 6.1.4 shows waveforms of light for each of these.

Another useful feature of this color model is that it can be used to explore other color models. Select any two points on the diagram and draw a line between them. Any color on that line

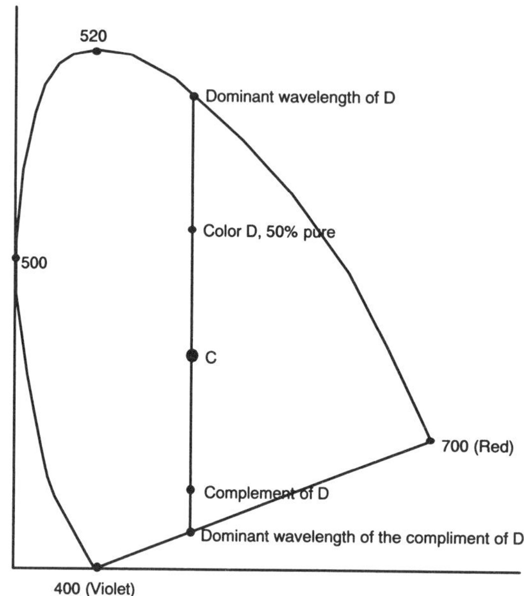

Fig. 6.1.3 Finding Information on the CIE Chromaticity Diagram

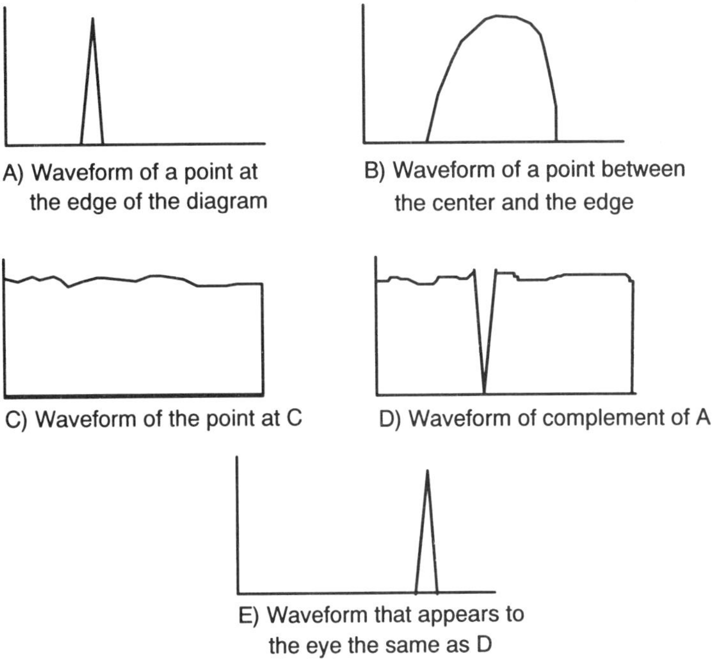

Fig. 6.1.4 Waveforms of Points on the CIE Chromaticity Diagram

can be produced by varying the amounts of the color of each end point. By selecting three points a triangle is formed. Any color inside the triangle can be produced by using the three corners in the correct amounts. This is the basis for the RGB color model. Red, green, and blue are at the farthest corners of the diagram, so this model can reproduce a large number of colors. But if the points are connected to make a triangle, there is still some space in the diagram, but outside the triangle, so not all colors can be reproduced with the RGB color model. Fig. 6.1.5 shows the RGB color model in the CIE diagram.

One drawback of this color model is the lack of shading information. The CIE diagram does not show what happens when the amount of color is reduced. There is no gray scale shown on the diagram. This diagram is shown in two dimensions. Eliminating the third dimension reduces the amount of information on the graph, and thus no gray scale.

One last point the reader might raise is why is the edge of the diagram the shape it is, and why isn't white in the center. This is because the eye is less sensitive to blue than to other colors. This tends to skew the shape of the diagram, and move white from the center.

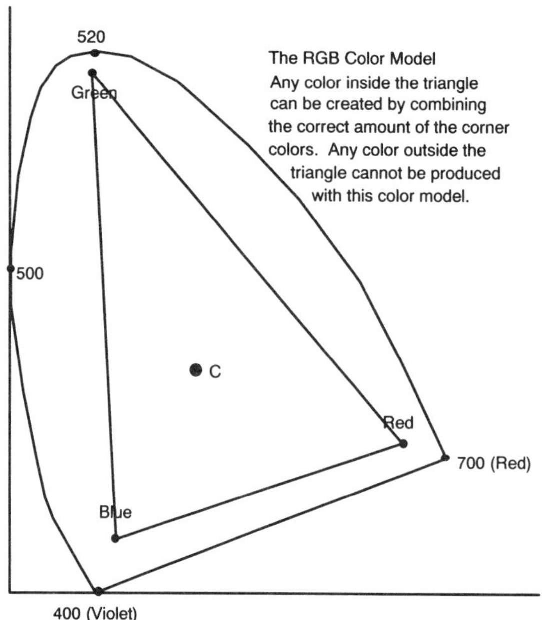

Fig. 6.1.5 The RGB Color Model on the CIE Chromaticity Diagram

The HSV Color Cone and HLS Double-Cone Models

One drawback of the RGB color model is that it is not very intuitive. When using RGB, how do you display orange, pink, or brown? The HSV and HLS models have been developed as a more intuitive approach.

The *HSV color cone* model uses three parameters, Hue, Saturation, and Value. These parameters are set up to form a hexagonal cone-shaped graph (see Fig. 6.1.6). *Hue* is an angle measure giving the color. Red is at 0 degrees, yellow at 60, green at 120, etc. *Saturation* gives the purity of the color. If the saturation is 1 then the color is the pure color given by Hue, if it is 0 then the color is white (or gray, depending on Value). *Value* gives the brightness of a color. At 1 the color is the brightest it can be. At 0 the color is black. To find bright red with this model the Hue is 0, Saturation = 1, and Value =1. To darken up the red, lower the value. To make pink, make Hue = 0, Saturation = 0.5, and Value = 1. As the value of Hue is increased, the color becomes more orange to about 30 degrees, when it starts becoming more yellow.

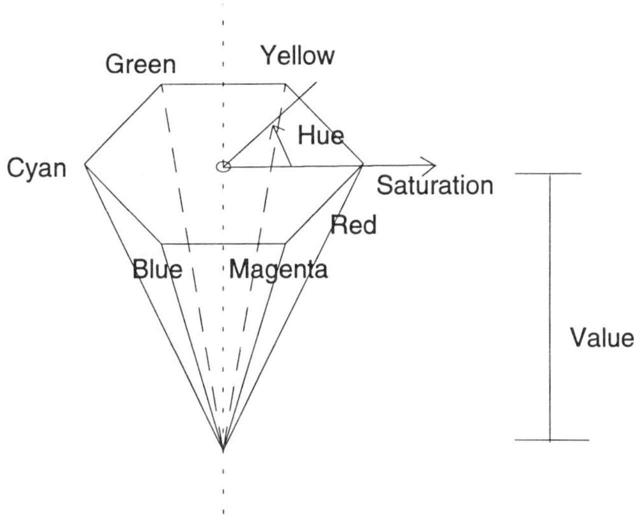

Fig. 6.1.6 The HSV Color Cone

The following function turns HSV parameters into RGB parameters. The RGB values returned are between 0 and 64, so they can be used in VGA color palettes. The methods involved in using VGA color palettes are described further along in this chapter. This function can easily be modified to give 16 or 24 bit values for SVGA monitors.

```
void HSV2RGB (int *R, int  *G, int  *B,
              int  H, float S, float V) {

  int   parm1, parm2, parm3;
  float fract, floathue;

  H = (H%360);
  floathue = (float)H/60;
  H /= 60;
  fract = floathue-(float)H;
  parm1 = (float)(V*(1.0-S))*63;
  parm2 = (float)(V*(1.0-(S*fract)))*63;
  parm3 = (float)(V*(1.0-(S*(1.0*fract))))*63;

  switch (H) {
    /* Hue = red */
    case 0 : *R=V; *G=parm3; *B=parm1; break;
    /* Hue = Yellow */
    case 1 : *R=parm2; *G=V; *B=parm1; break;
    /* Hue = Green */
    case 2 : *R=parm1; *G=V; *B=parm3; break;
```

```
        /* Hue = Cyan */
        case 3 : *R=parm1; *G=parm2; *B=V; break;
        /* Hue = Blue */
        case 4 : *R=parm3; *G=parm1; *B=V; break;
        /* Hue = Magenta */
        case 5 : *R=V; *G=parm1; *B=parm2; break;
      } /* end switch */
   } /* end HSV2RGB */
```

The *HLS double-cone* model (see Fig. 6.1.7) is quite similar to the HSV model. The three parameters it uses are Hue, Saturation, and Lightness. Hue and Saturation mean the same thing as in the HSV model. Lightness takes the place of Value. With this model the pure colors are found at L = 0.5, as opposed to V = 1 with the HSV model. The other difference is that H = 0 is blue, rather than red as in HSV. The order of the colors is the same.

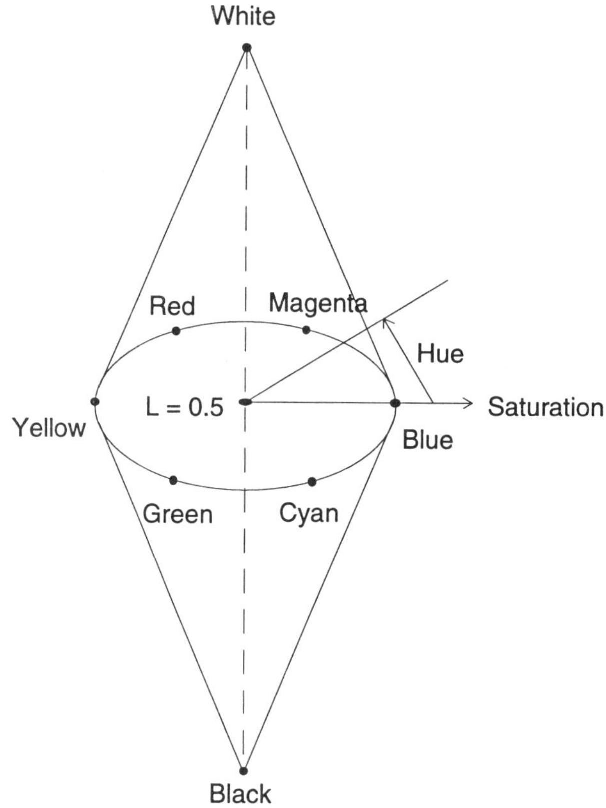

Fig. 6.1.7 HLS Double Cone

Changing the Palette

The VGA Monitor

Before applying the above information to the VGA monitor, let's quickly review Chapter 1. First of all, in a monochrome, or black and white, monitor there is an array of bits, one bit for each pixel. If the bit is set the pixel is lit, otherwise the pixel is dark. This array is called a *frame buffer*.

A more advanced monochrome monitor allows for a number of shades of gray. This means there must be more bits in the frame buffer for each pixel. If there are 2 bits per pixel then 4 shades of gray can be displayed. Of course black is included as one of those shades.

Now with a color monitor we need have three electron guns, one for each primary color. The simplest way to control them might be to have three numbers in the frame buffer for each pixel. But these are computers, and nothing can ever be done the simplest way. Instead, we set up an array of 16 elements, each element containing three sets of bits, one set for each gun. The number in the frame buffer is an index into this array, and the settings in the array tell the monitor how to set the electron guns. This array is called the *palette register array*. Each element is a palette register. Figure 6.2.1 is a picture recycled from Chapter 1 to help confuse things.

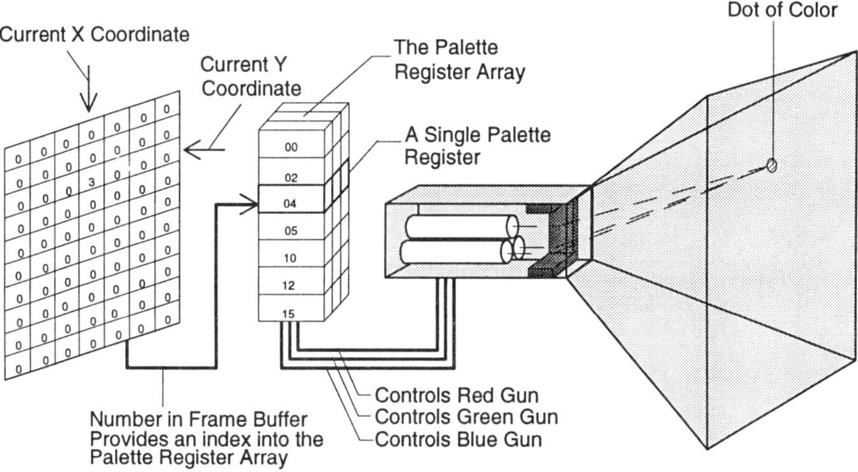

Fig. 6.2.1 Color Monitor with Frame Buffer and Palette Registers

The definition of the palette register array, if it were to be defined in C, might look something like:

```
struct color {
  unsigned bits   : 6;
};

struct palette_reg {
  struct color red, green, blue;
} palette_register_array[16];
```

This definition gives 6 bits of color resolution per color per palette. Since there are 3 color guns, there are $2^{(3\times6)}$=262,144 possible colors for each palette.

In the mode used by this chapter, the VGA 16-color mode, the palette array is defined from 0 to 15, giving 16 colors that can appear on the screen at one time. If a number greater than 15 is used, the higher bits are simply discarded, which gives the effect of a modulo operation. If we attempt to set color 16, we will end up setting color 0. There is also a 256 color mode supported by the VGA, but the BGI does not support that mode. Microsoft C does.

Borland provides several routines necessary to manipulate these data structures. The function setrgbpalette( ) is used to set palette registers. Its first parameter is the palette register to change. The next three parameters are the values to use for the red, green, and blue electron guns, in that order.

Before calling setrgbpalette( ), a call to getpalette( ) needs to be made. Internally, palette register data are stored differently than what might be expected. Function getpalette( ) returns a record with the following definition:

```
#define MAXCOLORS 15

struct palettetype {
    unsigned char size;
    signed   char colors[MAXCOLORS+1];
};
```

where size is the number of colors in the current mode. Colors is a little confusing. The way setrgbpalette( ) works, the locations of a certain palette are not always what you expect. In other words, to set palette 0, you do not always call setrgbpalette with a 0 for the register. Colors[0] will contain the actual number to use. This is done just to add a little more confusion to an already confused process. Here are the definitions for these procedures:

```
void setrgbpalette (int colornum, int red,
                    int green, int blue);
  /*
   * setrgbpalette is used to change the Red,
   * Green, and Blue settings for a given
   * palette register.
   *
   * Parameters:
   *   colornum - The palette number to
   *              change.
   *   red      - The value for the Red gun.
   *   green    - The value for the Green gun.
   *   blue     - The value for the Blue gun.
   */

void getpalette
             (struct palettetype far &palette);
  /*
   * getpalette will return information on
   * the current graphics setting
   *
   * Parameters:
   *   palette - Structure containing
   *     information on the current graphics
   *     setting.
```

```
  *
  * Note - This procedure is not supported
  *        on the IBM 1814 monitor.
  */
```

The concept of palette registers is confusing, but unfortunately little can be done up to this point but confuse the hapless reader. The following is a simple example to demonstrate the routines for setting the RGB palette registers. This program draws a series of bars on the screen while the palette registers contain their default settings. After the bars are drawn the palette registers are changed to show 16 shades of gray. As the palette registers change the bars on the screen change to match. Studying this program until you understand it, then running it will go a long way toward making palette registers understandable. This program is simple enough that it is not included in the distribution disk. It will take a trivial amount of time to type in.

```
#include <graphics.h>
#include <stdio.h>
#include <stdlib.h>
#include <conio.h>
#include <math.h>

/*============================================*/

void draw_bars() {
  /*
   * Draws a series of bars on the screen
   * using different colors
   */
  int i, j, Width;

  Width = getmaxx() / 15;

  for(i=1; i<=15; i++) {
    setcolor(i);
    for (j=1; j<=Width; j++)
      line (j+((i-1)*Width), 1,
            j+((i-1)*Width), getmaxy());
  } /* end loop */

} /* end draw_bars */

/*============================================*/

void change_palette(){
  /*
   * Set up palette with gray scale
   */
```

```
  int i;
  struct palettetype pal;

  getpalette(&pal);

  for (i=1; i<=15; i++)
    setrgbpalette(pal.colors[i],
                  i<<2, i<<2, i<<2);
} /* end change_palette() */

/*============================================*/

void main (void) {
  int   Driver, Mode, GraphError;

  Driver = DETECT;
  detectgraph(&Driver, &Mode);
  initgraph(&Driver, &Mode, '');

  GraphError = graphresult();
  if (GraphError != grOk) {
    printf("%s\n",grapherrormsg(GraphError));
    exit(-1);
  }

  /* Do Graphics Stuff Here */
  draw_bars();
  change_palette();

  getch();
  if (kbhit()) getch();

  closegraph();
}
```

Earlier in this chapter the question was asked: How do you get orange, pink, or brown from an RGB color model? Program BK0601.C answers that question, and also gives more practice with changing palettes. This program draws 14 gray bars across the top of the screen, each one using a different palette. The user can then use the keyboard to change the color content of each bar. The color guns can be manipulated until the desired color is achieved, and different colors can be compared.

This program is quite large for an example. The source is nearly nine pages long, so it is not presented in the text. But it is well worth studying for the information it gives on manipulating palette registers. In addition, it gives useful hints on using the PC keyboard. And so it is described here. If you wish to study it look at file BK0601.C on the distribution disk while you read. You might wish to try running it before looking at how it works. Instructions are printed on the screen as it runs.

The program has 2 main functions, draw_screen( ) and run_program( ). Function draw_screen( ) simply sets up the screen. The palette registers are all set to gray, which means equal amounts of red, green, and blue. Fourteen bars are drawn on the screen, each using a different palette register – previously what we referred to as colors. Calling them different colors now doesn't make sense since they all appear as the same shade of gray. But we refer to them as different colors anyhow. Only 14 colors are used because color 0 is needed for the background, and color 1 is needed for text.

Once the 14 bars are on the screen instructions are written. The second procedure is run_program( ). This procedure reads keystrokes, interprets those keystroke, and performs the correct action. Before we discuss how this is done a little background on the PC keyboard in necessary. The function getch( ) reads keys from the keyboard. Given the number of keys on the PC keyboard, including shifted keys, control keys, and alternate keys, there are far too many keys for one character of information. Function getch( ) returns an integer, but on the PC the top byte is always 0. Only one character of information is ever returned by getch( ) on a PC. Not all keys on the PC keyboard can be handled by getch( ). To overcome this certain keys, which we call "special" keys, return two characters worth of information. The first character is a 0 or null character. If getch( ) returns a 0 and another keystroke is waiting, then a special key has been pressed. Another call to getch( ) is required to find which special key was pressed. These keys include cursor keys, F keys, and some control and alternate keys. It should be noted that getch( ) can return a 0 if a special key has not been pressed by holding the alternate key, pressing the keypad 0 key, then releasing the alternate key. The function kbhit( ) is called to make sure a special key was really pressed.

The program uses a constant SPECKEY, which is equal to 0. If the character returned by getch( ) is SPECKEY and another keystroke is waiting, special character handling is invoked. The special character is read and the correct action is performed. If the key pressed is not a special key similar processing is performed, but a second call to getch( ) is not needed. Note that many keys, such as enter and escape, have constants defined to make the program more readable. The numeric values of all PC keys is given in Appendix I.

The functions raise( ) and lower( ) add color and subtract color from the current palette. The palette is retrieved, and the current value from the palette, which is currently on the screen, is erased. The palette value is incremented or decremented, and written back to the screen. Finally the new palette is set.

The functions next_block( ) and last_block( ) set the block on the screen that is being changed. They are quite simple. The pointer pointing at the current block is erased, the current block number incremented or decremented, and a new pointer is written.

The final function is change_color( ). This function does not change anything displayed on the screen, it changes the color gun that will be manipulated by raise( ) and lower( ). It works much the same as the last two functions. The pointer on the screen that indicates the current color is erased, the current_color variable is updated, and a new pointer written.

This is a very interesting and useful program. Spending some time with it to learn how colors work in the RGB color model is well worthwhile. The knowledge gained will save time later when you need to create pictures, and need to use orange.

Half-Toning and Dithering

If a gray scale is drawn on a VGA monitor it will not smoothly progress from black to white. Six bits per color does not provide enough color resolution. It is easy to tell by looking where one color stops and the next starts by a line that is visible between the shades. Dithering is a method of blending together two shades that are close together to eliminate the line between them. If a smooth shading is desired in 16-color mode, dithering must be used.

Sixteen colors is not a lot. For realistic looking pictures it is not enough. By taking several pixels of one color and adding in several pixels of another color, a third color can be made to appear on the screen. By doing this many more than 16 colors can be displayed. This technique is called *half-toning*.

The techniques of half-toning and dithering are so close that they almost seem like the same thing. The difference is that half-toning uses two different colors, while dithering uses two shades of the same color.

These techniques are not perfect. If a gray scale with dithering is displayed using 16 colors, differences can still be seen from one shade to the next. The VGA monitor uses 6 bits to control the electron guns. Studies have shown that 16 bits are needed if a smooth gray scale is to be created using dithering. We need at least 24 bits to create a smooth gray scale with no dithering. This why much is being written and said these days about monitors with 16-bit and 24-bit color resolution. Twenty four bit modes are sometimes called *true color* modes, since they can very nearly reproduce all shades the eye can detect. The BGI, however, does not support these SVGA modes. Techniques for programming them must wait for a future chapter (see Chapter 8).

Dithering

The idea behind dithering is this: If we take an area of the screen that is all one shade and sprinkle into pixels of a darker shade, the eye will not be able to pick up the pixels of the darker shade (if the shades are close together), but the entire area will be darkened. As the percentage of dark pixels is increased, the area becomes darker. The reverse can be used to lighten the area.

Several methods can be used for dithering. As the area is filled, a mathematical formula can be used to determine if a given pixel should be light or dark. This formula looks at the percentage of area to be light and the percentage to be dark. The light and dark pixels are then mixed for an even shading. This method has the drawback of introducing noticeable patterns into the fill area.

As an example, if you wish 1 pixel out of every 6 to be dark, and the rest light, you might modulo the Y position of the pixel by 6, and if the result is 0 use the dark color. Otherwise use the light color. This method is used in the demonstration program. There are other formulas that might be used. Some create patterns that are more obvious than others.

The next method is similar. A random number generator is used to determine if the pixel should be light or dark. If 1 out of 6 pixels is to be dark, the generator can be set to return a value between 0 and 5. If 0 is returned the pixel is dark. Otherwise the pixel is light. This method avoids the patterns introduced by the last method, but the shading is not as even. It is also presented in the demonstration program.

Both of the above methods can be clumsy in general programming situations, so a third method is often used. This method groups pixels together into squares or rectangles. Some of the pixels in the square are set to the lighter color, others to the darker color. A set of squares can be set up, with a different ratio of light to dark in each squares. Then a square and two colors can be selected when the dither routine is called. This method is demonstrated in the next section on half-toning.

In a future chapter we will be developing methods for filling various shapes. Any of these methods can be added to these functions to make a halftone or dither fill routine.

The following program draws a gray scale on the screen. The center third is dithered using a mathematical function. The bottom third is dithered with a random method. The top is left undithered for comparison.

```
/*
 * BK0602.C - Dithering Demo
 */

#include <graphics.h>
#include <stdio.h>
```

```
#include <stdlib.h>
#include <conio.h>
#include <math.h>

/*==========================================*/

void initialize_palette(){
  /*
   * Set up palette with gray scale
   */
  int i;
  struct palettetype pal;

  getpalette(&pal);

  for (i=1; i<=15; i++)
    setrgbpalette(pal.colors[i],
                  i<<2,i<<2,i<<2);
} /* end initialize_palette() */

/*==========================================*/

void undithered_bars() {
  /*
   * Draw the grayscale on the screen
   */
  int i, j, Width;

  Width = getmaxx() / 15;

  for(i=1; i<=15; i++) {
    setcolor(i);
    for (j=1; j<=Width; j++)
      line(j+((i-1)*Width), 1,
           j+((i-1)*Width),getmaxy());
  } /* end loop */

} /* end undithered_bars */

/*==========================================*/

void pattern_two_color_line (int Color1,
                             int Color2,
                             int D_Factor,
                             int X) {
  /*
   * Dither 2 colors using a mathematical
   * function to determine which color is used.
   *
```

```
     * Parameters:
     *   Color1    - The first color
     *   Color2    - The second color
     *   D_Factor - How many pixels of the first
     *     color should be used before a pixel of
     *     the second color is used.
     *   X         - X screen coordinate of
     *     dithered line.
     */
    int Y, i, Top, Bottom;

    Top    = (getmaxy() * 2) / 3;
    Bottom =  getmaxy() / 3;

    for (i=Bottom; i<=Top; i++)
      if (i % D_Factor == 0)
        putpixel (X, i, Color2);
      else
        putpixel (X, i, Color1);

  } /* end pattern_two_color_line() */

  /*-----------------------------------------------*/

  void pattern_dither() {
    /*
     * Dither the middle third of the gray scale
     * using a pattern dither
     */
    int i, j, width;

    width = getmaxx() / 15;

    for (i=1; i<=14; i++)
      for (j=1; j<=width >>1; j++) {
        pattern_two_color_line(i+1, i,
                               j+1, j+(i*width));
        pattern_two_color_line(i,   i+1,
                             j+1, 1+(i*width)-j);
      } /* end loop */
  } /* end pattern_dither */

  /*===============================================*/

  void random_two_color_line (int Color1,
                              int Color2,
                              int D_Factor,
                              int X) {
    /*
```

```
   * Dither 2 colors using a random number
   * generator to determine which color is
   * used.
   *
   * Parameters:
   *   Color1   - The first color
   *   Color2   - The second color
   *   D_Factor - The chance of having a pixel
   *     of color1 over color2
   *   X        - X screen coordinate of
   *     dithered line.
   */
  int Y, i, Stop;

  Stop = getmaxy();
  for (Y=(getmaxy()*2)/3; Y<=Stop; Y++)
    if (random(D_Factor) == 0)
      putpixel(X, Y, Color2);
    else
      putpixel(X, Y, Color1);

} /* end random_two_color_line() */

/*-------------------------------------------*/

void random_dither() {
  /*
   * Dither the last third of the gray scale
   * using a random dither
   */
  int i, j, width;

  width = getmaxx() / 15;

  for (i=1; i<=14; i++)
    for (j=1; j<=width >>1; j++) {
      random_two_color_line(i+1, i,
                            j+1, j+(i*width));
      random_two_color_line(i,   i+1,
                          j+1, 1+(i*width)-j);
    } /* end loop */
} /* end random_dither */

/*===========================================*/

void main (void) {
  int   Driver, Mode, GraphError;

  Driver = DETECT;
```

```
    detectgraph(&Driver, &Mode);
    initgraph(&Driver, &Mode, '');

    GraphError = graphresult();
    if (GraphError != grOk) {
        printf("%s\n",grapherrormsg(GraphError));
        exit(-1);
    }

    /* Do Graphics Stuff Here */
    randomize();
    initialize_palette();
    undithered_bars();
    pattern_dither();
    random_dither();

    getch();
    if (kbhit()) getch();

    closegraph();
}
```

This program draws a gray scale on the screen, then calls the function pattern_dither( ) to dither the middle third of the gray scale, and random_dither( ) to dither the bottom third. Both of these functions work the same way. Starting at the center of a bar, they dither to the right, constantly making the pattern lighter. At the same time they work from the center of the next bar to the left, constantly making the pattern darker. The actual work of dithering is done by calls to pattern_two_color_line( ) and random_two_color_line( ).

Function pattern_two_color_line( ) draws a dithered vertical line that covers the middle third of the screen. This function needs four parameters. The first two are the colors to be used, Color1 and Color2. Next is the amount of the first color over the second, as an integer, which is called D_Factor. The last parameter is the X location of the line. The function performs a modulo operation on the Y location of the pixel being drawn with D_Factor. If the result is 0, the second color is used, otherwise the first is used.

Function random_two_color_line( ) draws a dithered vertical line covering the bottom third of the screen. The parameters are the same as the last function. D_Factor is passed to the random number generator. If the result is 0 the second color is used, otherwise the first color is used.

Half-Toning

Half-toning is a form of color mixing. Two different colors are mixed in various amounts to produce other colors. Theoretically any colors between these two on the CIE chromaticity diagram can be created. The methods for mixing these colors are the same as for dithering. If blue pixels are sprinkled into an area filled with red, the area will start to appear purple. As more blue is added the area becomes more purple. If too much is added the area starts becoming more blue.

Methods used for half-toning are the same as for dithering. A mathematical formula can be used to determine if a pixel should be one color or the other. A random number generator can also be used. These two methods are illustrated in the programming example in the last section.

A third method uses blocks of pixels. This method groups pixels together into squares or rectangles. Some of the pixels in the block are set to the lighter color, others to the darker color. A set of blocks can be set up, with a different ratio of light to dark in each block. To use this method, two things must be done. The first is to set up the blocks, and the second is to write a function that lights pixels on the screen in a color determined by the block.

The blocks are made from a two-dimensional array of booleans. If an entry in the array is TRUE, the first color is used, otherwise the second is used. Different sizes can be used for the array. Common sizes are 2×2 and 3×3. Using a larger array allows for more colors, but either lowers resolution or complicates processing, depending on the algorithm used. This array is called a *mask*. A set of masks is needed, one for each final color that will appear on the screen. It is convenient to place the masks into an array.

Before we continue, we need to discuss booleans in C. The C language has no boolean type. We could use an entire character for one boolean, but since only one bit is needed, this wastes a tremendous amount of space. We can overcome this by using C's ability to manipulate individual bits. A data structure can be declared that assigns a certain number of bits to a field. We need a structure with only one field that is one bit long. This can then be typedef'ed to create a data type.

```
struct boolean {
    bit : 1;
};
typedef boolean;
```

We do not need the dot notation to access this field, since the only thing that will be assigned to it or read from it will be a single bit, which is the size of the entire data structure. Now all we have to do is declare a 3D array of these:

```
boolean Mask[10][3][3];
```

The first dimension is a mask for each final color. The next two dimensions form a 3 ×3 array of booleans. The entire array can be thought of as 10 blocks of 3×3 arrays of booleans. Fig. 6.3.1 shows how these will be initialized.

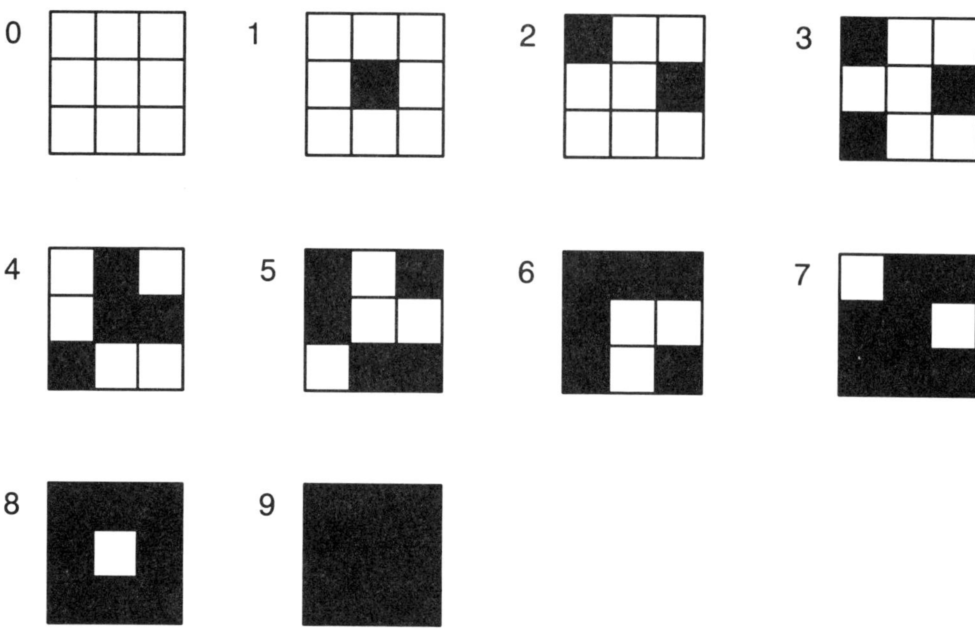

Fig. 6.3.1 Half-Toning Masks

Take note of the fact that you must be very careful to set up the masks so that no pattern is introduced. Sometimes these patterns can be quite subtle. On my first attempt at the demonstration program for this chapter, I accidentally introduced a pattern on mask six. Figure 6.3.2 shows what the mask looked like. Can you find the pattern? If not, try using this for mask 6 in the demo program. When the program is run the pattern really stands out.

Fig. 6.3.2 Mask with a Pattern

Now that the masks are defined, a procedure needs to be written to use them. This can be done in two ways. The most common is to divide the screen up into grids, so that the pixels in each grid match the pixels in the mask. Instead of lighting single pixels on the screen, groups of pixels are lit. If a 3×3 mask is used then 9 pixels are put on the screen at one time. This method lowers the resolution of the screen. With 2×2 masks the screen has half the resolution it would have. With a 3×3 mask the resolution is cut by a third!

The other method is to divide the screen up the same way, but still allow individual pixels to be set. The mask is checked to determine if the pixel being set is color one or color two. This lets the mask be quite large without lowering resolution, but checking the mask takes some time. The demonstration program uses the first method for simplicity.

The function that does this in the demonstration program is called plot_pixel( ). It actually plots a 3×3 grid of pixels. The XY coordinates are for the entire grid. Since only a third as many grids fit on the screen in each dimension, these parameters should have a third the value of a pixel that should be plotted at the same location. In other words, if the maximum X value for a pixel is 639, the maximum for this function is 213. This way the grid at (2,1) is exactly next to the grid at (1,1). A simple nested loop looks at each location of the mask and lights the corresponding pixel appropriately.

```
void plot_pixel (unsigned Mask_Num,
                 unsigned Color1,
                 unsigned Color2,
                 unsigned X,
                 unsigned Y) {

  int i, j, Index_X, Index_Y;

  X=(X*3)-1;
  Y=(Y*3)-1;
  for(i=0; i<3; i++) {
    for(j=0; j<3; j++) {
      if (Mask[Mask_Num][i][j])
        putpixel(X+i, Y+j, Color2);
      else
        putpixel(X+i, Y+j, Color1);
    } /* end inner loop */
  } /* end outer loop */

} /* end plot_pixel() */
```

Now the demonstration program. This program is not listed here because again it is quite large. The source can be found in BK0602.C This program not only demonstrates how to write half-toning code, but when run it can be used to sample half-toning effects. It works basically the same as the second palette program, the one where the color guns can be manipulated on the 14 bars. The only real differences involve the actual half-toning portion, which is described in fair detail before the listing. The method for initializing the array of masks is worth taking a second look at, however. Taking advantage of C's ability to pre-initialize arrays, we can come up with this compact, fast, yet readable method for setting up masks. If one is to be changed it is a simple matter to count down (remember to start at 0) to the correct mask, then change the needed values. If you want to try changing mask 6 to a block with a pattern, it is quite easy.

Programming the CGA

Although CGA monitors are obsolete, there are still a good number out there, and a few souls still have to program them. The CGA monitor is different than other systems. It cannot be programmed with the same methods. I have actually seen pretty good pictures on these monitors, using their high-resolution two-color mode and half-toning to create a gray scale.

The CGA has two graphics modes, a high resolution two-color mode, and a low-resolution four-color mode. The high-resolution mode is fairly straightforward to program. Program it as if it were a basic black and white monitor, with one bit per pixel.

The second mode uses four colors. Now it would be expected that the programmer could set each of four palette registers to determine the four colors. But alas, this is not how the CGA works. The palette registers are not as flexible as with other modes. Certain colors must be shown together.

There are four settings for the palette, each setting has three preselected colors, and a fourth color that the programmer can select. This fourth color is the background. The settings are changed by changing the mode the screen is in. The mode is not actually changed; it is the CGA low-resolution mode, but the colors displayed are changed. Table 6.4.1 gives the modes and the colors associated with them.

Table 6.4.1 CGA Palettes and Colors

Mode	Background Color	Color 1	Color 2	Color 3
CGAC0	User Selected	LightGreen	LightRed	Yellow
CGAC1	User Selected	LightCyan	LightMagenta	White
CGAC2	User Selected	Green	Red	Brown
CGAC3	User Selected	Cyan	Magenta	LightGray

Use initgraph( ) with one of the above modes to get the colors selected. To change from one color set to another use setgraphmode( ). Remember that setgraphmode erases the screen, so you will have to redraw it.

The background color is listed as user selectable for all palettes (in the CGA world, each of these modes is called a palette). The default for this color is black. To select the color use setbkcolor( ). The possible selections are: BLACK, BLUE, GREEN, CYAN, RED, MAGENTA, BROWN, LIGHTGRAY, DARKGRAY, LIGHTBLUE, LIGHTGREEN, LIGHTCYAN, LIGHTRED, LIGHTMAGENTA, YELLOW, and WHITE. There are constants defined for these values, so you can write them out in your program, or you can use the integer values that match. If the integer values are used, 0 is for black, 1 is for blue, etc.

The following program demonstrates how the CGA is programmed:

```
/*
 * BK0604.C - Demo program for CGA monitors
 */

#include <graphics.h>
#include <stdio.h>
#include <stdlib.h>
#include <conio.h>

/*============================================*/

void draw_screen() {
  /*
   * draw for blocks on the screen, each in a
   * different color.
   */
  int i;

  for (i=30; i<=100; i++) {
    setcolor (0);
```

```
      line (60, i, 160, i);
      setcolor (1);
      line (161, i, 260, i);
    } /* end forloop */

    for (; i<170; i++) {
      setcolor (2);
      line (60, i, 160, i);
      setcolor (3);
      line (161, i, 260, i);
    } /* end forloop */
  } /* end draw_screen() */

  /*=============================================*/

  #define ESC     27
  #define SPECKEY 0
  #define LEFT    75
  #define RIGHT   77
  #define UP      72
  #define DOWN    80
  #define BEEP    7
  #define ENTER   13

  void rotate_palettes() {
    /*
     * If UP or DOWN cursor keys are pressed, the
     * background color is changed.  If the space
     * bar is pressed the CGA palette is changed
     */
    char option;
    int  Cur_Pal_Num = 0, cur_bk = 0;

    do {
      option = getch();
      if (option == SPECKEY) {
        option = getch();
        switch (option) {
          case UP :
            cur_bk = (cur_bk + 1) % 16;
            setbkcolor (cur_bk);
            break;
          case DOWN :
            cur_bk = (cur_bk - 1);
            if (cur_bk < 0) cur_bk = 15;
            setbkcolor (cur_bk);
            break;
          default : putch(BEEP);
        } /* end switch */
```

```
    } /* end if */
    else {
      switch (option) {
        case ' ' :
          Cur_Pal_Num = (Cur_Pal_Num + 1) % 4;
          setgraphmode (Cur_Pal_Num);
          draw_screen();
          break;
        case ESC : break;
        default : putch(BEEP);
      } /* end switch */
    } /* end else */
  } while (option != ESC);
} /* end rotate_palettes() */

/*=============================================*/

void main (void) {
  int   Driver = CGA,
        Mode = CGAC0,
        GraphError;

  initgraph(&Driver, &Mode, '');

  GraphError = graphresult();
  if (GraphError != grOk) {
      printf("%s\n",grapherrormsg(GraphError));
      exit(-1);
  }

  /* Do Graphics Stuff Here */
  draw_screen();
  rotate_palettes();

  closegraph();
}
```

7

Three-Dimensional Graphics

One of the more interesting and popular branches of graphics programming is three dimensional-graphics. The challenge, of course, is how to represent the real three-dimensional world on a two-dimensional screen.

There are three methods that are used to make a two-dimensional image look three-dimensional. Most pictures use all three. The first is the proper use of perspective. Imagine a straight railroad track. The rails seem to meet in the distance, although they are parallel to each other. This is one example of perspective.

The next method is the proper use of shading. Imagine a ball. The part of the ball closest to the light appears the lightest. This shading can be modeled with the computer to add to the three-dimensional effect of your picture.

The third method is the use of texturing. Imagine that you are standing in a large field that hasn't been mown all summer. When you look at the grass close to yourself you see individual stalks. The field appears rough. As you look into the distance it smooths out. This texturing is a very effective means of giving your pictures a realistic look.

Perspective

The first step in drawing a three-dimensional picture is projecting the three-dimensional image onto the two-dimensional screen.

Projecting a 3D image onto a 2D screen

Since a cube is about the simplest 3D object there is, it is a good place to start. It would be useful if you have a computer drawing tool, or at least a pencil and paper handy so you can try this. We are going to draw a cube as if we are looking at it from slightly above and to the right of it.

First draw the front of the cube (Fig. 7.1.1).

Fig. 7.1.1 The Face of a Cube

That's easy enough. Now draw the right side. If we turned the cube so that side faced us it would appear square. But since we are looking at an angle it's distorted. The right angles do not appear 90°. We are slightly above the cube so the side seems to go upward as it goes back (Fig. 7.1.2).

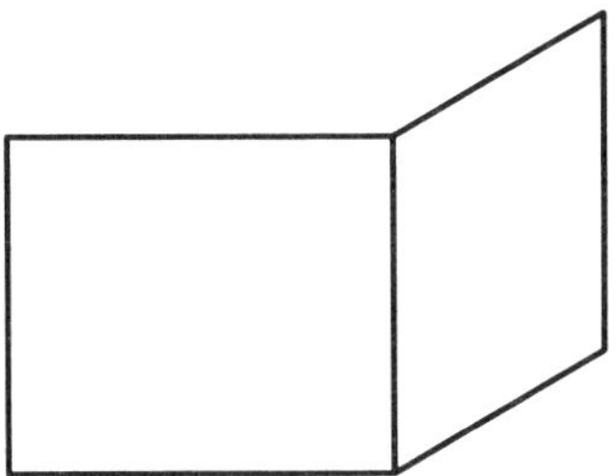

Fig. 7.1.2 Face and Right Side of a Cube

The line that makes the top of the right side is parallel to the line that makes the bottom. The line that makes the back is parallel to the line that forms the front. The top can now be put on easily by drawing a line across the back parallel to the top front line, and another line from the left side of the front parallel with the top of the right side (Fig. 7.1.3).

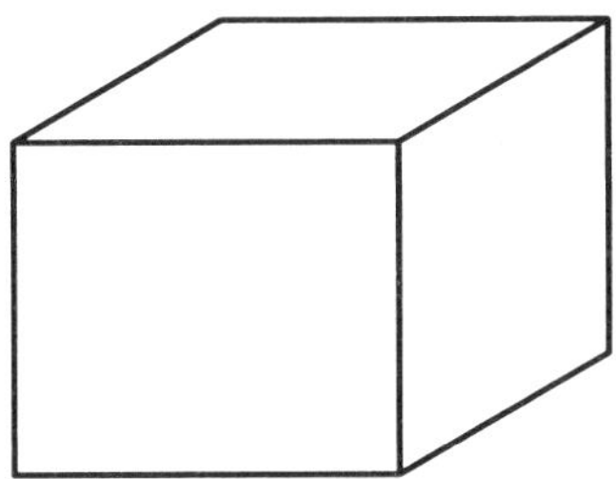

Fig. 7.1.3 All Visible Sides of a Cube

All sides on a cube are the same size, so all lines on the drawing should be the same length. But if drawn that way the cube will appear rectangular. The perspective is not what the eye would expect. For this reason when making professional type "working drawings" you should always draw lines the correct length and label their lengths, but when making artistic type drawings you should make adjustments so that it looks right. Looking carefully at Fig. 7.1.3, you might notice another distortion. The lines that make up the right side and top might not look parallel. This is another trick of perspective. At a distance parallel lines seem to converge. But these lines are parallel, so the eye is fooled into thinking they diverge. This is another adjustment that should be made to artistic works.

Look at Fig. 7.1.4 Which block appears to be higher? Why? Block B is drawn with the angles of the top and right side more distorted, as the would appear if the block is farther below eye level.

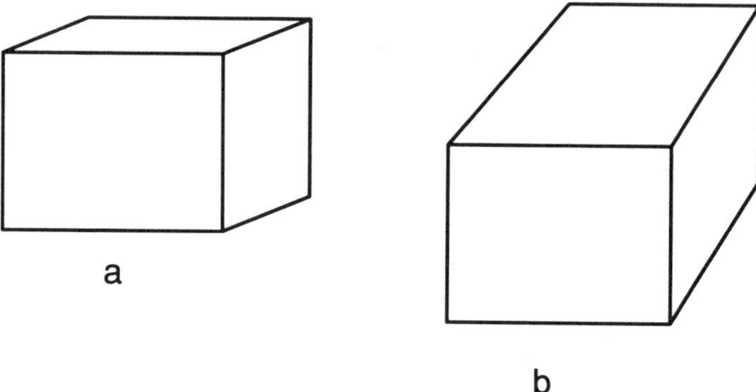

Fig. 7.1.4 3D Blocks

Now what happens when the block is rotated? If the block is turned counter-clockwise, when viewed from above, the right-hand edge rotates downward towards horizontal. The front edge rotates upward. When the block is rotated so the corner is facing forward, rather than the face, both edges make the same angle with the horizon. Usually when drawing this view the angle with the horizon is drawn at 30 degrees. This is called an isometric view, or the isometric perspective. Figure 7.1.5 shows this.

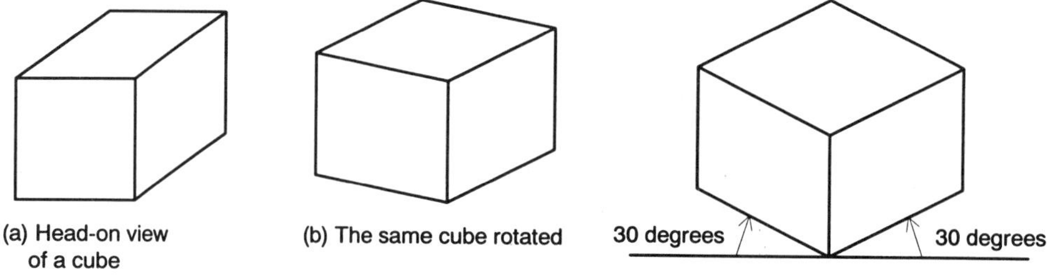

Fig. 7.1.5 Rotating a Cube

Now that we have a block, let's fancy it up by putting things on the surface. If we put a circle on the surface of an isometric cube it does not appear round. How annoying. Because the eye is already fooled into thinking this is a 3D image, it thinks the circle should also be distorted. Because of the perspective of the drawing, our eye thinks the circle must be an oval. To make what looks like a circle, we need to draw an oval. The narrow ends of the oval should be toward the sharper corners of the cube. Unfortunately with the BGI we cannot rotate ovals in the most convenient way. We must approximate the best we can. Figure 7.1.6 gives an example. You can see that these ovals still do not look perfect, but they do look better than perfectly round circles.

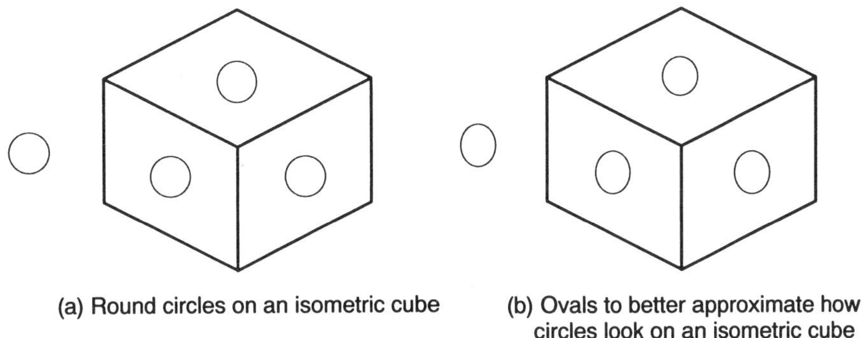

(a) Round circles on an isometric cube

(b) Ovals to better approximate how circles look on an isometric cube

Fig. 7.1.6 Cubes with Surface Markings

This method can be used to create sophisticated 3D drawings. Start with three views of what you want to draw, the front, side, and top. For every feature draw a box on your 3D drawing to serve as a guide. When all the major features are represented by boxes draw the details as they actually look inside the boxes, then erase the boxes. This method was used for many years by draftsmen. It take patience and practice, but results in great looking pictures. I know one artist who uses this method to create a line drawing of his pictures, then he paints in the colors and ends up with very realistic looking scenes.

This method is not presented here as a means of creating 3D graphics, only as a means to understand how to project a 3D object onto a 2D computer screen. To draw such things on a computer, using C, you might want to start by sketching on paper. Once you see how it looks on paper, you can transfer it directly to a program. Of course, a high-powered CAD program will do the same with a great deal less work.

A program has been included on the distribution disk to help you visualize how a 3D cube looks from different angles. Program BK0701.C draws a simple cube on the screen, then you can move it around with the cursor control keys. As it moves the perspective changes so that you seem to see it from different angles. Cntl left and cntl right will rotate the cube. There is a minor bug; after rotating, the cube ends up higher on the screen. The code for the program is rather simple, and there is little to be learned from it, so it is not presented. The important thing for this program is to see what effect moving and rotating the cube has on how it looks on a 2D screen. This program makes use of the BGI, as do all the examples in this chapter, so it will compile on Borland C, but will need modification to work with Microsoft C.

Single Vanishing Point Perspective

To understand perspective, we must think about how the eye works. The cornea of the eye is a lens that focuses light rays on the retina. And like all lenses it brings light in at an angle, not simply at a straight line (see Fig. 7.1.7).

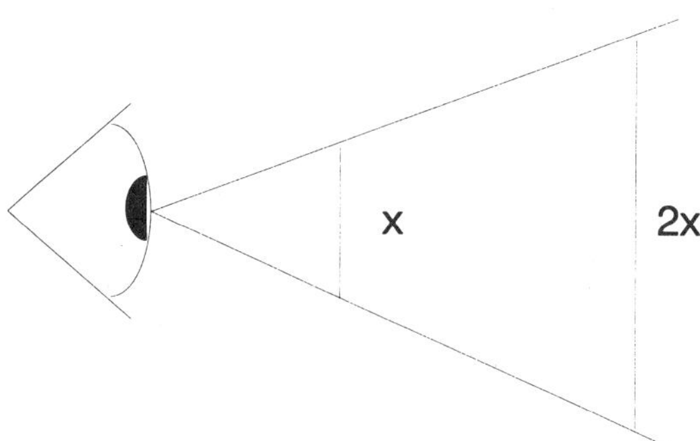

Fig 7.1.7 The Eye Sees an Angle

At a certain distance the eye sees a field of a certain width. At a farther distance the field of the eye is greater, since the field width is an angle. But this is not how we perceive things. We don't perceive our angle of vision getting wider as we look farther away, instead the brain perceives the width of the field of vision remaining the same, but things farther away become smaller and closer together.

This can lead to some interesting effects. The cubes drawn in the last section did not appear entirely cubical. This is because the closer part of the cube is drawn the same size as the far part of the cube. The information reaching the eye is ambiguous, so the picture is not interpreted entirely as expected. Pictures can be drawn where so much of the information is ambiguous the brain simply cannot interpret the picture consistently. Escher made an entire career out of such pictures.

But most people want to avoid these problems, and make realistic looking pictures. To avoid these problems, use vanishing point perspective. When we look into the distance everything seems to get smaller and converge on a single point. To see this, imagine a straight railroad track. The rails seem to meet in the distance. This effect can be drawn into pictures. When making the first rough sketch of the picture, draw a simple grid, such as the one in Fig. 7.1.8(a). Items that are farther away are smaller, but in proportion to the grids in the box. Notice that the lower lines in the grid are lying on the ground.

If you want a view from a hill, where the viewer is higher than the surroundings, move the horizon down. This will give the lines at the bottom of the box more of an angle [Fig. 7.1.8(b)]. If the perspective is from a valley, move the horizon up [Fig. 7.1.8(c)].

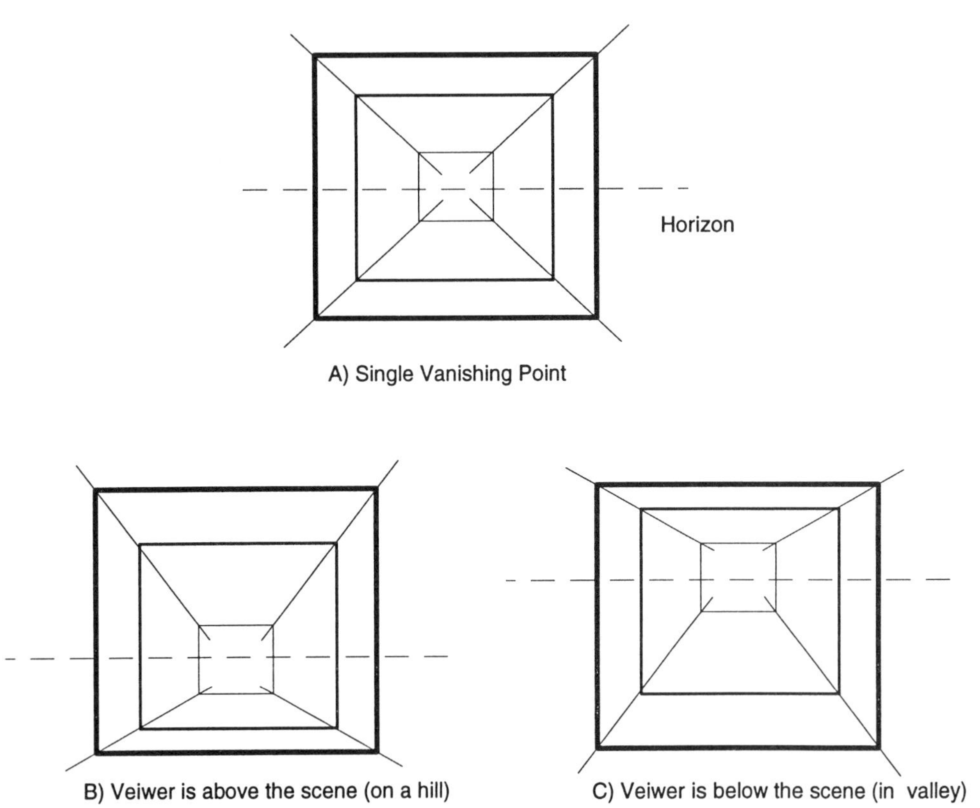

Fig. 7.1.8 Single Vanishing Point Perspective

Double Vanishing Point Perspective

When there is a large object, such as a building, in front of the viewer, single vanishing point perspective no longer works. There is no point in the distance in the center of the picture. There's a building there. If you look at one end of the building, lines seem to converge on one point, and if you look at the other end, lines seem to converge on a different point. This leads to the idea of double vanishing point perspective.

With double vanishing point perspective the viewer is generally at the level of the object being viewed. A corner of the object is facing the viewer. The bottom edges of the object on each side of the corner angles upward toward the appropriate vanishing point. The top edges angle downward. Fig. 7.1.9 shows an example of double vanishing point perspective.

A natural conclusion one might draw at this point is "infinite vanishing point perspective," where every large object in the scene converges on its own points. For instance, if you have three large buildings in the scene you might have six vanishing points, two for each building. There is an artistic reason not to do this, however. The vanishing point tends to draw the viewer's attention. This means the object of the scene will stand out clearly. If there are a number of objects in the scene, each vanishing to different points, the viewer will not have a clear indication what the object of the picture is. The picture becomes cluttered. Of course in art, as with computer programming, what works, works. If a scene is made of a number of different perspectives, and it looks good, no one can argue.

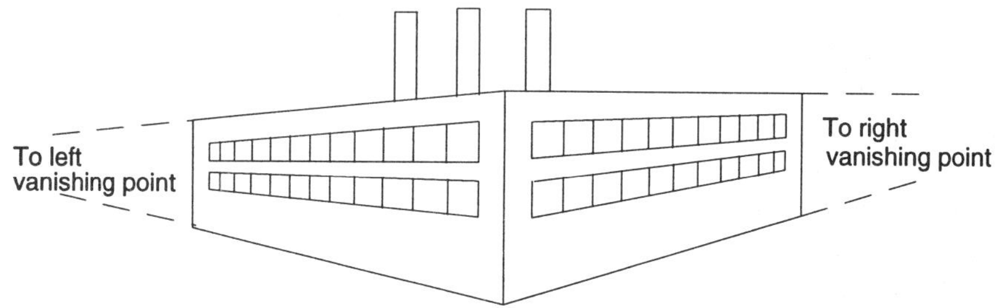

Factory without doors - A nonartist's sketch

Fig. 7.1.9 Double Vanishing Point Perspective

The following function draws the grid shown in Fig. 7.1.8(a) on the screen.

```
void perspective () {

   line (80,    0, 290, 210);
   line (560,   0, 350, 210);
   line (80,  479, 290, 270);
   line (560, 479, 350, 270);

   line (260, 180, 260, 300);
   line (260, 180, 380, 180);
   line (380, 180, 380, 300);
   line (260, 300, 380, 300);

   line (200, 120, 200, 360);
   line (200, 120, 440, 120);
   line (440, 120, 440, 360);
   line (200, 360, 440, 360);
```

```
    line (140,  60, 140, 420);
    line (140,  60, 500,  60);
    line (500,  60, 500, 420);
    line (140, 420, 500, 420);

    /* the horizon */
    setlinestyle(DASHED_LINE, 0, NORM_WIDTH);
    line (0, 240, 639, 240);
}
```

Shading

Shading makes an image appear more three dimensional by providing clues to the eye about how light falls on the object. Some surfaces of a three-dimensional object will be hidden from light and will be shaded, while light directly hits other parts, highlighting them.

Light travels as a ray. When that ray hits a smooth surface it reflects back. If the surface is perfectly shiny, what we call mirrored, all the different color components of the ray reflect. If the surface is not mirrored, but has a color, all the components but the color of the surface are absorbed. Only that color is reflected.

It is important to determine where the light ray goes after it is reflected. This relates to the angle at which it approaches the surface. To measure this angle, draw a line perpendicular to the surface. This line is called the *normal.* The angle between the ray of light and the normal is called the *angle of incidence*, and the incoming light is called *incident light.* The angle of the reflected light, called the *angle of reflection,* is measured from the opposite side of the normal from the angle of incidence. Both these angles are always the same. This way, given a surface and a source of light we can determine where the reflection goes. Figure 7.2.1 illustrates this concept.

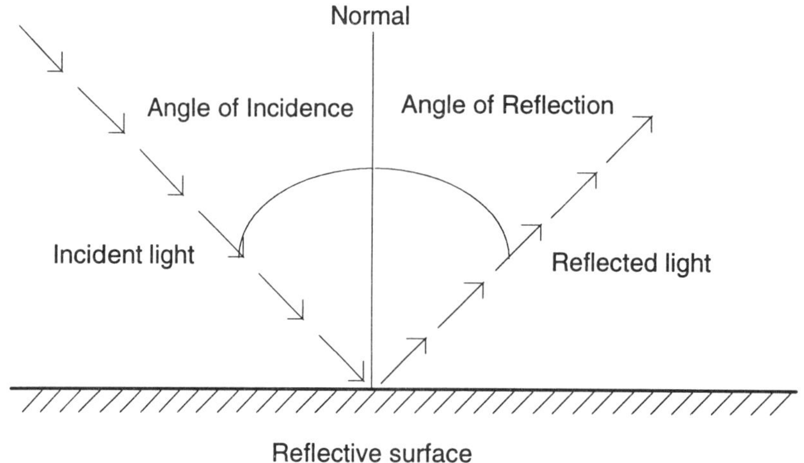

Fig. 7.2.1 The Direction of Reflected Light

If the reflected light is aimed straight at the viewer of the picture, the surface that is reflecting appears brighter than other surfaces. The surface loses its brightness as the reflected light misses the viewer by a larger distance. A surface that light does not hit is shaded and darker than the rest of the object.

These are general rules and guidelines that can be used to develop a picture. When a graphics programmer does ray tracing, he/she takes this concept to the limits. Every source of light is accounted for, and using the laws of physics, the computer traces every ray of light from the source until it exits the picture. Every surface that a ray is reflected from is shaded appropriately. This creates very realistic computer graphics.

When light hits a mirrored surface all colors in the light are reflected. A regular surface will absorb most wavelengths of light, and only reflect the light that matches the color of the surface. A dull surface will absorb some of the light even of the matching color, while a shiny surface will reflect most of that light.

If light hits a shiny surface and is reflected directly at the viewer, all colors in the light can be reflected. This phenomenon can be seen in a parking lot on a bright sunny day. When you look at the cars there is that annoying bright spot that shines right into your eyes. This is called glare by most people, but physicists call it *specular reflection.* The shinier the object, the larger the specular reflection. In other words, if the object is shinier, the angle of reflection can be larger and all light will still be reflected. The technical term for regular reflection is *diffuse reflection.*

So how do we put this on a computer? Imagine a shiny ball on the screen. Actually you don't imagine a 2D ball on the screen, but a 3D ball BEHIND the screen. Think of the "land behind the screen" as an extension of the real 3D world.

We call this a virtual world, and things in this world are virtual objects. So now we can talk about a virtual ball floating in virtual space.

Now imagine a shiny virtual ball floating behind the screen. Imagine this ball is illuminated by a light source over your left shoulder. This light source would be on the viewer's side of the screen, over his/her left shoulder, if it existed, but that does not matter. It still affects the ball. Certain areas of the ball are highlighted because of this source.

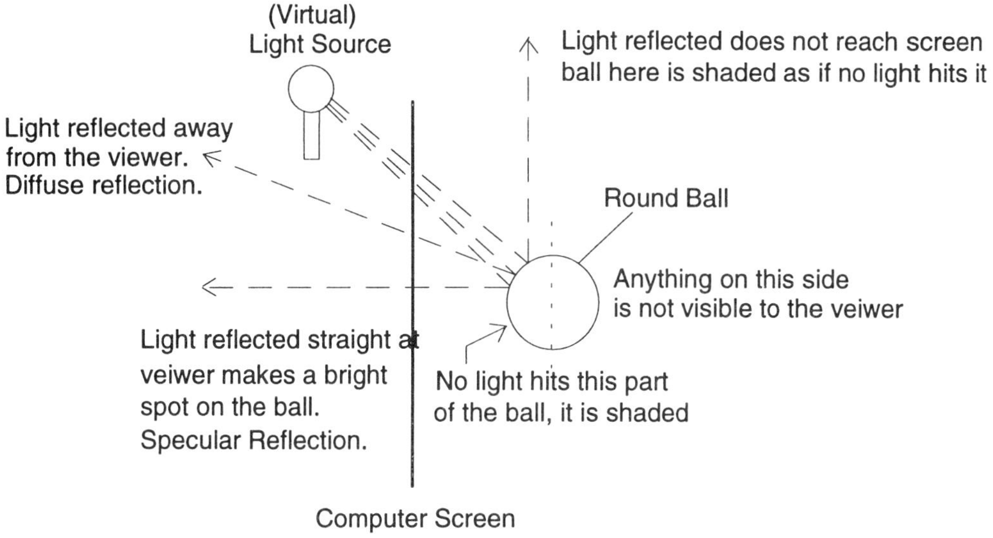

Fig. 7.2.2 Light Reflecting Off a Three-Dimensional Ball

Now imagine this entire scene from the side (Fig. 7.2.2). Rays come from the light source and reflect off the ball. Some hit the ball and reflect directly at the viewer, creating specular reflection. Other rays reflect out the screen, but not directly at the viewer. The farther away from the viewer the rays aim, the darker that part of the ball appears. Some parts of the ball are not hit by the light. These shaded parts appear the darkest. Light hits some parts of the ball, but the reflection does not go out the screen. These parts also appear as if they are in shade.

To project this ball onto a 2D screen use a dark color for the shaded parts. Use white or light gray for the specular reflection. The area just outside the boundary of the specular reflection should be the area of brightest diffuse reflection. Use a bright color for this, and shade it as smoothly as possible into the shaded areas. When using the 16-color mode supported by Borland, the shading cannot be made very smooth, unless you dither the colors as described in the last chapter.

Program BK0702.C draws a shiny 3D red balloon floating over a green field. This is done in the VGA 16-color mode, without worrying about dithering, to keep things simple. The program has three functions, each of which will be explained separately. The first is set_palette( ).

```
void set_palette () {
  struct palettetype pal;
  int i;

  getpalette(&pal);

  /* the sky */
  setrgbpalette(pal.colors[0],
                10<<2, 10<<2, 15<<2);

  /* ground */
  setrgbpalette(pal.colors[1],
                  0<<2, 13<<2, 0<<2);
  setrgbpalette(pal.colors[2],
                  0<<2, 15<<2, 0<<2);

  /* the balloon's shadow */
  setrgbpalette(pal.colors[3],
                   1<<2, 1<<2, 1<<2);

  /* the balloon */
  setrgbpalette(pal.colors[4],
                 11<<2,  2<<2, 2<<2);
  setrgbpalette(pal.colors[5],
                 12<<2,  2<<2, 2<<2);
  setrgbpalette(pal.colors[6],
                 13<<2,  2<<2, 2<<2);
  setrgbpalette(pal.colors[7],
                 14<<2,  3<<2, 3<<2);
  setrgbpalette(pal.colors[8],
                 15<<2,  4<<2, 4<<2);
  setrgbpalette(pal.colors[9],
                 15<<2,  5<<2, 5<<2);
  setrgbpalette(pal.colors[10],
                 15<<2,  6<<2, 6<<2);
  setrgbpalette(pal.colors[11],
                 15<<2,  7<<2, 7<<2);
  setrgbpalette(pal.colors[12],
                 15<<2,  8<<2, 8<<2);
  setrgbpalette(pal.colors[13],
                15<<2,  9<<2,  9<<2);
  setrgbpalette(pal.colors[14],
                15<<2, 10<<2, 10<<2);
```

```
    setrgbpalette(pal.colors[15],
                  15<<2, 15<<2, 15<<2);
}
```

The function of set_palette( ) is pretty obvious. It sets the palette registers, one at a time, to the desired values. The color used for the sky is 0, the ground uses 1 and 2, and the colors for the balloon are 4 through 15. Color 3 is black for the shadow of the balloon. The ground uses two shades of green, while the balloon uses various shades of red, with gray for the area of diffuse reflection.

The next function is draw_ground:

```
void draw_ground() {
  float width;
  int   x, y;
  int   MaxX, MaxY;
  int   cur_color = 2;

  MaxX = getmaxx();
  MaxY = getmaxy();
  set_palette();

  width=10.0;
  for (y=MaxY-150; y<MaxY; y++) {
    for (x=0; x<MaxX/2; x+=width) {
      line(x+(MaxX/2), y,
           x+(MaxX/2)+(int)width, y);
      if (cur_color == 1) {
        cur_color = 2;
      }
      else {
        cur_color = 1;
      }
      setcolor(cur_color);
      line((MaxX/2)-x, y,
           (MaxX/2)-(x+(int)width), y);
    }
    cur_color=1;
    setcolor(cur_color);
    width+=0.5;
  }
}
```

When color 0 is set the background changes to match. That is how the sky is drawn. The ground is drawn by drawing an alternating series of lines, some darker, some lighter, parallel to the horizon. As the series of lines moves down, the dark lines end up lying next to the dark lines drawn previously. This gives the impression of fields on the screen. Each time the Y coordinate is increased (the next line down on the screen) the lines are drawn a little longer. This gives the effect of lines meeting at a distance.

```
void draw_balloon() {
  int X_Center = getmaxx()/2-50,
      Y_Center = getmaxy()/2-50;

  setcolor(4);
  setfillstyle(SOLID_FILL, 4);
  fillellipse(X_Center, Y_Center, 50, 50);
  X_Center--;
  Y_Center--;

  setcolor(5);
  setfillstyle(SOLID_FILL, 5);
  fillellipse(X_Center, Y_Center, 46, 45);
  X_Center--;
  Y_Center-=2;

  setcolor(6);
  setfillstyle(SOLID_FILL, 6);
  fillellipse(X_Center, Y_Center, 42, 40);
  X_Center--;
  Y_Center-=2;

  setcolor(7);
  setfillstyle(SOLID_FILL, 7);
  fillellipse(X_Center, Y_Center, 38, 35);
  X_Center--;
  Y_Center-=2;

  setcolor(8);
  setfillstyle(SOLID_FILL, 8);
  fillellipse(X_Center, Y_Center, 36, 30);
  X_Center--;
  Y_Center-=2;

  setcolor(9);
  setfillstyle(SOLID_FILL, 9);
  fillellipse(X_Center, Y_Center, 32, 25);
  X_Center--;
  Y_Center-=2;

  setcolor(10);
  setfillstyle(SOLID_FILL, 10);
  fillellipse(X_Center, Y_Center, 28, 22);
  X_Center--;
  Y_Center-=2;
```

```
    setcolor(11);
    setfillstyle(SOLID_FILL, 11);
    fillellipse(X_Center, Y_Center, 24, 18);
    X_Center--;
    Y_Center-=2;

    setcolor(12);
    setfillstyle(SOLID_FILL, 12);
    fillellipse(X_Center, Y_Center, 21, 15);
    X_Center--;
    Y_Center-=2;

    setcolor(13);
    setfillstyle(SOLID_FILL, 13);
    fillellipse(X_Center, Y_Center, 18, 12);
    X_Center--;
    Y_Center-=2;

    setcolor(14);
    setfillstyle(SOLID_FILL, 14);
    fillellipse(X_Center, Y_Center, 15, 10);
    X_Center--;
    Y_Center-=2;

    setcolor(15);
    setfillstyle(SOLID_FILL, 15);
    fillellipse(X_Center, Y_Center, 4, 2);

    /* the shadow */
    setcolor (3);
    setfillstyle(SOLID_FILL, 3);
    fillellipse(X_Center+120, getmaxy()-120,
                45, 12);

  }
```

The balloon is drawn by drawing a series of filled ovals, each smaller than the last. As the ovals become smaller they are filled with a lighter color. This gives the effect of shading. The smallest oval uses light gray to show specular reflection. The center coordinates of each oval are moved up and to the left from the last oval to make the scene appear as if the light is coming from over the viewer's left shoulder. The last thing done is the shadow of the balloon is drawn in black on the field.

People often ask where does the shadow go in relation to the balloon, and questions such as that. Chapter 14, on ray tracing, shows how you can use the computer to give a full detailed analysis, and get everything mathematically perfect. But getting things mathematically perfect is a lot of bother. Most of the time it's easier to just experiment until the picture looks right.

Texturing

Different surfaces have different textures. Some are smooth and shiny, others are rough. For a picture to look realistic some care must be given to surface textures. Textures look smoother at a distance, and different textures reflect light differently.

Texturing and Reflection

The reflection discussed in the section on shading was for a smooth surface. A rough surface can be thought of as a number of smooth "micro-surfaces" put together at various angles. Light hits and is reflected in a number of directions, since there is a number of normals, one for each micro-surface. When light hits such a surface it is diffused (Fig. 7.3.1).

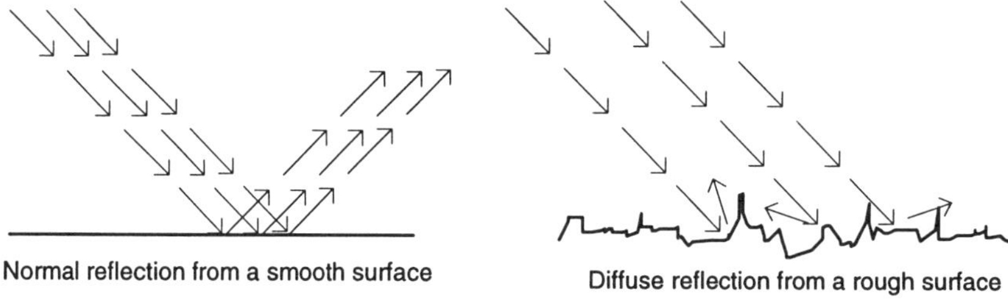

Fig. 7.3.1 Reflection from Smooth and Rough Surfaces

When light hits a smooth shiny object there is a bright center of reflection, called specular reflection, which appears white. A rough surface will not exhibit specular reflection. The smooth surface will show a wide area of diffuse reflection. The rough surface will have a much smaller area of diffuse reflection, and the brightest areas of this diffuse reflection will not be as bright as on the smooth surface.

Surface textures are not simply rough or smooth, there is a whole range in between. The top of a wooden table is not as smooth as the top of a glass table, but it is smoother than the surface of a blotter that might be on the table. These in between areas act pretty much as you would expect. The rougher the surface, the smaller the area of specular reflection, and the dimmer the diffuse reflection.

Many professional drawing packages allows the user to enter an index for the roughness of the surface. This allows the package to automatically add realistic lighting. The software user gives the location of a light source and the package uses ray tracing techniques and surface roughnesses to find how the light would look to the viewer. The general principles of this technique are outlined in Chapter 14, Ray Tracing.

Texturing and Perspective

Imagine a large unmowed field. The texture of this field is rough and grassy. As you look into the distance it seems to smooth out to a uniform green. Adding such distance clues can greatly enhance the realism of a picture. Fig. 7.3.2 shows this effect. As the distance increases the blades of grass get smaller, which makes the field appear smoother. This does not affect the reflectivity. A rough surface reflects poorly close up or at a distance; only the color becomes more uniform farther away.

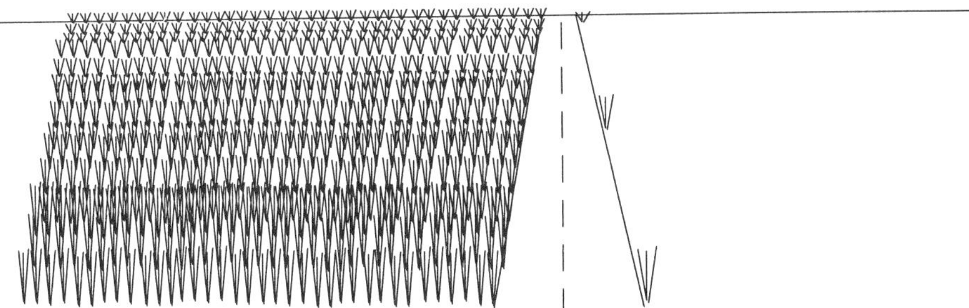

An unmowed field of grass shows that texture smooths out as distance increases
The left side of the road gives blades of grass at their relative sizes for comparison

Fig. 7.3.2 How Distance Affects Texturing

How is such a texture created on a computer? The method varies for each type of texture. Since there are an infinite variety of textures in the world, there is an infinite number of methods for modeling them. Instead of giving a generic method for all situations, several simple methods for specific situations will be presented.

After the picture given above, it seems natural to start with grass. Grass has long thin blades that give it its texture. First fill the background of the field with one shade of green. Make it a dark green for a lush field, or a lighter yellowish green for a dry field. Then draw a bunch of lines for the blades, using a different shade of green. I find that it's easiest to create a function that will draw a clump of grass of a given size at given location. The function can be called from a loop that creates the grass at the far end of the field. As the function works its way to the front of the field the size should be adjusted to make the grass appear larger.

There are many things in the world with a texture close enough to grass that this general technique can be applied. Hair, trees, fur, and certain types of high wispy clouds. Even texturing a road can be done this way. A road has a gravely, stony looking appearance. Use different shades of gray for the colors, and use the ellipse function instead of writing a function for grass. Using larger or smaller ellipses or just pixels, you can create a large number of textures this way. Leaves on a tree can be drawn the same way. It might well be worth an afternoon or two experimenting to see what textures you can create.

Many systems, such as games and simulators, need to create textures very quickly. The methods given above are not fast enough. These systems use a technique called filtering. Texture filters are used that automatically place the correct colors in the correct patterns for the desired texture. This method is too advanced to be explored here, but it is a fascinating advanced graphics topic.

Often systems that use texture filters only deal with the reflectivity of the texture. They do not actually model or display the real texture, they only show reflections as appropriate to the texture. This is okay for a system where the picture needs to change rapidly and constantly. For a picture where realism is more important than speed the texture needs to be displayed. The techniques given above are good as far as they go. For some pictures these are not realistic enough. In that case fractals can be used to create very realistic textures. The techniques of fractals are explained in Chapter 15.

8

The BIOS Graphics Interface

Neither Borland C nor Microsoft C can perform every graphics function that the user might need. As of this writing, neither compiler supports SVGA monitors, and neither compiler can create ellipses with the major axis at an angle. There are a whole number of things the experienced graphics programmer needs to be able to do that these compilers, or any others you might wish to purchase, cannot handle. This is part of the nature of graphics programming. There will always be something you need to do that is not supported by the compiler or graphics package you are using. It is quite complex, and no graphics programming system will do everything that everyone wants.

To be able to do everything you want as a graphics programmer, it is necessary to learn a great deal more about how the monitor works, and especially how the program interfaces to the monitor. That is, how the program lights a pixel in the proper color, how a line is drawn, how the palette is changed, and many other things that are usually taken care of by the compiler. Once the programmer understands how the compiler does these things, he/she can do them him/herself. Or more importantly, he/she can change how they are done to suit the present circumstance.

The first step to understanding what the compiler does when graphics are used is to understand DOS on a deeper level.

DOS and BIOS

Layers of DOS

One job of an operating system is to provide a consistent interface between the hardware and programs that run on the computer. The program does not need to worry about such details as whether the disk drive is IDE or RLL (two encoding schemes for data on a disk drive). The operating system does this by sitting between the hardware and the program. When the program wants to write to the disk, it does not do the writing itself, it tells the operating system what it wants written, and the operating system takes care of it (Fig. 8.1.1).

DOS does not actually perform all the work itself. DOS also must have compatibility between different hardware types. To provide this compatibility there is another layer between DOS and the hardware. This layer is called BIOS, for Basic Input/Output Services. BIOS is a set of software routines that resides in read-only memory (ROM) chips which are on the different devices on the computer. Software of this type, which is stored in ROM, and thus permanently bound to a certain device, is often called *firmware*. It is not really software, in the normal sense, but it certainly is not hardware.

BIOS is in ROM chips that are located on the hardware devices themselves, so when the device is replaced the BIOS is automatically replaced with it. In this way when a disk drive is replaced, the BIOS for that disk is replaced also. Because BIOS is bound to a certain piece of hardware, it can be written specifically for that piece of hardware. It does not have the worries that DOS and application programs do about being moved to another system with different hardware. So BIOS can be written to provide a consistent interface between devices. The way that BIOS operates for an IDE drive might be entirely different from that of an RLL drive. But the BIOS interface is consistent between them, so that DOS and the application programs do not care what type of drive is being used. There is also BIOS for the monitor, which resides on the adapter card.

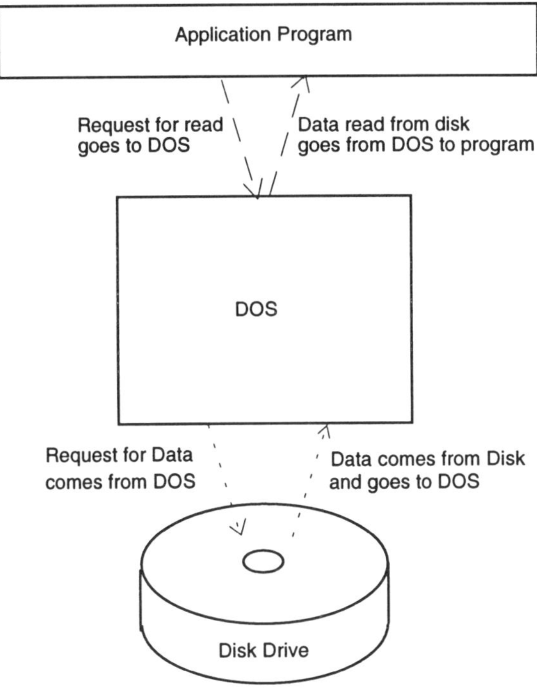

Fig. 8.1.1 Application Asks DOS for Disk Access

For many operations, such as writing to disk, DOS calls on BIOS to actually do the work. So when an application program needs to write something to disk it calls on DOS, which in turn calls on BIOS, which actually manipulates the computer hardware (Fig. 8.1.2).

One might wonder why DOS is there, if all it does is call BIOS. But that is not all DOS does. BIOS knows nothing of the file and directory structure on the disk. This is all created by DOS. When DOS calls BIOS to write to the disk DOS gives BIOS the data to be written, and a specific location on the disk. It is DOS's job to make sure that location on the disk is part of the correct file. Some tasks, such as drawing pixels on the screen, are simple enough for the application program to call BIOS directly.

MS-Windows™ and DOS fit together in much the same way as DOS and BIOS. MS-Windows sits on top of DOS, providing multitasking and graphics windowing services. Windows makes calls to DOS to perform many tasks (Fig. 8.1.3).

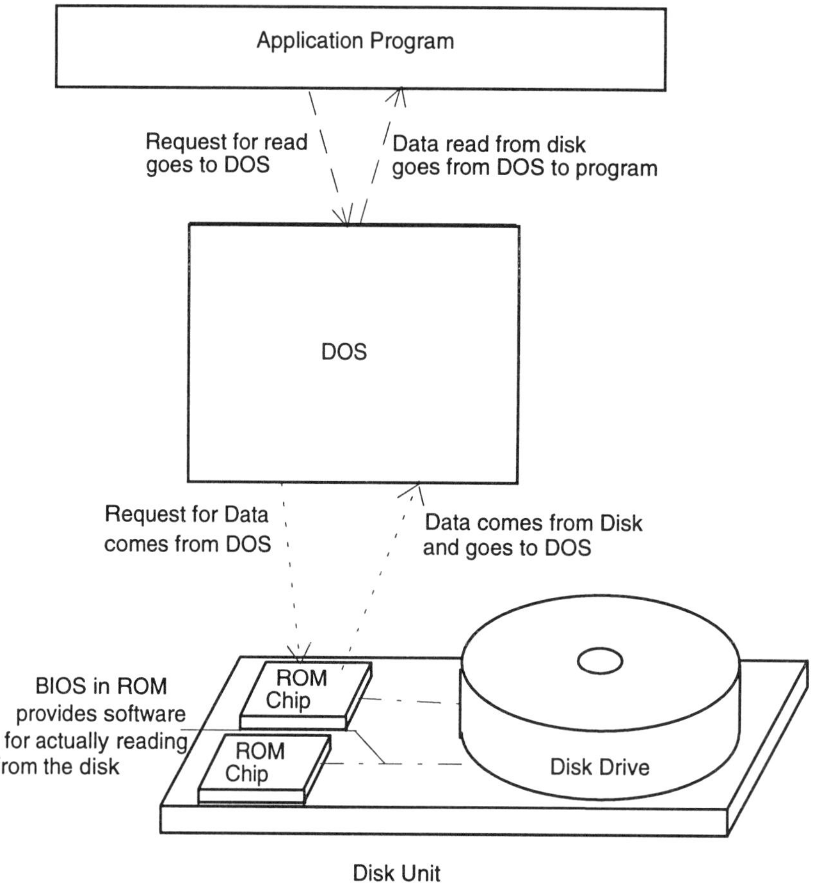

Fig. 8.1.2 DOS Calls BIOS, Which Is Actually on the Device

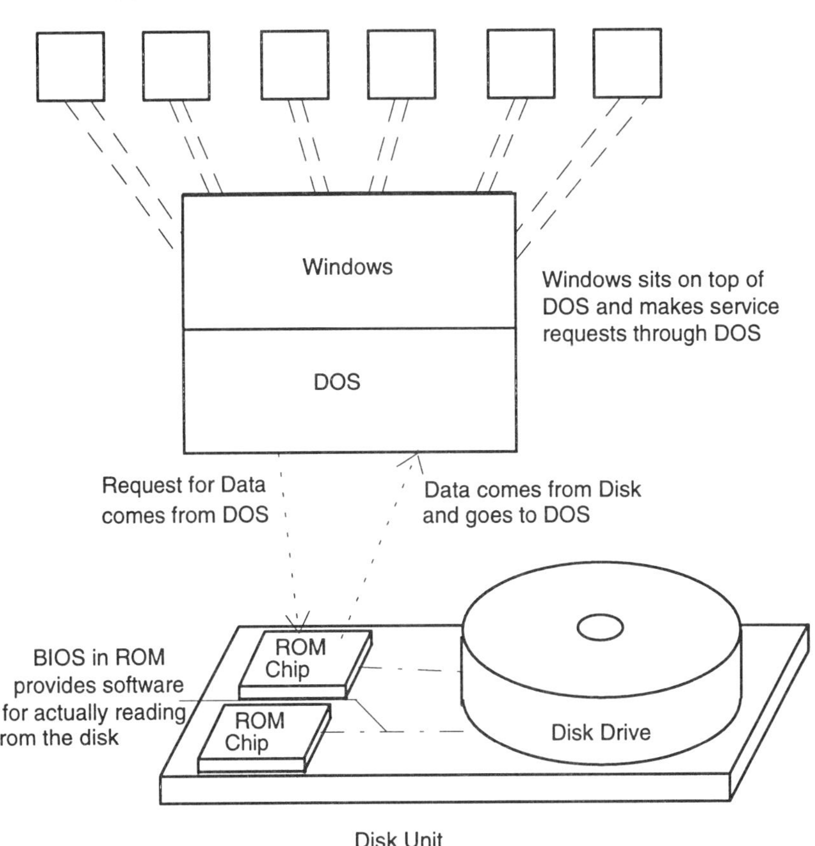

Fig. 8.1.3 Windows Sits on Top of DOS

Communicating with DOS and BIOS

Communication with DOS and BIOS is done using the assembly language interrupt command. While Borland and Microsoft provide inline assemblers, so that assembly language commands can be placed in normal C code, this method is inconvenient. Both of these compilers (and most other C compilers for DOS) provide a higher level command for dealing with interrupts. Both Borland and Microsoft happen to supply the same set of commands: int86( ), int86x( ), intdos( ), and intdosx( ). This allows program source code that uses BIOS for graphics to be compatible with both compilers.

Before discussing these commands, we need to discuss what happens when the assembly language interrupt command is used. An interrupt can be thought of as something like a function call. When an interrupt is called, execution of a program is transferred someplace else. When writing an application program the address of a function needs to be supplied when it is called. In a high level-language, such as C, this is done by providing the name of the function. The compiler then figures out the address. When using interrupts, we are calling functions provided by the hardware. We don't know where in memory these are located, and neither does the compiler, since after the program is compiled it might be moved to another computer with a different DOS version. When an interrupt is called the number of the interrupt is provided. This number is an index into an array of addresses that is located at the beginning of the computer's memory. This array is called the *interrupt vector table*. The address is taken from the interrupt vector table, and program execution is transferred there (Fig. 8.1.4).

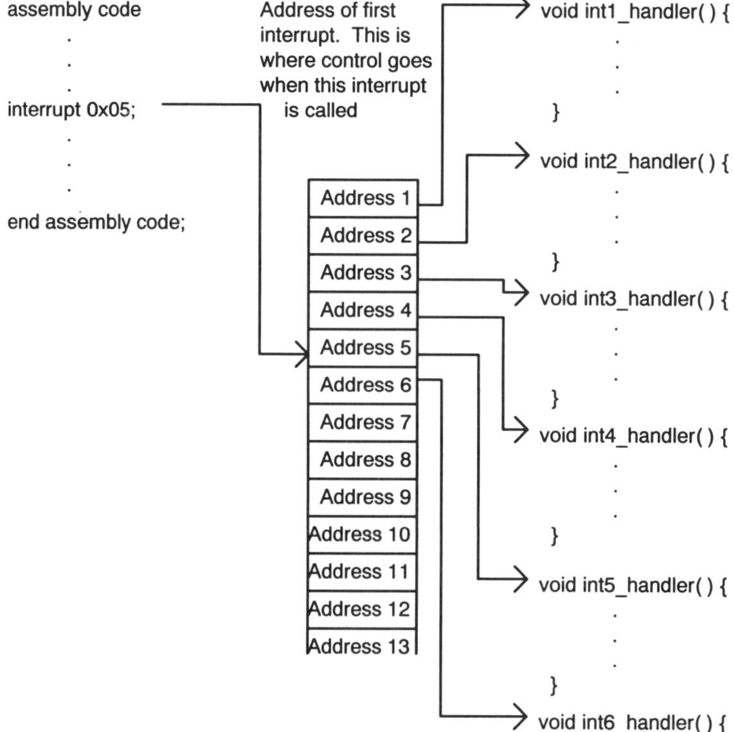

Fig. 8.1.4 The Interrupt Vector Table

All DOS services are provided by interrupt 0x21. DOS itself does not provide graphics services, however. These are provided by BIOS interrupt 10.

If interrupts are function calls then they need to have parameters. To understand how parameters are provided, we first need to understand something about assembly language programming and the architecture of the 8086 processor.

8086 Register Set

Processors contain special circuitry called registers. A register can be thought of as a special type of variable. The 8086 contains four general-purpose 16-bit registers, called AX, BX, CX, and DX. Each of these is divided into two 8-bit registers, the H and L registers. So the AX is made up of AH and AL registers (Fig. 8.1.5).

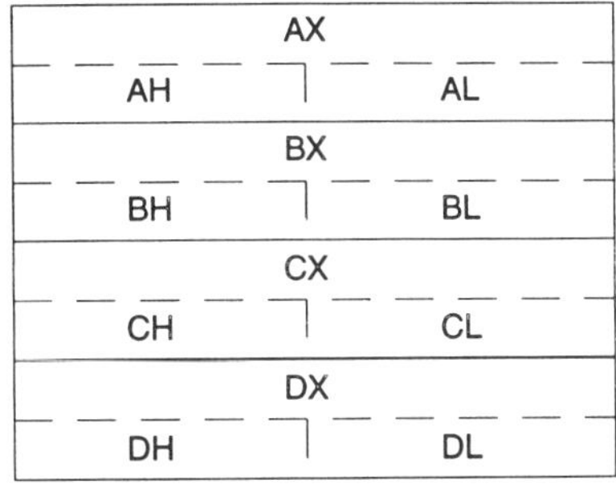

Fig. 8.1.5 8086 General Purpose Registers

In addition to the general-purpose registers, there are a number of special-purpose registers. Most of these hold various addresses, and are thus called *address registers*. Table 8.1.1 gives the special-purpose registers, with their function.

Table 8.1.1 8086 Special-Purpose Registers

Register type	Registers	Purpose
String Handling	SI	Start index of string
	DI	Destination index of string
Stack Segment Register	SS	Pointer to base of stack segment
Stack Pointers	SP	Pointer to top of system stack
	BP	Pointer into system stack
Code Segment Register	CS	Point to base of code segment
Instruction Pointer	IP	Point to current instruction in code segment
Data Segment Register	DS	Point to base of data segment
Extra Data Segment Rcgister	ES	Point to base of extra data segment
Flags Register	FLAGS	Condition flags

Some of the registers in Table 8.1.1 are called *segment registers.* These registers have special importance to the 8086 architecture. An in-depth knowledge of them is not needed for the intdos( ) function, but is needed for intdosx( ). These are discussed in the next section on intdosx( ).

Parameters for interrupts are contained in registers. Not all registers are used by every interrupt, and some registers are not used by any. No interrupt uses the CS, IP, or SS, since doing so would make a mess of program execution, and your computer would crash.

Now we can talk in greater detail about the interrupt commands. The simplest is intdos( ).

```
int intdos(union REGS *inregs,
           union REGS *outregs);
  /*
   * function for calling interrupt 21
   *   (DOS services);
   *
   * Parameters:
   *   inregs  - value of registers passed in
   *   outregs - value of registers after
   *             interrupt call.
   *
   * Returns: Value of AX register
   */
```

REGS is a union that holds the values of the registers for the interrupt call. Values are copied from REGS to the actual registers, then interrupt 21 is called. Here is the definition of REGS:

```
struct WORDREGS {
  unsigned int    ax, bx, cx, dx, si, di,
                  cflag, flags;
};

struct BYTEREGS {
  unsigned char    al, ah, bl, bh,
                   cl, ch, dl, dh;
};

union REGS {
  struct WORDREGS x;
  struct BYTEREGS h;
};
```

So if we wish to set the AH register to 3 we use the following:

```
union REGS regs;

regs.h.ah := 0x03;
```

The intdos( ) function prototype and REGS union are located in the file DOS.H, so whenever using this function be sure to use the line

```
#include <dos.h>
```

Some of the registers in the REGS union have not been discussed, but they are listed in Table 8.1.1. The flags register is a register of bits that are used to indicate when certain conditions arise. Table 8.1.2 shows the flags in the flags register.

Table 8.1.2 The 8086 Flags Register

Bit Number	ID	Purpose
0	CF	Carry Flag – set if an operation overflows a register
1	- -	not used by the 8086
2	PF	Parity Flag – set if result of operation has even number of bits set
3	- -	not used by the 8086
4	AF	Aux. Carry Flag – set if operation carried out of bit 3 (for BCD numbers)
5	- -	not used by the 8086
6	ZF	Zero Flag – set if result of an operation is 0
7	SF	Sign Flag – set if result of an operation is negative
8	TF	Trap Flag – used only by hardware. Software does not need to reference this flag.
9	IF	Interrupt Enable – if set all interrupts work. If cleared only certain absolutely necessary interrupts will work. These interrupts are called "non-maskable"
10	DF	Direction Flag – used for assembler string instructions. See an assembler manual for details.
11	OF	Overflow Flag - set if operation results in a carry into
12	- -	not used by the 8086
13	- -	not used by the 8086
14	- -	not used by the 8086
15	- -	not used by the 8086

The cflag field in the wordregs structure is not really a register in the 8086. It is a 16-bit field that contains the value of the carry flag from the flags register. This is useful since many interrupts use the carry flag to signal an error. The SI and DI registers are used most often used as pointers. This is useful when an interrupt needs to find something in memory. An example of this would be a DOS interrupt that writes a string to a disk file or to the screen. A string will not fit in registers, so these registers are used to point to the string in memory.

A simple example of the intdos( ) function is using the DOS interrupt to write a character to the screen. All DOS services are performed through interrupt 21. The DOS service that writes a character to the screen is 0x02, so this number is put in the AH register. The character to be written goes in the DL.

```
void write_char(char ch) {
  union REGS regs;

  regs.h.ah := 0x02;
  regs.h.dl := ch;
  intdos(&regs, &regs);
}
```

A somewhat more complex example is reading a character from the keyboard. The DOS service 0x06 will look to see if a character is available, and if one is, it is returned in the DL register. If no character is available the Zero Flag is set, otherwise it is cleared. This function will not wait for a key to be pressed, so it is not the same as getch( ). If a character is read it is not echoed to the monitor.

```
char get_char_nowait(char *keypressed) {
  /*
   * function to read a key from the keyboard.
   * This function will not wait if no key is
   * pressed.
   *
   * Parameter:
   *   keypressed - 1 if key was pressed,
   *                0 otherwise.
   *
   * Returns - character if key was pressed
   */
  union REGS regs;

  regs.h.ah := 0x06;
  intdos(&regs, &regs);

  /* check zero flag */
  if (0x0040 & regs.x.flags) {
    *keypressed := 0;
  } /* end if */
  else {
    *keypressed := 1;
    return (regs.h.dl);
  } /* end else */
} /* end get_char_nowait( ) */
```

To find a complete list of DOS services, consult any DOS programmer's guide.

Some DOS services require the use of segment registers. An understanding of what a segment register is, and its place in life, requires an in-depth understanding of 8086 architecture. The short explanation is this: The 8086 is a 16-bit machine. With 16 bits only 65,536 bytes can be addressed. This is a very small amount for today's software. To address more, two 16-bit registers need to be used together. The segment registers are used with other registers to point to memory locations.

A full address on the 8086 is 20 bits. Since two registers together hold 32 bits there is some overlap. If a segment register holds 0 it is pointing to the beginning of RAM. If it is incremented to 1 it points to byte number 16 in RAM. In 8086 terms every 16 bytes is a paragraph. The value in the segment register is often called the base, and the register it is teamed with holds the offset. If a segment register holding 0x0000 is teamed up with a register with 0x0020 (32 decimal) in it, together they point to byte number 32. If the base were 0x0001 and the offset is 0x0010 (16 decimal) they again point to byte 32. If the base is 0x0002 and the offset is 0x0000 then guess what? They point to byte number 32. This is what is meant by overlap. The base and offset are often written together as base:offset. So the second set of values above would become 0x0002:0x0020. The registers might be shown as ES:DX.

Segment Registers

The segment registers are special purpose, and each one points to a certain location in memory. The CS (code segment register) points to the start of program code. It is used along with the IP (instruction pointer) to point to the currently executing instruction. The SS (stack segment register) points to the base of the system stack. The SP (stack pointer register) is used with the SS to find the current top of the stack. The SP is usually only changed automatically by the CPU when items are pushed and popped. Sometimes the program itself needs to see what's on the stack, such as when parameters are accessed by a C function. This is done using the BP (byte pointer register). The DS (data segment register) is used for data. It works with the general-purpose registers. This is important for what we are now discussing, since many DOS services need the location of data items. The final segment register is the ES (extra segment register). This register acts like an extra DS. This is also important since many DOS services use the ES instead of the DS to locate things in memory.

The intdos( ) function does not allow for segment registers to be passed. This is the job of intdosx( ).

```
int intdosx(union REGS *inregs,
            union REGS *outregs,
            struct SREGS *segregs);
  /*
   * function for calling interrupt 21 (DOS
   *   services) for services requiring Segment
   *   Registers
   *
   * Parameters:
   *   inregs  - values of registers passed in
   *   outregs - values of registers after
   *             interrupt call.
   *   segregs - values of segment registers
   *
   * Returns: Value of AX register
   */
```

SREGS is defined as:

```
struct SREGS {
  unsigned int  es;
  unsigned int  cs;
  unsigned int  ss;
  unsigned int  ds;
};
```

A good example of this function is to write a string to the screen. The DOS service 0x40 is used for writing to files. DOS uses integer numbers called *file handles* to identify different files. Some file handles are reserved to special devices. File handle 0x01 is for output to the screen. The parameters for interrupt 21, service 0x40 are: AH = 0x40, BX = File handle, CX = Number of bytes to write, DS:DX = the location in memory of the string to write.

```
char *string = "Hello World\n\r";

void write_string() {
  union  REGS  regs;
  struct SREGS segregs;

  regs.h.ah := 0x40;
  regs.x.bx := 0x01;
  regs.x.cx := 13;
  regs.x.dx := FP_OFF(string);

  segregs.ds := FP_SEG(string);
```

```
    intdosx(&regs, &regs, &segregs);
};
```

Several things should be mentioned about the above code segment. The first is the string. It ends with "\n\r". This is because DOS service 0x40 does not process the string the way printf( ) does. The \n will move the cursor down to the next line, but \r is needed to move it to the beginning of the line. The next item is the FP_OFF( ) and FP_SEG( ) macros. These are defined in DOS.H, and are used for finding the address of a variable. Check the compiler library reference for details.

Calling BIOS

The intdos( ) and intdosx( ) are fine for calling DOS services, but we are more interested in BIOS services, since DOS services do not include graphics services. To access BIOS interrupts use int86( ) and int86x( ).

```
int int86(int intno, union REGS *inregs,
                     union REGS *outregs);
  /*
   * function for calling interrupts.
   *
   * Parameters:
   *   intno   - Interrupt number to be called
   *   inregs  - Register values going in
   *   outregs - Register values coming out
   *
   * Returns: Value in AX register
   */

int int86x(int intno, union  REGS  *inregs,
                      union  REGS  *outregs,
                      struct SREGS segregs);
  /*
   * function for calling interrupts that
   *   require segment registers.
   *
   * Parameters:
   *   intno   - Interrupt number to be called
   *   inregs  - Register values going in
   *   outregs - Register values coming out
   *   segregs - Segment register values going
   *             in
   *
   * Returns: Value in AX register
   */
```

Where DOS only uses a single interrupt, 0x21, BIOS uses a whole number. This means that different addresses in the interrupt vector table are used. We are most interested in interrupt 0x10, which provides video services. Some of interrupt 0x10's services are covered in detail in the next section of this chapter. Most BIOS interrupt 0x10 services are given in Appendix D, except for SVGA services which are listed separately in Appendix E.

Once intdos( ) is understood, there really is not a lot more to understanding int86( ), except that now an interrupt number must be provided. The int86( ) function can even do the same thing that intdos( ) does. Here is the example for intdos( ), rewritten using int86( ).

```
char get_char_nowait(char *keypressed) {
  /*
   * function to read a key from the keyboard.
   * This function will not wait if no key is
   * pressed.
   *
   * Parameter:
   *   keypressed - 1 if key was pressed,
   *                0 otherwise.
   *
   * Returns - character if key was pressed
   */
  union REGS regs;

  regs.h.ah := 0x06;
  int86(0x21, &regs, &regs);
  if (0x0040 & regs.x.flags) {
    *keypressed := 0;
  } /* end if */
  else {
    *keypressed := 1;
    return (regs.h.dl);
  } /* end else */
} /* end get_char_nowait( ) */
```

And the example for intdosx( ), converted to int86x( ):

```
char *string = "Hello World\n\r";

void write_string() {
  union  REGS  regs;
  struct SREGS segregs;
```

```
    regs.h.ah := 0x40;
    regs.x.bx := 0x01;
    regs.x.cx := 13;
    regs.x.dx := FP_OFF(string);
    segregs.ds := FP_SEG(string);
    int86x(0x21, &regs, &regs, &segregs);
  };
```

BIOS Interrupt 0x10 Graphics Services

The first thing we need to be able to do is to set the monitor to graphics mode. All graphics are handled through interrupt 0x10. The function call for setting the mode is 0x00, which means the value in AH is 0x00.

To use this function it is useful to know what type of monitor the program is running on. This is not easy as there is no interrupt service to tell you this for the older monitor types. There is one for SVGA monitors, but that is no good if you do not have an SVGA monitor. One approach that is often useful is to assume a monitor with minimum capabilities. As of this writing, pretty much anyone that runs graphics programs has at least a VGA monitor, and SVGA monitors are becoming quite common. It certainly seems justified to assume at least a VGA monitor. For a high-powered graphics program it seems reasonable to assume an SVGA monitor with at least 800 × 600 resolution. Modes supported by interrupt 0x10 function 0x00 are given in Table 8.2.1. Notice that there are no SVGA modes listed. SVGA modes are set by a different function. See Chapter 9 for details of SVGA programming.

No information is returned by interrupt 10, function 0. This means that there is no way to tell if the function failed. It would be nice if the interrupt returned an error code, so the program could keep trying modes until one worked. When a mode is successfully set the screen is cleared.

Table 8.2.1 Modes Supported by Interrupt 0x10

Mode Number	Minimum Adapter	Text/ Graphics	Resolution	Number of Colors
0x00	CGA	Text	40 × 25 characters	16
0x01	CGA	Text	40 × 25 characters	16
0x02	CGA	Text	80 × 25 characters	16
0x03	CGA	Text	80 × 25 characters	16
0x04	CGA	Graphics	320 × 200 pixels	4
0x05	CGA	Graphics	320 × 200 pixels	4
0x06	CGA	Graphics	640 × 200 pixels	2
0x07	EGA	Text	80 × 25 characters	4
0x0D	EGA	Graphics	320 × 200 pixels	16/64
0x0E	EGA	Graphics	640 × 200 pixels	16/64
0x0F	EGA	Graphics	640 × 350 pixels	4
0x10	EGA	Graphics	640 × 350 pixels	16/64
0x11	VGA	Graphics	640 × 480 pixels	2/256k
0x12	VGA	Graphics	640 × 480 pixels	16/256k
0x13	VGA	Graphics	320 × 200 pixels	256/256k

The following function will set the monitor to the specified graphics mode.

```
void set_mode(int mode) {
  union REGS regs;

  regs.h.ah = 0;
  regs.h.al = mode;
  int86(0x10,&regs,&regs);
}
```

It's that simple! The hard part is knowing what mode to use.

Setting Pixels Using BIOS

The next thing that we need to be able to do is set pixels. This is done with interrupt 0x10 function 0x0C (12 dec). Set AH to 0x0C, AL to the number of the color palette giving the color the pixel will be set to, BH to 0, CX to the X coordinate, and DX to the Y coordinate. Most of this is self-explanatory, except the BX. This register controls what page the pixel is set on. So far we've only used the default page, page number 0. We can write to other pages that are not visible, then switch that page to be visible, thus making the pixels we set suddenly appear. This is useful for animation and making windows. The technique is discussed in detail in Chapter 12 on animation.

The following function will plot pixels on monitors that support function 0x0C (12 dec)

```
void plot_pixel(int X, int Y, char Color) {
  union REGS regs;

  regs.h.ah = 0x0C;
  regs.h.al = Color;
  regs.x.bx = 0;
  regs.x.CX = X;
  regs.x.DX = Y;
  int86(0x10, &regs, &regs);
}
```

Here is a full program to demonstrate these functions. This is a very colorful program that sets a VGA monitor to mode 0x13, the medium-resolution, 256-color mode; it then draws lines on the screen using the default 256 colors. When a key is hit the program resets the monitor to character mode, then exits. Since this program does not really have much meat on it, it does not appear on the distribution disk. The program in the section on setting the palettes is the same, with more added on. It appears on the distribution disk as BK0801.C.

```
/*
 * BK0801.C -  Program to demonstrate BIOS
 * graphics functions. This program
 * will set the screen to VGA mode 13, draw
 * 256 lines in the 256 default colors, reset
 * monitor to text mode before exiting.
 */

#include <DOS.H>   /* contains union REGS
                      declaration */
#include <STDIO.H>
#include <CONIO.H>

void set_mode(int mode) {
/*
 *  This function sets the vga monitor to mode
 *  use on other monitors is undocumented
 */
```

```
    union REGS reg;

    reg.h.ah = 0;        /* set registers   */
    reg.h.al = mode;     /* for BIOS call   */
    int86 (0x10, &reg, &reg); /* call BIOS */
}

void setpix (int X, int Y, int Color) {
  union REGS regs;

  regs.h.ah = 0x0C;
  regs.h.al = Color;
  regs.x.bx = 0;
  regs.x.cx = X;
  regs.x.dx = Y;
  int86(0x10, &regs, &regs);
}


void drawscreen() {
  int i,j;
  int y = 200;

  for (i=0; i<256; i++)
    for (j=0; j<y; j++)
      setpix(i, j, i);

}

void main() {
/*
 * This Function sets VGA monitor to mode 19,
 *   displays 256 colors, waits for user to
 *   press a key, sets mode to text, and exits
 */
  FILE *screen;

  directvideo = 0;

  set_mode(19);  /* set monitor mode to 19 */
  drawscreen();
  getch();
  if (kbhit()) getch();

   /* reset monitor mode for text */
  set_mode(3);
  exit (0);    /* exit to DOS - no error */
}
```

This seems like such an obvious, useful, and necessary function, why would any monitor not support it? Well, BIOS tends to be rather slow. For many tasks, such as drawing circles and filling objects, this function is simply too slow.

Program BK0801.C uses BIOS interrupt 0x0C to plot a pixel. This can be quite slow if a lot of pixels are being plotted. The alternative is to write directly to screen memory. For modes with fewer than 256 colors, this is a somewhat complicated task, since 1 byte of screen memory is divided between several pixels in a rather complicated way. For these modes you might as well use the interrupt.

Writing directly to the frame buffer is much easier when using the VGA 256-color mode (mode 0x13). In this mode, 1 byte maps to exactly 1 pixel. The screen memory in this mode starts at 0xA000:0x0000. Each line of pixels is 320 bytes across and there are 200 lines from top to bottom. The following function will plot pixels by writing directly to screen memory in this mode.

```
void plot_pixel (int X, int Y, int Color) {
  char far *screen_mem = MK_FP(0xA000, 0000);

  *(screen_mem + 320*y + x) = Color;
}
```

The variable screen_mem is a pointer to the beginning of screen memory. Make sure that it is defined as a far pointer, because a far pointer is 32 bits while a near pointer is 16. The default pointer is a near pointer, which will not be able to hold the entire address. The MK_FP macro, which is defined in DOS.H, turns the given numbers into a far address. The first number is the base, the second number is the offset. The second line adds an offset to the start of the screen buffer, then puts Color in that location. In mode 0x13 there are 320 pixels in the X dimension. This function is highly mode dependent – it will not work in other modes.

The number in the variable color is the number of the palette register. For a complete description of palette registers see Chapter 6. For setting palette registers using BIOS see the next section in this chapter.

BK0802.C is the same as BK0801.C, except that the more efficient pixel plotting function given above is used. If you run the first then the second you will see a noticeable difference in speed.

```
/*
 * BK0802.C -  Program to demonstrate writing
 * directly to frame buffer. This program
 * will set the screen to VGA mode 13, draw
 * 256 lines in the 256 default colors, reset
 * monitor to text mode before exiting.
 */

/* contains union REGS declaration */
#include <DOS.H>
#include <STDIO.H>
#include <CONIO.H>

void set_mode(int mode){
/*
 *  This function sets the VGA monitor to mode
 *  use on other monitors is undocumented
 */
    union REGS reg;

    reg.h.ah = 0;          /* set registers  */
    reg.h.al = mode;       /* for BIOS call  */
    int86 (0x10, &reg, &reg); /* call BIOS   */
}

void setpix (int x, int y, int color) {

 /* locate screen buffer */
  char far *screenbuf = MK_FP(0xA000,0000);
  *(screenbuf + 320*y + x) = color;
}


void drawscreen() {
  int i,j;
  int y = 200;

  for (i=0; i<256; i++)
    for (j=0; j<y; j++)
      setpix(i, j, i);
}

void main() {
/*
 *  This Function sets VGA monitor to mode 19,
 *  displays 256 colors, waits for user to
 *  press a key, sets mode to text, and exits
```

```
  */
   FILE *screen;

   directvideo = 0;

   set_mode(19);  /* set monitor mode to 19 */
   drawscreen();
   getch();
   if (kbhit()) getch();

   /* reset monitor mode for text */
   set_mode(3);
   exit (0);    /* exit to DOS - no error */

}
```

Chapters 10 and 11 describe how to use the above routine to draw shapes and fill shapes, respectively. Once you have mastered these chapters you will be able to write all the graphics routines provided by the Borland and Microsoft compilers, and more importantly, you will be able to modify them to do just what you need.

Clearing the Screen using BIOS

There two ways of clearing the screen. The first is to reset the graphics mode using interrupt 10 function 0x00. This function clears the screen, but can be slow on some compatibles, and clears the screen to black. Often it is desired to set the entire screen to a single color other than black.

The second way is to set all pixels to the same color. There are two ways of doing this. The first is to use a nested loop with interrupt to function 0x0C. The following code sample clears the screen for VGA mode 0x13 hex.

```
void clear_screen() {
  int x, y;
  union REGS regs;

  for (y = 0; y < 200; y++)
    for (x = 0; x < 320; x++) {
      regs.h.ah = 0x0C;
      regs.h.al = Color;
      regs.x.bx = 0;
      regs.x.CX = X;
      regs.x.DX = Y;
      int86(0x10, &regs, &regs);
    } /* end for */
```

```
} /* end clear_screen() */
```

Needless to say, this is quite slow. Notice that all registers are reinitialized inside the loop. In general it is a bad idea to count on registers retaining their values after an interrupt call. Some interrupts are very good about not changing register values, others are not so good. Notice also that the program needs to be aware of what mode the screen is in, so it knows how many pixels are on the screen. This is generally true with all BIOS graphics functions. It helps to set up global variables with all the needed information, such as how many pixels there are in the X dimension and the Y dimension, how many colors are supported, etc. Another trick is to only allow one mode when using BIOS graphics. I generally only use BIOS graphics for programs that need 256 colors or SVGA graphics since these are not currently supported by Borland C.

The other method of clearing the screen is to use the memset( ) function to copy a single value to screen memory. This is the fastest way to clear the screen. Here you also need to know what mode you are in, and this is somewhat risky, since if you specify too many bytes you will wipe out another part of memory. The following function will clear the screen to a certain color when it is in mode 0x13.

```
void clear_screen(int color) {
  char screen_mem = MK_FP (0xA000, 0000);

  memset (screen_mem, 320*200*1, color);
}
```

The multiply here does not waste any time since it is a constant, and is done when the program is compiled.

Changing Color Palettes Using BIOS

Chapter 6 gives an in-depth overview of palette registers. If the term *palette register* is unfamiliar to you, you might want to go back and read this chapter before proceeding.

All the BIOS functions dealing with palette registers are provided by interrupt 0x10 function 0x10. This function is divided into a number of subservices for handling palette registers. For all the services supported by interrupt 0x10 see Appendix D. This appendix lists all services provided by interrupt 0x10, with descriptions of what they do, and register settings needed to call them. This interrupt provides quite a number of services, and they cannot all be described here in the text.

As mentioned above, the palette registers can be set one at a time or in blocks. To set them one at a time use subservice 0x10. The BX register is set to the palette number, CH holds the green value, CL holds the blue, and DH the red. The following function will set a single palette register.

```
void set_one_palette(int Pal_Nbr, int Red,
                                   int Green,
                                   int Blue) {
  union  REGS  regs;

  reg.h.ah = 0x10;
  reg.h.al = 0x10;
  reg.x.bx = Pal_Nbr;
  reg.h.ch = Green;
  reg.h.cl = Blue;
  reg.h.dh = Red;

  int86(0x10,&reg,&reg);
}
```

Use function 0x10 subservice 0x12 for setting a block of registers. Set AH to 0x10, AL to 0x12, BX to the number of the first palette to be set, CX to the number of palettes to be set, and ES:DX to a buffer that holds the settings for the registers. The buffer looks like this:

```
unsigned char palette[Number of Palettes][3];
```

To set the third palette to white you would do something like:

```
palette[2][0] = 63;
palette[2][1] = 63;
palette[2][2] = 63;
```

Remember that the array starts at 0, so 2 is the number of the third palette. It is helpful to define the following constants, to make the code more readable.

```
#define RED   0
#define GREEN 1
#define BLUE  2
```

So now the above code can be written as

```
palette[2][RED]   = 63;
palette[2][GREEN] = 63;
palette[2][BLUE]  = 63;
```

Remember that the entire array must be filled. If some palettes are not filled, you will not be able to predict the color of pixels on the screen using these palettes. The following function will change all the palette registers at once.

```
void set_all_palettes(int *palette) {
  union  REGS  regs;
  struct SREGS segregs;

  segread(&sreg);

  reg.h.ah = 0x10;
  reg.h.al = 0x12;
  reg.x.bx = 0;
  reg.x.cx = 256;
  reg.x.dx = FP_OFF(palette);

  sreg.es  = FP_SEG(palette);

  int86x(0x10,&reg,&reg,&sreg);
}
```

The program listed below uses both methods to set palettes. This shows how much faster setting all palettes at once is. First the monitor is set to the 256-color medium-resolution mode 0x13, using our function that calls BIOS for setting modes. Next a series of lines is drawn on the screen, from top to bottom, in the 256 default colors for this mode. These lines are drawn by setting pixels directly in memory. Next a function is called that sets the screen to a gray scale by setting each color palette individually using subservice 0x10. Then the screen is set to a "yellow" scale, by setting up a buffer, then calling subservice 0x12. Lastly the screen is reset to text mode, and the program exits. This program is BK0803.C on the distribution disk.

```
/*
 * BK0803.C - Program to demonstrate many
 * BIOS Graphics functions.  This program
 * will set the screen to VGA mode 13, draw
 * 256 lines in the 256 default colors, set
 * the palette registers one at a time to a
 * gray scale, then set the registers all at
 * once to a "yellow scale".  It resets the
 * monitor to text mode before exiting.
 */

#include <DOS.H>  /* contains union
```

```
                              REGS declaration */
#include <STDIO.H>
#include <CONIO.H>

#define RED   0
#define GREEN 1
#define BLUE  2


void set_mode(int mode) {
  /*
   * Set the mode of the monitor to the mode
   * number given as a parameter
   */
  union REGS reg;

  reg.h.ah = 0;
  reg.h.al = mode;
  int86 (0x10, &reg, &reg);

} /* end set_mode */

void newp() {
  /*
   * Set the colors on the screen to a
   *   grayscale using int 10, function 10,
   *   subservice 10 to set one register at a
   *   time.
   */
  int count, four;
  union  REGS  reg;

  /* This mode allows for 64 shades of gray  */
  /* since there is color definition of 6    */
  /* bits per color per pixel.  2**6 bits=64 */
  /* colors */
  for (count=0; count<64; count++)
    /* each shade of gray is for pixels wide */
    for(four = 0; four < 4; four++) {

    reg.h.ah = 0x10;
    reg.h.al = 0x10;
    reg.x.bx = count*4+four;
    reg.h.ch = count;
    reg.h.cl = count;
    reg.h.dh = count;

    int86(0x10,&reg,&reg);
  } /* end for loop */
```

```
}   /* end newp() */

void newp2() {
  /*
   * set colors on screen to "yellow scale"
   * using int 10, function 10 subservice 12
   * to set all registers at once.
   */
  unsigned char palette[256][3];
  int count, four=0;
  union  REGS  reg;
  struct SREGS sreg;

  /* This mode supports 64 shades of yellow */
  /* see comments in newp() for details     */
  for (count=0; count<64; count++)
    /* each shade is for pixels wide */
    for(four = 0; four < 4; four++) {
      palette[(count*4)+four][RED] = count;
      palette[(count*4)+four][GREEN] = count;
      palette[(count*4)+four][BLUE] = 0;
    } /* end for */

  segread(&sreg);

  reg.h.ah = 0x10;
  reg.h.al = 0x12;
  reg.x.bx = 0;
  reg.x.cx = 256;
  reg.x.dx = FP_OFF(palette);

  /* remember - we are trained professionals */
  /*   we do not recommend that you try this */
  /*   at home!                              */

  sreg.es = FP_SEG(palette);

  int86x(0x10,&reg,&reg,&sreg);
} /* end newp2() */

void setpix (int x, int y, int color) {
  /*
   * Set the pixel at screen coord (X, Y) to
   * Color.  This function only works for VGA
   * mode 0x13.
   */
  char far *screenbuf = MK_FP(0xA000,0000);
  *(screenbuf + 320*y + x) = color;
} /* end setpix() */
```

```
void drawscreen() {
  /*
   * Draw a series of lines down the screen
   * in 256 colors
   */
  int i,j;

  for (i=0; i<256; i++)
    for (j=0; j<200; j++)
      setpix(i, j, i);

} /* end drawscreen() */

void main() {
  FILE *screen;

  set_mode(0x13);
  drawscreen();
  getch();
  newp();
  getch();
  newp2();
  getch();

  set_mode(3);
  exit (0);
}
```

9

SVGA Programming

VESA

In the mid 1980s IBM developed the standard for the VGA monitor. After that, it seems, IBM lost its ability to control the imagination of PC manufacturers. In the late 1980s IBM developed the 8514 monitor, which provided higher resolution than the VGA, but this monitor never caught on as a standard. The industry was ripe for more advanced monitors, the technology was there. So many monitor manufacturers started building monitors with capabilities better than the VGA. But each was programmed differently.

An application using these monitors had to determine what brand of monitor it was running on, then provide separate routines to deal with each brand. Each monitor type uses different chips. Each chip set does things differently. Some have registers that need to be set in a certain way, others do not have those registers, but use ports instead. To give some idea of the scope of the problem, there are at least nine different chip sets commonly used to build monitors, and each chip set can be set up in different ways. So a program would have to support some 27 different methods to program these monitors. Either that or not support all monitors. Programming these was a real maze.

In the late 1980s a number of monitor manufacturers got together and formed a group to standardize these "Super VGA" (SVGA) monitors. A Super VGA monitor is one that supports the same modes as a VGA, plus other modes. This group is called the Video Electronics Standards Association (VESA®).[1] In 1989 VESA released its Super VGA BIOS Extension (VBE), version 1.0. This document describes a standard BIOS interface for SVGA monitors. Any monitor compatible with VESA VBE 1.0 will have a common BIOS level interface, which means that an application does not need to worry about setting registers that are specific to one monitor.

VESA VBE 1.0 set standards for resolutions up to 1280 × 1024 with 16 and 256 colors. Since then the standard has been updated twice. Version 1.1, released in 1990, defines a standardized interface for text modes with up to 60 lines on the screen, and 132 columns. Version 1.2, released in 1991, defines standards for 15-, 16-, and 24-bit color handling. As this is being written, VESA VBE 1.2 is the latest, although VESA has announced that it is working on version 2.0. All the material presented here on programming the SVGA is based on this standard. THIS MATERIAL WILL ONLY WORK FOR MONITORS THAT SUPPORT VESA VBE 1.2.

At first these standards did not carry much weight. When manufacturers did support them they did so half-heartedly, supplying drivers that might have bugs in them. But recently more and more companies have been throwing their weight behind the VBE standard. VESA now lists as members such companies as IBM, Microsoft, Intel, Apple, DEC, and a number of giants in the monitor business. Now just about every SVGA monitor supports the standards with solid bug-free code. If you have a monitor that does not seem to support the standard, or has supplied a

---

[1] The Video Electronics Standards Association is the international, non-profit organization which sets and supports industry-wide video graphics standards for the benefit of the end user. VESA's membership consists of manufacturers of monitors, peripherals, systems and software products. The VESA offices are located at 2150 North First Street, Suite 440, San Jose, CA 95131-2029, and can be reached at (408) 435-0333, FAX (408) 435-8225.

buggy driver, write to the manufacturer and chances are good that they have a VESA VBE driver that they will send you free.

SVGA Graphics Modes

VESA VBE 1.2 defines a number of text and graphics modes above and beyond those defined for VGA monitors. These modes have higher resolution and better color capability. Table 9.1.1 shows the modes defined by VBE. This table shows the VBE version that originally defined the mode. All modes defined in an earlier version of the VBE are supported in later versions. 100% upward compatibility is guaranteed.

Table 9.1.1 Video Modes Defined by VESA VBE 1.2

VESA VBE Version	Mode Number	Text/ Graphics	Resolution	Colors
1.0	0x100	Graphics	640 × 400 (pixels)	256
	0x101	Graphics	640 × 400	256
	0x102	Graphics	800 × 600	16
	0x103	Graphics	800 × 600	256
	0x104	Graphics	1024 × 768	16
	0x105	Graphics	1024 × 768	256
	0x106	Graphics	1280 × 1024	16
	0x107	Graphics	1280 × 1024	256
1.1	0x108	Text	80 × 60 (characters)	16
	0x109	Text	132 × 25	16
	0x10A	Text	132 × 43	16
	0x10B	Text	132 × 50	16
	0x10C	Text	132 × 60	16

VESA VBE Version	Mode Number	Text/ Graphics	Resolution	Colors
1.2	0x10D	Graphics	320 × 200 (pixels)	32k
	0x10E	Graphics	320 × 200	64k
	0x10F	Graphics	320 × 200	16.8m
	0x110	Graphics	640 × 480	32k
	0x111	Graphics	640 × 480	64k
	0x112	Graphics	640 × 480	16.8m
	0x113	Graphics	800 × 600	32k
	0x114	Graphics	800 × 600	64k
	0x115	Graphics	800 × 600	16.8m
	0x116	Graphics	1024 × 768	32k
	0x117	Graphics	1024 × 768	64k
	0x118	Graphics	1024 × 768	16.8m
	0x119	Graphics	1280 × 1024	32k
	0x11A	Graphics	1280 × 1024	64k
	0x11B	Graphics	1280 × 1024	16.8m

We will not be discussing the text modes in this book. The palettes for the 16-color and 256-color modes are handled the same as the VGA palettes for VGA 16- and 256-color modes.

The higher color modes do not make use of palette registers. The red, green, and blue values are placed directly in the frame buffer. The 32k and 64k color modes both use 16 bits to hold the color information, while the 16.8m color modes use 24 bits.

The 32k color modes use 5 bits each for red, green and blue, and leave 1 bit unused. Figure 9.1.1 shows the arrangements of bits for these modes. Information on the organization of bits can be gotten from the VBE service 0x01, return super VGA mode information service, which is described below.

Bit layout for 32k color modes

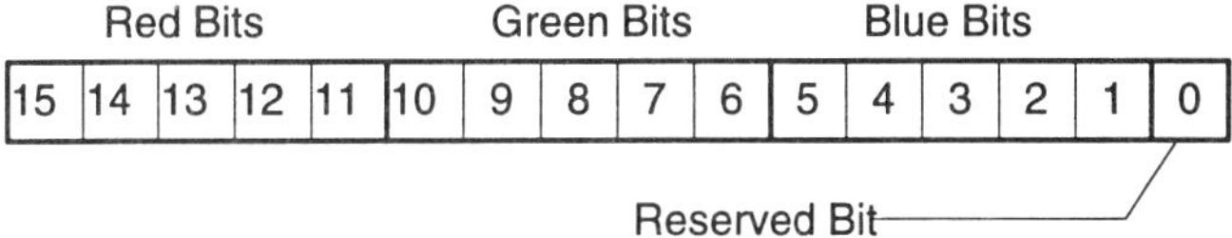

Bit layout for 64k color modes

Red Bits Green Bits Blue Bits

15	14	13	12	11	10	9	8	7	6	5	4	3	2	1	0

Bit layout for 16.8m color modes

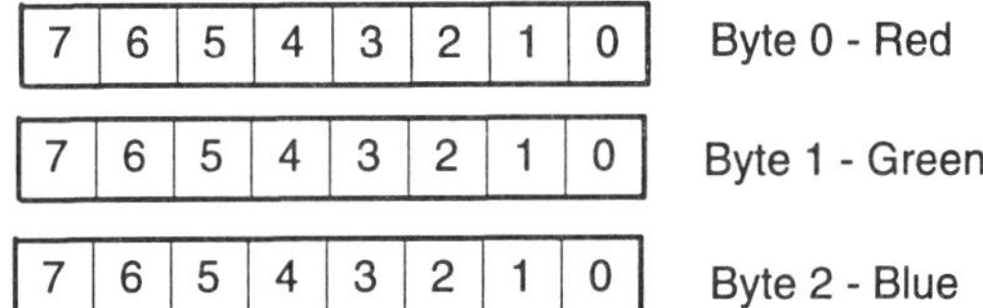

Fig. 9.1.1 Bit Layout in Direct Color Modes

Note that this is an example only, some manufactures do not use this same order. The 64k color modes use the reserved bit to give the green electron gun more resolution. In other words 6 bits are dedicated to the green gun, giving it 64 settings, rather than 32. This is because the human eye is slightly more sensitive to the green phosphor, so it can detect more shades of green.

The 16.8m color modes use 3 bytes for color information – the first for red, the second for green, and the third for blue.

For a more in-depth understanding, let's quickly review Chapter 6, on colors and color mixing. The human eye sees color by detecting wavelengths of light. The eye is sensitive to three wavelengths, and sees all colors as combinations of these. The detectors in the eye are sensitive enough to see quite a few shades. Studies have shown that if a gray scale is drawn using 16-bit color resolution (the 64k color modes described here) the eye can still see lines between the shades of gray. If those shades are dithered then the eye will no longer be able to see the lines, and it will look like a smooth shading from black through gray to white. With 24-bit color resolution (the 16.8m color modes) the eye can no longer see lines between the shades, and dithering is not needed.

SVGA BIOS Interrupts

All SVGA services are called through interrupt 10, service 0x4F. To specify the SVGA subservice, place the specific subservice number in the AL register. When the interrupt returns it will place status information in the AH and AL registers. For all SVGA services the AL will be set to 0x4F if the service is supported, and the AH will be set to 0 if the call was successful.

The following sections present code examples. For the most part these are psuedocode meant to clarify concepts. Many of the examples will not work the way they are presented. Examples of working code are given in the section entitled SVGALib.

SVGA BIOS Service 0x00 – Return SVGA Information

Service 0x00, Return SVGA Information, provides information on the SVGA adapter. This function returns a pointer to a buffer with the following structure:

```
struct VgaInfoBlock {
  char               VESASignature[4];
  unsigned char      VESAVersion[2];
  char      far     *OEMStringPtr;
  unsigned long      Capabilities;
  unsigned far      *VideoModePtr;
  unsigned           TotalMemory;
  char               Reserved[236];
};
```

The field VESASignature is set to hold the four characters "VESA". This is not a valid C string since it does not end with '\0', and the C string functions such as cmpstr( ) will not work on it.

VESAVersion gives the number of the VBE version supported by the monitor, with the higher byte giving the major number, and the lower byte giving the minor number. So for version 1.2 this field will be set to VESAVersion[0] = 01 and VESAVersion[1] = 02.

OEMStringPtr points to a string set up by the video card manufacturer. There are no restrictions on the format of this string, other than it that it is a valid C string and ends with the '\0' character.

The capabilities field gives hardware-specific information. As of VBE version 1.2 the only item defined in this field is the bit 0. If this bit is set the digital/analog converter that controls the electron guns is programmable. Programming this device is beyond the scope of this book.

VideoModePtr points to a list of supported SVGA modes. Table 9.1.1 lists the currently defined modes. It is guaranteed that all future VESA VBE standards will support these modes and these standards are guaranteed to be upwardly compatible. But just because a mode is in this list does not mean that it is currently available. A board might not have enough memory to support all the modes it could support if it had more memory, for instance. Service 0x01 can be used to find if a particular mode is supported. This service will be covered next.

TotalMemory gives the amount of memory on the board in 64k blocks. To find the number of bytes multiply this number by 65,536.

The register settings for this service are: AH=0x0F, AL=0x00, and ES:DI points to a buffer of type VGAInfoBlock. Here is an example of this function being called.

```
struct VGAInfoBlock G_SVGA_Info;

void get_SVGA_info() {
  union  REGS  regs;
  struct SREGS segregs;

  reg.h.ah = 0x4F;
  reg.h.al = 0x00;
  reg.x.dx = FP_OFF(G_SVGA_Info);

  sreg.es  = FP_SEG(G_SVGA_Info);

  int86x(0x10,&reg,&reg,&sreg);

  if (reg.h.al /= 0x4F) {
    printf ("Error: VESA VBE not supported ");
    printf ("by this monitor\n");
    exit();
  }
  if (reg.h.ah /= 0) {
    printf ("Error: Function call failed ");
    printf ("for unkown reason\n");
    exit();
  }

  if (strcmp(Info.VESASignature,"VESA") /= 0) {
    printf ("Error: VESA VBE not supported ");
    printf ("by this monitor\n");
    exit();
  }
}
```

This function should always be called first to determine if the VESA VBE is supported. The routine above tests to see if AL is equal to 0x4F. If not the standard is not supported, and the program exits. If it is and the AL is not set to 0, then an error occurred. If no error occurred the signature is checked. This is in case there is a service in place, but it is not a VESA VBE service. This is an unlikely event, but it could happen.

A similar routine is on the distribution disk in SVGALIB.C, called SVGA_Supported( ). SVGA_Supported( ) is described in full in the SVGALib section of this chapter.

SVGA BIOS Service 0x01 – Return Mode Information

The next service, 0x01, is called Return Mode Information. This function returns a great deal of mode specific information, such as whether the mode is supported, the number of colors supported in the mode, the number of pixels in each dimension, and much more. We will not cover all the information returned in detail, only what is immediately important for the tasks we want to perform – setting the mode, setting the color palettes, and plotting pixels.

This function makes use of a data structure with the following definition:

```
struct ModeInfoBlock {

  /* mandatory information */

  unsigned       ModeAttributes;
  char           WinAAttributes;
  char           WinBAttributes;
  unsigned       WinGranularity;
  unsigned       WinSize;
  unsigned       WinASegment;
  unsigned       WinBSegment;
  void      far (*WinFinctPtr)();
  unsigned       BytesPerScanLine;

  /* formerly optional
     now mandatory information */

  unsigned       XResolution;
  unsigned       YResolution;
  unsigned char  XCharSize;
  unsigned char  YCharSize;
```

```
    unsigned char   NumberOfPlanes;
    unsigned char   BitsPerPixel;
    unsigned char   NumberOfBanks;
    unsigned char   MemoryModel;
    unsigned char   BankSize;
    unsigned char   NumberOfImagePages;
    unsigned char   reserved1;

    /* New Direct Color Fields */

    unsigned char   RedMaskSize;
    unsigned char   RedFieldPosition;
    unsigned char   GreenMaskSize;
    unsigned char   GreenFieldPosition;
    unsigned char   BlueMaskSize;
    unsigned char   BlueFieldPosition;
    unsigned char   RsvdMaskSize;
    unsigned char   RsvdFieldPosition;
    unsigned char   DirectColorModelInfo;

    char            reserved[216];
  };
```

First some general background, before this structure is described in detail. VBE versions 1.0 and 1.1 listed the second grouping of fields as optional, and did not list the last grouping labeled New Direct Color Fields. The comment for the second group describes them as "formerly optional information (now mandatory)." That does not mean you can simply assume they will be filled in, since your program might run a monitor that supports version 1.0 or 1.1, but not 1.2. The version number should be checked, as described in the last section.

If the version number is lower than 1.2, you can determine whether the optional information is present by testing bit 2 of ModeAttributes. If it is set, the optional information is there.

To use this function set AH to 0x4F, AL to 0x01, CX to the mode number that you wish to obtain information on, and point ES:DI to the buffer that will hold the information. To find the number of a certain mode see Table 9.1.1 or Appendix E.

This function should only be used for modes supported by the adapter. These modes can be found with service 0, as described above. The VideoModePtr field points to an array listing the supported modes. This array ends with 0xFFFF. To determine if a particular mode is supported, first call VBE service 0x00, then search this array for the mode number. If it is not there, the mode is not supported. If it is there then use service 0x01 to determine if it is available. The array described here might contain modes that are not defined by the VBE. These are modes defined by the card manufacturer, but not supported by VESA VBE 1.2. The formerly optional fields are there primarily to deal with these modes.

To determine if a mode is supported, test the first bit of that same field.

```
if (ModeInfo.ModeAttributes & 0x0001) {
  Mode is supported
}
```

The various fields in VGAInfoBlock structure are described below.

ModeAttributes

The bits in the ModeAttributes field each describe a property of the mode passed to service 0x01. Table 9.1.2 gives the bit numbers and the properties they describe.

Table 9.1.2 Bits in ModeAttributes Field of ModeInfoBlock

Bit	Set/ Cleared	Attribute
0	Cleared	Mode not supported
	Set	Mode is supported
1	Cleared	v1.2 – reserved, v1.0 – v1.1 – optional information NOT present
	Set	v1.2 – reserved, v1.0 – v1.1 – optional information present
2	Cleared	Output functions not supported in BIOS
	Set	Output functions are supported in BIOS
3	Cleared	Monochrome mode
	Set	Color mode
4	Cleared	Text mode
	Set	Graphics mode
5-15		Reserved

Since we will be dealing almost exclusively in this book with the modes defined in VBE 1.2, the only bits we are really interested in are 0 and 1. The rest are predefined for modes defined by the VBE.

VBE Windows

Next we have to deal with the concept of windows as defined by the VBE. The segmented memory scheme used by the 8086 (see Chapter 8) causes problems when the monitor requires a large amount of memory. All modes defined by the VGA standard fit with one segment. This is not possible for SVGA modes. So VESA defined a similar idea to the 808g segment – the frame buffer window. Video memory is divided into separate banks, with only one bank in the address space of the CPU at one time. An interrupt, VBE service 0x02, is used to change the bank. By calling this interrupt the actual RAM at a certain address is changed.

This means pixels can be plotted only to a portion of the screen at one time. This portion of the screen is what the VBE calls a window. If you need to plot a pixel on a part of the screen that is not in the current window an interrupt is called to change the window.

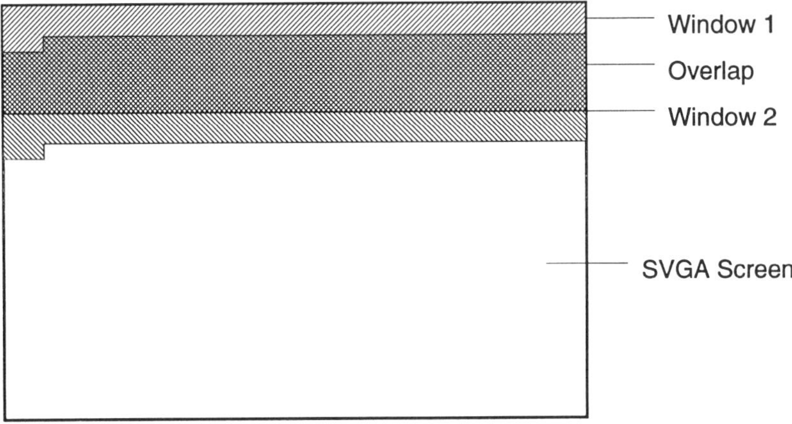

Fig. 9.1.2 Frame Buffer Windows on the Screen

Fig. 9.1.2 shows a SVGA screen with two windows highlighted. The first window starts at the upper left hand corner of the screen. The second window starts several lines below the first, but not at the start of the line. There are a number of overlapping windows all down the screen, each one starting farther from the start of the line. You can think of this as being like the segmented memory scheme of the 8086. Each window is a segment, and each starts on a paragraph boundary. If it is not convenient to use one window because the line you need for that window does not start at the beginning of the screen use an overlapping window. You can access most pixels through a number of windows.

Some systems have two windows, one for reading and the other for writing. The intention is that copying something from one portion of the screen to another can be made quick and easy by setting the read window where the object to be copied is, and setting the write window where it is to be copied too. This works, but in order to keep things simple we will ignore the fact that there are two windows as much as we can.

WinAAttributes and WinBAttributes

The WinAAttributes and WinBAttributes are bit masks. Table 9.1.3 gives the meanings of each field in the mask.

Table 9.1.3 WinAAttributes and WinBAttributes

Bit Number	Set/ Cleared	Meaning
0	Cleared	Window NOT supported
	Set	Window supported
1	Cleared	Window NOT readable
	Set	Window not readable
2	Cleared	Window NOT writeable
	Set	Window writeable
3-7	XXXX	reserved

Bit 0 gives information about whether the window is supported. Some systems allow two windows to be active at the same time. One window might be readable while another is writeable. The idea is that if you want to copy an object you set the readable window to the where the object is, and the writeable window to where it is going to, then copy. You do not have to keep setting and resetting the windows. Most monitors use only a single read/write window, but still it is important to look at these fields to make sure you can write to the window you think you can.

Granularity

The granularity gives the smallest boundary, in kilobytes, on which the window can be placed in video RAM. This is related to the window size, but also takes into account BytesPerScanLine, which is described below.

WinSize

The WinSize field gives the size, in kilobytes, of a window. That is, if this field is set to 64, the window is 64 kilobytes in size, or 65,536 bytes. All windows on one system are the same size.

WinASegment and WinBSegment

WinASegment and WinBSegment give the starting addresses of the two windows. This number stays the same when the window is switched, since the windows always occupy the same portion of the CPU's address space. To set up a frame buffer for a 24-bit mode you might use code like the following.

```
unsigned char *FrameBuffer[3] =
    MK_FP(WinASegment, 0x0000);
```

MK_FP is a macro defined by Borland C for creating far pointers. It is not defined by Microsoft C. The code above creates a pointer to an array of three byte blocks.

WinFuncPtr

WinFuncPtr is a pointer to the code that changes the window. The idea is that this can be called as a function, which is somewhat faster than using the interrupt. Unfortunately to call this from C requires setting up the registers first. Remember that the REGS construct does not hold actual registers, it is only a portion of normal RAM. A pointer to this RAM is passed to the int86( ) function, which then loads the actual register before calling the interrupt. To call the WinFuncPtr function from C requires that the programmer save the AX, BX and DX registers, set them up appropriately for the call, call the function, then restore the registers to their original values. How the registers need to be set up is described in a few paragraphs, when the interrupt is covered. Setting up the registers in Borland C can be done directly using the _AX, _BX, _CX, and _DX variables. Microsoft does not support these variables, however, so if you want your code to be portable between them you must use inline assembler language. Either way this is a tricky thing to do, and is only recommended for those that need the utmost speed out of their graphics software.

BytesPerScanLine

The BytesPerScanLine field gives the number of bytes for a row of pixels on the screen. This is not necessarily equal to the number of pixels, even for a 256-color mode where 1 byte represents 1 pixel. Some SVGA adapter manufacturers add pixels at the end of a scan line to make the next row start on an even number. For instance, in mode 0x114 the pixel resolution is 800 × 600, and there are 2 bytes per pixel, so the last pixel on the first scan line would be numbered 1599 (remember, the first is 0, not 1). Some manufacturers might add extra "ghost pixels" to the end so the next row starts at number 2048. Figure 9.1.3 shows graphically what these different fields mean on the screen.

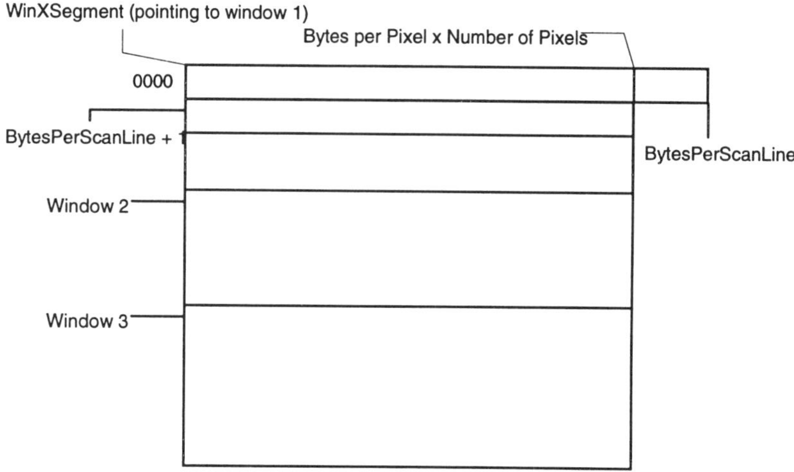

Fig 9.1.3 The BytesPerScanLine Field of the ModeInfoBlock.

Formerly Optional Information

Since we are not concerning ourselves with modes not defined by VBE 1.2, the formerly optional information will not be discussed in detail. Table 9.1.4 gives a brief description of each field

Table 9.1.4 Formerly Optional Information

Field Name	Purpose
XResolution	The number of pixels on the screen in the X dimension
YResolution	The number of pixels on the screen in the Y dimension
XCharSize	Number of pixels per character in the X dimension
YCharSize	Number of pixels per character in the Y dimension
NumberOfPlanes	Number of pixel planes.
BitsPerPixel	Total number of bits to define the color of a single pixel
MemoryModel	Memory models are described in Table 9.1.5
NumberOfBanks	Number of windows the system supports
BankSize	Number of bytes in a window
NumberOfImagePages	Number of full screens that will fit in video memory at one time (see Chapter 12 for an explanation of video pages)

Table 9.1.5 gives the MemoryModel field. These memory model types are described below.

Table 9.1.5 Memory Models

Model Number	Model
0x00	Text mode
0x01	CGA graphics
0x02	Hercules
0x03	4-plane planar
0x04	Packed pixel
0x05	Non-chain 4, 256 color
0x06	Direct Color
0x07	YUV
0x08 - 0x0F	Reserved, to be defined by VESA
0x10 - 0xFF	Reserved, to be defined by video adapter manufacturers

The TextMode memory model is the standard model. It uses 2 bytes per character, the first bit determines whether the character will blink or not, the next 3 bits are for the background color, the next 4 bits are the foreground color, and the second byte holds the ASCII code of the character to be displayed.

The CGA model is the 4-color palette model, which is described in Chapter 6. Hercules graphics are not covered here, since they are not supported by BIOS. The 4-plane planar is the model used by 16-color modes, with 16 palette registers. Non-chain 4, 256 color means 256-color modes with 256 palette registers. Packed Pixel and Direct Color modes are basically the same, and do not use palette registers. This model uses the bits in the frame buffer directly to determine the settings of the different electron guns. The direct color model is described in detail in the next section.

MaskSize and FieldPosition Fields

The final set of fields describes how to set pixels for modes that use the direct color model. The mask fields give the number of bits for each color, and the field position fields give the starting positions for the bits describing each color. The Rsvd fields are reserved, or in other words, bits in these fields do nothing. As an example, VBE 1.2 defines 0x10D to be a 16-bit color mode that supports 32k colors. To see how pixels are set up in 32k color modes see Fig. 9.1.4. For this mode, the fields might be set as follows:

```
RedMaskSize        =  5
RedFieldPosition   =  6

GreenMaskSize      =  5
GreenFieldPosition = 11

BlueMaskSize       =  5
BlueFieldPosition  =  1

RsvdMaskSize       =  1
RsvdFieldPosition  =  0
```

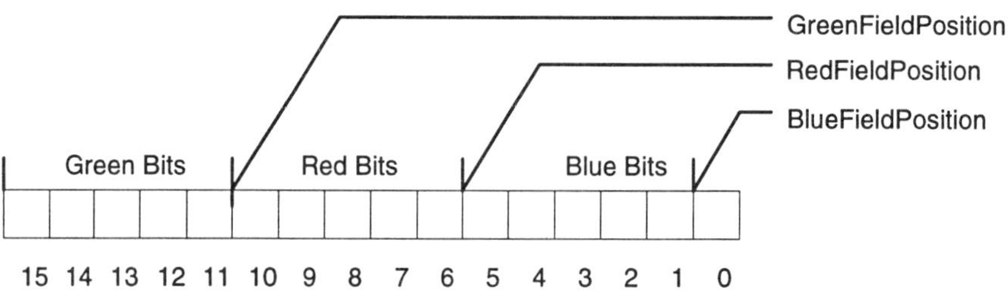

Fig. 9.1.4 Field Positions and Mask Sizes

This might not be quite what you'd expect. Not all manufacturers use the order Red Green Blue. For another example here is how a 64k color defined by VBE 1.2 mode would look (Fig. 9.1.5).

```
RedMaskSize         =  5
RedFieldPosition    = 11

GreenMaskSize       =  6
GreenFieldPosition  =  5

BlueMaskSize        =  5
BlueFieldPosition   =  0

RsvdMaskSize        =  0
RsvdFieldPosition   =  0
```

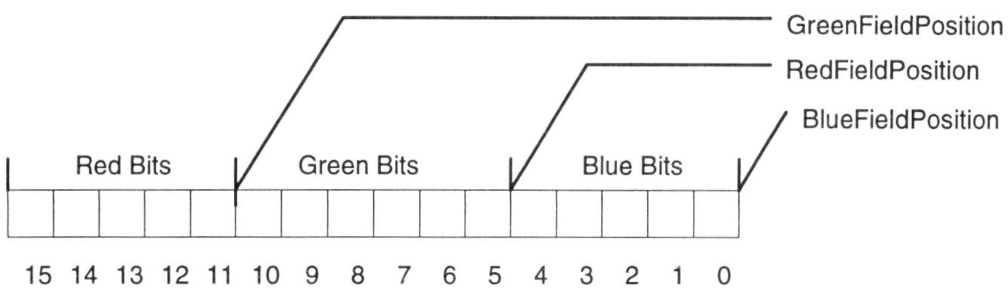

Fig. 9.1.5 Field Positions and Mask Sizes for a 64K Color Mode

On one card the first 5 bits might be red, while on another card the first 6 bits might be green. The field position and mask sizes can be used to shift bits to the proper location. Here is an example of how to do this:

```
void plot_pixel(int X, int Y,
                unsigned char Red,
                unsigned char Green,
                unsigned char Blue) {

  *(Frame_Buffer+(Y*BytesPerScanLine)+X) =
                         (Red   << RedMaskSize) +
                         (Green << GreenMaskSize) +
                         (Blue  << BlueMaskSize);
}
```

This code will set pixel (X,Y), provided the window is set correctly. In order for it to work properly FrameBuffer must be defined to be a pointer to an array, each element of which is the correct number of bits. For 15/16-bit modes this is easy since the array can be of unsigned integers (15-bit modes use a full unsigned integer, leaving one bit unused). For 24-bit modes this is tricky. The section on plotting pixels shows how to get around the problem of defining an array of 24 bit elements.

Here is an example of how to call VBE service 0x01. A variable of type ModeInfoBlock is global. This is consistent with other examples in this section, which look for information in this variable. It returns SUPPORTED if the mode is supported, or NOTSUPPORTED otherwise.

```
#define SUPPORTED    0
#define NOTSUPPORTED 1

struct ModeInfoBlock G_Mode_Info;

char get_mode_info (int mode_num) {
  union REGS L_Regs;
  struct SREGS L_Seg_Regs;

  L_Regs.h.ah = 0x4F;
  L_Regs.h.al = 0x01;
  L_Regs.x.cx = mode_num;
  L_Regs.x.di = FP_OFF(&G_Mode_Info);
  L_Seg_Regs.es = FP_SEG(&G_Mode_Info);

  int86x(0x10, &L_Regs, &L_Regs, &L_Seg_Regs);

  if (L_Regs.h.al != 0x4F) {
    printf("Unknown Error\n");
    exit (-1);
  else if (L_Regs.h.ah != 0) {
    return NOTSUPPORTED;
  }
  else if(!(G_Mode_Info.ModeAttributes&0x01)) {
    return NOTSUPPORTED;
  }
  else
    return SUPPORTED;

} /* end get_mode_info */
```

SVGA BIOS Service 0x02 – Setting the Video Mode

We know what modes the card can support by using service 0x00, and what modes are currently available by using service 0x01. Now we can set the mode using service 0x02. Set the AH to 0x4F, set the AL to 0x01, set the BX to the number of the mode desired, and call interrupt 0x10. On return, if the AL is equal to 0x4F and the AH is equal 0, then the call was successful. The different modes are given in

Table 9.1.1 at the beginning of the chapter, or in Appendix E. The following example assumes that service 0x01 has already verified that the mode is available.

```
void set_mode(int mode_num) {
  union REGS L_Regs;

  L_Regs.h.ah = 0x4F;
  L_Regs.h.al = 0x02;
  L_Regs.x.bx = mode_num;
  int86(0x10, &L_Regs, &L_Regs);

  if ((L_Regs.h.ah != 0) &&
      (L_Regs.h.al != 0x0f)) {
    printf("Unknown error occurred in set_mode()\n");
    exit(-1);
  }
} /* end set_mode() */
```

Plotting Pixels on SVGA Monitors

Setting the Correct Window

Monitor windows have already been described in the section on service 0x01. To determine which window the pixel falls into, in a 256-color mode, first multiply the Y coordinate by the BytesPerScanLine field of the ModeInfoBlock, then add the X coordinate to the result. For 15- or 16-color modes add 2*X, and for 24 bit modes add 3*X. This would be the byte location of the pixel in video memory, if there were no windows. If this number alone is used without regard to the window, and the number is past the end of the window, it will wrap to the beginning of the window. An attempt to show this graphically is made in Fig. 9.1.6.

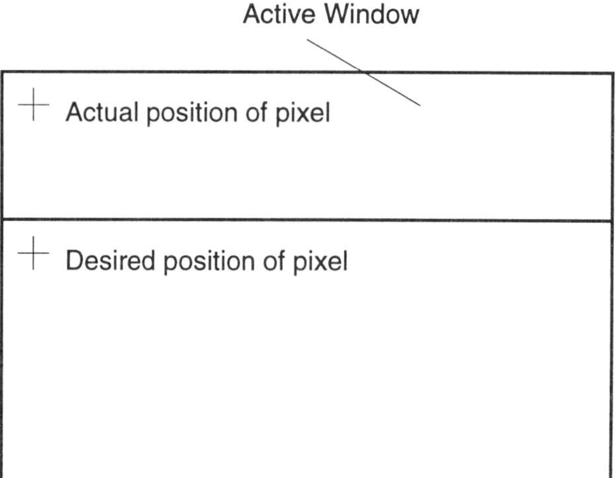

Attempt to plot a pixel at screen location (1, Y+1), where Y is the pixel size of the window in the Y dimension.

Fig. 9.1.6 SVGA Screen Windows

To make sure this doesn't happen, the window needs to be set to the correct portion of the screen. To find the correct portion, take the number found above, y*BytesPerScanLine+x, the screen position of the pixel, and divide by the window granularity. A word of warning, y*BytesPerScanLine can be quite large. Use long integers to prevent overflows. The window granularity is given in kilobytes, so this number needs to be multiplied by 1024 before the divide.

Now that we know the number of the window, use VBE service 0x05 to set the window. For this service set AH to 0x4F, AL to 0x05, BH to 0x00, BL to 0x00 for window A or 0x01 for window B, and DX to the number found in the last paragraph. Here is code to set the window given X,Y coordinates. This function uses the A window if it is writeable.

```
struct ModeInfoBlock G_Mode_Info;

void set_window(int X, int Y) {
  union REGS L_Regs;
  unsigned char L_Write_Win;
  long L_Win_Number;

  /* Find the window number */
  L_Win_Number =
    (((long)Y*(long)G_Mode_Info.BytesPerScanLine)+X)/
         (long)(G_Mode_Info.Win_Granularity * 1024);
```

```
    /* find write window */
    /* 0x03 = 0000 0011 binary.  This */
    /* tests bits 0 and 1.           */
    if (G_Mode_Info.WinAAttributes & 0x03)
      L_Write_Win = 0x00;
    else
      /* If A is not writeable B must be */
      L_Write_Win = 0x01;

    L_Regs.h.ah = 0x4F;
    L_Regs.h.al = 0x05;
    L_Regs.h.bh = 0x00;
    L_Regs.h.bl = L_Write_Win;
    L_Regs.x.dx = L_Win_Number;

    int86(0x10, &L_Regs, &L_Regs);

    if ((L_Regs.h.ah != 0) &&
        (L_Regs.h.al != 0x0f)) {
      printf("Unknown error occurred in set_window() \
  \n");
      exit(-1);
    }
  } /* end set_window() */
```

Service 0x05 can be used to find the current window. Use BH = 01, and the current window will be returned in DX. It is recommended that the application keep track of the current window in a variable, since looking at a variable is much faster than calling an interrupt.

Plotting Pixels in 8-Bit Modes

Now that we have the correct window, how do we find the correct place to put the pixel in the frame buffer? First we need to locate the frame buffer. The address is given in G_Mode_Info.WinASegment if A is the writeable window, or G_Mode_Info.WinBSegment otherwise. A frame buffer can be set up as an array of bytes as follows:

```
  unsigned char far *Frame_Buffer =
    MK_FP(G_Mode_Info.WinXSegment, 0x0000);
```

The MK_FP macros is supplied with the Borland C compiler, but unfortunately not with the Microsoft compiler. It creates a far pointer by using the first parameter as the segment and the second as the offset.

The offset into the frame buffer can be found by using the same method as finding the window, only modulo-ing by WinGranularity instead of dividing. The proper byte to set is found by adding the offset to the frame buffer pointer. This is quite similar to the method used for VGA 256-color mode. The following function will plot a pixel when an 8-bit color mode is used.

```
struct ModeInfoBlock G_Mode_Info;
int current_window = 0;

void plot_pixel (int X, int Y,
                 unsigned char Color) {
  unsigned char far *Frame_Buffer;
  long pixel_window

  /* First setup frame buffer */
  if (G_Mode_Info.WinAAttributes & 0x03)
    Frame_Buffer =
      MK_FP(G_Mode_Info.WinASegment, 0x0000);
  else
    Frame_Buffer =
      MK_FP(G_Mode_Info.WinBSegment, 0x0000);

  /* next find window */
  pixel_window =
   (((long)Y*(long)G_Mode_Info.BytesPerScanLine)+X) /
            (long)(G_Mode_Info.WinGranularity*1024);

  if (current_window /= pixel_window) {
    set_window(pixel_window);
    current_window = pixel_window;
  }

  /* now we can plot the pixel */
  *(Frame_Buffer +
    (((long)Y*(long)G_Mode_Info.BytesPerScanLine)+X)
          % long)(G_Mode_Info.WinGranularity*1024)) =
                                               Color;
} /* end plot_pixel() */
```

This function could be faster. A pixel plotting routine should be absolutely as fast as possible, since a great many pixels may need to be plotted quickly for such things as filling or clearing the screen. The routines presented in this book are generally simplified for the sake of understandability rather than made as fast as possible. I will leave it to the reader to upgrade these routines to make them as fast as possible.

Plotting Pixels in 15/16-Bit Modes

The plot_pixel( ) function listed above will only work for 8 bit modes. To make it work for a 15- or 16-bit mode, we need to redefine the frame buffer as an array of unsigned integers, rather than bytes:

```
unsigned int far *Frame_Buffer;
```

Pointing the frame buffer to the right location is the same. Now, given red, green, and blue values, we need to put them into an unsigned integer, so it can be put into the buffer. There is a trick to this, of course, because different cards put the red, green, and blue fields in different orders. The field positions in the ModeInfoBlock are used to set up an unsigned integer.

```
color = (Red   << G_Mode_Info.RedFieldPosition)   +
        (Green << G_Mode_Info.GreenFieldPosition) +
        (Blue  << G_Mode_Info.BlueFieldPosition);
```

This will put the fields in the correct order for plotting. There is a potential problem, however. If the variable Blue has 8 bits set and the blue field only uses 5 bits, the 3 extra bits could be added into the red or green field. If the programmer knows what type of monitor the program will run on, fine, but some programs will run on monitors supporting different modes. The MaskSize fields in the ModeInfoBlock can be used to prevent this problem. Shift the color to the left, then to the right, to make sure only the correct number of bits is set. The following assumes that Red, Green, and Blue are each 1 byte long (unsigned chars).

```
Red   =((Red  <<(8-G_Mode_Info.RedMaskSize))>>
                (8-G_Mode_Info.RedMaskSize));
Green=((Green<<(8-G_Mode_Info.GreenMaskSize))>>
                (8-G_Mode_Info.GreenMaskSize));
Blue  =((Blue <<(8-G_Mode_Info.BlueMaskSize))>>
                (8-G_Mode_Info.BlueMaskSize));
```

This code will work for either 15- or 16-bit modes. Now we have to find the place to put this in the frame buffer. We previously defined the frame buffer as a pointer to an array of bytes (unsigned chars). Since the compiler will index this array by integers instead of characters, our previous method for finding the location of the pixel in the frame buffer will put it twice as far into the buffer as we want. This can be corrected by dividing the screen position, once it is found, by 2. One final problem. Since in this mode there are 2 bytes per pixel, we still need to add an extra X to the offset. The following code puts it all together and sets a pixel to the correct RGB content.

```
struct ModeInfoBlock G_Mode_Info;
int current_window = 0;

void plot_pixel_16_bits (int X, int Y,
                         unsigned char Red,
                         unsigned char Green,
                         unsigned char Blue)
  unsigned int color;
  unsigned int far *frame_buffer;

  /* First setup frame buffer */
  if (G_Mode_Info.WinAAttributes & 0x03)
    Frame_Buffer =
      MK_FP(G_Mode_Info.WinASegment, 0x0000);
  else
    Frame_Buffer =
      MK_FP(G_Mode_Info.WinBSegment, 0x0000);

/* Next setup color mask */
Red  =((Red  <<(8-G_Mode_Info.RedMaskSize))>>
               (8-G_Mode_Info.RedMaskSize));
Green=((Green<<(8-G_Mode_Info.GreenMaskSize))>>
               (8-G_Mode_Info.GreenMaskSize));
Blue =((Blue <<(8-G_Mode_Info.BlueMaskSize))>>
               (8-G_Mode_Info.BlueMaskSize));

color = (Red  <<G_Mode_Info.RedFieldPosition)  +
        (Green<<G_Mode_Info.GreenFieldPosition)+
        (Blue <<G_Mode_Info.BlueFieldPosition);

  /* next find window */
  pixel_window =
   (((long)Y*(long)G_Mode_Info.BytesPerScanLine)+X+X)
        /((long)G_Mode_Info.WinGranularity*1024);

  if (current_window /= pixel_window) {
    set_window(pixel_window);
    current_window = pixel_window;
  }

  /* now we can plot the pixel */
  *(Frame_Buffer +
     ((((long)Y*long)G_Mode_Info.BytesPerScanLine)+
                                          X+X)/2) %
      (G_Mode_Info.WinGranularity*1024)) =
                                       Color;
} /* end plot_pixel_16_bits() */
```

Plotting Pixels in 24-Bit Modes

The above algorithm presents a problem when working with 24-bit modes. Some video cards add bytes to the end of a scanline to make the next scanline start on an even byte number. The idea is to simplify the math involved in plotting a pixel. These extra pixels do not appear on the screen. The structure of a 24-bit pixel is 3 bytes wide. Sometimes when extra bytes are added, the length of the entire scanline is not divisible by 3 (Fig. 9.1.7). This means starting at the next line, when we attempt to plot a pixel it will be shifted by a third or two-thirds of a pixel, which will throw the colors off. If we attempt to plot a white pixel, and it is shifted by a third, we will end up plotting two pixels, one red and the other cyan.

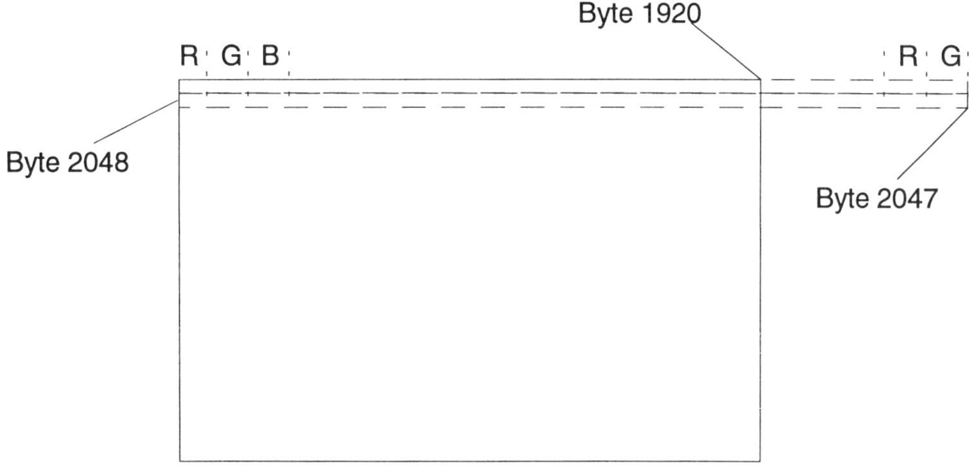

Fig. 9.1.7 The Scanline in a 24-Bit Mode Does Not Always End on a Pixel Boundary

So we need to modify the algorithm somewhat. Not all cards add these extra bytes at the end of the scanline, so the new algorithm we need must also be able to work like the old one. In other words we cannot simply add the bytes to get us to the next scanline; that will not work on all monitors.

The first thing to do is find the correct window. After that we need to find the byte on the scanline where the window starts. Next we find the Y coordinate of the pixel in the window, and the X coordinate *on the screen*. We can use these last two values to determine where we would plot the pixel if the window started at the left-hand side of the screen. We subtract the number of bytes between where the window starts and the left side of the screen from the byte where the pixel would start to determine where to plot the pixel.

To find where the window starts on the scanline takes a little effort. The first step is to find the number of lines per window. This is done by dividing the size of the window, in bytes, by the number of bytes per scanline. This value needs to be saved because it will be used in other places.

```
Lines_Per_Window = (1024*Mode_Info.Granularity)/
                        Mode_Info.BytesPerScanline;
```

We use this value to modulo the window size, giving the number of pixels each window moves from the left-hand side of the screen. In other words, if the value we get from the modulo is 8, then the first window will be 0 bytes from the left-hand side of the screen, the second window will be 8 bytes, the third window will be 16 bytes, etc. We multiply this by the current window number, so we know how many bytes from the left hand side the current window is, and then modulo this number by the bytes per scanline, since the number we found could be larger than the bytes per scanline. The value found, that is, the byte on the scanline where the window starts, is called Correction, since it is used to correct the pixel position.

```
Correction = (((1024*Mode_Info.Granularity) %
                Lines_Per_Window) * Current_Window) %
                                 Mode_Info.BytesPerScanLine;
```

Next we find the uncorrected position of the pixel. Modulo Y by the lines per window, and multiply by the bytes per scanline. This gives the first byte on the correct scanline where the pixel is to be plotted, if the window starts at the left-hand side of the monitor. Next multiply X by 3 and add it in, to get the correct position of the pixel. This value is WinPtr.

```
WinPtr = (X*3) + ((Y % Lines_Per_Window) *
                       Mode_Info.BytesPerScanLine);
```

The correct window can easily be found by dividing Y by Lines_Per_Window.

```
current_window = Y/Lines_Per_Window;
```

From this information we can easily find where in the frame buffer to plot the pixel, but putting the pixel there is not so easy. The 8086 does not support a 24-bit data type, so a structure of three unsigned chars can be used. A frame buffer is set up with this structure. A variable needs to be set up with this structure that will hold the RGB values and can be copied to the frame buffer. Unfortunately, bit operations won't work on this structure. This can be gotten around by creating a union with a long int and this structure. All the bit operations are performed on the long int, and the structure is set up automatically because they are in the same space in memory. Care must be taken that the correct bits are lined up.

```
struct Color24Bit_Struct {
  unsigned char c1;
  unsigned char c2;
  unsigned char c3;
};

union {
  unsigned long Holder;
  struct Color24Bit_Struct Actual_Color;
} color;
              .
              .
              .
color.Holder
    = ((long)Red  <<G_Mode_Info.RedFieldPosition)+
      ((long)Green<<G_Mode_Info.GreenFieldPosition)+
      ((long)Blue <<G_Mode_Info.BlueFieldPosition);
```

The variables Red, Green, and Blue are cast to longs to prevent the shift itself from overflowing. This will line the bits up correctly, but we cannot place the entire structure into the frame buffer at once. If we set the frame buffer up as an array of Color24Bit_Struct, and use pointers to place the pixel into the array, C will automatically increment the pointer by three bytes. So we will never be able to access byte 2048, since it is not divisible by 3. But all the hoops we just jumped through were because there is, or at least could be, a pixel that starts at byte 2048. So we need to set the frame buffer up as an array of bytes, just as it was for 8-bit modes, and copy in one color at a time.

```
 unsigned char far *Frame_Buffer;
              .
              .
              .
*(Frame_Buffer + WinPtr - Correction) =
                                 Color.Actual_Color.c1;
*(Frame_Buffer + WinPtr + 1 - Correction) =
                                 Color.Actual_Color.c2;
*(Frame_Buffer + WinPtr + 2 - Correction) =
                                 Color.Actual_Color.c3;
```

So all that business with the union is only to line bits up correctly. We did not run into this problem with other modes because in other modes the problem of the scanline ending at a fraction of a pixel does not exist. Here is the entire pixel plotting function for 24-bit modes:

```
struct ModeInfoBlock G_Mode_Info;
int current_window = 0;

void plot_pixel_24_bits (int X, int Y,
                         unsigned char Red,
                         unsigned char Green,
                         unsigned char Blue)

  unsigned Lines_Per_Window;
  unsigned Correction;
  unsigned WinPtr;
  unsigned char far *frame_buffer;

  struct Color24Bit_Struct {
    unsigned char c1;
    unsigned char c2;
    unsigned char c3;
  };

  union {
    unsigned long Holder;
    struct Color24Bit_Struct Actual_Color;
  } color;


  /* First setup frame buffer */
  if (G_Mode_Info.WinAAttributes & 0x03)
    Frame_Buffer =
      MK_FP(G_Mode_Info.WinASegment, 0x0000);
  else
    Frame_Buffer =
      MK_FP(G_Mode_Info.WinBSegment, 0x0000);

  Lines_Per_Window = (1024*Mode_Info.Granularity)/
                          Mode_Info.BytesPerScanline;

  Correction = (((1024*Mode_Info.Granularity) %
              Lines_Per_Window) * Current_Window) %
                               Mode_Info.BytesPerScanLine;

  WinPtr = (X*3) + ((Y % Lines_Per_Window) *
```

```
                                Mode_Info.BytesPerScanLine);

    pixel_window = Y/Lines_Per_Window;

    if (current_window /= pixel_window) {
      set_window(pixel_window);
      current_window = pixel_window;
    }

    color.Holder
        = ((long)Red  <<G_Mode_Info.RedFieldPosition)+
          ((long)Green<<G_Mode_Info.GreenFieldPosition)+
          ((long)Blue <<G_Mode_Info.BlueFieldPosition);

    *(Frame_Buffer + WinPtr - Correction) =
                                  Color.Actual_Color.c1;
    *(Frame_Buffer + WinPtr + 1 - Correction) =
                                  Color.Actual_Color.c2;
    *(Frame_Buffer + WinPtr + 2 - Correction) =
                                  Color.Actual_Color.c3;

  } /* end plot_pixel_24bits() */
```

Many of the things done in this example could be done when the mode is first set. That way they do not have to be redone every time a pixel is plotted, making the pixel plotting function more efficient. SVGALib does move these calculations out of the pixel plotting function and into the mode setting function.

The SVGA Library

Included on the distribution disk with this book are two files, SVGALib.C and SVGALib.H. These files contain the source code for a number of routines for programming SVGA monitors. These routines are meant to be fairly easy to understand and modify, as well as easy to use. They serve as both example code and as a graphics library that you can use in your programs. This section introduces this library and covers the routines that set up the monitor and data structures. More advanced functions are presented in the next two chapters. Of course this library, as well as any code in this book or on the distribution disk, is not guaranteed to operate as advertised due to bugs.

The SVGA library on the disk can be immediately compiled with Borland C, but a few minor modifications are needed for it to compile on Microsoft C. Borland's version of the FP_OFF and FP_SEG macros takes the address of a variable, while the Microsoft version takes the variable itself. The Borland version is called as:

```
L_Regs.es = FP_SEG(&Variable);
```

This is how these macros are used in the file. To compile this using Microsoft C remove the ampersand:

```
L_Regs.es = FP_SEG(Variable);
```

In addition, the Microsoft compiler does not support the MK_FP macro. This macro takes two 16-bit numbers and turns them into a 20-bit address. To create a far pointer in Microsoft set the pointer equal to the 16-bit segment, then shift the value in the variable 4 bits.

While the functions in the SVGALib are compatible with the compilers themselves, they may cause problems when used with other graphics libraries. For this reason you should not include Borland's GRAPHICS.H or Microsoft's GRAPH.H.

Functions in SVGALib

SVGALib provides a number of functions and useful variables. This section presents the basics of how to use the library. That is, how to set the monitor mode and how to plot pixels. The next section presents the internal organs of this much of the library. The primitives, such as line drawing and filling shapes, are presented in future chapters.

Before we start, something should be mentioned about the programming style used in the library. First of all, any function supplied by this library starts with the capital letters SVGA. This way when you are modifying your own code in 10 years, when you see SVGA_plot_pixel(X, Y) you know that is a routine from this library, rather than from Borland or from some other part of your code. This is quite useful in tracking down bugs, since you know where to look for the routine. For those of you who have never seen a program with a 100,000 lines of code, believe me, it helps!

The next item of style is the naming of variables. Certain variables, such as the number of pixels, are made globally available. While it is generally considered poor practice to use global variables, I have yet to see a program that does not. In some instances it even helps readability, since you don't have to pass 200 parameters to each and every function. All global variables exported by SVGALib start with the capital letters SVGA. You can tell global variables from functions because each first letter of a word in the variable name is capitalized. For instance

```
SVGA_MaxX
```

is a variable, while

```
SVGA_plot_pixel()
```

is a function.

Global variables used internally start with G_. While these don't affect the user of these routines, this is important when you want to make modifications. Parameters almost always start with P_ unless there is an overriding reason not to, and local variables always start with L_. You might have noticed this in the preceding sections, when regs suddenly turned into L_Regs. Again, each word in the variable name starts with a capital letter.

So far in the text I have been referring to some macros that return a constant value as constants themselves. While on a deep, compiler developer type level, this is not correct, I will continue this practice (as do many C programmers). Constants defined by SVGALib are all in capital letters. Exported constants do NOT start with the letters SVGA, although they probably should.

Files are organized so that all includes are at the top, followed by a mix of global variables, constants, and structure definitions, which are then followed by the functions. Constant definitions are generally meant to be used by one or several variables, and are defined right above those variables that use them.

Unrelated functions in the source file, as opposed to the header file, are separated by a line of equal signs in a comment. Related functions, or functions that are called exclusively by one "parent" function, are separated by a line of dashes in comments. These are the types of procedure that would be nested inside the parent in Pascal or Ada. The line of equal signs or dashes is meant to give that same feeling of nesting. All this organization really improves the maintainability of a large file by making it more readable and by making things easier to find.

It should be mentioned somewhere that graphics routines often need to be absolutely as fast as possible. When filling a large surface of the screen it simply does not do to have a fill routine running at less that 100% of what it can be. Unfortunately to make a routine as fast and efficient as possible often makes for difficult, complex, and completely unreadable code. Since the code in SVGALib is meant as much for demonstrating code as it is to be used, compromises are often made for the sake of readability. But efficiency has not been thrown to the wind, so you will find these routines usable, and in some cases understanding them will be a challenge.

Modify and enjoy. Of course you should not modify the copy on the distribution disk. Make a copy and keep the original as it is. This way you can always get back to the original.

Exported Variables

Before digging into the code, the basic exported variables functions in the library will be presented so the programmer can start using the library to draw graphics. At this point you might want a printout of SVGALib.H to make following the discussion easier.

As you look through SVGALib.H you will probably be surprised *not* to see any variables of type VGAInfoBlock or ModeInfoBlock. These are safely hidden inside the source file, and any needed information in them is accessed through function calls or exported variables.

A good place to start might be at the top of SVGALib.H. Constants FALSE and TRUE are defined as 0 and 1. This might conflict with other definitions you have lying around. If so one or the other should be gotten rid of. It is possible to use the #undef directive to undefine these, then define them again, but this is dangerous since in some places FALSE is expected to be one value, but in other places FALSE might be another value entirely. In fact it might be dangerous for SVGALib to use other definitions of FALSE and TRUE, since code similar to the following might be used:

```
if (situation1)
  L_Variable = FALSE;
else
  L_Variable = TRUE;

        .
        .
        .

if (L_Variable) {

        .
        .
        .
```

As you can see, if FALSE is defined to mean something other than 0, this code will not work.

Next is a list of errors. Every function returns error codes. Most errors are negative, with 0 generally meaning no error. This can be confusing if you use a function in an if statement, since FALSE is the same as no error, but this is consistent with DOS and BIOS. The BIOS routines defined by the VBE also return 0 for success. The constant VBESUPPORTED resides in this list and has a value of 1. This is because VBESUPPORTED is not an error, but it is returned by the function SVGA_supported. This function can then be used in an if statement with the result being quite readable:

```
if (SVGA_Supported() == VBESUPPORTED) {
  /* graphics code */

        .
        .
        .

}
else {
  printf ("No Dice!\n");
  exit   (-1);
}
```

This is the proverbial "no dice" error. SVGA_supported( ) is covered in detail further down in its proper place. Table 9.2.1 lists the available errors.

Table 9.2.1 SVGALib Errors

Constant	**Valu e**	**Message**
VBESUPPORTED	1	"Unknown Error"
NOERROR	0	"No Error"
UNKNOWNERROR	-1	"Unknown Error"
NOTINITIALED	-2	"Graphics system not initialized, use function SVGA_supported( )"
VBENOTSUPPORTED	-3	"System does not support VESA VBE"
NOTDIRECTCMODE	-4	"Graphics system is not in a direct color mode"
DIRECTCMODE	-5	"Graphics system IS in a direct color mode"
MODENOTSUPPORTED	-6	"Mode currently not supported by video adapter"
ONLYONEWINDOW	-7	"Graphics system supports only one access window"
NOWINDOW	-8	"Graphics system supports NO monitor access window"
NOMODESET	-9	"No supported mode has been found"
PIXELOUTOFRANGE	-10	"Attempt to plot a pixel off the screen fails"
OUTOFMEMORY	-11	"Out of memory"

Next is a bunch of constants for telling the system what mode you want. Most of these are the numbers of different modes. The first two are used when you want the highest resolution mode or the highest color mode, the next is for returning the screen to text mode, and the rest are for setting specific SVGA modes.

The first 8 cover the modes that use palette registers. The next 15 cover the 15-bit, 16-bit, and 24-bit modes. Each of these starts with the letters CO, then the number of bits, then the letter S for SVGA, then finally an abbreviation for the resolution. The resolution abbreviations are: VELORES (Very Extremely LOw RES) for 320 × 200, VLORES (Very LOw RES) for 640 × 400, LORES for 640 × 480, MEDRED for 800 × 600, HIRES for 1024 × 768, and VHIRES for 1280 × 1024. So if you want a 15-bit mode at resolution 1024 × 768 use CO15SHIRES. These names might seem clumsy, but you quickly get used to them. The modes supported by this library are given in Table 9.2.2.

Table 9.2.2 SVGALib Mode Constants

Type of Mode	Constant	Value	Meaning
Depends on Monitor	HIRESMODE	-0x100	Find the highest resolution
	HICOLORMODE	-0x101	Find the highest number of colors
Text	TEXT	-0x103	Return to text mode
Palette modes	CO8SVLORES	0x100	256 colors (8 bits), 640 × 400 res
	CO8SLORES	0x101	256 colors, 640 × 480 res
	CO4SMEDRES	0x102	16 colors, 800 × 600 res
	CO8SMEDRES	0x103	256 colors, 800 × 600 res
	CO4SHIRES	0x104	16 colors, 1024 × 768 res
	CO8SHIRES	0x105	256 colors, 1024 × 786 res
	CO4SVHIRES	0x106	16 colors, 1280 × 1024 res
	CO8SVHIRES	0x107	256 colors, 1280 × 1024 res
Direct Color	CO15SVELORES	0x10D	15 bit color, 320 × 200 res
	CO16SVELORES	0x10E	16 bit color, 320 × 200 res
	CO24SVELORES	0x10F	24 bit color, 320 × 200 res
	CO15SLORES	0x110	15 bit color, 640 × 480 res
	CO16SLORES	0x111	16 bit color, 640 × 480 res
	CO24SLORES	0x112	24 bit color, 640 × 480 res
	CO15SMEDRES	0x113	15 bit color, 800 × 600 res
	CO16SMEDRES	0x114	16 bit color, 800 × 600 res
	CO24SMEDRES	0x115	24 bit color, 800 × 600 res
	CO15SHIRES	0x116	15 bit color, 1024 × 786 res
	CO16SHIRES	0x117	16 bit color, 1024 × 786 res
	CO24SHIRES	0x118	24 bit color, 1024 × 786 res
	CO15SVHIRES	0x119	15 bit color, 1280 × 1024 res
	CO16SVHIRES	0x11A	16 bit color, 1280 × 1024 res
	CO24SVHIRES	0x11B	24 bit color, 1280 × 1024 res

At this time I might also suggest a few more modifications. The first is that this library does not support the VGA or earlier monitors. Nor does it support any

SVGA monitors other than those supporting the VESA VBE. And at the same time it does not let the graphics library that came with the compiler be used. In other words, if the monitor is not VBE compatible, you are stuck. But it would be possible to add support for VGA monitors. By doing this, if a monitor is found that does not support the VBE it could still use VGA graphics. This does not make the most of the monitor, but it does allow for graphics on almost any system purchased in the past 10 years.

Another modification is this: The VBE supports modes that use palette registers as well as modes that do not. There are constants for setting the highest resolution mode, or the highest number of colors, but these do not necessarily specify a direct color or palette mode. If you use HIRESMODE you will probably get a palette mode, and if you use HICOLORMODE you might get a 24-bit mode if the card is newer, or you might get a 16-bit mode on a somewhat older card, or on an even older card you might even get a palette mode. What if only the highest resolution direct mode will do?

Next we come to some exported variables. SVGA_Err holds the last error raised by a function. If a function call returns NOERROR, that will also be stored in this variable. SVGA_CurrentMode holds the constant for the mode that the monitor is currently set to. SVGA_DirectCMode is set to TRUE if the current mode is a direct color mode, or FALSE if not. This variable should be referenced before calling either set color function so you know which to use. If the direct color routine version is called when a palette mode is set the function will return an error and vice versa. SVGA_MaxX and SVGA_MaxY give the number of pixels on the screen.

SVGA_supported( )

Now we come to the actual functions. SVGA_Supported( ) returns VBESUPPORTED if the system has a monitor that supports the VESA VBE. This function also sets up the internal VGAInfoBlock structure, so it MUST be called first before calling any other SVGALib functions. Most functions will return NOTINITIALED if this function has not been called.

```
char SVGA_supported ();
  /*
   * detects if VESA VBE is supported, and
   * fills in important data structures if
   * it is.  Returns VBESUPPORTED if VESA
   * VBE is supported, or VBENOTSUPPORTED
   * otherwise.
   *
   * The routines in this library make use
   * of VBE defined BIOS services.  If they
   * are not supported these routines will
   * not work.
```

```
*
* ALWAYS CALL THIS ROUTINE BEFORE ANY
*   OTHERS IN THIS PACKAGE ARE CALLED!
*/
```

SVGA_set_mode( )

SVGA_set_mode( ) sets the monitor to a selected mode. The available modes are given in Table 9.2.2. This function must also be called before any graphics can be done, but after the call to SVGA_supported is made. Here is the prototype.

```
char SVGA_set_mode (int mode);
  /*
   * Sets the mode to one listed above.
   *
   * Parameter:
   *   mode - Mode to set the monitor to.  Use
   *     the modes #defined above.  If
   *     HIRESMODES is used the mode the
   *     highest resolution is set, if
   *     HICOLORMODE is used the mode
   *     with the most number of colors is
   *     used.
   *
   * Returns:
   *   The number of the mode set if no error,
   *   otherwise NOTINITIALED, if
   *   SVGA_supported has not been called,
   *   VBENOTSUPPORTED if the system has a
   *   monitor that does not support the VESA
   *   VBE, or MODENOTSUPPORTED if a mode has
   *   been listed that is not currently
   *   available.
   *
   *   If the return value is positive then no
   *   error occurred.
   */
```

If the HIRESMODE or HICOLORMODE constants were used you might not know if the monitor is in a direct color mode or a palette mode. The global variable SVGA_DirectCMode will be TRUE if the current mode is a direct color mode, FALSE otherwise. This is important to know since there are two different routines for setting the color, one for direct color modes, the other for palette modes. The global variable SVGA_CurrentMode holds the number of the current mode. This information is less important since the color setting routines work consistently for all color modes. The SVGA_MaxX and SVGA_MaxY will give the resolution of the screen.

SVGA_set_dc_color( )

The SVGA_set_dc_color( ) function is used to set the current drawing mode in direct color modes. This function takes as parameters 3 unsigned characters, one for each color gun. These 3 bytes should be set up the same way for 15- and 16-bit color modes as they are for 24-bit color modes. For example, if you want white in a 24-bit color mode you would use red = 0xFF, green = 0xFF, and blue = 0xFF. With these library functions, use the same values for white for all direct color modes. If a mode that is not 24 bits is used the values will be truncated so that the correct number of bits are used. This makes it easier to write programs that might run on any system. The trade-off is that on a 15 bit color system the color with the settings red=0x1D, green=0x83, blue=0xFF will look the same as the color red=0x1F, green=0x80, blue=0xFB. But these colors are very close anyway. It is easier to ignore the slight difference than it is to figure out if 0xFF, 0xFF, 0xFF makes white, or is it 0x1F, 0x1F, 0x1F (white on a 15-bit mode), or maybe 0x1F, 0x3F, 0x1F (white on a 16-bit system). Here is the prototype for SVGA_set_dc_color( ).

```
char SVGA_set_dc_color (unsigned char red,
                        unsigned char green,
                        unsigned char blue);
  /*
   * Set the color for direct color SVGA
   * routines.  This allows the user to be
   * unconcerned what order the color mask uses
   * (RGB, RBG, GRB, GBR, BGR, BRG), or how
   * many bits per pixel.
   *
   * Parameters:
   *   The RGB values for the current color.
   *   For 15 and 16 bit modes the MOST
   *   significant bits are used.
   *
   * Returns:
   *   NOERROR if no error, NOTINITIALED if
   *   mode is not set, NOTDIRECTCMODE if the
   *   current mode is not a direct color mode.
   */
```

SVGA_set_color( )

The SVGA_set_color( ) function sets the current drawing color for palette modes. What this function actually does is set the palette number that will be used. To get the color you really want, you need to set the palette register using SVGA_set_palette( ), which will be described next. For an in-depth description of palette registers see Chapter 6. Here is the prototype for SVGA_set_color( ).

```
char SVGA_set_color (unsigned char palettenum);
  /*
   * sets the current drawing color to
   * a palette.
   *
   * Parameter
   *   The palette number of the current
   *   drawing color
   *
   * Returns
   *   NOERROR if successful, NOTINITIALED if
   *   not mode is set, DIRECTCMODE if the
   *   current mode is a direct color mode.
   */
```

SVGA_set_palette( )

SVGA_set_palette is straightforward. It takes as parameters the number of the palette to set, and the RGB values to set it to. The color resolution, that is the number of bits per color, is 5, which is the same as for VGA mode 0x13.

```
char SVGA_set_palette (int palettenum,
                       unsigned char red,
                       unsigned char green,
                       unsigned char blue);
  /*
   * set a palette to represent a certain color
   *
   * Parameters:
   *   palettenum - The number of the palette
   *     to set
   *   red, green, blue - the amount of each
   *     color to set.
   */
```

SVGA_get_dc_color( ), SVGA_get_color( ) and SVGA_get_palette( )

There are two complementary functions for retrieving the current drawing color: SVGA_get_dc_color( ) and SVGA_get_color( ). The direct color routine passes back red, green, and blue values, while the palette mode routine passes back the current palette number. The function SVGA_get_palette( ) can then be called to find the RGB values for the palette. Here are the function prototypes:

```
char SVGA_get_dc_color (unsigned char *Red,
                        unsigned char *Green,
                        unsigned char *Blue);
  /*
   * Passes back RGB values of current drawing
   * color.  These values are always 24 bits
   * for consistancy with SVGA_set_dc_color().
   *
   * Parameters:
   *   Red
   *   Green
   *   Blue  - the RGB values of the current
   *     drawing color.
   *
   * Returns:
   *   NOERROR if no error has occured,
   *   NOTDIRECTCMODE if not a direct color
   *   mode NOTINITIALED if the graphics system
   *   is not initialized, or NOTSUPPORTED if
   *   the VBE is not supported by this
   *   monitor,
   */

char SVGA_get_color
            (unsigned char *P_Palette_Num);
  /*
   * Returns the palette number used for the
   * current drawing color.  For non direct
   * modes only.
   *
   * Parameter
   *   *P_Palette_Num - pointer to unsigned
   *     character the palette number used as
   *     the current color is put here
   *
   * Returns
   *   NOERROR if successful, NOTINITIALED if
   *   not mode is set, DIRECTCMODE if the
```

```
    *   current mode is a direct color mode.
    */


char SVGA_get_palette (int P_Palette_Num,
                       unsigned char *P_Red,
                       unsigned char *P_Green,
                       unsigned char *P_Blue);
  /*
   * Get RGB settings for a palette register
   *
   * Parameters:
   *   P_Palette_Num - Number of palette
   *   *P_Red
   *   *P_Green
   *   *P_Blue  - pointers to unsigned
   *     characters that will hold the RGB
   *     values
   *
   * Returns
   *   NOERROR if no error, NOTINITIALED if
   *   mode is not set, DIRECTCMODE if the
   *   current mode is a direct color mode.
   */
```

SVGA_plot_pixel( )

The next function is SVGA_plot_pixel( ). This function takes the X and Y values, in screen coordinates, and sets that pixel to the current drawing color. The programmer at this point does not have to worry about whether the screen is in a direct color mode or palette mode, nor does he/she have to worry about window details.

```
char SVGA_plot_pixel (int X, int Y);
  /*
   * sets a pixel to the current drawing
   * color.
   *
   * Parameters
   *   The coordinate of the pixel to set
   *
   * RETURNS
   *  NOERROR if successfull, NOTINITIALED
   *  if graphics mode not set.
   */
```

SVGA_return_err_msg( )

The final function we will cover is SVGA_return_err_msg( ). This function simply returns a pointer to a string containing a message appropriate for the current value SVGE_Err.

```
char *SVGA_return_err_msg():
  /*
   * Returns a string explaining the last
   * error raised
   */
```

The suggested method for using the library is to first call SVGA_supported( ) to determine if a suitable card is installed on the system. If the system does not have a card supporting VESA VBE, then the program could exit with an error message, or handle it some other way. Next the SVGA_set_mode( ) function is called to set a mode. The SVGA_DirectCMode global variable is tested to see if the mode uses direct color or uses palette registers. If the mode uses palette registers, a function might be called to set up the palette registers as desired. Then a call to SVGA_set_color( ) or SVGA_set_dc_color( ) would be made to set the current drawing color. After this initial set-up, calls would be made to the various functions in the package to draw images on the screen. When finished a call to SVGA_set_mode( ) with the mode TEXT should be made to return the system to text mode. The following is an example shell.

```
#include "SVGALib.h"

void setup_palettes(void) {

/* Your code here to set palette registers */
/*  as desired                             */

} /* end setup_palettes */

void main (void) {

  if (SVGA_supported() != VBESUPPORTED) {
    printf("%s",SVGA_return_err_msg());
    exit(-1);
  }

  if (SVGA_set_mode(HIRESMODE) != NOERROR) {
    printf("%s",SVGA_return_err_msg());
    exit(-1);
  }
```

```
    if (SVGA_DirectCMode) then
      SVGA_set_dc_color(Some_Red_Val,
                        Some_Green_Val,
                        Some_Blue_Val);
    else {
      setup_palettes();
      SVGA_set_color(Desired_Color);
    }

    /* Graphics stuff goes here */


    SVGA_set_mode(TEXT);
    exit(0);
  } /* end program */
```

Notice that the colors still need to be filled in. Other functions provided by the library, such as line drawing, ellipse drawing and filling routines, are covered in future chapters, as they are developed. The following section discusses the inner workings of these routines, so that they can be modified to suit your needs.

Inside SVGALib

The final section of this chapter covers the internals of SVGALib, hopefully making it understandable enough that the reader can make modifications and corrections him/herself. The code is quite complex, and it would aid greatly to have printouts of SVGALib.H and SVGALib.C. These files are quite large, and if the reader prefers, only the beginning portion need be printed at this time. There are convenient markers in the source code that divide the code into sections. For the rest of this chapter if you print out to the marker that says "END OF FIRST SECTION" you will have what is covered here. On the other hand you could simply call it up on the computer, and follow along there.

Global Variables

VgeInfoBlock and ModeInfoBlock

When one looks inside SVGALib.C the first thing one sees is a VgaInfoBlock called G_SVGA_Info, and then a ModeInfoBlock called G_Mode_Info. You should be familiar with these structures by now, and understand how and why they are used.

Internal Global Variables

Next is a bunch of internal global variables. The first, G_VBE_Supported, is used by various functions to see if the video adapter supports the VBE. When the system is brought up it has a value NOTINITIALED. When the function SVGA_supported( ) is called it will set this function to either VBESUPPORTED or VBENOTSUPPORTED.

The four constants MODE24BITS, MODE16BITS, MODE8BITS, and MODE4BITS are for the number of bits per pixel used by the current mode. The structure SVGA24BitColor, described in the section of this chapter titled **SVGA BIOS Interrupts**, is used to hold RGB information in 24-bit modes. The variable G_24Bit_Color, of this type, is the current drawing color in 24-bit modes. It is initialed to white. G_16Bit_Color is the current drawing color in 15- and 16-bit modes. The three variables G_Red, G_Green, and G_Blue give the color content of the current color for all direct color modes. The function SVGA_set_dc_color( ) sets the current color, although G_24Bit_Color is not used for 15- and 16-bit modes and G_16BitColor is not used for 24-bit modes. Color values passed to SVGA_set_dc_color( ) are always 8 bits each for red, green, and blue. For 15- and 16-bit modes not all bits are used. For these modes only the MOST significant bits are used, which makes dealing with colors more consistent between modes. For 15- and 16-bit color modes only the bits used to actually set the color are saved. This is sometimes annoying, since you might set the current drawing color to red=255, green=255 and blue=255, then find the values are actually set to 252, 253, and 252. Storing only the actual bits used makes other routines easier and more natural to implement, however. If you are writing a routine that has to compare the current color to a pixel that is already on the screen, this method of storing the colors makes things more straightforward.

The next item in SVGALib.C is a variable to hold the current drawing color for 4- and 8-bit modes, G_8BitColor. This actually holds the palette number that is currently being used. This is set by SVGA_set_color( ).

Next is a group of variables for dealing with the current window. Windows, as defined by the VBE, are presented in the section of this chapter titled **SVGA BIOS Interrupts**. G_Win_Size holds the window granularity * 1024, G_Cur_Window holds the number of the current window, and G_Write_Window holds 00 if window A is writeable, or 01 if window A is not writeable and window B is. G_Win_Size and G_Write_Window are set up by SVGA_set_mode( ). G_Cur_Window is set up by set_window( ). It is used by SVGA_plot_pixel, and since it is quite important that this function be as fast as possible it is important for this number to be available. The other way to find this number would be to call an interrupt, which is slower than looking at a variable by quite a bit. This should help you to see why the decision to sacrifice style for the sake of making these values available through global variables was made. G_Win_Size and G_Cur_Window are used by set_window( ), which is often called from SVGA_plot_pixel( ), so it is important that this information can be found as quickly as possible. It is important enough that making the granularity multiplied 1024 available actually makes the floodfill( ) routine run substantially faster than doing the multiply within floodfill( ). The next three variables in this section, G_8Bit_Win_Address, G_16Bit_Win_Address, and G_24Bit_Win_Address, each point to the frame buffer. There is one each for 4/8-bit modes, 15/16-bit modes and 24-bit modes. Having three separate pointers to the same array in memory makes it possible to give three different structures to that array, which makes it easier to handle the different modes. These pointers are also set up by SVGA_set_mode( ).

The next five variables, SVGA_Err, SVGA_CurrentMode, SVGA_DirectCMode, SVGA_MaxX and SVGA_MaxY, are exported, so they were explained in the last section.

SVGALib Functions

set_window( )

The function set_window( ) is meant to be called only by SVGALib functions, and it is not exported. It takes an integer as a parameter and sets the current window to that number. This is done by calling VESA VBE service 0x05.

SVGA_return_err_msg( )

The first exported routine is SVGA_return_err_msg( ). This function is simple and straightforward. SVGA_Err is used by a switch statement to return a string appropriate to the current error.

SVGA_supported( )

Next is the SVGA_supported( ) function. This calls VBE service 0x00 to fill in the VgaInfoBlock G_SVGA_Info. If the call is successful it looks at the VESASignature field of G_SVGA_Info to make sure it is set to "VESA". If it is, the function sets G_VBE_Supported and SVGA_Err to VBESUPPORTED, then returns this value. If either VESASignature is not set to "VESA" or the function call fails, G_VBE_Supported and SVGA_Err are set to VBENOTSUPPORTED, and this value is then returned.

SVGA_set_mode( )

One of the most complex functions in the SVGALib is SVGA_set_mode( ). It is complicated by having a great deal of flexibility. This function is responsible for finding and setting the highest resolution mode or the highest color mode. If the user were made to pick a mode and live with it this function would be simple, but writing portable programs with this package would not. To better deal with all its functionality, SVGA_set_mode( ) has been broken down into a number of subfunctions. The main function will be described first.

SVGA_set_mode( ) first looks to see if text mode is desired. If it is, a separate function is called to set it, since this requires a call to a different graphics service. Next, if the highest resolution mode is desired, a function, called set_hi_res_mode( ), is called to find the mode with the highest resolution. This function is rather misnamed, since it does not set the mode, it only finds the correct mode. If the mode with the most colors is desired, then set_hi_color_mode( ) is called. If instead of those three options a specific mode is requested the function card_supports_mode( ) is called to make sure the card does in fact support the requested mode. If that function returns FALSE, SVGA_Err is set to MODENOTSUPPORTED, and that value is returned as an error code. If card_supports_mode( ) returns TRUE then the function get_mode_info( ) is called. This function calls VBE service 01, which fills in the global variable G_Mode_Info. The ModeAttributes field is then tested to see if the mode is supported. If not the value MODENOTSUPPORTED is returned to SVGA_set_mode( ), which then fills in SVGA_Err and returns this value.

At this point either SVGA_set_mode( ) has returned an error or a mode has been found, one way or another. It then calls service 0x02 to actually set the mode. If that service now returns an error we have no idea what happened, since the card was tested to make sure it supports the mode. The value UNKNOWNERR is put into SVGA_Err, and returned. Otherwise, if all is well, the selected mode is placed into the SVGA_CurrentMode variable, and the function setup_mode_info( ) is called. This function sets up the frame buffer pointers, and other variables. The error value returned by that function is put into SVGA_Err and returned.

Now, on to the subfunctions. These will be covered in the order in which they appear in the source code, which is not necessarily the order they are called in. The function card_supports_mode( ) loops through the array of mode numbers supported, comparing each to the mode number passed in. If a match is found TRUE is returned; if the entire array is traversed without a match being found, FALSE is returned.

Next is get_mode_info( ). This function calls service 01 to fill in G_Mode_Info. The details of this structure, what is in it, and how it is used, were described previously.

The function setup_mode_info( ) takes useful information in G_Mode_Info and puts it into global variables where it is easily accessed. G_BitsColor is set to the number of bits per pixel. The frame buffer pointers are pointed to the proper frame buffer (window A or window B), and G_Write_Window is set to 00 or 01 as appropriate. This global variable is used by set_window( ), so it must be initialized before any window can be set. The current drawing window is now initialized to window 0. SVGA_DirectCMode is set to TRUE or FALSE as appropriate, and finally SVGA_MaxX and SVGA_MaxY are set to the proper values. The processing here looks ugly, but there really is not a good elegant way to do this. If a direct color mode is being set the current drawing color is set to white. This is done here since direct color modes need mode dependent information to properly set the colors. If a nondirect color mode is used the current drawing color is initialized to white when the program is loaded.

The next function is set_text_mode( ), which simply calls interrupt 0x10, service 0x00 to set the mode to 0x03, 25 rows by 80 characters text. A more sophisticated package would determine the mode when the graphics system is initialized, then restore that mode, rather than always setting mode 0x03. This can be annoying to those who set their screen to 43 rows, or to those who call your program from another graphics program. This change can be made by calling VBE service 0x03 in SVGA_supported( ), and saving the returned mode (see Appendix E for details on VBE service 0x03). Then the set_text_mode( ) function can be replaced with one that returns the mode to the one saved. When setting the mode, remember that if the mode is not one defined by the VBE use interrupt 0x10, service 0x00 (see Appendix D for this service).

The function set_hi_color_mode( ) passes back the number of the mode with the most colors supported by the card. This function does not actually set the mode. While the code is quite ugly, the idea is pretty simple. If you look carefully at the mode numbers of the direct color modes, you will notice that every third mode has the same number of bits color resolution. So first there is a loop to look at the 24-bit modes, starting from the highest resolution. Then there is a loop for 16-bit modes, then 15-bit modes. If no direct color mode is found, then the palette modes are looked at individually. Each of the above loops is pretty much the same. For each value the function card_supports_mode( ) is called. This function looks at the array of supported functions in G_SVGA_Info, and so is fairly fast. If the mode is found in that list, get_mode_info( ) is called to determine if the mode is currently available. This function calls service 0x01. If a supported mode is found the parameter P_Mode is set.

Function set_hi_res_mode( ) is similar to set_hi_color_mode( ). It looks at all the 1280 × 1024 modes, then the 1024 × 768 modes, on down to 640 × 480. It is assumed that a 640 × 480 palette mode will be found before a 320 × 200 direct color mode is, so the function stops there.

SVGA_get_mode( )

SVGA_get_mode( ) is quite simple. If the monitor has been set to a mode it passes back the mode number that was saved in G_CurrentMode. If the return value is negative then an error is raised.

SVGA_set_dc_color( )

SVGA_set_dc_color( ) is rather complex. It has already been described that the RGB values passed in should always be 8 bits, no matter what mode is being used. This simplifies the programmer's task when writing portable code. He/she might not know what modes will be available when the program runs. This function is responsible for taking the MOST significant bits. This makes different modes act more consistently. The program does not need to worry about details of setting different numbers of bits for different monitors. This can be accomplished by taking the number of bits in the RGB values, and subtracting the mask size for that color. The values are passed in as unsigned characters, which are 8 bits each. The lines

```
l_red   = P_Red   >> (8-G_Mode_Info.RedMaskSize);
l_green = P_Green >> (8-G_Mode_Info.GreenMaskSize);
l_blue  = P_Blue  >> (8-G_Mode_Info.BlueMaskSize);
```

truncate the unused bits. This same code works for 24-, 16-, and 15-bit modes. Next we have to put the RGB values into a holder or variable that makes it convenient to copy to the proper location in the frame buffer. It would be nice if code could be found to do this that does not depend on the number of bits or the order of the colors (some cards DO NOT use red first then green then blue last). Unfortunately the difference between 24 bits and 15 or 16 bits is rather too large to be able to reuse the same code with utmost efficiency and readability, so the code here is broken into two parts – for 15/16 bits and for 24 bits. The code for 15/16 bits is simpler so it will be covered first. The Field Position fields in the ModeInfoBlock structure are set up so that the color value can be shifted by the number in that field, to give the appropriate position in the bit field. Figure 9.3.1 shows this graphically. The lines of code given above will zero out all the bits not used by the particular color gun, so after performing the second shift, the three resulting values can simply be added for the final result. (A bitwise OR will work also.)

```
G_16Bit_Color =
      (l_red    << G_Mode_Info.RedFieldPosition) +
      (l_green << G_Mode_Info.GreenFieldPosition) +
      (l_blue << G_Mode_Info.BlueFieldPosition);
```

G_16Bit_Color holds the color for 15- or 16-bit color modes.

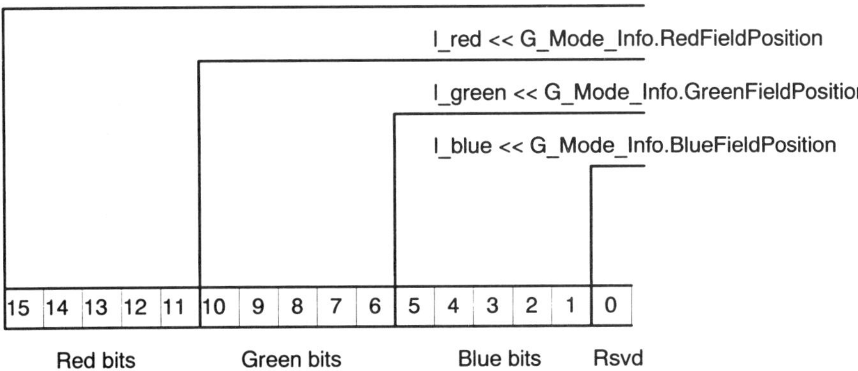

Fig. 9.3.1 Bits Shifted into Position on a 15-Bit Color Mode

Twenty-four-bit modes need a little more work. Unfortunately, there is no type that you can perform shift operations on that are 24 bits. Recall that a structure has been set up to handle 24-bit color modes, which is 24 bits wide. The compiler will not allow shift operations to be done on these. An easy way around this is create a union with that structure and a long integer.

```
union {
  struct SVGA24BitColor ActualColor;
  unsigned long         Holder;
} l_24bits;
```

All the fields in a union exist in the same memory space. This can be dangerous, not to mention difficult to read, and these should be used sparingly and only when really needed. Shift operations can be performed on the Holder field, and whatever happens to the bits in that field also happens to the bits in the ActualColor field, since they are the same bits. Of course the Holder field is 8 bits longer than the ActualColor field, so an extra shift needs to be done to the result to make this line up properly.

```
l_24bits.Holder =
    ((long)l_red   << G_Mode_Info.RedFieldPosition) +
    ((long)l_green << G_Mode_Info.GreenFieldPosition) +
    ((long)l_blue  << G_Mode_Info.BlueFieldPosition);
l_24bits.Holder = l_24bits.Holder << 8;
G_24Bit_Color   = l_24bits.ActualColor;
```

The final lines in this function save the truncate color values in global variables. The reason for saving truncated values is to make comparison to a pixel on the screen easier down the line. This might make certain tasks harder for the programmer, but these trade-offs sometimes must be made.

SVGA_get_dc_color( )

SVGA_get_dc_color( ) simply passes back the truncated color values saved by SVGA_set_dc_color( ).

SVGA_set_color( ) and SVGA_get_color( )

SVGA_set_color( ) will save the 8-bit value passed in. If a 4-bit mode is used the upper 4 bits are ignored. This number designates the palette number holding the color values to be used by SVGA_plot_pixel( ). For a complete discussion of palettes see Chapter 6. To set the RGB values of a palette, use SVGA_set_palette( ). This function uses interrupt 0x10, service 0x10, subservice 0x10, which is described in Chapter 8, to set the palette. This function simply uses the RGB values passed in with no massaging or filtering. It is the programmer's responsibility to make sure these are correct.

SVGA_get_color( ) will returns the current 4/8-bit drawing color, which is actually the number of a palette. SVGA_get_palette( ) uses interrupt 0x10, service 0x10, subservice 0x15 to get the current settings of the palette number passed in. See Appendix D for complete information on this service.

SVGA_plot_pixel( )

The final function we will cover in this chapter is SVGA_plot_pixel( ). First this function will test to make sure the pixel is on the screen, returning an error if not.

This check takes a little time, and can slow things down if large numbers of pixels are being plotted, but it can save a program from bombing out if an attempt is made to plot a pixel to executable code in RAM. Next is a switch statement that switches on the number of bits being used. Each branch is essentially the same, except for the 24-bit mode branch. The current window is tested to see if this is where the pixel will be plotted, and if not a new current window is set. The offset into the window is then found, and the frame buffer is updated. The 24-bit mode code uses code that is essentially the same, but the operates differently to account for problems discussed under the **plotting pixels** section of this chapter.

10

Creating Your Own Graphics Primitives

This chapter covers how graphics primitives work, so that you can write your own and modify those in SVGALib. All graphics primitives have certain characteristics in common. The all must work quickly and consistently. By consistent we mean that a line must always start at one of the given endpoints and stop at the other, be straight, and uniform in thickness. A circle must be round, with the correct radius. As with most things there are obvious ways of accomplishing the task, and more complex ways. When it comes to graphics the more complex methods often accomplish amazing results, being many times faster than the more obvious methods.

The trick is that the obvious methods rely on floating point math, while methods can be devised that use only integer math. Most of these methods owe their existence to a fellow named Bresenham, who, back in the 1960s, devised a method to derive integer-based graphics algorithms. These are not simple, but they are very efficient and are the most generally used algorithms for these primitives. It is not necessary to understand them to use SVGALib, but it is in order to make changes and correct bugs. It is also quite difficult to pass yourself off as a graphics programmer at a job interview if you don't have a least a passing acquaintance with these algorithms.

Drawing Lines

The Obvious Method

The screen is set up as a Cartesian coordinate system, so it sounds like drawing lines should be easy. The problem is that when drawing lines we often have to deal with fractions. If we build a function around the formula for a line:

$$y = {}^{\Delta y}\!/_{\Delta x}\, x + b$$

We need to do a divide, which results in fractional (floating point) numbers, which gives a slow algorithm. Bresenham's line drawing algorithm is much faster.

But before launching in on Bresenham's method it is instructive to look at the obvious line drawing function based on this formula. If we are given a starting X and Y value, we increment X, then multiply by Delta Y divided by Delta X, to get Y. Keep doing this until the endpoint is reached.

There are two things to notice. The first is that *b*, the *y* intercept, is not really used. Since we are given a starting point on the line, one of the endpoints, we do not need this information. We start at one end point and find other points on the line from there, using only the slope. The second thing to notice is that according to the algorithm above we are doing a divide inside the loop. But it should be pretty obvious that $\Delta y/\Delta x$ remains constant throughout the execution of the loop. So this can be brought outside the loop and only executed once. This leaves the following (pseudo)code:

```
void simple_line (int X1, int Y1,
                  int X2, int Y2) {
  float m = (Y2-Y1)/(X2-X1);
  int   i;

  for (i=X1; i<=X2; i++)
```

```
    plot_pixel(X1+i,(m*(X1+i))+Y1);
}
```

There, nice and simple. And it almost works. One problem is that if the line has an undefined[1] slope (x = a constant value c), then Δx is 0, causing the program to die with a divide by 0 error. This simply means we have to check for special cases. Another special case is if the line is horizontal (y = a constant value c), but this does not cause any real problems.

What does cause a problem is if the slope is greater than one. If we continue to increment X and solve for Y as the slope gets steeper, the Y's become farther apart than one pixel (Fig. 10.1.1).

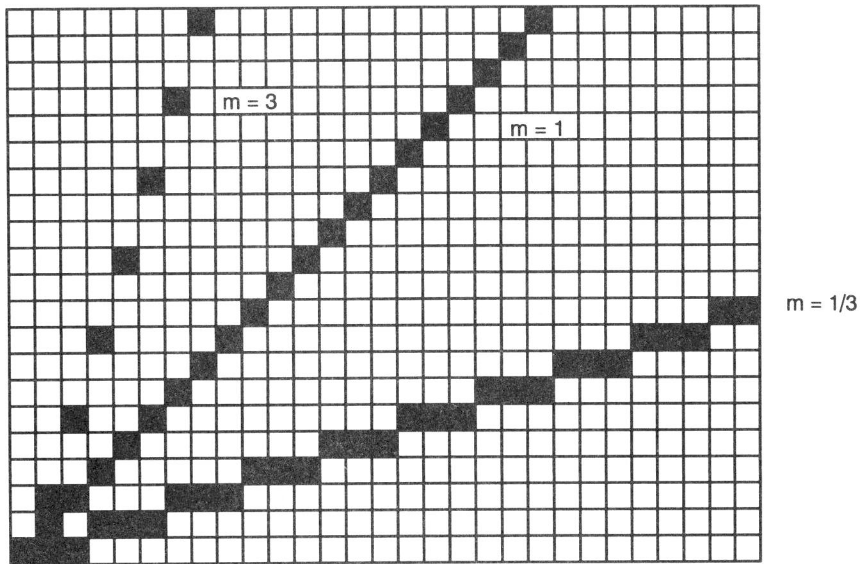

Fig. 10.1.1 As Slope Gets Steeper the *Y* Values Get Farther Apart

This problem arises because we increment X by 1 and the slope is greater than 1. If the slope were 3, for example, every time we increment X by 1, Y goes up by 3, leaving a 2 pixel gap between the first and the second pixels. If we increment by a smaller value the pixels will move closer together again. But what value should we

[1] Some people refer to this as an infinite slope. I prefer *undefined* because that term seems to prevent arguments with calculus professers. Here and there I refer to a slope as negative undefined. This of course means $-\infty$.

use? As the slope gets steeper the increment value gets smaller and smaller. We could figure out an increment value dependent on *X*, but a more efficient way is to check for a slope greater than 1 and if it is increment *Y* and solve for *X*. The formula for finding *X* from *Y* can easily be derived from the normal line formula.

$$X = \frac{Y - b}{m}$$

Here again, *b* can be ignored, since we are given a starting point. Here, then is the algorithm developed from the line equation.

```
void simple_line(int X1, int Y1,
                 int X2, int Y2) {

  float m;
  int   i;

  if ((X1-X2)==0)
    for (i=Y1; i<=Y2; i++)
      plot_pixel(X1, i);
  else if ((Y1-Y2)==0)
    for (i=X1; i<=X2; i++)
      plot_pixel(i, Y1);
  else if (abs(Y2-Y1)>abs(X2-X1)) {
    m=((Y2-Y1)/(X2-X1);
    for (i=Y1; i<=Y2; i++)
      plot_pixel((i+X1)/m, Y1+i);
  else
    m=((Y2-Y1)/(X2-X1);
    for (i=X1; i<=X2; i++)
      plot_pixel(X1+i,(m*(X1+i))+Y1);

} /* end simple_line() */
```

Before this algorithm will work, code needs to be added to make sure the start and end conditions are in the correct order. Once this is done you will have a working line function, but in many cases it will prove too slow to be useful. The problem is the floating point variable *m*. This will work well on machines equipped with a floating point processor, but on those without, this routine is a real dog. It is not used in general graphics programming, is not used by SVGALib, and is only presented here to show some of the problems involved with drawing a line.

Bresenham's Method

Bresenham's method of drawing lines involves some clever tricks to eliminate the floating point math. The first trick is to divide lines into categories by slope, either positive, negative, zero, or undefined (vertical). Zero and undefined slopes are handled the same as they are in the function given above. The neat thing about the other slopes is that by knowing if the slope is positive or negative you can narrow down the possible choices of the next point to 3 (Fig. 10.1.2).

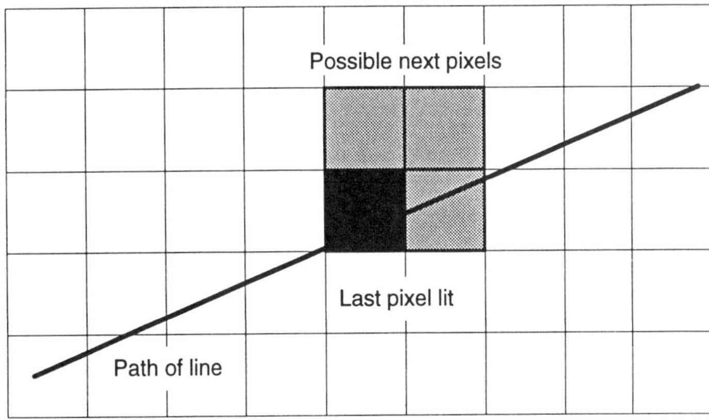

Fig. 10.1.2 Choice of 3 for the Next Point

In fact, if you further group the slopes into those with an absolute value greater that one or less than one, you can narrow down the choices to two points (Fig. 10.1.3).

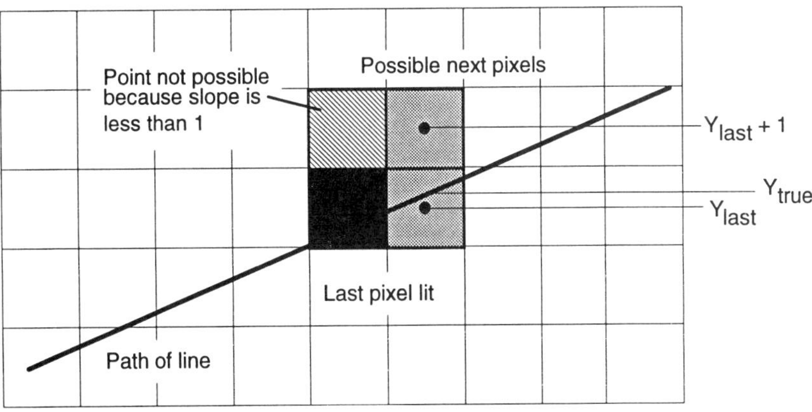

Fig. 10.1.3 Choice of 2 for the Next Point

Now how do we decide which of the two points? This is a little tricky, so follow carefully. First, start with the equation for a line.

$$y = mx + b = \frac{\Delta y}{\Delta x}x + b$$

Now we want to find which of the two possible points lies closer to the actual line defined by the equation. We know the x and y values of the point just plotted. To make things easier we will call this point the current point, and the next point to be plotted the next point. The x coordinate the next point is $x_{current}+1$. The y value will be either $y_{current}$ or $y_{current}+1$. The formula

$$y_{next} = m(x+1) + b$$

gives the true y value of the next point. Now we have to compare this to $y_{current}$ and $y_{current}+1$. The one that it is closer to is the y value of the point to be plotted. Two variables, d_1 and d_2, are created, d_1 being the distance from $y_{current}$ to y_{next}, and d_2 being the distance from $y_{current} + 1$ to y_{next}. It will be useful down the road to have the formulae for these distances written out. The distance from $y_{current}$ to y_{next} is

$$d_1 = y_{next} - y_{current} = m(x+1) + b - y_{current}$$

The distance from $y_{current}+1$ to y_{next} is

$$d_2 = (y_{current} + 1) - y_{next} = y_{current} + 1 - (m(x+1) + b)$$

Now we have two distances. A convenient way to compare them is to subtract the second from the first. If the result is positive the second distance is smaller, and the second point is the one to use. If the result is negative the first distance is smaller, and the first point is the one to use. A parameter p is defined to hold this value.

$$p = d_1 - d_2 = (m(x+1) + b - y_{current}) - (y_{current} + 1 - (m(x+1) + b))$$

Reducing this equation and replacing m with $\Delta y/\Delta x$ gives

$$p = 2\frac{\Delta y(x+1)}{\Delta x} + 2b - 2Y_{current} - 1$$

We're in the home stretch now. All we need is one final piece of magic to get rid of the fraction. If you followed everything to this point you know that we only care if p is positive or negative, and we don't care about p's actual value. If we are careful to arrange our endpoints so Δx is positive, then multiplying p by Δx will not change its sign. When we multiply both sides, the fraction falls out.

$$\Delta xp = 2\Delta y(x+1) + \Delta x(2b - 2y_{\text{current}} - 1)$$

This can be further simplified by incorporating Δx into p, in other words, $p = \Delta xp$. Again, this can be done because we only care about the sign of p, not about its value. Another simplification is to drop the constants $2b$ and -1. These are multiplied by Δx, but since Δx is constant for the entire line, these values are still constant. They can be ignored for the same reason b could be ignored in the simple line function. Because, at the start we are given an actual point, the y intercept is extra information. Here is the simplified formula.

$$p = 2\Delta y(x+1) - 2\Delta x \cdot y_{\text{current}}$$

In the code itself we will need to be able to find the next p (p_{next}) from p_{current}. This is done by relating p_{next} to p_{current}. Then p_{next} is found with the following formula.

$$p_{\text{next}} = 2\Delta y(x+2) - 2\Delta x \cdot y_{\text{next}}$$

Make a note that y_{next} is either y_{current} or $y_{\text{current}}+1$. We will see what this means to the algorithm in a little bit. Now to relate p_{next} to p_{current} we subtract the formula of one from the formula of the other.

$$p_{\text{next}} - p_{\text{current}} = 2\Delta y((x+2) - (x+1)) - 2\Delta x(y_{\text{next}} - y_{\text{current}})$$

which simplifies to

$$p_{\text{next}} = p_{\text{current}} + 2\Delta y - 2\Delta x(y_{\text{next}} - y_{\text{current}})$$

Now, given one p, we can find the next p. Because y_{next} is either y_{current} or $y_{\text{current}} + 1$, so the term $y_{\text{next}} - y_{\text{current}}$ either evaluates to 1 or 0. In the one case the last portion of the expression evaluates to $-2\Delta x$, in the other case it evaluates to 0. Now both multiplies are constant values that can be found BEFORE the loop. This makes for a very efficient algorithm. The parameter p needs to be initialized.

Use $p_{\text{first}} = 2\Delta y - \Delta x$, which is found by plugging x_1 and y_1 into the first formula for *p*, above.

Lots of math. Now we need to turn it into an algorithm. First of all arrange the points so that the lower *x* value is the one where the algorithm starts. Then find Delta_X and Delta_Y. Initialize p to 2*Delta_Y - Delta_X, plot the first pixel, then start the loop. We will be incrementing X1, so comparing it to X2 is a good end condition. When X1 = X2 the entire line is drawn. Inside the loop there is an if statement testing to see if p is greater than zero. The value of p being greater than 0 means that the next Y is one higher than this Y, so increment Y, then set p equal to p+Delta_Y × 2 - Delta_X × 2. It is good to figure these numbers before the loop. We will use _2_Delta_X and _2_Delta_Y for these values. If p is not greater than 0 then the next *y* is the same as the current *y*. Y1 is not incremented and p is set to p + _2_Delta_Y. Now the next point is plotted, X1 is incremented, and the loop ends. It would be good to compare this algorithm to the formulae above to see where each step comes from. For those who prefer to look at code rather than English or math, here it is.

```
void bresenhams_line (int X1, int Y1,
                      int X2, int Y2) {
/*
 * First cut - only handles slope of 0<m<=1
 */

  int temp;
  int p,      Delta_X,     Delta_Y,
           _2_Delta_X, _2_Delta_Y;

  if (X1>X2) {
    temp = X2;
    X2   = X1;
    X1   = temp;

    temp = Y2;
    Y2   = Y1;
    Y1   = temp;
  }

  Delta_X = X2-X1;
  Delta_Y = Y2-Y1;

  _2_Delta_X = 2*Delta_X;
  _2_Delta_Y = 2*Delta_Y;

  plot_pixel (X1, Y1);
```

```
    p=(_2_Delta_Y)-Delta_X;
    X1++;

    while (X1 < X2) {
      if (p>0) {
        p = p + _2_Delta_Y - _2_Delta_X;
        Y1++;
      }
      else {
        p= p+ _2_Delta_Y;
      }
      plot_pixel (X1, Y1);
      X1++;
    }
}
```

The comment at the top of the function points out that this version only handles slopes of $0<m<=1$. Remember that we also had this problem with the simple line algorithm. With Bresenham's method we've restricted the slope so that we narrowed the choice of pixels to 2 at each step. To make the method work for all cases, we need to divide things into a number of cases (Fig. 10.1.4).

To handle slopes greater than one it is necessary to rederive p. To start with, we will be incrementing y, so we need a formula to find x from y.

$$x = \frac{y-b}{m} = \frac{\Delta x(y-b)}{\Delta y}$$

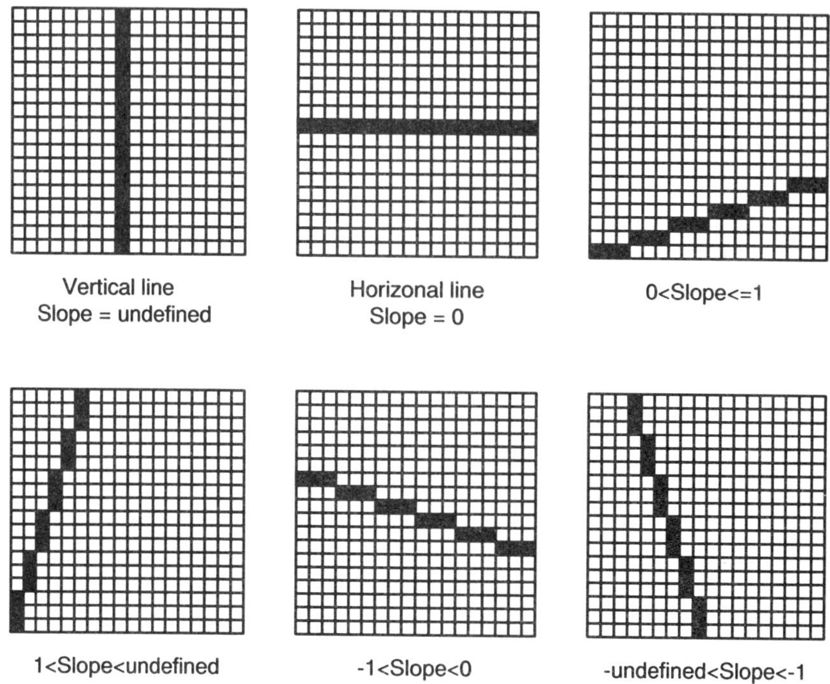

Fig. 10.1.4 Cases for Bresenham's Line Algorithm

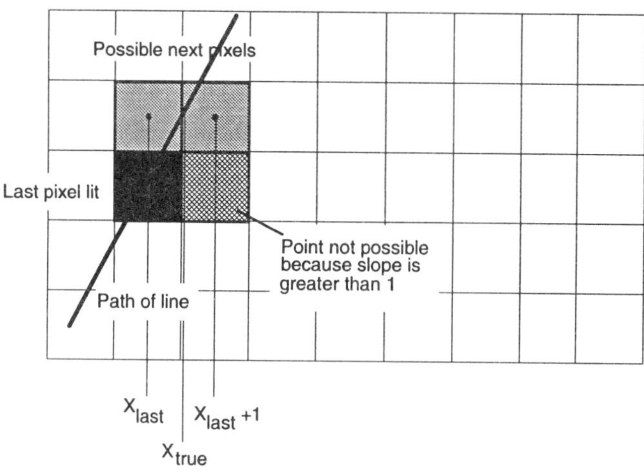

Fig. 10.1.5 Possible Pixel Choices for Line with Slope > 1

Figure 10.1.5 shows the situation when the slope is greater than one. We are stepping by y and we have a choice between two possible x values for the next point. So we proceed as before, first finding the distance from each possible x to the true x.

$$d_1 = x_{\text{true}} - x_{\text{last}} = \frac{y-b}{m} - x_{\text{last}}$$

$$d_2 = (x_{\text{last}} + 1) - x_{\text{true}} = (x_{\text{last}} + 1) - \frac{y-b}{m}$$

Now we subtract the two distances to get a distance parameter p. This works the same as before, if d_1 is smaller then p is negative, meaning x_{current} should be used.

$$p = d_1 - d_2 = x_{\text{true}} - x_{\text{last}} = \frac{y-b}{m} - x_{\text{last}} - \left[(x_{\text{last}} + 1) - \frac{y-b}{m}\right]$$

$$= 2\left(\frac{y-b}{m}\right) - 2x_{\text{last}} - 1$$

Here again we only care about the sign of p, not its value, so we can multiply both sides by a positive value without changing its meaning.

$$p = \Delta y(d_1 - d_2) = 2\Delta x\left(y-b\right) - 2\Delta y \cdot x_{\text{last}} - \Delta y$$

$$= 2\Delta x \cdot y - 2\Delta x \cdot b - 2\Delta y \cdot x_{\text{last}} - \Delta y$$

And as before, we can drop the constant values to simplify the expression.

$$p = 2\Delta x \cdot y - 2\Delta y \cdot x_{\text{last}}$$

Now we relate p_{next} to p_{current}, so that p_{next} can be found quickly and easily.

$$p_{\text{next}} - p_{\text{current}} = 2\Delta x(y+1) - 2\Delta y \cdot x_{\text{current}} - \left[2\Delta x \cdot y - 2\Delta y \cdot x_{\text{last}}\right]$$

Add the formula for p_{current} to both sides, and we get

$$p_{\text{next}} = p_{\text{current}} + 2\Delta x \cdot y - 2\Delta y(x_{\text{current}} - x_{\text{last}})$$

The last term, $x_{current} - x_{last}$, will either evaluate to 0 or 1, which causes the last expression to drop out or be equal to $2\Delta y$. All that is left is to initialize p. Use $p = 2\Delta y + \Delta x$.

The previous derivation had a description of how all this is turned into C code. By using the above formulas for p with that same description you get the following code.

```
void slope_gt_one (int X1, int Y1,
                   int X2, int Y2) {
/*
 * bresenham's line method
 * for slope of m>1
 */

  int temp;
  int p,    Delta_X,     Delta_Y,
      _2_Delta_X, _2_Delta_Y;

  if (Y1>Y2) {
    temp = X2;
    X2   = X1;
    X1   = temp;

    temp = Y2;
    Y2   = Y1;
    Y1   = temp;
  } /* end if */

  Delta_X = X2-X1;
  Delta_Y = Y2-Y1;

  _2_Delta_X = 2*Delta_X;
  _2_Delta_Y = 2*Delta_Y;

  plot_pixel (X1, Y1);
  p=_2_Delta_X-Delta_Y;
  Y1++;

  while (Y1 < Y2) {
    if (p>0) {
      p=p+(_2_Delta_X-_2_Delta_Y);
      X1++;
    } /* end if */
    else {
      p=p+_2_Delta_X;
    } /* end else */
```

```
      plot_pixel (X1, Y1);
      Y1++;
    } /* end while */
  } /* end slope_gt_one */
```

Two cases have been presented here, to give a feel for the derivation. The other two cases are in SVGALib.C on the distribution disk. Search for slope_0_to_one. The function you find is for the case $0<m<1$. The other line drawing functions for other slopes follow this function and are named appropriately. The function that you call to draw lines is called SVGA_line( ).

The code in SVGALib has one more (simple) trick to it. It would be useful to be able to draw patterned lines – dotted lines, dashed lines, etc. Borland and Microsoft graphics packages have this ability, and so does SVGALib. This is done by using a bit mask, called G_Bit_Mask, which is an unsigned integer. This bit mask is ANDed with an unsigned int, G_CurBit, with only one bit set. If the result is not 0 a pixel is plotted. G_CurBit is then shifted one bit to the left. If the set bit is shifted out G_CurBit is reset to 0x8000. Note: Borland supplies a function, rot( ), for the binary rotation operation, but it does not seem to work correctly. It seems to shift, rather than rotate.

A very simple function is provided for setting the line pattern bit mask.

```
  void SVGA_line_pattern
                    (unsigned int P_Bit_Mask) {
    G_BitMask = P_Bit_Mask;
  } /* end SVGA_line_pattern */
```

There are a number of useful routines that make use of the line function. One is for drawing polygons. This uses an unsized array to hold points. Either the array can be ended with a value that is not a possible pixel location, such as -1, or the number of points can be passed to the function as a parameter. Both Borland and Microsoft use this second technique, so we will also. This function groups each two integers in the array into a point, and loops through the points, drawing lines from one point to the next. After exiting the loop, it closes the polygon automatically by drawing a line from the last point to the first. Borland's polygon routine does not do this, but programs that use Borland's will work with this routine anyway. Microsoft's version does close the polygon.

```
void SVGA_polygon (int P_Num_Pts,
                   int *P_Pt_Array) {
  int i;

  P_Num_Pts *= 2;
  for (i=0; i<P_Num_Pts-2; i+=2) {
    SVGA_line(P_Pt_Array[i],
              P_Pt_Array[i+1],
              P_Pt_Array[i+2],
              P_Pt_Array[i+3]);
  }

  SVGA_line(P_Pt_Array[P_Num_Pts-2],
            P_Pt_Array[P_Num_Pts-1],
            P_Pt_Array[0],
            P_Pt_Array[1]);
} /* end SVGA_polygon */
```

Another useful routine is one equivalent to Borland's lineto( ). SVGALib uses two global variables, G_Cur_X and G_Cur_Y, to hold the current screen location. The function SVGA_set_loc_abs( ) will set these variables to absolute screen coordinates, SVGA_set_loc_rel( ) will set them to a location relative to the current location. SVGA_line_to_abs( ) and SVGA_line_to_rel( ) draw lines from the current location to the location passed in, in absolute and relative coordinates, respectively. The code for these routines is quite trivial, so it is not presented here. If you wish to review it, look at SVGALIB.C.

Drawing Circles

Bresenham's method can also be applied to circles. But before presenting it, there is a trick that simplifies circles. Figure 10.2.1 shows that circles have a symmetry that allows us to reflect one point to eight different parts of the circumference of a circle. This means we need to plot only one-eighth of the circle, and the rest can be plotted by reflection.

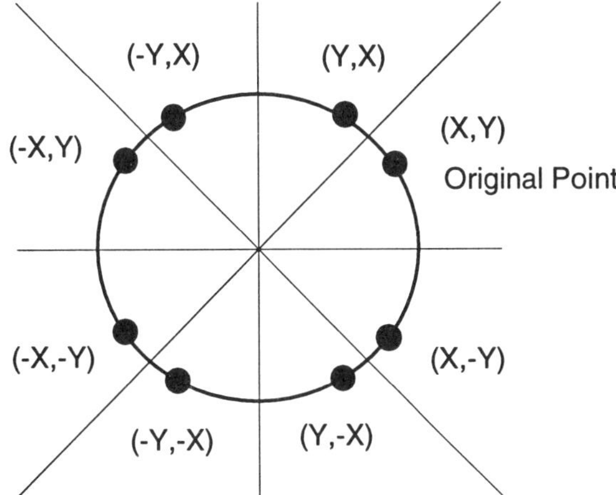

Fig. 10.2.1 Eight-Way Symmetry of a Circle

Figure 10.2.1 shows that given a point (X,Y) on the circumference of a circle the point (-X, Y) is also on the circle, and so is (X, -Y), as well as (-X, -Y). This is fourfold symmetry. The eightfold symmetry comes by reversing X and Y. We can do this because a circle is round. So if (X,Y) is on the circle so is (Y, X), (-Y,X), (Y, -X) and (-Y,-X). Most of the time the circle will not be on the origin, but we can add and subtract X and Y from the center coordinates for the same effect when it is not. This gives rise to the following function.

```
void circle_plot (int X, int X_center, int Y,
                  int Y_center, char Palette) {

    SVGA_plot_pixel (X_center+X,Y_center+Y);
    SVGA_plot_pixel (X_center-X,Y_center+Y);
    SVGA_plot_pixel (X_center+X,Y_center-Y);
    SVGA_plot_pixel (X_center-X,Y_center-Y);
    SVGA_plot_pixel (X_center+Y,Y_center+X);
    SVGA_plot_pixel (X_center-Y,Y_center+X);
    SVGA_plot_pixel (X_center+Y,Y_center-X);
    SVGA_plot_pixel (X_center-Y,Y_center-X);
} /* end circle_plot() */
```

Now all we have to do is find the points for one-eighth of the circle. This also eliminates the slope problem we had with lines. If we start drawing the circle at the right-hand position on the X axis (0°) and draw up, we must increment Y and determine what the new X coordinate is. When we reach 45 degrees we need to reverse our method, incrementing X and finding Y. But if we use the above pixel plotting function, we will find that the points in this section are already filled in. This saves us a derivation and makes the circle code quite clean and compact. The slope problem will reappear with ellipse, which only possess a 4-way symmetry. When we draw an ellipse, when the 45-degree point is reached we need to switch from incrementing Y to incrementing X.

The math for drawing circles is quite similar to that for drawing lines. We start with a point on the arc of the circle. Since we are only finding points in the first eighth of the circle we can narrow the choice of the next point to two possibilities (Fig. 10.2.2).

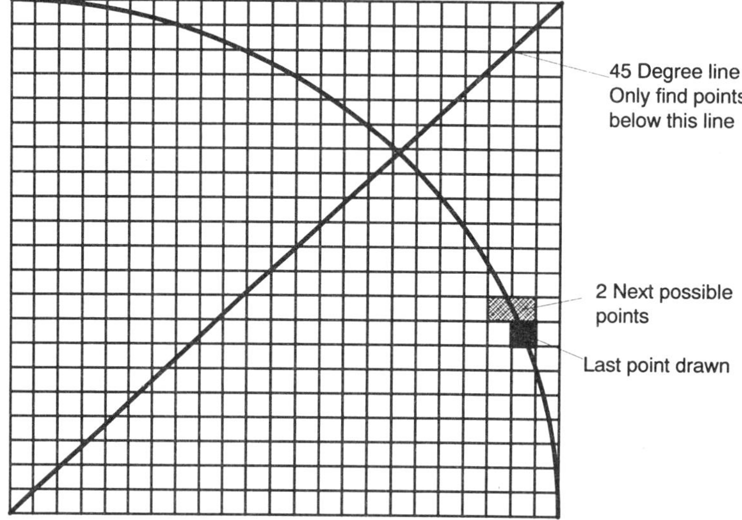

Fig. 10.2.2 Two Choices for Next Pixel when Drawing a Circle

The idea once again is to find which point is actually closer to the arc by finding the distance between each possible point and the true arc, and subtracting the distances. We start with the formula for a circle.

$$\frac{X^2 + Y^2}{r^2} = 1$$

Since we are finding points in the eighth of the circle starting at 0°, we will be incrementing Y and finding the appropriate X. With a little simple rearranging we find a formula for X dependent on Y:

$$X^2 = r^2 - Y^2$$

The closer point can now be found by finding the distances from each possible point to the true point (X_{true}, Y_{true}), then subtracting one distance from the other. By testing the sign of the result we find which point should be used. Here is the formula for the distance from the true point on the circle to the point on the right, which is X_{last}.

$$d_1 = X_{last}{}^2 - X_{true}{}^2 = X_{last}{}^2 - r^2 + (Y_{last} + 1)^2$$

And the point to the left, which is X_{last} - 1.

$$d_2 = X_{true}{}^2 - (X_{last} - 1)^2 = r^2 - (Y_{last} + 1)^2 - (X_{last} - 1)^2$$

Subtracting d_2 from d_1 yields

$$\begin{aligned} p &= d_1 - d_2 \\ &= X_{last}{}^2 - r^2 + (Y_{last} + 1)^2 - \left[r^2 - (Y_{last} + 1)^2 - (X_{last} - 1)^2\right] \\ &= 2(Y_{last} + 1)^2 + X_{last}{}^2 + (X_{last} - 1)^2 - 2r^2 \end{aligned}$$

We might call this $p_{current}$. To find p_{next} we plug the next point, ($X_{current}$,$Y_{current}$) into this formula. $Y_{current}$ is Y_{last}+1, $X_{current}$ is either X_{last} or X_{last} + 1. Because we don't know which yet we will simply refer to it as $X_{current}$.

$$p_{next} = 2[(Y_{last} + 1) + 1]^2 + X_{current}{}^2 + (X_{current} - 1)^2 - 2r^2$$

Now we subtract $p_{current}$ from p_{next}.

$$\begin{aligned} p_{next} - p_{current} = {} & 2[(Y_{last} + 1) + 1]^2 + X_{current}{}^2 + (X_{current} - 1)^2 - 2r^2 - \\ & \left[2(Y_{last} + 1)^2 + X_{last}{}^2 + (X_{last} - 1)^2 - 2r^2\right] \end{aligned}$$

Pretty ugly. But if we expand all the terms, most will cancel. This is not a basic algebra book, although it may be starting to look like one, so we will jump straight to the finished product. After canceling we add $p_{current}$ to both sides and end up with the following surprising simple formula.

$$p_{\text{next}} = p_{\text{current}} + 4Y_{\text{last}} + 6 + 2\left(X_{\text{current}}{}^2 - X_{\text{last}}{}^2\right) - 2\left(X_{\text{current}} - X_{\text{last}}\right)$$

Depending on which point is closer to the line, $X_{current}$ - X_{last} is 0 or -1. So the last term can be taken out and the constant becomes either 6 or 4. In the case where $X_{current}$ is equal to X_{last} the second to the last term also drops out and we are left with a nice simple formula.

$$p_{\text{next}} = p_{\text{current}} + 4Y_{\text{last}} + 6$$

Which is what we need to find p_{next} when the point being plotted has the same X value as the last point. The other case is just a tad harder. The formula still has squares in it, and it would be really nice if we could get rid of these. In this case $X_{\text{current}}{}^2$ can be replaced by $\left(X_{\text{last}} - 1\right)^2$, which can be expanded to $X_{\text{last}}{}^2 - 2X_{\text{last}} + 1$. Now the formula can be simplified to

$$p_{\text{next}} = p_{\text{current}} + 4\left(Y_{\text{last}} - X_{\text{last}}\right) + 10$$

We still have a multiply in each case. But in both cases it is a multiply by 4, which is equivalent to shifting 2 bits to the left. So, once we have a point we call circle_plot( ). Then we check p. If p < 0 the X value of the next point is the same as for this point, and we use the first formula. Otherwise we use the second formula and decrement X. Then, either way, we increment Y. This of course goes into the loop. But how do we start? We need to set p to its initial value. If we plug X and Y into our original p formula for X_{last} and Y_{last} we find it simplifies right on down to

$$p = 3 - 2r$$

So now we are ready to look at the actual code.

```
void circle_plot (int X, int X_center,
                  int Y, int Y_center) {

  SVGA_plot_pixel (X_center + X, Y_center + Y);
  SVGA_plot_pixel (X_center - X, Y_center + Y);
  SVGA_plot_pixel (X_center + X, Y_center - Y);
  SVGA_plot_pixel (X_center - X, Y_center - Y);
  SVGA_plot_pixel (X_center + Y, Y_center + X);
  SVGA_plot_pixel (X_center - Y, Y_center + X);
  SVGA_plot_pixel (X_center + Y, Y_center - X);
```

```
    SVGA_plot_pixel (X_center - Y, Y_center - X);

  } /* end circle_plot() */

  void SVGA_circle (int X_center, int Y_center,
                    int Radius) {

    int Y = 0;
    int X = Radius;
    int p = 3 - 2 * Radius;

    while (Y <= X) {
      circle_plot (X, X_center, Y, Y_center);

      if (p < 0)
        p = p + (Y<<2) + 6;
      else {
        p = p + ((Y - X)<<2) + 10;
        X--;
      } /* end else */
      Y++;
    } /* end while loop */
  } /* end SVGA_circle() */
```

This code is quite quick, but, as always, there is a problem. Due to aspect ratio, in some modes the circles appear tall and thin. This is because the pixels in those modes are not square. Most of the SVGA modes use square pixels, as does the VGA high-resolution mode, but the lower resolution modes sometimes do not.

To make circles appear round in other modes, use the ellipse routine given on the next page. The parameter r1 is the radius in the X dimension and r2 is the radius in the Y dimension. To make circles appear round, first use the radius of the circle for r1, then take the number of pixels in the X dimension, divide by the number of pixels in the Y dimension, then multiply by 0.75 (the ratio of the depth of the screen to its width). Divide the radius by the result and use that number for r2.

Drawing Ellipses

Drawing ellipses with Bresenham's method is similar to circles. The same process is used of finding the true position based on the equation of an ellipse, then finding the closer pixel. But ellipses are somewhat more complicated than circles. Ellipses only have a four-way symmetry (Fig. 10.3.1).

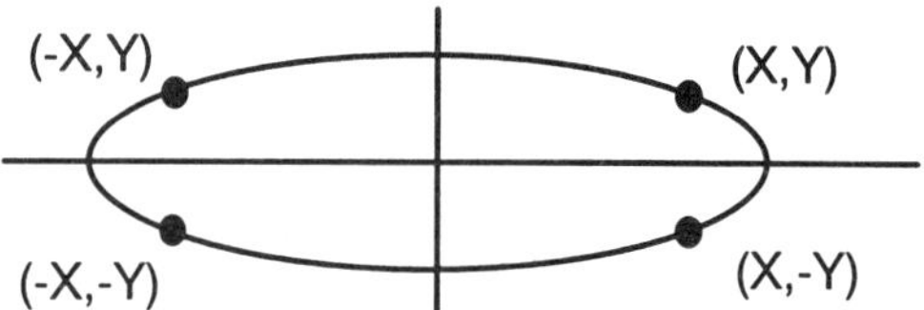

Fig 10.3.1 Ellipses Have Four-way Symmetry

So we start plotting at the X axis, incrementing Y to draw the curve for the first quadrant. We reflect each point to the four quadrants, and an ellipse appears. For plotting we can use and ellipse_plot( ) function similar to the circle_plot function given in the last section.

```
void ellipse_plot (int X, int X_center,
                   int Y, int Y_center) {

  SVGA_plot_pixel (X_center + X, Y_center + Y);
  SVGA_plot_pixel (X_center - X, Y_center + Y);
  SVGA_plot_pixel (X_center + X, Y_center - Y);
  SVGA_plot_pixel (X_center - X, Y_center - Y);

} /* end ellipse_plot() */
```

At some point the slope of the curve becomes too shallow to increment Y. When this happens gaps start to appear in the ellipse (Fig. 10.3.2), just like when drawing a line with slope greater than 1.

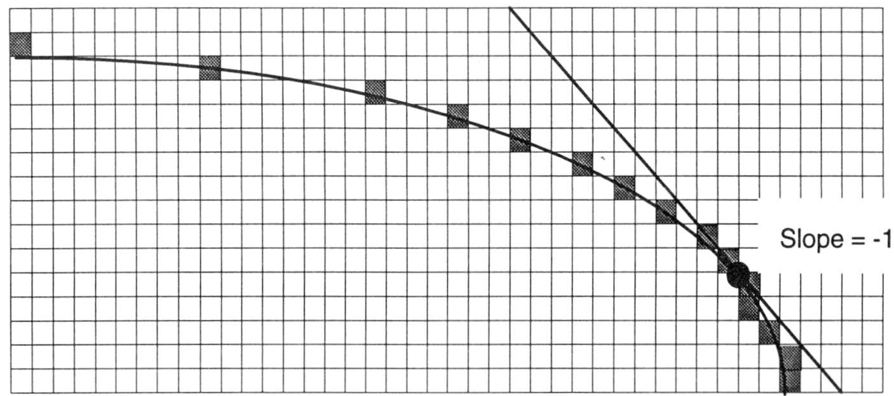

Fig. 10.3.2 Pixels on an Ellipse

The slope of an ellipse in the first quadrant varies from negative infinite at the X axis to 0 at the Y axis. At some point it is equal to -1. Gaps start appearing when the slope becomes greater than -1, that is, when the slope is closer to 0 than -1. So when the point is reached where the slope is greater than -1 we need to stop incrementing Y, and start over at the Y axis, decrementing X.

But how do we find, quickly and efficiently, the point where the slope becomes -1? Well calculus was invented for just such situations, so I hope the reader will forgive a brief resort to this black art. The formula for an ellipse is

$$\frac{X^2}{r_1^2} + \frac{Y^2}{r_2^2} = 1$$

where r_1 and r_2 are radii along the X and Y axes. This is a simplified version. This version only allows for ellipses with the major axis on the X or Y axis, and centered on the origin. The problem of being centered on the origin is handled by the ellipse_plot( ) function, same as circles. The problem of having the major axis aligned with the X or Y axis is a limitation shared with both the Borland and Microsoft ellipse routines, so we will live with it.[2]

Calculus tells us that the derivative of a formula gives the slope of the formula at each point. The derivative of the ellipse formula is

$$\frac{2X}{r_1^2} + \frac{2YY'}{r_2^2} = 0$$

and since we want to find the point where the slope is -1, we make $y' = -1$. This gives the formula

$$\frac{2X}{r_1^2} - \frac{2Y}{r_2^2} = 0$$

Solving for X we get

$$X = \frac{Yr_1^2}{r_2^2}$$

---

[2] Chapter 13 on linear transformations gives a way around this limitation.

Which we now substitute for X in the ellipse formula

$$\frac{\left(Yr_1^{\,2} \big/ r_2^{\,2} \right)^2}{r_1^{\,2}} + \frac{Y^2}{r_2^{\,2}} = 1$$

and solve for Y.

$$Y = \frac{r_2^{\,2}}{\sqrt{r_1^{\,2} + r_2^{\,2}}}$$

Now this might look pretty ugly, with all the squares and the radical sign, but r_1 and r_2 are constants, so the whole expression is a constant that can be found once before the loop is entered.

Now we need to perform the same derivations that we did for the line and the circle, this time for two cases: Slope less than −1 and slope greater than −1. First we will find the formulas for the first case, where we are incrementing Y each iteration (Fig 10.3.3).

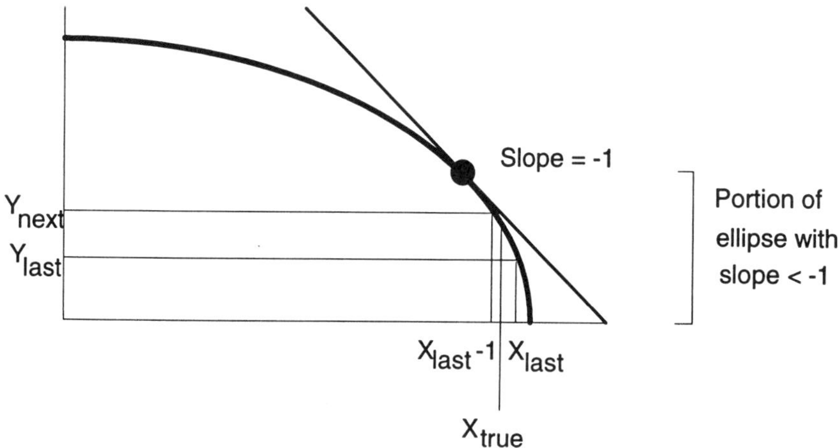

Fig. 10.3.3 Finding the Next Point on an Ellipse

So we need to find the distance $X_{true} - X_{next}$, and the distance $X_{last} - X_{true}$. We first start by taking the ellipse equation and solving for X^2.

$$X^2 = r_1^2\left(1 - \frac{Y^2}{r_2^2}\right)$$

The next several steps should be quite familiar by now. First find the distances between the true point on the ellipse and each of its neighboring pixels, as given by the next two formulas.

$$d_1 = X_{\text{true}}^{\ \ 2} - \left(X_{\text{last}} - 1\right)^2 = r_1^2\left(1 - \frac{Y_{\text{current}}^{\ \ 2}}{r_2^2}\right) - \left(X_{\text{last}} - 1\right)^2$$

$$d_2 = X_{\text{last}}^{\ \ 2} - X_{\text{true}}^{\ \ 2} = X_{\text{last}}^{\ \ 2} - r_1^2\left(1 - \frac{Y_{\text{current}}^{\ \ 2}}{r_2^2}\right)$$

Variable d_1 here is the distance from X_{true} to $X_{\text{current}} - 1$, while d_2 is the distance from the X_{current} to X_{true}. Keep this in mind, as it may seem backwards. But by using these values everything comes out positive.

Next find the distance parameter by subtracting one distance from the other. If the first distance is smaller the parameter will be negative, and the first point should be used.

$$\begin{aligned} p = d_1 - d_2 &= 2X_{\text{true}}^{\ \ 2} - X_{\text{last}}^{\ \ 2} - \left(X_{\text{last}} - 1\right)^2 \\ &= 2r_1^2\left(1 - \frac{Y_{\text{current}}^{\ \ 2}}{r_2^2}\right) - X_{\text{last}}^{\ \ 2} - \left(X_{\text{last}} - 1\right)^2 \end{aligned}$$

Now it would be nice to eliminate fractions from the formula for p. This can be done by multiplying r_2^2 across the formula.

$$p_{\text{current}} = r_2^2 p = 2r_1^2\left(r_2^2 - Y_{\text{current}}^{\ \ 2}\right) - r_2^2\left(X_{\text{last}}^{\ \ 2} - \left(X_{\text{last}} - 1\right)^2\right)$$

Next we need a formula for the next p. Use the preceeding formula, and plug in the next pixel.

$$p_{\text{next}} = 2r_1^2\left(r_2^2 - \left(Y_{\text{current}}+1\right)^2\right) - r_2^2\left(X_{\text{last}}^2 - \left(X_{\text{last}}-1\right)^2\right)$$

Subtract p_{current} from p_{next}, to find a way of finding p_{next} from p_{current}.

$$p_{\text{next}} - p_{\text{current}} = 2r_1^2\left(r_2^2 - Y_{\text{current}}^2\right) - r_2^2\left(X_{\text{last}}^2 - \left(X_{\text{last}}-1\right)^2\right) -$$
$$\left[2r_1^2\left(r_2^2 - \left(Y_{\text{current}}+1\right)^2\right) - r_2^2\left(X_{\text{next}}^2 - \left(X_{\text{next}}-1\right)^2\right)\right]$$

Add p_{current} to both sides, and simplify.

$$p_{\text{next}} = p_{\text{current}} - 2r_1^2\left(2Y_{\text{current}}^2 + 3\right)$$
$$-2r_2^2\left(X_{\text{next}}^2 - X_{\text{last}}^2 + X_{\text{next}} - X_{\text{last}}\right)$$

Now we can substitute X for X_{last}, for the case where p is greater than 0. When p greater than 0 then d_2 is smaller, and X_{current} is plotted. X_{current} is also plugged into the above formula to find the p_{next}.

$$p_{\text{next}} = p_{\text{current}} - r_1^2\left(4Y_{\text{current}} + 6\right)$$

This formula contains a multiply, which we've been able to avoid in the past. The ellipse formula is somewhat more complicated than that for circles or lines, so we can no longer find p without resorting to multiplies. An integer multiply is only one machine instruction, however, so using multiplies is not that bad, as long as they can be kept to a minimum. At first glance it also looks like there might be a variable raised to a power, but r_1^2 is a constant and can be found before the loop is started.

Now, for the case where p is less than 0, we substitute $X - 1$ for X_{last}. Variable p being negative means that d_1 was the smaller distance, and this is the value to plot. The next p formula with $X - 1$ substituted simplifies to

$$p_{\text{next}} = p_{\text{current}} - 4\left(r_1^2 Y_{\text{current}} - r_2^2 X_{\text{last}}\right) - 6r_1^2$$

Now all we need to do is find the starting p. The loop will start by plotting the point at 0°. The coordinates for this point are $(r_1,0)$, so plug $Y_{\text{current}}=0$ and $X_{\text{last}}=r_1$ into the original p formula. This will give the following for the starting p:

$$p_{\text{start}} = 2r_1^{\,2}\left(r_2^{\,2} - 1\right) - r_2^{\,2}\left(2r_1^{\,2} - 2r_2^{\,2} + 1\right)$$

The code for this portion of the ellipse will be presented here, so this math will not get confused with the math for the next portion. The formula we have uses a number of squares and multiplies. Because of this numbers can get quite large. Look at the formula above for the initial *p*. Imagine that this function is being used to draw a circle with a radius of 100 pixels. This is not even that large of a circle, but the first thing we have to do is

$$100^2\left(100^2 + (100 - 1)^2\right)$$

This comes from the first half of the initial *p* formula, before the minus sign. This evaluates to 198,010,000, which does not quite fit into a 16-bit register. So when we implement the function all internal variables except *X* and *Y* should be declared as longs to prevent overflow. The squares of r_1 and r_2 should be declared as longs, since it is reasonable for the function to be called with values for r_1 and r_2 greater than 182, which is larger than the square root of 32,767.

Other than that, translating the above formulas into code is straightforward. Find r1_squared and r2_squared before the loop. Find the point for ending the loops, which is called chgpt in the code below, according to the formula from the derivative of the ellipse formula. Set X to r1, set Y to 0. Loop. The code inside the loop should look quite familiar by now. It comes directly from the *p* formulas.

```
void SVGA_ellipse (int X_center, int Y_center,
                   int r1,       int r2) {

  int Y = 0;
  int X = r1;
  long r1_squared = (long)r1*(long)r1;
  long r2_squared = (long)r2*(long)r2;
  long p = 2*r1_squared*(r2_squared-1)-
           r2_squared*(2*(r1_squared-r1+1));
  long chgpt = r2_squared/
              sqrt(r1_squared+r2_squared);

  while (Y <= chgpt) {
    ellipse_plot (X, X_center, Y, Y_center);

       if (p >= 0)
      p = p - r1_squared*((Y<<2)+6);
    else {
```

```
        p = p - ((r1_squared*Y)-
                (r2_squared*X)<<2)
               -6*r1_squared;
        X--;
      } /* end else */
      Y++;
    } /* end while loop */

                    .
                    .
                    .
```

Next we have the portion of the ellipse with a slope greater than –1. We use a second loop for this portion of the ellipse. The end condition for this loop is the same as for the first loop, since that is the point where the two curves meet, closing the ellipse (Fig. 10.3.4).

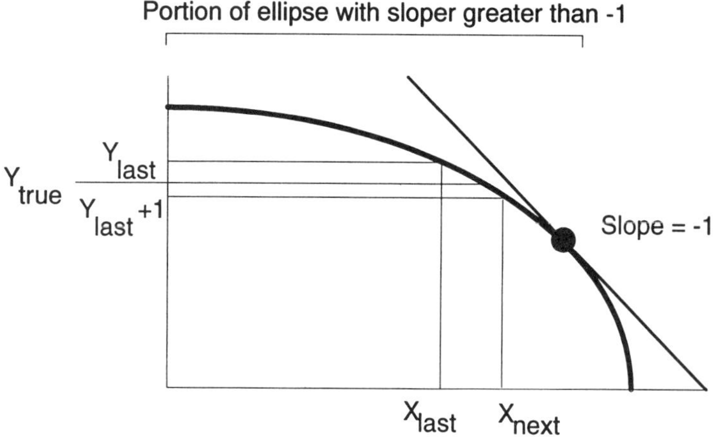

Fig. 10.3.4 Finding the Next Point on an Ellipse when the Slope is Greater Than -1

The descriptions of the math by now are probably getting quite repetitive. You should be able, by now, to figure out these derivations with little help. So this derivation will only be skimmed lightly.

First take the ellipse formula and solve for Y, since we are incrementing X.

$$Y = r_2^{\,2}\left(1 - \frac{X^2}{r_1^{\,2}}\right)$$

Next find the distances between the true Y value and it's neighboring pixels.

$$d_1 = Y_{\text{last}}{}^2 - Y_{\text{true}}{}^2 = Y_{\text{last}}{}^2 - r_2{}^2\left(1 - \frac{X_{\text{current}}}{r_1{}^2}\right)$$

$$d_2 = Y_{\text{true}}{}^2 - \left(Y_{\text{last}} - 1\right)^2 = r_2{}^2\left(1 - \frac{X_{\text{current}}{}^2}{r_1{}^2}\right) - \left(Y_{\text{last}} - 1\right)^2$$

Subtract d_2 from d_1 to find p.

$$p = d_1 - d_2 = Y_{\text{last}}{}^2 + \left(Y_{\text{last}} - 1\right)^2 - 2r_2{}^2\left(1 - \frac{X_{\text{current}}{}^2}{r_1{}^2}\right)$$

Get rid of fractions in the p formula.

$$p_{\text{current}} = r_1{}^2 p = r_1{}^2\left(Y_{\text{last}}{}^2 + \left(Y_{\text{last}} - 1\right)^2\right) - 2r_2{}^2\left(r_1{}^2 - X_{\text{current}}{}^2\right)$$

Plug in Y_{next} and $X_{\text{current}}+1$ to find p_{next}.

$$p_{\text{next}} = r_1^2\left(Y_{\text{next}}{}^2 + \left(Y_{\text{next}} - 1\right)^2\right) - 2r_2^2\left(r_1^2 - \left(X_{\text{current}} + 1\right)^2\right)$$

Subtract the formula for p_{current} from the formula for p_{next} and add p_{current} to find p_{next} from p_{current}.

$$p_{\text{next}} = p_{\text{current}} + 2r_1^2\left(Y_{\text{next}}{}^2 - Y_{\text{last}}{}^2 - Y_{\text{next}} + Y_{\text{last}}\right)$$
$$+2r_2^2\left(2X_{\text{current}} + 3\right)$$

If p is less than 0 then d_2 is the smaller and the current Y value is the Y for the pixel that will be plotted. Plug this into the next p formula.

$$p_{\text{next}} = p_{\text{current}} + r_2^2\left(4X_{\text{current}} + 6\right)$$

If p is greater than 0 then d_1 is smaller and $Y - 1$ is the Y for the pixel to be plotted. Plug this value into the next p formula.

$$p_{next} = p_{current} + r_2^{\,2}\left(4X_{current} + 6\right) - 4r_1^{\,2}\left(Y_{last} - 1\right)$$

Now for the starting *p*. We start plotting at the *Y* axis. The coordinate for this point is $(0,r_2)$. Plug these in for $X_{current}$ and Y_{last} in the original *p* formula.

$$p_{start} = r_1^{\,2}\left(r_2^{\,2} + \left(r_2 - 1\right)^2\right) - 2r_2^{\,2}\left(r_1^{\,2} - 1\right)$$

When the first loop is finished set X to 0, Y to r_2 and reset *p* using the second initial *p* formula. Loop again. The code for the second loop is quite similar to the first. This code is in SVGALib, in the function called SVGA_ellipse( ).

Drawing Arcs

The basic algorithm for drawing arcs is Bresenham's circle algorithm, but with start and stop angles added to the parameter list. The XY coordinates of the start and stop can be found with a little simple trigonometry Take the sine of the start angle, and multiply by the radius for the X value of the start coordinate, and take the cosine of the start angle multiplied by the radius for the Y value. The XY coordinates of the end angle can be found the same way. When we draw the arc we find points, and we have to determine if each point is inside the arc. Given an X,Y coordinate pair, how do you determine if it is inside the arc or not? Bresenham's circle algorithm uses the symmetry of a circle to divide it into eight sections. The method for finding if a point is in the arc depends on which eighth of the circle the point is in (Fig. 10.4.1).

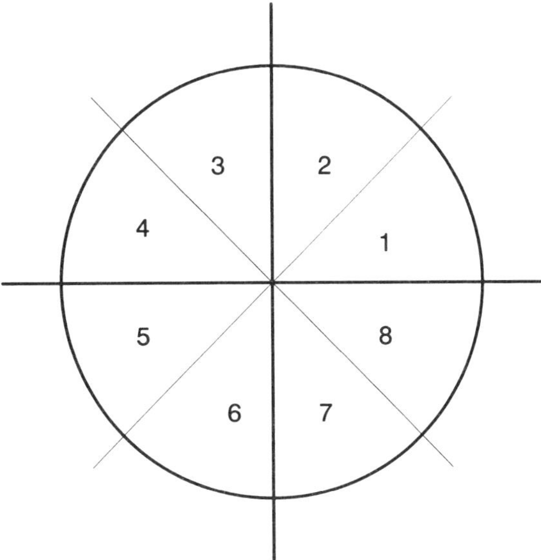

Fig. 10.4.1 Eight Sections of a Circle

For section 1 the starting Y must be less than the Y of the point we are drawing. But this can also occur if the start angle is in the second quadrant (sections 3 and 4), and it will definitely be true if the start angle is in either the third or fourth quadrants. So we need to prove that the start angle is in the first quadrant. This can be done simply by making sure that X and Y are positive. So far we have three conditions to check to draw a point in section 1. Now we have to look at the endpoint. To start with, if the endpoint is in any sector other than the first the point can be drawn. We can test to see if either X or Y is negative, and if so the end angle is past the first quadrant, and the point can be drawn. What if both are positive? If Y of the endpoint is greater than Y of the point being drawn, then the point can be drawn. The following code shows these checks:

```
if (((StartY <= Y)  &&
     (StartY >= 0)  &&
     (StartX <= 0)) &&
    ((EndY   >= Y)  ||
     (EndY   <  0)  ||
     (EndX   <  0))) {
  SVGA_plot_pixel(X_center+X, Y_center+Y);
}
```

Now we have six comparisons for each pixel. For each iteration of the loop, 8 pixels are plotted. If for each there are six comparisons then there are 48 extra comparisons for each iteration. This will slow the algorithm significantly. Things can be simplified by breaking the algorithm up into eight sections and computing each separately. This way the start and end angles can be checked and if the region being computed does not contain a portion of the arc it is skipped entirely. But is this more efficient? That depends on the size of the arc. If the arcs being drawn are small, in an angular sense, large numbers of computations and compares are simply skipped. Then dividing the algorithm up like this is more efficient. If the arcs are large, then it would be better to keep all calculations together and put up with extra comparisons.

Is it simpler? If you divide the circle up you can make quick simple checks of the original angles to determine if the section contains a portion of the arc. This eliminates the need for certain checks inside the loop, and makes the code easier and more readable. But the function is now eight times longer. Since we are dividing the routine up to calculate sections of the circle separately the circle_plot routine is no longer useful. Each point is now plotted from within the loop.

It sounds like a compromise is in order. The function supplied with SVGALib divides the circle into quadrants. If the arc starts somewhere in the first quadrant the code for that quadrant is called. If the arc starts in the second quadrant, the code for the first quadrant is not called. This does require a little thought, however. If the start angle is at the end of the second quadrant, the code for the second quadrant still needs to be called. If the end angle is toward the beginning of the fourth quadrant, the fourth quadrant code must be drawn. Keep this in mind, since it makes some of the start and stop conditions seem rather strange.

Once we know that the angle starts in the first quadrant we know that code needs to be called, regardless of any other condition. Once the first quadrant code is running there is no reason to check if the start angle is in the first quadrant. Thus we eliminate two of the six checks from the first loop, by moving them outside the loop. We can eliminate one more check by comparing the end angle itself, rather than its XY coordinates. So we end up with

```
if (St_Angle < 90) {
  while (X <= Y) {
    if ((StartY <= Y) &&
        ((EndY >= Y) || (End_Angle >= 90)))
      SVGA_plot_pixel(X_center+X, Y_center+Y);
```

This code eliminates three checks from the previous example. This is about the most efficient I've been able to get it, and it seems to draw circles in a reasonable amount of time.

Bresenham's algorithm plots the second section by interchanging X and Y coordinates. So we could try interchanging X and Y in the three remaining checks.

```
    if ((StartY <= X) &&
        ((EndY >= X) || (End_Angle >= 90)))
      SVGA_plot_pixel(X_center+Y, Y_center+X);
```

But this doesn't work. The problem is that we are drawing our circles with integer math only. We perform a sin operation to find StartY and EndY, then we truncate the results. The real X coordinate of a point is at some mathematical point between 2 pixels, but because of Bresenham's method, we only have whole number approximations. This means that the true end might be at X = 4.9, but it gets truncated to 4. The true point we are drawing might be X = 3.5, but Bresenham's approximates it as 4. The arc just terminated several degrees before it should have. This is similar to the slope problem in the line and ellipse algorithms. It doesn't take many degrees to be noticeable.

Why didn't this happen in section 1? Because we increment Y each iteration of the loop, so the true Y coordinate of the loop IS a whole number. So when we draw the pixel for section 2 we still need to compare to the Y value. In fact we always need to compare to the Y value of the pixel being drawn for all parts of the circle. We switch some values but not all. Compare the code below to the code above, and to the code given for section 1.

```
    if ((StartX <= Y) &&
        ((EndX >= Y) || (End_Angle >= 90)))
      SVGA_plot_pixel(X_center+Y, Y_center+X);
```

So here is the complete code for the first quadrant:

```
void SVGA_arc (int X_center, int Y_center,
               int Radius,
               int St_Angle, int End_Angle) {

  int Y = 0;
  int X = Radius;
  int p = 3 - 2 * Radius;
  int StartX, StartY, EndX, EndY;

  if (St_Angle >=360) St_Angle %=360;
  if (St_Angle < 0)   St_Angle  =St_Angl-360;
  if (End_Angle> 360) End_Angle%=360;
  if (End_Angle< 0)   End_Angle =St_Angle-360;
  if (St_Angle > End_Angle) {
```

```
    int  temp = St_Angle;
    St_Angle  = End_Angle;
    End_Angle = temp;
  }

  StartX = cos((St_Angle*M_PI)/180.0)*
                              (float)Radius;
  StartY = sin((St_Angle*M_PI)/180.0)*
                              (float)Radius;
  EndX   = cos((End_Angle*M_PI)/180.0)*
                              (float)Radius;
  EndY   = sin((End_Angle*M_PI)/180.0)*
                              (float)Radius;

  /* first Quadrant */
  if (St_Angle < 90) {
    while (Y <= X) {
      if ((StartY <= Y) &&
          ((EndY >= Y) || (End_Angle >= 90)))
        SVGA_plot_pixel (X_center+X,
                         Y_center+Y);
      if ((StartX >= Y) &&
          ((EndX <= Y) || (End_Angle >= 90)))
        SVGA_plot_pixel (X_center+Y,
                         Y_center+X);

      if (p < 0)
        p = p + (Y<<2) + 6;
      else {
        p = p + ((Y - X)<<2) + 10;
        X--;
      } /* end else */
      Y++;
    } /* end while loop */
  } /* end if */
```

There is code here to make sure that the start and end angles are between 0° and 360°, and to make sure the start angle is less than the end angle. This simplifies the algorithm, but introduces a quirk. If you were to call this function with a start angle of 359° and an end angle of 361° almost the entire circle would be drawn. Borland and Microsoft arc functions suffer from this same quirk, so we will put up with it here (Fig 10.4.2).

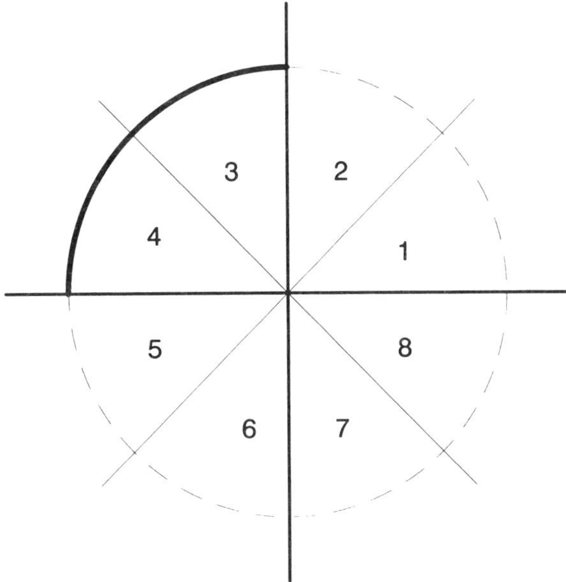

Fig. 10.4.2 Quadrant II

For points in the second quadrant to be plotted the start angle must be less than 180°, and the end angle must be greater than 90°. Notice the overlap. For points in section 4 StartY must be greater than Y, if the arc starts in quadrant II. But the start angle could be in the first quadrant, with a StartY less than Y and the point will still need to be plotted. So we need to check for a StartY greater than Y or a start angle in the first quadrant. The end angle needs to be at least 90°, but this is already checked as part of the start condition. So all we need to check is that the Y value of the end angle is less than the Y value of the point being plotted.

```
if (((StartY>=Y)||(St_Angle<=90)) &&
    (EndY < Y))
  SVGA_plot_pixel (X_center-X,
                   Y_center+Y);
```

Section 3 has a trick to it. The X and Y values are reversed to plot the point, but in quadrant II, X values are negative. We find positive X's and Y's, as for quadrant I, but we subtract Y from X_center to find the X coordinate to plot. So this means we have to compare with negative Y's. In this section, as long as StartX is greater than -Y, the start angle is before this point. EndX must be less than negative Y, or in the third or fourth quadrants.

```
    if ((StartX>=-Y) &&
        ((EndX<-Y) || (End_Angle>=180)))
      SVGA_plot_pixel (X_center-Y,
                       Y_center+X);
```

Here is the code for quadrant II:

```
/* Second Quadrant */
if ((St_Angle <= 180) && (End_Angle >= 90)) {
  Y=0;
  X=Radius;
  while (Y <= X) {
    if (((StartY>=Y)||(St_Angle<=90)) &&
        (EndY < Y))
      SVGA_plot_pixel (X_center-X,
                       Y_center+Y);
    if ((StartX>=-Y) &&
        ((EndX<-Y) || (End_Angle>=180)))
      SVGA_plot_pixel (X_center-Y,
                       Y_center+X);

    if (p < 0)
      p = p + (Y<<2) + 6;
    else {
      p = p + ((Y - X)<<2) + 10;
      X--;
    } /* end else */
    Y++;
  } /* end while loop */
} /* end if */
```

In the third quadrant (Fig. 10.4.3) both X and Y coordinates are negative, so all our comparisons are with negative numbers.

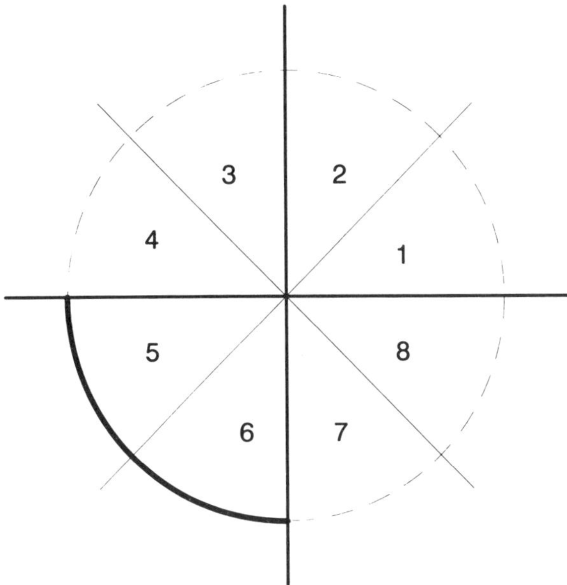

Fig. 10.4.3 Quadrant III

In section 5, StartY must be greater than -Y, and either EndY must be less than -Y or End_Angle must be in the fourth quadrant.

```
if ((StartY >= -Y) &&
    ((EndY <= -Y) || (End_Angle >= 270)))
  SVGA_plot_pixel (X_center-X,
                   Y_center-Y);
```

For section 6, StartX must be less than -Y, or the start angle must be before the third quadrant. EndX must be greater than -Y.

```
if (((StartX<=-Y)||(St_Angle<=180)) &&
    (EndX >= -Y))
  SVGA_plot_pixel (X_center-Y,
                   Y_center-X);
```

The complete code for the third and fourth quadrants is not given, since it is quite similar to the first and second. See SVGALib for the actual code. In the fourth quadrant Y is negative, but X is positive.

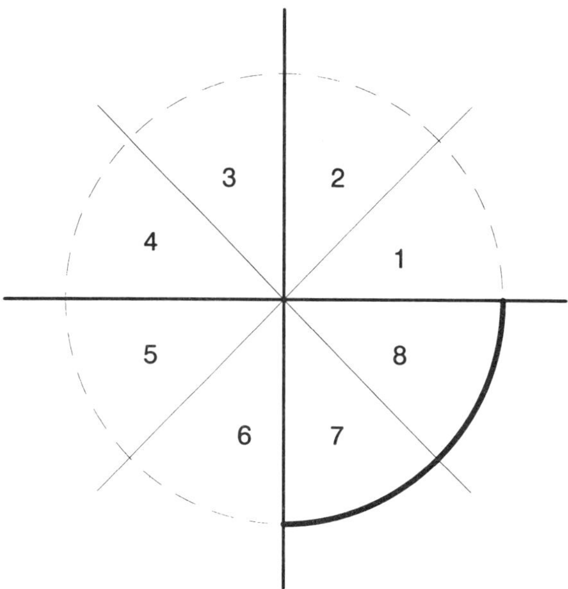

Fig. 10.4.4 Quadrant IV

In section 8 we use –Y to compare with (Fig. 10.4.4). StartY must be less than –Y, or the start angle must be in one of the previous quadrants. Notice that if the start angle is in quadrant III, StartY can be either greater or less than -Y, but the current point will always be after the start angle. Note also that if the start angle is in either of the first two quadrants StartY must be greater than -Y. EndY must also be greater than
-Y. If the end angle is not in this quadrant we would not be executing this code, so we don't need to even consider what happens to Y in other quadrants.

```
if (((StartY<=-Y)||(St_Angle<=270)) &&
    (EndY >= -Y))
  SVGA_plot_pixel (X_center+X,
                   Y_center-Y);
```

In section 7, we compare with positive Y, since Y's in this section replace X's, and X's in the fourth quadrant are positive. StartX must be less than Y, or the start angle must be in a previous quadrant. EndX must be greater than Y. Again we don't need to concern ourselves with end angles in other quadrants.

```
if (((StartX<Y)||(St_Angle<=270)) &&
    (EndX >= Y))
```

```
        SVGA_plot_pixel (X_center+Y,
                         Y_center-X);
```

The pieces of code presented above have some quirks in them. Some places there are greater than equal (>=) or less than equal (<=) operators; in other places there are only greater than (>) or less than (<) operators. This is because the code to find StartX, StartY, EndX, and EndY truncates any decimal portion. In some cases this creates inaccuracies in starting and stopping the arc. Substituting greater than for greater than equals helps, but it is not perfect. Actually all operators should have the equal signs, and code should be put in place to round. In Chapter 5 on charts and graphs, we rounded by adding 0.5 to the number, then truncating. But this method only works for positive numbers. If you have -1.2, and you add 0.5 and truncate you end up with -1. It is difficult to come up with a simple rounding function that works in all cases.

11

Filling Primitives

The next step in creating a useful library is to create fill routines. The most useful fill routines are for filling ellipses and polygons, plus one routine is needed for odd shapes that are not ellipses or polygons. SVGALib also includes a function for filling rectangles, since a rectangle filling function is quite trivial to implement.

It is useful for filling primitives to support pattern fill. The functions provided by SVGALib allow the user to set up a pattern much the same way that Microsoft graphics functions do. A bit map in the form of an array of unsigned characters is set up and passed to SVGALib through the SVGA_set_fill_pattern( ) function.

Most fill routines draw horizontal lines to actually do the filling. Because these lines are horizontal we know that the SVGA window only needs to be set once for each line. A separate function for drawing horizontal lines is useful here, so that we can eliminate the overhead of checking if the window needs to be set at each pixel, and also eliminate the overhead of determining the slope and deciding which of Bresenham's line routines is appropriate. This horizontal line function also gives us one central place to implement pattern filling.

The color used for filling is the current drawing color. If you wish to change the color used for filling, use SVGA_set_color( ) or SVGA_set_dc_color( ), as appropriate.

SVGA_set_fill_pattern( )

The method for defining a fill is the same basic method used by both Borland (for defining a user fill pattern) and Microsoft. The method is to define an array of 8 bytes (unsigned char's in C) that is used as a bit map to hold the pattern. The first line that is filled will take the first byte to use as a bit map, and repeat the bit pattern in that byte over and over, until the end of the line is reached. The next line uses the second byte, and so on. The ninth line will start over using the first byte for its bit map.

The array used by the fill routines is safely hidden inside SVGALIB.C, with a default value of all bits set, so the default fill pattern is solid fill. A simple function is provided to allow the user to set his/her own fill patterns. Here is the array and function defined:

```
unsigned char G_FillPattern[8] = {0xFF,
                                  0xFF,
                                  0xFF,
                                  0xFF,
                                  0xFF,
                                  0xFF,
                                  0xFF,
                                  0xFF };

void SVGA_set_fill_pattern
            (unsigned char P_FillPattern[8]) {
  memcpy(G_FillPattern, P_FillPattern, 8);
}
```

The fill_line( ) function

The fill_line( ) function draws horizontal lines for filling shapes more efficiently than by calling SVGA_line( ). It also allows for one place to implement the pattern fill method. The pattern fill code is not repeated in each fill function.

Since this function only draws horizontal lines it only needs one Y coordinate, plus the beginning and ending X coordinates.

```
char fill_line (int X1, int X2, int Y);
```

Because there is only one Y coordinate we only need to set the SVGA window once each time the function is called, which is a major time saver. This is done basically the same way as for SVGA_plot_pixel( ). At first glance it does not look like that would work for a horizontal line since windows do not necessarily start at the first pixel of a scan line (Fig. 11.1.1)

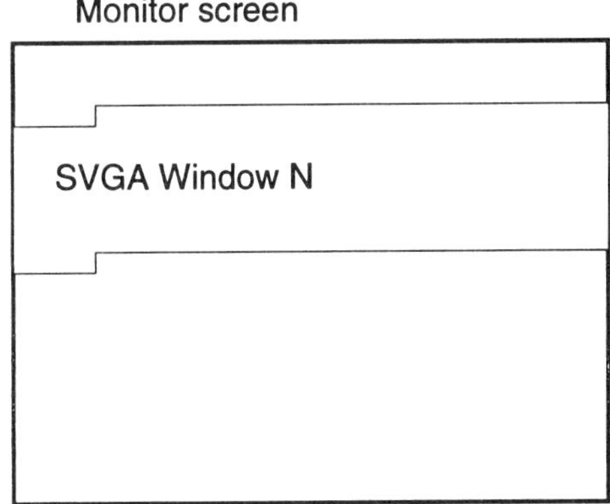

Fig. 11.1.1 An SVGA Window Does Not Always Start at the First Pixel of the Scan Line

But the window is found based on the first pixel in the fill line, so if necessary, an overlapping window that started some lines above will be used. This happens automatically, since the window used is based on the first pixel of the fill line. This pixel will be in the window we want to use. Once the window is set all we have to do is plot pixels one after the other. This is done using essentially the same method as SVGA_plot_pixel( ).

This method is fine if all we need is a solid fill. If we need to fill an object with patterns we need to add a little more code. A global variable, G_FillPattern, is an 8-byte array that holds the fill pattern. If a bit in this array is set, the corresponding pixel is filled on the screen. Otherwise it is left as is. The pattern can be set with the function SVGA_set_fill_pattern( ).

We would prefer this pattern to always start at the same point relative to the screen, no matter where the object starts. That means that if a fill object is drawn over another one with the same pattern, the patterns of the two objects will overlap, with only the background showing through. This is necessary because of the independent nature of fill_line( ). Imagine SVGA_fill_ellipse( ). For each scan line, it makes a call to fill_line( ). Function fill_line( ) does not know if this is the first time its been called for one ellipse, or the seventh. We cannot start the fill pattern over at the beginning each time the function is called, or all we will get as a fill pattern is straight lines up and down.

The first step in drawing a pattern fill is to select the correct byte from G_FillPattern. This is done by modulo-ing the Y coordinate by 8. As we draw the line we AND this byte with the X value of the pixel we are plotting modulo 8.

Only the code for 15- and 16-bit modes is shown, since for other modes the code is a combination of this and the pixel plotting code shown in Chapter 9. If you understood that code you can understand this.

```
char fill_line (int X1, int X2, int Y) {
  unsigned char L_LinePattern = G_FillPattern[Y%8];
  unsigned char L_CurBit;
  long L_ScreenPos;
  int  L_Window;
  int  i;
  int  temp;

  if (G_VBE_Supported == NOTINITIALED) {
    SVGA_Err = NOTINITIALED;
    return       NOTINITIALED;
  }
  if (G_VBE_Supported == VBENOTSUPPORTED) {
    SVGA_Err = VBENOTSUPPORTED;
    return       VBENOTSUPPORTED;
  }

  if (X1 > X2) {
    temp = X1;
    X1   = X2;
    X2   = temp;
  }

  L_ScreenPos =
        ((long)Y*(long)G_Mode_Info.BytesPerScanLine)+X1;

  L_CurBit = 1<<X1%8;
```

```
    switch (G_BitsColor) {
              .
              .
              .
      case MODE16BITCOLOR :
        L_ScreenPos += X1;

        L_Window = L_ScreenPos / G_Win_Size;

        if (G_Cur_Window != L_Window)
          set_window(L_Window);

        for(i=0; i<X2-X1; i++) {
          if (L_LinePattern & L_CurBit) {

            *(G_16Bit_Win_Addr +
                      ((L_ScreenPos%G_Win_Size)/2) +i) =
                                              G_16Bit_Color;

          } /* end if */
          L_CurBit <<= 1;
          if (!L_CurBit) L_CurBit = 1;
        } /* end loop */
        break;
              .
              .
              .
    } /* end switch */

    SVGA_Err = NOERROR;
    return NOERROR;
  } /* end fill_line() */
```

SVGA_fill_rectangle( ) and SVGA_fill_ellipse( )

Both of these functions are quite simple, so both are presented here in one section. The SVGA_fill_rectangle( ) function takes as parameters the coordinates of the upper left and lower right corners. First the boundary of the rectangle is drawn, then a for loop is used to call fill_line( ) for each scan line between the top and the bottom of the rectangle.

```
char SVGA_fill_rectangle (int X1, int Y1,
                          int X2, int Y2) {
  int i;
  int temp;

  if (G_VBE_Supported == NOTINITIALED) {
    SVGA_Err = NOTINITIALED;
    return     NOTINITIALED;
  }
  if (G_VBE_Supported == VBENOTSUPPORTED) {
    SVGA_Err = VBENOTSUPPORTED;
    return     VBENOTSUPPORTED;
  }

  if (Y1 > Y2) {
    temp = Y1;
    Y1   = Y2;
    Y2   = temp;
  }

  SVGA_line (X1,Y1,X2,Y1);
  SVGA_line (X2,Y1,X2,Y2);
  SVGA_line (X2,Y2,X1,Y2);
  SVGA_line (X1,Y2,X1,Y1);

  for (i=Y1; i<=Y2; i++)
    fill_line(X1, X2, i);

  SVGA_Err = NOERROR;
  return     NOERROR;
} /* end SVGA_fill_rectangle() */
```

Although the code for SVGA_ellipse_fill( ) is rather more involved, most of it is recycled from SVGA_ellipse( ). In that routine, Bresenham's method was used to find a point somewhere on the arc of the ellipse, then that point was reflected to three other points on the ellipse. In this way only points for the first quadrant needed to be calculated. SVGA_fill_ellipse( ) uses exactly the same code for finding the original point. When a point on the ellipse is reflected across the Y axis of the ellipse, a fill line is defined. The point and the reflected point are passed to fill_line( ). The code for doing this is in a function called ellipse_fill( ).

```
void ellipse_fill (int X, int X_center,
                   int Y, int Y_center) {

  SVGA_plot_pixel (X_center + X, Y_center + Y);
  SVGA_plot_pixel (X_center - X, Y_center + Y);
  SVGA_plot_pixel (X_center + X, Y_center - Y);
```

All graphics in this section were created with programs on the distribution disk. All of these programs are described in the text.

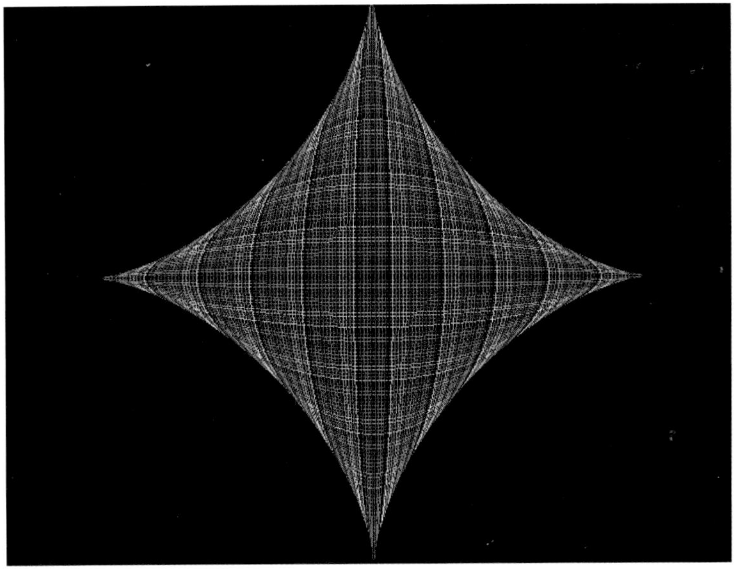

Color Plate I. Demonstration of the BGI's ellipse ( ) function from Chapter 2. Program BK0202.C, Chapter 2.

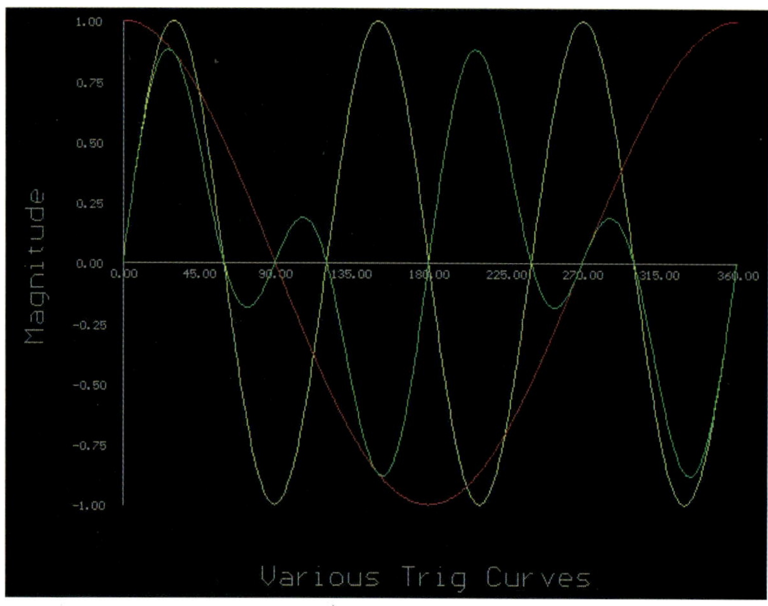

Color Plate II. Various trig curves plotted with "generic" plotting functions defined in BK0502.C. Program BK0502D.C, Chapter 5.

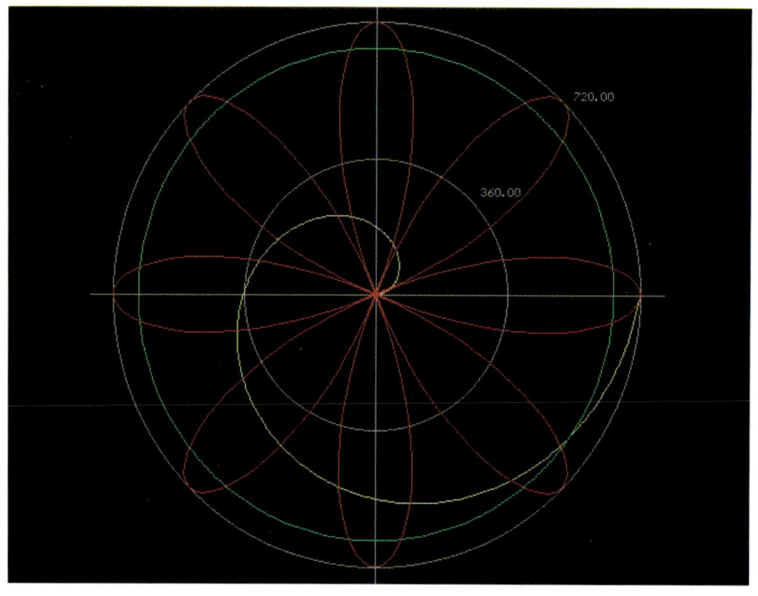

Color Plate III. Various polar curves plotted with "generic" polar plotting functions defined in BK0503.C. Program BK0503D.C, Chapter 5

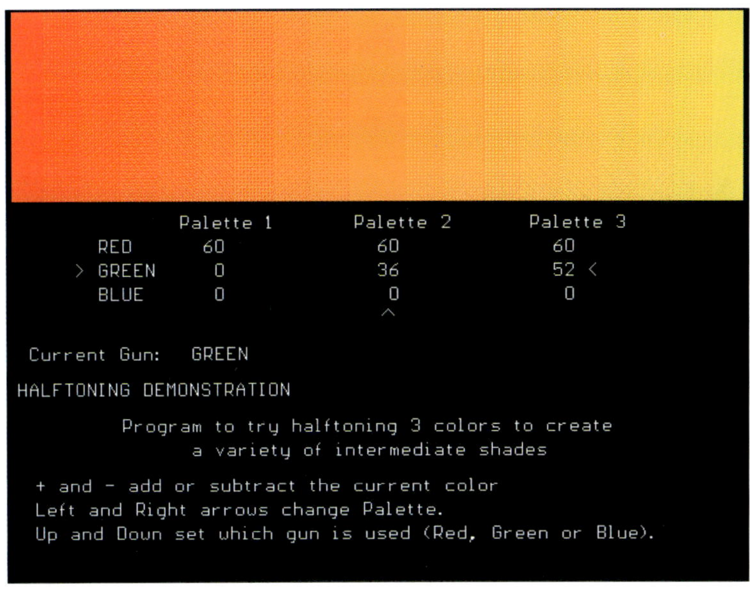

Color Plate IV. Red fading to yellow, using halftoning technique. Program BK0603.C, Chapter 6.

Color Plate V. A shiny balloon floating over a field. Demonstration of perspective and shading. Program BK0702.C, Chapter 7.

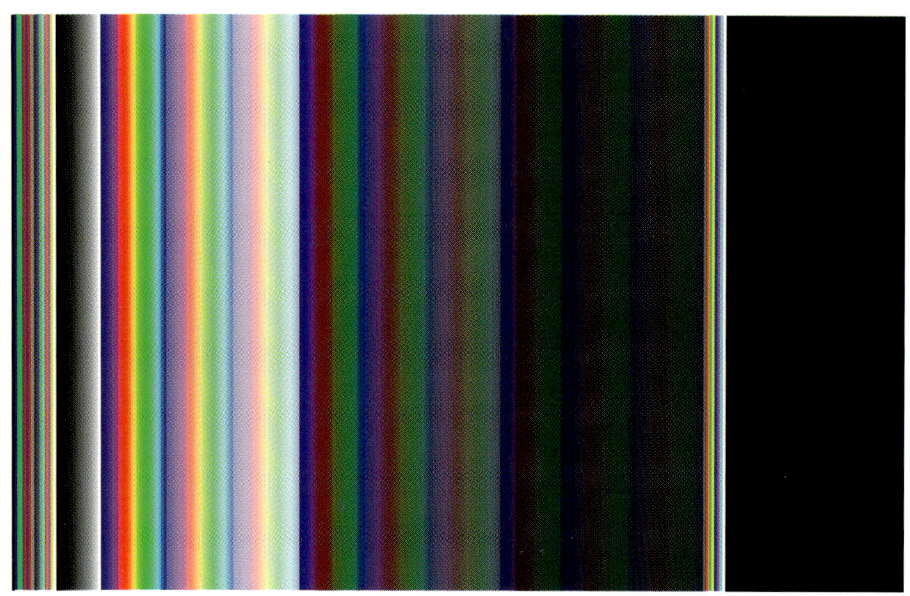

Color Plate VI. 256 default colors. Program BK0802.C, Chapter 8.

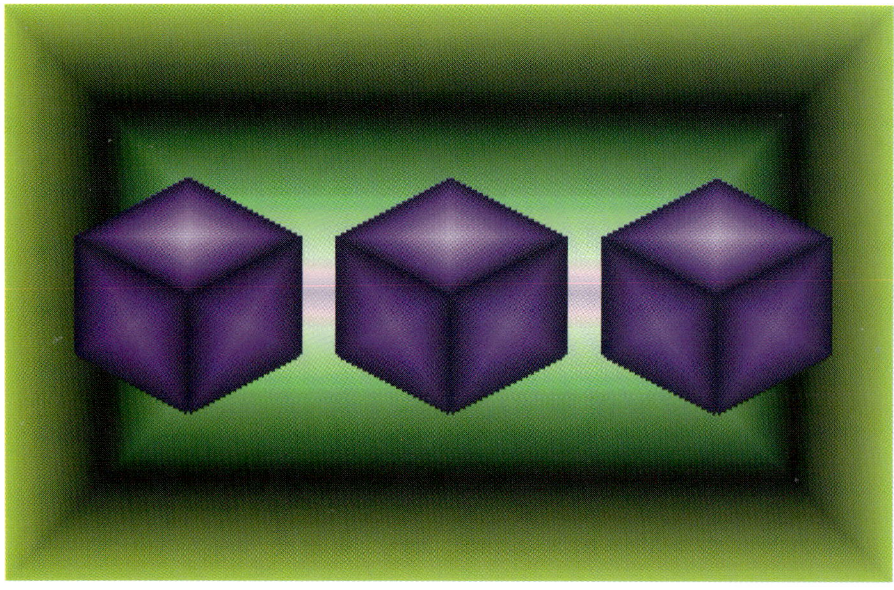

Color Plate VII. Colorful animation effects can be created by manipulating palette registers. Program Demo.C, Chapter 12.

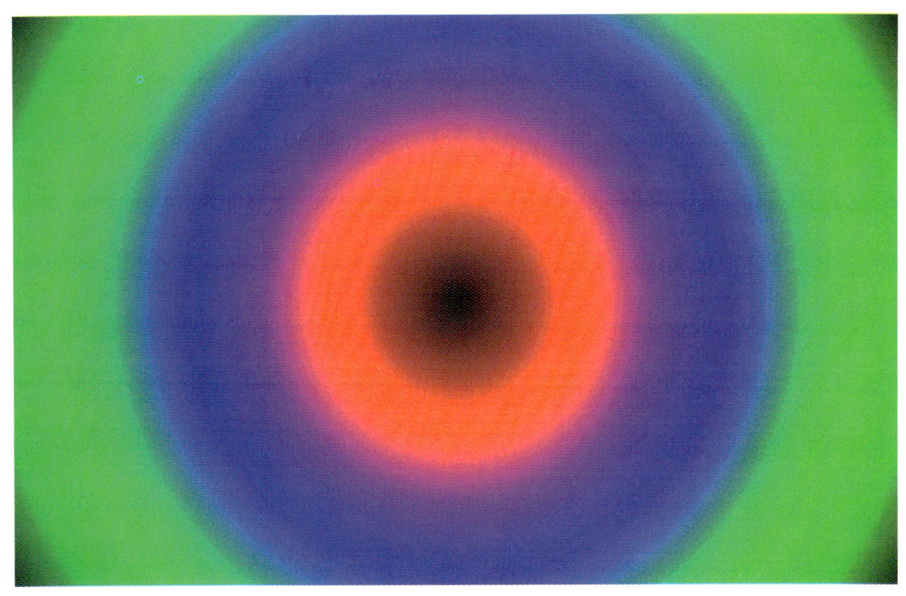

Color Plate VII continued

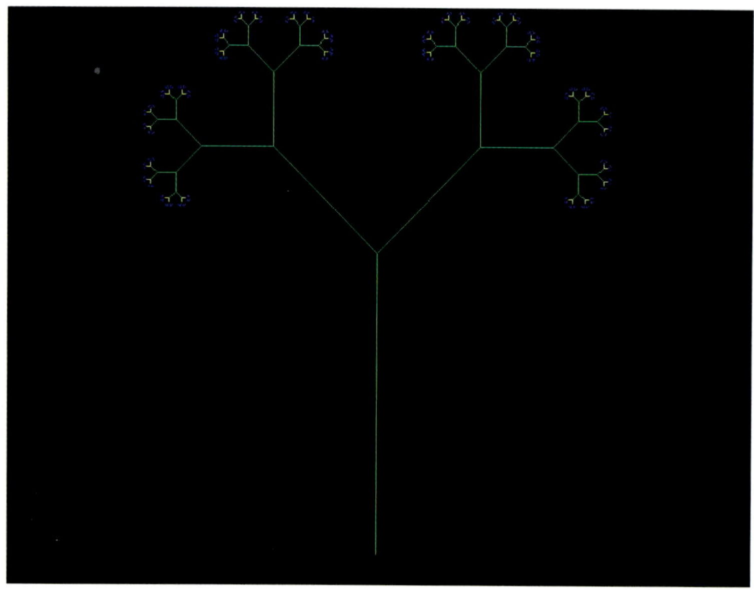

Color Plate VIII. Even simple fractals create lifelike pictures. Lindenmeyer's Plant. Program BK1501.C, Chapter 15.

Color Plate IX. The Mandelbrot Set displays infinite detail. The farther in you zoom, the more detail you see. Program Mandel.C, Chapter 15.

Color Plate IX continued.

Color Plate IX continued.

```
    SVGA_plot_pixel (X_center - X, Y_center - Y);

    fill_line (X_center + X,
               X_center - X, Y_center + Y);
    fill_line (X_center + X,
               X_center - X, Y_center - Y);

  } /* end ellipse_fill() */
```

Bresenham's ellipse code is reproduced in SVGA_fill_ellipse( ), but it is not presented here in the text.

SVGA_floodfill( )

This function is used for filling general shapes, that is shapes that are not ellipses or polygons. It is presented before SVGA_polyfill( ) because the concepts behind it are simpler, so this function is easier to understand.

The flood fill algorithm works on any closed shape. A pixel inside the shape is passed to the routine. The routine checks to see if that point is the color of the border or the fill color. If not, the pixel is set to the fill color and the flood fill algorithm calls itself recursively for the next pixel above, below, to the right, and to the left. Nice and simple. But the odd handling of SVGA monitors leads to complications. First, pseudocode to illustrate the basic function:

```
  Flood_Fill (int X, int Y, color Border,
                            color FillColor);

    color : color_of_cur_pixel =
      get_color (X, Y);

    if NOT((color_of_cur_pixel == Border) or
           (color_of_cur_pixel == FillColor))then
      plot_pixel (X, Y, FillColor);
      Flood_Fill (X+1, Y,   Border, FillColor);
      Flood_Fill (X-1, Y,   Border, FillColor);
      Flood_Fill (X,   Y+1, Border, FillColor);
      Flood_Fill (X,   Y-1, Border, FillColor);
    end if;

  end Flood_Fill;
```

SVGA monitors might be in either direct or palette modes. Locating the border must be done differently for each, so the flood fill function has been broken into two parts, one for direct color modes, the other for palette modes. To simplify calling this function, from a user standpoint, only one function is exported, SVGA_floodfill( ), which determines the type of mode the monitor is currently in, and calls the appropriate flood fill function.

Since the same function is called for both direct and palette modes, we cannot pass the border color to the function. Two other auxiliary functions are supplied for setting the border color, one for direct modes, the other for palette modes. These functions set global variables. G_8Bit_Border_Color is set by SVGA_set_border_color( ), and SVGA_set_dc_border_color( ) sets G_Border_Red, G_Border_Green, and G_Border_Blue; plus G_16Bit_Border_Color or G_24Bit_Border_Color as appropriate. The definitions for the global variables are:

```
struct SVGA24BitColor G_24Bit_Border_Color =
                              {0xFF, 0xFF, 0xFF};

unsigned int G_16Bit_Border_Color = 0xFFFF;

unsigned char G_Border_Red   = 0xFF;
unsigned char G_Border_Green = 0xFF;
unsigned char G_Border_Blue  = 0xFF;

unsigned char G_8Bit_Border_Color = 0xFF;
```

The code for SVGA_set_border_color is quite simple, since all it does is set G_8Bit_Border_Color.

```
char SVGA_set_border_color
                   (unsigned char palettenum) {
  /*
   * sets the fill color to
   * a palette.
   *
   * Parameter
   *   The palette number of the current
   *   drawing color
   *
   * Returns
   *   NOERROR if successful, NOTINITIALED if
   *   not mode is set, DIRECTCMODE if the
   *   current mode is a direct color mode.
   */
```

```
    if (G_VBE_Supported == NOTINITIALED) {
      SVGA_Err = NOTINITIALED;
      return       NOTINITIALED;
    }

    if (G_VBE_Supported == VBENOTSUPPORTED) {
      SVGA_Err = VBENOTSUPPORTED;
      return       VBENOTSUPPORTED;
    }

    if (SVGA_DirectCMode == TRUE) {
      SVGA_Err = DIRECTCMODE;
      return     DIRECTCMODE;
    }
    G_8Bit_Border_Color = palettenum;

    SVGA_Err = NOERROR;
    return     NOERROR;
  } /* end SVGA_set_border_color() */
```

The SVGA_set_dc_border_color( ) function is a little trickier. The same issues that applied to setting the drawing color apply here. We want the same RGB value to produce colors as much alike as possible, regardless of the number of bits being used. This relieves the programmer from having to create code to determine what mode the monitor is in and then use different values depending on that mode.

Since the same issues drive the design of this function as the SVGA_set_dc_color( ) function the code is the same. First we truncate the bits that are not used. Next we deal with the 24-bit mode. In G_Mode_Info there are three fields that mark the starting bit for each color. If we could shift the RGB fields into a data structure that is 24 bits long, life would be good. But we cannot do that with 24 bits. So we create a union of our 24-bit structure, SVGA24BitColor, with a 32-bit unsigned long integer. We can now shift into the 32-bit unsigned long field of the union, shift over 8 bits to align the value with the structure, and then, because the fields overlap in a union, take the value from the SVGA24BitColor field and copy into the G_24Bit_Border_Color variable. If we are using a 15- or 16-bit mode, things are easier. We shift the values into an unsigned integer, which is 16 bits, then put that into G_16Bit_Border_Color. Finally we store the RGB values in G_Border_Red, G_Border_Green, and G_Border_Blue. Care must be taken that bits used here will be the same as the bits used by SVGA_get_dc_pixel( ), so that values can be compared in a meaningful way.

```
  char SVGA_set_dc_border_color (
                         unsigned char P_Red,
                         unsigned char P_Green,
```

```
                      unsigned char P_Blue) {
/*
 * Set the fill color for all SVGA fill
 * routines.  This allows the user to be
 * unconcerned what order the color mask uses
 * (RGB, RBG, GRB, GBR, BGR, BRG), or how
 * many bits per pixel.
 *
 * Parameters:
 *   The RGB values for the fill color.  For
 *   15 and 16 bit modes the MOST significant
 *   bits are used.  This means that for a 15
 *   bit mode color 1:1:1 looks the same as
 *   color 2:2:2, but color 32:32:32 looks as
 *   one would expect.  If the least
 *   significant bits were used color
 *   31:31:31 would be bright white, and
 *   color 32:32:32 would have no signicant
 *   bits set, so this would appear BLACK.
 *
 * Returns:
 *   NOERROR if no error, NOTINITIALED it
 *   mode is not set, NOTDIRECTCMODE if the
 *   current mode is not a direct color mode.
 */
unsigned char  l_red, l_green, l_blue;
union {
  struct SVGA24BitColor ActualColor;
  unsigned long         Holder;
} l_24bits;

unsigned char L_Byte;

if (G_VBE_Supported == NOTINITIALED) {
  SVGA_Err = NOTINITIALED;
  return     NOTINITIALED;
}

if (G_VBE_Supported == VBENOTSUPPORTED) {
  SVGA_Err = VBENOTSUPPORTED;
  return     VBENOTSUPPORTED;
}

if (SVGA_DirectCMode == FALSE) {
  SVGA_Err = NOTDIRECTCMODE;
  return     NOTDIRECTCMODE;
}

/* get trunced values */
```

```
l_red   =
  P_Red   >> (8 - G_Mode_Info.RedMaskSize);
l_green =
  P_Green >> (8 - G_Mode_Info.GreenMaskSize);
l_blue  =
  P_Blue  >> (8 - G_Mode_Info.BlueMaskSize);

if (G_BitsColor == MODE24BITCOLOR) {
   /* 24 bit stuff */

  l_24bits.Holder =
      l_red   << G_Mode_Info.RedFieldPosition
    + l_green << G_Mode_Info.GreenFieldPosition
    + l_blue  << G_Mode_Info.BlueFieldPosition;
  l_24bits.Holder = l_24bits.Holder << 8;
  G_24Bit_Border_Color =
                  l_24bits.ActualColor;
}
else if (G_BitsColor == MODE16BITCOLOR) {
 /* 16 bit stuff */
  G_16Bit_Border_Color =
      l_red   << G_Mode_Info.RedFieldPosition
    + l_green << G_Mode_Info.GreenFieldPosition
    + l_blue  << G_Mode_Info.BlueFieldPosition;
}
G_Border_Red   =
  l_red   << (8 - G_Mode_Info.RedMaskSize);
G_Border_Green =
  l_green << (8 - G_Mode_Info.GreenMaskSize);
G_Border_Blue  =
  l_blue  << (8 - G_Mode_Info.BlueMaskSize);

SVGA_Err = NOERROR;
return     NOERROR;
} /* end SVGA_set_dc_border_color() */
```

Functions are provided to get the current border colors. These functions are quite simple, so they will not be presented here.

What is needed next are functions to find the color of a given pixel. The non-direct mode version is fairly straightforward. It sets the window, then pulls the correct number of bits, 4 or 8, from the correct frame buffer.

```
char SVGA_get_pixel (int X, int Y,
               unsigned char *P_Palette) {
  int L_Window;
  int L_ScreenPos =
       (Y*G_Mode_Info.BytesPerScanLine)+X;
```

```
    if (G_VBE_Supported == NOTINITIALED) {
      SVGA_Err = NOTINITIALED;
      return       NOTINITIALED;
    }

    if (G_VBE_Supported == VBENOTSUPPORTED) {
      SVGA_Err = VBENOTSUPPORTED;
      return       VBENOTSUPPORTED;
    }

    if (((X < 0) || (X > SVGA_MaxX)) ||
        ((Y < 0) || (Y > SVGA_MaxY))) {
      SVGA_Err = PIXELOUTOFRANGE;
      return       PIXELOUTOFRANGE;
    }

    L_Window = L_ScreenPos / G_Win_Size;

    if (G_Cur_Window != L_Window)
      set_window(L_Window);

    switch (G_BitsColor) {
      case MODE4BITCOLOR : {
        int PixNum_In_Window =
                       L_ScreenPos % G_Win_Size;

        *P_Palette = *(G_8Bit_Win_Addr +
                       PixNum_In_Window);
        break;
      } /* end block */
      case MODE8BITCOLOR :
        *P_Palette = *(G_8Bit_Win_Addr +
                       L_ScreenPos % G_Win_Size);
        break;
      default :
        SVGA_Err = DIRECTCMODE;
        return     DIRECTCMODE;
    } /* end switch */

    SVGA_Err = NOERROR;
    return     NOERROR;
  } /* end SVGA_get_pixel() */
```

And of course the direct color version is more complicated. Care must be taken that RGB values returned are formatted the same way as the stored border colors in G_Border_Red, G_Border_Green, and G_Border_Blue, so that when these variables are compared to the pixel color the comparison will be meaningful.

First the window is set. We deal with the 24-bit case first. This is the inverse of the code for setting the 24-bit border color. A union is declared with an unsigned long integer, and a SVGA24BitColor field. The frame buffer is set, then the 24-bit value is copied from the frame buffer to the SVGA24BitColor field. The long int field is then shifted 8 bits, after which the 8-bit RGB fields are extracted with shift operations. This will work since the each field in the frame buffer is 8 bits.

```
if (G_BitsColor == MODE24BITCOLOR) {
  union {
    struct SVGA24BitColor ActualColor;
    unsigned long         Holder;
  } L_24Bits;

  L_ScreenPos += X+X;
  L_Window = L_ScreenPos / G_Win_Size;

  if (G_Cur_Window != L_Window)
    set_window(L_Window);

  L_24Bits.ActualColor
      = *(G_24Bit_Win_Addr +
          ((L_ScreenPos/3)+X+X) % G_Win_Size);

  L_24Bits.Holder = L_24Bits.Holder >> 8;
  *P_Red   = L_24Bits.Holder >>
              G_Mode_Info.RedFieldPosition;
  *P_Green = L_24Bits.Holder >>
            G_Mode_Info.GreenFieldPosition;
  *P_Blue  = L_24Bits.Holder >>
             G_Mode_Info.BlueFieldPosition;
} /* end if 24 bit mode */
```

The 15- and 16-bit modes need a little more work. We can define an unsigned integer to copy the value into from the frame buffer, and this can be shifted. But we need a little extra work to make sure that only the correct bits are set in the RGB parameters and that these are the same bits set in G_Border_Red, G_Border_Green, and G_Border_Blue.

What we need to do is move the bits for each field into the most significant bits of the appropriate parameter (Fig. 11.2.1). Then the least significant bits must be cleared, so that when these values are compared to the G_Border colors the comparison will be meaningful. It is a simple thing to shift the bits into the least significant bits, using the field positions:

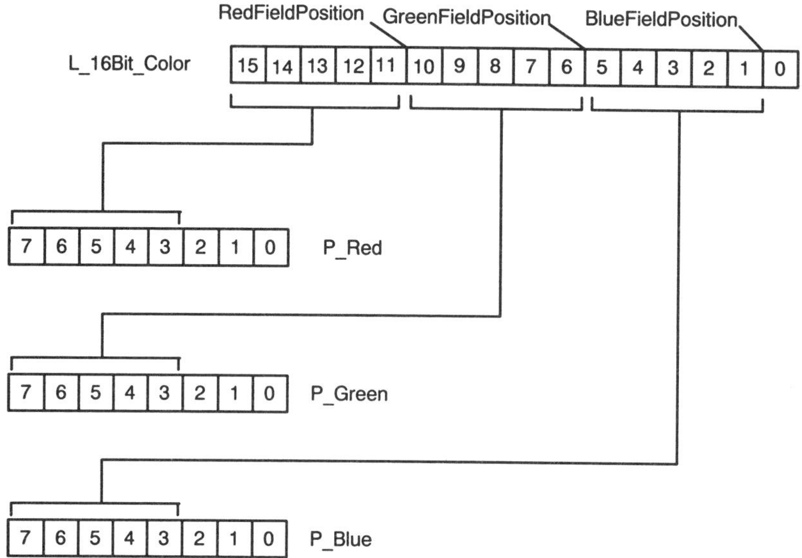

Fig. 11.2.1 Bits in Frame Buffer Need to be Moved to Three Individual Bytes

```
P_Color = L_16Bit_Color >>
            G_Mode_Info.ColorFieldPosition;
```

Now all we have to do is shift the bits into the most significant bit position. This will leave the least significant bits cleared. The correct number of bits to shift by can be found by subtracting the total number of bits, 8, from the size of the field.

```
P_Color = (L_16Bit_Color >>
           G_Mode_Info.ColorFieldPosition) <<
              (8 - G_Mode_Info.ColorMaskSize);
```

where *color* is Red, Green, or Blue. This works for both 15- and 16-bit modes. Here is the final code.

```
char SVGA_get_dc_pixel (int X, int Y,
                        unsigned char *P_Red,
                        unsigned char *P_Green,
                        unsigned char *P_Blue){
  int L_Window;
  int L_ScreenPos =
         (Y*G_Mode_Info.BytesPerScanLine)+X;

  if (G_VBE_Supported == NOTINITIALED) {
```

```
  SVGA_Err = NOTINITIALED;
  return      NOTINITIALED;
}

if (G_VBE_Supported == VBENOTSUPPORTED) {
  SVGA_Err = VBENOTSUPPORTED;
  return      VBENOTSUPPORTED;
}

if (G_BitsColor == MODE24BITCOLOR) {
  union {
    struct SVGA24BitColor ActualColor;
    unsigned long         Holder;
  } L_24Bits;

  L_ScreenPos += X+X;
  L_Window = L_ScreenPos / G_Win_Size;

  if (G_Cur_Window != L_Window)
    set_window(L_Window);

  L_24Bits.ActualColor
      = *(G_24Bit_Win_Addr +
           ((L_ScreenPos/3)+X+X) % G_Win_Size);

  L_24Bits.Holder = L_24Bits.Holder >> 8;
  *P_Red   = L_24Bits.Holder >>
              G_Mode_Info.RedFieldPosition;
  *P_Green = L_24Bits.Holder >>
            G_Mode_Info.GreenFieldPosition;
  *P_Blue  = L_24Bits.Holder >>
             G_Mode_Info.BlueFieldPosition;
} /* end if 24 bit mode */
else if (G_BitsColor == MODE16BITCOLOR) {
  unsigned int L_16BitColor;

  L_ScreenPos += X;
  L_Window = L_ScreenPos / G_Win_Size;

  if (G_Cur_Window != L_Window)
    set_window(L_Window);

  L_16BitColor  = *(G_16Bit_Win_Addr +
             ((L_ScreenPos/2)+X) % G_Win_Size);

  *P_Red   = (L_16BitColor >>
             G_Mode_Info.RedFieldPosition) <<
               (8 - G_Mode_Info.RedMaskSize);
  *P_Green = L_16BitColor >>
```

```
                   G_Mode_Info.GreenFieldPosition <<
                    (8 - G_Mode_Info.GreenMaskSize);
      *P_Blue   = L_16BitColor >>
                   G_Mode_Info.BlueFieldPosition <<
                    (8 - G_Mode_Info.BlueMaskSize);
    } /* end else if 15/16 bit mode */
    else {
      SVGA_Err = MODENOTSUPPORTED;
      return     MODENOTSUPPORTED;
    } /* end else */

    SVGA_Err = NOERROR;
    return     NOERROR;
  } /* end SVGA_get_dc_pixel() */
```

The flood fill algorithm is fairly compact and elegant. But the need to use one or another function to find the pixel color really makes a mess of it. To avoid this mess SVGALib divides flood fill into two separate functions, non_dc_floodfill( ) for palette modes and dc_floodfill( ) for direct color modes. These functions are not called directly, but rather the exported function SVGA_floodfill( ) determines the type of mode, direct color or palette, and calls the correct one. The code for non_dc_floodfill( ) is simple and straightforward:

```
  void non_dc_floodfill (int X, int Y) {
    unsigned char L_This_Color;

    /* break the recursion if */
    /* we've gone off the screen */
    if (X > SVGA_MaxX) return;
    if (Y > SVGA_MaxY) return;

    SVGA_get_pixel (X, Y, &L_This_Color);
    if ((L_This_Color != G_8Bit_Color)  &&
        (L_This_Color != G_8Bit_Border_Color)) {
      SVGA_plot_pixel(X, Y);
      non_dc_floodfill(X-1, Y);
      non_dc_floodfill(X,   Y-1);
      non_dc_floodfill(X+1, Y);
      non_dc_floodfill(X,   Y+1);
    } /* end if */

  } /* end non_dc_floodfill() */
```

But there are still things that need to be said about this function. The two if statements at the beginning are quite important. If the figure being filled is not closed the algorithm will "leak out." If there is nothing to detect the end of the screen the algorithm will keep recursing, going off into "no man's land." The

SVGA_plot_pixel routine is protected so that it should not write to memory beyond the screen, but the recursion will still cause the stack to fill up and overflow.

Speaking of stacks, this brings up another point. This routine will often recurse quite deeply while filling an object. The default stack size for most compilers is fairly small (for Borland it's 4K, for Microsoft it's about the same). Most compilers have way of increasing the stack size. SVGALib contains the line

```
extern unsigned _stklen = 60000;
```

in order to accomplish this. If the compiler you are using does not accept this, check your programmer's guide. The stack size given here is large enough for medium-sized objects, but in high-resolution modes larger objects have to be broken into pieces, with each piece filled separately.

The final point is that this function does not use fill_line( ). Nor does it have any provision for pattern filling. The reason is this: If you attempt to fill with a pattern, the algorithm will first work its way left until an edge is found. It will then start working its way to the right. If the point to the right is not filled because of a space in the pattern the call to the right will be successful, and the function will call itself with the point to the left, which is the edge. That call being successful, the function will then start to the right again, and then again to the left. This is a really nifty infinite loop. The problem is that the routine needs to mark the pixels where it has been already.

One way to do this would be to create some sort of table or tree structure, where the point passed in is placed in the table. If that point is already found in the table exit the function. This can use a tremendous amount of memory. A method that might prove to be less memory intensive might be to create a 2D array of bits large enough that there is a bit for each pixel in the object. The bit for a pixel can be checked when the function is entered. If it is not set then set it and continue; if it is set we have already visited this pixel, so exit the function. This would involve a bit of coding. Another way around would be to have a call to flood fill first fill the object with a third color with no pattern. Then a second call to flood fill would put the pattern in place, actually putting the background color in where the fill color is not used. This version would also look to make sure a pixel is not the background color. This would probably be quite slow, plus the user would see the object being filled with a third color and wonder what is going on.

The code for dc_floodfill( ) is essentially the same as non_dc_floodfill( ), except for the color handling, and one other exception. For SVGA_get_dc_pixel( ) to pass back RGB values, it needs something to pass them back into. So we need to declare local variables to hold these values. When local variables are declared in C, they are allocated space on the stack. Because of the recursive nature of the algorithm, stack space is already at a premium. We want to do all that we can to use as little stack space as possible. So what we do is at the beginning of the function we declare a byte, which is the smallest amount of space we can allocate on the stack, which can be used as a flag.

Further down in the code a block is started using the "curly brace" character "{". In C you can start a block anywhere inside a function, and variables can be declared any time you start a block. The variables declared here are also put on the stack, but when the block is closed the stack space is freed. So we declare the local RGB variables inside the block, and compare them to the G_Border variables. We set the flag and close the block. Now we look at that flag to see if we should recurse. Here is the code.

```
void dc_floodfill (int X, int Y) {
  unsigned char L_Continue;

  /* break the recursion if */
  /* we've gone off the screen */
  if (X > SVGA_MaxX) return;
  if (Y > SVGA_MaxY) return;

  { /* declare things in such a way that they
       can be taken off the stack before
       recursion */
    unsigned char L_Red,  L_Blue,  L_Green;

    SVGA_get_dc_pixel (X, Y,
                &L_Red, &L_Green, &L_Blue);

       /* Are we at the border? */
    if (!((L_Red   == G_Red)    &&
          (L_Green == G_Green)  &&
          (L_Blue  == G_Blue))      &&

      /* Have we visited this pixel already? */
        !((L_Red   == G_Border_Red)    &&
          (L_Green == G_Border_Green)  &&
          (L_Blue  == G_Border_Blue)))   {
      L_Continue = TRUE;
    } /* end if */
    else
      L_Continue = FALSE;
  } /* take local declarations off stack */

  if (L_Continue == TRUE) {
    SVGA_plot_pixel(X, Y);
    dc_floodfill(X-1, Y);
    dc_floodfill(X,   Y-1);
```

```
    dc_floodfill(X+1, Y);
    dc_floodfill(X,   Y+1);
  }

} /* end dc_floodfill() */
```

SVGA_polyfill( )

Filling polygons is not an easy thing for computers to do. Human beings can look at a polygon and see whether a pixel is inside the polygon or not. A computer does not have access to this world view.

So the polyfill algorithm needs to start at the left-hand side of the polygon and scan across, looking for the right side of the polygon. This is a good first step, but there is a problem. With a polygon of the shape shown in Fig. 11.3.1(a), the next edge reached will halt the scan, leaving large portions unfilled [Fig. 11.3.1(b)]. So what we can do is continue scanning, and if we find another edge in the polygon, start filling again. If the edge we start at is considered the first edge, then every time we cross an even-numbered edge we stop filling and every time we cross an odd-numbered edge we start filling again. For this to work we must be sure that the polygon is closed.

But at a corner point where the polygon doubles back on itself the fill will stop at the corner point, then the algorithm will scan until another edge is found, and start the fill again. But at this point it will be filling outside the polygon [Fig. 11.3.1(c)]. The scan has become confused, and is now filling the outside areas instead of the inside. This problem is fixed by tracking the slope of the lines. Whenever two lines with a common endpoint have slopes with different signs, the common end-point is placed a second time in the data structure. This means the algorithm will attempt to fill between the two points, which have the same X and Y coordinates. But that's okay, fill_line( ) can handle that.

That's the basic idea. The code that implements this is quite complex. The interface is much like SVGA_polygon( ). An array of corner points is passed in, along with an integer to indicate the number of points in the array. The corner points are used to find the boundary lines of the polygon, very much like SVGA_polygon( ). For each line in the polygon a function that closely resembles Bresenham's line function is called. The big difference is that this function stores the points on the line as well as draws the line. After all the points on the boundary are stored the data structure is traversed in such a way that the polygon can be scanned as described above.

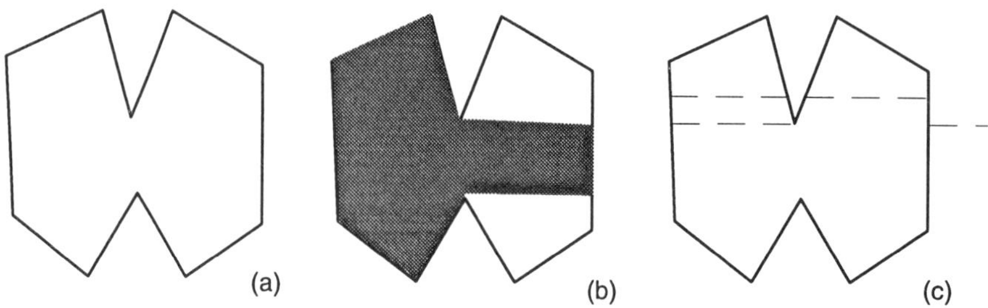

Fig. 11.3.1 Problems with Filling a Polygon

The data structure used by SVGA_polyfill( ) is a binary tree with the key field being the Y coordinate. Each node in the tree contains a sorted list of X values. The Y values are not needed in the list, since they all use the same Y value, which is the key field for the tree. This structure will allow us to traverse the tree, and at each node pull points out of the list in pairs, and draw a fill line between the pair. Pairs of points will be pulled out of the list until there are no more, which should be the edge of the polygon. If the first point of the pair is pulled out without a matching second point an error must have occurred, since the SVGA_polyfill( ) automatically closes the polygon. Here are the structure definitions:

```
struct pointlist {
  int X;
  struct pointlist *Next;
};

struct pointtree {
  int Y; /* this is the key field */
  struct pointlist *pts;
  struct pointtree *Left;
  struct pointtree *Right;
} *G_PolyFill_Tree = NULL;
```

Support functions for the linked lists are needed to create the list, add points, and retrieve points. These functions are all pretty standard. Remember that the list is ordered from lowest X to highest. Note that remove_from_list( ) takes the first point then deallocates the space for that point. When all points are removed all nodes in the list have been deallocated.

```
void create_list (struct pointlist **P_List) {
  *P_List = NULL;
} /* create_list */
```

```
char insert_in_list (struct pointlist **P_List,
                     int X) {

  if (*P_List == NULL) {
    if ((*P_List =
          malloc(sizeof(struct pointlist)))
                                      == NULL) {
      SVGA_Err = OUTOFMEMORY;
      return     OUTOFMEMORY;
    }
    (*P_List)->X    = X;
    (*P_List)->Next = NULL;
    SVGA_Err = NOERROR;
    return     NOERROR;
  }
  else if ((*P_List)->X > X) {
    struct pointlist *temp;
    if ((temp =
           malloc(sizeof(struct pointlist)))
                                      == NULL) {
      SVGA_Err = OUTOFMEMORY;
      return     OUTOFMEMORY;
    }
    temp->X    = X;
    temp->Next = *P_List;
    *P_List    = temp;
    SVGA_Err = NOERROR;
    return     NOERROR;
  }
  else /*  (*P_List)->X <= X */
    return (insert_in_list(
                       &((*P_List)->Next), X));
} /* end insert_in_list() */

void remove_from_list
              (unsigned char *P_Found,
               struct pointlist **P_List,
               int *X) {

  struct pointlist *L_Temp;
  if (*P_List != NULL) {
    *P_Found = TRUE;
    L_Temp   = *P_List;
    *P_List  = (*P_List)->Next;
    *X       = L_Temp->X;
    free (L_Temp);
  }
  else
```

```
      *P_Found = FALSE;
} /* end remove_from_list() */
```

Several comments: The first is that the insert routine is recursive. This makes the code much cleaner and simpler. If you prefer nonrecursive code feel quite free to change it. Another comment is on the use of malloc( ). This routine can be quite dangerous, especially on unprotected operating systems such as DOS. It is imperative to verify that it returned a valid pointer, and to stop program execution otherwise. If this is not checked you could easily write into a portion of memory, oftentimes the interrupt vector table, and cause the computer to "crash." Also always verify that all lists end with a null pointer, so you don't "run off the end." Finally, make sure that you are including alloc.h or stdlib.h to make the prototype of malloc( ) visible. Without this malloc( )'s behavior is quite unpredictable.

The tree routines needed are for inserting points and traversing the tree. The traversal routine is responsible for drawing the fill lines and for deallocating the nodes as they are traversed. More on this later. There is no need for a create routine, since there is only one global tree, which is set to null from the start. The insert routine is the normal binary tree insert. Note the call to create_list( ). Also note that the return value of malloc( ) is carefully checked.

```
char insert_in_tree (struct pointtree **P_Tree,
                     int X, int Y) {

  if (*P_Tree == NULL) {
    if ((*P_Tree =
           malloc(sizeof(struct pointlist)))
                                      == NULL) {
      SVGA_Err = OUTOFMEMORY;
      return     OUTOFMEMORY;
    }
    (*P_Tree)->Y = Y;
    create_list (&(*P_Tree)->pts);
    insert_in_list(&(*P_Tree)->pts, X);
    (*P_Tree)->Left  = NULL;
    (*P_Tree)->Right = NULL;
    SVGA_Err = NOERROR;
    return     NOERROR;
  }
  else if ((*P_Tree)->Y > Y)
    return (insert_in_tree(&(*P_Tree)->Left,
                                         X, Y));
  else if ((*P_Tree)->Y < Y)
    return (insert_in_tree(&(*P_Tree)->Right,
                                         X, Y));
  else {
```

```
      insert_in_list(&(*P_Tree)->pts, X);
      SVGA_Err = NOERROR;
      return     NOERROR;
    }
  } /* end insert_in_tree() */
```

The tree traversal function is called traverse_tree_destruct( ), since it traverses the tree and deallocates the nodes as it goes. This routine traverses the tree, and at each node it pulls out a point from the list. It then goes into a loop, pulling a point, using the two points to call fill_line( ), the pulling another point. If there are no more points in the list the loop is exited. If the first point of the pair of points is pulled, and there is no matching second point this indicates a rather serious bug in the routine, rather than a user error, so program execution is halted, the screen is returned to text mode, and an error message is written on the screen. After the traversal the current node is deallocated. This must only be done after the traversal in both directions, and after all points have been removed from the list. Otherwise you will be left with dangling pointers. The order of traversal is not important, but this function uses an in-order traversal for the sake of convention, which results in the polygon being filled from the top down.

```
  void traverse_tree_destruct
                    (struct pointtree **P_Tree) {
    if (*P_Tree != NULL) {
      traverse_tree_destruct (&(*P_Tree)->Left);

      { /* declare here to control
            stack growth */
        unsigned char L_Found;
        int X1, X2;

        remove_from_list (&L_Found,
                          &(*P_Tree)->pts, &X1);
        while (L_Found != FALSE) {
          remove_from_list (&L_Found,
                          &(*P_Tree)->pts, &X2);
          if (L_Found == FALSE) {
            /* this is a bad error -
               don't return a code,
               bring down the program */
            SVGA_set_mode (3);
            printf ("UNKOWN FATAL ERROR  IN ")
            printf ("SVGA_Polyfill\n\n");
            exit(-1);
          } /* end if */
          fill_line(X1, X2, (*P_Tree)->Y);
```

```
        remove_from_list(&L_Found,
                         &(*P_Tree)->pts, &X1);
      } /* end while loop */
    } /* end declare */

    traverse_tree_destruct (&(*P_Tree)->Right);
    free (*P_Tree);
  } /* end if (*P_Tree ... */
} /* end traverse_tree_destruct() */
```

Now that all the support functions and data structures are taken care of we can take a quick look at polyfill_line( ), which is called from SVGA_polyfill( ), and is responsible for putting most points into the above data structure. This function is almost exactly like Bresenham's line algorithm, except that whenever the Y coordinate changes the point is inserted into G_PolyFill_Tree. When a horizontal line is drawn there is no need to place points in the tree.

```
void polyfill_line(int X1, int Y1,
                   int X2, int Y2) {
  float m;
  int   i;

  if (X2-X1 == 0) /* slope is infinite */
    if (Y1<Y2) {
      for (i=Y1; i<=Y2; i++) {
        SVGA_plot_pixel (X1, i);
        insert_in_tree (&G_PolyFill_Tree,
                                         X1, i);
        if (SVGA_Err != NOERROR) return;
      } /* end for */
    } /* end if */
    else {
      for (i=Y2; i<=Y1; i++) {
        SVGA_plot_pixel (X1, i);
        insert_in_tree (&G_PolyFill_Tree,
                                         X1, i);
        if (SVGA_Err != NOERROR) return;
      } /* end for */
    } /* end else */
  else if (Y2-Y1 == 0) /* slope is 0 */
    if (X1<X2) {
      for (i=X1; i<=X2; i++) {
        SVGA_plot_pixel (i, Y1);
      } /* end for */
    } /* end if */
    else {
      for (i=X2; i<=X1; i++) {
```

```
        SVGA_plot_pixel (i, Y1);
      } /* end for */
    } /* end else */
  else {            /* other slopes */
    m=(float)(Y2-Y1)/(float)(X2-X1);
    if (m > 1.0)
      polyfill_slope_gt_one
                          (X1, Y1, X2, Y2);
    else if (m > 0)
      polyfill_slope_0_to_one
                          (X1, Y1, X2, Y2);
    else if (m < -1)
      polyfill_slope_lt_neg_one
                          (X1, Y1, X2, Y2);
    else polyfill_slope_neg_one_to_0
                          (X1, Y1, X2, Y2);
  } /* end else */
} /* end polyfill_line() */
```

Since this function is taken from SVGA_line( ), which did not return error codes properly, it also does not return error codes properly. To help fill in for this, it detects errors by checking SVGA_Err, which is filled in by the support routines, and if SVGA_Err indicates an error this function is exited. SVGA_polyfill( ) checks SVGA_Err, and returns whatever code that variable holds. In this way SVGA_polyfill( ) can let the program know that it is out of memory, even though the polyfill_line( ) routine does not properly communicate errors.

Function polyfill_line( ) makes calls to a number of functions that implement Bresenham's line algorithm, and stores points whenever there is a change in the Y value. Since these are so much like the Bresenham's line functions presented in the last chapter they will not be presented in detail here. For more discussion on these functions, as well as the function shown above, see the discussion in Chapter 10. The code for one of these functions is shown next, as a representative sample. Notice the calls to insert_in_tree( ).

```
void polyfill_slope_0_to_one (int X1, int Y1,
                              int X2, int Y2) {
/*
 * bresenham's line method
 * for slope of 0<M<1
 */

  int temp;
  int p,    Delta_X,    Delta_Y,
         _2_Delta_X, _2_Delta_Y;
```

```
    if (X1>X2) {
      temp = X2;
      X2   = X1;
      X1   = temp;

      temp = Y2;
      Y2   = Y1;
      Y1   = temp;
    } /* end if */

    Delta_X = X2-X1;
    Delta_Y = Y2-Y1;

    _2_Delta_X = 2*Delta_X;
    _2_Delta_Y = 2*Delta_Y;

    if (G_BitMask & G_CurBit)
      SVGA_plot_pixel (X1, Y1);
    G_CurBit = G_CurBit >> 1;
    if (G_CurBit == 0) G_CurBit = 0x8000;
    p=_2_Delta_Y-Delta_X;
    X1++;

    while (X1 < X2) {
      if (p>0) {
        p=p+(_2_Delta_Y-_2_Delta_X);
        insert_in_tree (&G_PolyFill_Tree,
                                      X1, Y1);
        if (SVGA_Err != NOERROR) return;
        Y1++;
      } /* end if */
      else {
        p=p+_2_Delta_Y;
      } /* end else */
      if (G_BitMask & G_CurBit)
        SVGA_plot_pixel (X1, Y1);
      G_CurBit = G_CurBit >> 1;
      if (G_CurBit == 0) G_CurBit = 0x8000;
      X1++;
    } /* end while */
  } /* end polyfill_slope_0_to_one() */
```

And finally we come to SVGA_polyfill( ) itself. This function is similar to SVGA_polygon( ). It takes as parameters an unsized array of integers representing the X and Y values of the vertices, and an integer which gives the number of points in the array. This function makes calls to polyfill_line( ) to draw the outline of the polygon and fill G_PolyFill_Tree. It also tracks the slope of each line, and if the sign of the slope changes between two lines it puts the common end-point into the structure so that it will be there twice. Note the special handling to check the slopes between the last and the first lines. Here is the code.

```
char SVGA_polyfill (int P_Num_Pts,
                    int *P_Pt_Array) {
  int i;
  float L_Last_Slope, L_Next_Slope;

  if (G_VBE_Supported == NOTINITIALED) {
    SVGA_Err = NOTINITIALED;
    return     NOTINITIALED;
  }
  if (G_VBE_Supported == VBENOTSUPPORTED) {
    SVGA_Err = VBENOTSUPPORTED;
    return     VBENOTSUPPORTED;
  }

  L_Next_Slope = P_Pt_Array[3]-P_Pt_Array[1] /
                 P_Pt_Array[2]-P_Pt_Array[0];

  P_Num_Pts *= 2;
  for (i=0; i<P_Num_Pts-2; i+=2) {
    L_Last_Slope = L_Next_Slope;
    L_Next_Slope =
      P_Pt_Array[i+3]- P_Pt_Array[i+1] /
                 P_Pt_Array[i+2]-P_Pt_Array[i];

    if (((L_Last_Slope>0)&&(L_Next_Slope<0))
                        ||
        ((L_Last_Slope<0)&&(L_Next_Slope>0))) {
       insert_in_tree(&G_PolyFill_Tree,
                      P_Pt_Array[i],
                      P_Pt_Array[i+1]);
    } /* end if */

    polyfill_line(P_Pt_Array[i],
                  P_Pt_Array[i+1],
                  P_Pt_Array[i+2],
                  P_Pt_Array[i+3]);

    if (SVGA_Err != NOERROR) return SVGA_Err;
  } /* end loop */

  L_Last_Slope = L_Next_Slope;
  L_Next_Slope =
        P_Pt_Array[1]-P_Pt_Array[i+1] /
               P_Pt_Array[0]-P_Pt_Array[i];
```

```
    /* automagically close the polygon */
    if (((L_Last_Slope>0)&&(L_Next_Slope<0))
                                ||
        ((L_Last_Slope<0)&&(L_Next_Slope>0))){
       insert_in_tree(&G_PolyFill_Tree,
                      P_Pt_Array[i],
                      P_Pt_Array[i+1]);
    }
    polyfill_line(P_Pt_Array[P_Num_Pts-2],
                  P_Pt_Array[P_Num_Pts-1],
                  P_Pt_Array[0],
                  P_Pt_Array[1]);

    if (SVGA_Err != NOERROR) return SVGA_Err;

    /* if sign of slope of last line is different
       from sign of slope of first line, add
       first point to structure, again! */
    L_Last_Slope = L_Next_Slope;
    L_Next_Slope = P_Pt_Array[3]-P_Pt_Array[1] /
                   P_Pt_Array[2]-P_Pt_Array[0];

    if (((L_Last_Slope>0)&&(L_Next_Slope<0))
                                ||
        ((L_Last_Slope<0)&&(L_Next_Slope>0))) {
       insert_in_tree(&G_PolyFill_Tree,
                      P_Pt_Array[0],
                      P_Pt_Array[1]);
    } /* end if */
    if (SVGA_Err != NOERROR) return SVGA_Err;

    traverse_tree_destruct (&G_PolyFill_Tree);

    SVGA_Err = NOERROR;
    return     NOERROR;

}
```

It should be pointed out here that this implementation of polyfill( ) is somewhat nonstandard. To save on RAM and time, the more standard implementation uses a simple array instead of the complex data structure given here. This data structure however makes the processing more clear. The array is generally an array of records, each record containing one X and Y pair. As processing proceeds the points are added to the array in the order that they are found. After processing finishes, the array is sorted, then the points are taken out two at a time, and lines are drawn between them.

The arguments for one data structure or the other are rather complex. The data structure shown requires many more pointers than the array implementation. Since the size of each node is small the overhead needed for pointers constitutes a large percentage of the RAM used by the algorithm. Also there is time needed to find the location for points being inserted, and to allocate the memory. The array implementation will use less memory if the array is fitted to the number of points needed. To do this the number of points needed needs to be found first or estimated. The routine can be run without storing points, but with a counter tracking the number of points needed, after which an array of the proper size is allocated and the routine is run again, this time storing points in the allocated array. This takes time. The size can be estimated by looking at the distance between each vertex. This will generally allocate more space than needed, since points are only stored when the Y value changes, but that is better than allocating too little. A quick analysis indicates that this will generally save some RAM. A small amount of processing can be done to make the estimate even better. For instance, we know that if the line between two vertices is at an angle greater than 45° every point will be stored, while lines with angles less than this store fewer and fewer points until the angle reaches 0, when no points are stored. Thus a fair amount of RAM can be saved by looking at the angle of each line.

But what is the time cost of using an array? Inserting in a binary tree has a big O time of log(n), while inserting in the sorted list has a big O of $n/2$. In both of these measures n is the number of points. For the array storage method the time is dependent on the number of lines and the number of points. But the array needs to be sorted, which is an $n*\log(n)$ operation. So, except for very small polygons the data structure used by SVGALib is somewhat faster but uses rather more RAM. The array implementation is the more often used. The main reason the more complicated data structure is used here is because it makes the processing more straightforward and easier to understand.

12

Animation

Animation is the term used for graphics in motion. Any time something on the screen shows movement it is animated. PC BIOS supports several methods of animation. Unfortunately none of these methods is very good for the smooth, sophisticated animation required by games and multimedia. The reasons for this will be explained as we investigate these methods. They do serve as a useful introduction to animation, however.

For really good animation effects the programmer must directly program the graphics adapter, rather than going through BIOS or the high-level routines provided by Microsoft and Borland. So far I have made a point of avoiding this kind of low-level programming in this book, since it is an introductory book. But at the end of this chapter there is a program that directly changes the palette registers in VGA mode 0x13, which serves as a simple example of what professional graphics programmers working with animation do with their time.

Simple Animation

The way an animation is usually created, both on computers and on film, is to take a series of similar pictures and flash them rapidly on the screen. The items in the picture that are the same do not change, the items that are different seem to move. Imagine a square drawn on the computer screen. The square is erased, then drawn again at an angle, then erased and drawn at more of an angle (Fig. 12.1.1). This is repeated continuously. If this is done rapidly enough the eye cannot detect that the square is being erased and redrawn. It looks as if the square were moving, spinning on its axis. If done properly the movement looks very smooth and natural. This is implemented in program BK1201.C on the distribution disk. This program is not presented, since it is quite simple and straightforward.

Fig. 12.1.1 Shapes Used by Program BK1201.C

Program BK1201.C demonstrates animation with simple line drawings. As the image becomes more complex this method rapidly becomes too slow. Program BK1201.C suggests that quite a lot can be done with line drawings, however, since there is a lengthy delay between drawing the square and erasing it again.

If an animation becomes too complex for the simple line drawing method, arrays can be used to hold bit maps of the images. The bit map can be copied to the frame buffer at the appropriate place. This is especially good for VGA and SVGA screen modes where each pixel is a whole number of bytes. If a mode is being used where this is not true a loop can be used to call putpixel( ) to set the appropriate pixels on the screen. This is quite slow.

Using getimage( ) and putimage( ) for Animation

For modes where each pixel is not a whole number of bytes Borland and Microsoft have both supplied routines that allow programmers to capture bit maps and replace them on the screen. To use these functions the image must be drawn on the screen first. It is then copied from the screen to a buffer in RAM or captured, from where it can be copied back to the screen any number of times. This is also useful for saving bit maps to a file. The Borland functions are called getimage( ) to capture the bit map, imagesize( ) to find the size of the bit map required, and putimage( ) to replace the image on the screen. The Microsoft functions are called _getimage( ), _imagesize( ), and _putimage( ). Microsoft also supplies versions for use with its windowing and xycoord systems (see Chapter 4 on Microsoft Graphics programming).

Parameters for both compilers' functions are the same. Function getimage( ) takes coordinates of the upper left corner, the lower right corner, and a pointer to a buffer. The function imagesize( ) takes the coordinates of the upper left corner and the lower right corner, and returns the size needed for the buffer. Function putimage( ) takes the coordinates of the upper left corner, a pointer to the buffer where the image is stored, and an action. The buffer stores information the size of the image, so the lower right corner is not needed. The action parameter takes an enumeration, the possible values for which are listed with the function prototypes. The use of this parameter is explained later. The prototypes for both Borland and Microsoft functions are given below (see also Tables 12.1.1 and 12.1.2):

Borland

```
void getimage(int left,  int top,
              int right, int bottom,
              void far *bitmap);
  /*
   * getimage() will copy a rectangular bit
   *   map from the screen.
   *
   * Parameters:
   *   left   - left hand border of bit map
   *   top    - top border of bit map
   *   right  - right hand border of bit map
   *   bottom - bottom border of bit map
   *   bitmap - pointer to buffer that will
   *     hold the bitmap
   */

unsigned far imagesize(int left,  int top,
                       int right, int bottom);
  /*
   * imagesize() will return the size buffer
   *   needed to store a screen image
   *
   * Parameters:
   *   left   - the left border of the image
   *   top    - the top of the image
```

```
    *   right  - the right hand side
    *   bottom - the bottom of the image
    */

void far putimage(int left, int top,
                  void far *bitmap, int op);
   /*
    * putimage() puts an image previously saved
    *   with getimage() on the screen.
    *
    * Parameters:
    *   left   - the left hand location of the
    *            image
    *   top    - the top of the image
    *   bitmap - buffer containing the bitmap
    *   op     - logical operation for putting
    */
```

Table 12.1.1 Possible actions for Borland's putimage( )

Enumeration	Value	Description
COPY_PUT	0	Copy to screen
XOR_PUT	1	Exclusive OR with what is on screen
OR_PUT	2	OR with what is on screen
AND_PUT	3	AND with what is on screen
NOT_PUT	4	Copy inverse of source

Microsoft

```
void _getimage(short x1, short y1,
               short x2, short y2,
               char _huge *image);
   /*
    * function to copy a block from the frame
    *   buffer.
    *
    * Parameters:
    *   x1, y1 - the upper Left hand corner of
    *            the block
    *   x2, y2 - the lower right hand corner
    *   image  - buffer that the portion of the
    *            frame buffer is copied to
    */
```

```
long _imagesize(short x1, short y1,
                short x2, short y2);
  /*
   * Function to return the amount of memory
   * needed to hold an image
   *
   * Parameters:
   *   x1, y1 - the upper left corner of the
   *            image on the screen
   *   x2, y2 - the lower right corner
   *
   * Returns:  The number of bytes needed to
   *   store the image
   */

void _putimage(short x, short y,
               char *huge image,
               short action);
  /*
   * Function to put an image on the screen
   *   that has previously been saved with
   *   _getimage()
   *
   * Parameters:
   *   x, y   - the upper left corner where the
   *            image is to be placed.
   *   image  - buffer holding the image
   *   action - bitwise action for copying the
   *            buffer to the screen
   */
```

Table 12.1.2 Possible Actions for Microsoft's _putimage( )

Constant	Meaning
_GAND	AND the graphic with the screen
_GOR	OR the graphic with the screen
_GPRESET	Uses the logical negative of the graphic
_GPSET	Place the graphic on the screen as it is
_GXOR	XOR the graphics with what is on the screen

The parameter *op* [action for Microsoft's _putimage( )] describes the action used for writing the image to the screen. The image can be combined with what is already on the screen by using logic operations. The operations available include AND, OR,

XOR, NOT, and simply writing over what is on the screen. The operation is carried out on each bit of each pixel on the screen and the corresponding bit in the bit map.

XOR_PUT (_GXOR) is the most interesting action. If an image is placed on the screen using XOR_PUT the background shows through. If the image is then put on the screen again, using XOR_PUT, at exactly the same place, the image will be removed but the background will be left as it was. This is often useful, but the fact that the background shows through often creates a mess. For this reason the example program for this section makes a copy of the background first, then uses COPY_PUT (_GPSET) to place the object on the screen. To erase the object, it is overwritten by the image that has the background saved in it.

The proper way to use these functions is to first set the mode you will be using, then decide the xy coordinates that will bound the region where the image will be captured from. Use imagesize( ) to find the size of the needed buffer and malloc( ) to allocate a buffer of that size. Next draw the image on the screen, then use getimage( ) to capture the image. Now the buffer can be written to a disk file, or written to the screen as many times as desired, using putimage( ). Program BK1202.C on the distribution disk demonstrates this.

Program BK1201.C has a green ball bouncing around the screen. First an area of background is captured, then the ball is drawn and captured. The ball is then erased by putting the area of background over the ball. The ball is then put to the screen a little distance from its starting point. The process repeats until the ball hits a wall, when its direction is changed. This continues until a key is pressed.

```
/*
 * BK1202 - Animation using getimage() and
 *  putimage() - A ball bouncing around the
 *  screen
 */

#include <graphics.h>
#include <stdlib.h>
#include <stdio.h>
#include <alloc.h>

void main(void) {
    int Mode, Driver, GraphError;
    int X, Y, MaxX, MaxY;
    int Size;
    void far *Blank, *Ball;
    int Dir_X = 3, Dir_Y = 3;
    int i;

    Driver = DETECT;
    detectgraph(&Driver, &Mode);
```

```
initgraph(&Driver, &Mode, '');

GraphError = graphresult();
if (GraphError != grOk) {
  printf("%s\n",grapherrormsg(GraphError));
  exit(-1);
}

/* Do Graphics Stuff Here */
/* Upper left corner of image */
MaxX = getmaxx();
MaxY = getmaxy();
X = MaxX/2-20;
Y = MaxY/2-20;

/* First get a black square
   to be used to erase image */

Size = imagesize(X, Y, X+40, Y+40);
if ((Blank = farmalloc(Size)) == NULL) {
  closegraph();
  printf("Not Enough Memory");
  exit(-1);
}
getimage(X, Y, X+40, Y+40, Blank);

/* Next get a green ball */
setcolor(GREEN);
setfillstyle(SOLID_FILL, GREEN);

fillellipse(X+20, Y+20, 20, 20);
if ((Ball = farmalloc(Size)) == NULL) {
  closegraph();
  printf("Not Enough Memory");
  exit(-1);
}
getimage(X, Y, X+40, Y+40, Ball);

/* move ball around screen
   by erasing with black square
   then replacing ball a small
   distance from where it started */
while (!kbhit()) {
  putimage(X, Y, Blank, COPY_PUT);
  X += Dir_X, Y += Dir_Y;
  putimage(X, Y, Ball, COPY_PUT);

  /* Boundries of ball's travel */
  if (X >= MaxX - 30) Dir_X = -3;
```

```
        if (X <= 30)          Dir_X =  3;
        if (Y >= MaxY - 30) Dir_Y = -3;
        if (Y <= 30)          Dir_Y =  3;
    }

    getch();
    if (kbhit()) getch();

    closegraph();
}
```

When this program runs the ball seems to flicker. The reason for this is that the putimage( ) function is rather slow, compared to screen retrace. The period of time while the electron guns are sweeping the screen is called *screen retrace* or *refresh*. In between each retrace there is a small amount of time while the gun is repositioned from the lower left of the screen to the upper right. If getimage( ) were timed to do its work between retraces the one image would be finished before the next started and there would be no flicker. But putimage( ) is not so timed, and indeed it may simply be too slow. If putimage( ) takes more time to copy the image to the frame buffer than the time between retraces then there will be flicker. This is only a problem in animation, where the image is erased then redrawn rapidly and repeatedly. If the image were just put on the screen and left there, flicker would not be a problem.

Using Paging

The method described in the last section can be inadequate for more complex images. If a number of items have to be put on the screen all at the same time, but all in different places, simply using putimage can become a mess.

Certain monitor modes require more memory for the frame buffer than other modes. Modes that require less memory can use the excess as a secondary frame buffer. An image can be set up in the excess memory, then a switch can be set to make that memory the active frame buffer used by the screen. This technique is called *paging*. Each separate section of memory that can be used as a frame buffer is called a page.

When a page is being displayed on the screen it is called the visual page. Only one page at a time can be the visual page. A page that is not the visual page is said to be in the background. Usually graphics routines write to the visual page, but they can be changed to write to any page, background or foreground. The page that is being written to is called the active page. A complex scene can be constructed on a background page, then it can be switched to be the active page, causing the entire complex screen to become visible at once. Again Borland and Microsoft both supply very similar routines for setting the active and visual pages.

Borland

```
void far setactivepage(int page);
  /*
   * setactivepage() will make page the active
   *   page.  All graphics output will be
   *   written to that page.
   *
   * Parameter:
   *   Page - the number of the page to make
   *          active
   */

void setvisualpage (int page);
  /*
   * Function to set the visual page
   *
   * Parameter
   *   page - the page to make the visual page
   *
   * Returns: The previous visual page, or
   *   a negative value on error.
   */
```

Microsoft

```
short _setactivepage(short page);
  /*
   * Function to set the active video page.
   *
   * Parameter:
   *   page - The new active page
   *
   * Returns: the previous active page
   */

short _setvisualpage(short page);
  /*
   * Function to set the visual page
   *
   * Parameter
   *   page - the page to make the visual page
```

```
 *
 * Returns: The previous visual page, or
 *   a negative value on error.
 */
```

Remember that these functions should only be used for modes that support more than one page (see Appendix F on PC monitor modes for a list of modes and how many pages they support). The example for this section is not really complex enough to show why paging might be used, since such an example would be too complex to really make an effective example. This example is basically the same as the one for the last section, except that paging has been added.

First the background page is set as the active page, so the original ball can be drawn without being seen. Next a piece of background is captured, same as the last program. After that a ball is drawn and captured in the background. Next the visual page is switched, making the ball visible. The new background page is now made the active page, and where the ball would be on that page is cleared. Notice that the ball is drawn on one page in the same place that it is drawn on the other, then on the other it is moved. This is done to minimize flicker. Note also that the mode is hard-wired to make sure the monitor uses a mode that supports paging. The source for this program is in file BK1203.C on the distribution disk.

```
/*
 * BK1203 - A ball bouncing
 *  around the screen using paging
 */

#include <graphics.h>
#include <stdlib.h>
#include <stdio.h>
#include <alloc.h>

void main(void) {
    /* use VGA medium mode, since it has
       more than 1 page */
    int Mode = VGAMED, Driver = VGA,
        GraphError;
    int X, Y, X_Old, Y_Old, MaxX, MaxY;
    int Size;
    void far *Blank, *Ball;
    int Dir_X = 6, Dir_Y = 6;
    int i;

    initgraph(&Driver, &Mode, '');

    GraphError = graphresult();
```

```
if (GraphError != grOk) {
  printf("%s\n",grapherrormsg(GraphError));
  exit(-1);
}

/* Do Graphics Stuff Here */
/* Upper left corner of image */
MaxX = getmaxx();
MaxY = getmaxy();
X    = MaxX/2-20;
Y    = MaxY/2-20;

/* first set active page to 1
   so objects will not be
   displayed as they are drawn */
setactivepage(1);

/* Next get a black square
   to be used to erase image */
Size = imagesize(X, Y, X+40, Y+40);
if ((Blank = farmalloc(Size)) == NULL) {
  closegraph();
  printf("Not Enough Memory");
  exit(-1);
}
getimage(X, Y, X+40, Y+40, Blank);

/* Next get a green ball */
setcolor(GREEN);
if ((Ball = farmalloc(Size)) == NULL) {
  closegraph();
  printf("Not Enough Memory");
  exit(-1);
}
setfillstyle(SOLID_FILL, GREEN);

fillellipse(X+20, Y+20, 20, 20);
getimage(X, Y, X+40, Y+40, Ball);

/* move ball around screen
   by erasing with black square
   then replacing ball a small
   distance from where it started */
while (!kbhit()) {
  /* display set up page */
  setvisualpage(1);

  /* set up next page */
  setactivepage(0);
```

```
        putimage(X, Y, Blank, COPY_PUT);
        X_Old = X,  Y_Old = Y;
        X += Dir_X, Y += Dir_Y;
        putimage(X, Y, Ball, COPY_PUT);

        /* Boundries of ball's travel */
        if (X >= MaxX - 30) Dir_X = -3;
        if (X <= 30)        Dir_X =  3;
        if (Y >= MaxY - 30) Dir_Y = -3;
        if (Y <= 30)        Dir_Y =  3;

        /* display set up page */
        setvisualpage(0);

        /* set up next page */
        setactivepage(1);
        putimage(X_Old, Y_Old, Blank, COPY_PUT);
        putimage(X, Y, Ball, COPY_PUT);

      }

      getch();
      if (kbhit()) getch();

      closegraph();
  }
```

Although an attempt was made to minimize flickering this program still does. One would think that since it is only a switch being set it would be easy enough to squeeze in between the retrace. The trouble is that the setvisualpage( ) function uses BIOS, which is not timed to the retrace. The answer is to avoid BIOS, and go directly to the video board and monkey with its registers. As explained in the introduction to this chapter, that type of programming is not covered since it is beyond the scope of an introductory-level graphics book. The professional graphics programmer spends a good deal of his/her time avoiding retrace.

Animation by Manipulating Colors

Chapter 6 on color covers palette registers, in case you are a little fuzzy on this subject. Another way of creating an animation effect is by manipulating the color palette registers. This is less common, but I've had a great deal of luck with it in the past three years, and so I wanted to go into in some detail here.

The idea is to set up a pattern on the screen, then change the palette registers to make the pattern move. It is easier to demonstrate than to explain in any more detail.

Program BK1204.C is actually part of a physics demonstration on waves that was written some years ago. A series of concentric circles is drawn so that the color at the center is 1 (in 16-color mode) and the color increments until it reaches 15, when it starts over again. This pattern is repeated a number of times. Remember that colors in non-direct modes only describe which palette register is being used, and the register describes what color is being shown. The registers are set to a gray scale in the following way: Color 1 is very dark gray, almost black. The colors smoothly and rapidly get whiter until color 7, which is bright white. The colors then start getting darker, smoothly and rapidly, until color 15, which is set the same as color 1. Color 0 is not touched, since it is the background and must remain black. As the concentric circles are drawn they look like waves spreading out on the surface of a pond.

Now comes the real magic. A loop is entered that "moves" the color settings from one register to the next. Before the loop is entered color 7 is bright white. The first time through the loop color 8 becomes bright white, while color 7 becomes a slightly darker shade. The color that was in 15 gets put into 1, 1 gets put into 2, etc. At this point watching the program run might make things clearer. This program can be found in BK1204.C on the distribution disk.

```
/*
 * BK1204 - wave demonstration.  Waves are made to
 *   wave by changing palette registers.  Left over
 *   from physics wave demo package.
 */

#include <DOS.H>
#include <GRAPHICS.H>
#include <STDLIB.H>
#include <ALLOC.H>

void set_palette () {
  int i,j;
  struct palettetype pal;

  getpalette(&pal);

  for (i=1; i<8; i++) {
    setrgbpalette (pal.colors[i],
                   i<<3, i<<3, i<<3);
    setrgbpalette (pal.colors[16-i],
                   i<<3, i<<3, i<<3);
  }
  setrgbpalette(pal.colors[8],
```

```
                15<<2, 15<<2, 15<<2);
}

void main(void) {
  int x=320,y=200;
  int driver = DETECT, mode;
  int i,j;
  int temp;
  struct palettetype pal;

  initgraph(&driver, &mode, "");
  set_palette();

  x = getmaxx()/2;
  y = getmaxy()/2;

  for (i=0; i<x/2; i++) {
    setcolor((i%15)+1);
    circle (x, y, i);
  }

  getpalette(&pal);

  i=0;
  while (!kbhit()) {
    for (j=0;j<15;j++) {

      for (i=1; i<8; i++) {
        setrgbpalette
           (pal.colors[((i+j)%15)+1],
            i<<3, i<<3, i<<3);
      }
      setrgbpalette (pal.colors[((8+j)%15)+1],
                     15<<2, 15<<2, 15<<2);
      for (i=7; i>0; i--) {
        setrgbpalette
          (pal.colors[(((16-i)+j)%15)+1],
           i<<3, i<<3, i<<3);
      }
    }
  }

  getch();
  if (kbhit()) getch();
  closegraph();
}
```

This type of animation really lights up in 256-color modes. Changing 256 color registers one at a time, however, takes a little bit of time. If you look carefully at the program above, while it runs, you can see that even changing 16 registers one at a time slows the program noticeably. Fortunately BIOS provides a function for setting a block of color registers all at once. Table 12.4.1 shows how to set up the registers for this function call. The interrupt number is 0x10.

Table 12.4.1 Register Setup for BIOS Service 0x10, Function 0x10 Subservice 0x12, Set Block of Palette Registers

Register	Value
AH	0x10
AL	0x12
BX	Number of first color register to set
CX	Number of registers to set
DS	Offset of buffer holding register values
ES	Segment of buffer holding register values

A complete example of how to use this function for animation effects will not be given, but an example of how to call it will be.

```
void newpal (unsigned char palette[256][3]) {
  union  REGS  reg;
  struct SREGS sreg;

  segread(&sreg);

  reg.h.ah = 0x10;
  reg.h.al = 0x12;
  reg.x.bx = 0;
  reg.x.cx = 256;
  reg.x.dx = FP_OFF(palette);

  sreg.es = FP_SEG(palette);

  int86x(0x10,&reg,&reg,&sreg);
}
```

The array passed in shows how to set up the new values for the color register. The first dimension is the number of the color register, the second is the RGB values in that order. To set the 24th color register to a yellow you would use:

```
register_array[24][0] = 63;  /* red value   */
register_array[24][1] = 63;  /* green value */
register_array[24][2] = 0;   /* blue value  */
```

There is also a function for reading a block of registers. This function is covered in Appendix D on BIOS interrupt 0x10. When I use this form of animation, however, I generally set up all 256 color registers at once, to make sure they have the values I want them to have. For details on using BIOS with your programs see Chapter 8.

Unfortunately this interrupt suffers from the same problem as the interrupt for changing the visual page. It is not timed to the video retrace. Up to now I have attempted to avoid low-level programming in this book. However I have had so much success with one program that I have included it (in one of its many variations) on the distribution disk. The name of the program is simply DEMO.C, since it is set up as a monitor demonstration program. I highly recommend that you run it since it is one of the most colorful and interesting programs on the distribution disk. Since it is on the distribution disk I should explain how I got around the flicker problem.

The basic idea is to set up three buffers, one each with the red, the green, and the blue values, then pump those buffers into the RGB color registers as quickly as possible. The values are sent to the registers through a byte-sized port, 0x03C9. The value at port 0x03C8 gives the register number that will go to the port. Once the register number has been sent to port 0x03C8, port 0x03C9 expects values for red, green, and blue in that order.

A pointer to each buffer is passed to the function. A loop sends the register value to port 0x03C8, then sends the value from the red buffer to port 0x03C9 and points the pointer to the next item in that buffer. The green and blue values are sent to the same port and there pointers are set to the next item. This is a very fast and efficient algorithm. There is no timing done to make sure the retrace is off, but I have not seen any flicker on any monitors I've run this on. On some monitors I have seen some snow, but this is not nearly as annoying as the flicker, and it has been on few enough monitors that I elected to ignore it rather than investigate and fix it.[1]

```
unsigned char rpalette[256];
unsigned char gpalette[256];
unsigned char bpalette[256];

void newpal (unsigned char *rpalette,
             unsigned char *gpalette,
             unsigned char *bpalette) {
```

[1] I am indebted to Mr. Lance Wulfers, currently with CSC Inc, Endwell, New York, for this method of setting palette registers without flicker.

```
    register unsigned char i;

    for(i=0;i<255;i++) {
       outportb(0x03c8, i);
       outportb(0x03c9, *(rpalette++));
       outportb(0x03c9, *(gpalette++));
       outportb(0x03c9, *(bpalette++));
    }

    outportb(0x03c8, 255);
    outportb(0x03c9, *rpalette);
    outportb(0x03c9, *gpalette);
    outportb(0x03c9, *bpalette);

}
```

The method for manipulating the color buffers used by DEMO.C is interesting and worth looking at. An array of unsigned characters is defined called color_tube, and initialed so both the ends are 0 and the middle is 64, similar to the wave program. The reason it is called color_tube is the idea that colors are supposed to flow along the color_tube. The RGB color buffers are then initialized so that color 0 is black for the background, and color 1 is white for text. The next 96 colors are set from the color tube so that there is a gray scale starting from dark gray going to bright white, then going back to dark gray again. The colors above are also set from the color tube so that all colors are initialized. Function initial_colors( ), given later, should be studied to see how the color tube is set up. Studying how the color buffers are set from the color tube might also give some insight as to how the color tube is used.

```
unsigned char color_tube[96];

void initial_colors (void) {
    int count;

    for (count = 0; count < 48; count++) {
        color_tube[count]    = count+16;
        color_tube[95-count] = count+16;
    }

    rpalette[0] = 0;
    gpalette[0] = 0;
    bpalette[0] = 0;

    rpalette[1] = 63;
    gpalette[1] = 63;
    bpalette[1] = 63;
```

```
    for (count=0; count<95; count++) {
      rpalette[count+2] = color_tube[count];
      gpalette[count+2] = color_tube[count];
      bpalette[count+2] = color_tube[count];

      gpalette[count+95]  = color_tube[count];
      rpalette[count+95]  = color_tube[count];
      bpalette[count+160] = color_tube[count];
    }

    newpal(rpalette, gpalette, bpalette);
}
```

When using this type of animation, drawing the screen is a fairly trivial task, and the real magic is in the color manipulation. After the color tube and the RGB buffers are set up some sort of repeating pattern is drawn on the screen, then the colors are changed. The code for changing the colors is given here, followed by an explanation.

```
void cascade_colors (char *option,
                     char *spec_key) {
    long Start, Stop;
    unsigned int  delay;
    unsigned int  i;
    char done = FALSE;
    int  loop_ctrl, loop_end;
    int  red_start, green_start, blue_start;
    int  red_pos,   green_pos,   blue_pos;
    time_t curr_time, start_time;

    time(&start_time);
    do {

      switch (random(3)) {
        case 0 : red_start = 0;
                 green_start = random(95);
                 blue_start  =
                    random(green_start+95);
                 break;
        case 1 : green_start = 0;
                 blue_start = random(95);
                 red_start  =
                   random(blue_start+95);
                 break;
        case 2 : blue_start = 0;
                 red_start = random(95);
                 green_start  =
                   random(red_start+95);
```

```
            break;
    }

    red_pos     = 0;
    green_pos   = 0;
    blue_pos    = 0;

    if (red_start > green_start)
        loop_end = red_start+95;
    else if (green_start > blue_start)
        loop_end = green_start+95;
    else
        loop_end = blue_start+95;

    for (loop_ctrl=0; loop_ctrl<loop_end;
                             loop_ctrl++) {

        for (i = 255; i > 2; i--){
          rpalette[i] = rpalette[i-1];
          gpalette[i] = gpalette[i-1];
          bpalette[i] = bpalette[i-1];
        }

        if ((loop_ctrl >= red_start) &&
            (red_pos < 96)) {
            rpalette[2] =
                    color_tube[red_pos];
            red_pos++;
        }
        if ((loop_ctrl >= green_start) &&
            (green_pos < 96)) {
            gpalette[2] =
                color_tube[green_pos];
            green_pos++;
        }
        if ((loop_ctrl >= blue_start) &&
            (blue_pos < 96)) {
            bpalette[2] =
                     color_tube[blue_pos];
            blue_pos++;
        }
        newpal(rpalette, gpalette, bpalette);

        if (kbhit()) {
            *option = my_getch(&(*spec_key));
            done = TRUE;
            break;
        }
```

```
            time(&curr_time);
            if (difftime(curr_time, start_time) >
                                                420) {
              *spec_key = FALSE;
              *option   = RANDOM_SELECT;
              return;
            }

            /* timer loop */
            for (delay=0; delay<G_Delay; delay++);
        }
      } while (!done);
  }
```

First I'll get the trivial stuff out of the way. As the colors cascade the program needs to check for key presses. If a key is pressed the program returns that key to the calling function, so that function can act on it. In this case the calling function makes use of F keys, so this function must also return whether a "special" key was pressed. The PC keyboard is covered in Chapter 6, where a program for studying colors is given, and in Appendix I. The version of the program on the distribution disk is set up as a monitor demonstration program, for showing off the capabilities of VGA monitors. Such a program is better if it changes the screen every so often. So after 7 minutes, if no keys have been pressed, this function exits and passes back a code to show that the calling function should draw a new screen. The rest of the function is dedicated to cascading colors.

The idea for cascading colors is first to take all the values in the three buffers and move them up one position, so the value that was in rpalette[23] will next be in rpalette[24]. The value that was in that last position falls off the end. After this is accomplished we need something to go into the first slot. This is where the color tube comes in. If all three buffers took colors from the color tube at the same spot then all that would be displayed would be shades of gray. So each buffer starts feeding from the color tube at a different time.

The switch statement at the beginning of the function uses a random number generator to decide when each buffer starts feeding from the color tube. The if statement after that decides when all the buffers are finished feeding from the tube and the process can start over. At each cycle each buffer feeds, but from different positions in the color tube. If the system does not wait until all buffers are finished before resetting there will be a harsh line when one or more buffers are suddenly cut off. Next there is a nested loop that executes until all buffers are finished. Inside this loop is another loop that causes the cascade. This is a triply nested loop, which we were all taught was a bad thing in school, but if you set this program to the fastest it can go, you will see that it is not a problem. After that loop is a series of if statements that decide if a value should be read from the color tube. The last value in the color tube is 0, so after a buffer finishes reading from the tube a 0 will be cascaded up and, eventually, if the system did not reset, the entire buffer would be 0.

Finally, I can give an example of an interesting screen. This function is called after the color initialization function, before the cascade function. It simply draws a set of concentric circles out from the center of the screen, in increasingly higher colors.

```
void fcircle1() {
    int  Radius;
    char Palette;

    setpix(160, 100, 2);
    for (Radius = 1; Radius < 189; Radius++) {
      Palette = Radius+1;
      bcircle (160, 100, Radius, Palette);
    }
    setpix(160, 100, 2);
} /* end fcircle1() */
```

The bcircle( ) function is Bresenham's circle function, as described in Chapter 10, but this one plots the circle doubly wide so that no pixels are left unplotted. To see this in action, run the program DEMO on the distribution disk and press key F2. One last note. This program uses some pretty ugly logic to control the speed of the color cascade. I tried Borland's delay( ) function, but it does not operate smoothly. So I used the code now present to control the speed. It seems to work for a wide range of machines, speeds, and tastes. If you are interested in this type of animation you might want to study the other screens available to get a feel for the possibilities.

13

Linear Transformations in Computer Graphics

Linear transformations are matrix operations that describe movements of points in a space. The coordinates of a point make up a 2×1 matrix. A 2×2 matrix that describes the transformation is multiplied with the coordinate matrix, resulting in a 1×2 matrix that holds the coordinates of the transformed point. If you wish to work in 3- space, for transforming 3D images, you would use a 3×1 matrix to hold the coordinates and a 3×3 matrix to describe the transformation. Linear transformations provide a powerful set of tools for such things as rotating an object, moving it around the screen (translating it), shearing it, flipping it, etc.

Matrices for C Programmers (not for math majors)

This section introduces basic matrix operations. The notation used here is not the standard mathematical notation. Instead the notation has some minor modifications to make it more understandable for those people trained as computer programmers. Most people trained in math tend to view a matrix as an abstract object, while computer programmers tend to view it as a type of array. Matrices are accessed by an index giving the X and Y positions of the desired element. Standard mathematical notation puts the Y index first, then the X index. To a graphics programmer, who is used to accessing pixels and 2D arrays with the X index first, this is confusing. To avoid this confusion the X index is always given first. This means the first index indicates the column, since X coordinates refer to columns, and the second indicates the row. Unfortunately, this will confuse any math people reading this chapter. The notation used here does match the computer examples given with this chapter.

To facilitate this chapter some very simple matrix functions have been included on the distribution disk. These can be found in the file MATRIX.C. To use this file in your programs include the header file MATRIX.H. I would not encourage you to use this package for professional quality software since it not of very high quality. Most of the functions need more error checking, and several of the functions are not nearly as efficient as they could be. Also, for a good high quality matrix package you would need more functions, for such things as finding a matrix inverse and other standard matrix functions.

The file MATRIX.H defines a structure for matrices:

```
struct matrix {
  int   DimX;
  int   DimY;
  float *Mat;
};
```

This structure holds the matrix itself in an unsized 1D array. This is easier to define than an unsized 2D array. To access the correct elements we can look at the DimX and DimY fields to find the correct dimensions, then with a little simple math we can translate 2D space to 1D space to find the correct position in the array. This is no less efficient that using a 2D array in the first place, since a computer's memory is actually a 1D array. For any multidimensional array this math must be performed. The only difference is we are doing it by hand rather than letting the compiler do it. With any good optimizing compiler the binary code produced will be just as good as if a 2D array were used. The following function prototypes are also defined in MATRIX.H:

```
void Mat_alloc(int DimX, int DimY,
               struct matrix *Mat);

void Mat_dealloc(struct matrix *Mat);

void Mat_insert(struct matrix *Mat,
                int X, int Y, float number);
/*
 * function for inserting a number into
 * a matrix
 */

float Mat_read(struct matrix Mat,
               int X, int Y);

void Mat_Mult (struct matrix Mat1,
               struct matrix Mat2,
               struct matrix *result);
```

There is also a macro defined to enter numbers into a matrix without the overhead of a procedure call. The macro also does not check to make sure the coordinate of the item being entered is in fact in the matrix. This has the advantage of saving overhead, but the disadvantage of allowing overflows.

```
#define MAT_INSERT(matrix, X, Y) /
    (matrix).Mat[((matrix).DimY*(X-1))+(Y-1)]
/*
 * alternate macro for inserting a number
 * into a matrix.  Use the syntax
 * MAT_INSERT(MyMatrix, X, Y) = MyNumber;
 * This has the advantage of lower overhead
 * than the function call, plus looks something
 * like what you would expect an insertion into
 * a matrix to look like
 */
```

An example using this macro is given in the code for multiplying matrices. A similar macro for reading from a matrix could also be set up. It would be a good idea as the macro is quite a bit more efficient than the equivalent function.

The source for the matrix package is covered briefly. Mat_alloc( ) allocates a new matrix. A matrix is defined as the size in the X dimension, the size in the Y dimension, and a pointer to a float, which can be used as an array of floats. When a matrix is allocated the array of floats needs to be allocated and the DimX and DimY fields are filled in. The array of floats is zeroed out, so that after a matrix is allocated the program can assume all initial values are zero. A loop is used to zero the array, since readability is more important in an example than efficiency. It would be more efficient to use memset( ) or a related function to zero the array.

```
void Mat_alloc(int DimX, int DimY,
               struct matrix *Mat) {
  int i, size;

  (*Mat).DimX = DimX;
  (*Mat).DimY = DimY;

  if (((*Mat).Mat =
    malloc(sizeof(float)*DimY*DimX)) == NULL) {
    printf("Out of Memory in Mat_alloc()\n\n");
    exit(-1);
  }

  size = DimY * DimX;
  for (i=0; i<size; i++)
    (*Mat).Mat[i] = 0.0;

}
```

The function Mat_dealloc( ) deallocates an array when there is no more use for it. It is a good idea to deallocate matrices when they are no longer needed, to preserve RAM, and to deallocate all matrices before the program finishes. Otherwise the DOS memory manager could have problems and the computer could "crash."

```
void Mat_dealloc(struct matrix *Mat) {

  (*Mat).DimX = 0;
  (*Mat).DimY = 0;

  free((*Mat).Mat);
}
```

Mat_insert( ) is used to insert a number into the array. First the X,Y coordinates of the item in the table are decremented because arrays in C start at 0, but we want the upper left corner of the table to be (1,1). Next the bounds are checked and the number is put into the array. The proper location in the array is found with the following formula:

$$DimY * X + Y$$

This is called *column major order*, since all the elements of one column are adjacent in memory, then all the elements of the next column, etc. It could also have been organized in *row major order* with all the elements of one row adjacent in memory, then all the elements of the next row, etc.

```
void Mat_insert(struct matrix *Mat,
                int X, int Y, float number) {

  X--;
  Y--;
  if (((*Mat).DimX < X) ||
      ((*Mat).DimY < Y)) {
    printf
       ("Out of Bounds error in Mat_insert");
    exit(-1);
  }

  (*Mat).Mat[(*Mat).DimY*X+Y] = number;
}
```

The macro version for insertion works basically the same way, without the checks. The Mat_read( ) function also works basically the same.

```
float Mat_read
         (struct matrix Mat, int X, int Y) {

  X--;
  Y--;
  if ((Mat.DimX < X) ||
      (Mat.DimY < Y)) {
    printf ("Out of Bounds error in Mat_read");
    exit(-1);
  }

  return (Mat.Mat[Mat.DimY*X+Y]);
}
```

The following formula is used to multiply two matrices:

$$C[j,k] = \sum_{i=1}^{n} A[i,k] \times B[j,i]$$

This formula says that for the element of matrix C indexed by $[j,k]$, take the first element of the row k in matrix A and multiply it by the first element of column j of matrix *B*. Then multiply the next element in the same row of matrix *A* and the next element of the same column of matrix *B*, then add the results of the two multiplies. Keep multiplying and adding until you get to the end of the row and column. This is shown graphically in Fig. 13.1.1. In this figure there is a dashed box around the elements of *A* and the elements of *B* that are used to find *C*[1,1].

Matrix A

Row 1	$A[1,1]$	$A[2,1]$
Row 2	$A[1,2]$	$A[2,2]$
Row 3	$A[1,3]$	$A[2,3]$
Row 4	$A[1,4]$	$A[2,4]$

Matrix B

Col 1	Col 2	Col 3
$B[1,1]$	$B[2,1]$	$B[3,1]$
$B[1,2]$	$B[2,2]$	$B[3,2]$

Matrix C = A x B

$$\begin{bmatrix} C[1,1] & C[1,1] & C[1,1] \\ C[1,1] & C[1,1] & C[1,1] \\ C[1,1] & C[1,1] & C[1,1] \\ C[1,1] & C[1,1] & C[1,1] \end{bmatrix}$$

Fig. 13.1.1 Matrix Multiplication

The following are examples of how to find two specific elements of matrix *C*, given matrices *A* and *B* as they are defined in Fig. 13.1.1.

$$C[1,1] = A[1,1] \times B[1,1] + A[2,1] \times B[1,2]$$
$$C[3,2] = A[1,2] \times B[3,1] + A[2,2] \times B[3,2]$$

The code for multiplying two matrices does the following: When multiplying matrices, the X dimension of the first matrix must be equal to the Y dimension of the second, so there is check in the code. Next a matrix to hold the result needs to be allocated. The resulting matrix will have an X dimension the same as the second matrix, and a Y dimension the same as the first. And then the actual multiply can be done. This requires three nested loops, one for *j* in our sigma equation, one for *k*, and one for *i*. These loops do just what the sigma equation says to do for each element in the resultant matrix. Note that for each i we read from the resultant matrix. This means the resultant matrix must be zeroed out before the loops can be entered, or we will get garbage values for our results. Fortunately we took care of this in the matrix allocation function.

```
void Mat_mult (struct matrix Mat1,
               struct matrix Mat2,
               struct matrix *result) {
  int i, j, k;

  if (Mat1.DimX != Mat2.DimY) {
    printf
      ("Incompatible matrices in Mat_mult");
    exit (-1);
  }

  Mat_alloc(Mat2.DimX, Mat1.DimY, &(*result));

  for (k = 1; k <= (*result).DimY; k++)
    for (j = 1; j <= (*result).DimX; j++)
      for (i = 1; i <= Mat1.DimX; i++)
        MAT_INSERT(*result, j, k) =
          Mat_read (*result, j, k) +
          Mat_read (Mat1, i, k)*
          Mat_read(Mat2, j, i);
}
```

There are probably ways to make this function more efficient. Another way of making matrix multiplication more efficient is to pay attention to the order of multiplications when a number of matrices are to be multiplied. When a series of matrices are multiplied the order of multiplication can make a great deal of difference in how many operations are done, so a function could be provided for multiplying a list of matrices. This function would determine the best order for multiplying the matrices, then perform the multiplications in that order. Note that matrix multiplication is associative, but it is not symmetric. In other words

$$A \cdot B \neq B \cdot A$$

but

$$(A \cdot B) \cdot C = A \cdot (B \cdot C)$$

So we can perform the multiplications in any order, as long as we do not change which side of the multiplication sign each matrix is on.

Linear Transformations in Graphics

There are a number of transformations available to transform, or reshape, graphics objects. Specific transformations for specific tasks are presented later in the chapter. Right now an example transformation for rotating an object is presented, so that we have an example to work with.

To rotate an object on a Cartesian grid we can use the following formulas on each point:

$$x_{rot} = x \cdot \sin(\Theta) + y \cdot \cos(\Theta)$$
$$y_{rot} = -x \cdot \sin(\Theta) + y \cdot \cos(\Theta)$$

We can represent these equations with the following matrix:

$$\begin{bmatrix} \cos(\Theta) & \sin(\Theta) \\ -\sin(\Theta) & \cos(\Theta) \end{bmatrix}$$

Place one point of the object to be rotated into a row vector and multiply that vector by the above matrix. Repeat for each point in the object. The result will be the original object rotated about the origin.

$$\begin{bmatrix} X_{\text{rot}} \\ Y_{\text{rot}} \end{bmatrix} = \begin{bmatrix} X & Y \end{bmatrix} \begin{bmatrix} \cos(\Theta) & \sin(\Theta) \\ -\sin(\Theta) & \cos(\Theta) \end{bmatrix}$$

This transformation rotates the object about the origin. If the object is not on the origin it will not rotate as you would expect (Fig. 13.2.1).

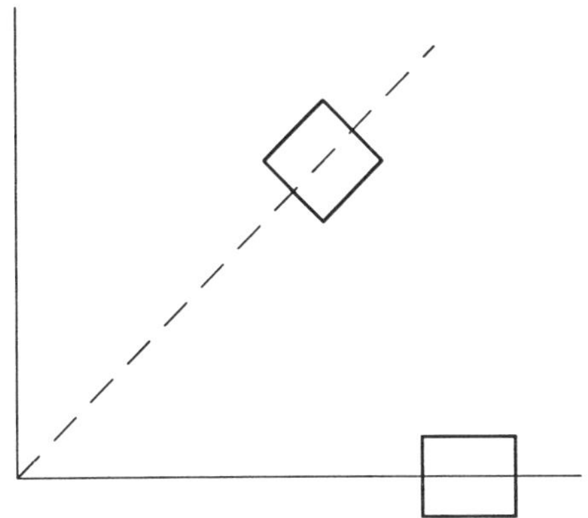

Fig. 13.2.1 Object Rotated About the Origin When It Is Not on the Origin

To rotate an object properly it must be moved to the origin, rotated, then moved back. A transformation for translation is given later.

Linear transformations use square matrices, so an efficient way to perform multiple transformations on an object is to multiply the transformation matrices together. The result is a square matrix of the proper size. When the resulting transformation is carried out each primary transformation is carried out in the order it was multiplied into the result.

An Example: Rotating an Ellipse

Rotated ellipses are useful for isometric 3D drawing (see Chapter 7). If a circle is drawn on an isometric surface it will appear distorted. To make it look round an ellipse is needed with one axis at the same angle as the isometric angle.

I will not go over the entire rotated ellipse algorithm, since most of it is the same as Bresenham's ellipse algorithm (see Chapter 10). A modification to the main algorithm is to set up a matrix to represent the rotation linear transformation. The angle to use is passed into the function as a parameter. After setting up the transformation matrix the normal Bresenham's algorithm is executed.

The transformation matrix is passed to the ellipse_plot( ) function. This function takes advantage of the four way symmetry of an ellipse to plot four points when only one is calculated. Each one of these points is put into a matrix, which is then multiplied by the transformation matrix. The result of the multiply is the location to plot the pixel. Unfortunately this must be done for each of the four pixels being plotted, rather than performing one matrix multiply and projecting the result. If you attempted to use only one matrix multiply and project the result all you would end up with is a distorted ellipse, rather than a rotated one. Notice that the X_center and Y_center values are added on after the matrix multiply. This way the points of the oval are centered on the origin when the multiply is performed. The following code can be found in file BK1301.C.

```
void ellipse_plot (int X, int X_center,
                   int Y, int Y_center,
                   struct matrix xform) {
  struct matrix cur_pt, xformed_pt;

  Mat_alloc (2, 1, &cur_pt);

  MAT_INSERT(cur_pt, 1, 1) = +X;
  MAT_INSERT(cur_pt, 2, 1) = +Y;
  Mat_mult  (cur_pt, xform, &xformed_pt);
  putpixel
    (X_center +
            (int)Mat_read(xformed_pt, 1, 1),
     Y_center +
            (int)Mat_read(xformed_pt, 1, 2),
     WHITE);
  Mat_dealloc(&xformed_pt);

  MAT_INSERT(cur_pt, 1, 1) = -X;
  MAT_INSERT(cur_pt, 2, 1) = +Y;
  Mat_mult  (cur_pt, xform, &xformed_pt);
  putpixel
    (X_center +
            (int)Mat_read(xformed_pt, 1, 1),
     Y_center +
            (int)Mat_read(xformed_pt, 1, 2),
     WHITE);
  Mat_dealloc(&xformed_pt);

  MAT_INSERT(cur_pt, 1, 1) = +X;
  MAT_INSERT(cur_pt, 2, 1) = -Y;
  Mat_mult  (cur_pt, xform, &xformed_pt);
  putpixel
    (X_center +
          (int)Mat_read(xformed_pt, 1, 1),
     Y_center +
          (int)Mat_read(xformed_pt, 1, 2),
     WHITE);
  Mat_dealloc(&xformed_pt);
```

```
  MAT_INSERT(cur_pt, 1, 1) = -X;
  MAT_INSERT(cur_pt, 2, 1) = -Y;
  Mat_mult  (cur_pt, xform, &xformed_pt);
  putpixel
    (X_center +
           (int)Mat_read(xformed_pt, 1, 1),
     Y_center +
           (int)Mat_read(xformed_pt, 1, 2),
     WHITE);
  Mat_dealloc(&xformed_pt);

  Mat_dealloc(&cur_pt);
} /* end ellipse_plot() */

void rotated_ellipse
           (int X_center, int Y_center,
            int r1,       int r2,
            int Theta) {

  long Y = 0;
  long X = r1;
  long r1_squared = r1*r1;
  long r2_squared = r2*r2;
  long p = 2*r1_squared*(r2_squared-1)-
           r2_squared*(2*(r1_squared-r1+1));
  long chgpt =
     r2_squared/sqrt(r1_squared+r2_squared);
  struct matrix xform;

  Mat_alloc(2, 2, &xform);

  MAT_INSERT(xform, 1, 1) =
                     cos(Theta*M_PI/180);
  MAT_INSERT(xform, 2, 1) =
                     sin(Theta*M_PI/180);
  MAT_INSERT(xform, 1, 2) =
                    -sin(Theta*M_PI/180);
  MAT_INSERT(xform, 2, 2) =
                     cos(Theta*M_PI/180);

  while (Y <= chgpt) {
    ellipse_plot (X, X_center,
                  Y, Y_center, xform);

    if (p >= 0)
      p = p - r1_squared*((Y<<2)+6);
    else {
      p = p - ((r1_squared*Y)-
             (r2_squared*X)<<2)-6*r1_squared;
```

```
        X--;
      } /* end else */
      Y++;
    } /* end while loop */

    X=0, Y=r2;
    p = r1_squared*((r2_squared<<1)-(r2<<1)+1) -
        ((r2_squared*(r1_squared-1))<<1);

    while (Y >= chgpt ) {
      ellipse_plot (X, X_center,
                    Y, Y_center, xform);

      if (p < 0)
        p = p + r2_squared*((X<<2)+6);
      else {
        p = p + (r2_squared*((X<<2)+6))-
                ((r1_squared*(Y-1))<<2);
        Y--;
      } /* end else */
      X++;
    } /* end while loop */

    Mat_dealloc(&xform);

  } /* end SVGA_ellipse() */
```

This code is quite inefficient. For every single point plotted a matrix is allocated, initialized to 0.0, and deallocated. This overhead can be saved by doing away with the matrix package and performing the matrix operations "inline." The matrix package is used here to keep the example readable.

Other Transformations

A number of transformations are possible. Here are several.

Translation

The following are general equations to define a translation and a rotation together. These two equations are the basis for most of the transformations we will look at.

$$x_{\text{final}} = x \cdot \cos(\Theta) + y \cdot \sin(\Theta) + x_{\text{trans}}$$
$$y_{\text{final}} = -x \cdot \sin(\Theta) + y \cdot \cos(\Theta) + y_{\text{trans}}$$

Where X and Y are points in the object, X_{trans} and Y_{trans} are the distance to translate the object in the X dimension and the Y dimension, and X_{final} and Y_{final} are the xy coordinates of point after being transformed. If there is no rotation then theta is 0 and we have the following:

$$x_{\text{final}} = x \cdot 1 + 0 + x_{\text{trans}}$$
$$y_{\text{final}} = 0 + y \cdot 1 + y_{\text{trans}}$$

Linear transformations need to be square matrices in order to make the matrix multiplication come out right. So we use the following matrix:

$$\begin{bmatrix} 1 & 0 & x_{\text{trans}} \\ 0 & 1 & y_{\text{trans}} \\ 0 & 0 & 1 \end{bmatrix}$$

But now our vector needs to have three elements for the multiplication:

$$\begin{bmatrix} x_{\text{final}} \\ y_{\text{final}} \\ 1 \end{bmatrix} = \begin{bmatrix} x & y & 1 \end{bmatrix} \begin{bmatrix} 1 & 0 & x_{\text{trans}} \\ 0 & 1 & y_{\text{trans}} \\ 0 & 0 & 1 \end{bmatrix}$$

The rest of the transformations will be presented in this 3 × 3 format, for ease of combining them with the translation.

Rotation with a 3 × 3 Matrix

Here is the matrix to use for rotation, in 3 × 3 format.

$$\begin{bmatrix} \cos(\Theta) & \sin(\Theta) & 0 \\ -\sin(\Theta) & \cos(\Theta) & 0 \\ 0 & 0 & 1 \end{bmatrix}$$

Scaling

Scaling means resizing. If we scale by the same amount in both X and Y dimensions the object remains proportional. We can also scale by different amounts in either dimension.

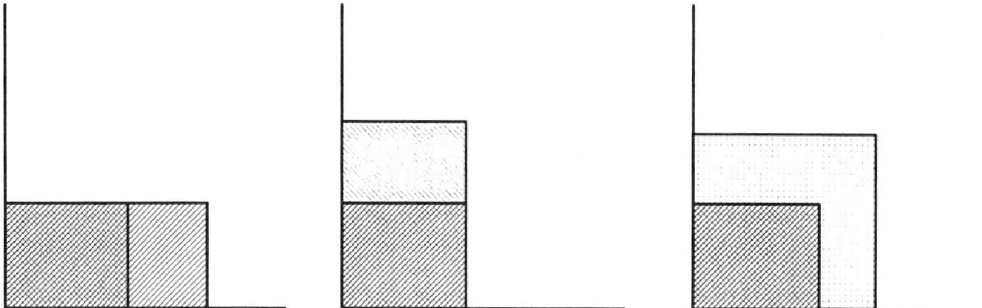

(a) Resize Object in X Dimension (b) Resize Object in Y Dimension (c) Resize Object in X and Y Dimension

Fig. 13.4.1 Resizing an Object

The matrix for scaling is easy to find. Start with general equations.

$$
\begin{aligned}
x_{\text{final}} &= x \cdot \cos(\Theta) + y \cdot \sin(\Theta) + x_{\text{trans}} \\
y_{\text{final}} &= -x \cdot \sin(\Theta) + y \cdot \cos(\Theta) + y_{\text{trans}}
\end{aligned}
$$

Use a translation of 0 and a rotation of 0, and multiply the remaining X's by the amount of X scaling desired and the remaining Y's by the amount of Y scaling desired. This gives the following equations:

$$
\begin{aligned}
x_{\text{final}} &= x \cdot x_{\text{scale}} + 0 + 0 \\
y_{\text{final}} &= 0 + y \cdot y_{\text{scale}} + 0
\end{aligned}
$$

which gives the following matrix:

$$
\begin{bmatrix} x_{\text{scale}} & 0 & 0 \\ 0 & y_{\text{scale}} & 0 \\ 0 & 0 & 1 \end{bmatrix}
$$

If these values are both 1 the X and Y values will be unchanged after the multiplication. This is the identity matrix. If these values are larger than 1 the object being sized will grow, and if they are smaller than 1 the object will shrink.

The object can be scaled in the X dimension and Y dimension independently. To scale only in the X dimension make $y_{scale} = 1$, and to scale in the Y dimension only make $x_{scale} = 1$. To scale in both dimensions use the same value for x_{scale} and y_{scale}.

As with rotation, before scaling an object it should be centered on the origin. Otherwise it will scale unevenly. The object can be moved to the origin by using the translation matrix. Multiply the matrix to translate the object to the origin by the scale matrix, then multiply the result by a translation matrix that moves the object back. Use the result as the matrix to multiply each point.

Shear in X

A shear means that the portion of the object farthest from the origin is moved away at right angles to origin. One way to picture this is with a stack of CDs that has been pushed so that they no longer line up (Fig 13.4.2).

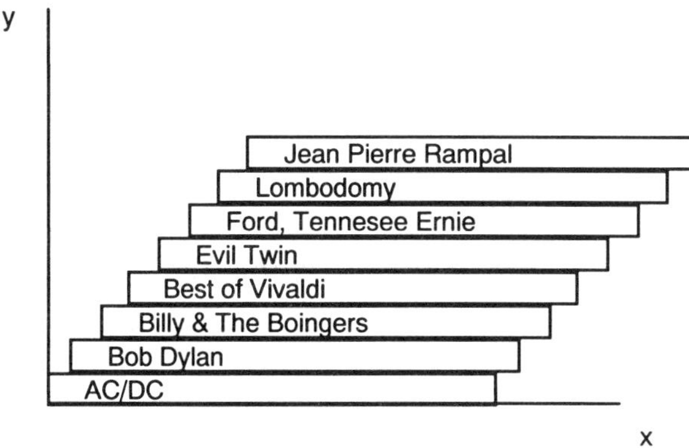

Fig. 13.4.2 A stack of CDs that Has Been Sheared

Figure 13.4.1 has a shear in the X dimension. The matrix to accomplish this is:

$$\begin{bmatrix} 1 & 0 & 0 \\ x_{\text{shear}} & 1 & 0 \\ 0 & 0 & 1 \end{bmatrix}$$

Shear in Y

To shear in the Y dimension use:

$$\begin{bmatrix} 1 & y_{\text{shear}} & 0 \\ 0 & 1 & 0 \\ 0 & 0 & 1 \end{bmatrix}$$

Mirror Across the X Axis

Mirroring reflects an object across one of the axes.

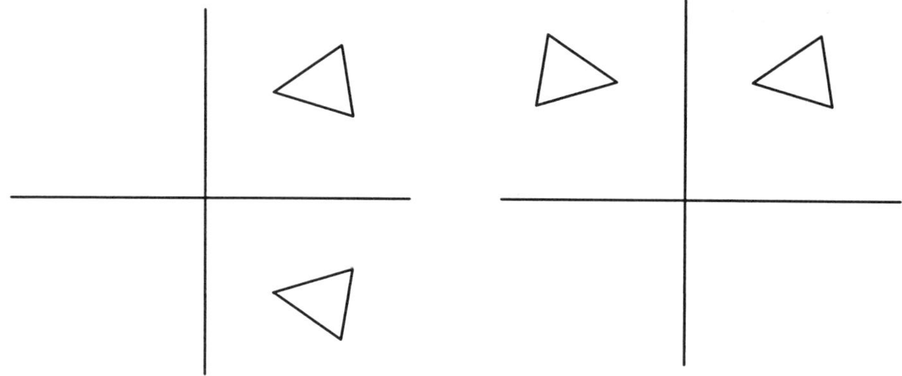

(a) Object Reflected Across X Axis

(b) Object Reflected Across Y Axis

An object can be mirrored across the X axis by using the following:

$$\begin{bmatrix} 1 & 0 & 0 \\ 0 & -1 & 0 \\ 0 & 0 & 1 \end{bmatrix}$$

This transformation can be used to flip an item top to bottom by centering it on the origin, mirroring it, then translating it back again.

Mirror Across the Y Axis

An object can be mirrored across the Y axis by using the following:

$$\begin{bmatrix} -1 & 0 & 0 \\ 0 & 1 & 0 \\ 0 & 0 & 1 \end{bmatrix}$$

This transformation can be used to flip an item side to side by centering it on the origin, mirroring it, then translating it back again.

Mirror Across Both Axes

If we multiply both of the above preceeding matrices together we get:

$$\begin{bmatrix} -1 & 0 & 0 \\ 0 & -1 & 0 \\ 0 & 0 & 1 \end{bmatrix}$$

We can also flip an object around the line $y = x$:

$$\begin{bmatrix} 0 & 1 & 0 \\ 1 & 0 & 0 \\ 0 & 0 & 1 \end{bmatrix}$$

To flip on the line $y = -x$ use:

$$\begin{bmatrix} 0 & -1 & 0 \\ -1 & 0 & 0 \\ 0 & 0 & 1 \end{bmatrix}$$

Miscellaneous

At this point it might be interesting and informative for the reader to consider how these transformations might be implemented and used in a drawing tool. If the tool is object oriented then each object can have its own origin, or anchor point. The object itself is made of one or more primitive shapes. Not every pixel needs to be stored, only an enumeration indicating which primitive should be used to create the shape, where the shape is in relation to the object's origin, and various shape-specific information. For instance, a primitive shape might be a polygon, in which case it stores the enumeration POLYGON, the X,Y coordinates of the upper left-hand corner, in relation to the object itself, and a list of vertices storing where each vertex is in relation to the upper left corner. An ellipse would store the enumeration ELLIPSE, the center in relation to the object, and the length in the X direction and the length in the Y direction, in relation to the object's origin.

The object itself would have a location in relation to the origin of the picture. When the object is drawn it's drawn as if it were at the origin, but a translation is applied to each point to move it to the proper location on the picture. To draw the object simply draw each primitive. The primitives are drawn as if they are at the center of the object, but a translation is used to move the primitive to its proper location. The translation for the object as a whole is combined with the translation for each primitive that it is made from before that primitive is drawn. So at each and every point in the object only one matrix multiplication needs to be performed.

For an interactive graphics system if you want to resize the object you would highlight it. This would put a bounding box around the object. You would then resize the bounding box with a mouse. The difference between the sizes of the final bounding box and the original bounding box gives the values for the resize transformation. Then the resize transformation would be applied. To rotate you might highlight the object, then enter an angle.

Adding linear transformations to a drawing package allows many powerful features to be added easily and efficiently.

14

Ray Tracing

Ray tracing is used to create very realistic looking 3D pictures on a computer. It makes use of the physical laws of light, reflection, and refraction to model a setting in the real world.

In Chapter 7 we touched on the subject of light rays, and how they can be traced to produce shading. Ray tracing takes this concept to the extreme. A 3D simulation of the area being drawn is set up in the computer. Then each and every light source affecting the scene is cataloged. These light sources send rays in many different directions. Each ray is traced to the point where it is either absorbed by the objects in the scene, it exits the scene completely, or it hits the viewer's eye. Each time the ray hits an object part of it is reflected, and part is absorbed. If the object is translucent part is also refracted. At this point it should be obvious that writing a program to do this is quite complex and time-consuming. Creating such a program is, unfortunately, quite a complex task and beyond what we have room for in a book such as this. The idea of this chapter, then, will be to present the basic theory and some practical considerations for developing a ray tracing program. This should give the reader some feel for what goes on in a ray tracing program, and what he/she is in for if the decision is made to pursue this very fascinating topic.

Theory of Ray Tracing

Tracing a Ray in Two Dimensions

A good place to start might be with a review of ray tracing in two dimensions. This topic is covered in many introductory physics courses, and is covered briefly in Chapter 7 of this book.

Light travels outward from its source in straight lines, until it hits a surface. When it hits a surface it is either absorbed or reflected, depending on the properties of the surface, as shown in Fig. 14.1.1.

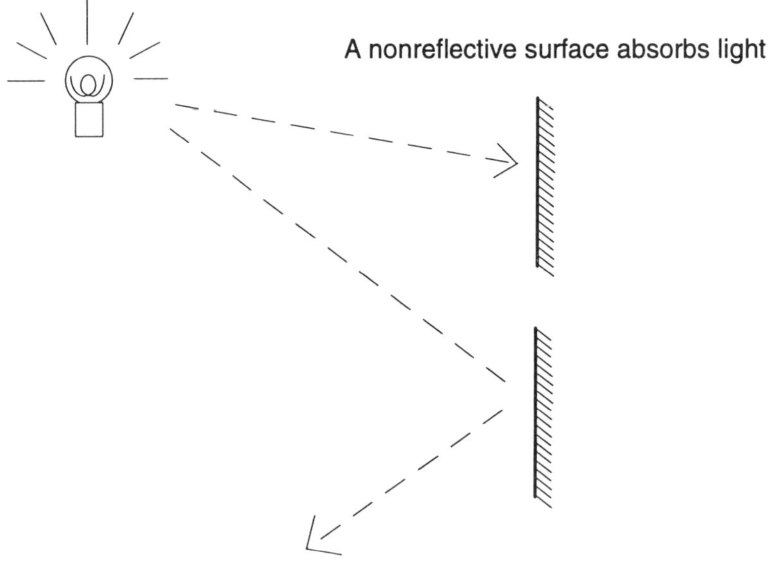

Fig. 14.1.1 Reflection and Absorption

If the surface is dark and rough light is absorbed, if it is smooth and shiny light is reflected.

White light contains all colors. If the surface it reflects off of has a color then only that color is reflected, while the other colors of the light are absorbed (Fig. 14.1.2). This happens even if the surface is not smooth and shiny.

A mirrored surface will reflect all light rays as they are. You might say that a mirrored surface has no color of its own.

If a colored surface is smooth and shiny then light reflected directly at the viewer will be reflected with all its colors and will appear white, while the rest of the surface will reflect only the color of the surface. This white area is glare, or as scientists call it, *specular reflection*. The reflection of ambient light is called *diffuse reflection.*

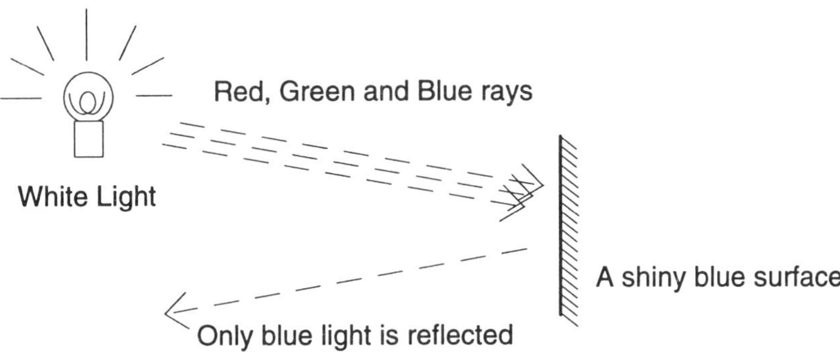

Fig. 14.1.2 Reflection from a Colored Surface

This much was covered in Chapter 7. Now we need to formalize our ideas and provide a mathematical basis, so that we can model reflection with a computer. When light is reflected off of a surface the angle it reflects at is the same as that of its approach, only in the opposite direction. This angle is usually measured from a reference 90° to the surface. This reference is called the *normal.* If we lay the light source and the surface on a Cartesian grid we can use line equations for the light rays (Fig. 14.1.3). We can then use Bresenham's line algorithm to trace the path of the light ray from it's source until it hits a surface. When a surface is encountered we can find another line formula from the laws of reflection, and trace that ray. This is done until the ray is either absorbed or exits the scene. If it exits the scene through the computer monitor we use it to set the color of the last object it reflected off.

If the surface lines up with one of the axes, then finding the equation of the reflection is easy. If the surface does not line up with an axis we need to do a little more work. The following formula gives the angle of reflection, relative to the X axis, off of a surface that has angle s with the X axis.

$$r = i + 2s - 180°$$

where r is the angle the reflected ray makes with the X axis, i is the angle between the initial ray and the X axis, and s is the angle between the surface and the X axis.

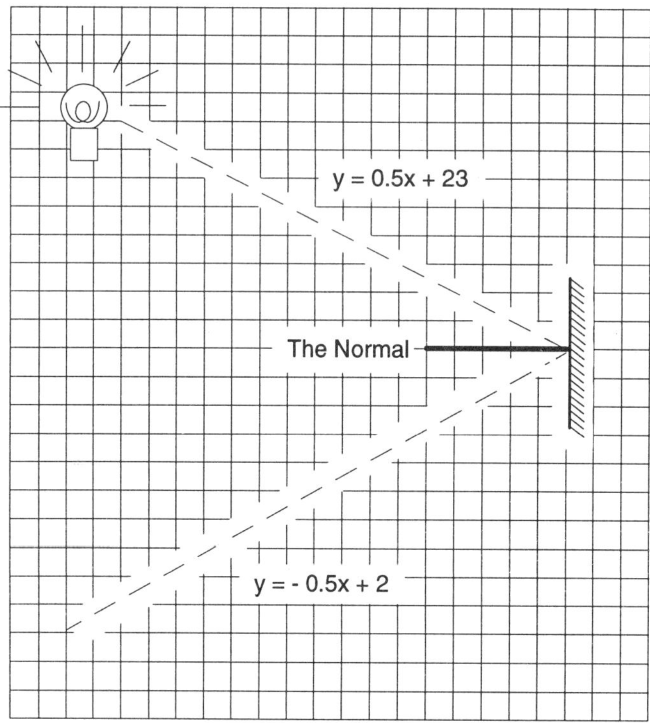

3D Cartesian Geometry

3D Coordinate Space

2D Cartesian space is a grid formed by two graduated lines at right angles to each other. Any point on the grid can be specified by giving the distance along each axis. Add a third axis at right angles to the other two, and you have a 3D coordinate space. This coordinate space is used like the 2D space, except that for each point a third index is added. If the original two axes are X and Y, then it makes sense that the third would be Z.

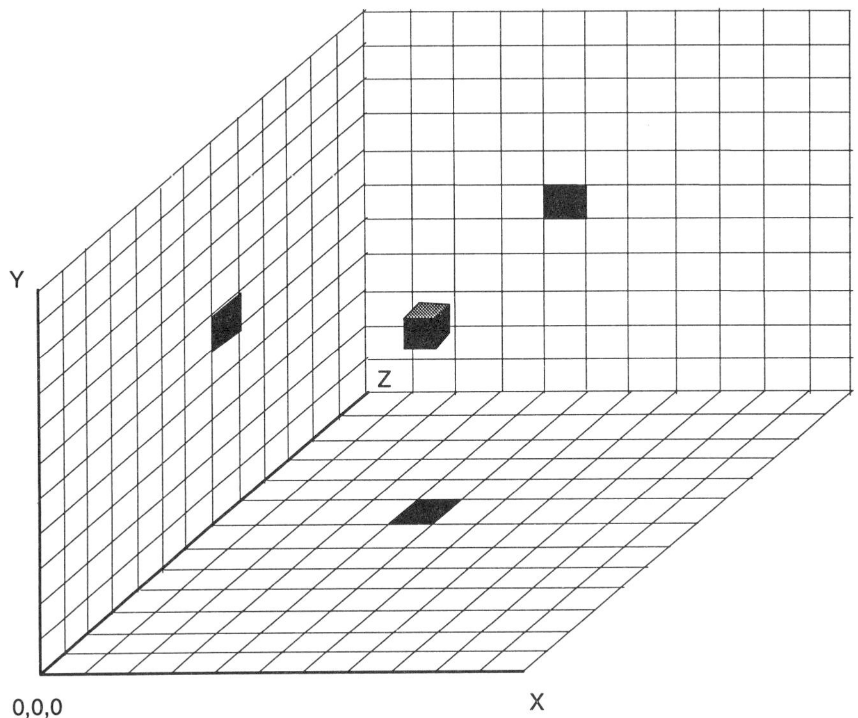

Fig. 14.2.1 A Voxel in 3D Space

That much is standard and straightforward. But computers always do things differently. A computer screen is divided into a 2D coordinate grid, but we don't look at the intersections of the grid lines. Instead we look at the squares formed by the intersections, and we number these instead of the grid lines. We refer these squares as pixels. When dealing with 3D space in computer graphics it's convenient to do the same. The grid lines of a 3D space split the 3D space into cubes. These cubes are sometimes referred to as *voxels*, which is a sort of contraction of volume pixels (Fig. 14.2.1). The particular voxel that is filled in is at 3D coordinates (4, 5, 7), with the X coordinate listed first, then the Y, then Z. You might at first glance think the coordinates (5,6,8), but remember the origin, (0,0,0), takes up the entire first voxel.

Lines in 3 Dimensions

We can use two equations to represent a line on a 3D grid:

$$y = mx + b$$
$$y = nz + b$$

The first equation looks familiar. This equation defines the line relative to the XY plane. The second equation defines the line relative to the YZ plane. In this equation n is the slope of the line on the YZ plane, or $\Delta Y/\Delta Z$, and b is the familiar Y intercept, which is equal to b in the first equation. The Y coordinate for each of these equations is the same, so another way to write this would be:

$$y = mx + b = nz + b$$

This shows that for each Y there is a single X and a single Z. We can represent a line in 3D as two lines in two 2D planes, each plane at 90° to the other (Fig. 14.2.2). This is really interesting because it means we can use a very simple variation of the standard Bresenham's algorithm to draw lines in 3D. To find each triple representing a point, first find the double for the XY dimension, then find the double for the ZY dimension. The Y for each is the same. Each plane should be done separately, since the line might be shorter on one plane than on the other. To see this imagine a 3D line that goes straight into the YZ plane (X = a constant value c). The representation this line will have on the YZ plane is a point. This looks like it runs counter to what is said above, but is in fact a special case, equivalent to the 2D case where m is infinite.

Surfaces in 3 Dimensions

Most shapes in the typical ray tracing system are represented as flat surfaces. Even if the object being modeled is round, for efficiency's sake, it will often be broken into a series of flat surfaces.

Surfaces have several properties that must be modeled. They are two-dimensional, with size, shape, and orientation. They also reflect light differently, but that will be dealt with later. At this point we are only worried about geometric properties. The size, shape, and orientation are defined by the vertices of the surface.

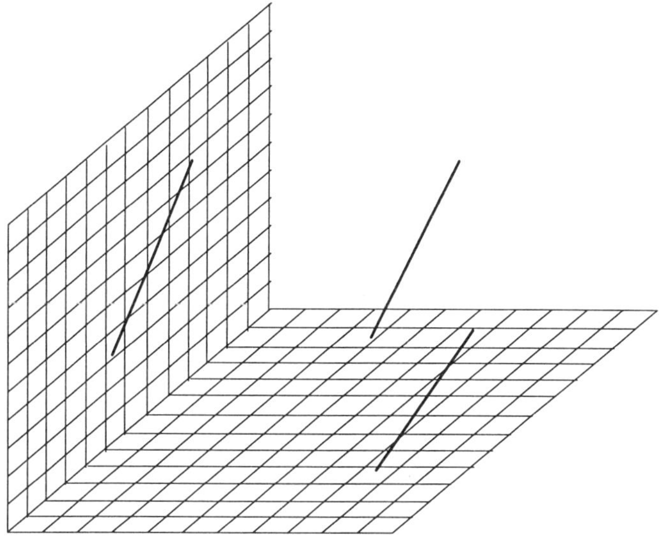

Fig. 14.2.2 A 3D Line Represented as Two 2D Lines

We are used to dealing with size and shape from 2D graphics. 3D orientation is new. *Orientation* is the property that tells us what direction a light ray will reflect after hitting the surface. In two dimensions, orientation is the angle that a line makes with the X axis. The angle of the line with the X axis also defines the angle it makes with the Y axis. The orientation of a 2D surface in 3D space can be defined by using two angles, one for the XY plane, the other for the YZ plane. Remember that our lines have two components, one for each of these planes. If we trace the XY component, it will reflect off the surface only in the XY plane. Its direction is only affected by the XY angle component of the surface's orientation. Then trace the YZ component of the light ray. Its reflection is only effected by the YZ angle. The two reflected components provide all the information needed to trace a ray in three dimensions.

Ellipses in 3 Dimensions

To create spheres and 3D ellipses, an algorithm similar to Bresenham's ellipse can be used. I like to refer to this algorithm as Bresenham's football algorithm.

As Fig. 14.2.3 shows, an ellipse in 3D (or a football) can be defined by three normal 2D ellipses at right angles to each other. If the radii of all three ellipses are the same the 3D ellipse is a sphere or ball. If the three axes of the football are aligned with the axes of the Cartesian grid the process of drawing the football is greatly simplified. If another alignment is desired a 3D transformation can be applied just as it can for 2D ellipses. In this figure 1 is a 2D ellipse aligned with the XY axis, 2 is a 2D ellipse aligned with the YZ axis and 3 is a 2D ellipse aligned with the XZ axis. These numbers are used by the psuedocode example of Bresenham's football algorithm below.

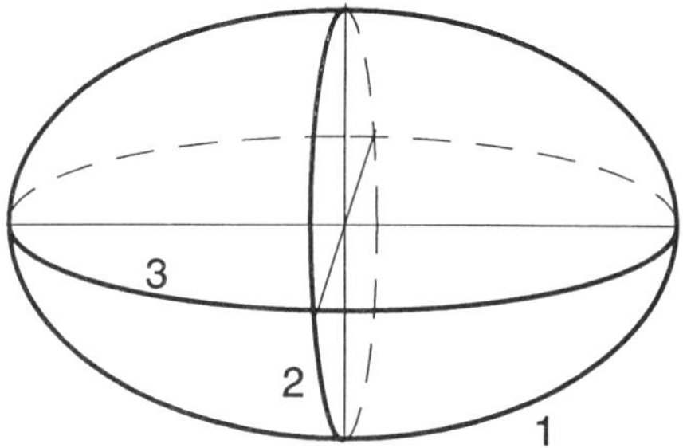

Fig. 14.2.3 A 3D Ellipse, or "Football"

A football can be drawn by starting at the center, or "waist," of the object and drawing ever smaller 2D ellipses outward toward the ends. Drawing these 2D ellipses can be done with the standard Bresenham's ellipse algorithm, with a parameter added for the third dimension. Since the axis of the football is aligned with the coordinate system's axis this parameter is constant for the 2D ellipse. Simply give that value as the value for the third dimension.

We need the to find the two radii for the 2D ellipse. This can be done by applying Bresenham's algorithm to each of the ellipse's at right angles to the one being drawn. Each point found on each of these ellipses is the length and width of the next 2D ellipse to be drawn. The following psuedocode might clarify:

```
procedure 3D_Ellipse (int x,  int y,  int z,
                      int r1, int r2, int r3) is

  variables for Bresenham's ellipse algorithm
  defined here.

  procedure ellipse_plot (int x, int y, int z,
                          int x_ctr, int z_ctr) is
  begin
    /* plotting a voxel requires 3 coordinates */
    plot_voxel (x_ctr + x, y, z_ctr + z);
    plot_voxel (x_ctr - x, y, z_ctr + z);
    plot_voxel (x_ctr + x, y, z_ctr - z);
    plot_voxel (x_ctr - x, y, z_ctr - z);
  end ellipse_plot;
```

```
  procedure Draw_2D_Ellipse (int x,  int y, int z,
                             int r1, int r2) is

    variables for Bresenham's ellipse algorithm
    defined here.

  begin draw_2D_Ellipse

    while (y <= chgpt) do
      ellipse_plot (calculated_x,
                    y,  /* same y as passed in as a
                           parameter */
                    calculated_z,
                    x,  /* same x and z passed in */
                    z);

      normal 2D Bresenham's ellipse processing
    end loop;

    rest of processing for Bresenham's ellipse
  end draw_2D_ellipse;

begin 3D_Ellipse

  while (y <= chgpt) do
    Draw_2D_Ellipse(x, /* as passed in */
                    y, /* processing shown */
                    z, /* as passed in */
                    point on ellipse 1 becomes
                         becomes r1,
                    point on ellipse 2 becomes
                         becomes r2);
    processing for Bresenham's ellipse for
       both ellipses 1 and 2.
    y--;
  end loop;

  rest of processing for both ellipse1 and 2.
end 3D_Ellipse;
```

Figure 14.2.4 shows this algorithm graphically.

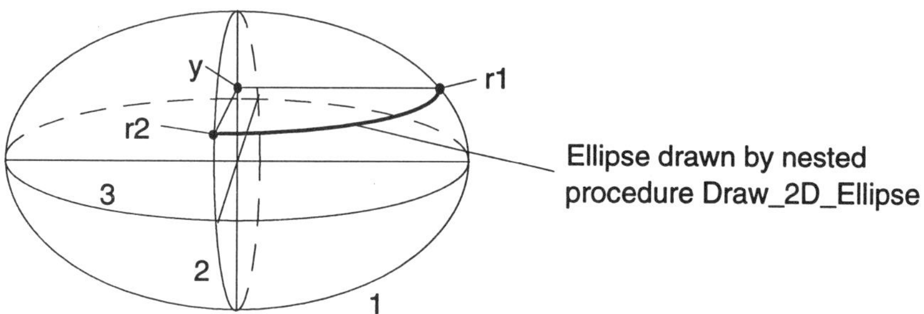

Fig 14.2.4 Bresenham's Football Algorithm

The parent procedure, 3D_Ellipse, is a derivation of Bresenham's ellipse algorithm, which finds points on both ellipse 1 and ellipse 2. The nested procedure Draw_2D_Ellipse is Bresenham's ellipse algorithm, which simply draws ellipses aligned with the XY plane. The points on ellipse 1 and ellipse 2 that 3D_Ellipse found are passed to Draw_2D_Ellipse as the two radii for the 2D ellipse drawn by Draw_2D_Ellipse. The nested procedure ellipse_plot is a simple derivation of the procedure of the same name from Chapter 10, made to work in 3D space. The algorithm first plots the ellipse at the "waist" of the football—the ellipse that is numbered 3 on Fig. 14.2.4—then works its way up drawing smaller and smaller ellipses.

Bresenham's algorithm is quite efficient, however there is quite a lot of data needed for a football. This algorithm, in practice, is quite slow. For this reason most of the time the complete football is not drawn. Instead a number of voxels are skipped between each ellipse, making a series of concentric rings. This is then repeated at right angles. The result is a wire mesh object. These meshes define a series of surfaces that can be used to reflect rays.

This method produces spheres that look something like the mirrored ball in a dance club – they are broken into separate surfaces instead of being truly round. Many 3D graphics systems just live with this. But there are things that can be done to improve on it. The first and most obvious is to make the surfaces smaller. This of course requires more calculations and is slow. There is a more sophisticated method. If the angles of each corner point are stored, the light rays that reflect from them can be traced. Since the actual angles of these points are used the light that is reflected will be what would actually reflect off the real object. Next the values of reflected light for points on the surface are interpolated from the values at the corners. This is far more efficient than tracing every point on the surface, and some interpolation algorithms do a very good job. They look quite realistic.

Refraction

So far we have concerned ourselves with reflection only. Many ray tracing scenes also include transparent objects, such as a window or a glass of water. Such objects cause the rays of light to bend, or refract. If you plan on modeling transparent objects then the information for each surface must include an index of refraction. The index of refraction is defined as

$$n = \frac{\sin(i)}{\sin(r)}$$

where n is the index of refraction, i is the angle of incidence, and r is the angle of refraction. This is Snell's law. When light hits a refracting surface we know the angle the light is coming in at and the angle the surface is at. We need to find the angle it has inside the transparent object, or the angle of refraction. To do this, we solve the formula from Snell's law for r.

$$r = \sin^{-1}\left(\frac{\sin(i)}{n}\right)$$

When the light exits the transparent object we have the angle the light is now at from the preceeding formula, and the angle the surface it exits from is at. We now need to find the angle it will take when it exits. To do this use Snell's law solved for i.

$$i = \sin^{-1}(n \cdot \sin(r))$$

If the surface where the light exits the object is parallel to the surface where the light entered, the rays before and after will be parallel. But if the sides are not parallel, such as if the object is a lens or a bottle, the ray will leave the object at a different angle than the one it entered at.

Note that most transparent objects reflect a certain amount of light. The light ray that hits the eye after coming from a glass object is often not just the light refracted through the object, but is combined with a small amount of light, or glare, that is reflected from another source.

Ray Tracing in 3 Dimensions

We have been describing a process where a light ray exits its source and is traced to the point where it is finally absorbed or exits the scene through the screen. If we did this we would have quite a large number of rays to trace, most of which would be absorbed and not contribute to the final image. What is actually done is rays are traced backward from each pixel on the screen. As the ray reflects off surfaces the reflectivity of each surface is recorded. When the light ray is traced to its source the pixel can be set by determining the color of the light source and subtracting out any light that has been absorbed on the way. The math needed to trace the ray backward is exactly the same as for tracing it forward.

Representing a 3D World in the Computer

A 3D coordinate system is created inside the computer. This could be a 3D array of voxels, each voxel containing a pointer to the surface that voxel is part of. If the pointer is null, the voxel is floating in air and is not part of any surface.

Each surface has properties that need to be saved. The orientation is needed so the direction of the reflected ray can be found. We also need information on how the surface reflects. We can use three integers, one each to indicate how much red, green, and blue the surface reflects. If all three are set to the maximum value the surface will be a mirror and reflect any light that hits it. If all three are 0 the surface will absorb all light and be black. This scheme raises a problem with representing white objects. If having the RGB reflection values at max represents a mirrored surface, how do we represent a white surface? So we also need a diffusion or roughness index. A smoother or shinier object will have a higher value, and will reflect light more cohesively. This would be represented by reflecting the rays exactly as they hit, where for a more diffuse surface the rays hitting the entire surface might be averaged, and the entire surface given the same value.

When we create our 3D world we use the line and ellipse algorithms outlined above. Much of the time the algorithms only create outlines of the surfaces of each object. After a surface is created another piece of code needs to create the surface information itself, or what the voxel points to, using reflection and refraction information entered by the artist and angle information from the outlines of the surface. Then the voxels that make up the surface need to be pointed to that surface information. Here are some example structures.

```
struct surface {
  int XY_Angle;
```

```
    int ZY_Angle;
    int Red_Reflexivity;
    int Green_Reflexivity;
    int Blue_Reflexivity;
    int Diffusion_Index;
    int Refraction_Index;
  };

  struct surface far *world[x][y][z];
```

Practical Concerns

The preceeding data structures suffer from being RAM hungry. Imagine if the scene were to be 1000 pixels by 1000 pixels on the screen. To make things simple we make voxels the same size as the screen pixels, and make the scene 1000 voxels deep. Each voxel is a pointer, and on PCs pointers take 4 bytes. This is for far pointers, since there is no way enough information could fit in the near heap. And so we have 1000 × 1000 × 1000 × 4 bytes, or 4 Gigabytes! And that's without even considering surface information yet. That simply won't work.

But in most scenes most space is completely empty. There really is no reason for each and every voxel to have an empty pointer allocated to it.

It sounds like some sort of dynamic data structure is in order. Voxels should only be allocated as needed. As we trace the ray, each time it hits a new voxel the data base of voxels could be searched, and if a match is not found the ray continues on its way. This sounds extremely slow. At each step we need to determine where the voxel is, then we need to perform a search in the data base. Even if a binary tree is used, which is quite efficient speedwise, we would likely need to search 10 nodes for each voxel.[1] Now we need to do this for each and every ray, and for each and every voxel hit by each and every array. You could probably get a good night's sleep while this processing is being done, even on the fastest PowerPC™.

So how about a hybrid data structure? Perhaps a 2D array of binary trees would work. The indices of the array represent the XY coordinates of objects in the scene; the lookup field in the binary trees would be the Z coordinate.

---

[1] This is if we can somehow use one index, that index being the coordinate in one dimension. Each dimension has 1000 and the average search in a binary tree with 1000 items requires 10 nodes to be visited. In reality it seems likely that there will be a number of voxels in the tree with the same key. This means further searching is required, and this representation will be even slower than the estimate given here.

```
struct surface_tree {
  int z_coord;
  struct surface      *surface_ptr;
  struct surface_tree *right;
  struct surface_tree *left;
};

struct surface_tree *world[x][y];
```

This representation gets the RAM requirement down to 4 megabytes for the "world." A considerable improvement, but surface information still is not stored. As far as speed is concerned, you would trace each ray, and look at each voxel in each ray (this is a given, you can't get around it), then look at that proper location in the world array. If that location is a null pointer you go on your way, otherwise you search the tree pointed to by that voxel. There will still be some searching, but far less than if all voxels are kept in a single binary tree.

You will still need quite sophisticated memory management to handle a data structure of this size, at least on a PC running DOS. With a little thought it should be possible to come up with another compromise better suited to PCs. Perhaps all voxels that are part of a surface could be put into a data base, as described above, and a 2D array of bits could be set up. If the bit is cleared there are no voxels set for that particular XY coordinate, otherwise a search of the data base will need to be made. This lowers the memory requirement of the array to 1/2 megabyte, and is probably the best compromise between speed and RAM usage.

Other Suggestions

At the beginning of this chapter I said I would not give examples for this material, since it is quite complex. Even the smallest example would probably overwhelm most readers. I do, however, encourage you to spend some time thinking about it and even developing your own programs.

If you do develop your own ray tracing programs there are some helpful tips you might keep in mind. First of all keep the scene as simple as you can. This means limiting the size of the scene to a reasonable number of voxels, as well as not putting to many objects into it. Anything outside the scene should appear as some neutral background color. If walls are put around the scene, as if it's in a room, then the walls will take up space in the data structures. Not only will this use RAM, but will slow processing since walls will cause all bits in the voxel usage array, the "world" array, to be set. Finally use a distant diffuse light source, rather than a point source in the scene. Sunlight as opposed to a lamp in a room. All the incoming rays from the light source will then be parallel and uniformly white.

I've seen some scenes like this that were quite effective. One very interesting program I've seen had a scene with three silver balls floating stationary over a colorful surface. You could see the surface reflected in each ball, and you could see the balls reflected in each other. When the program was first called up all the rays were traced out and the balls were colored. The colors were then left as they were and the palette registers were changed. As the palette registers were changed all the colors in the scene changed appropriately, and no more tracing had to be done. The effect was quite striking.

It would be really neat to write a ray tracing system that allows you to input objects interactively, but that would require a tremendous amount of work. It would be much easier for a first try to simply set up the data structures and hard-wire the objects.

15

Fractals

Fractals and fractal geometry are one of the most fascinating areas of computer graphics. Fractal geometry was first introduced by a mathematician working for IBM, Benoit Mandelbrot, in 1975. Since then it has been found that fractals can be used to draw very realistic looking images of just about everything. Computer-generated images of trees, clouds, mountains, and even moons and planets made with the use of fractals are now starting to appear on calendars, in movies, and just about everywhere you look. I recently attended a rock concert given by the Steve Miller Band, where the backdrop throughout the whole concert was a constantly expanding view of one particular fractal, called the Mandelbrot set.

The History of Fractals

What is a fractal? Not an easy question to answer. With questions like this I often find the easiest way to answer is by presenting the history of the subject. This lets the reader see the developments that led to the present understanding of that subject, and gives him/her an intuitive feel that is otherwise hard to develop.

While the term *fractals* has only been used since 1975, when it was introduced by Dr. Mandelbrot, the discoveries and developments that led to this new science can be traced back to second half of the nineteenth century.

Problems with Conventional Math

At that time calculus had already been known for more than 200 years, and it had been used to study a large chunk of what was then known with good success. Mathematicians of the day were convinced that by more and more sophisticated applications of calculus pretty much everything could be understood and modeled. But such was not the case.

A Polish mathematician, named Sierpinski, took a triangle, drew lines from the center of each side to the centers of the other sides, defining a smaller triangle inside the first. He then cut this smaller triangle out. The corners of the original triangle now made three triangles, so he repeated the process on each of these. He then repeated this process an infinite number of times (Fig. 15.1.1), which is something mathematicians can do. He then attempted to find the area of the resulting shape.

Fig. 15.1.1 Sierpinsky's Triangle

To find the area, consider that at each step you cut out a definite amount of area. The area that you remove gets smaller at each step, but still if you do this an infinite number of times you must remove all area. So the resulting shape has no area. QED.

Or we can look at it another way. At each step we remove no more that a quarter of the remaining area. Since we never remove more than a quarter of the area at each step, there must always be a finite area left. So the result is a finite area larger that 0. QED. Wait a minute!

As the years progressed a number of such troubling shapes emerged. One is known as Cantor's Dust. Imagine a line segment. Cut out the center third. You are now left with two line segments, each one third the length of the original. Cut out the center third of each of these segments. Repeat this process an infinite number of times. What are we left with? There must be an infinite number of them, since at each step we double the number we have. They do not take up an infinite amount of space, and therefore they must be infinitely small. Points. The result is a bunch of points. But we started with a line segment with one dimension. Now we have points with 0 dimensions. When did we switch dimensions?

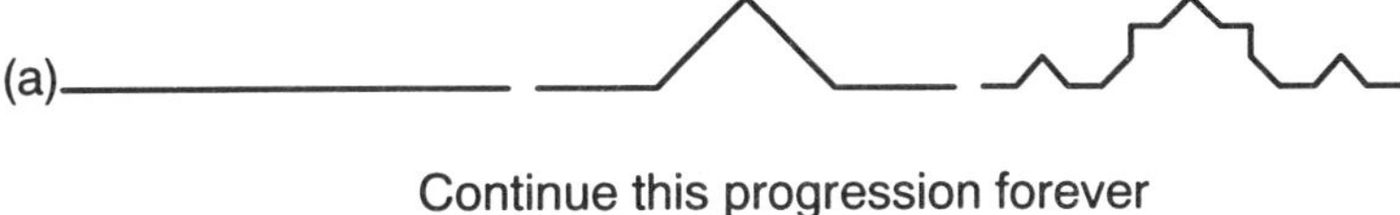

Continue this progression forever

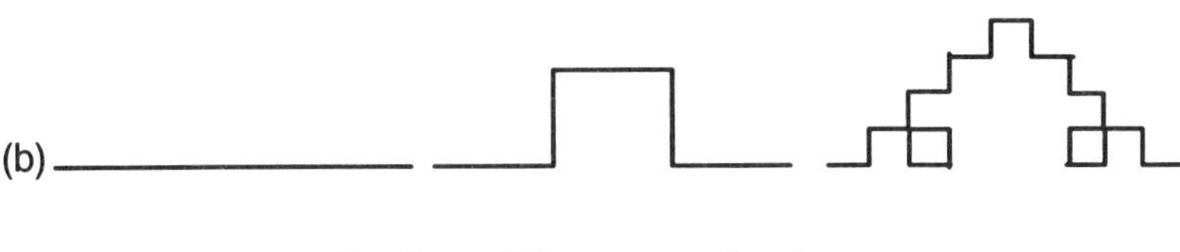

Continue this progression forever

Which one is longer?

Fig. 15.1.2 Koch's Coastlines

A third troubling shape is called Koch's Coastline. Start with a line segment. Remover the center third and replace it with two segments the same length as the portion removed. The two new lines should be positioned so that their ends touch on one end, and join the original shape on the other [Fig. 15.1.2(a)]. Now you have a shape with four line segments. Repeat the above with each line segment. Repeat an infinite number of times. How long is the shape? Since we add length at each step, and we have an infinite number of steps, the length must be infinitely long.

Now do the same again, only instead of adding two lines at each step, add three [Fig. 15.1.2(b)]. Now how long is this shape? Since we also repeat an infinite number of times this must also be an infinite length. But we add more to this shape at each step, so isn't it longer? Can we speak of different sized infinities?

Fractional Dimensions

At first such shapes were seen as mathematical curiosities not worthy of real study. But as the number of these troublesome shapes grew mathematicians started to take notice. Early in the twentieth century a mathematician named Hausdorff started investigating, and was later joined by another mathematician name Besicovitch. Besicovitch proposed that these problem shapes should be considered to have fractional dimensions. The method of measuring dimension developed by Hausdorff and Besicovitch, the Hausdorff/Besicovitch dimension, is defined as the ratio between the log of the number of copies and the log of the size of the seed relative to each copy. For instance the dimension of the first Koch Coastline would be $\log(4)/\log(3) \cong 1.26186$. The dimension of the second coastline would be $\log(5)/\log(3) \cong 1.46497$. The greater Hausdorff/Besicovitch dimension shows the longer length of the second coastline.

Cellular Automata

The astute reader will have noticed that all the shapes just discussed involve performing an operation an infinite number of times. This is not easy to do. Back in the 1920s even performing these operations enough to get a good idea of the shape was a very tedious and time-consuming task. And so research into these shapes died out until computers made practical performing a large number of iterations.

Even after computers came along it was some time before anyone thought of using them to study these odd shapes. This branch of mathematics just did not receive that much attention. The first to put the computer to such a use was a biologist named Lindenmeyer. Lindenmeyer used a method called *cellular automata* to study plant growth. Like those odd shapes with fractional dimensions, cellular automata often take a great deal of labor to draw by hand, and are much more easily studied on a computer.

A cellular automata is a mathematical system that is given a start state and a set of rules to follow. One method of representing a cellular automata is with strings of letters. A typical such system might be:

```
start    ->  A;
rule 1   ->  A => ABA;
rule 2   ->  B => BB;
```

which means we start with the letter A, and at each iteration all A's turn to the string ABA, and all B's turn back into the string BB. From the given start you'd get the following progression:

```
A
ABA
ABABBABA
ABABBABABBBBABABBABA
```

The string will continue to grow. This is not a very interesting cellular automata. One that is quite interesting is called The Game of Life, developed by a fellow named Conway. Start with a grid. Each square in the grid can either be alive (colored in) or dead (background color). If a square is dead and three of its neighbors are alive the square comes to life. If the square if alive and two or three of its neighbors are alive it remains alive, otherwise it dies. These rules sound quite simple, but they lead to behavior that is quite complex. In fact it is so fascinating a number of programs have been written to implement this automata. I have included a version on the distribution disk with this book. The program is called LIFEGAME.C, and was written with the Borland compiler. It uses BIOS calls instead of the BGI (see Chapter 2), however, so it should not be terribly difficult to make it Microsoft compatible. Since it is programmed this way it will only run on monitors that support IBM mode 19, 256 colors by 480 × 320 pixels. This is the standard VGA 256 color mode, so any SVGA monitor will work, as well as VGA and MCGA monitors.

The LifeGame program will allow the user to set the original grid up with random squares filled in, or it will allow the user to set up the original screen him/herself. If you use the random set up the first screen you will see has a number of lit squares (in this version each square is one pixel). The computer will grind away for a few seconds, because this program is rather slow, and suddenly the second generation will pop up, with most of the original squares having died. At the third generation interesting things start to happen. In some places you can start to see "signs of life," where a number of squares are close enough to support each other. In these areas old squares are constantly dying, but new ones are constantly coming to life. Sometimes the living area will grow for quite some time, other times it will die out completely in a few generations.

If the user chooses to set up the starting screen him/herself there are a number of interesting patterns that might be tried. A simple box of nine squares is an interesting shape. Figure 15.1.3 shows several other interesting shapes. Shape A will actually move across the screen at about a 45 degree angle in the direction of the notch in the upper right-hand corner. These "floaters" can be constructed to float in one of four different directions. Shape B simply rocks back and forth. This is useful to tell if a shape is still evolving. Some shapes can be stable and not change from one generation to the next. If you put a shape like B in one corner you can see the generations change, and see if other things on the screen have reached a stable state which will not change. Shape D just happens to be such a stable shape. A wall like this can be extended for quite a length. So what's so interesting about a stationary wall? Anyone who has played the game of life at some point has sent a floater crashing into one of these walls. Try it, it's quite entertaining! I'll leave you to see for yourself what shapes C and E evolve into. A word about E. I've found that most any rectangular shape that's larger than a certain size is quite entertaining. The shape shown here has beveled corners. It does not seem to matter how the corners are made, with bevels, standard corners, or even leaving a square or two of space in between makes minor differences in the evolution of the shape, but they are all quite fascinating. Another one to try is simply a long line.

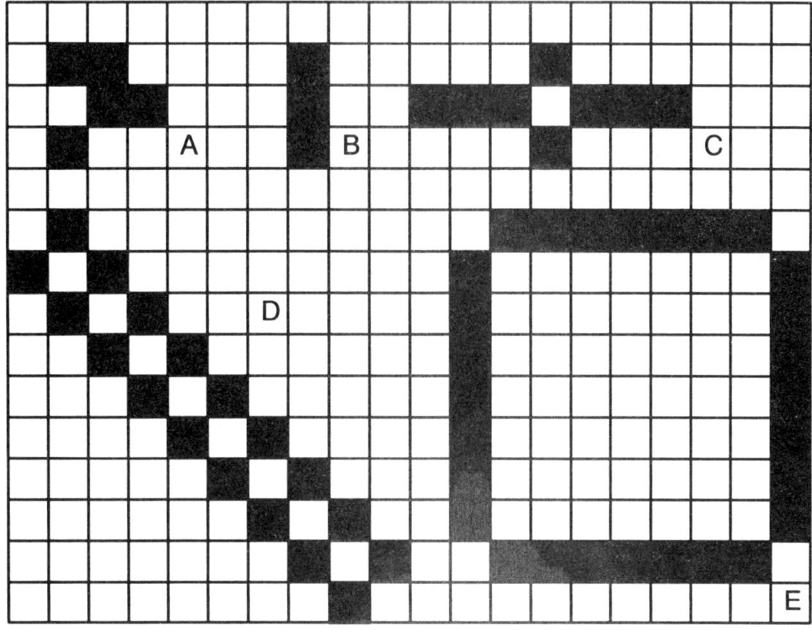

Fig. 15.1.3 Interesting "Life Forms" for the Game of Life

I will not present the code for this program here because it is somewhat complicated and does not really contribute to an understanding of fractals. It might be worth looking at the use of pointers and macros to make the program more efficient, however.

Another example of a cellular automata is shown in Fig 15.1.4. Start with a horizontal line segment. At the end draw two line segments half the length of the original, at 45 degrees to the original and 90 degrees to each other. Repeat. After a few iterations you start to see a plant-like shape. This is one thing that Lindenmeyer did, along with creating other similar plant-like shapes. These are often referred to as Lindenmeyer's plants. What is the Hausdorff/Besicovitch dimension of this shape?

File BK1501.C provides the source code for a program that draws Lindenmeyer's plant. This code does use the BGI. An explanation of the code is not presented here, but it works almost exactly the same as the code for the simplified symmetric tree presented under the section called Practical Fractals. For such a simple thing it looks startlingly like a real plant. Now we are on the very edge of fractals.

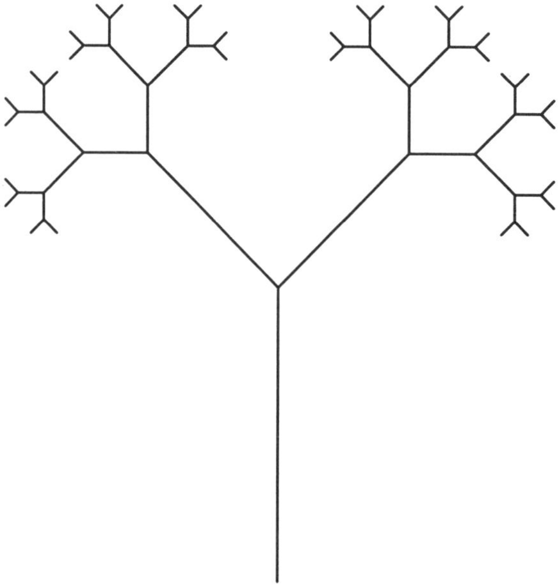

Fig. 15.1.4 Lindenmeyer's Plant

Chaos

Now enters Dr. Mandelbrot. In the 1950s he had studied the price of cotton for the last several hundred years. Accurate cotton prices are available from a very long time ago, making this study possible. He had noticed a peculiar trait of these prices. They show a cyclic and yet unpredictable nature. They rise and fall fairly regularly, but there is no pattern and no way to predict when the price will be the same again, when it will next rise or fall, or how high or low it will get. Moreover these variations seem independent of time. The prices rise and fall on a yearly basis, but they also fall on a ten yearly basis, as well as on a hundred yearly basis. And at each step they show the same amount of detail and the same unpredictability. Most peculiar.

In 1968 Dr. Mandelbrot began a study of Nile River levels. In this study he noticed the same cyclic yet unpredictable nature. In fact he started noticing it everywhere – the stock market, the path of rivers, the shape of mountains. Dr. Mandelbrot called systems that show this cyclic yet unpredictable behavior *chaotic*.

Dr. Mandelbrot at this time was employed by IBM, so what could come more naturally than to study this phenomenon with computers? Through the seventies, eighties, and up to today he used iterative methods like those employed by Lindenmeyer, as well as Koch and Sierpinski long ago, to study chaos. In his studies he found the computer unexpectedly drawing many surprising shapes, from clouds to trees to mountains. In 1982 he published *The Fractal Geometry of Nature*, which describes what fractals are and how they can produce such detailed and realistic pictures of natural things, with a very small amount of computer code.

The Mandelbrot Set

The Mandelbrot Set is probably the most famous fractal of all time. It was not originally discovered by Dr. Mandelbrot, but he did discover interesting things about it, and made it popular.

The Mandelbrot Set is a graph of a certain equation: $z_2 = z_1^2 + c$, where c, z_1, and $z_2$are complex numbers. If you take a Cartesian grid with the imaginary numbers as the Y axis and the real numbers as X axis, and iterate this formula, oh say, 200 times, at each point on the coordinate system, you will find that at some places the formula diverges to infinity, while at other places it stabilizes and converges on a certain value. Now if you were to color in the points on the grid where it diverges with, oh say, white, and color the points that converge with maybe blue, you might think you'd get a more or less random scattering of blue and white dots. But surprisingly enough you will see a shape.

Once you get over the initial surprise of seeing a shape, you will not be surprised to learn that the shape has an inside and an outside. After all, isn't that part of being a shape? The outside of the shape is not very interesting. Neither is the inside. But the edge of the shape is quite interesting indeed – it is chaotic. If you look at it you can see quite a bit of detail. If you zoom in and look closer you see more detail. If you keep zooming you keep seeing more detail. Forever. While the area of the shape is quite finite, the length of the edge is infinite. And in fact you can do this with the program MANDEL.C on the distribution disk.

This program makes use of the BGI, but it is a fairly simple program, and the only use made of the BGI is to set the mode, plot pixels, and return the screen to text mode. In fact there are only two lines that plot pixels, and these are only five lines apart, so translating this program to Microsoft C should not be too bad.

When you run the program it will first plot the Mandelbrot Set, as described above. This takes a little bit of time since the program must iterate 200 times on each pixel, and it uses the highest resolution your monitor and the BGI support. In fact it can easily take an hour or more, depending on the processor in your computer and the clock speed. Be patient, the program is working. Once the shape is finished a small red cursor appears in the center of the screen. You can move this cursor with the arrow keys, the Tab key, and PGUP and PGDN. Use the cursor to select the upper left corner of an interesting area and press enter. A green spot will appear to mark that corner. Now move the cursor to the lower right corner of the interesting looking area and press enter. The box you just marked will now be expanded on the screen. Again this takes a while. I've seen other programs that are faster, but it always seems to be at the expense of lower detail. This may be a necessary trade-off: speed for detail.[1]

I will not go into details on the complete program, most of which is just help screens and moving the cursor around. But I will present the mandel( ) function, which does the work of drawing. The code for this is listed later, and can be found in the program MANDEL.C on the distribution disk.

The general logic of the program is to look at each pixel, use the ScaleX( ) and ScaleY( ) function to find the real and imaginary components of the imaginary number associated with that pixel, and run the Mandelbrot Set algorithm on these values.

Now looking at the code, we see a loop on y, which is, of course, the Y axis. First thing inside the loop is a call to ScaleY( ), which returns the imaginary portion of *c*. Just inside this loop is a check to see if a key has been pressed. This is not done inside the nested loop since it is a rather slow function, and the entire thing is already quite slow. Next is a nested loop on x, which is the X axis, and inside this is a call to ScaleX( ), which returns the real portion of *c*. We then initialize the imaginary and real parts of *z*, and start iterating the Mandelbrot set formula.

The math at this point requires some explanation. The formula we are iterating is $z_2 = z_1^2 + c$, where c, z_1, and z_2 are complex numbers. A complex number is a number in the format $x + yi$, where i is the square root of -1. So if $z = x + yi$, then $z^2 = (x + yi)(x + yi)$. Break z into its XY components and you get z0 = $x' = x^2 + y^2$ and z1 = $y' = 2xy$. The components of c are the imaginary portion i and the real portion R. So to bring it together z0 = $x^2 + y^2 + R$ and z1 = $2xy + i$. In the program the order is reversed from the explanation in order to not save a value in a temporary variable. Because of the number of iterations this simple step saves a significant amount of time. Finally the components are added and the value found is compared to 4. If it is larger the series diverged, a white point is plotted and we go to the next point. If the value found is less than 4, after 200 iterations the series does not diverge and the pixel is plotted as blue. Here is the code.

[1] This program was written by my brother and myself. My brother requested at this point that I say this program definitely works by the brute force method and more sophisticated and faster methods are probably available. As for myself, I feel this version gives the best views of any Mandelbrot program I've seen. - JAF

```
float ScaleX (float RLow, float RHigh, int X) {
  return RLow + ((X*(RHigh-RLow))/MaxX);
}

float ScaleY (float ILow, float IHigh, int Y) {
  return ILow + ((Y*(IHigh-ILow))/MaxY);
}

void Mandel (float ILow, float IHigh,
             float RLow, float RHigh) {
  float Z0=0, sqr_Z0,
        Z1=0, sqr_Z1;
  int n; /* n so we don't confuse it with I */
  float I, R;
  int x, y;
  unsigned char done = FALSE;
  char option = 0;

  for (y=0; y<MaxY; y++) {
    I = ScaleY(ILow, IHigh, y);
    if (kbhit()) {
      option = getch();
      if (option == ESC) {
        closegraph();
        display_close();
        exit(0);
      }
      else if (option == ENTER) return;
      if (kbhit()) getch();
    }
    for (x=0; x<MaxX; x++) {
      R = ScaleX(RLow, RHigh, x);
      Z0=0, Z1=0;
      for (n=0; n<ITERATIONS; n++) {
        sqr_Z0 = Z0*Z0;
        sqr_Z1 = Z1*Z1;
        Z1 = 2*Z1*Z0 + I;
        Z0 = sqr_Z0 - sqr_Z1 + R;
        if (sqr_Z0 + sqr_Z1 > 4.0) {
          done = TRUE;
          putpixel(x, y, WHITE);
          break;
        }
      } /* end for loop */
      if (done == FALSE)
        putpixel(x, y, BLUE);
      else
```

```
         done = FALSE;
      } /* end inner for loop */
    } /* end outer for loop */
  } /* end Mandel */
```

Fractals

In 1975 Dr. Mandelbrot coined the term *fractal* to mean any shape that has a Hausdorff/Besicovitch dimension larger than the traditional topological dimension. Mandelbrot's studies have shown that a number of natural shapes look the way they do because they have this property. This explains how fractals can be used by computers to draw very realistic looking pictures using fairly small compact code.

Practical Fractals

In this section we look at how you can use fractals to create realistic images. The idea is that shapes in nature often show a certain amount of *self-similarity*, or Mandelbrot's chaotic behavior. If you look at a river from a high altitude you see that it winds around. If you move closer you see that on a smaller scale it winds in the same way – winds within winds, so to speak. If you look at a tree you see another self-similarity. The trunk grows out of the ground, branches grow out of the trunk, and more branches grow out of those branches.

Trees are a good place to start. All code presented in the following sections can be found on the distribution disk in file BK1502.C.

A Simplified Symmetric Tree

The code presented here represents a simplified model of some sort of generic tree. It starts by drawing a trunk as a straight line up and down. The function that draws the trunk then calls itself twice, recursively, to draw a branch on the left and right of the trunk, each growing from the same place in the trunk, each of the same length, and each coming from the trunk at a 45-degree angle. The function then thinks of the branch it just drew as the trunk, so it goes and draws two more branches off of the branch just drawn. This process continues until it reaches a predetermined number of levels in the recursion.

To write this recursive function we need the starting coordinates of the branch to be drawn, the length of the branch, and the angle to draw it at. Remember that

Borland C uses radians to measure angles, the angle defined as 0.645 radians is approximately 45 degrees. We use the length and angle to find the end-point of the line for the line( ) function. Next we have to find the beginning point for the branches, which is the halfway point on the line just drawn. We multiply the length by 0.8 so that the branches will be shorter than the trunk. Finally we add or subtract the angle of change from the angle of the trunk, and make the recursive call. This function is not fast, but it is fun to watch in action.

```
#include <graphics.h>
#include <math.h>
#include <stdlib.h>

#define ANGLE  0.645

void symma_tree (float X1, float Y1,
                 float R,  float Theta,
                 int   Level) {

  float SX, SY, EX, EY;

  if (Level > 0) {
    EX = X1 + (R * cos(Theta));
    EY = Y1 + (R * sin(Theta));

    line (X1+(getmaxx()/2), Y1+getmaxy()-25,
          EX+(getmaxx()/2), EY+getmaxy()-25);

    SX = X1 + ((R * 0.5) * cos(Theta));
    SY = Y1 + ((R * 0.5) * sin(Theta));
    symma_tree (SX, SY, R*0.8,
                Theta-ANGLE, Level-1);
    symma_tree (SX, SY, R*0.8,
                Theta+ANGLE, Level-1);
  } /* end if */
} /* end symma_tree() */

void main(void) {
  int Mode, Driver, GraphError;

  Driver = DETECT;
  detectgraph(&Driver, &Mode);
  initgraph(&Driver, &Mode, '');

  GraphError = graphresult();
  if (GraphError != grOk) {
    printf(
      "%s\n",grapherrormsg(GraphError));
```

```
        exit(-1);
    }

    /* Do Graphics Stuff Here */
    setbkcolor(WHITE);
    setcolor(GREEN);

    symma_tree(0, 0, 150, -1.5707963, 14);
    outtextxy (50, 50, "Symma Tree");
    getch();

    if (kbhit()) getch();
    closegraph();
}
```

Figure 15.2.1 shows the basic shape of the "symma tree." The trunk is drawn first, then the two branches. Picture in your mind two more branches being drawn from each branch, then two more branches from each of those. This is what the symma_tree( ) function does.

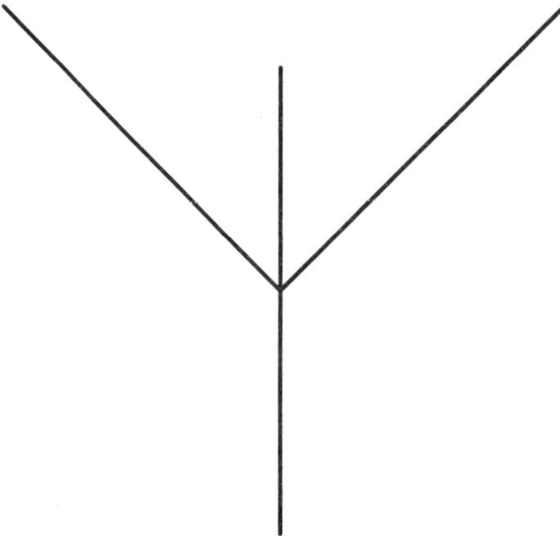

Fig. 15.2.1 Basis of the "Symma Tree"

A Less Simplified Asymmetric Tree

The symma tree is interesting, but it hardly looks realistic. One problem is that trees do not display that much symmetry. Variations on the above theme would be to change the angle of one branch, change where it grows from the trunk, or change how much the next branch is shortened. The function given here changes the first two of these parameters, giving a rather more realistic look to the tree. Notice how the side with the shallower angle is given a fuller look. If you can explain why then you are starting to develop an understanding of fractals.

This code will not be covered in detail since the only differences between this and the last function is the change in one angle and the change in placement of one branch. The original call is the same as above.

```
#define RT_ANGLE    0.645
#define LFT_ANGLE   0.9

void non_symma_tree (float X1, float Y1,
                     float R,  float Theta,
                     int   Level) {

  float SX, SY, EX, EY;

  if (Level > 0) {
    EX = X1 + (R * cos(Theta));
    EY = Y1 + (R * sin(Theta));

    line (X1+(getmaxx()/2), Y1+getmaxy()-50,
          EX+(getmaxx()/2), EY+getmaxy()-50);

    SX = X1 + ((R * 0.4) * cos(Theta));
    SY = Y1 + ((R * 0.4) * sin(Theta));
    non_symma_tree (SX, SY, R*0.8,
                    Theta-RT_ANGLE, Level-1);

    SX = X1 + ((R * 0.6) * cos(Theta));
    SY = Y1 + ((R * 0.6) * sin(Theta));
    non_symma_tree (SX, SY, R*0.8,
                    Theta+LFT_ANGLE, Level-1);
  } /* end if */
} /* end non_symma_tree() */
```

Figure 15.2.2 shows the original trunk and first two branches of this tree. After repeating the process 12 more times can you guess what it would look like?

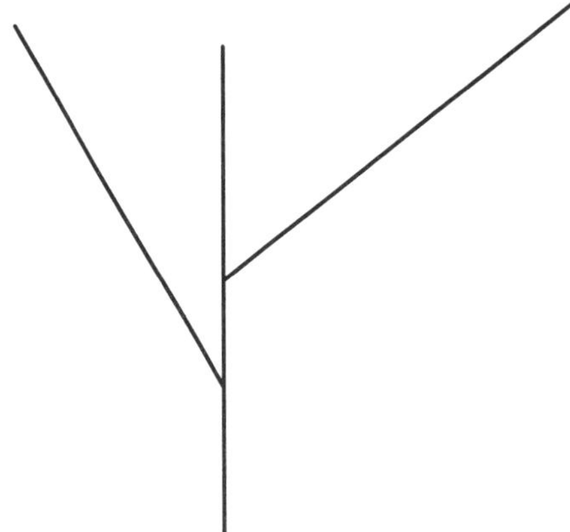

Fig. 15.2.2 Basis for the Asymmetric Tree

A Surprisingly Realistic Tree

With the last two sections you should have started to see that what we are trying to do here is model how a tree grows. Not in a realistic sense of the trunk growing, and branches sprouting from the trunk but with the trunk continuing to grow. These simplified models work as if the trunk grows, then after the trunk stops growing the branches grow.

The branches of a real tree do not always sprout from the same spot on the parent branch or trunk, nor do they always grow to the same length as other branches on the same trunk, or at the same angle. To make a tree more realistic it helps to add an element of randomness. Once that element of randomness is added, however, it needs to be controlled. Branches must be smaller than the trunk, and angles must be within a certain range, or the resulting tree is not realistic. The function here limits the length of a branch to between 0.5 and 0.9 times the length of the trunk. The new length is then used in the determination of the angle and start position. On a real tree a branch that starts lower on the trunk will be longer, but will often make a more acute angle with the trunk. If a long branch grew near the top of the trunk it would be too heavy for the trunk to support. These are the types of things the fractal designer looks at.

```
void random_symma_tree (float X1, float Y1,
                        float R,  float Theta,
                        int   Level) {

  float SX, SY, EX, EY, length, angle;

  if (Level > 0) {
    EX = X1 + (R * cos(Theta));
    EY = Y1 + (R * sin(Theta));

    line (X1+(getmaxx()/2), Y1+getmaxy()-50,
          EX+(getmaxx()/2), EY+getmaxy()-50);

    length = (((float)rand()/(float)RAND_MAX) *
                                    0.4) + 0.5;
    angle = (((float)rand()/(float)RAND_MAX) *
                                 length) + 0.4;
    SX = X1 + ((R * length) * cos(Theta));
    SY = Y1 + ((R * length) * sin(Theta));
    random_symma_tree (SX, SY, R*0.78,
                       Theta-angle, Level-1);

    length = (((float)rand()/(float)RAND_MAX) *
                                    0.2) + 0.4;
    angle = (((float)rand()/(float)RAND_MAX) *
                                 0.2) + length;
    SX = X1 + ((R * length) * cos(Theta));
    SY = Y1 + ((R * length) * sin(Theta));
    random_symma_tree (SX, SY, R*0.78,
                       Theta+angle, Level-1);
  } /* end if */
} /* end random_symma_tree() */
```

The tree drawn by this code is a surprisingly realistic looking tree. Certain things could be done better. A trunk and branches on a real tree are not thin lines, they have thickness that diminishes as the tree grows outward. A real tree does not always have two smaller branches growing from each branch, sometimes there are several, other times there are none. One thing to watch as you add detail, however, is speed. It is surprising how quickly these recursive routines slow down.

These trees are also quite rounded on top, somewhat like a weeping willow. If you want a tree that is more pointed at the top, such as a pine, try adding a branch growing from the top, as an extension of the trunk (see the maple leaf and fern below).

A Windblown Tree

The windblown tree is a simple attempt to model what happens if a tree grows where it is constantly being blown by winds from one direction. When you look at such a tree you see that it is thinner on the upwind side, and the branches tend to point toward the downwind side. To model this, fewer branches are drawn on the upwind side, and the angles are made to favor the downwind. Notice how the levels are handled. Twice as many downwind branches are drawn as upwind, but the level is taken down by 2 instead of 1. Otherwise the downwind side would look impossibly thick and full.

```
void wind_blown_tree (float X1, float Y1,
                      float R,  float Theta,
                      int   Level) {

  float SX, SY, EX, EY, length, angle;

  if (Level > 0) {
    EX = X1 + (R * cos(Theta));
    EY = Y1 + (R * sin(Theta));

    line (X1+(getmaxx()/2), Y1+getmaxy()-50,
          EX+(getmaxx()/2), EY+getmaxy()-50);

    length = (((float)rand()/(float)RAND_MAX) *
                                   0.1) + 0.3;
    angle = (((float)rand()/(float)RAND_MAX) *
                                   0.1) + 0.3;
    SX = X1 + (0.3 * R * cos(Theta));
    SY = Y1 + (0.3 * R * sin(Theta));
    wind_blown_tree (SX, SY, R*0.8,
                     Theta-angle, Level-3);

    length = (((float)rand()/(float)RAND_MAX) *
                                   0.3) + 0.3;
    angle = (((float)rand()/(float)RAND_MAX) *
                                   0.3) + 0.3;
    SX = X1 + ((R * length) * cos(Theta));
    SY = Y1 + ((R * length) * sin(Theta));
    wind_blown_tree (SX, SY, R*0.8,
                     Theta+angle, Level-2);

    length = (((float)rand()/(float)RAND_MAX) *
                                   0.3) + 0.3;
    angle = (((float)rand()/(float)RAND_MAX) *
                                   0.3) + 0.3;
    SX = X1 + ((R * length) * cos(Theta));
    SY = Y1 + ((R * length) * sin(Theta));
```

```
    wind_blown_tree (SX, SY, R*0.8,
                     Theta+angle, Level-2);

  } /* end if */
} /* end wind_blown_tree() */
```

Other Shapes

This section covers code for drawing a fern and a maple leaf. The code for these very different shapes is surprisingly similar. This is because from a fractal point of view, the forces that shape these objects are quite similar. They are affected little by the elements, and show very little randomness.

For the maple leaf, branches come out close to the base, one on each side of the trunk, at the same angle. Another branch is added growing straight up from the trunk. This becomes part of the trunk, and causes other smaller branches to grow from the trunk. As the branch that grows upward gets smaller with each recursive call the branches growing from the sides become proportionately smaller. This is worth studying. The shape of the maple leaf after two iterations is shown in Fig. 15.2.3(a).

```
#define LEAF_ANGLE  0.645

void maple_leaf (float X1, float Y1,
                 float R,  float Theta,
                 int   Level) {

  float SX, SY, EX, EY;

  if (Level > 0) {
    EX = X1 + (R * cos(Theta));
    EY = Y1 + (R * sin(Theta));

    line (X1+(getmaxx()/2), Y1+getmaxy()-75,
          EX+(getmaxx()/2), EY+getmaxy()-75);

    SX = X1 + ((R * 0.1) * cos(Theta));
    SY = Y1 + ((R * 0.1) * sin(Theta));
    maple_leaf (SX, SY, R*0.8,
                Theta-LEAF_ANGLE, Level-1);
    maple_leaf (SX, SY, R*0.8,
                Theta+LEAF_ANGLE, Level-1);
    SX = X1 + ((R * 0.7) * cos(Theta));
    SY = Y1 + ((R * 0.7) * sin(Theta));
    maple_leaf (SX, SY, R*0.5, Theta, Level-1);
  } /* end if */
} /* end maple_leaf() */
```

The fern is similar, only the branches are actually drawn at a somewhat downward angle, and the branch growing up from the trunk (or in this case the stem) grows at a slight angle [Fig. 15.2.4(b)]. As the levels of recursion increase this angle becomes more apparent. The angle remains the same but the branches become smaller, which tends to magnify the angle. When this program is run notice how the stalk curls slightly at the top, and also notice how each branch curls, mirroring the stalk.

```
#define FERN_ANGLE1 1.7
#define FERN_ANGLE2 1.8
#define STALK_ANGLE 0.05

void fern (float X1, float Y1,
           float R,  float Theta, int Level) {

  float SX, SY, EX, EY;

  if (Level > 0) {
    EX = X1 + (R * cos(Theta));
    EY = Y1 + (R * sin(Theta));

    line (X1+(getmaxx()/2), Y1+getmaxy()-75,
          EX+(getmaxx()/2), EY+getmaxy()-75);

    SX = X1 + ((R * 0.5) * cos(Theta));
    SY = Y1 + ((R * 0.5) * sin(Theta));
    fern (SX, SY, R*0.5,
          Theta-FERN_ANGLE1, Level-1);
    SX = X1 + ((R * 0.55) * cos(Theta));
    SY = Y1 + ((R * 0.55) * sin(Theta));
    fern (SX, SY, R*0.5,
          Theta+FERN_ANGLE2, Level-1);
    SX = X1 + ((R * 0.53) * cos(Theta));
    SY = Y1 + ((R * 0.53) * sin(Theta));
    fern (SX, SY, R*0.8,
          Theta+STALK_ANGLE, Level-1);
  } /* end if */
} /* end fern() */
```

Figure 15.2.3 shows the first two iterations of each of these shapes. The dashed lines show that a line comes up from the trunk, extending it. This line is not dashed in the actual program.

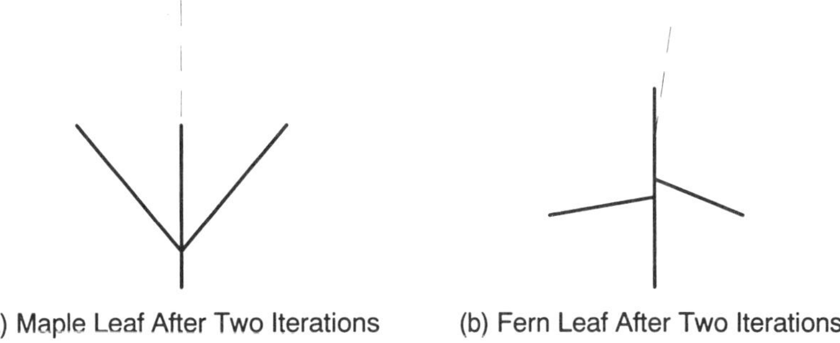

(a) Maple Leaf After Two Iterations (b) Fern Leaf After Two Iterations

Fig. 15.2.3 Basis of Maple Leaf and Fern

How Fractals Model Nature

Fractals model nature by taking advantage of self-similarity. Many natural objects show some degree of self similarity. The above sections should make it clear that many trees and other plants do. To make a realistic image of your favorite tree start by looking for how the parts of the tree mirror the whole. Look at the angles of the branches: How many branches are there growing from the trunk and is the number of branches from each branch the same, or is it a function of the length of the branch?, etc. Flowers can easily be modeled using the same techniques.

Mountains, the flow of rivers, clouds, and a number of other natural objects lend themselves to the same techniques. Look the line of a mountain from the distance. Then look closer. From a distance the mountain has a peak. Closer up that peak has a number of smaller local peaks on it. Even closer, each of these peaks has even more smaller peaks on it. Rivers, as discussed at the opening of the chapter, wind around to the left and the right, and each wind has its own little winds left and right. Edges of clouds are rough. Look closely at the edge, and you see that each portion of the edge mirrors the roughness of the whole.

All these types of self-similarity can be modeled with computers. A function could be written that takes a curve, breaks it apart, and adds or subtracts a smaller version of the whole to the part. Call the function recursively for each part, and when the function returns you have a nice neat model of a river bed. Make the original curve rougher, with a sharp peak in the middle, and the function returns a mountain peak. Make the original curve very rough and closed, and it might just return something that looks like a cloud.

Iterated Function Systems

One problem with the traditional method for generating fractals is speed. Recursive programs are not known for their speed, especially when they involve an activity as slow as drawing lines. Bresenham's method for drawing lines spends little time calculating where each pixel should be plotted, but plotting each individual pixel still takes some time. Compound that with the fact that the functions given previously often plot the same point over and over, and one must start to wonder if there is not a faster way.

In 1985 a pair of mathematicians, one named Barnsley, the other with the rather unlikely name of John Elton, showed the world a faster method of generating fractal images. Not only is this method faster, since it eliminates the recursion, but it is also more flexible, since only one procedure is used to make nearly any shape that shows the property of self-similarity.

Sierpinsky's Triangle Again

Take a piece of paper. On this paper draw three dots to form the corners of a triangle. In the center of these three dots draw another dot. Now pick any one of the corners randomly, and draw a dot halfway between the center dot and that corner. Pick another corner at random (it could be the same corner), and draw a dot halfway between your latest dot and that corner. Repeat this process, oh say, 10,000 times, and an amazing thing happens. Sierpinsky's Triangle appears. How odd. Must be Sierpinsky was really on to something with this strange triangle of his. Repeating the process might not be such an easy thing to do by hand, but program BK1503.C will do it for you.

Okay, so we have a mathematical curiosity. So what? Well, it turns out that this program makes use of Barnsley and Elton's method, in a rather crude form.

A Deeper Look at Self-Similarity

To understand why the Sierpinsky's Triangle program draws Sierpinsky's Triangle, it is helpful to develop a more mathematical understanding of self-similarity. An object displays self-similarity if any part of the object can be obtained by applying any number of affine transformations to the whole object. An affine transformation is a linear transformation that is made of a combination of rotation, sizing, and translation. Linear transformations are discussed in Chapter 13.

Sierpinsky's Triangle shows a high degree of self-similarity since each and every part is the same as the starting triangle, only scaled much smaller and translated to various parts of the original. The Sierpinsky's Triangle program starts with a point on the triangle, then scales and translates that point to another part of the triangle. Scales a point? Points have no size, how can they be scaled? Actually the transformations are not applied to the point itself, but to the relation with the point to the randomly selected corner point. If you look carefully at the code for this program you will not see anything that looks like linear transformations. It so happens that with Sierpinsky's Triangle the transformations can be simplified to the code given.

Notice that the loop is run 10 times before any points are plotted. The starting point in the center of the triangle is not actually in Sierpinsky's Triangle because of the white space in the center. If the first several points are plotted they will appear in this white space. Iterating 10 times without plotting allows the system to stabilize so that all plotted points will definitely be in the triangle. The following code for Sierpinsky's Triangle is in file BK1503.C on the distribution disk.

```
void sierpinsky(void) {
  int L_Vertex1_X = getmaxx()/2,
      L_Vertex1_Y = 50,
      L_Vertex2_X = 50,
      L_Vertex2_Y = getmaxy()-150,
      L_Vertex3_X = getmaxx()-150,
      L_Vertex3_Y = getmaxy()-50;
  int L_CurrPt_X, L_CurrPt_Y;
  unsigned int i, j;

  /* plot vertices */
  for (i=L_Vertex1_X-1; i<=L_Vertex1_X+1; i++)
    for (j=L_Vertex1_Y-1;
         j<=L_Vertex1_Y+1;
                      j++)
      putpixel(i, j, DARKGRAY);
  for (i=L_Vertex2_X-1; i<=L_Vertex2_X+1; i++)
    for (j=L_Vertex2_Y-1;
         j<=L_Vertex2_Y+1;
                      j++)
      putpixel(i, j, DARKGRAY);
  for (i=L_Vertex3_X-1; i<=L_Vertex3_X+1; i++)
    for (j=L_Vertex3_Y-1;
         j<=L_Vertex3_Y+1;
                      j++)
      putpixel(i, j, DARKGRAY);

  /* approximate center of triangle */
  L_CurrPt_X = ((L_Vertex3_X-L_Vertex2_X)/2)
                                +L_Vertex2_X;
  L_CurrPt_Y = ((L_Vertex2_Y-L_Vertex1_Y)/2)
```

```
                                        +L_Vertex1_Y;


    /* find first 10 points, but don't plot  */
    /* give the system a chance to stabilize */
    randomize();
    for (i=1; i<=10; i++) {
      switch (random(3)) {
        case (0) :
          L_CurrPt_X = ((L_CurrPt_X-L_Vertex1_X)/
                                   2)+L_Vertex1_X;
          L_CurrPt_Y = ((L_CurrPt_Y-L_Vertex1_Y)/
                                   2)+L_Vertex1_Y;
          break;
        case (1) :
          L_CurrPt_X = ((L_CurrPt_X-L_Vertex2_X)/
                                   2)+L_Vertex2_X;
          L_CurrPt_Y = ((L_CurrPt_Y-L_Vertex2_Y)/
                                   2)+L_Vertex2_Y;
          break;
        case (2) :
          L_CurrPt_X = ((L_CurrPt_X-L_Vertex3_X)/
                                   2)+L_Vertex3_X;
          L_CurrPt_Y = ((L_CurrPt_Y-L_Vertex3_Y)/
                                   2)+L_Vertex3_Y;
          break;
      } /* end switch */
    } /* end loop */

    /* Do a long loop where the one of the
       vertices are selected and the current
       point is placed halfway between that
       vertex and the current point */
    for (i=0; i<=60000; i++) {
      switch (random(3)) {
        case (0) :
          L_CurrPt_X = ((L_CurrPt_X-L_Vertex1_X)/
                                   2)+L_Vertex1_X;
          L_CurrPt_Y = ((L_CurrPt_Y-L_Vertex1_Y)/
                                   2)+L_Vertex1_Y;
          break;
        case (1) :
          L_CurrPt_X = ((L_CurrPt_X-L_Vertex2_X)/
                                   2)+L_Vertex2_X;
          L_CurrPt_Y = ((L_CurrPt_Y-L_Vertex2_Y)/
                                   2)+L_Vertex2_Y;
          break;
```

```
      case (2) :
        L_CurrPt_X = ((L_CurrPt_X-L_Vertex3_X)/
                                    2)+L_Vertex3_X;
        L_CurrPt_Y = ((L_CurrPt_Y-L_Vertex3_Y)/
                                    2)+L_Vertex3_Y;
        break;
    } /* end switch */
    putpixel(L_CurrPt_X, L_CurrPt_Y, DARKGRAY);
  } /* end loop */

} /* end sierpinsky() */
```

The Iterated Function System

The magic of Elton and Barnsley's discovery is that any self-similar image can be reproduced with the same set of six linear transformations: translation in the X dimension, translation in the Y dimension, scaling in X, scaling in Y, rotation in X, and rotation in Y. Four values are given for each transformation, and one set of values is picked randomly. The set of values is applied to the current point to find the next point, which is then plotted. Each set of values is given a weight, so that a particular set is more or less likely to be used depending on the area it covers. For instance, the stalk of a fern has fewer points in it than the leaves, so the values relating to the stalk should be called less often. Here is the code for the iterated function system, which can be found in BK1504.C:

```
/* set up for fern */

float trns_x[4] = { 0.0,  0.0,  0.0,  0.0 };
float trns_y[4] = { 0.0,  1.6,  0.44, 1.6 };
float size_x[4] = { 0.0,  0.20,-0.15, 0.85 };
float size_y[4] = { 0.16, 0.22, 0.24, 0.85 };
float rot_x[4]  = { 0.0, -0.26, 0.28,-0.04 };
float rot_y[4]  = { 0.0,  0.23, 0.26,-0.04 };
float prob[4]   = { 382;  2615, 4915, 32767 };

void ifs_proc () {

  float x = 0.0, y = 0.0, next_x;

  int k, j, px, py, i;

  randomize();

  /* find first 10 points without plotting
     to let the system stabilize */
```

```
    for (i=0; i < 10; i++) {
      j = random(32767);
      if (j < prob[0])
        k = 0;
      else if (j < prob[1])
        k = 1;
      else if (j < prob[2])
        k = 2;
      else
        k = 3;

      next_x = size_x[k]*x+rot_x[k]*y+trns_x[k];
      y      = size_y[k]*y+rot_y[k]*x+trns_y[k];
      x      = next_x;
      px     = x * 25 + getmaxx()/2;
      py     = getmaxy() - y*25 - 100;
    } /* end for loop */

    /* Now find and plot pixels */
    for (; i < 20000; i++) {
      j = random(32767);
      if (j < prob[0])
        k = 0;
      else if (j < prob[1])
        k = 1;
      else if (j < prob[2])
        k = 2;
      else
        k = 3;

      next_x = size_x[k]*x+rot_x[k]*y+trns_x[k];
      y       = size_y[k]*y+rot_y[k]*x+trns_y[k];
      x      = next_x;
      px     = x * 25 + getmaxx()/2;
      py     = getmaxy() - y*25 - 100;

      putpixel (px, py, DARKGRAY);
    } /* end for loop */
  } /* end ifs_proc() */
```

So how does it work? Start with a set of six numbers: *a* representing X translation, *b* for Y translation, *c* for X scaling, *d* for Y scaling, *e* for X rotation, and *f* for Y rotation. Now we use matrix multiplication to combine the six linear transformations, as described in Chapter 13, so that only one transformation needs to be applied while the program is running. This gives the following formulas:

$$x_2 = c*\cos(e) - d*\sin(f) + e$$
$$y_2 = c*\sin(e) - d*\cos(f) + f$$

But we don't like to have all those sines and cosines in a loop, so we figure the sines and cosines into our data set and they become constants. This gives the siz variables from the program:

trns_x = a
trns_y = b
size_x = c*cos(e)
size_y = d*sin(f)
rot_x = -c*sin(e)
rot_y = d*cos(f)

The names used in the program are rather misleading. This is due to legacy code – in the original version of this program the sines and cosines were still in the loop, so the names were more meaningful. The sines and cosines were removed from the loop and put into the data set to speed things up. (For an example for this book I attempted to put them back in, but then I could no longer plot anything reasonable.) Two data sets for drawing interesting fractals are:

```
/* set up for fern */

float trns_x[4] = { 0.0,  0.0,  0.0,  0.0 };
float trns_y[4] = { 0.0,  1.6,  0.44, 1.6 };
float size_x[4] = { 0.0,  0.20,-0.15, 0.85 };
float size_y[4] = { 0.16, 0.22, 0.24, 0.85 };
float rot_x[4]  = { 0.0, -0.26, 0.28,-0.04 };
float rot_y[4]  = { 0.0,  0.23, 0.26,-0.04 };
float prob[4]   = { 382;  2615, 4915, 32767 };

/* Sierpinksy's triangle */
float trns_x[4]  = { -5.0,  5.0,  2.5,  0.0 };
float trns_y[4]  = {  1.5,  0.0,  6.0,  0.0 };
float size_x[4]  = {  0.5,  0.5,  0.5,  0.0 };
float size_y[4]  = {  0.5,  0.5,  0.5,  0.0 };
float rot_x[4]   = {  0.0,  0.0,  0.0,  0.0 };
float rot_y[4]   = {  0.0,  0.0,  0.0,  0.0 };
int prob[4] = { 10922, 21845, 32767, 32767 };
```

These have been included with BK1504.C. Fractal geometry is a fascinating and challenging field in computer graphics. What is presented here is only the tip of the iceberg. Three-dimensional fractals are being used more and more to create stunningly beautiful pictures everywhere from calendars to movies. To learn more about fractals, including 3D fractals, AP Professional offers a book, *Fractals Everywhere*, written by the fellow who devised the iterated function system, Michael Barnsley. This book is considered one of the classic books on fractals, and is highly recommended.

Appendix A
Borland Graphics Functions

This appendix covers most, if not all, of the graphics routines supplied by the Borland Graphics Interface (BGI). Graphics programmers often need to communicate with BIOS, so the functions needed to do that are also listed here. Function prototypes for most of the functions listed here are given in the file GRAPHICS.H, but the prototypes for the functions used to call BIOS are in DOS.H. Because not all functions are prototyped in the same place, this appendix lists the header file where each function is prototyped.

This appendix only lists the Borland functions for calling DOS and BIOS. It does not list BIOS functions themselves. For a listing of BIOS graphics functions see Appendix D.

A table of contents is given here to aid in finding appropriate functions and related information.

Borland Graphics Functions

Borland Graphics Functions

arc( )

```
void far arc (int x, int y, int stangle,
              int endangle, int radius);
  /*
   * arc() draws an arc of a circle
   *
   * Parameters:
   *   x - X coordinate of the center
   *   y - Y coordinate of the center
   *   stangle - angle to start at - 0 is at 3
   *             o'clock
   *   endangle - angle to stop at - arc is
   *              drawn counter-clockwise
   *   radius - the radius of the circle
   */
```

arc( ) will draw an arc of a circle, centered at screen coordinate (x,y), with the given radius, starting at angle stangle, ending at angle endangle.

Prototype in GRAPHICS.H
Covered in Chapter 2, page 35
Related functions: circle( ), ellipse( ), fillellipse( ), pieslice( ),
getarccoords( )

bar( )

```
void far bar (int left,  int top,
              int right, int bottom);
  /*
   * bar() will draw a filled in rectangle.
   *
   * Parameters:
   *   left   - coordinate of left side
   *   top    - coordinate of top
   *   right  - coordinate of right side
   *   bottom - coordinate of bottom
   */
```

bar( ) will draw a filled-in rectangle with the upper left corner at screen coordinate (left, top) and the lower right corner at (right,bottom). The rectangle does not need to be on the screen first. The rectangle will not be outlined; if an outlined rectangle is desired call rectangle( ) with the same coordinates.

Prototype in GRAPHICS.H
Covered in Chapter 5, page 147
related functions: rectangle( ), fillellipse( ), fillpoly( ), floodfill( ), setfillstyle( ), bar3d( )

bar3d( )

```
void far bar3d (int left,  int top,
                int right, int bottom,
                int depth, int topflag);
  /*
   * bar3d() will draw a 3 dimensional box
   *   and fill the front face.
   *
   * Parameters:
   *   left   - coordinate of left side
   *   top    - coordinate of top
   *   right  - coordinate of right side
   *   bottom - coordinate of bottom
   *   depth  - number of pixels deep the
   *     box will be
   *   topflag - if 0 no top will be put on
   *     the box, otherwise a top will be put
   *     on.
   */
```

bar3d( ) will draw a 3D box on the screen with the upper left corner of the front face at screen coordinate (left,top) and the lower right corner of the front face at (right,bottom). The box is outlined and the front face is filled. If topflag is 0 no top will be put on the box. Any other value for this parameter will cause a top to be put on the box.

Prototype in GRAPHICS.H
Not covered in detail in this book
related functions: bar( ), rectangle( ), setfillstyle( )

circle( )

```
void far circle (int x, int y, int radius);
  /*
   * circle() draws a circle on the screen
   *
   * Parameters:
   *   x - X coordinate of the center
   *   y - Y coordinate of the center
   *   radius - the radius of the circle
   */
```

circle( ) will draw a circle centered at screen coordinate (x,y), with the given radius.

Prototype in GRAPHICS.H
Covered in Chapter 2, page 35
Related functions: arc( ), ellipse( ), fillellipse( )

cleardevice( )

```
void cleardevice(void);
  /*
   * cleardevice() clears the graphics screen
   */
```

cleardevice( ) will clear the graphics screen. That is, it will set all bytes in the frame buffer to 0, causing the entire screen to take on the background color. The current position, used by lineto( ) and related functions, is set to screen coordinate (0,0).

Prototype in GRAPHICS.H
Covered in Chapter 2, page 29
Related functions: clearviewport( )

clearviewport( )

```
void clearviewport(void);
  /*
   * clear current viewport
   */
```

Borland C has the ability to set up viewports. When this is done all graphics output is performed in coordinates relative to the viewport, with no output outside the viewport being displayed. Details of using viewports are covered in Chapter 4.

clearviewport( ) will clear the contents of the viewport.

Prototype in GRAPHICS.H
Not covered in detail in this book
Related functions: setviewport( ), cleardevice( ), getviewsettings( )

closegraph( )

```
void closegraph(void);
  /*
   * closegraph() sets the monitor to text
   *   mode.
   */
```

closegraph( ) will set the monitor to it's native text mode, usually 80 × 25, 16 color text mode. To return the monitor to the mode it was in before initgraph( ) was called, use restorecrtmode( ).

Prototype in GRAPHICS.H
Covered in Chapter 2, page 26
Related functions: initgraph( ), restorecrtmode( ), detectgraph( )

detectgraph( )

```
void far detectgraph (int far *graphdriver,
                      int far *mode);
  /*
   * detectgraph() will determine what type of
   *   monitor the system has.  It will then
   *   determine the mode with the highest
   *   resolution.
   *
   * Parameters:
   *   graphdriver - The type of monitor being
   *     used.  If DETECT (0) is used, the type
   *     of monitor is detected and passed
   *     back.
   *   mode - The mode with the highest
   *     resolution for the selected monitor.
   */
```

If detectgraph( ) is given a graphics driver it will find the highest resolution mode for that driver. If the number 0 is given instead of a graphics driver it will find the available graphics driver with the highest resolution supported by the hardware, and the highest resolution mode supported by that driver. Table A.1 gives the graphics drivers supplied with Borland C, the numeric value assigned to that driver, and the constant defined in GRAPHICS.H with that value. Table A.2 gives the names and properties of modes supported by each driver.

Prototype in GRAPHICS.H
Covered in Chapter 2, page 18
Related functions: initgraph( )

Table A.1

Constant Name	Numeric Value	BGI Driver Needed
DETECT	0 (Request Autodetection)	Depends on monitor type
CGA	1	CGA.BGI
MCGA	2	CGA.BGI
EGA	3	EGAVGA.BGI
EGA64	4	EGAVGA.BGI
EGAMONO	5	EGAVGA.BGI
IBM8514	6	IBM8514.BGI
HERCMONO	7	HERC.BGI
ATT400	8	ATT.BGI
VGA	9	EGAVGA.BGI
PC3270	10	PC3270.BGI

Table A.2

Graphics Driver	Mode Name	Numeric Value	Cols	Rows	Palette	Pages
CGA	CGAC0	0	320	200	C0	1
	CGAC1	1	320	200	C1	1
	CGAC2	2	320	200	C2	1
	CGAC3	3	320	200	C3	1
	CGAHI	4	640	200	2 Colors	1
MCGA	MCGAC0	0	320	200	C0	1
	MCGAC1	1	320	200	C1	1
	MCGAC2	2	320	200	C2	1
	MCGAC3	3	320	200	C3	1
	MCGAMED	4	640	200	2 Colors	1
	MCGAHI	5	640	480	2 Colors	1
EGA	EGAHI	0	640	200	16 Colors	4
	EGAHI	1	640	350	16 Colors	2

Graphics Driver	Mode Name	Numeric Value	Cols	Rows	Palette	Pages
EGA64	EGA64LO	0	640	200	16 out of 64 Colors	1
	EGA64HI	1	640	350	4 out of 64 Colors	1
EGA MONO	EGAMONOHI	3	640	350	2 Colors	1 or 2
HERC MONO	HERC MONOHI	0	720	348	2 Colors	2
ATT400	ATT400C0	0	320	200	C0	1
	ATT400C1	1	320	200	C1	1
	ATT400C2	2	320	200	C2	1
	ATT400C3	3	320	200	C3	1
	ATT400MED	4	640	200	2 Color	1
	ATT400HI	5	640	400	2 Color	1
VGA	VGALO	0	640	200	16 Color	2
	VGAMED	1	640	350	16 Color	2
	VGAHI	2	640	480	16 Color	1
PC3270	PC3270HI	0	720	350	2 Color	1
IBM8514	IBM8514LO	0	640	480	256 Color	1
	IBM8514HI	1	1024	768	256 Color	1

drawpoly( )

```
void far drawpoly (int numpoints;
                   int far *polypoints);
  /*
   * drawpoly() draws a polygon
   *
   * Parameters:
   *   numpoints  - The number of vertices in
   *     the polygon.
   *   polypoints - array of integers
   *     containing the coordinates of the
   *     vertices.
   */
```

drawpoly( ) will draw a polygon with numpoints number of vertices. The coordinates of the vertices are given by an array of integers, with the x coordinates indexed by the even indices of the array, and the y coordinates by the odd.

Prototype in GRAPHICS.H
Covered in Chapter 2, page 39
Related functions: fillpoly( ), rectangle( )

ellipse( )

```
void far ellipse (int x, int y,
                  int stangle, int endangle,
                  int xradius, int yradius);
    /*
     * ellipse() draws an arc of an ellipse
     *
     * Parameters:
     *   x - X coordinate of the center
     *   y - Y coordinate of the center
     *   stangle - angle to start at - 0 is at
     *             3 o'clock
     *   endangle - angle to stop at - arc is
     *              drawn counter-lockwise
     *   XRadius - the radius of the ellipse in
     *             the X dimension
     *   YRadius - the radius of the ellipse in
     *             the Y dimension
     */
```

ellipse( ) will draw an arc of an ellipse on the screen, centered on screen coordinate (x,y), starting at angle stangle, ending at endangle, with the radius along the X axis of xradius, and the radius along the Y axis of yradius.

Prototype in GRAPHICS.H
Covered in Chapter 2, page 36
Related functions: fillellipse( ), arc( ), circle( ), pieslice( ), sector( )

fillellipse( )

```
void far fillellipse (int x, int y,
                      int xradius,
                      int yradius);
  /*
   * fillellipse() draws a filled ellipse on
   *   the screen
   *
   * Parameters:
   *   x       - X coordinate of the center
   *   y       - Y coordinate of the center
   *   xradius - the radius of the ellipse in
   *     the X dimension
   *   yradius - the radius of the ellipse in
   *     the Y dimension
   */
```

fillellipse( ) will draw a filled ellipse on the screen. The ellipse does not have to be on the screen when this function is called. The ellipse is centered on screen coordinate (x,y), with a radius along the X axis of length xradius, and a radius along the Y axis of length yradius.

Prototype in GRAPHICS.H
Covered in Chapter 2, page 48
Related functions: ellipse( ), sector( ), setfillstyle( ), fillpoly( ), bar( ), floodfill( )

fillpoly( )

```
void far fillpoly(int numpoints,
                  int far *polypoints);
  /*
   * fillpoly() draws a filled polygon.
   *
   * Parameters:
   *   numpoints  - the number of vertices in
   *     the polygon
   *   polypoints - array of integers
   *     containing the coordinates of the
   *     vertices
   */
```

fillpoly( ) will draw a filled polygon on the screen. The polygon does not need to be on the screen when this function is called. The number of vertices in the polygon is numpoints, the coordinates of the vertices are given by an array of integers, with the x coordinates indexed by the even indices of the array, and the y coordinates indexed by the odd.

Prototype in GRAPHICS.H
Covered in Chapter 2, page 48
Related functions: fillellipse( ), drawpoly( ), floodfill( ), setfillstyle( )

floodfill( )

```
void far floodfill (int x, int y, int border);
  /*
   * floodfill() fills an irregularly shaped
   *   closed shape.
   *
   * Parameters:
   *   x      - X coordinate of the seed
   *            point.
   *   Y      - Y coordinate of the seed
   *            point.
   *   Border - Border color of the shape to
   *            be filled.
   */
```

floodfill( ) will fill a closed irregular shape on the screen. This shape **must** be on the screen before floodfill( ) is called. Screen coordinate (x,y) is any point within the shape, and border is the color of the border bounding the shape. Care must be taken that the border of the shape is actually closed (and all the same color), or floodfill will "leak out" and fill the entire screen. The algorithm used by floodfill( ) is a rather innefficient recursive algorithm (see Chapter 11 for details on the algorithm) and for this reason it is recommended that fillpoly( ) or fillellipse( ) be used wherever possible.

Prototype in GRAPHICS.H
Covered in Chapter 2, page 49
Related functions: fillellipse( ), fillpoly( ), setfillstyle( )

getarccoords( )

```
void far getarccoord (struct arccoordstype
                        far *arccoords);
  /*
   * getarccoords() gets information on the arc
   * drawn by the last call to arc()
   *
   * Parameter:
   *   arccoords - information on last arc
   *               drawn
   */
```

getarccoords( ) is used to translate beginning and ending angles of the last arc drawn to X,Y coordinates, so that lines can be made to connect to them. The center point of the arc is also given. The structure of arccoordstype is

```
struct arccoordstype {
  int x, y;
  int xstart, ystart, xend, yend;
};
```

where x and y are the coordinates of the center of the arc, xstart and ystart give the pixels at the start of the arc, and xend and yend give the pixels at the end of the arc.

Prototype in GRAPHICS.H
Not covered in detail in this book
Related functions: arc( ), line( )

getaspectratio( )

```
void far getaspectratio(int far *xasp,
                        int far *yasp);
  /*
   * getaspectratio() gets the current aspect
   *   ratio of the screen.  The yasp parameter
   *   is normalized to 10,000.
   *
   * Parameters
   *   xasp, yasp - the size of the x and y
   *     dimensions of the pixels, relative to
   *     each other.
   */
```

getaspectratio( ) will get the aspect ratio of the current screen mode. Parameter yasp is normalized to 10,000, and xasp is the size of the pixel in the x dimension, relative to 10,000. On VGA high-resolution modes xasp should be equal to yasp, since in these modes pixels are square. In all other modes xasp should be less than yasp. This function is useful if you wish to implement your own circle routines, or for similar things, but most Borland-supplied routines take the aspect ratio into account so the programmer does not need to worry about it.

Prototype in GRAPHICS.H
Not covered in detail in this book
Related functions: setaspectratio( ), circle( ), ellipse( )

getbkcolor( )

```
int far getbkcolor(void);
  /*
   * getbkcolor() returns the background color
   */
```

The background color of the graphics screen is always color 0, but 0 can represent any color. This function returns the constant value of the background color.

Prototype in GRAPHICS.H
Covered in Chapter 2, page 32
Related functions: setbkcolor( ), getcolor( ), setcolor( )

getcolor( )

```
int far getcolor(void) : Word;
  /*
   * getcolor() will return the default
   *   drawing color
   */
```

getcolor( ) will return the current drawing color. This color is used for drawing lines, arcs, etc, and filling. It is not used by putpixel( ).

Prototype in GRAPHICS.H
Covered in Chapter 2, page 31
Related functions: setcolor( ), setbkcolor( ), getbkcolor( ), line( ), putpixel( )

getdefaultpalette( )

```
struct palettetype *far getdefaultpalette(void);
  /*
   * getdefaultpalette() returns a pointer to
   *   a buffer with the values of the default
   *   palette used when the monitor is first
   *   put into graphics mode.
   */
```

getdefaultpalette( ) will return a pointer to a palette containing the values the original palette contained when the monitor was first set to graphics mode. This allows the programmer to return the palette to the default colors at any time.

Prototype in GRAPHICS.H
Not covered in detail in this book
Related functions: getpalette( ), setpalette( )

getfillpattern( )

```
void far getfillpattern(char far *pattern);
  /*
   * getfillpattern() gets the user defined
   *   fill pattern
   *
   * Parameter:
   *   pattern - pointer to 8 byte array that
   *     will contain the user defined pattern
   */
```

getfillpattern( ) will get the current user defined fill pattern. See setfillpattern( ) for details on how user-defined fill patterns are created. If a user-defined pattern is not being used do not use this function. Use getfillsettings( ) to determine if a user-defined fill pattern is being used, and to find the pattern being used if it is not user-defined.

Prototype in GRAPHICS.H
Not covered in detail in this book
Related functions: getfillstyle( ), setfillpattern( ), setfillstyle( )

getfillsettings( )

```
void far getfillsettings
   (struct fillsettingstype far *fillinfo);
  /*
   * getfillsettings will get information on
   *   the current fill settings
   *
   * Parameter:
   *   fillinfo - information on the fill
   *     current fill settings
   */
```

getfillsettings( ) will get the current settings used by the fill routines. The structure fillsettingstype has the following structure:

```
struct fillsettingstype {
  int pattern;
  int color;
};
```

If pattern is equal to USER_FILL then use getfillpattern to return the pattern. For a table with the available predefined fill patterns see setfillstyle.

Prototype in GRAPHICS.H
Not covered in detail in this book
Related functions: setfillstyle( ), getfillpattern( )

getgraphmode( )

```
int far getgraphmode(void);
  /*
   * getgraphmode() returns the mode that the
   *   monitor is currently in.
   */
```

getgraphmode( ) will return the number of the current graphics mode. For a table of graphics modes and their properties see detectgraph( ).

Prototype in GRAPHICS.H
Covered in Chapter 2, page 25
Related functions: detectgraph( ), initgraph( ), setgraphmode( )

getimage( )

```
void getimage(int left,  int top,
              int right, int bottom,
              void far *bitmap);
  /*
   * getimage() will copy a rectangular bit
   *   map from the screen.
   *
   * Parameters:
   *   left   - left hand border of bit map
   *   top    - top border of bit map
   *   right  - right hand border of bit map
   *   bottom - bottom border of bit map
   *   bitmap - pointer to buffer that will
   *     hold the bitmap
   */
```

getimage( ) will copy a rectangular area of the frame buffer into a buffer pointed to by bitmap. The first two words of this buffer contain the width and the height of the area copied. The function imagesize( ) can be used to get the size of the buffer needed. This function is useful for saving graphic images in files or for moving them from one part of the screen to another.

Prototype in GRAPHICS.H
Covered in Chapter 12, page 360
Related functions: imagesize( ), putimage( ), setactivepage( ), setvisualpage ( )

getlinesettings( )

```
void far getlinesettings
  (struct linesettingstype far *lineinfo);
  /*
   * linesettingstype() will get the current
   *   information used by line routines to
   *   draw lines
   *
   * Parameter:
   *   lineinfo - structure containing
   *     information used to draw lines.
   */
```

getlinesettings( ) will get parameters used by line routines. The parameter lineinfo has the following structure:

```
struct linesettingstype {
  int linestyle;
  unsigned upattern
  int thickness;
};
```

For a table showing predefined line styles see setlinestyle( ). The upattern parameter is only used if linestyle is USERBIT_PATTERN.

Prototype in GRAPHICS.H
Not covered in detail in this book
Related functions: setlinestyle( ), line( ), lineto( )

getmaxcolor( )

```
int far getmaxcolor(void);
  /*
   * getmaxcolor() returns the number of the
   *   highest color available
   */
```

getmaxcolor( ) returns the maximum number of colors available in the current graphics mode. For a table on colors available in different modes see detectgraph( ). For a table on constants defined for different colors see setcolor( ).

Prototype in GRAPHICS.H
Covered in Chapter 2, page 28
Related functions: setgraphmode( ), getgraphmode( ), initgraph( ), detectgraph( ), getmaxx( ), getmaxy( )

getmaxmode( )

```
int far getmaxmode(void);
  /*
   * getmaxmode() will return the maximum mode
   *   number available
   */
```

getmaxmode( ) will return the maximum mode number supported for the currently loaded driver. It can be used with drivers that have not been supplied by Borland.

Prototype in GRAPHICS.H
Not covered in detail in this book
Relate functions: getmoderange( ), getmodename( ), detectgraph( ), initgraph( )

getmaxx( )

```
int far getmaxx(void);
  /*
   * getmaxx() returns the maximum X
   *   coordinate.
   */
```

getmaxx( ) will return the maximum number of points available in the X dimension for the current graphics mode. For a table of modes and the resolution of those modes see detectgraph( ).

Prototype in GRAPHICS.H
Covered in Chapter 2, page 28
Related functions: setgraphmode( ), getgraphmode( ), initgraph( ), detectgraph( ), getmaxy( )

getmaxy( )

```
int far getmaxy(void);
  /*
   * getmaxy() returns the maximum Y
   *   coordinate.
   */
```

getmaxy( ) will return the maximum number of points available in the Y dimension for the current graphics mode. For a table of modes and the resolution of those modes see detectgraph( ).

Prototype in GRAPHICS.H
Covered in Chapter 2, page 28
Related functions: setgraphmode( ), getgraphmode( ), initgraph( ), detectgraph( ), getmaxx( )

getmodename( )

```
char *far getmodename(int mode_number);
  /*
   * getmodename() returns a string with the
   *   name for the mode number passed in.
   *
   * Parameter:
   *   mode_number - The number of the mode
   *                 being named
   */
```

getmodename( ) will return a string with a name for the mode given by mode_number. See detectgraph( ) for a table of modes.

Prototype in GRAPHICS.H
Not covered in detail in this book
Related functions: getmoderange( ), detectgraph( ), initgraph( )

getmoderange( )

```
void far getmoderange (int graphdriver,
                       int far *lomode,
                       int far *himode);
  /*
   * getmoderange will return the modes
   *   available for the given driver
   *
   * Parameters:
   *   graphdriver - BGI driver
   *   lomode      - lowest mode available
   *   himode      - highest mode available.
   */
```

getmoderange( ) will get the range of modes available for the given BGI driver. It should be noted that this function will only work with Borland-supplied drivers. If you are using a third-party driver use getmaxmode( ) instead. For a table of modes available for Borland-supplied drivers see detectgraph( ).

Prototype in GRAPHICS.H
Not covered in detail in this book
Related functions: getmaxmode( ), getmodename( ), detectgraph( ).

getpalette( )

```
void getpalette (struct palettetype far &palette);
  /*
   * getpalette will return information on
   * the current graphics setting
   *
   * Parameters:
   *   palette - Structure containing
   *     information on the current graphics
   *     setting.
   *
   * Note - This procedure is not supported
   *        on the IBM 1814 monitor.
   */
```

getpalette( ) will return information on the palette registers. This function needs to be called before calling setrgbpalette. See Chapter 6 for details. The parameter palette has the following structure:

```
struct palettetype {
    unsigned char size;
    signed   char colors[MAXCOLORS+1];
};
```

Prototype in GRAPHICS.H
Covered in Chapter 6, page 175
Related functions: setrgbpalette( ), setcolor( )

getpalettesize( )

```
int far getpalettesize(void);
  /*
   * getpalettesize() will return the number of
   *   colors in the current mode
   */
```

getpalettesize( ) will return the number of colors, that is, the number of palette registers, available in the current mode. For information on the number of colors available in different modes see detectgraph( ).

Prototype in GRAPHICS.H

Not covered in detail in this book
Related functions: getpalette( ), setrgbpalette( ), setcolor( )

getpixel( )

```
unsigned far getpixel(int x, int y);
  /*
   * returns the color of the pixel at (x,y)
   */
```

getpixel( ) will return the color of the pixel at screen coordinate (x,y).

Prototype in GRAPHICS.H
Not covered in detail in this book
Related functions: putpixel( )

gettextsettings( )

```
void gettextsettings (struct textsettingstype
                          far *texttypeinfo);
  /*
   * gettextsettings() will return the various
   *   parameters for graphics text settings
   *
   * Parameter:
   *   texttypeinfo - Data structure holding
   *     parameters for graphics text.
   */
```

gettextsettings( ) will return information on current graphics text settings. The information is returned in a structure textsettingstype, defined below.

```
struct textsettingstype {
  int font;
  int direction;
  int charsize;
  int horiz;
  int vert;
};
```

font is the current font being used, direction is 0 = horizontal or 1 = vertical, charsize is described below, horiz and vert are the justifications in the horizontal and vertical directions. Table A.3 gives the available justifications depending on direction.

The field charsize is a multiplier, so that if it is 1 the displayed characters will 8 pixels by 8 pixels, if it is 2 the displayed characters will be 16 pixels by 16 pixels, etc. If it is 0, a user-defined character size is being used.

Prototype in GRAPHICS.H
Covered in Chapter 3, page 70
Related functions: settextstyle( ), settextjustify( ), textheight( ), textwidth( ), setusercharsize( ),

Table A.3

Text Direction	**Name**	**Value**	**Action**
Horizontal	LEFT_TEXT	0	Left justify text
	CENTER_TEXT	1	Center text
	RIGHT_TEXT	2	Right justify text
Vertical	BOTTOM_TEXT	0	Justify from the bottom
	CENTER_TEXT	1	Center text
	TOP_TEXT	2	Justify from the top

getviewsettings( )

```
void far getviewsettings
         (struct veiwporttype far *veiwport);
  /*
   * getviewsettings() will get information
   *   on the current veiwport
   *
   * Parameter:
   *   viewport - contains info on the current
   *     viewport.
   */
```

getviewsettings( ) will get information on the current viewport. The parameter viewport has the following structure:

```
struct viewporttype {
  int left, top, right, bottom;
  int clip;
};
```

Fields left, top, right and bottom give the borders of the viewport. Clip is set to 0 if clipping is disabled, or some other value is clipping is enabled.

Prototype in GRAPHICS.H
Not covered in detail in this book
Related functions: clearviewport( ), setviewport( )

getx( )

```
int far getx(void);
  /*
   * getx() returns the x coordinate of the
   *   current screen coordinate
   */
```

getx( ) will return the x coordinate of the current screen coordinates, used by lineto( ), moveto( ) and related functions. The returned coordinate is relative to the viewport.

Prototype in GRAPHICS.H
Not covered in detail in this book
Related functions: gety( ), moveto( ), lineto( )

gety( )

```
int far gety(void);
  /*
   * gety() returns the x coordinate of the
   *   current screen coordinate
   */
```

gety( ) will return the y coordinate of the current screen coordinates, used by lineto( ), moveto( ), and related functions. The returned coordinate is relative to the viewport.

Prototype in GRAPHICS.H
Not covered in detail in this book
Related functions: getx( ), moveto( ), lineto( )

graphdefaults( )

```
void far graphdefaults(void);
  /*
   * graphdefaults() resets all graphics
   *   settings to their defaults
   */
```

graphdefaults( ) resets all graphics settings to their defaults. It sets the viewport to the entire screen, moves current position to (0,0), resets the default palette, default background and drawing colors, the default fill and line styles and patterns, and resets the text font and justifications.

Prototype in GRAPHICS.H
Not covered in detail in this book.
Related functions: initgraph( ), setgraphmode( ), getdefaultpalette( )

grapherrormsg( )

```
char * far grapherrormsg (int errorcode);
  /*
   * grapherrormsg() returns a string
   *   describing the error associated with the
   *   error code passed in.
   *
   * Parameter:
   *   errorcode - integer of error returned by
   *     graphresult.
   */
```

grapherrormsg( ) will return a string containing a message related to the error code passed in. To find the proper code to pass in when a function fails use graphresult( ). For a table containing error codes and their meanings see graphresult( ). The meanings given in this table are similar to the messages returned by this function, but are not word for word the same.

Prototype in GRAPHICS.H
Covered in Chapter 2, page 23
Related functions: graphresult.

_graphfreemem( )

```
void far _graphfreemem (void far *ptr,
                        unsigned size);
  /*
   * _graphfreemem() deallocates memory
   *   allocated with _graphgetmem().
   *
   * Parameters:
   *   ptr  - pointer to buffer being
   *          deallocated
   *   size - size of buffer being deallocated
   */
```

_graphfreemem( ) is a special graphics memory management routine. It deallocates memory allocated with _graphgetmem( ). The default version calls free( ). The programmer can define a new version to take advantage of his/her memory manager. The prototype of the new function must appear exactly as it does here.

Prototype in GRAPHICS.H
Not covered in detail in this book
Related functions: _graphgetmem( )

_graphgetmem( )

```
void far _graphgetmem (void far *ptr,
                       unsigned size);
  /*
   * _graphgetmem() allocates memory for the
   *   graphics system
   *
   * Parameters:
   *   ptr  - pointer to buffer being allocated
   *   size - size of buffer being allocated
   */
```

_graphgetmem( ) is a special graphics memory management routine. It allocates memory for the graphics system. The default version calls malloc( ). The programmer can define a new version to take advantage of his/her memory manager. The prototype of the new function must appear exactly as it does here.

Prototype in GRAPHICS.H

Not covered in detail in this book
Related functions: _graphfreemem( )

graphresult( )

```
int far graphresult(void);
  /*
   * graphresult() returns an error code for
   *   the last graphics routine called, and
   *   resets the error level to grOk.
   */
```

graphresult( ) returns an error code describing what happened with the last graphics function called. If the last call was successful the constant grOk (0) is returned, otherwise an error code will be returned. See Table A.4 for error codes, what they mean, and constants defined in GRAPHICS.H that are associated with them. To obtain a text string describing an error code use geterrormsg( ). When this function is called, the internal error code is reset to grOk, so a second call to this routine will always return grOk.

Prototype in GRAPHICS.H
Covered in Chapter 2, page 23
Related functions: geterrormsg( ).

Table 1.4

Error Code	Constant	Meaning
0	grOk	No error
-1	grNoInitGraph	(BGI) graphics not installed (use InitGraph)
-2	grNotDetected	Graphics hardware not detected
-3	grFileNotFound	Device driver not found
-4	grInvalidDriver	Invalid device driver file
-5	grNoLoadMem	Not enough memory to load driver
-6	grNoScanMem	Out of memory in scan fill
-7	grNoFloodMem	Out of memory in flood fill
-8	grFontNotFound	Font file not found
-9	grNoFontMem	Not enough memory to load font
-10	grInvalidMode	Invalid graphics mode for selected driver
-11	grError	Graphics error
-12	grIOerror	Graphics I/O error
-13	grInvalidFont	Invalid font file
-14	grInvalidFontNum	Invalid font number
-15	grInvalidDeviceNu m	Invalid device number
-18	grInvalidVersion	Invalid version number

imagesize( )

```
unsigned far imagesize(int left,  int top,
                       int right, int bottom);
  /*
   * imagesize() will return the size buffer
   *   needed to store a screen image
   *
   * Parameters:
   *   left   - the left border of the image
   *   top    - the top of the image
   *   right  - the right hand side
   *   bottom - the bottom of the image
   */
```

imagesize( ) will return the number of bytes needed to store an image on the screen. The upper left corner of the image is at screen coordinate (left,top) and the lower right corner is at screen coordinate (right,bottom). This function is used with malloc( ) to allocate a buffer that getimage will copy the image to.

Prototype in GRAPHICS.H
Covered in Chapter 12, page 360
Related functions: getimage( ), putimage( ), setactivepage( ), setvisualpage ( )

initgraph( )

```
void far initgraph (int  far *graphdriver,
                    int  far *mode,
                    char far *pathtodriver);
  /*
   * initgraph() will load the proper BGI
   *   driver, then set the monitor to the
   *   proper mode.
   *
   * Parameters:
   *   graphdriver  - BGI driver to be used
   *   mode         - What mode should be used.
   *   pathtodriver - location of BGI file on
   *                  the hard disk.
   */
```

initgraph( ) will load a graphics driver from a file and set a graphics mode. For a table with graphics drivers and modes associated with those drivers see detectgraph( ). 0 should NOT be used for a graphics driver with this function. If you want the computer to tell you the best driver to use, use detectgraph( ) find it. Parameter pathtodriver is a DOS path to the graphics driver. For a detailed discussion of DOS paths see Chapter 2. If this function cannot find a graphics driver on the disk it will set the graphics error code. Call graphresult( ) to find out if it failed. Table A.5 gives the graphics drivers supplied with Borland C.

The problem with initgraph( ) not being able to find the needed graphics driver can be quite annoying. It is possible to link graphics drivers with your program. Details are given in Chapter 2.

Prototype in GRAPHICS.H
Covered in Chapter 2, page 18
Related functions: detectgraph( ), setgraphmode( ), getgraphmode( ), closegraph( ), registerbgidriver( ), registerbgifont( )

Table A.5

Driver File	Constant Name
CGA	CGA_driver
EGAVGA	EGAVGA_driver
HERC	Herc_driver
ATT (for the AT&T 400 monitor)	ATT_driver
PC3270	PC3270_driver
IBM8514	IBM8514_driver

installuserdriver( )

```
int far installuserdriver
    (char far *name, int huge (*detect)(void));
  /*
   * installuserdriver() is used to install a
   *   vendor supplied BGI driver
   *
   * Parameters:
   *   name   - the name of the BGI file
   *   detect - optional autodetect function
   *
   * Returns:  The number initgraph() uses
   *   to select this driver manually
   */
```

installuserdriver( ) is used to install BGI drivers that come from sources other than Borland.

Prototype in GRAPHICS.H
Not covered in detail in this book
Related functions: initgraph( ), registerbgidriver( ), installuserfont( )

installuserfont( )

```
int far installuserfont(char far *name);
  /*
   * installuserfont() installs a vendor
   *   supplied font
   *
   * Parameter:
   *   name - name of the .CHR file containing
   *          the font
   *
   * Returns: the number settextstyle() uses to
   *   select this font
   */
```

installuserfont( ) installs a font file (a .CHR file) supplied by a source other than Borland.

Prototype in GRAPHICS.H
Not covered in detail in this book
Related functions: initgraph( ), registerbgidriver( ), installuserfont( )

int86( )

```
int int86(int intno, union REGS *inregs,
                     union REGS *outregs);
  /*
   * function for calling interrupts.
   *
   * Parameters:
   *   intno   - Interrupt number to be called
   *   inregs  - Register values going in
   *   outregs - Register values coming out.
   *
   * Returns: Value in AX register
   */
```

int86( ) provides an interface to BIOS level interrupts. For a complete list of BIOS graphics functions covering CGA through VGA monitors, see Appendix D. For BIOS functions covering SVGA monitors, see Appendix E. The structure of REGS is:

```
struct WORDREGS {
  unsigned int    ax, bx, cx, dx, si, di,
```

```
                  cflag, flags;
};

struct BYTEREGS {
  unsigned char    al, ah, bl, bh,
                   cl, ch, dl, dh;
};

union REGS {
  struct WORDREGS x;
  struct BYTEREGS h;
};
```

Prototype in DOS.H
Covered in Chapter 8, page 224
Related functions: int86x( ), intdos( ), intdosx( )

int86x( )

```
int int86x(int intno, union  REGS  *inregs,
                      union  REGS  *outregs,
                      struct SREGS segregs);
  /*
   * function for calling interrupts that
   *   require segment registers.
   *
   * Parameters:
   *   intno   - Interrupt number to be called
   *   inregs  - Register values going in
   *   outregs - Register values coming out.
   *   segregs - Segment register values going
   *             in.
   *
   * Returns: Value in AX register
   */
```

int86x( ) provides an interface to BIOS level interrupts that require access to segment registers. For a complete list of BIOS graphics functions covering CGA through VGA monitors, see Appendix D. For BIOS functions covering SVGA monitors, see Appendix E. The structure of REGS is:

```
struct WORDREGS {
  unsigned int    ax, bx, cx, dx, si, di,
                  cflag, flags;
};
```

```
struct BYTEREGS {
  unsigned char    al, ah, bl, bh,
                   cl, ch, dl, dh;
};

union REGS {
  struct WORDREGS x;
  struct BYTEREGS h;
};
```

The structure of SREGS is:

```
struct SREGS {
  unsigned int  es;
  unsigned int  cs;
  unsigned int  ss;
  unsigned int  ds;
};
```

Prototype in DOS.H
Covered in Chapter 8, page 224
Related functions: int86( ), intdos( ), intdosx( )

intdos( )

```
int intdos(union REGS *inregs,
           union REGS *outregs);
  /*
   * function for calling interrupt 21
   *   (DOS services);
   *
   * Parameters:
   *   inregs  - value of registers passed in
   *   outregs - value of registers after
   *             interrupt call.
   *
   * Returns: Value of AX register
   */
```

intdos( ) provides an interface to DOS level interrupts. This function is not generally useful for graphics programming since DOS does not provide graphics functions. This function is presented here because it is covered in the book. For low-level graphics functions use interrupt 0x10. Interrupt 0x10 can be called with the C function int86( ). Union REGS is defined as follows:

```
struct WORDREGS {
  unsigned int    ax, bx, cx, dx, si, di,
                  cflag, flags;
};

struct BYTEREGS {
  unsigned char    al, ah, bl, bh,
                   cl, ch, dl, dh;
};

union REGS {
  struct WORDREGS x;
  struct BYTEREGS h;
};
```

Prototype in DOS.H
Covered in Chapter 8, page 215
Related functions: int86( ), int86x( ), intdosx( )

intdosx( )

```
int intdosx(union REGS *inregs,
            union REGS *outregs,
            struct SREGS *segregs);
  /*
   * function for calling interrupt 21 (DOS
   *   services) for services requiring Segment
   *   Registers
   *
   * Parameters:
   *   inregs  - values of registers passed in
   *   outregs - values of registers after
   *             interrupt call.
   *   segregs - values of segment registers
   *
   * Returns: Value of AX register
   */
```

intdosx( ) provides an interface to DOS level interrupts that require access to segment registers. This function is not generally useful for graphics programming since DOS does not provide graphics functions. This function is presented here because it is covered in the book. For low-level graphics functions use interrupt 0x10. Interrupt 0x10 can be called with the C function int86( ). Union REGS is defined as follows:

```
struct WORDREGS {
  unsigned int    ax, bx, cx, dx, si, di,
                  cflag, flags;
};

struct BYTEREGS {
  unsigned char    al, ah, bl, bh,
                   cl, ch, dl, dh;
};

union REGS {
  struct WORDREGS x;
  struct BYTEREGS h;
};
```

The structure of SREGS is:

```
struct SREGS {
  unsigned int  es;
  unsigned int  cs;
  unsigned int  ss;
  unsigned int  ds;
};
```

Prototype in DOS.H
Covered in Chapter 8, page 222
Related functions: int86( ), intdos( ), intdosx( )

line( )

```
void far line (int x1, int y1, int x2, int y2);
  /*
   * line() will draw a line from one
   *   coordinate to another
   *
   * Parameters:
   *  x1 - X of the first coordinate.
   *  y1 - Y of the first coordinate.
   *  x2 - X of the second coordinate.
   *  y2 - Y of the second coordinate.
   */
```

line( ) will draw a line from screen coordinate (x1,y1) to screen coordinate (x2,y2), using the current drawing color.

Prototype in GRAPHICS.H
Covered in Chapter 2, page 31
Related functions: lineto( ), linerel( ), setcolor( ), getcolor( )

lineto( )

```
void far lineto (int x, int y);
  /*
   * lineto() draws a line from the current
   *  position to coordinates (X,Y) then sets
   *  the current position to (X, Y)
   *
   * Parameters:
   *   x - X coordinate to start drawing at
   *   y - Y coordinate to start drawing at
   */
```

lineto( ) will draw a line from the current screen coordinate to screen coordinate (x,y), in the current drawing color. It will then reset the current screen coordinate to (x,y). If point (x,y) is off the screen the line is drawn and the current location is set any way. Use moveto( ) to set the original screen location.

Prototype in GRAPHICS.H
Covered in Chapter 2, page 32
Related functions: line( ), linerel( ), moveto( ), moverel( ), setcolor( ), getcolor( )

linerel( )

```
void far linerel (int x, int y);
  /*
   * linerel() draws a line from the current
   *   position to a position specified by
   *   Dx, Dy; relative to the current
   *   position.  This is then made the new
   *   current position.
   *
   * Parameters:
   *   x - distance in the X dimension.
   *   y - distance in the Y dimension.
   */
```

linerel( ) will draw a line from the current screen coodinate to screen coordinate (currentx+x, currenty+y), where (currentx, currenty) is the current screen coordinate, using the current drawing color. It will then reset the current screen coordinate to (currentx+x, currenty+y). If point (currentx+x, currenty+y) is off the screen the line is drawn and the current location is set anyway. Use moveto( ) to set the original screen location.

Prototype in GRAPHICS.H
Covered in Chapter 2, page 32
Related functions: line( ), linerel( ), moveto( ), moverel( ), setcolor( ), getcolor( )

moveto( )

```
void far moveto (int x, int y);
  /*
   * moveto() will set the current drawing
   *    location
   *
   * Parameters:
   *    x - X coordinate to start drawing at
   *    y - Y coordinate to start drawing at
   */
```

moveto( ) will set the current screen coordinate for use with lineto( ) and linerel( ). The current screen coordinate can be set so that it is off the screen.

Prototype in GRAPHICS.H
Covered in Chapter 2, page 32
Related functions: line( ), lineto( ), linerel( ), moverel( ), setcolor( ), getcolor( )

moverel( )

```
void far moverel (int x, int y);
  /*
   * moverel() changes the current drawing
   *   position by the number of pixels
   *   specified by DX and DY
   *
   * Parameters:
   *   x - Number of pixels to move the
   *        current position in X dimension.
   *   y - Number of pixels to move the
   *        current position in Y dimension.
   */
```

moverel( ) resets the current screen coordinate to (currentx+x, currenty+y) where (currentx, currenty) is the current screen coordinate. The current screen coordinate can be set so that it is off the screen.

Prototype in GRAPHICS.H
Covered in Chapter 2, page 32
Related functions: line( ), lineto( ), linerel( ), moveto( ), setcolor( ), getcolor( )

outtext( )

```
void outtext (char far *textstring);
  /*
   * outtext() will write a string of text to
   *   the screen at the current position using
   *   parameters selected by SelectTextStyle.
   *
   * Parameter:
   *   textstring - String of text to be
   *                written.
   */
```

outtext( ) will write a string of text on the screen, starting at the current screen coordinate, using the current graphics font. The current screen coordinate is set to be at the end of the string. Use moveto( ) to set the screen coordinate before calling outtext( ).

Prototype in GRAPHICS.H

Covered in Chapter 3, page 68
Related functions: moveto( ), outtextxy( )

outtextxy( )

```
void outtextxy (int x, int y,
                char far *textstring);
  /*
   * outtextxy() will write a string of text to
   *   the screen using parameters selected by
   *   SelectTextStyle, at the screen
   *   coordinates given by X and Y.
   *
   * Parameters:
   *   x          - X coordinate of text
   *   y          - Y coordinate of text
   *   textstring - String of text to be
   *                written.
   */
```

outtextxy( ) will write a string of text on the screen, starting at that coordinate (x, y), using the current graphics font. The current location is then set to be at the end of the string.

Prototype in GRAPHICS.H
Covered in Chapter 3, page 68
Related functions: moveto( ), outtext( )

pieslice( )

```
void far pieslice (int x, int y,
                   int stangle, int endangle,
                   int Radius);
  /*
   * pieslice() will draw a filled portion of a
   *   pie chart
   *
   * Parameters:
   *   x        - X coordinate of center
   *   y        - Y coordinate of center
   *   stangle  - Angle to start drawing at
   *   endangle - Angle to stop drawing at
   *   radius   - radius of arc
   */
```

pieslice( ) draws a filled arc of a circle.

Prototype in GRAPHICS.H
Covered in Chapter 5, page 148
Related functions: arc( ), fillellipse( ), arccoords( ), setfillstyle( ), setfillpattern( )

putimage( )

```
void far putimage(int left, int top,
                  void far *bitmap, int op);
  /*
   * putimage() puts an image previously saved
   *   with getimage() on the screen.
   *
   * Parameters:
   *   left   - the left hand location of the
   *            image
   *   top    - the top of the image
   *   bitmap - buffer containing the bitmap
   *   op     - logical operation for putting
   */
```

putimage( ) places an image saved by getimage( ) on the screen. The upper left corner of the replaced image will be screen coordinate (left, top). The parameter op specifies a logical operation used to place the image. Available operations are shown in Table A.6. If COPY_PUT is used the image will overwrite what is on the screen. If XOR_PUT is used each bit in the image is XORed with each bit on the screen. If the image is then XORed again the image on the screen is removed, leaving what was there originally. The following table gives possible values of parameter op.

Table A.6

Enumeration	Value	Description
COPY_PUT	0	Copy to screen
XOR_PUT	1	Exclusive OR with what is on screen
OR_PUT	2	OR with what is on screen
AND_PUT	3	AND with what is on screen
NOT_PUT	4	Copy inverse of source

Prototype in GRAPHICS.H
Covered in Chapter 12, page 360
Related functions: getimage( ), imagesize( ), setactivepage( ), setvisualpage( )

putpixel( )

```
void far putpixel (int x, int y, int color);
  /*
   * putpixel() lights a pixel on the screen
   *
   * Parameters:
   *   x     - the x coordinate of the pixel.
   *   y     - the Y coordinate of the pixel.
   *   color - the color the pixel will be
   *           displayed in.
   */
```

putpixel( ) will plot a pixel at screen coordinate (x,y), using the given color.

Prototype in GRAPHICS.H
Covered in Chapter 2, page 27
Related functions: getpixel( ), getpalette( ), setpalette( ), getmaxx( ), getmaxy( )

rectangle( )

```
void far rectangle (int x1, int y1,
                    int x2, int y2);
  /*
   * rectangle() draws a rectangle on the
   *   screen
   *
   * Parameters:
   *   x1 - The X coordinate of the upper
   *        left corner
   *   y1 - The Y coordinate of the upper
   *        left corner
   *   x2 - The X coordinate of the lower
   *        right corner
   *   y2 - The Y coordinate of the lower right
   *        corner
   */
```

rectangle( ) will draw a rectangle on the screen with the upper left-hand corner at screen coordinate (x1,y1) and the lower left corner at (x2,y2).

Prototype in GRAPHICS.H

Covered in Chapter 2, page 39
Related functions: drawpoly( ), fillpoly( ), bar( ), bar3d( )

registerbgidriver( )

```
int registerbgidriver(void (*driver)(void));
  /*
   * registerbgidriver will register a
   *   graphics driver that has been linked
   *   into the executable file.
   *
   * Parameters:
   *   driver - symbolic constant for the
   *            driver being registered.
   */
```

registerbgidriver( ) is used to tell the graphics system that the driver passed in was included at link time. This is part of the process for linking graphics drivers into the executable file so that they do not need to be supplied in a separate file. The entire process of linking BGI drivers into the executable is covered in Chapter 2.

Prototype in GRAPHICS.H
Covered in Chapter 2, page 62
Related functions: registerfarbgidriver( ), initgraph( ), registerbgifont( )

registerbgifont( )

```
int registerbgifont(void (*font)(void));
  /*
   * registerbgifont will register a
   *   graphics font that has been linked
   *   into the executable file.
   *
   * Parameters:
   *   font - symbolic constant for the
   *          font being registered.
   */
```

registerbgifont( ) is used to tell the graphics system that the font passed in was included at link time. This is part of the process for linking graphics fonts into the executable file so that they do not need to be supplied in a separate file. The process for doing this is not covered in this book, but it is similar to linking graphics drivers. Linking graphics drivers is covered in detail in Chapter 2.

Prototype in GRAPHICS.H
Not covered in detail in this book
Related functions: registerbgidriver( ), settextstyle( )

registerfarbgidriver( )

```
int far registerfarbgidriver(void *__driver);
  /*
   * registerfarbgidriver will register a
   *   graphics driver that has been linked
   *   into the executable file, but only
   *   when it has been converted using
   *   BGIOBJ's /F option
   *
   * Parameters:
   *   driver - symbolic constant for the
   *            driver being registered.
   */
```

registerfarbgidriver( ) is used to tell the graphics system that the driver passed in was included at link time. The functions in the driver must be far procedure calls. In this manner the graphics driver does not take up space in the 64K segment used by the main program code. The programmer should be familiar with Intel 8086 architecture before using this function. This function is used as part of the process for linking graphics drivers into the executable file so that they do not need to be supplied in a separate file. The entire process of linking BGI drivers into the executable file is covered in Chapter 2.

Prototype in GRAPHICS.H
Covered in Chapter 2, page 63
Related functions: registerbgidriver( ), initgraph( ), registerbgifont( )

restorecrtmode( )

```
void far restorecrtmode(void);
  /*
   * restorecrtmode() will restore the monitor
   *   to the mode it was in before initgraph()
   *   was called
   */
```

restorecrtmode( ) will restore the monitor to the mode it was in before initgraph( ) was called. This function can be used with setgraphmode( ) to switch between text and graphics modes.

Prototype in GRAPHICS.H
Not covered in detail in this book
Related functions: initgraph( ), closegraph( ), setgraphmode( )

sector( )

```
void far sector (int x, int y,
                 int stangle, int endangle,
                 int xradius, int yradius);
    /*
     * sector() draws and fills an arc of an
     *   ellipse
     *
     * Parameters:
     *   x - X coordinate of the center
     *   y - Y coordinate of the center
     *   stangle - angle to start at - 0 is at
     *             3 o'clock
     *   endangle - angle to stop at - arc is
     *              drawn counter-clockwise
     *   XRadius - the radius of the ellipse in
     *             the X dimension
     *   YRadius - the radius of the ellipse in
     *             the Y dimension
     */
```

sector( ) will draw and fill an arc of an ellipse.

Prototype in GRAPHICS.H
Covered in Chapter 2, page 37
Related functions: ellipse( ), fillellipse( ), setfillstyle( ), setfillpattern( ), pieslice( )

setactivepage( )

```
void far setactivepage(int page);
  /*
   * setactivepage() will make page the active
   *   page.  All graphics output will be
   *   written to that page.
   *
   * Parameter:
   *   Page - the number of the page to make
   *          active
   */
```

setactivepage( ) will switch the active page, redirecting output of graphics routines to a different page. This is useful in animation. An image can be drawn on a page, then the page is displayed. While that page is displayed the next image can be drawn on another page. When the second page is displayed the picture seems to move. Pages are not supported on CGA or MCGA cards. For a table of modes with how many pages each mode supports see detectgraph( )

Prototype in GRAPHICS.H
Covered in Chapter 12, page 367
Related functions: setvisualpage( ), setgraphmode( ), initgraph( ), detectgraph( )

setallpalette( )

```
void far setallpalette(struct palettetype
                           *far palette);
  /*
   * setallpalette() sets all colors at once
   *
   * Parameter:
   *   Palette - the new palette settings
   */
```

setallpalette( ) will set all colors at once. For a list of available colors see setcolor( ). The stucture of palettetype is:

```
#define MAXCOLORS 15

struct palettetype {
  unsigned char size;
  signed   char colors[MAXCOLORS+1];
};
```

Prototype in GRAPHICS.H
Not covered in detail in this book
Related functions: setcolor( ), getcolor( ), setbkcolor( ), getbkcolor( )

setaspectratio( )

```
void far setaspectratio(int xasp, int yasp);
  /*
   * setaspectratio() changes the aspect ratio
   *   that the BGI uses for making sure
   *   circles are round, etc.
   *
   * Parameters:
   *   xasp - new x aspect
   *   yasp - new y aspect
   */
```

setaspectratio( ) will change the internal software variables used to make sure circles appear round even when pixels are rectangular, not square. This can be used to compensate for a monitor being out of alignment, causing the hardware aspect ratio to be off. First obtain the aspect ratio with getaspectratio( ), then adjust xasp by adding or subtracting increments of 5. After each adjustment call setaspectratio( ) and draw a circle. If the circle appears round the aspect ratio is correct.

Prototype in GRAPHICS.H
Not covered in this book in detail
Related functions: getaspectratio( ), circle( )

setbkcolor( )

```
void setbkcolor (int Color);
  /*
   * setcolor() sets the background color
   *
   * Parameters:
   *   Color - The color that the background
   *           will be set to
   */
```

setbkcolor( ) will set palette 0 to display the appropriate color.

Prototype in GRAPHICS.H
Covered in Chapter 2, page 32
Related functions: getbkcolor( ), cleardevice( )

setcolor( )

```
void far setcolor (int Color);
  /*
   * setcolor will set the default drawing
   *  color
   *
   * Parameters:
   *   Color - The color that the default
   *           will be set to
   */
```

setcolor( ) will set the color used by most graphics primitives, including line( ) and related functions, and ellipse( ) and related functions. Table A.7 gives constants defined in GRAPHICS.H to name colors in 16 color modes, and their associated values.

Prototype in GRAPHICS.H
Covered in Chapter 2, page 31
Related functions: getcolor( ), setbkcolor( ), getbkcolor( ), setallpalette( )

Table A.7

Dark Colors	Numeric Value	Light Colors	Numeri c Value
BLACK	0	DARKGRAY	8
BLUE	1	LIGHTBLUE	9
GREEN	2	LIGHTGREEN	10
CYAN	3	LIGHTCYAN	11
RED	4	LIGHTRED	12
MAGENTA	5	LIGHTMAGENTA	13
BROWN	6	YELLOW	14
LIGHTGRAY	7	WHITE	15

setfillpattern( )

```
void setfillpattern (char far *pattern,
                     int color);
  /*
   * setfillpattern() defines a pattern to be
   *   used by the fill procedures
   *
   * Parameters:
   *   Pattern - array of 8 bytes, used as a
   *     2D array of bits. The pattern in the
   *     array is used as the fill pattern
   *   Color   - Color used for filling
   */
```

setfillpattern( ) will set a user-defined pattern to be used by filling routines. The pattern is in an array of 8 bytes, which is viewed as a two-dimensional array of bits. When a bit in the pattern is set, the corresponding pixel on the screen is set to the current filling color, as set by calling setfillstyle( ). When a bit is cleared, the corresponding pixel on the screen is set to the background color. Note that before the fill routine is called it is necessary to call setfillstyle( ) with a pattern of USER_FILL.

Prototype in GRAPHICS.H
Covered in Chapter 2, page 56
Related functions: setfillstyle( ), fillellipse( ), fillpoly( ), floodfill( ), getfillpattern( ), getfillstyle( )

setfillstyle( )

```
void far setfillstyle (int Pattern, int Color);
  /*
   * setfillstyle() sets the fill pattern used
   *   by fillpoly(), fillellipse() and
   *   floodfill().
   *
   * Parameters:
   *   Pattern - Number of the pattern used to
   *             fill things.
   *   Color   - Color that will be used to
   *             fill things.
   */
```

setfillstyle( ) will set the pattern that fill routines use. Table A.8 gives a list of fill styles defined in GRAPHICS.H. To use a user-defined fill pattern, first call this function with the pattern set to USER_FILL, then use setfillpattern( ).

Prototype in GRAPHICS.H
Covered in Chapter 2, page 53
Related functions: setfillpattern( ), fillellipse( ), fillpoly( ), floodfill( ), getfillpattern( ), getfillstyle( )

Table A.8

Name	Value	Description
EMPTY_FILL	0	Fill with the background color
SOLID_FILL	1	Solid Fill
LINE_FILL	2	Fill with horizontal lines
LTSLASH_FILL	3	Fill with ///
SLASH_FILL	4	Fill with ///, thick lines
BKSLASH_FILL	5	Fill with \\\, thick lines
LTBKSLASH_FILL	6	Fill with \\\, thin lines
HATCH_FILL	7	Light hatch fill
XHATCH_FILL	8	Heavy crosshatch fill
INTERLEAVE_FILL	9	Interleaving line fill
WIDE_DOT_FILL	10	Widely spaced dot fill
CLOSE_DOT_FILL	11	Closely spaced dot fill
USER_FILL	12	User-defined fill patterns

setgraphbufsize( )

```
unsigned far setgraphbufsize(unsigned bufsize);
  /*
   * setgraphbufsize() resets the size of the
   *   internal buffer used by the graphics
   *   system
   *
   * Parameter:
   *   bufsize - the new size of the buffer
   *
   * Returns:  the previous size
   */
```

setgraphbufsize( ) resizes the internal graphics buffer used by floodfill( ). This buffer is allocated when initgraph( ) is called, with a size of 4K bytes. Function initgraph( ) makes a call to _graphgetmem( ) to allocate memory. More memory might be needed if floodfill( ) (or other graphics functions) return error -7 (out of flood memory), less memory might be needed if the program is using all memory available and floodfill( ) is not being used.

NOTE: This function must be called before calling initgraph( ).

Prototype in GRAPHICS.H
Not covered in detail in this book
Related functions: _graphgetmem( ), initgraph( ), floodfill( )

setgraphmode( )

```
void far setgraphmode (int Mode);
  /*
   * setgraphmode() will change the mode that
   *   the monitor is currently in.
   */
```

setgraphmode( ) is used to change the graphics mode without reloading the BGI graphics driver. This function is faster than initgraph since no disk reads are involved. For a table of drivers and modes available for each driver see detectgraph( ).

Prototype in GRAPHICS.H
Covered in Chapter 2, page 25

Related functions: initgraph( ), detectgraph( ), closegraph( )

setlinestyle( )

```
void far setlinestyle (int linestyle,
                       unsigned upattern,
                       int thickness);
  /*
   * setlinestyle() will set the thickness
   *   and patterns of dots and dashes used
   *   to draw a line.
   *
   * Parameters:
   *   lineStyle - Identifies the style the
   *     line is drawn in.
   *   upattern  - User defined bit pattern
   *     used to draw lines if LineStyle is 4
   *     (User defined Style)
   *   thickness - The thickness of the line.
   */
```

setlinestyle( ) will set the pattern used by line( ), lineto( ), and related functions. Table A.9 gives a list of line patterns defined in GRAPHICS.H. The parameter upattern is used to give setlinestyle( ) a user defined pattern. It is only used if linestyle is set to USERBIT_LINE. If thickness is thrcc, lines will be drawn 3 pixels wide, otherwise they will be 1 pixel wide.

Prototype in GRAPHICS.H
Covered in Chapter 2, page 44
Related functions: line( ), lineto( ), linerel( )

Table A.9

Name	Value	Description
SOLID_LINE	0	Solid Line
DOTTED_LINE	1	Dotted Line
CENTER_LINE	2	Centered Line
DASHED_LINE	3	Dashed Line
USERBIT_LINE	4	User defined line style

setpalette( )

```
void far setpalette(int colornum, int color);
  /*
   * setpalette() sets a palette to a certain
   *   color
   *
   * Parameters:
   *   colornum - the palette number
   *   color    - the color to set it to
   */
```

setpalette( ) will set one palette to a certain color when using a 16-color mode. For available colors see setcolor( ).

Prototype in GRAPHICS.H
Not covered in detail in this book
Related functions: setcolor( ), setrgbpalette( ), setallpalette( ), getpalette( )

setrgbpalette( )

```
void setrgbpalette (int colornum, int red,
                    int green, int blue);
  /*
   * setrgbpalette is used to change the Red,
   * Green, and Blue settings for a given
   * palette register.
   *
   * Parameters:
   *   palette - The palette number to
   *             change.
   *   red     - The value for the Red gun.
   *   green   - The value for the Green gun.
   *   blue    - The value for the Blue gun.
   */
```

setrgbpalette( ) is used to set the red, green and blue palette registers for a given color. This gives complete control over the displayed colors.

Prototype in GRAPHICS.H
Covered in Chapter 6, page 175
Related functions: getpalette( ), setpalette( ), setallpalette( )

settextjustify( )

```
void settextjustify (int horiz, int vert);
    /*
     * settextjustify() will set the text
     *   justification for vertical or
     *   horizontal text.
     *
     * Parameters:
     *   horiz - Text justification for
     *           horizontal text.
     *   vert  - Text justification for
     *           vertical text.
     */
```

settextjustify( ) will set the justification for text written to the screen with outtext( ) or outtextxy( ). The available justifications are given in Table A.10.

Prototype in GRAPHICS.H
Covered in Chapter 3, page 70
Related functions: settextstyle( ), outtext( ), gettextsettings( )

Table A.10

Text Direction	Name	Value	Action
Horizontal	LEFT_TEXT	0	Left justify text
	CENTER_TEXT	1	Center text
	RIGHT_TEXT	2	Right justify text
Vertical	BOTTOM_TEXT	0	Justify from the bottom
	CENTER_TEXT	1	Center text
	TOP_TEXT	2	Justify from the top

settextstyle( )

```
void settextstyle (int font, int direction,
                   int charSize);
  /*
   * settextstyle() will set the font,
   *   direction and size for graphics text.
   *   The proper .CHR file must be present.
   *
   * Parameters:
   *   font      - What font will be loaded.
   *   direction - 0 for horizontal, 1 for
   *               vertical.
   *   charsize  - Size to multiply character
   */
```

settextstyle( ) will set the font, direction, and size of graphics text. Fonts supplied with Borland C are given in Table A.11. Direction is either HORIZ_DIR for horizontal text, or VERT_DIR for vertical text. The parameter charsize is a multiplier with 1 producing characters that are 8 × 8 pixels, 2 producing characters that are 16 × 16 pixels, etc. If it is desired to scale text in other ways use setusercharsize( ). To write graphics text to the screen use outtext( ), or outtextxy( ), since standard C output functions such as printf( ) or putch( ) use only the standard bit-mapped font.

Prototype in GRAPHICS.H
Covered in Chapter 3, page 67
Related functions: gettextsettings( ), settextjustify( ), setusercharsize( ), textheight( ), textwidth( ), outtext( ), outtextxy( )

Table A.11

Font Name	Value	Description
DEFAULT_FONT	0	8 × 8 bit-mapped font
TRIPLEX_FONT	1	Stroked triplex font
SMALL_FONT	2	Stroked small font
SANS_SERIF_FONT	3	Stroked sans-serif font
GOTHIC_FONT	4	Stroked gothic font

setusercharsize( )

```
void setusercharsize (int multx, int divx,
                      int multy, int divy);
  /*
   * setusercharsize() will set the size that
   *   graphics text will be written, and
   *   reproportion graphics text.
   *
   * Parameters:
   *   multx - Multiply value for X
   *   divx  - Divide value for X
   *   multy - Multiply value for Y
   *   divy  - Divide value for Y
   */
```

setusercharsize( ) is used to scale stroked text. The X and Y dimensions are treated independently, with each dimension being multiplied by the multiply value for that dimension and then being divided by the divide value for that dimension. The base size (all parameters being 1) varies with the font.

Prototype in GRAPHICS.H
Covered in Chapter 3, page 68
Related functions: gettextscttings( ), settextjustify( ), settextstyle( ), textheight( ), textwidth( )

setvisualpage( )

```
void setvisualpage (int page);
  /*
   * Function to set the visual page
   *
   * Parameter
   *   page - the page to make the visual page
   *
   * Returns: The previous visual page, or
   *   a negative value on error.
   */
```

setvisualpage( ) selects a video page to be displayed. The visual page is the one displayed on the monitor; the active page is the one that graphics functions will write to. If the active page and visual page are not the same, new graphics will not show on the screen. This allows for a complete graphics screen to be set up in the background then rapidly displayed. This is useful for animation.

Prototype in GRAPHICS.H
Covered in Chapter 12, page 367
Related functions: getimage( ), putimage( ), setactivepage( )

setwritemode( )

```
void far setwritemode(int mode);
  /*
   * setwritemode() will change the method for
   *   outputting graphics between copying and
   *   xor'ing
   *
   * Parameter:
   *   mode - COPY_PUT or XOR_PUT
   */
```

setwritemode( ) allows graphics routines to XOR with what's on the screen rather than copying over the screen. If XORing is enabled and an item is placed on the screen it can be removed by repeating the call that put it there. This is useful for such things as "rubber band lines."

Prototype in GRAPHICS.H
Not covered in detail in this book
Related functions: putpixel( ), putimage( )

textheight( )

```
int far textheight (char far *textstring);
    /*
     * textheight() will return the height of a
     *   string in pixels, given the current
     *   graphics text settings
     *
     * Parameter:
     *   textstring - String to be measured.
     */
```

textheight( ) will return the number of pixels in the Y dimension needed to write the given string, using the current font and size.

Prototype in GRAPHICS.H
Covered in Chapter 3, page 71
Related functions: gettextsettings( ), settextjustify( ), setusercharsize( ), textwidth( ), outtext( ), outtextxy( )

textwidth( )

```
int far textwidth (char far *textstring);
    /*
     * textwidth() will return the width of a
     *   string in pixels, given the current
     *   graphics text settings
     *
     * Parameter:
     *   textstring - String to be measured.
     */
```

textwidth( ) will return the number of pixels in the X dimension needed to write the given string, using the current font and size.

Prototype in GRAPHICS.H
Covered in Chapter 3, page 71
Related functions: gettextsettings( ), settextjustify( ), setusercharsize( ), textheight( ), outtext( ), outtextxy( )

wherex( )

```
int wherex(void);
  /*
   * returns the current X screen coordinate
   */
```

wherex( ) returns the current x position, used for writing text in graphics mode or by lineto( ) and related functions.

Prototype in GRAPHICS.H
Not covered in detail in this book
Related functions: wherey( ), moveto( ), moverel( ), lineto( ), linerel( ), outtext( )

wherey( )

```
int wherey(void);
  /*
   * returns the current Y screen coordinate
   */
```

wherey( ) returns the current y position, used for writing text in graphics mode or by lineto( ) and related functions.

Prototype in GRAPHICS.H
Not covered in detail in this book
Related functions: wherex( ), moveto( ), moverel( ), lineto( ), linerel( ), outtext( )

Appendix B
Microsoft Graphics Functions

Most of the graphics functions included with the Microsoft QuickC compiler 2.5 for DOS are covered in this appendix. These functions should be compatible with other Microsoft C compilers for DOS. This library of functions is powerful and flexible, and provides most of the graphics functions the average programmer will ever need. On occasion, however, the graphics programmer will need to communicate BIOS to perform lower level graphics functions. The functions Microsoft C provides for this are directly compatible with Borland functions for the same purpose. These are covered in Appendix A. All functions covered in this appendix are prototyped in GRAPH.H. The contents of this appendix are listed below to aid in finding information.

Microsoft Graphics Functions

Microsoft's Approach to Graphics

Microsoft's approach to graphics is to implement fewer functions with each function doing more. Because of this, one function usually is used to both draw a filled object and draw the outline of an object. These routines take a parameter `short control`, which specifies whether the object is to be filled or not. Table B.1 shows the possible values of control.

Table B.1

Constant	Value	Meaning
_GFILLINTERIOR	2	Fill interior with current fill mask
_GBORDER	3	Do not fill interior

Another aspect of Microsoft's approach is that often very similar functions are provided for using absolute coordinates and for using window coordinates. Absolute coordinates are those used by the physical screen. These coordinates are the same as the ones used by the Borland and the BIOS graphics functions. The Microsoft graphics library allows for the coordinates to be remapped to fit the application. The screen coordinates can be redefined so that the distance between adjacent pixels is any interval, even fractional. This is covered in detail in Chapter 4.

The version of a function that uses window coordinates uses the same name as the regular version with _w appended. Window coordinates are specified with double float, rather than an int, since window coordinates can be scaled to a high degree.

Microsoft also provides an alternate form for specifying screen coordinates, the structure xycoord.

```
struct xycoord {
  short xcoord;
  short ycoord;
};
```

Functions that use xycoord use the name of the main function with _xy appended.

There is a separate form of xycoord for use with windows, _wxycoord:

```
struct _wxycoord {
  double wx;
  double wy;
};
```

Functions that use this have _wxy appended to the name. The large number of similar functions allows for different programmer styles and tastes while keeping the number of functions to remember manageable.

_arc( )

```
short far _arc(short x1, short y1,
               short x2, short y2,
               short x3, short y3,
               short x4, short y4);
  /*
   * function for drawing an arc
   *
   * Parameters:
   *   x1, y1 - the upper left corner of the
   *            bounding box.
   *   x2, y2 - the lower right corner of the
   *            bounding box.
   *   x3, y3 - start vector
   *   x4, y4 - end vector
   */
```

_arc( ) draws an arc of an ellipse. The ellipse fits in a bounding box with (x1, y1) marking the upper left corner, and (x2, y2) marking the lower right. The start of the arc is marked by a line from the center of the bounding rectangle to the point (x3,y3). Where this line crosses the bounding rectangle the arc begins. A line from the center to (x4, y4) is used to mark the end of the arc. If you wish the arc to appear on the other side of the line reverse points (x3,y3) and (x4,y4).

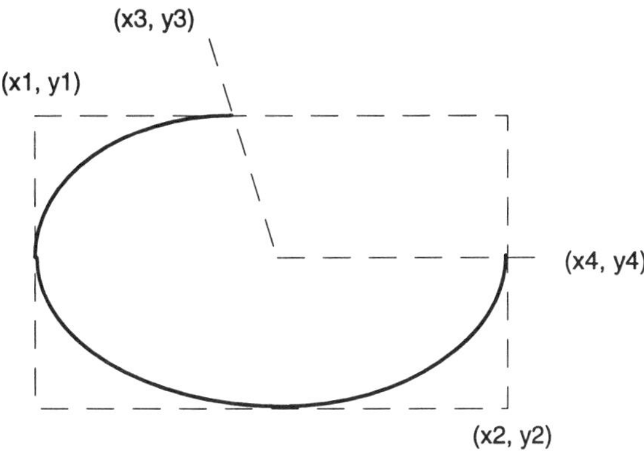

Alternate functions:

```
arc_wxy (struct _wxycoord pwxy1,
         struct _wxycoord pwxy2,
         struct _wxycoord pwxy3,
         struct _wxycoord pwxy4);
```

Covered in Chapter 4, page 113
Related functions: ellipse( ), pie( ), getarcinfo( )

circles

Microsoft does not support a separate circle function. Use the ellipse function for drawing circles.

_clearscreen( )

```
void _far _clearscreen(short area);
  /*
   * function for clearing all or part of the
   *   screen
   *
   * Parameter:
   *   area - part of the screen to be cleared.
   */
```

_clearscreen( ) clears the graphics screen, a viewport, or a window. Three constants are defined for use with this function: _GCLEARSCREEN for clearing the entire screen, _GVIEWPORT for clearing a viewport, and _GWINDOW for clearing a window.

Alternate functions: none
Covered in Chapter 4, page 108
Related functions: _getbkcolor( ), _setbkcolor( )

_displaycursor( )

```
short _far _displaycursor(short toggle);
  /*
   * function to determine whether graphics
   * cursor will remain on or off when graphics
   * functions are exitted
   *
   * Parameter:
```

```
 *   toggle - _GCURSORON to leave cursor on.
 *            _GCURSOROFF to turn cursor off.
 *
 * Returns: Previous state of toggle
 */
```

_displaycursor( ) is used to determine whether the cursor will be left on when graphics mode is exited.

Alternate functions: none
Not covered by this book
Related functions: _gettextcursor( ), _settextcursor( )

_ellipse( )

```
short _far _ellipse (short control,
                     short x1, short y1,
                     short x2, short y2);
  /*
   * function for drawing ellipses.
   *
   * Parameters:
   *   control - whether the ellipse should be
   *             filled or not.
   *   x1, y1  - coordinates of upper left
   *             corner
   *   x1, y1  - coordinates of lower right
   *             corner
   */
```

_ellipse( ) draws an ellipse on the screen. The ellipse fits within a bounding box that has (x1, y1) as the upper left corner and (x2, y2) as the lower right. Control determines if the ellipse will be filled. Use _GFILLINTERIOR to fill the ellipse, or _GBORDER for an unfilled ellipse. To draw a circle use a square bounding rectangle.

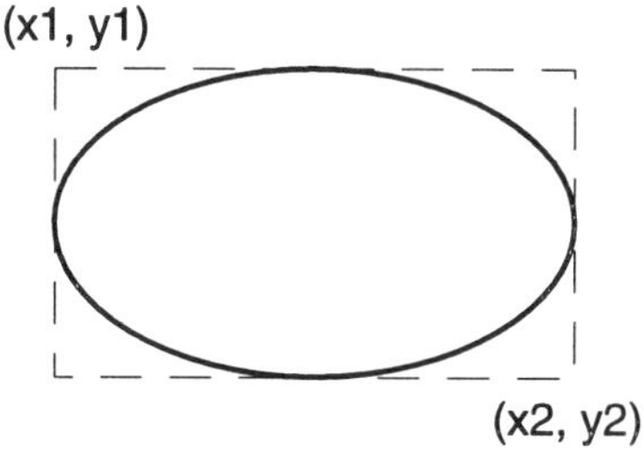

Alternate functions:

```
_ellipse_w(short control,
           double wx1, double wy1,
           double wx2, double wy2);

_ellipse_wxy(short control,
             struct _wxycoord *pwxy1,
             struct _wxycoord *pwxy2);
```

Covered in Chapter 4, page 111
Related functions: _arc( ), _pie( )

_floodfill( )

```
short _floodfill (short x, short y,
                  short boundary);
  /*
   * Routine for filling shapes that are not
   *   ellipses or polygons
   *
   * Parameters:
   *   x, y - location of any point inside the
   *          object being filled.
   *   boundary - the color of the border of
   *              the shape.
   */
```

_floodfill( ) is used to fill oddly shaped objects that are not ellipses or polygons. The object must have a closed border of a single color. This color is passed to the function as the parameter boundary. The function then fills in all directions until a pixel of this color is found. If the border is not closed, or if part is not the correct color, the algorithm will "leak out" and fill the entire screen. The nature of the floodfill algorithm causes this function to be less efficient than other filling methods. It is therefore recommended that drawing filled ellipses or polygons be done where possible. The floodfill algorithm is covered in detail in Chapter 11.

Alternate functions:

```
_floodfill_w(double wx1, double wy1,
             short boundary);
```

Covered in Chapter 4, page 117
Related functions: _ellipse( ), _polygon( ), rectangle( )

_getactivepage( )

```
short _far _getactivepage(void);
  /*
   * gets the active video page
   *
   * Returns:  The number of the active video
   *   page.
   */
```

_getactivepage( ) returns the number of the video page that is currently being written to. Most video modes support more than one frame buffer, but the contents of only one is displayed on the screen at one time. These buffers are called pages. The active page is the page where graphics are written; the visual page is the page being displayed. If the active page and visual page are not the same, new graphics will not show on the screen. This allows for a complete graphics screen to be set up in the background and then rapidly displayed. This is useful for animation. To see how many pages are supported by different modes see _setvideomode( ).

Alternate functions: none
Not covered in this book
Related functions: _setactivepage( ), _getvisualpage( ), _setvisualpage( ), _getimage( ), setimage( )

_getarcinfo( )

```
short _far _getarcinfo
           (struct xycoord _far *start,
            struct xycoord _far *end,
            struct xycoord _far *fillpoint);
  /*
   * Find the start and end points, and a point
   * that can be used by floodfill to fill the
   * last arc drawn
```

```
 *
 * Parameters:
 *   start - coordinate of the start point
 *   end   - coordinate of the end point
 *   fillpoint - point used by floodfill to
 *     fill the arc.
 *
 * Returns: 0 on error.
 */
```

_getarcinfo( ) is a very useful routine that passes back the points where the last arc drawn starts, where it ends, and a point that can be passed to floodfill to fill the arc. This is useful for connecting lines to arcs in order to create more complex shapes.

Alternate functions: none
Not covered by this book
Related functions: _arc( ), _floodfill( ), _pie( )

_getbkcolor( )

```
long _far _getbkcolor(void);
  /*
   * function to get the background color in
   *   graphics mode
   *
   * Returns: the back ground color
   */
```

_getbkcolor( ) will return the current graphics back ground color. This is the color the screen will be set to when _clearscreen( ) is called.

The RGB values for the new back ground color passed in are in a long, which is 32 bits. Figure B.1 shows how the bits are set up to describe the color for MCGA 256 color mode (also supported by VGA). For EGA 64 color mode the lower 1 bits of the RGB fields are ignored.

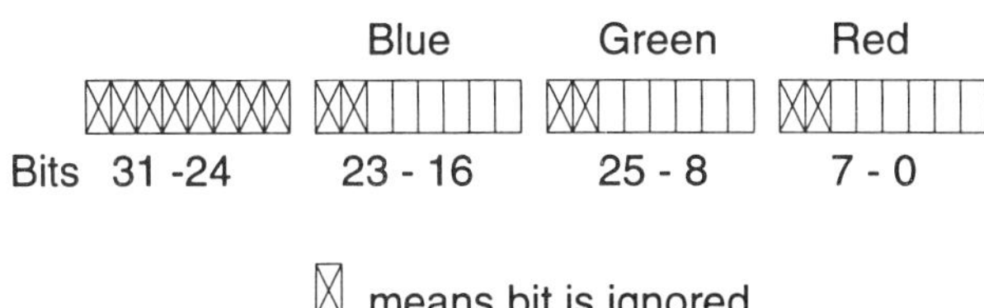

Fig. B1

Some functions use these constants, which work for 256 color mode. Other functions use 4 bit colors.

Table B.2 gives predefined constants for colors.

Table B.2

Dark Colors	Numeric Value	Light Colors	Numeric Value
_BLACK	0x000000L	_GRAY	0x151515L
_BLUE	0x2A0000L	_LIGHTBLUE	0x3F1515L
_GREEN	0x002A00L	_LIGHTGREEN	0x153F15L
_CYAN	0x2A2A00L	_LIGHTCYAN	0x3F3F15L
_RED	0x00002AL	_LIGHTRED	0x15153FL
_MAGENTA	0x2A002AL	_LIGHTMAGENTA	0x3F153FL
_BROWN	0x00152AL	_YELLOW	0x153F3FL
_WHITE	0x2A2A2AL	_BRIGHTWHITE	0x3F3F3FL

Alternate functions: none
Covered in Chapter 4, page 105
Related functions: _getcolor( ), _clearscreen( )

_getcolor( )

```
short far _getcolor(void);
  /*
   * function for getting the current drawing
   *   color.
   *
   * returns:
   *   The current drawing color
   */
```

_getcolor( ) returns the color currently used to draw objects.

Alternate functions: none
Covered in Chapter 4, page 104
Related functions: _getbkcolor( ), _clearscreen( )

_getcurrentposition( )

```
struct xycoord _far _getcurrentposition(void);
  /*
   * function to return the current position
   *
   * Returns:  The current position
   */
```

_getcurrentposition( ) returns the current position used by _lineto( ), _moveto( ), and _outgtext( ). The current position is the screen coordinate where _lineto( ) starts drawing, and where _outgtext( ) starts writing text. The definition of xycoord is

```
struct xycoord {
  short xcoord;
  short ycoord;
};
```

Alternate functions: none
Not covered in this book
Related functions: _lineto( ), _moveto( ), _outgtext( )

_getfillmask( )

```
unsigned char _far * _far _getfillmask
                   (unsinged char _far *mask);
  /*
   * function to find the current fill mask
   *
   * Parameter:
   *   mask - 8 byte array used as the current
   *          fill mask
   *
   * Returns:  0 if mask is not set
   */
```

_getfillmask( ) is used to retrieve the current fill mask. This mask is an 8-byte array used to determine a pattern with which shapes are filled. If a bit in the array is set, the corresponding pixel on the screen is set to the current drawing color, otherwise it is set to the background color.

Alternate functions: none
Not covered in this book
Related functions: _setfillmask( ), _ellipse( ), _polygon( )

_getfontinfo( )

```
short _getfontinfo
              (struct _fontinfo _far *fontbuffer);
  /*
   * function to retrieve information on the
   * current font settings
   *
   * Parameter:
   *   fontbuffer - A structure containing font
   *     information
   *
   * Returns: A negative value if no font has
   *   been loaded or registered.
   */
```

_getfontinfo( ) is used to retrieve information on current font settings. The structure _fontinfo is defined as

```
struct _fontinfo {
  int  type;
  int  ascent;
  int  pixwidth;
  int  pixheight;
  int  avgwidth;
  char filename[81];
  chat facename[32];
};
```

If bit 0 of the type is set then the current font is a vector font, otherwise it is bit mapped. Field ascent gives the height from the top to the baseline in pixels. Fields pixwidth and pixheight give the width and height of the characters, with pixwidth set to 0 for proportional fonts. Field avgwidth gives the average width of characters. Field filename gives the full DOS pathname of the file in which the font is located. Field facename gives the name of the font.

Alternate functions: none
Not covered in this book
Related functions: _setfont( ), _outgtext( )

_getgtextextent( )

```
short _getgtextextent(char *text);
  /*
   * Function to return the width of a string
   *   in pixels, using the current font.
   *
   * Parameter:
   *   text - string to measure
   *
   * Returns: Number of pixels needed for
   *   string
   */
```

_getgtextextent( ) returns the number of pixels needed for a string

Alternate functions: none
Not covered in this book
Related functions: _gettextinfo( ), _registerfonts( ), _setfont( ), _outgtext( ), _getgtextvector( )

_getgtextvector( )

```
struct xycoord _getgtextvector(void);
  /*
   * function to return the current text
   *  vector
   *
   * Returns:  The current text vector in
   *   an xycoord structure
   */
```

_getgtextvector( ) returns information describing the direction text is written in. This information is stored as two numbers, the meaning of which is given in the Table B.3:

Table B.3

Vector	Meaning
(0,0)	Unchanged
(1,0)	Horizontal (default)
(0,1)	Rotated 90 degrees counterclockwise
(-1, 0)	Rotated 180 degrees
(0, -1)	Rotated 270 degrees counterclockwise

The definition of xycoord is

```
struct xycoord {
  short xcoord;
  short ycoord;
};
```

Alternate functions: none
Not covered in this book
Related functions: _gettextinfo( ), _registerfonts( ), _setfont( ), _outgtext( ), _gettextextent( ), _setgtextvector( )

_getimage( )

```
void _getimage(short x1, short y1,
               short x2, short y2,
               char _huge *image);
  /*
   * function to copy a block from the frame
```

```
 *   buffer.
 *
 * Parameters:
 *   x1, y1 - The upper left hand corner of
 *            the block
 *   x2, y2 - The lower right hand corner
 *   image  - buffer that the portion of the
 *            frame buffer is copied to
 */
```

_getimage( ) will copy a block from the frame buffer to a buffer in memory. This function is useful in animation, where an object can be copied to a buffer and then erased from the screen. The object can then be copied from the buffer to the frame buffer at a slightly different position. If this is done repeatedly the object will seem to move about the screen. This function is also useful for saving images.

Alternate functions:

```
void _getimage_w(double wx1, double wy1,
                 double wx2, double wy2,
                 char _huge *image);

void _getimage_wxy
               (struct _wxycoord _far *pwxy1,
                struct _wxycoord _far *pwxy2,
                char _huge *image);
```

Covered in Chapter 12, page 362
Related functions: _imagesize( ), putimage( )

_getlinestyle( )

```
unsigned short _far _getlinestyle (void);
  /*
   * Function to return pattern line will
   *   be drawn with
   *
   * Returns: bitmap used for drawing lines
   */
```

_getlinestyle( ) returns the current bit map used to create patterns when drawing lines. When a bit is set in the bit map the corresponding pixel on the line is set to the current drawing color, otherwise it is not set.

Alternate functions: none
Not covered in this book
Related functions: _setlinestyle( ), _lineto( )

_getphyscoord( )

```
struct xycoord _far _getphyscoord
                         (short x, short y);
  /*
   * Function to translate view coordinates
   *   to physical screen coordinates
   *
   * Parameters:
   *   x, y - view coordinates
   *
   * Returns: xycoord structure with physical
   *   screen coordinates
   */
```

_getphyscoord( ) returns an xycoord structure with the physical screen coordinates that are the same as the view coordinates passed in. Microsoft C allows the programmer to set view coordinates so that the origin is not the upper left corner of the screen. See Chapter 4 for a discussion of view coordinates. The definition of xycoord is

```
struct xycoord {
  short xcoord;
  short ycoord;
};
```

Alternate functions: none
Not covered in this book
Related functions: _setviewport( ), _setvieworg( ), _getviewcoord ( )

_getpixel( )

```
short _far _getpixel(short x, short y);
  /*
   * function for finding the color of a pixel
   *
   * parameters:
   *   x - x coordinate of pixel being gotten
   *   y - y coordinate of pixel being gotten
   *
```

```
 * returns:
 *    The color of the pixel
 */
```

_getpixel( ) returns the color of the pixel at coordinate (x,y)

Alternate functions:

```
_getpixel_w (double wx, double wy);
```

Covered in Chapter 4, page 104
Related functions: _setpixel( )

_getviewcoord( )

```
struct xycoord _far _getviewcoord
                        (short x, short y);
  /*
   * Return view coordinates of point on
   *   physical screen
   *
   * Parameters:
   *   x, y - physical coordinates
   *
   * Returns: equivalant view coordinates in
   *   xycoord structure
   */
```

_getviewcoord( ) translates physical screen coordinates to view coordinates, _getviewcoord_w( ) translates window coordinates to view coordinates, getviewcoord_wxy( ) translates window coordinates in _wxycoord format to view coordinates.

Alternate functions:

```
struct xycoord _far _getviewcoord_w
                        (double x, double y);

struct xycoord _far _getviewcoord_wxy
               (struct _wxycoord _far *pwxy1);
```

Not covered in this book
Related functions: _setviewport( ), _setvieworg( ), _getphyscoord ( )

_getvideoconfig( )

```
struct videoconfig _far * _far _getvideoconfig
             (struct videoconfig _far *config);
  /*
   * Function to get the current video
   *   configuration
   *
   * Parameter:
   *   config - information on the current
   *     video configuration
   *
   * Returns: information on the current
   *     video configuration
   */
```

_getvideoconfig( ) returns information on the current video configuration, in a structure videoconfig, which is defined as:

```
struct videoconfig {
  short numxpixels;
  short numypixels;
  short numtextcols;
  short numtextrows;
  short numcolors;
  short bitsperpixel;
  short numvideopages;
  short mode;
  short adapter;
  short monitor;
  short memory;
};
```

Fields numxpixels and numypixels are the number of pixels in the x and y dimensions, numtextcols and numtextrows are the number of rows and columns for text modes, numcolors is the number of colors available in the current mode, bitsperpixel gives the number of bits required for a pixel, numvideopages gives the number of pages available with the current card and memory, adapter and monitor types are given in Tables B.4 and B.5, respectively, and memory is the amount of RAM available in kilobytes.

Table B.4 Adapter Types

Constant	Value	Adapter Type
_MDPA	0x0001	Monochrome Display Adapter
_CGA	0x0002	Color Graphics Adapter
_EGA	0x0004	Enhanced Graphics Adapter
_VGA	0x0008	Video Graphics Array
_MCGA	0x0010	MultiColor Graphics Array
_HGC	0x0020	Hercules Graphics Adapter
_OCGA	0x0042	Olivetti Color Graphics Adapter
_OEGA	0x0044	Olivetti Enhanced Graphics Adapter
_OVGA	0x0048	Olivetti Video Array

Table B.5 Monitor Types

Constant	Value	Monitor Type
_MONO	0x0001	Monochrome
_COLOR	0x0002	Color or Enhanced emulating Color
_ENHCOLOR	0x0004	Enhanced Color
_ANALOGMONO	0x0008	Analog Monochrome only
_ANALOGCOLOR	0x0010	Analog Color only
_ANALOG	0x0018	Analog Monochrome and Color modes

Alternate functions: none
Covered in Chapter 4, page 96
Related functions: _setvideomode( )

_getvisualpage( )

```
short _far _getvisualpage(void);
  /*
   * Function to return the current visual page
   *   (page being displayed)
   *
   * Returns: The number of the current visual
   *   page
   */
```

_getvisualpage( ) returns the number of the video page that is currently being displayed. Most video modes support more than one frame buffer, but the contents of only one is displayed on the screen at one time. These buffers are called pages. The active page is the page where graphics are written; the visual page is the page being displayed. If the active page and visual page are not the same, new graphics will not show on the screen. This allows for a complete graphics screen to be set up in the background then rapidly displayed. This is useful for animation. To see how many pages are supported by different modes see _setvideomode( ).

Alternate functions: none
Not covered in this book
Related functions: _setactivepage( ), _getvisualpage( ), _setvisualpage( ), _getimage( ), setimage( )

_getwindowcoord( )

```
struct wxycoord _getwindowcoord
                    (short x, short y);
  /*
   * Function to translate physical coordinates
   *   to window coordinates
   *
   * Parameters:
   *   x, y - physical coordinates to be
   *          translated
   *
   * Returns:  The equivelant window coordinate
   *   in a wxycoord structure
   */
```

_getwindowcoord( ) translates physical screen coordinates to view coordinates.

Alternate functions: none
Not covered in this book
Related functions: _setviewport( ), _setvieworg( ), _getphyscoord ( )

_getwritemode( )

```
short _far _getwritemode (void);
  /*
   * Function to get the current mode for
   *   plotting graphics
   *
   * Returns current mode for plotting graphics
   */
```

_getwritemode( ) is used to find the current mode for plotting graphics used by _lineto( ), _rectangle( ), and _polygon( ). The graphic can be written directly to the screen, or it can be combined with what is currently on the screen using logical operators. For example, if the current mode is XOR and a line is drawn each pixel in the line will be XORed with the pixel already on the screen. If the same line is then XORed again it will be completely removed from the screen, leaving what was there previously. This technique is covered in detail in Chapter 12 on animation. The possible modes are given in Table B.6.

Table B.6

Constant	Meaning
_GAND	AND the graphic with the screen
_GOR	OR the graphic with the screen
_GPRESET	Uses the logical negative of the graphic
_GPSET	Place the graphic on the screen as it is (default)
_GXOR	XOR the graphics with what is on the screen

Alternate functions: none
Not covered in this book
Related functions: _getimage( ), _putimage( ), _lineto( ), setwritemode( )

_imagesize( )

```
long _imagesize(short x1, short y1,
                short x2, short y2);
  /*
   * Function to return the amount of memory
   * needed to hold an image
   *
```

```
* Parameters:
*   x1, y1 - the upper left corner of the
*            image on the screen
*   x2, y2 - the lower right corner
*
* Returns:  The number of bytes needed to
*   store the image
*/
```

_imagesize( ) will return the number of bytes needed to store the portion of the graphics screen bounded by the box with (x1, y1) as its upper left corner and (x2, y2) as its lower right, given the current graphics mode. This number can be used with malloc( ) to allocate a buffer of the appropriate size.

Alternate functions:

```
long _imagesize_w(double wx1, double wy1,
                  double wx2, double wx2);

long _imagesize_wxy
              (struct _wxycoord _far *pwxy1,
               struct _wxycoord _far *pwxy2);
```

Covered in Chapter 12, page 362
Related functions: _getimage( ), _putimage( )

_lineto( )

```
short far _lineto(short x, short y);
  /*
   * function for drawing a line.  The start
   *   of line is set with _moveto()
   *
   * Parameters:
   *   x - x coordinate where the line will end
   *   y - y coordinate where the line will end
   *
   * Returns: A nonzero value on success
   */
```

_lineto( ) draws a line from the current location to the point (x, y), then makes that the current position. Lines drawn with this function can be patterned (dotted, dashed, etc) by calling _setlinestyle( ) first.

Alternate functions:

```
short _lineto_w(double wx, double wy);
```

Covered in Chapter 4, page 109
Related functions: _getcurrentposition( ), _getlinestyle( ), moveto( ), setlinestyle( )

_moveto( )

```
struct xycoord far _moveto(short x, short y);
  /*
   * function for setting the current location
   *   where the next line will be drawn from.
   *
   * Parameters:
   *   x - x coordinate of current location
   *   y - y coordinate of current location
   *
   * Returns: The previous current location
   */
```

_moveto( ) sets the current position, which is the position where the next call to _lineto( ) will start drawing from, and the position where outgtext will start writing.

Alternate functions:

```
struct _wxycoord _moveto_w(double wx,
                           double wy);
```

Covered in Chapter 4, page 109
Related functions: _getcurrentposition( ), _getlinestyle( ), lineto( ), setlinestyle( ), _outgtext( )

_outgtext( )

```
void _outgtext(unsigned char *text);
  /*
   * function for outputting text using
   *   graphics fonts
   *
   * Parameter:
   *   text - string of text
   */
```

_outgtext( ) is used to write strings in graphics fonts. Graphics modes allow for a great deal of flexibility with text. Text can be written using different typefaces and sizes. Text written with this function starts at the current position, which can be changed with _moveto( ). After the text is written the current position is updated. No formatting is provided for this function.

Alternate functions: none
Covered in Chapter 4, page 128
Related functions: _moveto( ), _registerfont( ), _unregisterfont( ), _setfont( )

_pie( )

```
short far _pie(short control,
               short x1, short y1,
               short x2, short y2,
               short x3, short y3,
               short x4, short y4);
  /*
   * function for drawing pie slices.
   *
   * Parameters:
   *   Control - whether the pie slice should
   *              be filled or not.
   *   x1, y1 - the upper left corner of the
   *             bounding box.
   *   x2, y2 - the lower right corner of the
   *             bounding box.
   *   x3, y3 - start vector
   *   x4, y4 - end vector
   *
   * Returns: A nonzero value on success
   */
```

_pie( ) draws a pie slice, that is an arc of an ellipse with lines from the endpoints of the arc to the center of the ellipse. The control parameter is used to determine if the pie slice is filled or not. Use _GFILLINTERIOR for a filled slice or _GBORDER for an unfilled slice. The ellipse fits in a bounding box with (x1, y1) marking the upper left corner, and (x2, y2) marking the lower right. The start of the arc is marked by an imaginary line from the center of the bounding rectangle to the coordinates (x3,y3). The arc starts where this line crosses the bounding rectangle. The end of the arc is marked by a line from the center of the bounding rectangle to point (x4, y4).

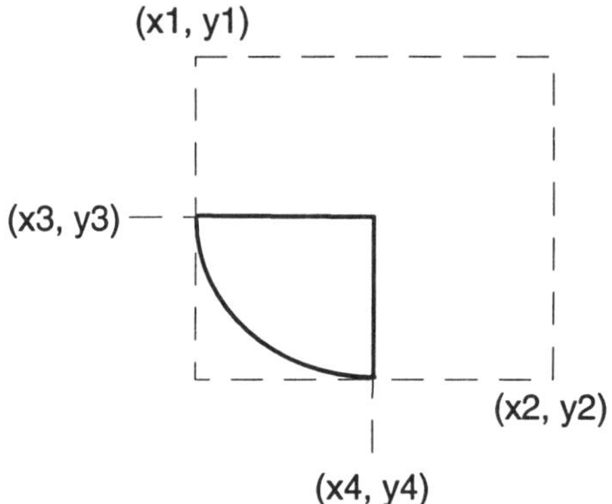

Alternate functions:

```
short far _pie_wxy
               (short control,
                struct _wxycoord _far *pwxy1
                struct _wxycoord _far *pwxy2
                struct _wxycoord _far *pwxy3
                struct _wxycoord _far *pwxy4);
```

Covered in Chapter 4, page 114
Related functions: _arc( ), _ellipse( )

_polygon( )

```
short far _polygon(short control,
                   struct xycoord far *points,
                   short numpoints);
  /*
   * function for drawing polygons
   *
   * Parameters:
   *   control   - whether the polygon should
   *               be filled
   *   points    - array of points, each is a
   *               corner of the polygon
   *   numpoints - the number of corner points
   *
   * Returns:  A nonzero value if successful
   */
```

_polygon( ) is used to draw polygons. The control parameter is used to determine if the polygon is filled or not. Use _GFILLINTERIOR for a filled polygon or

_GBORDER for an unfilled polygon. Parameter points is an array of points, each point being a vertex of the polygon; numpoints gives the number of points in the polygon. The definition of xycoord is

```
struct xycoord {
  short xcoord;
  short ycoord;
};
```

Alternate functions:

```
short far _polygon_w(short control,
                     double _far *points,
                     short numpoints);

short far _polygon_wxy
                (short control,
                 struct _wxycoord far *points,
                 short numpoints);
```

Covered in Chapter 4, page 114
Related functions: _ellipse( ), _rectangle( )

_putimage( )

```
void _putimage(short x, short y,
               char *huge image,
               short action);
  /*
   * Function to put an image on the screen
   *   that has previously been saved with
   *   _getimage()
   *
   * Parameters:
   *   x, y   - the upper left corner where the
   *            image is to be placed.
   *   image  - buffer holding the image
   *   action - bitwise action for copying the
   *            buffer to the screen
   */
```

_putimage( ) places an image saved with _getimage on the screen. By using _getimage( ) and _putimage( ) together a graphic can be animated. Draw the image on the screen, use _getimage( ) to copy it into a buffer, then erase if from the screen. Repeatedly put it on the screen with _putimage then erase it, moving it slightly each time. The graphic will seem to move across the screen. These functions are also useful for saving graphics on disk.

Parameters x and y give the upper left-hand corner of the location where the graphic will be placed. Function _getimage( ) stores the height and width of the graphic, so this information is not needed to place the image. Parameter image is a pointer to the buffer that holds the graphic. Parameter action determines how the image is to be copied to the screen. The graphic can be written directly to the screen, or it can be combined with what is currently on the screen using logical operators. For example, if the current action is XOR and an image is put, each pixel in the image will be XORed with the pixel already on the screen. If the same image is then XORed again it will be completely removed from the screen, leaving what was there previously. The possible actions are given in Table B.7.

Table B.7

Constant	Meaning
_GAND	AND the graphic with the screen
_GOR	OR the graphic with the screen
_GPRESET	Uses the logical negative of the graphic
_GPSET	Place the graphic on the screen as it is
_GXOR	XOR the graphics with what is on the screen

Alternate functions:

```
void _putimage_w(double wx, double wy,
                 char *huge image,
                 short action);
```

Covered in Chapter 12, page 362
Related functions: _getimage( ), _imagesize( )

_rectangle( )

```
short far _rectangle(short control,
                     short x1, short y1,
                     short x2, short y2);
  /*
   * function for drawing rectangles
   *
   * Parameters:
   *   control - whether the rectangle is
```

```
 *              filled
 *   x1, y1  - the upper left corner
 *   x2, y2  - the lower right corner
 *
 * Returns: A nonzero value on success
 */
```

_rectangle( ) will draw a rectangle on the screen. The parameter control is used to determine if the rectangle is filled or not. Use _GFILLINTERIOR for a filled polygon or _GBORDER for an unfilled rectangle. Parameters x1 and y1 give the upper left hand corner of the rectangle, x2 and y2 give the lower right.

Alternate functions:

```
short far _rectangle_w(short control,
                       double x1, double y1,
                       double x2, double y2);

short far _rectangle_wxy
                  (short control,
                   struct _wxycoord _far *pwxy1,
                   struct _wxycoord _far *pwxy2)
```

Covered in Chapter 4, page 114
Related functions: _polygon( ), _ellipse( )

_registerfonts( )

```
short _registerfonts(unsigned char *pathname)
  /*
   * Function to register available fonts for
   *   using text in graphics modes
   *
   * Parameter:
   *   pathname - path of font files.  Wild
   *              cards are accepted.
   *
   * Returns:
   *   A value less than 0 if an error occurs,
   *   otherwise the number of fonts registered
   */
```

_registerfonts( ) loads font files from the disk and makes them available for use. Parameter pathname is the full DOS pathname of the file containing the font. Wild cards can be used to load a number of fonts at one time. This function can be called repeatedly to load more than one font. Table B.8 lists six fonts that are supplied with Microsoft C. Other fonts are available.

Table B.8

Font	Mapping	Sizes	Spacing	File Name
Courier	Bit	13 × 8, 16 × 9, 20 × 12	Fixed	COURB.FON
Helv	Bit	13 × 5, 16 × 7, 20 × 8, 13 × 15, 16 × 6, 19 × 8	Fixed	HELVB.FON
Tms Rmn	Bit	10 × 5, 12 × 6, 15 × 8 16 × 9, 20 × 12, 26 × 16	Fixed	TMSRB.FON
Modern	Stroked	Scaled	Proportional	MODERN.FON
Script	Stroked	Scaled	Proportional	SCRIPT.FON
Roman	Stroked	Scaled	Proportional	ROMAN.FON

Alternate functions: none
Covered in Chapter 4, page 125
Related functions: _setfont( ), _outgtext( ), _getfontinfo( )

_remapallpalette( )

```
short _far _remapallpalette
                    (const long _far *colors);
  /*
   * Change all palette registers with one call
   *
   * Parameter:
   *   colors - array of new color mappings.
   *
   * Returns: 0 if successful
   */
```

_remapallpalette( ) changes all palette registers with one call. An array is passed in with the new color values. If the array is too large the extra values are ignored; if it is not large enough the function will read junk past the array. The RGB values for the new colors are in an array of longs, which are 32 bits. Figure B.2 shows how the bits are set up to describe the color for MCGA 256-color mode (also supported by VGA) for each element of the array. For EGA 64-color mode the lower 1 bits of the RGB fields are ignored.

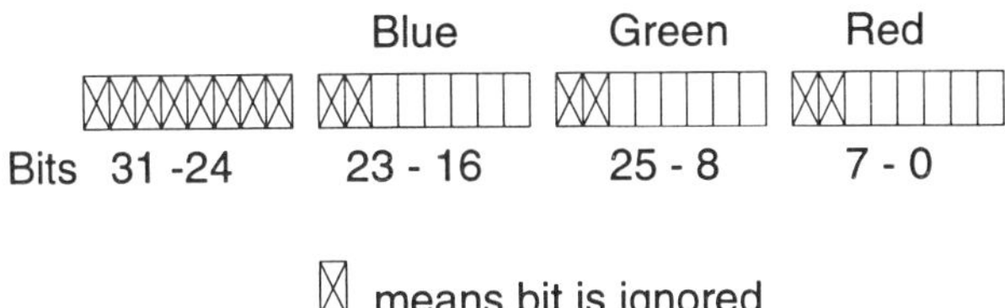

Fig. B.2

Table B.9 gives predefined constants for colors.

Table B.9

Dark Colors	Numeric Value	Light Colors	Numeric Value
_BLACK	0x000000L	_GRAY	0x151515L
_BLUE	0x2A0000L	_LIGHTBLUE	0x3F1515L
_GREEN	0x002A00L	_LIGHTGREEN	0x153F15L
_CYAN	0x2A2A00L	_LIGHTCYAN	0x3F3F15L
_RED	0x00002AL	_LIGHTRED	0x15153FL
_MAGENTA	0x2A002AL	_LIGHTMAGENTA	0x3F153FL
_BROWN	0x00152AL	_YELLOW	0x153F3FL
_WHITE	0x2A2A2AL	_BRIGHTWHITE	0x3F3F3FL

Alternate functions: none
This function is not covered in this book, but palette registers are covered in Chapter 6, and the method of changing palette registers to create animation effects is covered in Chapter 12.
Related functions: _remappalette( )

_remappalette( )

```
long _far _remappalette (short index,
                         long color);
  /*
   * Function to change a single color palette
   *
   * Parameters:
   *   index - palette register to change
   *   color - new color value for the register
   *
```

```
* Returns: Previous color value, or -1 on
*          error
*/
```

_remappalette( ) changes a single color register. The RGB values for the new color passed in are in a long, which is 32 bits. Figure B.3 shows how the bits are set up to describe the color for MCGA 256-color mode (also supported by VGA). For EGA 64-color mode the lower 1 bits of the RGB fields are ignored.

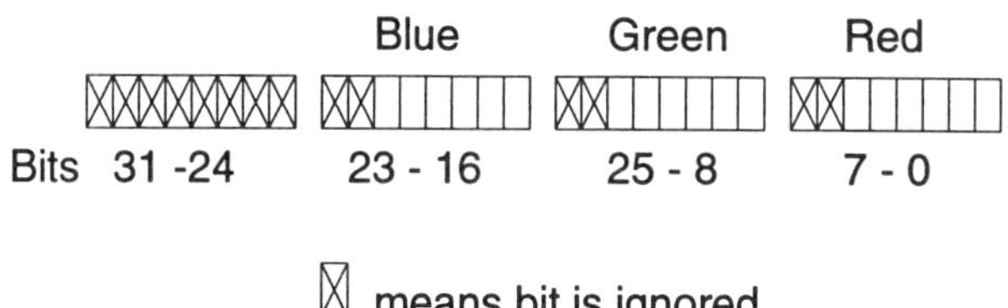

Fig. B.3

Table B.10 gives predefined constants for colors.

Table B.10

Dark Colors	Numeric Value	Light Colors	Numeric Value
_BLACK	0x000000L	_GRAY	0x151515L
_BLUE	0x2A0000L	_LIGHTBLUE	0x3F1515L
_GREEN	0x002A00L	_LIGHTGREEN	0x153F15L
_CYAN	0x2A2A00L	_LIGHTCYAN	0x3F3F15L
_RED	0x00002AL	_LIGHTRED	0x15153FL
_MAGENTA	0x2A002AL	_LIGHTMAGENTA	0x3F153FL
_BROWN	0x00152AL	_YELLOW	0x153F3FL
_WHITE	0x2A2A2AL	_BRIGHTWHITE	0x3F3F3FL

Alternate functions: none
Not covered in this book, but palette registers are covered in Chapter 6, and the method of changing palette registers to create animation effects is covered in Chapter 12.
Related functions: _remapallpalette( )

_selectpalette( )

```
short _far selectpalette(short number);
  /*
   * Select CGA palette
   *
   * Parameter:
   *   number - new CGA palette
   *
   * Returns: The number of the previous
   *          palette
   */
```

_selectpalette( ) sets a CGA palette. CGA monitors support four color palettes, with three colors being predetermined, and the fourth, the background, being user selectable. Use setbkcolor( ) with colors 0 to 15 to set the user-selectable background.

Alternate functions: none
Not covered in this book, but CGA programming is covered in Chapter 6.
Related functions: _remapallpalette( ), _remapalette( ), _setcolor( ), setbkcolor( )

_setactivepage( )

```
short _setactivepage(short page);
  /*
   * Function to set the active video page.
   *
   * Parameter:
   *   page - The new active page
   *
   * Returns: the previous active page
   */
```

_setactivepage( ) sets the number of the video page that is currently being written to. Most video modes support more than one frame buffer, but the contents of only one is displayed on the screen at one time. These buffers are called pages. The active page is the page where graphics are written; the visual page is the page being displayed. If the active page and visual page are not the same, new graphics will not show on the screen. This allows for a complete graphics screen to be set up in the background then rapidly displayed. This is useful for animation. To see how many pages are supported by different modes see _setvideomode( ).

Alternate functions: none
Covered in Chapter 12, page 366
Related functions: _getactivepage( ), _getvisualpage( ), _setvisualpage( )

_setbkcolor( )

```
long far _setbkcolor(long color);
  /*
   * function for setting the background color
   *   in graphics mode.
   *
   * Parameters
   *   color - the color the background will be
   *           set to
   *
   * Returns: The previous back ground color
   */
```

_setbkcolor( ) sets a new background color. The RGB values for the new back ground color passed in are in a long, which is 32 bits. Figure B.4 shows how the bits are set up to describe the color for MCGA 256-color mode (also supported by VGA). For EGA 64-color mode the lower 1 bits of the RGB fields are ignored.

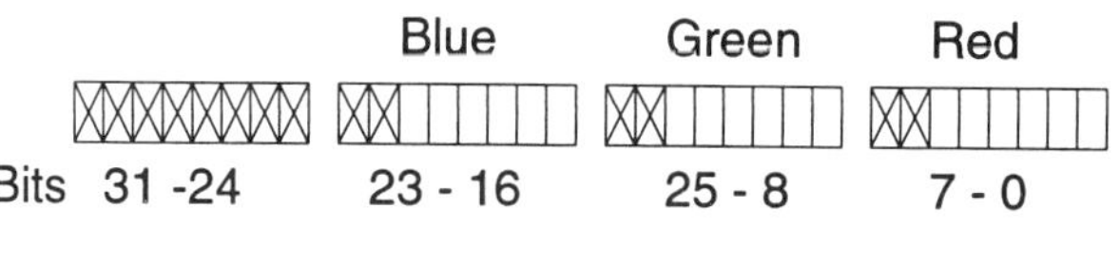

Fig. B.4

Table B.11 gives predefined constants for colors.

Table B.11

Dark Colors	Numeric Value	Light Colors	Numeric Value
_BLACK	0x000000L	_GRAY	0x151515L
_BLUE	0x2A0000L	_LIGHTBLUE	0x3F1515L
_GREEN	0x002A00L	_LIGHTGREEN	0x153F15L
_CYAN	0x2A2A00L	_LIGHTCYAN	0x3F3F15L
_RED	0x00002AL	_LIGHTRED	0x15153FL
_MAGENTA	0x2A002AL	_LIGHTMAGENTA	0x3F153FL
_BROWN	0x00152AL	_YELLOW	0x153F3FL
_WHITE	0x2A2A2AL	_BRIGHTWHITE	0x3F3F3FL

Alternate functions: none
Covered in Chapter 4, page 105
Related functions: _setcolor( ), _getbkcolor( ), _getcolor( ), _selectpalette( )

_setcliprgn( )

```
void far _setcliprgn(short x1, short y1,
                     short x2, short y2);
  /*
   * function for setting a clipping region
   *
   * Parameters:
   *   x1 - left side of clipping region
   *   y1 - top of clipping region
   *   x2 - right side of clipping region
   *   y2 - bottom of clipping region
   */
```

_setcliprgn( ) will set a clipping region on the screen outside of which most graphics routines will not write.

Alternate functions: none
Covered in Chapter 4, page 106
Related functions: _arc( ), _ellipse( ), _polygon( ), _ellipse( ), _lineto ( ), _setvieworg( )

_setcolor( )

```
short far _setcolor(short color);
  /*
   * function for setting the current drawing
   *   color.
   *
   * Parameters:
   *   color - color the current drawing color
   *           will be set to.
   *
   * Returns: -1 if error, else the previous
   *          color
   */
```

_setcolor( ) sets the current drawing color.

Alternate functions: none
Covered in Chapter 4, page 101
Related functions: _arc( ), _ellipse( ), _polygon( ), _ellipse( ), _lineto ( )

_setfillmask( )

```
void _setfillmask(unsigned char *mask);
  /*
   * Function to set fill pattern
   *
   * Parameter:
   *   mask - array of 8 characters giving
   *          bit pattern for filling
   */
```

_setfillmask( ) is used to set fill patterns. An 8 byte array is used as a bitmask to determine pixels to be turned on or off. If a bit is set in the bitmask the corresponding pixel on the screen is set to the current color, otherwise it is set to the background color. The default is solid fill.

Alternate functions: none
Covered in Chapter 4, page 117
Related functions: _ellipse( ), _polygon( ), _ellipse( ), _getfillmask( )

_setfont( )

```
short _setfont (unsigned char *options)
  /*
   * Function for setting the current font
   *
   * Parameter:
   *   options - String describing font desired
   *
   * Returns:
   *   Number of the font when successful, or a
   *   negative value otherwise.
   */
```

_setfont( ) sets the graphics font used by outgtext( ). Graphics modes allow for a great deal of flexibility with text. Text can be written using different typefaces and sizes. The options parameter is a string with option codes imbedded in it. The option codes give different characteristics of the desired font, and allow the user to select a font that comes close or only a font that matches the given characteristics perfectly. Table B.12 gives fonts supplied with Microsoft C; Table B.13 gives option codes that can be used in the options parameter.

Table B.12 MicroSoft C fonts

Font	Mapping	Sizes	Spacing	File Name
Courier	Bit	13 × 8, 16 × 9, 20 × 12	Fixed	COURB.FON
Helv	Bit	13 × 5, 16 × 7, 20 × 8, 13 × 15, 16 × 6, 19 × 8	Fixed	HELVB.FON
Tms Rmn	Bit	10 × 5, 12 × 6, 15 × 8 16 × 9, 20 × 12, 26 × 16	Fixed	TMSRB.FON
Modern	Stroked	Scaled	Proportional	MODERN.FON
Script	Stroked	Scaled	Proportional	SCRIPT.FON
Roman	Stroked	Scaled	Proportional	ROMAN.FON

Table B.13 Option Codes

Option Code	Meaning
b	Select best fit
f	Fixed space font only
h*y*	Character height – *y* is height in pixels
n*x*	Font number, where *x* is less than the number returned by _registerfonts( )
p	Proportional font only
r	Raster mapped (bit mapped) font only
t'fontname'	Name typeface, in single quotes
v	Vector mapped (stroked) font only
w*x*	Character width – *x* is the width in pixels

Alternate functions: none
Covered in Chapter 4, page 125
Related functions: _getfontinfo( ), _outgtext( ), _registerfonts( )

_setgtextvector( )

```
struct xycoord _setgtextvector(short x, short y);
  /*
   * function to return the current text vector
   *
   * Returns:  The current text vector in
   *    an xycoord structure
   */
```

_setgtextvector( ) sets the direction text is written in. This information is stored as two numbers, the meaning of which is given in Table B.14.

Table B.14

Vector	Meaning
(0,0)	Unchanged
(1,0)	Horizontal (default)
(0,1)	Rotated 90 degrees counterclockwise
(-1, 0)	Rotated 180 degrees
(0, -1)	Rotated 270 degrees counterclockwise

This function reads the sign of the number rather than the value, so (-3, 0) is the same as (-1, 0). What happens with two positive or two negative values is not documented.

Alternate functions: none
Not covered in this book
Related functions: _gettextinfo( ), _registerfonts( ), _setfont( ), _outgtext( )

_setlinestyle( )

```
void _setlinestyle(unsigned short mask);
  /*
   * Function to set the style that future
   * lines will be drawn with.
   *
   * Parameter:
   *   Mask - bit pattern to describe pattern
   *          of line
   */
```

_setlinestyle( ) sets the style of line to be drawn by _lineto( ). This function takes a byte that will be used as a bitmask. When a bit is set in the bitmask the corresponding pixel on the line is lit.

Alternate functions: none
Covered in Chapter 4, page 116
Related functions: _lineto( ), _setfillpattern( )

_setpixel( )

```
short far _setpixel(short x, short y);
  /*
   * function for setting a pixel
   *
   * parameters:
   *   x - x coordinate of pixel being set
   *   y - y coordinate of pixel being set
   *
   * Returns: The pixels previous value, or
   *   -1 on error
   */
```

_setpixel( ) lights a single pixel on the screen. The pixel lit is the one at coordinates (x, y). The color used is the current drawing color.

Alternate functions:

```
short far _setpixel_w(double x, double y);
```

Covered in Chapter 4, page 101
Related functions: _getpixel( ), _getcolor( ), setcolor( )

_setvieworg( )

```
struct xycoord far _setvieworg (short x, short y);
  /*
   * function for moving the origin to another
   *   part of the screen
   *
   * Parameters:
   *   x - x coordinate of the origin, as
   *       measured from the upper left corner
   *   y - y coordinate of the origin, as
   *       measured from the upper left corner
   *
   * Returns: The previous origin
   */
```

_setvieworg( ) sets the origin to the screen coordinates specified by (x, y). The values passed to this function are always measured from the upper left-hand corner.

Alternate functions: none
Covered in Chapter 4, page 106
Related functions: _getphyscoord( ), getviewcoord( ), setviewport( )

_setviewport( )

```
void _far _setviewport(short x1, short y1,
                       short x2, short y2);
  /*
   * Function to define a viewport
   *
   * Parameters
   *   x1, y1 - upper left corner of viewport
   *            in screen coordinates
   *   y1, y2 - lower left corner of viewport
   */
```

_setviewport( ) sets a viewport. It defines a clipping region then sets the origin to the upper left corner of the clipping region.

Alternate functions: none
Covered in Chapter 4, page 106
Related functions: _getphyscoord( ), getviewcoord( ), setvieworg( )

_setvideomode( )

```
short _far _setvideomode(short mode);
  /*
   * Function to set video mode
   *
   * Parameter:
   *   mode - the number desired mode
   *
   * Returns: 0 on error
   */
```

_setvideomode( ) is used to set the screen to graphics mode, or back to text mode. This function can automatically detect the best available mode in terms of either resolution or number of colors. Table B.15 gives constants defined for supported modes.

Table B.15

Constant	Value	Number of Pixels	Number of Colors	Monitor Types
_MAXRESMODE	-3	Depends on monitor	Depends on monitor	All
_MAXCOLORMODE	-2	Depends on monitor	Depends on monitor	All
_DEFAULTMODE	-1	Restore to original	Restore to original	All
_TEXTBW40	0	40 col text	16 grey	All
_TEXTC40	1	40 col text	16 for/8 back	Color only
_TEXTBW80	2	80 col text	16 grey	All except PCjr.
_TEXTC80	3	80 col text	16 for/8 back	All color exc. PCjr.
_MRES4COLOR	4	320 × 200	4	CGA
_MRESNOCOLOR	5	320 × 200	4 grcy	CGA
_HRESBW	6	640 × 200	2 (B&W)	CGA
_TEXTMONO	7	80 col text	2 (B&W)	Hercules
_HERCMONO	8	720 × 348	2 (B&W)	Hercules
_MRES16COLOR	13	320 × 200	16	EGA
_HRES16COLOR	14	640 × 200	16	EGA
_ERESNOCOLOR	15	640 × 350	2 (B&W)	EGA
_ERESCOLOR	16	640 × 350	4 or 16	EGA
_VRES2COLOR	17	640 × 480	2 (B&W)	VGA
_VRES16COLOR	18	640 × 480	16	VGA
_VRES256COLOR	19	320 × 200	256	VGA
_ORESCOLOR	64	640 × 400	1/16	Olivetti

Alternate functions: none
Covered in Chapter 4, page 96
Related functions: _getvideoconfig( )

_setvisualpage( )

```
short _setvisualpage(short page);
  /*
   * Function to set the visual page
   *
   * Parameter
   *   page - the page to make the visual page
   *
   * Returns: The previous visual page, or
   *   a negative value on error.
   */
```

_setvisualpage( ) sets the number of the video page that is currently being displayed. Most video modes support more than one frame buffer, but the contents of only one is displayed on the screen at one time. These buffers are called pages. The active page is the page where graphics are written; the visual page is the page being displayed. If the active page and visual page are not the same, new graphics will not show on the screen. This allows for a complete graphics screen to be set up in the background then rapidly displayed. This is useful for animation. To see how many pages are supported by different modes see _setvideomode( ).

Alternate functions: none
Covered in Chapter 12, page 366
Related functions: _getactivepage( ), _getvisualpage( ), _setvisualpage( )

_setwindow( )

```
void far _setwindow (short finvert,
                     double wx1, double wy1,
                     double wx2, double wy2);
  /*
   * function for setting a graphics window
   *
   * Parameters:
   *   finvert - should the y coordinates be
   *     reversed from the normal screen.  A
   *     value of 1 reverses the coordinates,
   *     0 does not.
   *   wx1 - the new x coordinate of the left
   *     hand side of the window.
   *   wy1 - the new y coordinate of the top
   *     of the window.
   *   wx2 - the new x coordinate of the right
```

```
    *     hand side of the window.
    *   wy2 - the new y coordinate of the bottom
    *     of the window.
    */
```

_setwindow( ) redefines the coordinate system of a viewport. This function allows the y axis to be flipped so that it will correspond to standard cartesian coordinates. It also allows the number of the axes to be scaled to better match the work the computer is doing.

Alternate functions: none
Covered in Chapter 4, page 107
Related functions: _setviewport( ), _setvieworg( )

_setwritemode( )

```
short _far _setwritemode(short action);
  /*
   * Set the action for graphics functions that
   *   write to the screen.
   *
   * Parameter:
   *   action - the action that graphics functions
   *     will use when plotting on the screen.
   *
   * Returns - previous action
   */
```

_setwritemode( ) will set the action used by graphics functions when they plot pixels on the screen. Normally pixels are simply written to the screen overwriting what is already there. But the color of the pixel on the screen can be combined with the new color using logical operations. For example, a line can be drawn by XORing each pixel on the line with what is already on the screen. If the same line is then redrawn, again XORing with what is already on the screen, the line drawn with the first call will be removed and the original contents of the screen will be left untouched. This technique is covered in detail in Chapter 12 on animation. The possible modes are given in Table B.16.

Table B.16

Constant	Meaning
_GAND	AND the graphic with the screen
_GOR	OR the graphic with the screen
_GPRESET	Uses the logical negative of the graphic
_GPSET	Place the graphic on the screen as it is (default)
_GXOR	XOR the graphics with what is on the screen

Alternate functions: none
Not covered in this book
Related functions: _getimage( ), _putimage( ), _lineto( ), getwritemode( )

_unregisterfonts( )

```
void _unregisterfonts(void);
  /*
   * Function to remove all fonts from font
   *   registry
   */
```

_unregisterfonts( ) removes all fonts from registry, allowing an entirely new set of fonts to be registered. This is useful when the registry runs out of space.

Alternate functions: none
Not covered in this book
Related functions: _registerfonts( ), _setfont( )

struct xycoord

See paragraph at start of Appendix B

struct _wxycoord

See paragraph at start of Appendix B.

Appendix C

SVGALib Constants and Functions

SVGALib is a library of functions for programming VESA VBE compatible monitors. This library was written for this book and included on the distribution disk. The source code is in file SVGALIB.C on the distribution disk, and prototypes for exported functions are in SVGALIB.H.

This library is fairly new, and though as much testing as possible has been performed, there are bound to be some minor bugs here and there. The source code for these routines is completely explained in Chapters 9, 10 and 11. This appendix documents how the functions in this library should work. If a function does not work as described here consult the appropriate chapter and make corrections to the source code. The contents of this appendix are listed below to aid in finding information.

SVGA_arc( )

```
void SVGA_arc (int X_center, int Y_center,
               int Radius,
               int St_Angle, int End_Angle);
  /*
   * Draw an arc of a circle
   *
   * Parameters:
   *  X_Center,
   *  Y_Center  - center of circle
   *  Radius    - radius of circle
   *  St_Angle  - starting angle of arc
   *  End_Angle - ending angle of arc
   *
   * Notes - St_Angle and End_Angle are taken
   * modulo 360.  If End_Angle < St_Angle the
   * angles are reversed, i.e. End_Angle becomes
   * St_Angle, and Vica Versa.  This has the
   * unfortunate effect that if St_Angle is 359
   * and End_Angle is 361 almost the entire
   * circle is drawn, rather than a small
   * portion as would be expected.  Note also
   * that the Borland arc routine has this same
   * quirk.
   */
```

SVGA_arc( ) draws an arc of a circle. The circle is centered on coordinate (X_center, Y_center), with a radius of Radius. The arc is drawn from St_Angle to End_Angle. These angles are taken modulo 360 to simplify the algorithm. The start angle must be smaller than the end angle AFTER the modulo operation, or the angles will be reversed. That means if St_Angle 359 and End_Angle is 361, End_Angle will be moduloed by 360 to become 1. Since End_Angle is now smaller than St_Angle the angles are reversed and the algorithm draws an arc from 1 to 359. The aspect ratio is not taken into account by this function. Most SVGA modes use square pixels, so this is usually not a problem.

Covered in Chapter 10, page 318
Related functions: SVGA_circle( ), SVGA_ellipse

SVGA_circle( )

```
void SVGA_circle (int X_center, int Y_center,
                  int Radius);
  /*
   * draw a circle with radius Radius, centered
   *   on point (X_Center,Y_Center)
   */
```

SVGA_circle( ) draws a circle on the screen, centered on screen coordinate (X_center, Y_center), with a radius of Radius. This function does not take into account aspect ratio, and so only draws round circles in modes with square pixels; in other modes the circles are elongated toward the top and bottom. To correct this use SVGA_ellipse with the Y radius multiplied by the aspect ratio. Most SVGA modes use square pixels, so the aspect ratio usually is not a problem. There is no separate function for drawing filled circles. To draw a filled circle use SVGA_fill_ellipse( ).

Covered in Chapter 10, page 304
Related functions: SVGA_arc( ), SVGA_ellipse( ), SVGA_fill_ellipse( )

SVGA_CurrentMode (Global Variable)

```
extern int  SVGA_CurrentMode;
```

SVGA_CurrentMode holds the current mode the screen is in. On startup its value is NOTINITIALED. Table C.1 lists the modes supported by SVGALib. Palette modes make use of palette registers; for direct modes, values for controlling the RGB color guns are placed directly in the frame buffer.

Table C.1

Type of Mode	Constant	Value	Meaning
Palette modes	CO8SVLORES	0x100	256 colors (8 bits), 640 × 400 res
	CO8SLORES	0x101	256 colors, 640 × 480 res
	CO4SMEDRES	0x102	16 colors, 800 × 600 res
	CO8SMEDRES	0x103	256 colors, 800 × 600 res
	CO4SHIRES	0x104	16 colors, 1024 × 768 res
	CO8SHIRES	0x105	256 colors, 1024 × 786 res
	CO4SVHIRES	0x106	16 colors, 1280 × 1024 res
	CO8SVHIRES	0x107	256 colors, 1280 × 1024 res
Direct Color	CO15SVELORES	0x10D	15 bit color, 320 × 200 res
	CO16SVELORES	0x10E	16 bit color, 320 × 200 res
	CO24SVELORES	0x10F	24 bit color, 320 × 200 res
	CO15SLORES	0x110	15 bit color, 640 × 480 res
	CO16SLORES	0x111	16 bit color, 640 × 480 res
	CO24SLORES	0x112	24 bit color, 640 × 480 res
	CO15SMEDRES	0x113	15 bit color, 800 × 600 res
	CO16SMEDRES	0x114	16 bit color, 800 × 600 res
	CO24SMEDRES	0x115	24 bit color, 800 × 600 res
	CO15SHIRES	0x116	15 bit color, 1024 × 786 res
	CO16SHIRES	0x117	16 bit color, 1024 × 786 res
	CO24SHIRES	0x118	24 bit color, 1024 × 786 res
	CO15SVHIRES	0x119	15 bit color, 1280 × 1024 res
	CO16SVHIRES	0x11A	16 bit color, 1280 × 1024 res
	CO24SVHIRES	0x11B	24 bit color, 1280 × 1024 res

Covered in Chapter 9, page 274
Related functions: SVGA_set_mode( ), SVGA_DirectCMode

SVGA_DirectCMode (Global Variable)

```
extern char SVGA_DirectCMode;
```

SVGA_DirectCMode contains TRUE (defined as 1) if the current mode is a direct color mode. If the current mode uses palette registers SVGA_DirectCMode contains FALSE (defined as 0).

Covered in Chapter 9, page 274
Related functions: SVGA_set_mode( ), SVGA_CurrentMode

SVGA_ellipse( )

```
void SVGA_ellipse(int X_Center, int Y_Center,
                  int r1,       int r2);
  /*
   * Draw an ellipse with radius along the X axis of
   *   of r1, and a radius along the Y axis of r2;
   *   centered at point (X_Center, Y_Center)
   *
   * Parameters:
   *   X_Center - center of ellipse on X axis
   *   Y_Center - center of ellipse on Y axis
   *   r1       - length of ellipse on X axis
   *   r2       - length of ellipse on Y axis
   */
```

SVGA_ellipse( ) will draw an ellispe on the screen at location (X_Center, Y_Center), with a length of r1 and a width of r2.

Covered in Chapter 10, page 309
Related functions: SVGA_circle( ), SVGA_arc( ), SVGA_line( )

SVGA_Err (Global Variable)

```
extern char SVGA_Err;
```

SVGA_Err contains the error value of the last function call to the SVGALib. Every function call in the SVGALib sets SVGA_Err, so to find an error make sure this variable is read immediately, or it will be reset. Table C.2 lists possible errors, plus the string returned by SVGA_return_err_msg( ).

Table C.2

Constant	Valu e	Message
VBESUPPORTED	1	"Unknown Error"
NOERROR	0	"No Error"
UNKNOWNERROR	-1	"Unknown Error"
NOTINITIALED	-2	"Graphics system not initialized, use function SVGA_supported( )"
VBENOTSUPPORTED	-3	"System does not support VESA VBE"
NOTDIRECTCMODE	-4	"Graphics system is not in a direct color mode"
DIRECTCMODE	-5	"Graphics system IS in a direct color mode"
MODENOTSUPPORTED	-6	"Mode currently not supported by video adapter"
ONLYONEWINDOW	-7	"Graphics system supports only one access window"
NOWINDOW	-8	"Graphics system supports NO monitor access window"
NOMODESET	-9	"No supported mode has been found"
PIXELOUTOFRANGE	-10	"Attempt to plot a pixel off the screen fails"
OUTOFMEMORY	-11	"Out of memory"

Covered in Chapter 9, page 274
Related functions: SVGA_return_err_msg( )

SVGA_fill_ellipse( )

```
char SVGA_fill_ellipse (int X_center,
                        int Y_center,
                        int r1, int r2);
  /*
   * Draw a filled ellipse on the screen
   *
   * Parameters:
   *   X_center - x coordinate of ellipse
   *              center
   *   Y_center - y coordinate of ellipse
   *              center
```

```
 *   r1        - x radius of ellipse
 *   r2        - y radius
 *
 * Returns
 *  NOERROR if successful, NOTINITIALED
 *  if graphics mode not set.
 */
```

SVGA_fill_ellipse( ) draws a filled ellipse on the screen, centered on screen coordinate (X_center, Y_center), with r1 as the x radius and r2 as the y radius. The ellipse does not need to be on the screen before this function is called. The current drawing color is used to fill.

Covered in Chapter 11, page 333
Related functions: SVGA_ellipse( ), SVGA_floodfill( ), SVGA_polyfill( ), SVGA_set_fill_pattern( )

SVGA_fill_rectangle( )

```
char SVGA_fill_rectangle (int X1, int Y1,
                          int X2, int Y2);
  /*
   * Draw a filled rectangle on the screen
   *
   * Parameters
   *  X1, Y1 - the upper left corner of
   *           the rectangle
   *  X2, Y2 - the lower right
   *
   * Returns
   *  NOERROR if successful, NOTINITIALED
   *  if graphics mode not set.
   */
```

SVGA_fill_rectangle( ) draws a filled rectangle on the screen with screen coordinate (X1, Y1) as the upper left corner and screen coordinate (X2, Y2) as the lower right. The rectangle does not need to be on the screen before this function is called. The current drawing color is used to fill.

Covered in Chapter 11, page 333
Related functions: SVGA_polyfill( ), SVGA_polygon( ), SVGA_set_fill_pattern( )

SVGA_floodfill( )

```
char SVGA_floodfill (int X, int Y);
  /*
   * Fill an object that is on the screen
   *
   * Parameters:
   *   X, Y - seed point of floodfill
   *
   * Returns
   *  NOERROR if successful, NOTINITIALED
   *  if graphics mode not set.
   *
   * Note:  This function uses a recursive
   * algorithm.  If stack space is used up
   * it may behave unpredictably.  To use
   * this function increase stack space to
   * its maximum and enable stack checking
   *
   * Note: This function DOES NOT support
   * pattern filling.
   */
```

SVGA_floodfill( ) implements the floodfill algorithm, with screen coordinate (X, Y) as the seed. This algorithm is useful for filling objects that are not ellipses or polygons. The object being filled must have a closed border of one single color. The seed value is any point inside that border. The algorithm will fill in all directions until a pixel of the border color is found. If the border is not closed or all the same color the algorithm will "leak out" and fill the entire screen. The version of floodfill included with this book does not implement pattern filling. It does use a recursive algorithm, so when using this consider increasing stack space to its maximum. Check your compiler manuals for instructions on how to do this. The floodfill algorithm is known for its inefficiency, so consider using another fill algorithm where possible. The current drawing color is used to fill.

SVGA_floodfill( ) needs to know what border color to look for. Two functions are provided, SVGA_set_border_color( ) for palette register modes and SVGA_set_dc_border_color( ) for direct color modes.

Covered in Chapter 11, page 335
Related functions: SVGA_fill_ellipse( ), SVGA_polyfill( ), SVGA_fill_rectangle( ), SVGA_set_border_color( ), SVGA_set_dc_border_color( ), SVGA_get_border_color( ), SVGA_get_dc_border_color( )

SVGA_get_border_color( )

```
char SVGA_get_border_color
                (unsigned char *P_Palette_Num);
  /*
   * Find the border color for
   *   SVGA_floodfill(), when using palette
   *   color modes.
   *
   * Parameters:
   *   P_Red   - Red content of border color
   *   P_Green - Green content of border color
   *   P_Blue  - Blue content of border color
   *
   * Returns:
   *  NOERROR if successful, NOTINITIALED
   *  if graphics mode not set, DIRECTCMODE
   *  if a direct color mode.
   */
```

SVGA_get_border_color( ) will pass back in P_Palette_Num the border color used by SVGA_floodfill( ), when using a palette mode. When not in a palette mode this function returns DIRECTCMODE.

Covered in Chapter 11, page 335
Related functions: SVGA_floodfill( ), SVGA_get_dc_border_color( ), SVGA_set_border_color( ), SVGA_set_dc_border_color( )

SVGA_get_dc_border_color( )

```
char SVGA_get_dc_border_color
                       (unsigned char *P_Red,
                        unsigned char *P_Green,
                        unsigned char *P_Blue);
  /*
   * Find the border color for
   *   SVGA_floodfill(), when using direct
   *   color modes.
   *
   * Parameters:
   *   P_Red   - Red content of border color
   *   P_Green - Green content of border color
   *   P_Blue  - Blue content of border color
   *
```

```
 * Returns:
 *  NOERROR if successful, NOTINITIALED
 *  if graphics mode not set, NOTDIRECTCMODE
 *  if not a direct color mode.
 */
```

SVGA_get_dc_border_color( ) will return the border color used by SVGA_floodfill( ), when using a direct color mode. When not in a direct color mode this function returns NOTDIRECTCMODE.

SVGA_get_dc_border_color( ) gets the RGB components of the current border color used by SVGA_floodfill( ). The SVGA_set_dc_border_color( ) function is set up to be as mode independent as possible. In other words it should use close to the same values whether using 15-, 16-, or 24-bit color modes. This is done by truncating the low-order bits of the RGB values when using 15- or 16-bit modes. This function will return the TRUNCATED values. So if a new color is set the values returned by this function might not match the values used to set the color, but they will match the values returned by SVGA_get_dc_pixel( ). These values are the ones needed by SVGA_floodfill( ) to find the border.

Covered in Chapter 11, page 335
Related functions: SVGA_floodfill( ), SVGA_get_border_color( ), SVGA_set_border_color( ), SVGA_set_dc_border_color( )

SVGA_get_color( )

```
char SVGA_get_color
              (unsigned char *P_Palette_Num);
  /*
   * Returns the palette number used for the
   * current drawing color.  For nondirect
   * modes only.
   *
   * Parameter
   *   *P_Palette_Num - pointer to unsigned
   *     character.  Passes back the palette
   *     number of the current color
   *
   * Returns
   *   NOERROR if successful, NOTINITIALED if
   *   not mode is set, DIRECTCMODE if the
   *   current mode is a direct color mode.
   */
```

SVGA_get_color( ) returns the palette register number being used as the current drawing color.

Covered in Chapter 9, page 278; and Chapter 11, page 335
Related functions: SVGA_set_color( ), SVGA_get_dc_color( ), SVGA_set_dc_color( ), SVGA_get_pixel( ), SVGA_get_dc_pixel( ), SVGA_get_palette( )

SVGA_get_dc_color( )

```
char SVGA_get_dc_color (unsigned char *P_Red,
                        unsigned char *P_Green,
                        unsigned char *P_Blue);
  /*
   * Passes back the RGB values of
   * the current drawing color.  For direct
   * color modes only.
   *
   * Parameters
   *   *P_Red
   *   *P_Green
   *   *P_Blue  - pointers to unsigned
   *     characters that will hold the RGB
   *     values
   *
   * Returns
   *   NOERROR if no error, NOTINITIALED if
   *   mode is not set, NOTDIRECTCMODE if the
   *   current mode is not a direct color mode.
   */
```

SVGA_get_dc_color( ) gets the RGB components of the current drawing color. The SVGA_set_dc_color( ) function is set up to be as mode independent as possible. In other words it should use close to the same values whether using 15-, 16-, or 24-bit color modes. This is done by truncating the low order bits of the RGB values when using 15- or 16-bit modes. This function will return the TRUNCATED values. So if a new color is set the values returned by this function might not match the values used to set the color, but they will match the values returned by SVGA_get_dc_pixel( ).

Covered in Chapter 9, page 278; and Chapter 11, page 335
Related functions: SVGA_set_color( ), SVGA_get_color( ), SVGA_set_dc_color( ), SVGA_get_pixel( ), SVGA_get_dc_pixel( ), SVGA_get_dc_border_color( )

SVGA_get_palette( )

```
char SVGA_get_palette (int P_Palette_Num,
                       unsigned char *P_Red,
                       unsigned char *P_Green,
                       unsigned char *P_Blue);
  /*
   * Get RGB settings for a palette register
   *
   * Parameters:
   *   P_Palette_Num - Number of palette
   *   *P_Red
   *   *P_Green
   *   *P_Blue  - pointers to unsigned
   *     characters that will hold the RGB
   *     values
   *
   * Returns
   *   NOERROR if no error, NOTINITIALED if
   *   mode is not set, DIRECTCMODE if the
   *   current mode is a direct color mode.
   */
```

SVGA_get_palette( ) will get the RGB components of a palette register.

Covered in Chapter 9, page 279
Related functions: SVGA_set_color( ), SVGA_get_color( ), SVGA_get_pixel( ), SVGA_set_palette( )

SVGA_get_pixel( )

```
char SVGA_get_pixel (int X, int Y,
                     unsigned char *P_Palette);
  /*
   * Get the RGB components used to color
   *   the pixel at coordinate (X, Y), when
   *   using palette color modes
   *
   * Parameters:
   *   X, Y      - the screen coordinate of
   *               the pixel
   *   P_Palette - the palette number of
   *               that pixel
   *
   * Returns:
   *  NOERROR if successful, NOTINITIALED
```

```
 *  if graphics mode not set, DIRECTCMODE
 *  if a direct color mode.
 */
```

SVGA_get_pixel( ) gets the palette register number used to color the given pixel, when using palette register modes.

Covered in Chapter 11, page 339
Related functions: SVGA_set_color( ), SVGA_get_color( ), SVGA_get_dc_pixel( ), SVGA_get_palette( ), SVGA_set_palette( )

SVGA_get_dc_pixel( )

```
char SVGA_get_dc_pixel (int X, int Y,
                        unsigned char *P_Red,
                        unsigned char *P_Green,
                        unsigned char *P_Blue);
  /*
   * Get the palette number used to color
   *   the pixel at coordinate (X, Y), when
   *   using direct color modes
   *
   * Parameters:
   *   X, Y      - the screen coordinate of
   *               the pixel
   *   P_Red   - Red content of pixel color
   *   P_Green - Green content of pixel color
   *   P_Blue  - Blue content of pixel color
   *
   * Returns:
   *  NOERROR if successful, NOTINITIALED
   *  if graphics mode not set, NOTDIRECTCMODE
   *  if not a direct color mode.
   */
```

SVGA_get_dc_pixel( ) gets the RGB components of the pixel at (x,y). The RGB values are normalized so that they will be as close as possible for the same color independent of the mode. See SVGA_get_current_dc_color( ) for details. See also the explanation of this function in Chapter 11.

Covered in Chapter 11, page 342
Related functions: SVGA_set_color( ), SVGA_get_color( ), SVGA_get_dc_pixel( ), SVGA_get_palette( ), SVGA_set_palette( )

SVGA_line( )

```
void SVGA_line (int X1, int Y1,
                int X2, int Y2);
  /*
   * Draws a line from point (X1,Y1) to
   *   point (X2,Y2)
   */
```

SVGA_line( ) draws a patterned line from screen coordinate (X1, Y1) to screen coordinate (X2, Y2). The default pattern is solid; the color used is the current color. Use SVGA_line_pattern( ) to set the line pattern to something other than a solid line.

Covered in Chapter 10, page 292
Related functions: SVGA_line_pattern( ), SVGA_line_to_abs( ), SVGA_line_to_rel( ), SVGA_set_loc_abs( ), SVGA_set_loc_rel( )

SVGA_line_to_abs( )

```
void SVGA_line_to_abs (int X, int Y);
  /*
   * Draw line from current location to point
   *   (X,Y) make point (X,Y) new current
   *   location
   */
```

SVGA_line_to_abs( ) draws a patterned line from the current point to the screen coordinate specified by (X, Y). The default pattern is solid; the color used is the current color.

Covered in Chapter 10, page 304
Related functions: SVGA_line_pattern( ), SVGA_line_to_rel( ), SVGA_set_loc_abs( ), SVGA_set_loc_rel( )

SVGA_line_to_rel( )

```
void SVGA_line_to_rel (int X, int Y);
  /*
   * draw line from current location to point
   *   X pixels and Y pixels from the the
   *   current location.  Make the location the
   *   new current location.
   */
```

SVGA_line_to_rel( ) draws a patterned line starting at the current point. X is added to the current X position and Y is added to the current Y position to find the end point. The default pattern is solid; the color used is the current color.

Covered in Chapter 10, page 304
Related functions: SVGA_line_pattern( ), SVGA_line_to_abs( ), SVGA_set_loc_abs( ), SVGA_set_loc_rel( )

SVGA_line_pattern( )

```
void SVGA_line_pattern (unsigned int P_Bit_Mask);
  /*
   * set the bit mask used by line drawing functions for the
   *   line pattern
   */
```

SVGA_line_pattern( ) is used to set a bit mask used by the line drawing functions to determine the pattern to draw a line. For each bit set in the bit mask, a pixel is plotted on the line. When the pixel on the line corresponds to a cleared bit, the pixel is left as it is.

Covered in Chapter 10, page 303
Related functions: SVGA_line( ), SVGA_line_to( ), SVGA_line_to_abs( )

SVGA_MaxX, SVGA_MaxY (Global Variables)

```
extern int MaxX;
extern int MaxY;
```

SVGA_MaxX and SVGA_MaxY hold the maximum X and Y coordinates for pixels in the current mode.

Covered in Chapter 9, page 274
Related functions: SVGA_plot_pixel( )

SVGA_plot_pixel( )

```
char SVGA_plot_pixel (int X, int Y);
  /*
   * sets a pixel to the current drawing
   * color.
   *
   * Parameters
   *   The coordinate of the pixel to set
   *
   * RETURNS
   *  NOERROR if successful, NOTINITIALED
   *  if graphics mode not set.
   */
```

SVGA_plot_pixel( ) sets the pixel at screen coordinate (X, Y) to the current drawing color. If the (X, Y) coordinate is off the screen the pixel is not plotted. This check means that there is a time penalty, but it is safer since RAM will not be overwritten. This one function is used for both direct color and palette register modes. No color is passed to this function, since that would require RGB values for direct modes but a single number for palette modes. To simplify the graphics interface the current color is set using either SVGA_set_color( ) or SVGA_set_dc_color( ), then SVGA_Plot_pixel( ) determines the mode and which current color to use – the direct mode color or the palette mode color.

Covered in Chapter 9, page 279
Related functions: SVGA_MaxX, SVGA_MaxY, SVGA_set_color( ), SVGA_set_dc_color( ), SVGA_get_color( ), SVGA_get_dc_color( )

SVGA_polyfill( )

```
char SVGA_polyfill (int P_Num_Pts,
                    int *P_Pt_Array);
  /*
   * Draw a filled polygon on the screen
   *
   * Parameters:
   *   P_Num_Pts - the number of vertices
   *               in the polygon
   *   P_Pt_Array - array of vertices
   *
   * Returns:
   *  NOERROR if successful, NOTINITIALED
```

```
 *  if graphics mode not set, OUTOFMEMORY
 *  if there is not enough heap space to
 *  finish execution of function.
 */
```

SVGA_polyfill( ) draws a filled polygon on the screen. The polygon does not have to be on the screen before this function is called. P_Num_Pts gives the number of points in the polygon. The coordinates of the vertices are given by an array of integers, with the x coordinates indexed by the even indices of the array and the y coordinates by the odd.

Covered in Chapter 11, page 347
Related functions: SVGA_polygon( ), SVGA_fill_ellipse, SVGA_floodfill( ), SVGA_set_color( ), SVGA_set_dc_color( ), SVGA_set_fill_pattern( )

SVGA_polygon( )

```
void SVGA_polygon (int P_Num_Pts,
                   int *P_Pt_Array);
  /*
   * Draw a polygon on the screen
   *
   * Parameters:
   *   P_Num_Pts - Number of corner points in
   *     the polygon
   *   P_Pt_Array - Array of corner points
   */
```

SVGA_polygon( ) draws a polygon on the screen. P_Num_Pts gives the number of points in the polygon. The coordinates of the vertices are given by an array of integers, with the x coordinates indexed by the even indices of the array and the y coordinates by the odd.

Covered in Chapter 10, page 303
Related functions: SVGA_polyfill( ), SVGA_rectangle( )

SVGA_return_err_msg( )

```
char *SVGA_return_err_msg(void);
  /*
   * Returns a string explaining the last
   * error raised
   */
```

SVGA_return_err_msg( ) returns a string with a message explaining the last error. The string contains a new line character at the end. The strings for each error are listed in Table C.3.

Table C.3

Constant	Value	Message
VBESUPPORTED	1	"Unknown Error"
NOERROR	0	"No Error"
UNKNOWNERROR	-1	"Unknown Error"
NOTINITIALED	-2	"Graphics system not initialized, use function SVGA_supported( )"
VBENOTSUPPORTED	-3	"System does not support VESA VBE"
NOTDIRECTCMODE	-4	"Graphics system is not in a direct color mode"
DIRECTCMODE	-5	"Graphics system IS in a direct color mode"
MODENOTSUPPORTED	-6	"Mode currently not supported by video adapter"
ONLYONEWINDOW	-7	"Graphics system supports only one access window"
NOWINDOW	-8	"Graphics system supports NO monitor access window"
NOMODESET	-9	"No supported mode has been found"
PIXELOUTOFRANGE	-10	"Attempt to plot a pixel off the screen fails"
OUTOFMEMORY	-11	"Out of memory"

Covered in Chapter 9, page 280
Related functions: SVGA_Err

SVGA_set_border_color( )

```
char SVGA_set_border_color
                    (unsigned char palettenum);
  /*
   * Set the border color for SVGA_floodfill(),
   *   when using palette color modes.
   *
```

```
 * Parameters:
 *   palettenum - the palette number of the
 *                border color
 *
 * Returns:
 *  NOERROR if successful, NOTINITIALED
 *  if graphics mode not set, DIRECTCMODE
 *  if a direct color mode.
 */
```

SVGA_set_border_color( ) is used to set the border color for SVGA_floodfill( ) when using palette color modes.

Covered in Chapter 11, page 336
Related functions: SVGA_set_dc_border_color( ), SGVA_floodfill( ), SVGA_DirectCMode

SVGA_set_dc_border_color( )

```
char SVGA_set_dc_border_color
                       (unsigned char P_Red,
                        unsigned char P_Green,
                        unsigned char P_Blue);
  /*
   * Set the border color for SVGA_floodfill(),
   *   when using direct color modes.
   *
   * Parameters:
   *   P_Red   - Red content of border color
   *   P_Green - Green content of border color
   *   P_Blue  - Blue content of border color
   *
   * Returns:
   *  NOERROR if successful, NOTINITIALED
   *  if graphics mode not set, NOTDIRECTCMODE
   *  if not a direct color mode.
   */
```

SVGA_set_border_dc_color( ) is used to set the border color that SVGA_floodfill( ) will look for when using direct color modes. The SVGA_set_dc_color( ) function is set up to be as mode independent as possible. In other words the RGB values should be close to the same whether using 15-, 16-, or 24-bit color modes. This is done by truncating the low-order bits of the RGB values when using 15- or 16-bit modes. This function will return the TRUNCATED values. So if a new color is set the values returned by this function might not match the values used to set the color, but they will match the values returned by SVGA_get_dc_border_color( ), which SVGA_floodfill( ) uses to find the border.

Covered in Chapter 11, page 337
Related functions: SVGA_set_border_color( ), SGVA_floodfill( ), SVGA_DirectCMode

SVGA_set_color( )

```
char SVGA_set_color (unsigned char palettenum);
  /*
   * set the current drawing color to
   * a palette.
   *
   * Parameter
   *   The palette number of the current
   *   drawing color
   *
   * Returns
   *   NOERROR if successful, NOTINITIALED if
   *   not mode is set, DIRECTCMODE if the
   *   current mode is a direct color mode.
   */
```

SVGA_set_color( ) is used to set the number of the palette that holds the RGB values of the current drawing color, when using palette color modes.

Covered in Chapter 9, page 277; and Chapter 11, page 335
Related functions: SVGA_set_dc_color( ), SVGA_get_color( ), SVGA_plot_pixel( )

SVGA_set_dc_color( )

```
char SVGA_set_dc_color (unsigned char red,
                        unsigned char green,
                        unsigned char blue);
  /*
   * Set the color for direct color SVGA
   * routines.  This allows the user to be
   * unconcerned what order the color mask
   * uses (RGB, RBG, GRB, GBR, BGR, BRG), or
   * how many bits per pixel.
   *
   * Parameters:
   *   The RGB values for the current color.For
```

```
     *   15 and 16 bit modes the MOST significant
     *   bits are used.  This means that for a 16
     *   bit mode color 1:1:1 looks the same as
     *   color 2:2:2, but color 32:32:32 looks as
     *   one would expect.  If the least
     *   significant bits were used color 31:31:31
     *   would be bright white, and color
     *   32:32:32 would have no signicant bits
     *   set, so this would appear BLACK.
     *
     * Returns:
     *   NOERROR if no error, NOTINITIALED if
     *   mode is not set, NOTDIRECTCMODE if the
     *   current mode is not a direct color mode.
     */
```

SVGA_set_dc_color( ) is used to set the RGB values of the current drawing color, when using direct color modes. This function is set up to be as mode independent as possible. In other words the RGB values should be close to the same whether using 15-, 16-, or 24-bit color modes. This is done by truncating the low-order bits of the RGB values when using 15- or 16-bit modes.

Covered in Chapter 9, page 276; and Chapter 11, page 335
Related functions: SVGA_set_color( ), SVGA_get_dc_color( ), SVGA_plot_pixel( )

SVGA_set_fill_pattern( )

```
  void SVGA_set_fill_pattern
              (unsigned char P_FillPattern[8]);
    /*
     * Set the current fill pattern
     *
     * Parameters:
     *   P_FillPattern - Array of 8 bytes used as
     *     bitmask.  If a bit in P_FillPattern is
     *     set the corresponding pixel is set,
     *     otherwise it is not touched
     */
```

SVGA_set_fill_pattern( ) will set a user-defined pattern to be used by filling routines. The pattern is in an array of eight bytes, which is viewed as a two dimensional array of bits. When a bit in the pattern is set, the corresponding pixel on the screen is set to the current filling color, as set by calling setfillstyle( ). When a bit is cleared the corresponding pixel on the screen is set to the background color. The function SVGA_floodfill( ) does not support pattern filling, but all other fill routines do.

Covered in Chapter 11, page 330
Related functions: SVGA_polyfill( ), SVGA_fill_ellipse( )

SVGA_set_loc_abs( )

```
void SVGA_set_loc_abs (int X, int Y);
  /*
   * Set current drawing location in absolute
   * screen coordinates
   */
```

SVGA_set_loc_abs( ) sets the current position in absolute screen coordinates. This point is used by SVGA_line_to_abs( ) and SVGA_line_to_rel( ) as the starting point of the line they will draw.

Covered in Chapter 10, page 304
Related functions: SVGA_line_to_abs( ), SVGA_line_to_rel( ), SVGA_set_loc_rel( )

SVGA_set_loc_rel( )

```
void SVGA_set_loc_rel (int X, int Y);
  /*
   * Set new drawing location relative to
   *   current drawing location
   */
```

SVGA_set_loc_rel( ) moves the current position relative to its current location. This point is used by SVGA_line_to_abs( ) and SVGA_line_to_rel( ) as the starting point of the line they will draw.

Covered in Chapter 10, page 304
Related functions: SVGA_line_to_abs( ), SVGA_line_to_rel( ),
SVGA_set_loc_abs( )

SVGA_set_mode( )

```
char SVGA_set_mode (int mode);
  /*
   * Set the mode to one listed above.
   *
   * Parameter:
   *   mode - Mode to set the monitor to.  Use
   *     the modes #defined above.  If
   *     HIRESMODES is used the mode the
   *     highest resolution is set, if
   *     HICOLORMODE is used the mode with
   *     the most number of colors is used.
   *
   * Returns:
   *   The number of the mode set if no error,
   *   otherwise NOTINITIALED, if
   *   SVGA_supported
   *   has not been called, VBENOTSUPPORTED if
   *   the system has a monitor that does not
   *   support the VESA VBE, or
   *   MODENOTSUPPORTED
   *   if a mode has been listed that is not
   *   currently available.
   *
   *   If the return value is positive then no
   *   error occurred.
   */
```

SVGA_set_mode( ) is used to set the monitor to a graphics mode or set it back to text mode. A specific mode can be selected or the function can be told to use the highest resolution mode available, or the mode with the most colors. Constants have been defined for each graphics mode that the SVGALib supports, for text mode, and for finding the highest color and highest resolution modes. These constants are given in Table C.4. **Before this function is called a call must be made to SVGA_supported( )** to determine if the VESA VBE is supported by the monitor and what modes are supported by the monitor.

Table C.4

Type of Mode	Constant	Value	Meaning
Depends on Monitor	HIRESMODE	-0x100	Find the highest resolution
	HICOLORMODE	-0x101	Find the highest number of colors
Text	TEXT	-0x103	Return to text mode
Palette Modes	CO8SVLORES	0x100	256 colors (8 bits), 640 × 400 res
	CO8SLORES	0x101	256 colors, 640 × 480 res
	CO4SMEDRES	0x102	16 colors, 800 × 600 res
	CO8SMEDRES	0x103	256 colors, 800 × 600 res
	CO4SHIRES	0x104	16 colors, 1024 × 768 res
	CO8SHIRES	0x105	256 colors, 1024 × 786 res
	CO4SVHIRES	0x106	16 colors, 1280 × 1024 res
	CO8SVHIRES	0x107	256 colors, 1280 × 1024 res
Direct Color	CO15SVELORES	0x10D	15 bit color, 320 × 200 res
	CO16SVELORES	0x10E	16 bit color, 320 × 200 res
	CO24SVELORES	0x10F	24 bit color, 320 × 200 res
	CO15SLORES	0x110	15 bit color, 640 × 480 res
	CO16SLORES	0x111	16 bit color, 640 × 480 res
	CO24SLORES	0x112	24 bit color, 640 × 480 res
	CO15SMEDRES	0x113	15 bit color, 800 × 600 res
	CO16SMEDRES	0x114	16 bit color, 800 × 600 res
	CO24SMEDRES	0x115	24 bit color, 800 × 600 res
	CO15SHIRES	0x116	15 bit color, 1024 × 786 res
	CO16SHIRES	0x117	16 bit color, 1024 × 786 res
	CO24SHIRES	0x118	24 bit color, 1024 × 786 res
	CO15SVHIRES	0x119	15 bit color, 1280 × 1024 res
	CO16SVHIRES	0x11A	16 bit color, 1280 × 1024 res
	CO24SVHIRES	0x11B	24 bit color, 1280 × 1024 res

Covered in Chapter 9, page 275
Related functions: SVGA_supported( ), SVGA_err

SVGA_set_palette( )

```
char SVGA_set_palette (int palettenum,
                       unsigned char red,
                       unsigned char green,
                       unsigned char blue);
  /*
   * Set a palette to represent a certain color
   *
   * Parameters:
   *   palettenum - The number of the palette
   *     to set
   *   red, green, blue - the amount of each
   *     color to set.
   */
```

SVGA_set_palette( ) sets a palette register to hold a certain RGB content, when using palette register modes.

Covered in Chapter 9, page 277
Related functions: SVGA_set_color( ), SVGA_set_dc_color( )

SVGA_supported( )

```
char SVGA_supported ();
  /*
   * Detects if VESA VBE is supported, and
   * fills in important data structures if
   * it is.  Returns VBESUPPORTED if VESA
   * VBE is supported, or VBENOTSUPPORTED
   * otherwise.
   *
   * The routines in this library make use
   * of VBE defined BIOS services.  If they
   * are not supported these routines will
   * not work.
   *
   * ALWAYS CALL THIS ROUTINE BEFORE ANY
   *   OTHERS IN THIS PACKAGE ARE CALLED!
   */
```

SVGA_supported( ) is used to determine if the video adapter supports the VESA Video Bios Extension. SVGALib uses the VESA VBE exclusively and will not work if it is not supported.

SVGA_supported( ) also fills in important data structures without which other routines will not be able to work. For this reason it is important to **always call this routine before any other calls are made to SVGALib.**

Covered in Chapter 9, page 274
Related functions: SVGA_set_mode( ), SVGA_err

Appendix D
Interrupt 0x10, BIOS Graphics Interface

BIOS interrupt 0x10 provides many I/O functions, not just graphics. In spite of what this appendix is called, interrupt 0x10 provides functions for controlling the monitor in text and graphics modes. An attempt is made to cover as many functions here as possible, but there are quite a few. Some newer functions that are only supported by newer adapter cards might have been missed, as well as lesser used functions. The SVGA programming functions have been separated into their own appendix, E. Mouse functions use interrupt 0x33, which is also covered in its own appendix, G.

BIOS interrupt 0x10 covers many functions. The contents of this appendix are provided to aid in finding the correct function.

Interrupt 0x10, BIOS Graphics Interface

Function 0x00 – Set Video Mode

This function is used to set text modes as well as CGA, EGA, MCGA, and VGA modes. For setting SVGA modes use function 0x4F, which is covered in Appendix E. Modes supported by this function are given in Table D.1.

Table D.1 Monitor Modes Supported by Interrupt 0x10

Mode	Minimum Adapter	Text/ Graphics	Pixels/ Characters	Colors	Pages
0	CGA	Text	40 × 25	16 fore/ 8 back	
1	CGA	Text	40 × 25	16 fore/ 8 back	
2	CGA	Text	80 × 25	16 fore/ 8 back	
3	CGA	Text	80 × 25	16 fore/ 8 back	
4	CGA	Graphics	320 × 200	4 (CGA palette)	1
5	CGA	Graphics	320 × 200	4 (CGA palette)	1
6	CGA	Graphics	640 × 200	2	1
7	EGA	Text	80 × 25	4 (CGA palette)	
13	EGA	Graphics	320 × 200	16 out of 64 16/256K (VGA)	1
14	EGA	Graphics	640 × 200	16 out of 64 16/256K (VGA)	4
15	EGA	Graphics	640 × 350	4	1
16	EGA	Graphics	640 × 350	16 out of 64 16/256K (VGA)	2
17	VGA	Graphics	640 × 480	16 out of 256K	1
18	VGA	Graphics	640 × 480	16 out of 256K	1
19	VGA	Graphics	320 × 200	256 out of 256K	1

Input Register Values

Register	Value
AH	0x00
AL	Mode Number

Output Register Values

Register	Value
none	

Function 0x01 – Set Cursor Size (Text Modes)

This function is used to set the size of the text mode cursor. The cursor can use any number of lines, up to the full height of a character. Monochrome, EGA and VGA adapters use 14 lines per character, CGA uses 8. Lines are numbered from top to bottom starting at 0. The starting line and ending line of the cursor are designated. If the starting line is greater than the ending line the cursor will start toward the top of the character, then wrap around to the bottom, creating a two part cursor. If the start and end of the cursor are set to -1 the cursor will be turned off. This is not the recommended method for turning the cursor off; instead use function 0x02. For VGA monitors a graphics cursor can be used by calling service 0x12, subservice 0x34.

Input Register Values

Register	Value
AH	0x01
CH	Start line of cursor
CL	Ending line of cursor

Output Register Values

Register	Value
none	

Function 0x02 – Set Cursor Position

This function sets the cursor position using screen coordinates. Screen coordinates start with (0,0) as the upper left corner. The cursor can be set to a location that is off the screen, which is a good way to turn the cursor off. When this function is called register BH holds the video page number. See Chapter 12 for a description of video pages.

Input Register Values

Register	Value
AH	0x02
BH	Video page number
DH	Row (Y coordinate)
DL	Column (X coordinate)

Output Register Values

Register	Value
none	

Function 0x03 – Get Cursor Position and Size

Find the current cursor position and size.

Input Register Values

Register	Value
AL	0x03
BH	Video page number

Output Register Values

Register	Value
CH	Cursor starting line
CL	Cursor ending line
DL	Row (Y coordinate)
DH	Column (X coordinate)

Function 0x04 – Read Light Pen Position

This function is used to find the position of a light pen. Not supported by VGA monitors.

Input Register Values

Register	Value
AH	0x04

Output Register Values

Register	Value
AH	0 if not triggered; 1 if triggered
BX	Pixel column number (X coordinate)
CX	Pixel line number (Y coordinate)
DH	Character row (Y coordinate)
DL	Character column (X coordinate)

Function 0x05 – Set Active Video Page

This function sets the number of the active display page. Most modes support multiple pages. The visual page is the one displayed on the monitor; the active page is the one that graphics functions will write to. If the active page and visual page are not the same, new graphics will not show on the screen. This allows for a complete graphics screen being set up in the background then rapidly being displayed. This is useful for animation. Most video output functions take a parameter indicating what page output should go to.

Input Register Values

Register	Value
AH	0x05
AL	Active Page Number

Output Register Values

Register	Value
none	

Function 0x06 – Create a Window or Scroll Window Up

This function can be used to define a window, scroll a window up a given number of lines, or clear the window. The entire screen can be cleared by setting the window size to be the entire screen.

Input Register Values

Register	Value
AH	0x06
AL	Number of lines to scroll - 0 to clear the window
BH	Attribute of new lines
CH	Top row of window (Y coordinate)
CL	Left side of window (X coordinate)
DH	Bottom of window (Y coordinate)
DL	Right side of window (X coordinate)

Output Register Values

Register	Value
none	

Function 0x07 – Create a Window or Scroll Window Down

This function can be used to define a window, scroll a window down a given number of lines, or clear the window. The entire screen can be cleared by setting the window to be the size of the entire screen.

Input Register Values

Register	Value
AH	0x07
AL	Number of lines to scroll - 0 to clear the window
BH	Attribute of new lines
CH	Top row of window (Y coordinate)
CL	Left side of window (X coordinate)
DH	Bottom of window (Y coordinate)
DL	Right side of window (X coordinate)

Output Register Values

Register	Value
none	

Function 0x08 – Read Character and Attribute at Cursor

The frame buffer in text mode contains 2 bytes for each character on the screen. The first holds the attribute, or foreground and background color of the character, the second holds the extended ASCII code of the character. Figure D.1 shows how the attribute byte is set up. This function will return the attribute and character at the current cursor position.

Background				Foreground			
Intensity	Red	Green	Blue	Bright	Red	Green	Blue

Fig. D.1

Input Register Values

Register	Value
AH	0x08
BH	Active page

Output Register Values

Register	Value
AH	Attribute
AL	Extended ASCII code of character

Function 0x09 – Write Character and Attribute at Cursor

The frame buffer in text mode contains 2 bytes for each character on the screen. The first holds the attribute, or foreground and background color of the character, the second holds the extended ASCII code of the character. Figure D.2 shows how the attribute byte is set up. This function will write the attribute and character at the current cursor position. The character will be repeated the number of times that CX is set to. If this is set to 0 the character will not appear.

Background				Foreground			
Intensity	Red	Green	Blue	Bright	Red	Green	Blue

Fig. D.2

Input Register Values

Register	Value
AH	0x09
AL	Extended ASCII code of character
BH	Active display page
BL	Attribute
CX	Number of times to repeat character

Output Register Values

Register	Value
none	

Function 0x0A – Write Character at Cursor

Similar to function 0x09, except that it does take an attribute in text mode.

Input Register Values

Register	Bit #	Value
AH		0x0A
AL		Extended ASCII code of character
BL	0	Blue on (graphics modes only)
	1	Green on (graphics modes only)
	2	Red on (graphics modes only)
BH		Active page (not used in graphics modes)
CX		Number of times to repeat character.

Output Register Values

Register	Value
none	

Function 0x0B – Set CGA Color Palette

This function is used to set the special palettes used by CGA modes. See Chapter 6 for details on CGA color palettes.

Input Register Values

Register	When BH is	Value
AH		0x0B
BH		0 - Set border in text modes or set background in graphics CGA 4 color modes 1 - Set palette
BL	0	Border color in text modes Background color in graphics CGA 4 color modes
	1	Palette number (0 or 1)

Output Register Values

Register	Value
none	

Function 0x0C – Plot a Pixel

Plot a pixel on the screen. This function is valid for CGA, EGA, and VGA monitors, but it is slow. Writing directly to the frame buffer is the preferred method. The number of colors and pixels depends on the graphics mode. See Appendix F for this information. If bit 7 of AL is set, the new pixel will be XORed with the screen contents, otherwise the new pixel will replace the old.

Input Register Values

Register	Value
AH	0x0C
AL	Pixel color
BH	Display page
CX	Column (X coordinate)
DX	Row (Y coordinate)

Output Register Values

Register	Value
none	

Function 0x0D – Read Pixel from Screen

This function reads the color of the pixel at a given screen coordinate. This function is valid for CGA, EGA, and VGA monitors, but it is slow. Reading directly from the frame buffer is preferred. The number of colors and pixels depends on the graphics mode. See Appendix F for this information.

Input Register Values

Register	Value
AH	0x0D
BH	Display page
CX	Column (X coordinate)
DX	Row (Y coordinate)

Output Register Values

Register	Value
AL	Pixel color

Function 0x0E – Write Character at Cursor Position with No Processing (Raw Mode)

The function writes a character to the screen at the current cursor position without processing. The bell, backspace, carriage return, and linefeed are recognized and processed; all other characters are written directly to the screen. Note that when a carriage return is written the cursor will go to the beginning of the line, but the line will not be incremented. When a linefeed is written the cursor will go to the next line, but will not be returned to the beginning of the line.

Input Register Values

Register	Value
AH	0x0E
AL	ASCII code of character to be written
BH	Active display page (text modes only)
BL	Foreground color (graphics modes only)

Output Register Values

Register	Value
none	

Function 0x0F – Get Current Video Mode

This function gets the current video mode, plus the number of characters per line. See function 0x00 (set mode) for a listing of supported modes.

Input Register Values

Register	Value
AH	0x0F

Output Register Values

Register	Value
AL	Current display mode
AH	Number of characters per line
BH	The active display page

Function 0x10 - EGA/VGA Graphics Services
Subservice 0x00 – Set EGA Palette Register

This function is used to set a single EGA/VGA palette register. For 16-color modes only. This function does not set the values in the register directly; it copies the value from another register. The register to copy the value from is passed in the register.

Input Register Values

Register	Value
AH	0x10
AL	0x00
BH	Color (0 - 15)
BL	Palette nmber

Output Register Values

Register	Value
none	

Function 0x10
Subservice 0x01 – Set EGA/VGA Overscan Border Color

This function sets the overscan border register on EGA/VGA monitors to display a certain color.

Input Register Values

Register	Value
AH	0x10
AL	0x01
BH	Color

Output Register Values

Register	Value
none	

Function 0x10
Subservice 0x02 – Set All EGA Palette Registers

This function copies 17 bytes to the EGA palette registers and the overscan register, allowing a program to change all registers with one command. It is suggested that the 17-byte buffer be set up with a call to function 0x10 subservice 0x17 to read the registers, then edit the buffer to give the colors desired.

Input Register Values

Register	Value
AH	0x10
AL	0x02
DS	Offset of 17-byte buffer of register values
ES	Segment of 17-byte buffer of register values

Output Register Values

Register	Value
none	

Function 0x10
Subservice 0x03 – Toggle EGA Blinking/Intensity
(VGA/EGA only)

This function toggles the blinking bit or the intensity bit, for VGA/EGA monitors only.

Input Register Values

Register	Value
AH	0x10
AL	0x03
BL	0 - Toggle intensity
	1 - Toggle blink

Output Register Values

Register	Value
none	

Function 0x10
Subservice 0x07 – Read Individual Palette Register
(VGA minimum)

Read a single palette register.

Input Register Values

Register	Value
AH	0x10
AL	0x07
BL	Register number

Output Register Values

Register	Value
BH	Palette register value

Function 0x10
Subservice 0x08 – Read Overscan Register
(VGA minimum)

Read the color of the overscan border.

Input Register Values

Register	Value
AH	0x10
AL	0x08

Output Register Values

Register	Value
BH	Overscan register value

Function 0x10
Subservice 0x09 – Read All Palette Registers
(VGA minimum)

Read RGB values for all palette registers. ES:DX points to a table in RAM. This table should be defined as:

```
unsigned char palette[256][3];
```

This defines RGB values for each of 256 palettes. The first index gives the palette number, the second gives the RGB values, so that

```
palette[82][0];
```

is the red value of the eighty-second palette register.

Input Register Values

Register	Value
AH	0x10
AL	0x09
DX	Offset of buffer to hold 256 RGB colors
ES	Segment of buffer

Output Register Values

Register	Value
ES:DX	RGB values are returned in buffer

Function 0x10
Subservice 0x10 – Set Individual VGA Palette Register
(VGA minimum)

Set one single VGA palette register to the given RGB values. Only the lower 6 bits of each value are used.

Input Register Values

Register	Value
AH	0x10
AL	0x10
BX	Palette register number
CH	Green value
CL	Blue value
DH	Red value

Output Register Values

Register	Value
none	

Function 0x10
Subservice 0x12 – Set Block of VGA Registers
(VGA minimum)

Set a block of palette registers to user-defined RGB values. The ES:DX register combination points to a buffer containing the RGB values to be set. This buffer should be defined as:

```
unsigned char palette[N][3];
```

where N is the number of palette registers to be set. The first index gives the palette number, the second gives the RGB values so that

```
palette[24][0]
```

gives the red value for the 24th palette register. This function is not timed to the screen retrace, and so can cause a slight flicker on the monitor.

Input Register Values

Register	Value
AH	0x10
AL	0x12
BX	Number of first color register to set
CX	Number of registers to set
DS	Offset of buffer holding register values
ES	Segmenet of buffer holding register values

Output Register Values

Register	Value
none	

Function 0x10
Subservice 0x15 – Read Individual Color Register
(VGA minimum)

Read the RGB values of an individual color register.

Input Register Values

Register	Value
AH	0x10
AL	0x15
BX	Number of palette register

Output Register Values

Register	Value
CH	Green value
CL	Blue value
DH	Red value

Function 0x10
Subservice 0x17 – Read Block of Color Registers
(VGA minimum)

Read a block of color registers. ES:DX points to a table in RAM. This table should be defined as:

```
unsigned char palette[X][3];
```

where X is the number of palette registers that will be read. The first index gives the palette number, the second gives the RGB values, so that

```
palette[82][0];
```

is the red value of the eighty-second palette register.

Input Register Values

Register	Value
AH	0x10
AL	0x17
BX	Number of first palette register
CX	Number of palette registers to read
DX	Offset of buffer of RGB values
ES	Segment of buffer of RGB values

Output Register Values

Register	Value
ES:DX	RGB values are returned in buffer pointed to by ES:DX

Function 0x10
Subservice 0x1B – Sum Color Values to Gray Scale
(VGA minimum)

Translate RGB values in palette registers to gray scale. Useful for graphics software that might run on laptop computers. This function takes the RGB values in the register, takes a weighted sum of the values, and places the result in each of the three values in the register, overwriting the current register contents. The result is that the RGB values are all the same, creating a shade of gray that depends on the original color value. The formula for developing the shade of gray is 0.3*Red + 0.59*Green + 0.11*Blue.

Input Register Values

Register	Value
AH	0x10
AL	0x1B
BX	First Register to Sum
CX	Number of Registers to Sum

Output Register Values

Register	Value
none	

Function 0x11 – EGA/VGA Font Services
Subservice 0x00 – Load User Definable Font
(EGA minimum)

Load a user character font into the loadable character generator.

Input Register Values

Register	Value
AH	0x11
AL	0x00
BH	Number of bytes per character
BL	Block to load
CX	Number of characters
DX	Character offset into table
BP	Offset of character table
ES	Segment of character table

Output Register Values

Register	Value
none	

Function 0x11
Subservice 0x01 – Load ROM Monochrome (8 × 14) Character Set
(EGA minimum)

Loads the 8 × 14 character set. This set is the default for monochrome monitors.

Input Register Values

Register	Value
AH	0x11
AL	0x01
BL	Block to load

Output Register Values

Register	Value
none	

Function 0x11
Subservice 0x02 – Load ROM 8 × 8 Double Dot Character Set
(EGA minimum)

Loads the 8 × 8 Double Dot character set.

Input Register Values

Register	Value
AH	0x11
AL	0x02
BL	Block to load

Output Register Values

Register	Value
none	

Function 0x11
Subservice 0x03 – Set Block Specifier
(EGA minimum)

EGA/VGA monitors can set to display two character sets at a time. If both sets are the same, bit 3 of the attribute byte sets the foreground of the character to high intensity, if the character sets are not the same this bit sets the character set. IBM recommends that function 0x10 subservice 0x00 be called with BX = 0712 before a call to this function is made.

Input Register Values

Register	Bits	Value
AH		0x11
AL		0x03
BL	0, 1, 4	Character set to use when attribute bit 3 is cleared
	2, 3, 5	Character set to use when attribute bit 3 is set

Output Register Values

Register	Value
none	

Function 0x11
Subservice 0x04 – Load ROM 8 × 16 Character Set
(EGA minimum)

Load the ROM 8 × 16 character set.

Input Register Values

Register	Value
AH	0x11
AL	0x04
BL	Block to load

Output Register Values

Register	Value
none	

Function 0x11
Subservice 0x10 – Load User Definable Font
(EGA minimum)

Load a user character font into the loadable character generator. A call to MODE SET must be issued immediately before this function is called, page 0 must be the active page, and the character height will be recalculated. Other than that, this function operates the same as function 0x11, subservice 0x00.

Input Register Values

Register	Value
AH	0x11
AL	0x00
BH	Number of Bytes per Character
BL	Block to Load
DX	Character Offset into Table
BP	Offset of Character Table
ES	Segment of Character Table

Output Register Values

Register	Value
none	

Function 0x11
Subservice 0x11 – Load ROM Monochrome (8 × 14) Character Set
(EGA minimum)

Loads the 8 × 14 character set. This set is the default for monochrome monitors. A call to MODE SET must be issued immediately before this function is called, page 0 must be the active page, and the character height will be recalculated. Other than that, this function operates the same as function 0x11, subservice 0x01.

Input Register Values

Register	Value
AH	0x11
AL	0x01
BL	Block to load

Output Register Values

Register	Value
none	

Function 0x11
Subservice 0x12 – Load ROM 8 × 8 Double Dot Character Set
(EGA minimum)

Loads the 8 × 8 Double Dot character set. A call to MODE SET must be issued immediately before this function is called, page 0 must be the active page, and the character height will be recalculated. Other than that, this function operates the same as function 0x11, subservice 0x02.

Input Register Values

Register	Value
AH	0x11
AL	0x02
BL	Block to Load

Output Register Values

Register	Value
none	

Function 0x11
Subservice 0x13 – Load ROM 8 × 16 Character Set
(EGA minimum)

Load the ROM 8 × 16 character set. A call to MODE SET must be issued immediately before this function is called, page 0 must be the active page, and the character height will be recalculated. Other than that, this function operates the same as function 0x11, subservice 0x04.

Input Register Values

Register	Value
AH	0x11
AL	0x04
BL	Block to load

Output Register Values

Register	Value
none	

Function 0x11
Subservice 0x20 – Set High Order Character Pointer
(EGA minimum)

The standard ASCII set only defines 128 characters. When the original PC was designed IBM defined 128 more characters to make an extended ASCII code of 256 characters. The EGA and VGA monitors allow for the upper 128 to be redefined by the program.

Input Register Values

Register	Value
AH	0x11
AL	0x20
BP	Offset of table of 128 character definitions
ES	Segment of table of 128 character definitions

Output Register Values

Register	Value
none	

Function 0x11
Subservice 0x21 – Set Character Pointer

(EGA minimum)

Set a pointer to table of graphics characters.

Input Register Values

Register	Value	Meaning
AH	0x11	
AL	0x21	
BL	1	14 rows on screen
	2	25 rows on screen
	3	43 rows on screen
CX		Bytes per Character
BP		Offset of Table of Characters
ES		Segment of Table of Characters

Output Register Values

Register	Value
none	

Function 0x11
Subservice 0x22 – Load ROM Monochrome (8 × 14) Character Set
(EGA minimum)

Loads the 8 × 14 character set.

Input Register Values

Register	Value	Meaning
AH	0x11	
AL	0x22	
BL	1	14 rows on screen
	2	25 rows on screen
	3	43 rows on screen

Output Register Values

Register	Value
none	

Function 0x11
Subservice 0x23 – Load ROM 8 × 8 Double Dot Character Set
(EGA minimum)

Loads the 8 × 8 Double Dot character set.

Input Register Values

Register	Value	Meaning
AH	0x11	
AL	0x23	
BL	1	14 rows on screen
	2	25 rows on screen
	3	43 rows on screen

Output Register Values

Register	Value
none	

Function 0x11
Subservice 0x24 – Load ROM 8 × 16 Character Set
(EGA minimum)

Load the ROM 8 × 16 character set.

Input Register Values

Register	Value	Meaning
AH	0x11	
AL	0x24	
BL	1	14 rows on screen
	2	25 rows on screen
	3	43 rows on screen

Output Register Values

Register	Value
none	

Function 0x11
Subservice 0x30 – Get Character Generation Data

Get various data used by the system for generating characters on the screen.

Input Register Values

Register	Value	Meaning
AH	0x11	
AL	0x21	
BL	0	Get Int 0x1F pointer
	1	Get Int 0x43 pointer
	2	Get ROM 8 × 14 character table pointer
	3	Get ROM 8 × 8 character table pointer
	4	Get ROM 8 × 8 upper 128 character table pointer
	5	Get ROM alpha supplement 9x14 pointer
	8	Get ROM 8x16 character table pointer
	9	Get ROM alpha supplement 9x16 pointer

Output Register Values

Register	Value
CX	Bytes per character
DL	Number of rows on the screen - 1
BP	Offset of requested pointer
ES	Segment of requested pointer

Function 0x12 – EGA/VGA Services
Subservice 0x10 – Get EGA/VGA Information

(EGA Minimum)

Returns status of EGA or VGA display, including configuration switch settings. The VGA does not use physical switches; instead it uses RAM memory and uses this function to read virtual switch settings. Meanings of switch settings are given in Table D.2.

Table D.2

Switch Number				Enhanced Adapter	Mono-chrome	Color Graphics
1	**2**	**3**	**4**			
1	1	1	1	Secondary Color Display 40 × 25	Primary	
0	1	1	1	Secondary Color Display 80 × 25	Primary	
1	0	1	1	Secondary enhanced display emulation mode	Primary	
0	0	1	1	Secondary enhanced display high-res mode	Primary	
1	0	0	1	Primary color display 40 × 25	Secondary	
0	0	0	1	Primary color display 80 × 25	Secondary	
1	1	0	1	Secondary Monochrome		Primary 40 × 25
0	1	0	1	Secondary Monochrome		Primary 80 × 25
1	1	1	0	Primary enhanced display emulation mode	Secondary	
0	1	1	0	Primary enhanced display high-res mode	Secondary	
1	0	1	0	Primary monochrome		Secondary 40 × 25
0	0	1	0	Primary monochrome		Secondary 80 × 25

Input Register Values

Register	Value
AH	0x10
BL	0x10

Output Register Values

Register	Value	Meaning
BH	0	Color mode
	1	Monochrome mode
BL		Memory value
	0x00	64 Kilobytes
	0x01	126 Kilobytes
	0x10	192 Kilobytes
	0x11	256 Kilobytes
CH		Feature bits
CL		Switch settings (see Table D.2)

Function 0x12
Subservice 0x20 – Select Alternate Print Screen Function
(EGA minimum)

Redirect the print screen interrupt to call a function that is compatible with EGA/VGA monitors.

Input Register Values

Register	Value
AH	0x12
BL	0x20

Output Register Values

Register	Value
none	

Function 0x12
Subservice 0x30 – Set Scan Lines for Alphanumeric Modes
(VGA minimum)

Set the number of scan lines for VGA alphanumeric modes. Does not take effect until next mode set operation (function 0x00).

Input Register Values

Register	Value	Meaning
AH	0x12	
AL	0	200 scan lines
	1	350 scan lines
	2	400 scan lines
BL	0x30	

Output Register Values

Register	Value
none	

Function 0x12
Subservice 0x31 – Default Palette Loading During Set Mode Operation
(VGA minimum)

Determines if the default palette should be loaded during a set mode operation. If default palette loading is disabled the palette will remain as is during the next set mode call (funct 0x00).

Input Register Values

Register	Value	Meaning
AH	0x12	
AL	0	Enable default palette loading
	1	Disable default palette loading
BL	0x31	

Output Register Values

Register	Value
none	

Function 0x12
Subservice 0x36 – Enable/Disable Video Output
(VGA minimum)

Enable or disable video output.

Input Register Values

Register	Value	Meaning
AH	0x12	
AL	0	Enable video output
	1	Disable video output

Output Register Values

Register	Value
none	

Function 0x13 – String Output
Subservice 0x00 – Write Character String

Write string to screen independent of cursor position. The cursor position is not updated. An attribute is specified for the entire string.

Input Register Values

Register	Value
AH	0x13
AL	0x00
BH	Page number
BL	Attribute
CX	Number of characters in string
DH	Row (Y coordinate)
DL	Column (X coordinate)
BP	Offset of string
ES	Segment of string

Output Register Values

Register	Value
none	

Function 0x13
Subservice 0x01 – Write Character String

Write string to screen independent of cursor position. The cursor position is updated to the end of the string after write. An attribute is specified for the entire string.

Input Register Values

Register	Value
AH	0x13
AL	0x00
BH	Page number
BL	Attribute
CX	Number of characters in string
DH	Row (Y coordinate)
DL	Column (X coordinate)
BP	Offset of string
ES	Segment of string

Output Register Values

Register	Value
none	

Function 0x13
Subservice 0x02 – Write Character String

Write string to screen independent of cursor position. The cursor position is updated to the beginning of the string after write. Attributes for each character are imbedded in the string.

Input Register Values

Register	Value
AH	0x13
AL	0x00
BX	Page number
CX	Number of characters and attributes in string
DH	Row (Y coordinate)
DL	Column (X coordinate)
BP	Offset of string
ES	Segment of string

Output Register Values

Register	Value
none	

Function 0x13
Subservice 0x03 – Write Character String

Write string to screen independent of cursor position. The cursor position is updated to the end of the string after write. Attributes for each character are imbedded in the string.

Input Register Values

Register	Value
AH	0x13
AL	0x00
BX	Page number
CX	Number of characters and attributes in string
DH	Row (Y coordinate)
DL	Column (X coordinate)
BP	Offset of string
ES	Segment of string

Output Register Values

Register	Value
none	

Function 0x1A – Read/Write Display Combination

Read or write display combination. This function is a system's function and is not meant to be called by application programs.

Input Register Values

Register	Value	Meaning
AH	0x1A	
AL	0	Read DCC
	1	Write DCC
BH		Alternate display code (when AL is 1)
BL		Active display code (when AL is 1)

Output Register Values

Register	Value
AL	0x1A (when call is valid
BH	Alternate display code (when AL was 1 on call)
BL	Active display code (when AL was 1 on call)

Function 0x1B – Get Functionality/State Information

(VGA minimum)

Read the functionality/state table from the VGA adapter. This function can be used to determine if a VGA monitor is present.

Input Register Values

Register	Value
AH	0x1B
BP	Offset of buffer to hold functionality/state information
ES	Segment of buffer to hold functionality/state information

Output Register Values

Register	Value
AL	0x1B if call was valid
	Information in table pointed to by ES:BP

Function 0x1C – Save/Restore Video State

(EGA minimum)

This function is used to save or restore the current video state. Before saving the video state this same function is called to find the buffer size needed to store the current state. Set the registers appropriately for what information is to be saved, and set AL to 0. BX will contain the size needed for the buffer. A buffer is allocated then the call is repeated with ES:BP pointing to the buffer and AL set to 1. Make sure CX is set the same as for the previous call, or the buffer could overflow.

Input Register Values

Register	Value	Meaning
AH	0x1C	
AL	0x00	Return size of buffer needed
	0x01	Save video state
	0x02	Restore video state
CX	0x01	Video hardware state
	0x02	Video data areas
	0x04	DAC state and color registers
BP		Offset of save/restore buffer
ES		Segment of save/restore buffer

Output Register Values

Register	Value
AL	0x1C if valid
BX	Size of buffer (if AL was 0 on call)
	Information in buffer (if AL was 1 on call)

Appendix E

VESA VBE 1.2 SVGA Data Structures and Functions

On October 1, 1989, the Video Electronics Standards Association (VESA ®)[1] released its first standard for a software interface for super VGA monitors, the Video BIOS Extension (VBE). Until then no standardized software interface existed. Software had to be aware of what chip set was used by the monitor card, and had to have code for each separate chip set. There are maybe nine different chip sets currently being used to build SVGA adapters, and each chip set has several different ways it could be set up. Before the VESA standard was introduced, software had to

---

[1] The Video Electronics Standards Association is the international, non-profit organization that sets and supports industry-wide video graphics standards for the benefit of the end user. VESA's membership consists of manufacturers of monitors, peripherals, systems, and software products. The VESA offices are located at 2150 North First Street, Suite 440, San Jose, CA 95131-2029, and can be reached at (408) 435-0333, FAX (408) 435-8225.

either support some 27 different monitor types individually, or not support SVGA features.

The VESA VBE has been updated several times since 1989. As of this writing, the most recent is VESA VBE 1.2, dated October 22, 1991. This is the version of the standard covered in this appendix. This version covers support for palette register modes with resolutions greater than those supported by VGA, plus a number of text modes, plus direct color modes using 15, 16, and 24 bits. One item that is missing from this standard is a mouse interface for these modes (see Appendix G on mouse programming). For a detailed discussion on programming graphics on SVGA monitors see Chapters 9 through 11.

A table of contents for this appendix is provided to aid in finding information.

Modes defined by VESA VBE 1.2 are given in table E.1.

Table E.1 Video Modes Defined by VESA VBE 1.2

VESA VBE Version	Mode	Graphics/ Text	Pixels/ Characters	Colors
1.0	256	Graphics	640 × 400	256 out of 256K
	257	Graphics	640 × 480	256 out of 256K
	258	Graphics	800 × 600	16 out of 256K
	259	Graphics	800 × 600	256 out of 256K
	260	Graphics	1024 × 768	16 out of 256K
	261	Graphics	1024 × 768	256 out of 256K
	262	Graphics	1280 × 1024	16 out of 256K
	263	Graphics	1280 × 1024	256 out of 256K
1.1	264	Text	80 × 60	8
	265	Text	132 × 25	8
	266	Text	132 × 43	8
	267	Text	132 × 50	8
	268	Text	132 × 60	8
1.2	269	Graphics	320 × 200	15 bit
	270	Graphics	320 × 200	16 bit
	271	Graphics	320 × 200	24 bit
	272	Graphics	640 × 480	15 bit
	273	Graphics	640 × 480	16 bit
	274	Graphics	640 × 480	24 bit
	275	Graphics	800 × 600	15 bit
	276	Graphics	800 × 600	16 bit
	277	Graphics	800 × 600	24 bit
	278	Graphics	1024 × 768	15 bit
	279	Graphics	1024 × 768	16 bit
	280	Graphics	1024 × 768	24 bit
	281	Graphics	1280 × 1024	15 bit
	282	Graphics	1280 × 1024	16 bit
	283	Graphics	1280 × 1024	24 bit

VESA VBE Data Structures

VESA VBE defines several data structures. The structure definitions are given here. For a detailed discussion of these structures see Chapter 9.

VgaInfoBlock

```
struct VgaInfoBlock {
  char              VESASignature[4];
  unsigned char     VESAVersion[2];
  char     far     *OEMStringPtr;
  unsigned long     Capabilities;
  unsigned far     *VideoModePtr;
  unsigned          TotalMemory;
  char              Reserved[236];
};
```

Function 0x00, return super VGA information, fills in a buffer with the structure of VGAInfoBlock. This function is used to determine if the VESA VBE is supported, and which version is supported. After the call the field VESASignature contains the four characters "VESA". Note that this is not a proper C string, since it does not end with '\0'. The C string operations such as cmpstr( ) will not work on it. VESAVersion contains the VBE version that the card supports, with the major version in the first byte and the minor version in the second byte. OEMStringPtr is a string containing whatever information the adapter manufacturer wants to put in it. Capabilities defines what capabilities the hardware has. As of this writing only one bit has been defined in this field. If bit 0 is set, the digital/analog converter, which translates digital values in the frame buffer to the analog signals that control the electron guns, is programmable. VideoModePtr points to an array of mode numbers supported by this card. It is possible that not all modes listed will be available due to the amount of RAM on the adapter card or for other reasons. Once the desired mode is found in the list, call function 0x01, return super VGA mode information, to determine if the mode is available. TotalMemory is the number of 64K memory blocks on the card. To find the actual amount of memory multiply this value by 65,536.

ModeInfoBlock

```
struct ModeInfoBlock {

  /* mandatory information */

  unsigned        ModeAttributes;
  char            WinAAttributes;
  char            WinBAttributes;
  unsigned        WinGranularity;
  unsigned        WinSize;
  unsigned        WinASegment;
  unsigned        WinBSegment;
  void     far (*WinFinctPtr)();
  unsigned        BytesPerScanLine;

  /* formerly optional
     now mandatory information */

  unsigned        XResolution;
  unsigned        YResolution;
  unsigned char   XCharSize;
  unsigned char   YCharSize;
  unsigned char   NumberOfPlanes;
  unsigned char   BitsPerPixel;
  unsigned char   NumberOfBanks;
  unsigned char   MemoryModel;
  unsigned char   BankSize;
  unsigned char   NumberOfImagePages;
  unsigned char   reserved1;

  /* New Direct Color Fields */

  unsigned char   RedMaskSize;
  unsigned char   RedFieldPosition;
  unsigned char   GreenMaskSize;
  unsigned char   GreenFieldPosition;
  unsigned char   BlueMaskSize;
  unsigned char   BlueFieldPosition;
  unsigned char   RsvdMaskSize;
  unsigned char   RsvdFieldPosition;
  unsigned char   DirectColorModelInfo;

  char            reserved[216];
};
```

VESA VBE 1.2 SVGA Data Structures and Functions

Function 0x01, return super VGA mode information, fills in a buffer with the structure of ModeInfoBlock. Note that this is how this structure is defined for VBE v1.2. For older version the fields marked "Formerly Optional, Now Mandatory" may or may not be filled in, since these fields were optional for older standards. The fields marked "New Direct Color Fields" will not be filled in by an adapter supporting a version of the VBE older than 1.2. The fields in this structure are covered in detail in Chapter 9. Space limitations will not allow that information to be repeated here.

Status Information

Each VBE function returns status information in the AX register. If the AL register is not set to 0x4F the function is not supported. If the AH is set to 0x01 the function call failed. If AH is set to 0x00 the function call was successful.

VESA VBE 1.2 Interrupts

SVGA functions defined by the VESA VBE are accessed through BIOS interrupt 0x10, function 0x4F. Interrupt 0x10 is the same BIOS interrupt as is used for all monitor functions (see Appendix D). Function 0x4F is undefined by older IBM standards. Most SVGA manufacturers have not defined functions for 0x4F either, so the use of this function does not interfere with most existing monitor systems. The VESA function number is placed in the AL register.

The functions defined by VESA VBE 1.2 are covered very briefly below. For more detailed discussions and examples see Chapter 9.

Function 0x00 – Return Super VGA Information

This function fills in a variable of structure VgaInfoBlock, the definition of which was given earlier. To find out if the VESA VBE is supported call this function, then test the AL register for 0x4F to make sure the function is supported, and AH for 0x00 to make sure the call was successful. If AL is not 0x4F chances are the VBE is not supported. If the call was successful it is probable that the VBE is supported, but it is a good idea to verify this by testing the VESASignature field. It should contain the four letters "VESA". Note that the VESASignature field is not a valid C string and does not end with a '\0'. The C string functions, such as cmpstr, will not work on this field. For a more detailed discussion of this structure and its fields see Chapter 9.

Input Register Values

Register	Value
AH	0x4F
AL	0x00
ES	Segment of structure of type VgaInfoBlock
DS	Offset of structure of type VgaInfoBlock

Output Register Values

Register	Value
AL	0x4F if function supported
	!0x4F otherwise
AH	0x00 if call successful
	0x01 otherwise

Function 0x01 – Return Super VGA Mode Information

This function fills in a variable of type ModeInfoBlock, the definition of which was given earlier, in the section labeled **ModeInfoBlock**. There is a great deal of information in this block, which is used to determine if a given mode is supported and how to access a pixel in the given mode. If the mode is a direct color mode the number of bits per color per pixel is given, along with the starting bit number for each color. For a more detailed discussion on how to use this information see Chapter 9.

The easiest way to determine if a mode is supported by the graphics adapter is to call function 0x00 to make sure the VESA VBE is supported, then call function 0x01 with the desired mode number in the CX register. On return, test bit 0 of the ModeAttributes field. If it is set the mode is supported.

Input Register Values

Register	Value
AH	0x4F
AL	0x01
CX	Mode number
ES	Segment of structure of type ModeInfoBlock
DS	Offset of structure of type ModeInfoBlock

Output Register Values

Register	Value
AL	0x4F if function supported
	!0x4F otherwise
AH	0x00 if call successful
	0x01 otherwise

Function 0x02 – Set Super VGA Video Mode

Once a supported mode is found it can be set with this function. To find a supported mode use function 0x01. If this function fails, due to the selected mode not being supported or for other reasons, the monitor will remain in the mode it was in before the call, and the AH register will contain a value other than 0x00. Not all VESA VBE compatible cards support the same modes. For a list of possible modes see Table E.1 at the beginning of this appendix. A list of modes supported by the card can be obtained from function 0x00. It is possible that not all of these modes will be available, due to memory constraints of the video adapter or other reasons. To determine if a mode is available use function 0x01.

Input Register Values

Register	Bit #	Value
AH		0x4F
AL		0x02
BX	0-14	Mode number
	15	Clear memory flag - 0 to clear memory, 1 otherwise

Output Register Values

Register	Value
AL	0x4F if function supported
	!0x4F otherwise
AH	0x00 if call successful
	0x01 otherwise

Function 0x03 – Return Current Video Mode

This function returns the mode number to which the adapter is set.

Input Register Values

Register	Value
AH	0x4F
AL	0x0

Output Register Values

Register	Value
AL	0x4F if function supported
	!0x4F otherwise
AH	0x00 if call successful
	0x01 otherwise
BX	Mode number

Function 0x04 – Save/Restore Super VGA Video State

This function has three purposes: (1) Save the video state, (2) find the amount of memory needed to save the desired information, and (3) restore saved information. Four different sets of information can be stored: hardware information, BIOS data, DAC state, SVGA state. The digital/analog converter (DAC) is a device used to convert digital values from the frame buffer into analog values for controlling the electron guns in the monitor. The DAC can be reprogrammed to make the electron guns more or less sensitive.

First call this function with DL set to 0x00 to find the size of the buffer. Then allocate a buffer of the correct size. Next call the function again with DL set to 0x01, to retreive the desired data and store it in the allocated memory. Make sure when you call the function the second time that CX contains the same value as for the first call, so the correct amount of memory is needed. The current state can then be restored at any time, but when it is, again make sure that the CX register contains the proper value.

Input Register Values

Register	Bit #	Value
AH		0x4F
AL		0x04
DL		0x00 - find buffer size 0x01 - save state 0x02 - restore state
CX	0	Save/restore video hardware state
	1	Save/restore video BIOS state
	2	Save/restore video DAC state
	3	Save/restore super VGA state
ES		Segment of buffer (if DL is 1 or 2 only)
DS		Offset of buffer (if DL is 1 or 2 only)

Output Register Values

Register	Value
AL	0x4F if function supported
	!0x4F otherwise
AH	0x00 if call successful
	0x01 otherwise
BX	Number of 64 byte blocks needed to store info. (if DL was for call 0 only)

Function 0x05 – CPU Video Memory Window Control

This function sets or gets the position of window A or window B in the frame buffer. For a detailed discussion of SVGA windows A and B see Chapter 9. Before using this function a call should be made to function 0x01 to determine the size, location, and granularity of the windows.

This function can also be accessed through a far call, which is faster. The address to use for the far call is available from function 0x01. For the far call version register AH and AL need not be loaded, but BH, BL, and DX must be. Registers AX and DX are destroyed by the call, so the values of these registers need to be saved before the call.

Input Register Values

Register	Value
AH	0x4F
AL	0x05
BH	0x00 - Set window position 0x01 - Get window position
BL	0x00 for window A, 0x01 for window B
DX	Window position in granularity units (only if BH is 0x00)

Output Register Values

Register	Value
AL	0x4F if function supported
	!0x4F otherwise
AH	0x00 if call successful
	0x01 otherwise
DX	Window position in granularity units (only if BH was 0x01 for call)

Function 0x06 – Set/Get Logical Scan Line Length

This function is used to set or get the logical scan line length, allowing a program to set up a logical frame buffer that is wider than the display area. Due to hardware considerations the desired width may not be available. In this case the next larger available size will be chosen. Therefore it is advised that after this function is called the information passed back be read to determine the actual width set.

Input Register Values

Register	Value
AH	0x4F
AL	0x06
BH	0x00 - Set scan line length 0x01 - Get scan line length
CX	Desired width in pixels (if BH is 0x00 only)

Output Register Values

Register	Value
AL	0x4F if function supported
	!0x4F otherwise
AH	0x00 if call successful
	0x01 otherwise
BX	Bytes per scanline (always)
CX	Actual pixels per scan line (always)
DX	Maximum pixels per scan line (always)

Function 0x07 – Set/Get Display Start

When function 0x06 is called, it is possible for a logical screen to be larger than the physical screen, in which case some pixels will be plotted off the screen. This function can be used to pan around the screen by setting what pixel will be displayed in the upper left corner. This function can also be used to switch rapidly from one display area to another for a paging effect. This is useful in animation.

Input Register Values

Register	Value
AH	0x4F
AL	0x07
BH	0x00 (reserved, must always be 0x00)
BL	0x00 - Set display start 0x01 - Get display start
CX	First pixel in scan line to display (X coordinate) (when BL is 0x00 only)
DX	First scan line to display (Y coordinate) (when BL is 0x00 only)

Output Register Values

Register	Value
AL	0x4F if function supported
	!0x4F otherwise
AH	0x00 if call successful
	0x01 otherwise
CX	First pixel on scan line being displayed (X coordinate) (when BL was 0x01 for call only)
DX	First scan line being displayed (Y coordinate) (when BL was 0x01 for call only)

Function 0x08 – Set/Get DAC Palette Control

The digital/analog converter (DAC) is a device used to convert digital values from the frame buffer into analog values for controlling the electron guns. The DAC can be reprogrammed to make the electron guns more or less sensitive.

The standard VGA setting for DACs is 6 bits of color definition per electron gun. When function 0x02 (set video mode) is called, the DAC is reset to this. Some DACs can be reconfigured to provide 8 bits of color definition or more per color gun. Details on how this is done are beyond the scope of this book.

To determine if the DAC is configurable, function 0x00 should be used (see Chapter 9). If the selected number of pixels per color gun is not available the next lower available number is used.

Input Register Values

Register	Value
AH	0x4F
AL	0x08
BL	0x00 - Set pixels per gun 0x01 - Get pixels per gun
BH	Number of bits per color gun (6 default) (When BL is 0x00 only)

Output Register Values

Register	Value
AL	0x4F if function supported
	!0x4F otherwise
AH	0x00 if call successful
	0x01 otherwise
BH	The number of bits per color gun set (6 default) (always)

Appendix F
PC Monitor Modes

Table F.1 gives most of the important information on modes supported by the CGA, EGA, VGA and SVGA adapters. When using direct color modes (those modes that use 15, 16, or 24 bits) SVGA adapter cards vary quite widely in how color data are represented. To obtain this information it is necessary to call SVGA interrupts to fill in SVGA data structures. The information on how to do this is given in Appendix E. A detailed discussion is given in Chapter 9.

Table F.1

Mode	Minimum Adapter	Text/ Graphics	Pixels/ Characters	Colors	Pages
0x00	CGA	Text	40 × 25	16 fore/ 8 back	1
0x01	CGA	Text	40 × 25	16 fore/ 8 back	1
0x02	CGA	Text	80 × 25	16 fore/ 8 back	1
0x03	CGA	Text	80 × 25	16 fore/ 8 back	1
0x04	CGA	Graphics	320 × 200	4 (CGA palette)	1
0x05	CGA	Graphics	320 × 200	4 (CGA palette)	1
0x06	CGA	Graphics	640 × 200	2	1
0x07	EGA	Text	80 × 25	4 (CGA palette)	
0x0D	EGA	Graphics	320 × 200	16 out of 64 16/256K (VGA)	1
0x0E	EGA	Graphics	640 × 200	16 out of 64 16/256K (VGA)	4
0x0F	EGA	Graphics	640 × 350	4	1
0x10	EGA	Graphics	640 × 350	16 out of 64 16/256K (VGA)	2
0x11	VGA	Graphics	640 × 480	16 out of 256K	1
0x12	VGA	Graphics	640 × 480	16 out of 256K	1
0x13	VGA	Graphics	320 × 200	256 out of 256K	1
0x100	SVGA	Graphics	640 × 400	256 out of 256K	1
0x101	SVGA	Graphics	640 × 480	256 out of 256K	1
0x102	SVGA	Graphics	800 × 600	16 out of 256K	1
0x103	SVGA	Graphics	800 × 600	256 out of 256K	1
0x104	SVGA	Graphics	1024 × 768	16 out of 256K	1
0x105	SVGA	Graphics	1024 × 768	256 out of 256K	1
0x106	SVGA	Graphics	1280 × 1024	16 out of 256K	1
0x107	SVGA	Graphics	1280 × 1024	256 out of 256K	1
0x108	SVGA	Text	80 × 60	8	1
0x109	SVGA	Text	132 × 25	8	1
0x10A	SVGA	Text	132 × 43	8	1
Bx10B	SVGA	Text	132 × 50	8	1
Dx10C	SVGA	Text	132 × 60	8	1

Mode	Minimum Adapter	Text/ Graphics	Pixels/ Characters	Colors	Pages
0x10D	SVGA	Graphics	320 × 200	15 bit	1
0x10E	SVGA	Graphics	320 × 200	16 bit	1
0x10F	SVGA	Graphics	320 × 200	24 bit	1
0x110	SVGA	Graphics	640 × 480	15 bit	1
0x111	SVGA	Graphics	640 × 480	16 bit	1
0x112	SVGA	Graphics	640 × 480	24 bit	1
0x113	SVGA	Graphics	800 × 600	15 bit	1
0x114	SVGA	Graphics	800 × 600	16 bit	1
0x115	SVGA	Graphics	800 × 600	24 bit	1
0x116	SVGA	Graphics	1024 × 768	15 bit	1
0x117	SVGA	Graphics	1024 × 768	16 bit	1
0x118	SVGA	Graphics	1024 × 768	24 bit	1
0x119	SVGA	Graphics	1280 × 1024	15 bit	1
0x11A	SVGA	Graphics	1280 × 1024	16 bit	1
0x11B	SVGA	Graphics	1280 × 1024	24 bit	1

Appendix G

Mouse BIOS Functions

Although this book does not cover mouse programming in depth, it is not difficult, and once a programmer is familiar with interfacing with BIOS routines, he/she can get quite far simply by reading this appendix. It is suggested that if the programmer is not familiar with mouse programming he/she read the entire appendix first before designing his/her code. A table of contents for this appendix is provided to help the programmer to find information.

General Concepts of Mouse Programming

There are two basic ways to interface with a mouse. The first is to look at the mouse every once in a while to see what it's doing. This technique is called *polling*. The second technique is to set up a function that is called whenever a mouse interrupt occurs. This technique is called *event-driven* and the function is called the *mouse handler*. Polling is easier for the programmer, but event-driven is more efficient, since the program does not need to keep looking for something to happen. When something happens the mouse handler takes care of it, otherwise the program is free to do its processing. Since polling is easier, this appendix will concentrate on that. Setting up the mouse handler is complex and takes an in-depth knowledge of how interrupts work. There are a number of good books on the market that cover event-driven programming.

Note that Microsoft only supports certain graphics modes with its mouse driver. To use the mouse in other modes is not as easy and involves a great deal of low-level programming. We will not be covering how to use the mouse in unsupported modes here. The modes that are supported are mostly standard CGA/EGA/VGA modes. It is hoped that the VESA group will soon come out with standards for a mouse interface that will be compatible with VBE SVGA modes. See Table G.1 for supported modes.

Mouse Movement

The mouse is a pointing device, meaning that moving the mouse moves a pointer, the mouse cursor, on the screen. The mouse programmer needs to understand how the movement of the mouse is passed to the program, how the cursor moves, and how the two relate.

A mouse is a device that translates linear movement into discrete chunks and tells the computer how many discrete movements in a certain direction the mouse made. Each discrete movement is called a mickey. If the mouse is moved one inch it might send the number 200 to the computer, in which case we would say the mouse has a resolution of 200 mickeys per inch, a common resolution.

The Mouse Screen

The pointer on the screen is set and measured using a system of virtual pixels. Most screen modes use a virtual screen of 640 × 200 pixels. So if the screen is in a mode with 320 × 200 pixels, every virtual pixel in the Y dimension maps to one pixel on the screen, but a virtual pixel in X dimension maps to one-half of a pixel on the screen. If the cursor is at pixel (0,0) and the mouse tells it to move to (1,0) it will not move on the screen. If the mouse tells it to move to (2,0) it will then move one real pixel. In text modes that have 80 × 25 character resolution the cursor needs to move 8 virtual pixels horizontally before it moves one real character. Table G.1 gives the dimensions of the virtual screen for a number of the supported graphics modes. Other modes are supported by the Microsoft mouse, but those modes are not standard graphics modes and are only supported by one or at most a few video card manufacturers.

Table G.1

Mode	Adapter	Text/ Graphics	Virtual Screen Size	Actual Screen Size	Mouse Cursor Size
0	CGA	Text	640 × 200	40 × 25	1 character
1	CGA	Text	640 × 200	40 × 25	1 character
2	CGA	Text	640 × 200	80 × 25	1 character
3	CGA	Text	640 × 200	80 × 25	1 character
4	CGA	Graphics	640 × 200	320 × 200	8 × 16
5	CGA	Graphics	640 × 200	320 × 200	8 × 16
6	CGA	Graphics	640 × 200	640 × 200	16 × 16
7	EGA	Text	640 × 200	80 × 25	1 character
13	EGA	Graphics	640 × 200	320 × 200	16 × 16
14	EGA	Graphics	640 × 200	640 × 200	16 × 16
15	EGA	Graphics	640 × 350	640 × 350	16 × 16
16	EGA	Graphics	640 × 350	640 × 350	16 × 16
17	VGA	Graphics	640 × 480	640 × 480	16 × 16
18	VGA	Graphics	640 × 480	640 × 480	16 × 16
19	VGA	Graphics	640 × 200	320 × 200	16 × 16

As the mouse moves it tells the mouse driver how many mickeys in each dimension it has moved and the mouse driver then moves the cursor automatically. The programmer can set how many mickeys are needed to move the mouse 8 pixels in either dimension. The dimensions are controlled independently, so it can be set so that a small movement of the mouse in the X dimension results in a large movement of the screen cursor, but a large movement in the Y dimension results in only a small movement of the cursor.

If the mouse is moved rapidly the number of mickeys needed to move cursor 8 pixels is halved, resulting in a more rapid sweep of the cursor across the screen. This gives the mouse a more natural feel. The speed at which this happens can be changed by the program.

The Mouse Cursor

The next thing that needs to be discussed is setting the shape of the cursor. Setting the cursor in text mode is easier to understand, so we will start there. First we need to look at how data are stored in the text mode frame buffer. Each character on the screen takes 2 bytes of data, the first being the color of the character and the second being the extended ASCII code of the character. The color byte is set up as shown in Fig. G.1.

Two unsigned integers are passed to the interrupt that sets the text cursor. The first is ANDed with frame buffer, the second XORed with it. So to set the mouse cursor to be the same character as the one it is over with inverse color use 0xFFFF for the first integer and 0xFF00 for the second. This is the default cursor.

Background				Foreground			
Intensity	Red	Green	Blue	Bright	Red	Green	Blue

Fig G.1 Color Information in Text Mode Frame Buffers

The Graphics Mouse Cursor

The graphics cursor takes an area of the screen that is usually 16 × 16 virtual pixels. For these modes, to set the shape two bitmasks are used. Each bit mask is made of 16 unsigned integers. The first is ANDed with what is on the screen, the second is XORed. Pixels take more than one bit of data, so each bit in the mask cannot be directly ANDed with a pixel. Each bit in the mask is expanded so that all bits in the frame buffer for the one pixel are ANDed with the same value. The second bitmask must be adjacent to the first in RAM. The first is used to turn off pixels under the cursor, the second is used to turn on the pixels that make up the cursor.

For modes 4 and 5 the graphics cursor is 8 × 16 virtual pixels. These modes still use the same size bitmasks to set the cursor, but the bits no longer need to be expanded.

When the mouse is polled to see where the cursor is, only one (X,Y) coordinate pair is returned. Since the cursor itself could be a block that is 16 × 16 pixels, that naturally leads to the question "Which coordinate is returned?" This can be set. The coordinate that is returned is called the *hot spot* of the cursor. The hot spot is measured from the upper left corner of the cursor, so that that location is 0 when setting the hot spot. The hot spot can be from -127 to 127 virtual pixels from the upper left corner of the cursor in either dimension, which means it does not need to be on the cursor.

Is a Mouse Present on the System?

Many PCs even today do not have mouses, or use mouse drivers that are not compatible with the Microsoft driver. An application should test for a mouse before assuming one is present. Even an application that requires a mouse should test for one, then raise an error if one is not present.

First look at interrupt vector table at interrupt 0x33. Each entry in the vector table is a far address. A far address uses 2 unsigned integers, one being the segment, the other being the offset. So each entry in the interrupt vector table takes 4 bytes. To find the proper entry in the table for int 0x33 multiply 0x33 by 4. This is at memory location 0x0000:0x00CC. If the value there is 0000,0000 (each entry is 2 unsigned ints) the mouse driver is not present. But just because there is a valid address there does not mean a mouse is present. If there is a valid address then call int 0x33, function 0x00 (reset mouse). If the mouse is present this function will return -1 in the AX register. This function should be called before any other mouse functions.

Miscellaneous

Microsoft lists several considerations for mouse programming. One important consideration is that any program using a mouse should not program video hardware directly. Programming video hardware directly is too advanced to be covered in this book, but a number of programmers prefer it to using BIOS for graphics programming since it is faster. In this book we do touch on directly manipulating palette registers and the frame buffer, but this should not interfere with the mouse.

The next consideration deals with making changes to the screen. The mouse software saves what was under the cursor, then restores it when the mouse is moved. Consider what would happen if the program writes over the cursor. When the mouse is moved what was on the screen previously is restored, overwriting the new graphics. For this reason the mouse cursor should be turned off, using function 0x02, before writing to the screen location where the mouse cursor is. Microsoft also recommends turning the mouse cursor off before changing screen modes, since the way memory is used is quite different between modes. It is quite unpredictable what will be put on the screen when the mouse attempts to restore information saved in a different mode.

Mouse Interrupts

All mouse interfacing is done through interrupt 0x33. The different functions are accessed by placing the function number in the AX register.

Microsoft defines a large number of functions, not all of which are supported by Logitech or other mouse manufacturers. The functions listed below are the most important, and are supported by most mouse manufacturers.

Function 0x00 – Reset Mouse

Reset all internal mouse variables to default values. It can also be used to detect if a mouse exists and how many buttons the mouse has.

Input Register Values

Register	Value
AX	0x0000

Output Register Values

Register	Value
AX	0xFFFF if mouse is supported
BX	Number of buttons

Function 0x01 – Show Cursor

An internal counter in the mouse driver is used to determine if the mouse cursor should be shown or not. If this counter is 0 the cursor is shown; if it is a negative value the cursor is hidden. Hide Cursor decrements the counter, Show Cursor increments the cursor if it is not 0. This allows more flexibility than using one bit for on/off. Suppose there is a procedure that hides the mouse cursor. It calls another procedure that also hides the mouse cursor, then shows it before returning to the parent. If the counter were simply one bit it would suddenly show up on the parent procedure. By using a counter, the first procedure would set it to -1, hiding the cursor. The second procedure would decrement the counter again to -2, perform its processing, then increment the counter on leaving. The cursor is now set to -1 and is still hidden.

Input Register Values

Register	Value
AX	0x0001

Output Register Values

Register	Value
none	

Function 0x02 – Hide Cursor

An internal counter in the mouse driver is used to determine if the mouse cursor should be shown or not. If this counter is 0 the cursor is shown; if it is a negative value the cursor is hidden. Hide Cursor decrements the counter, Show Cursor increments the cursor if it is not 0. This allows more flexibility than using one bit for on/off. Suppose there is a procedure that hides the mouse cursor. It calls another procedure that also hides the mouse cursor, then shows it before returning to the parent. If the counter were simply one bit it would suddenly show up on the parent procedure. By using a counter, the first procedure would set it to -1, hiding the cursor. The second procedure would decrement the counter again to -2, perform its processing, then increment the counter on leaving. The cursor is now set to -1 and is still hidden.

Input Register Values

Register	Value
AX	0x0002

Output Register Values

Register	Value
none	

Function 0x03 – Poll Mouse

Return the mouse cursor position and button press status.

Input Register Values

Register	Value
AX	0x0003

Output Register Values

Register	Bit #	Value
BX	0	Left button pressed
	1	Right button pressed
	2	Middle button pressed
CX		Current X coordinate in virtual pixels
DX		Current Y coordinate in virtual pixels

Function 0x04 – Set Mouse Cursor Position

Set the mouse cursor to a new position on the screen. Position is specified in virtual pixels. The cursor cannot be made to appear outside the cursor limits set with functions 0x07 and 0x08 (set X and Y limits). If the cursor is moved to a protected area or the cursor is hidden, it will not show at the new location. Some older mouse drivers do not show the mouse immediately at it's new location. To ensure against this problem, an immediate call to function 0x02 then 0x01 (hide then show cursor) is recommended.

Input Register Values

Register	Value
AX	0x0004
CX	X coordinate in virtual pixels
DX	Y coordinate in virtual pixels

Output Register Values

Register	Value
none	

Function 0x05 – Button Press Information

Find the number of times the polled button has been pressed, and reset the count. Also gives the location of the mouse cursor when the polled button was last pressed. Only the count for the polled button is reset. The current button pressed status is returned for all buttons.

Input Register Values

Register	Bit #	Value
AX		0x0005
BX	0	Find left button status
	1	Find right button status
	2	Find middle button status

Output Register Values

Register	Bit #	Value
AX	0	Left button currently pressed
	1	Right button currently pressed
	2	Middle button currently pressed
BX		Button counter
CX		Cursor's X position at last button press
DX		Cursor's Yposition at last button press

Function 0x06 – Button Release Information

Find the number of times the polled button has been released, and reset the count. Also gives the location of the mouse cursor when the polled button was last released. Only the count for the polled button is reset. The current button pressed status is returned for all buttons.

Input Register Values

Register	Bit #	Value
AX		0x0005
BX	0	Left button released
	1	Right button released
	2	Middle button released

Output Register Values

Register	Bit #	Value
AX	0	Left button released
	1	Right button released
	2	Middle button released
BX		Button counter
CX		Cursor's X position at last button press
DX		Cursor's Yposition at last button press

Function 0x07 – Set X Limits

Restrict the mouse cursor to a certain range, in the X dimension.

Input Register Values

Register	Value
AX	0x0007
CX	Minimum X coordinate
DX	Maximum X coordinate

Output Register Values

Register	Value
none	

Function 0x08 – Set Y Limits

Restrict the mouse cursor to a certain range, in the Y dimension.

Input Register Values

Register	Value
AX	0x0008
CX	Minimum Y coordinate
DX	Maximum Y coordinate

Output Register Values

Register	Value
none	

Function 0x09 – Set Graphics Cursor and Hot Spot

Sets the graphics mouse cursor's bit mask and hot spot. Two bit masks are used, the first is ANDed with the screen contents and the second is ORed. Each bit mask is 16 unsigned integers. The location of the hot spot is measured from the top left-hand corner of the cursor, and can be from -128 to 127 pixels from that point in either dimension.

Input Register Values

Register	Value
AX	0x0009
BX	X coordinate of hot spot, relative to upper left of cursor. Value between -128 .. 127
CX	X coordinate of hot spot, relative to upper left of cursor. Value between -128 .. 127
DX	Offset of bit mask
ES	Segment of bit mask

Output Register Values

Register	Value
none	

Function 0x0A – Set Text Cursor

Sets the text mouse cursor. When the software cursor is used two unsigned integers are used, the first of which is ANDed with the contents of the screen, the second is XORed. See text at the start of this appendix for detailed information on setting the text cursor.

Input Register Values

Register	Value
AX	0x000A
BX	0 for mouse cursor, 1 for hardware cursor
CX	AND bit mask if BX is 0, start line if BX is 1
DX	XOR bit mask if BX is 0, start line if BX is 1

Output Register Values

Register	Value
none	

Function 0x0C – Set Mouse Event Handler

Sets the address of the mouse event handler. The mouse event handler is called as a far function by the mouse driver when certain mouse events occur. Mouse events include buttons being pressed or released, or the mouse moving. Since this routine is called by the mouse driver and not by the program's own code it needs to follow the same rules as programming interrupts or terminate and stay resident programs. No registers can be modified, it cannot call DOS or BIOS interrupts, including the mouse interrupts, and it must be a DOS far procedure, with far return. The events on which the event handler is called can be set by passing an event mask to the BIOS call. The definition of this mask is given in Table G.2. Information is passed to the event handler in registers. Table G.2 gives the information in each register.

Mouse BIOS Functions

Table G.2 Information Available to the Mouse Event Handler

Register	Bit #	Meaning
AX		Event flag (See table G.3)
BX		Button status
	0	Left button pressed
	1	Right button pressed
	2	Middle button pressed
CX		X coordinate of mouse cursor in virtual pixels
DX		Y coordinate of mouse cursor in virtual pixels
DI		X dimension mickeys
SI		Y dimension mickeys
DS		Data segment of driver

Table G.3 Mouse Event Flags

Bit #	Meaning
0	Motion
1	Left button pressed
2	Left button released
3	Right button pressed
4	Right button released
5	Left button pressed
6	Left button released

Input Register Values

Register	Value
AX	0x000C
CX	Event mask
DX	Offset of mouse event handler
ES	Segment of mouse event handler

Output Register Values

Register	Value
none	

Function 0x0F – Set Mouse Sensitivity

Set the number of mickeys of mouse movement needed to move the cursor 8 pixels in either dimension. The default is 8 mickeys in the X dimension and 16 in the Y.

Input Register Values

Register	Value
AX	0x000F
CX	Number of mickeys to move mouse cursor 8 mickeys in X dimension
DX	Number of mickeys to move mouse cursor 8 mickeys in X dimension

Output Register Values

Register	Value
none	

Function 0x10 – Protect Area

Define an area of the screen protected from the mouse cursor. If the mouse cursor is moved over a protected area it becomes invisible.

Input Register Values

Register	Value
AX	0x0010
CX	Left of protected area
DX	Top of protected area
SI	Right of protected area
DI	Bottom of protected area

Output Register Values

Register	Value
none	

Function 0x13 – Set Double Speed Threshold

Set the speed at which the cursor will move twice the number pixels for a given number of mickeys of mouse movement.

Input Register Values

Register	Value
AX	0x0013
DX	Threshold speed in mickeys/second

Output Register Values

Register	Value
none	

Function 0x24 – Get Mouse Information

Get information on the mouse. Not all mouse drivers support this function. To determine if the function is supported load BX with 0xFFFF before calling. If the call returns 0xFFFF in the BX register, this function is not supported.

Input Register Values

Register	Value
AX	0x0024

Output Register Values

Register	Bit #	Value
BH		Major version number
BL		Minor version number
CH		Mouse type
	1	Bus mouse
	2	Serial mouse
	3	Inport mouse
	4	PS/2 mouse
	5	HP mouse
CL		Mouse IRQ (0 for PS/2)

Appendix H

IBM PC Extended ASCII Codes

IBM PCs use the ASCII (American Standard Code for Information Interchange) encoding to store character data. This encoding was developed by ANSI (American National Standards Institute) with the help of several industrial organizations, particularly AT&T, at a time when 7-bit machines were common. Due to AT&T's influence many of the lower ASCII codes are specialized for telecommunications. Due to the number of 7-bit machines in use, the ASCII code only defines the first 128 characters. The PC is an 8-bit machine with 256 possible combinations for each character. IBM defined an extension to the ASCII code for the extra 128 characters. The full extended ASCII code is given in table H.1. Some of the telecommunications symbols in the first 32 encodings are rather cryptic. The meanings of these are given in Table H.2.

Table H.1 Extended ASCII Codes

Hex	Dec	ASCII	Hex	Dec	ASCII	Hex	Dec	ASCII
0x00	0	Null	0x56	86	V	0xAC	172	¼
0x01	1	SOH	0x57	87	W	0xAD	173	¡
0x02	2	STX	0x58	88	X	0xAE	174	«
0x03	3	ETX	0x59	89	Y	0xAF	175	»
0x04	4	EOT	0x5A	90	Z	0xB0	176	░
0x05	5	ENQ	0x5B	91	[	0xB1	177	▒
0x06	6	ACK	0x5C	92	\ (Back Slash)	0xB2	178	▓
0x07	7	Bell	0x5D	93	]	0xB3	179	│
0x08	8	BKSP	0x5E	94	^	0xB4	180	┤
0x09	9	Tab	0x5F	95	_	0xB5	181	╡
0x0A	10	Line Feed	0x60	96	`	0xB6	182	╢
0x0B	11	Vert Tab	0x61	97	a	0xB7	183	╖
0x0C	12	Form Feed	0x62	98	b	0xB8	184	╕
0x0D	13	Car Retn	0x63	99	c	0xB9	185	╣
0x0E	14	Shift out	0x64	100	d	0xBA	186	║
0x0F	15	Shift In	0x65	101	e	0xBB	187	╗
0x10	16	DL Esc	0x66	102	f	0xBC	188	╝
0x11	17	DC1	0x67	103	g	0xBD	189	╜
0x12	18	DC2	0x68	104	h	0xBE	190	╛
0x13	19	DC3	0x69	105	i	0xBF	191	┐
0x14	20	DC4	0x6A	106	j	0xC0	192	└
0x15	21	NAK	0x6B	107	k	0xC1	193	┴
0x16	22	SYN	0x6C	108	l	0xC2	194	┬
0x17	23	ETB	0x6D	109	m	0xC3	195	├
0x18	24	CAN	0x6E	110	n	0xC4	196	─
0x19	25	EM	0x6F	111	o	0xC5	197	┼
0x1A	26	SUB	0x70	112	p	0xC6	198	╞

Hex	Dec	ASCII	Hex	Dec	ASCII	Hex	Dec	ASCII
0x1B	27	ESC	0x71	113	q	0xC7	199	╟
0x1C	28	FS	0x72	114	r	0xC8	200	╚
0x1D	29	GS	0x73	115	s	0xC9	201	╔
0x1E	30	RS	0x74	116	t	0xCA	202	╩
0x1F	31	US	0x75	117	u	0xCB	203	╦
0x20	32	space	0x76	118	v	0xCC	204	╠
0x21	33	!	0x77	119	w	0xCD	205	═
0x22	34	"	0x78	120	x	0xCE	206	╬
0x23	35	#	0x79	121	y	0xCF	207	╧
0x24	36	$	0x7A	122	z	0xD0	208	╨
0x25	37	%	0x7B	123	{	0xD1	209	╤
0x26	38	&	0x7C	124	|	0xD2	210	╥
0x27	39	'	0x7D	125	}	0xD3	211	╙
0x28	40	(	0x7E	126	~	0xD4	212	╘
0x29	41	)	0x7F	127	△	0xD5	213	╒
0x2A	42	*	0x80	128	Ç	0xD6	214	╓
0x2B	43	+	0x81	129	ü	0xD7	215	╫
0x2C	44	,	0x82	130	é	0xD8	216	╪
0x2D	45	-	0x83	131	â	0xD9	217	└
0x2E	46	.	0x84	132	ä	0xDA	218	┌
0x2F	47	/	0x85	133	à	0xDB	219	█
0x30	48	0	0x86	134	å	0xDC	210	▄
0x31	49	1	0x87	135	ç	0xDD	221	▌
0x32	50	2	0x88	136	ê	0xDE	222	▐
0x33	51	3	0x89	137	ë	0xDF	223	▀
0x34	52	4	0x8A	138	è	0xE0	224	α
0x35	53	5	0x8B	139	ï	0xE1	225	β
0x36	54	6	0x8C	140	î	0xE2	226	Γ
0x37	55	7	0x8D	141	ì	0xE3	227	π
0x38	56	8	0x8E	142	Ä	0xE4	228	Σ
0x39	57	9	0x8F	143	Å	0xE5	229	σ
0x3A	58	:	0x90	144	É	0xE6	230	µ
0x3B	59	;	0x91	145	æ	0xE7	231	τ

Hex	Dec	ASCII	Hex	Dec	ASCII	Hex	Dec	ASCII
0x3C	60	<	0x92	146	Æ	0xE8	232	Φ
0x3D	61	=	0x93	147	ô	0xE9	233	Θ
0x3E	62	>	0x94	148	ö	0xEA	234	Ω
0x3F	63	?	0x95	149	ò	0xEB	235	δ
0x40	64	@	0x96	150	û	0xEC	236	∞
0x41	65	A	0x97	151	ù	0xED	237	ϕ
0x42	66	B	0x98	152	ÿ	0xEE	238	ε
0x43	67	C	0x99	153	ö	0xEF	239	∩
0x44	68	D	0x9A	154	ü	0xF0	240	≡
0x45	69	E	0x9B	155	¢	0xF1	241	±
0x46	70	F	0x9C	156	£	0xF2	242	≥
0x47	71	G	0x9D	157	¥	0xF3	243	≤
0x48	72	H	0x9E	158	Pt	0xF4	244	⌠
0x49	73	I	0x9F	159	ƒ	0xF5	245	⌡
0x4A	74	J	0xA0	160	á	0xF6	246	÷
0x4B	75	K	0xA1	161	í	0xF7	247	≈
0x4C	76	L	0xA2	162	ó	0xF8	248	°
0x4D	77	M	0xA3	163	ú	0xF9	249	●
0x4E	78	N	0xA4	164	ñ	0xFA	250	•
0x4F	79	O	0xA5	165	Ñ	0xFB	251	√
0x50	80	P	0xA6	166	ª	0xFC	252	^{n}
0x51	81	Q	0xA7	167	º	0xFD	253	^{2}
0x52	82	R	0xA8	168	¿	0xFE	254	■
0x53	83	S	0xA9	169	¬	0xFF	255	null
0x54	84	T	0xA A	170	⌐			
0x55	85	U	0xAB	171	½			

Table H.2 Symbol Abbreviations Meanings

Abbr	Meaning	Abbr	Meaning
SOH	Start Of Heading	DC4	Device Control 4
STX	Start Of Text	NAK	Negative AcKnowledge
ETX	End Of Text	SYN	SYNchronous idle
EOT	End Of Transmission	ETB	End Transmission Block
ENQ	ENQuiry	CAN	CANcel
ACK	ACKnowledge	EM	End Medium
BKSP	BacKSPace	SUB	SUBstitute
Vert Tab	Vertical Tab	ESC	ESCape
Car Retn	Carriage Return	FS	File Separator
DL Esc	Data Link Esc	GS	Group Separator
DC1	Device Control 1	RS	Record Separator
DC2	Device Control 2	US	Unit Separator
DC3	Device Control 3		

Appendix I
The IBM PC Keyboard

Reading keystrokes from the PC keyboard presents a problem. The type char contains 8 bits, which allows for 256 characters. The average PC keyboard has 103 keys, each of which can be used alone, with the shift key, with the alt key, or with the ctrl key. All in all there are more than 400 possible characters that can be generated by the keyboard. They cannot all be represented with one byte.

What the designers of the PC decided to do was use 2 bytes, but only for special lesser used characters. The getch( ) function returns a character (the prototype shows it returning an integer, but the high-order byte of that integer is empty). If one of the special keys has been pressed getch( ) will return 0. A second call to getch( ) immediately after the first will read a code telling what key was pressed. The trouble is it is possible for a regular key to return 0 without having a second byte. In this case the second call to getch( ) will hang, waiting for more input from the keyboard. A call to kbhit( ) can be made to determine if there is a second character waiting. With this information it is possible to write a special getch( ) function for use when it is expected that the user will press a special key. It would look something like:

```
#define FALSE 0
#define TRUE  1

char spec_getch(char *special) {
  char key = getch();
  if ((key == 0) && (kbhit())) {
    *special = TRUE;
    key = getch();
    return (key);
  }
  else {
    *special = FALSE;
    return (key);
  }
} /* end spec_getch() */
```

Table I.1 gives the scan codes for most of the keys on the IBM PC keyboard.

Appendix I

Table I.1 IBM PC Keyboard Scan Codes

Key	Normal		Shifted		Ctrl		Alt	
F1	0	59	0	84	0	94	0	104
F2	0	60	0	85	0	95	0	105
F3	0	61	0	86	0	96	0	106
F4	0	62	0	87	0	97	0	107
F5	0	63	0	88	0	98	0	108
F6	0	64	0	89	0	99	0	109
F7	0	65	0	90	0	100	0	110
F8	0	66	0	91	0	101	0	111
F9	0	67	0	92	0	102	0	112
F10	0	68	0	93	0	103	0	113
F11	0	133	0	135	0	137	0	139
F12	0	134	0	136	0	138	0	140
Left	0	75		255	0	115	0	155
Right	0	77		255	0	116	0	157
Up	0	72		255	0	141	0	152
Down	0	80		255	0	145	0	160
Home	0	71		255	0	119	0	151
End	0	79		255	0	117	0	159
PGUP	0	73		255	0	132		9
PGDN	0	81		255	0	118	0	81
Ins	0	82		255		255		none
Del	0	83		255		255	0	83
ESC		27		27		27	0	1
BACK		8		8		127	0	14
TAB		9	0	15	0	148	0	165
Enter		13		13		10	0	28
A		97		65		3	0	46
B		98		66		2	0	48
C		99		67		3	0	46
D		100		68		4	0	32
E		101		69		5	0	18
F		102		70		6	0	33
G		103		71		7	0	34
H		104		72		8	0	35
I		105		73		9	0	23
J		106		74		10	0	36
K		107		75		11	0	37
L		108		76		12	0	38
M		109		77		13	0	50
N		110		78		14	0	49
O		111		79		15	0	24
P		112		80		16	0	25

Key	Normal	Shifted	Ctrl	Alt
Q	113	81	17	Echo output to prn
R	114	82	18	0 19
S	115	83	19	0 31
T	116	84	20	0 20
U	117	85	21	0 22
V	118	86	22	0 47
W	119	87	23	0 17
X	120	88	24	0 45
Y	121	89	25	0 21
Z	122	90	26	0 44
0	48	41	none	0 129
1	49	33	none	0 120
2	50	64	break	0 121
3	51	35	none	0 122
4	52	36	none	0 123
5	53	37	none	0 124
6	54	94	30	0 125
7	55	38	none	0 126
8	56	42	none	0 127
9	57	40	none	0 128
[	91	123	27	0 26
]	93	125	29	0 27
'	39	34	none	0 40
`	96	126	none	0 41
-	45	95	31	0 130
\	92	124	28	0 43
;	59	58	none	0 39
=	61	43	none	0 131

Keypad keys

Key	Normal	Shifted	Ctrl	Alt
+	43	43	0 144	0 78
-	45	45	0 142	0 74
/	47	47	0 149	0 164
*	42	42	0 150	0 55

Index

D

E

F

G

H

I

K

L